International Economics

OWL

RY

i

INTERNATIONAL ECONOMICS

Bo Södersten

and

Geoffrey Reed

Third Edition

First published in the USA 1970
First published in the UK 1971
Reprinted eight times
Second edition 1980
Reprinted eleven times
Third edition 1994

Published by
MACMILLAN PRESS LTD
Houndmills, Basingstoke, Hampshire RG21 6XS
and London
Companies and representatives
throughout the world

 ISBN 0–333–48981–0 hardcover
ISBN 0–333–61216–7 paperback

International edition 0–333–76365–3

A catalogue record for this book is available
from the British Library.

This book is printed on paper suitable for recycling and
made from fully managed and sustained forest sources.

10   9   8   7   6   5
03   02   01   00   99

Copy-edited and typeset by Povey–Edmondson
Okehampton and Rochdale, England

Printed in Hong Kong

To Anna, Henrik, Erika and Viktor

To Sandra

1001662920

Acknowledgements

The authors and publishers are grateful to the following for permission to use copyright material:

Blackwell Publishers, Oxford, for tables from I. Trela and J. Whalley (1990) 'Global Effects of Developed Country Trade Restrictions on Textiles and Apparel', *Economic Journal*, 100, pp. 1190–205; from F. Brown and J. Whalley (1980) 'Equilibrium Evaluations of Tariff Cutting Proposals in the Tokyo Round and Comparisons with More Extensive Liberalisations of World Trade', *Economic Journal*, 90, pp. 836–66; and from C. T. Ennew, D. Greenaway and G. V. Reed (1990) 'Further Evidence on Effective Tariffs and Effective Protection', *Oxford Bulletin of Economics and Statistics*, 52, pp. 69–78.

GATT (General Agreement on Tariffs and Trade) for a table from GATT (1979) *The Tokyo Round of Multilateral Trade Negotiations* (Geneva).

Harvester-Wheatsheaf and New York University Press for a table from V. N. Balasubramanyam and D. R. Basu (1990) 'India: Export Promotion Policies and Export Performance' in C. R. Milner (ed.), *Export Promotion Strategies*.

International Monetary Fund for tables from K. Pilbeam (1992) *International Finance* (London: Macmillan), originally published in the IMF's *Balance of Payments Yearbook* (1990); and from G. C. Hufbauer and J. Schott (1985) *Trading for Growth: The Next Round of Trade Negotiations* (Washington, DC: Institute for International Economics), originally published in the IMF's *International Financial Statistics: Yearbook*.

Trade Policy Research Centre, University of Reading, for tables from D. Greenaway (1985) 'Clothing from Hong Kong and Other Developing Countries' in D. Greenaway and B. Hindley, *What Britain Pays for Voluntary Export Restraints*, Thames Essay No. 43 (London).

Oxford University Press for a table from W. M. Corden (1974), *Trade Policy and Economic Welfare*, and for a table from I. Little, T. Scitovsky and M. Scott (1970), *Industry and Trade in Some Developing Countries: A Comparative Study*.

The United States Department of Commerce for a table from *The Survey of Current Business*.

The World Bank for a table based on Tables A8.3 and A8.4 in Finger, J. M. and Olechowski, A. (1987), *The Uruguay Round: A Handbook for the Multilateral Trade Negotiations*.

Helbing & Lichtenhahn Verlag AG for a table from Greenaway, D. and Nam, C-H. (1988), 'Industrialisation and Macroeconomic Performance in Developing Countries under Alternative Liberalisation Scenarios', *Kyklos*, 41.

Professor A.O. Krueger and the National Bureau for Economic Research for a table based on Tables 6.2 and 6.3 in Krueger, A.O. (1978), *Foreign Trade Regimes and Economic Development: Liberalization Attempts and Consequences*.

Every effort has been made to contact all the copyright-holders, but if any have been inadvertently overlooked the publishers will be pleased to make the necessary arrangement at the first opportunity.

Contents

List of Figures

List of Tables

Preface to the Third Edition

The first edition of *International Economics*, written by Bo Södersten, was published in Swedish in 1969, with the American and British editions following in 1970 and 1971. The second edition was published in 1980. This third edition has been extensively rewritten by Bo Södersten and Geoffrey Reed.

The first and second editions were well received, and used in many countries. Their aim was to present a reasonably rigorous treatment of international economics in a way that would be accessible both to undergraduate students and to others with a general interest in economics and international affairs. The emphasis was on theory, although problems of economic policy were discussed throughout. The intention was to provide the reader with theoretical tools that could be applied to various kinds of problems, not just those that happened to be topical when the book was published.

This intention has been maintained in the third edition. There have, however, been many new developments in both economic theory and the institutional setting since the second edition, and the new edition has been substantially revised to take account of these.

Part I is concerned with the pure theory of international trade. It starts with the classical and neo-classical models of inter-industry trade that have been the mainstay of trade theory since the early nineteenth century, and are still much in use today. Such theories are concerned with explaining the determinants of what was, for many years, the dominant pattern of trade, with each country exporting the output of some industries and importing the output of others. More recently it has become apparent that much trade, at least between developed countries, is intra-industry in nature: that is, countries simultaneously import and export the same type of good. A major feature of recent trade theory has been the development of models explaining this phenomenon, usually in terms of product differentiation and economies of scale, and a discussion of such theories is included in Part 1. The gains from international trade, and the adjustment problems faced when a country opens its market to foreign competition, are discussed in the context of both types of trade.

Part II deals with trade policy. The reduction since the Second World War in the 'old' forms of protection, notably tariffs and quotas, has been to some extent restraints, accompanied by the development of regional trading blocs that combine free trade among members while maintaining barriers to trade with other countries. Part II examines the arguments for and against both the old and the new protectionism, including an account of the contribution made by the renewed interest in the political economy of protection, and the role of the General Agreement on Tariffs and trade in securing and maintaining trade liberalisation. It deals also with the question of the best trade strategies to be followed by developing countries, and with the influences of foreign investment and multi-national enterprises.

Part III concentrates on international macroeconomics, discussing both international monetary problems and the implementation of macroeconomic policy in an open economy. There have been major changes in the institutional setting in the last two decades, and it is arguable that further changes are inevitable. Such changes have provided the stimulus for both new economic theories and the revival of some others.

There has been a significant increase in empirical studies in all areas of international economics in recent years. This reflects the development of new theories, and the wish to test them against both each other and the older theories, and is made possible by the availability of more comprehensive and reliable data and the development of econometric and other quantitative techniques. Discussions of empirical analyses form an important part of the third edition.

The structure and contents of the third edition are in many ways similar to those of the second edition, and so the acknowledgements made there still apply. There is, however, much new material, and we are grateful to Kevin Dowd, David Greenaway, Robert Hine and Mervyn Lewis for their willingness to read earlier efforts.

Bo Södersten
Lund

Geoffrey Reed
Nottingham

Introduction: International Economics and Economic Theory

Today the national state is the dominant political entity. Most countries, from an economic point of view, are still intimately linked with others. Two – the United States and China – could conceivably withdraw from the world economy without disastrous consequences to themselves. For other countries such an act would border on the unthinkable. It would bring about not only a drastic lowering of economic welfare but also a complete change of ways of life. For practical purposes, all countries must accept the fact that they are part of a world economy. No country can escape its role in the system of interdependent trading nations.

There now seems little doubt that the degree of interdependence among nations has increased markedly over the last two decades or more. World trade has grown exceptionally fast in the post-war years, both absolutely and relative to national incomes. The forces behind the internationalisation process have been strong. Technical progress in transport and communication has played an important role. Increased returns to scale in production and high income elasticities for differentiated products have also had their impact. These and many other factors have favoured international specialisation and trade, both in tangible goods and in services. The forces working for economic interdependence among nations seem irresistible.

Although the nation-state is still in the 1990s the dominant entity, the increasing interdependence between countries has meant the loss of some degree of sovereignty. Some countries have surrendered a good part of their sovereignty willingly, for example the members of the European Community (although even there we see fierce debate over the degree to which sovereignty should be ceded to a central institution). Others, while unwilling to surrender sovereignty, are nevertheless constrained in how they can exercise their autonomy. Even the United States must nowadays take account of the reactions of other countries when formulating its economic policies.

Although governments are generally aware of the losses that would be incurred if they were to isolate themselves completely from the world economy, they are still often tempted to adopt policies that reduce the degree of dependence. Governments in the advanced industrial countries are often concerned to limit the impact on their own economies of changes in the rest of the world, whether these be 'shocks', such as the increase in oil prices in 1973, or 'structural changes', such as the threat to domestic industries of imports from newly industrialising countries. Many less developed countries have also tried to establish a policy of self-reliance. They have tried to isolate themselves from international influences by a policy of import-substitution. It may however be argued that those countries, whether developed or developing, that have grown most quickly in the last few decades have been those that have not attempted to isolate themselves from the world economy.

Whether the degree of interdependence will continue to increase or not, and if so on what lines, is a matter for debate. On the one hand we see increasing interdependence between groups of countries, either formally, as in the European Community or the North American Free Trade Area, or informally, as in the 'Pacific Rim' countries. On the other hand, there is evidence of increasing friction over economic matters, as between the United States, the European Community, and Japan. The 'free trade versus fair trade' debate is important here, providing an impetus towards unilateral action. Some observers have suggested that the world economy will move towards a system of economic blocs, within which there will be free trade, but between which there will not. The forces working for a national identity – perhaps a new type of identity, be it from dominating neighbours or a new type of changed social and political system – are also strong in many countries. Whether existing trends toward internationalisation or new forms of nationalism will get the upper hand is impossible to say. This is primarily a political question.

■ *International economics as a subject*

Even if most people are agreed that international economic relations are of great importance for most countries, it does not necessarily follow that international economics should be studied as a subject independent of other branches of economics.

There are certainly many policy problems and problems within international economics that the use of economic theory can elucidate. At the same time, it is becoming less tenable for economists to discuss the policy options open to a government as though the economy were closed from the rest of the world, so that much of 'domestic economics' is necessarily discussed in an international setting. However, there are more deep-seated reasons why international economics has a long tradition as a subject in its own right.

Many theorems and insights central to economic theory have been developed by economists working within international economics. The theory of comparative advantage and the factor-price equalisation theorem are examples. Both belong to the area usually called the *pure theory* of international trade. The pure theory of trade can be said to be part of price theory, the terms used in a broad sense. But price theory or micro theory *per se* seldom pursues the subject to such a degree that all the aspects of the theory which are of interest to a trade theorist are revealed in its full implications. Trade theory is a distinct part of modern economic theory with a rich body of theorems.

Analogous conditions hold for the macroeconomic parts of international economic theory. Some of its results, for instance those about income determination in open economies, are quite straightforward applications of the corresponding parts of the theory for closed economies. But other parts, for instance exchange-rate theory, can hardly be obtained except from a study of the specific theory.

When it comes to the policy aspects of the subject, it is quite obvious that the policy problems faced by an open economy are quite different to those faced by the closed economy. While the assumption that an economy is closed may be tenable for some problems (such as whether to impose a tax on a non-traded good that makes up a minor part of national output), in most cases the discussion must recognise the openness of the economy. The nation is however not only a distinct political entity: it also has many important economic characteristics that set it apart from the larger integrated areas that make up the world economy: the mobility of the factors of production is much larger within the nation than among nations, there are tariffs and taxes on imported goods, different currencies give rise to specific problems, etc. All these lead to international economic policy problems that must be considered in the context of many countries rather than one country.

There are, therefore, from both theoretical and policy points of view, good reasons why international economics is dealt with as a specific branch of economics. Modern economics is a large and diversified subject. A training in general economic theory is the best background for a study of international economics. But it can only be regarded as a background. To obtain a real understanding of the field, the student will have to study international economics directly.

Now we shall now consider briefly five areas in which international economics has had something important to contribute to economics in general, and preview some of the problems and results.

■ *Comparative advantage and pure theory*

One of the basic questions facing international trade theory is: Why does trade take place? The classical economists saw labour as the only factor of production and said that differing labour productivity among countries caused trade. More recent economists have seen the source of trade as being differences in countries' endowments of factors of production. The most recent development has been to explain trade flows in terms of imperfectly competitive markets, so-called intra-industry trade.

A closely linked question is: Why do countries gain by trading? The classical economists said that as long as cost conditions differ between countries, at least one and probably both will gain by trading. The modern theory of intra-industry trade tends to focus as much on the role played by consumers' tastes.

These questions, and their answers, contain the essence of the theory of comparative advantage. The first can be said to state the positive side and the second the normative side. The normative aspect is perhaps the most interesting to the modern student. It demonstrates, on very weak assumptions, that trade will be beneficial to all countries involved in trade. It is important to understand the nature of this theory. It has often been attacked and is often misunderstood. It is still frequently argued that trade is detrimental to countries, today especially in connection with less-developed countries (LDCs). Right from the outset, therefore, we will enter disputed territory. Whatever the student's final opinion is, he will have to undertake a certain amount of theoretical work before he can reach an informed judgement.

One of the central assumptions of the classical economist was that factors of production were fully mobile within countries but not at all mobile between countries. Labour could move freely from New York to Arizona, but it could not cross the border into Mexico. This is an assumption that modern trade theorists have stuck to in elaborating the modern theory of trade. It might seem to be too strong. Within Western Europe, for instance, there have been substantial movements of workers, largely north from Portugal, Spain, southern Italy, Greece and Turkey to France, Germany and Switzerland. But the movements of labour have taken place primarily between somewhat integrated areas. The movement of workers between the United States and Europe, for example, is still insignificant.

For many purposes the assumption that labour is immobile between countries is valid. Using this (and some other fairly stringent assumptions), modern trade theory has proved some startling theorems. One is that trade alone will lead to a complete equalisation of factor prices. Even in the absence of factor movements, if only goods can be traded freely, wages will be equalised.

A study of modern trade theory will also help the student understand one of the basic principles of economics, that of *general equilibrium*. Trade theory is essentially a branch of general-equilibrium analysis. It is firmly embedded in the Walrasian tradition. From there stems the preoccupation with creating a theory that is self-contained, where all variables of importance enter and where all variables are interdependent. Such a theory will of necessity be of an abstract and simplified nature. It works with a few well-defined variables and relies on simplifying assumptions, some of which are of a drastic nature. Its strength lies in the fact that it creates a picture of the world which in important ways is complete.

At the heart of general-equilibrium theory are the notions of determinateness and completeness: the relations which describe an economy must form a complete whole where all the variables of the system can be determined. The viewpoint that all factors which make up an economy hang together and are dependent on one another has had a very strong place in economic theorising. It might even be said to have been *the* distinctive feature of economics as a science. It had also had important policy implications as it has forced policy-makers to try to view the economy as a whole and not simply try to focus the attention on the effect of a parameter change on one or two obvious variables. The pure theory of trade offers the student an excellent illustration of one of the basic notions of economics as a science.

■ *Comparative statics: the question of change*

The pure theory of trade is fundamentally a static theory. It studies some aspects of trading economies in the setting of static equilibrium. It abstracts from one fundamental aspect, that of change.

The simplest way to study the effects of change is by the use of comparative statics. We take an economy in a given equilibrium and then introduce a change in some of the basic variables. This is done, for example, in the study of the effects of economic growth on international trade. Growth of production and trade in the world economy has been very rapid in the post-war years. The more precise theory of growth and trade was also primarily developed during this period. From a methodological point of view, this type of theory is also interesting because it illustrates clearly how the static models of pure trade theory can be developed in a comparative–static way. It clearly demonstrates also some of the basic effects of economic growth on the variables in the trade model. One question it answers is the following. Let us assume that economic growth occurs in two trading economies. What will be the effects on the terms of trade (the ratio of export prices to import prices) and on national income? The answer will depend on which sectors growth occurs in and what the income elasticities are.

The effects of increases in factor endowments and technical progress are also studied. These effects can be handled clearly by the use of geometry.

An understanding of this type of theory therefore does not involve very advanced or difficult methods. The effects of technical progress, for instance, are quite striking. An understanding of this kind of theory is essential also for a broad group of problems outside the field of international trade, so it seems appropriate to treat the theory of economic growth and trade rigorously and explicitly.

■ *Trade policy: is trade good or bad?*

The book is based on the principle of decreasing abstraction. The most theoretical parts are in the beginning, especially in Part I; then, as the exposition develops, it becomes more and more policy oriented – it assumes more of an 'applied' nature. This is because theory is needed to appreciate all the facets of a policy problem. It is logical to start with theory and then proceed to policy, though it perhaps seems that policy problems are sometimes 'easier' to deal with than theoretical questions.

Part 2 is devoted to problems of trade policy. It both demonstrates principles of trade policy, for example the effects of tariffs on trade, and analyses the factual development of trade policy, and in particular the political dimension of the formulation of that policy. One thing Part 2 shows is that free trade, in a world of sovereign states, is usually the best policy except in the case of the few large countries, but that the political pressure to restrict trade may be difficult to resist. However, since some trade is always better than no trade, it is unlikely that trade will ever be eliminated.

The trade problems of the developed countries and the LDCs are seldom of the same kind. One of the trade problems confronting LDCs is the stabilisation of commodity prices. Together with the question of tariff preferences, this problem has dominated the UNCTAD conferences held so far. These questions are also intimately linked with the strivings for a new economic world order.

The proposals for stabilisation of commodity prices are of different kinds. The object of some is to stabilise terms of trade between LDCs and industrial countries; others, less far-reaching, aim at stabilising export prices or export proceeds. To understand the true nature of some of these plans, they must be considered against the models of growth and trade developed earlier. These models show explicitly the basic factors that determine the development of commodity prices in international trade. Therefore, they show clearly which factors have to be controlled if international prices are to be controlled. They give an example of how recent developments in trade theory can be used to elucidate long-standing policy problems.

■ *Macroeconomic aspects: different currencies*

One of the obvious differences between trade within a country and international trade is that the latter involves different currencies. If a New Yorker trades with a Californian, they both use the same currency, but trade between a New Yorker and a Canadian involves different currencies.

One essential complication in connection with foreign trade is that the relative values of currencies change. One year, £1 sterling could be worth $2.00 US, the next, 1.50. This concerns the balance of payments between countries.

Disequilibria in the external balances of countries give rise to changes in exchange rates. The policy problems surrounding disequilibria in the balance of payments and changes in exchange rates are among the most pertinent ones in the world economy. If anything, they have become more important and attracted increasing attention as domestic capital markets have become increasingly integrated.

The first chapters in Part 3 are devoted to these macroeconomic aspects of international economics. The basic principles of foreign exchange markets are discussed and an explanation is given of how a country's balance of payments can be in disequilibrium and how it can be kept in equilibrium.

International monetary matters have been at the forefront of economic theory in recent years, and important reformulations of theory have taken place. They centre around what is commonly called the *monetary approach to the balance of payments*. This theory states (to put it somewhat bluntly) that in the long run the exchange rate will primarily be determined by changes in the money supply. An increase in the money supply will cause inflation. This in turn will cause a depreciation of the exchange rate. This is an illustration of 'the law of one price': if the price level increases, the value of the currency will fall proportionately.

■ *The international monetary system and international policy co-ordination*

The international monetary system underwent great changes in the 1970s. Up until 1971 the Bretton Woods system reigned, which meant that exchange rates were fixed. During the 1960s this system was put under greater and greater strain. Finally, it broke down. It has now been replaced by a system of floating exchange rates, but one within which some countries attempt to link their currency to those of other countries.

A system of floating rates does not, however, solve all balance-of-payments problems. Exchange-rate changes have been very large, and international capital flows of increasing importance. Some might argue that the problems posed for economies by the current problems may best be solved by the international co-ordination of macroeconomic policies, others that there should be a return to the pegged exchange rate system of Bretton Woods, yet others that international capital movements should once more be regulated. The closing chapters of Part 3 discuss these questions.

■ PART 1 ■
THEORIES OF INTER- AND INTRA-INDUSTRY TRADE

■ *Chapter 1* ■

The Basic Geometry of Comparative Advantage and the Gains from Trade

■ *1.1* Introduction

Two of the basic questions that the theory of international trade has to answer are what determines the pattern of trade and who gains from trade. Economics does have answers to these questions – ones that go back more than 150 years – in the theories of comparative advantage and the gains from trade. These theories, formulated around 1815, are usually connected with the name of David Ricardo.[1] The theory of comparative advantage or, as it is sometimes called, the theory of comparative costs, is one of the oldest, still unchallenged theories of economics. Before exploring the basic theory of comparative advantage and the gains from trade, which is usually done geometrically, we shall take a brief look at its historical background.

The economic doctrine that prevailed during the first two centuries of the development of the modern nation-state – the seventeenth and eighteenth centuries – was *mercantilism*. The doctrine of mercantilism had many modern features: it was highly nationalistic, viewing the well-being of the home nation as of prime importance; it favoured the regulation and planning of economic activity as an efficient means of fostering the goals of the nation; and it generally viewed foreign trade with suspicion.

The most important way in which a nation could grow rich, according to the doctrine of mercantilism, was by acquiring precious metals, especially gold. Single individuals, however, were not to be trusted: they might also like gold, but perhaps they liked other things even more. Left to themselves, they might exchange gold for satin and linen, spices from India, or sugar from Cuba, or indulge in whatever private pleasures they preferred, to the detriment of the stock of precious metals stored in the nation. To prevent such undertakings, the nation had to control foreign trade. Exports were viewed favourably as long as they brought in gold, but imports were viewed with apprehension, as depriving the country of its true source of richness – precious metals. Therefore, trade had to be regulated and restricted, no specific virtue being seen in having a large volume of trade.

It was against this background that English classical economics developed, for mercantilism was the credo that Adam Smith and David Ricardo rebelled against.[2] English classical economics was an offspring of liberalism and the Enlightenment – of a general philosophy that stressed the importance of the individual and viewed the nation as nothing more than the sum of its inhabitants.

For Smith, as for Ricardo, the supreme subject of economics was the consumer: man laboured and produced in order to consume. And anything that could increase consumption, or, to use Ricardo's phrase, 'the sum of enjoyments', ought to be viewed with favour.

■ 1.2 Absolute and comparative advantage

Adam Smith and the absolute advantage of trade

Adam Smith saw clearly that a country could gain by trading. The tailor does not make his own shoes; he exchanges a suit for shoes. Thereby both the shoemaker and the tailor gain. In the same manner, Smith argued, a whole country could gain by trading with other countries.

For example, suppose it takes 10 units of labour to manufacture 1 unit of good X in country A but 20 labour units in country B, and it takes 20 units of labour to manufacture 1 unit of good Y in country A but only 10 labour units in country B. Country A has the absolute advantage in producing good X, country B the absolute advantage in producing good Y. If the two countries were to exchange the two goods at a ratio of one to one, i.e. 1 unit of good X for 1 unit of good Y, country A could get a unit of good Y by using 10 units of labour to produce 1 unit of good X and trading that with B for 1 unit of good Y, whereas if it produced that unit of good Y itself then it would have to give up 20 units of labour. The 10 units of labour 'saved' can then be used to produce another unit of X for home consumption.

The symmetry of the example makes it obvious that country B may make a similar gain by producing 2 units of Y, using 20 labour units, and exporting 1 unit in exchange for 1 unit of X, rather than using the 20 units of labour to produce 1 unit of *X* itself. The implication is clearly that both countries could have more of both goods, with a given effort, by trading.

This is a simple and powerful illustration of the benefits of trade, and on it Adam Smith rested his plea for non-interference – for free trade as the best policy for trade between nations. Smith's argument seems convincing, but it is not very deep. It was left to Torrens[3] and Ricardo to produce the stronger and more subtle argument for the benefits from trade contained in the theory of comparative advantage.

David Ricardo and the theory of comparative advantage

Ricardo did not object to Smith's analysis. It is obvious that if one country has an absolute advantage over the other in one line of production and the other country has an absolute advantage over the first in a second line of production, both countries can gain by trading. A great deal of trade, perhaps most trade, is governed by such differences.

But what if one country is more productive than another country in all lines of production? If country *A* can produce all goods with less labour cost than country *B*, does it still benefit the countries to trade? Ricardo's answer was yes. So long as country *B* is not equally less productive in all lines of production, it still pays both countries to trade.

We shall spend some time elucidating this principle, as it is of basic importance to the theory of trade. We shall start with Ricardo's own model before going on to consider more modern means of demonstration.

Ricardo used England and Portugal as examples in his demonstration, the two goods they produced being wine and cloth, with Portugal assumed to be more efficient in making both cloth and wine. Table 1.1 shows how Ricardo summed up the cost conditions in the two countries. These costs are assumed to apply irrespective of the scale of production of a good.

According to this model, Portugal has an *absolute advantage* in the production of wine as well as in the production of cloth, because the labour cost of production for each unit of the two commodities is less in Portugal than in England.

To demonstrate that trade between England and Portugal will, even in this case, lead to gains for both countries, it is useful to introduce the concept of *opportunity cost*. The opportunity cost of a good *X* is the amount of another good, *Y*, that has to be given up in order to produce an additional unit of *X*. Table 1.2 gives the opportunity costs of producing wine and cloth in Portugal and England. These costs have been constructed on the basis of the information given in Table 1.1.

Table 1.1   *Cost comparisons*

	Labour cost of production (in hours)	
	1 unit of wine	*1 unit of cloth*
Portugal	80	90
England	120	100

Table 1.2   *Opportunity costs*

	Opportunity cost of production	
	1 unit of wine	*1 unit of cloth*
Portugal	80/90 = 8/9	90/80 = 9/8
England	120/100 = 12/10	100/120 = 10/12

A country has a *comparative advantage* in producing a good if the opportunity cost of producing the good is lower at home than in the other country. Table 1.2 shows that Portugal has the lower opportunity cost of the two countries in producing wine, while England has the lower opportunity cost in producing cloth. Thus Portugal has a comparative advantage in the production of wine and England has a comparative advantage in the production of cloth.

We should now further clarify the meaning of the term 'comparative advantage'. In order to speak about comparative advantage there must be at least two countries and at least two goods. We compare the opportunity costs of the production of each good in both countries. As long as the two countries' opportunity costs for one good differ, one country has a comparative advantage in the production of one of the two goods, while the second country has a comparative advantage in the production of the other. In such a case both countries will gain from trade, regardless of the fact that one of the countries might have an absolute disadvantage in both lines of production.

☐ *Ricardo on the gains from trade*

Let us assume that Portugal and England do not trade but produce and consume in isolation – a state usually referred to as *autarky*. Given the assumption that the labour input required to produce 1 unit of either good is constant in both countries, the prices of wine and cloth in the two countries must then be determined by their respective costs of production (i.e. by their labour inputs).

If in England it takes 120 hours of labour to produce 1 unit of wine, while it takes 100 hours to make 1 unit of cloth, wine must then be more expensive per unit than cloth – 1 unit of wine will cost 120/100 or 1.2 units of cloth. If in Portugal it takes 80 hours of labour to make 1 unit of wine and 90 hours to make 1 unit of cloth then cloth will be more expensive than wine – 1 unit of wine will cost 80/90, or 0.89, units of cloth. Let us now introduce the possibility of trade. If England could import 1 unit of wine at a cost of less than 1.2 units of cloth then she would gain by doing so. If Portugal could import more than 0.89 units of cloth in exchange for 1 unit of wine then she too would gain. Therefore, if 1 unit of wine can be exported to England from Portugal in exchange for something between 1.2 and 0.89 units of cloth, both countries will gain from trading.

Let us assume that in the international market 1 unit of wine exchanges for 1 unit of cloth. It is then advantageous for England to export cloth and import wine, because in the absence of trade England would have to give up the production and consumption of 1.2 units of cloth in order to produce and consume each additional unit of wine she wants. By trading, she need only give up 1 unit of cloth in order to consume that additional unit of wine, and can either consume the additional 0.2 units of cloth herself, or export some of it in order to consume more imported wine, or can enjoy the same levels of consumption of cloth and wine as under autarky while the workers enjoy more leisure.

Portugal will also gain by trading. In isolation she would have to use 90 units of labour to produce 1 unit of cloth. Now she can make 1 unit of wine with 80 hours of labour and exchange this unit of wine for 1 unit of cloth in the international market. Every 10 hours of labour freed by this process can then be used for either increased production and consumption or increased leisure.

Thus trade offers each country the opportunity of specialising in the production of the good in which it has the comparative advantage and then exchanging some of this production for the good in which it has the comparative disadvantage. Both countries can reallocate their labour to the line where their comparative advantage lies, export this good and import the other. In short, with a given amount of labour resources each country can consume more by trading than in isolation. This possibility is usually referred to as the *gains from trade*.

Note that in working through this example we have not found it necessary to introduce money into the system, nor have we considered the question of the wages paid to workers. Furthermore, we have not asked how such trade flows will arise – we have implicitly treated each country as though it were an individual, rather than a group of individuals. Neither have we made any explicit assumptions about the way in which the markets, if any, operate within our two countries. Finally, we have assumed that there is only one factor of production – labour – and that the average product of labour is constant in both sectors in each country.

In the simple two-country, two-good, one-factor world we have been considering, national currencies are in effect irrelevant, and as we shall see later, all we need assume concerning wages is that so long as a country is producing both goods then all workers in both industries are paid the same money wage. We may demonstrate the irrelevance of national currencies and of the money wage rate under autarky, while providing one possible explanation of why trade in the directions suggested may occur, by introducing them into the model. To simplify the presentation, we shall, for the moment at least, also assume perfect competition in all markets.

Suppose that the wage rate in England under autarky is £1 per hour. Given our assumptions, the cost of producing 1 unit of cloth, and hence its price, will thus be £100, while the cost and price of 1 unit of wine will be £120. Note that 1 unit of wine would then exchange for 1.2 units of cloth, as in our original example. Suppose also that under autarky the wage rate in Portugal is 2 escudos per hour, so that the cost and price of 1 unit of wine is 160 escudos and of 1 unit of cloth is 180 escudos, so that again 1 unit of wine costs 0.89 units of cloth.

Consider now an individual in Portugal with 1600 escudos and the opportunity to export and import goods. He can use that money to purchase 10 units of wine, which he can then export to England. There, he can sell those 10 units of wine for £1200, and can then use that sum of money to purchase 12 units of cloth at English prices. If he then imports those 12 units of cloth to Portugal he can sell them at Portuguese prices for 2160 escudos, making a profit of 560 escudos. This is of course an example of *arbitrage* between two markets with different (relative) prices. Such profits are of course an inducement to trade!

It should be obvious that doubling the wage rate in England would not alter the essential details of this transaction; that we could equally well have started by assuming an individual in England with money to invest in such trade; and that we have no need to make any assumption about the exchange rate between the two currencies. It should be equally obvious that an individual exporting cloth from Portugal to England and wine from England to Portugal must make a loss in money terms.

It is also apparent that this example raises other questions which we must seek to answer. The additional demand for wine in Portugal arising from its export will tend to increase its price in Portugal, with the same happening for cloth in England, while the additional supply of cloth in Portugal and of wine in England due to their import must reduce their prices in those countries. However, as long as there is a difference in relative prices between the two countries there must be opportunities for individuals to gain by trading, so that the volume of trade will continue to grow. Moreover, the price changes and the ensuing changes in the profitability of producing the two goods must cause the expansion of the export sector and the contraction of the import sector in both countries, with labour having to move from the latter to the former. Will then the new state of affairs lead to an equilibrium situation, and if so, what will be the characteristics of that equilibrium?

We may deduce that in an equilibrium we must have the same relative prices in both countries, as otherwise the volume of trade will change, but with our present assumptions we cannot determine what that equilibrium price ratio will be. We know that in each country the import industry will contract, but will it disappear so that the country specialises completely in the production of its export good? In either event, what will be the volumes of trade in cloth and wine? We know that labour must move from the import-competing sector to the export sector, but what will happen to its money wage or, more importantly, to its real wage? Finally, while we have seen that some individuals may profit from arbitrage between the two markets, does this mean that other individuals may lose, and if so, can we say that the country is better off?

A wider set of questions concerns the extent to which our conclusion that countries gain from free trade is dependent upon the particular assumptions we have made. We shall extend this original classical model to cases where there are two or more factors of production, and in particular examples to cases where there are more than two countries and more than two goods, and we shall consider what happens when markets are not perfectly competitive. In order to do so we shall go deeper into the questions of what determines which country has a comparative advantage in a given good, and how we can judge whether a country does gain from trade. In most cases we shall conclude that free trade is superior to autarky.

For the moment we shall examine how the differences in opportunity costs between the two countries, and the possibilities of gains from trade, may be analysed geometrically using the concepts of the *production-possibility curve* and the *community indifference map*, without attempting to tackle these wider questions.

■ *1.3* Production, consumption and trade

□ *The production-possibility curve*

The quantity of each good a country produces will depend on her factor endowments and on her technical knowledge. By 'factor endowments' we mean the amounts of factors of production the country possesses – usually assumed to be fixed. If we were to continue thinking in Ricardian terms, there would be only one factor of production – labour – and the technology assumption would be that each additional unit of labour produces the same increase in output – constant marginal and average products. This would ensure that the opportunity costs of production would be constant. We shall pursue the development of this Ricardian model in Chapter 2. Here we shall consider the more general case of the increasing opportunity cost or concave production-possibility curve.

The production-possibility curve is the boundary of all those combinations of the two goods which the country can produce. By definition then, the country can, with its given factor endowments and technology, produce anywhere inside or on the production-possibility curve, but cannot produce outside it. An example of a concave production-possibility curve is given in Figure 1.1. A country producing inside its production-possibility curve, say at point F, must be using its resources inefficiently, since by moving out towards the boundary, to point E for example, it could produce more of at least one good. The conditions necessary for the efficient use of resources (the Pareto efficiency conditions) are discussed later. For the moment we shall assume that these conditions are met.

Suppose now that the country is producing at point E, on the production-possibility curve. It can increase its output of cloth only by switching factors of production from the wine sector to the cloth sector, and if it does so efficiently then it will move along the production-possibility curve from E to, say, E'. The opportunity cost of increasing its

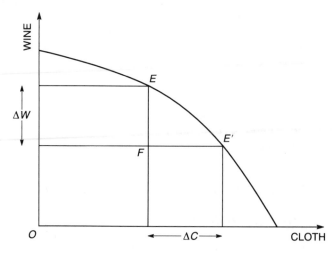

Figure 1.1   *A concave production-possibility curve*

cloth production is of course the reduction in wine production, and we would measure this by the slope of the line drawn from E to E', $\Delta W / \Delta C$.

If we consider only very small increases in the production of cloth then we would measure the opportunity cost of cloth production at point E by the slope of the tangent to the production-possibility curve at that point. Note that since the production-possibility curve in Figure 1.1 is concave the opportunity cost of cloth increases as we increase the production of cloth (the slope of the production-possibility curve is greater at E' than at E). A concave production-possibility curve, frequently assumed in trade theory, is referred to as an increasing cost production-possibility curve. Such a relationship could arise in an economy with only one factor, say labour, if some workers are especially efficient in the production of cloth, others in the production of wine, and we transfer workers so that we obtain the greatest increase in the output of cloth for a given reduction in the output of wine. Alternatively, we could obtain such a production-possibility curve with two or more factors even if the factors are homogeneous, as in the Heckscher–Ohlin model discussed in Chapter 3.

As we shall see in Chapter 2, the assumptions of the Ricardian model are such that the production-possibility curve is a straight line – the constant opportunity cost case. We may under certain conditions, such as strongly increasing returns to scale, obtain a decreasing cost production-possibility curve, which must then be convex towards the origin. Discussion of this case is postponed until Chapter 4.

The shape of the production-possibility curve may differ between the short and the long run if some factors are more difficult to move between

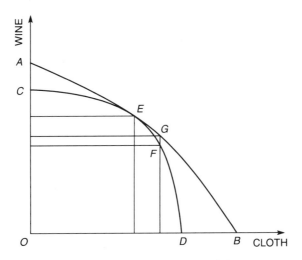

Figure 1.2   *Long- and short-run production-possibility curves*

sectors than others. We shall explore this in more depth in Chapter 4, where we consider the Specific Factors Model as a shorter run version of the Heckscher–Ohlin model. Here it is sufficient to note that the short-run production-possibility curve may lie inside the long-run curve, as in Figure 1.2, where AB is the long-run, CD the short-run production-possibility curve and point E shows the current output mix. We would expect such an outcome if in the short run the adaptability of the economy is low, say because it is difficult to transfer capital between sectors or because workers are specialised, so that we would have to give up a large amount of wine in order to obtain a given increase in cloth production (the move from E to F in Figure 1.2). If the adaptability is higher in the long run, because, say, capital is now more easily transferred or workers may be retrained, then less wine may need be foregone in order to obtain the given increase in cloth production (the move from E to G in Figure 1.2).

Relative commodity prices will determine the production mix, i.e. where we are on the production-possibility curve. If we assume perfect competition in the factor markets then we may show that the economy will operate on the production-possibility curve, and that the slope of the curve at any point is the ratio of marginal costs at that production mix (and of course the opportunity cost of production). If there is also perfect competition in the goods market then firms will produce where price is equal to marginal cost. Hence, for any given price ratio for the two goods we know that production must take place at that point on the production-possibility curve where it has slope equal to the price ratio for the two goods. Thus, if the ratio of the price of cloth to the price of wine is that shown by the (negative of) the slope of the line $P_0 P_0$ in Figure 1.3, the production mix must be the point shown as A.

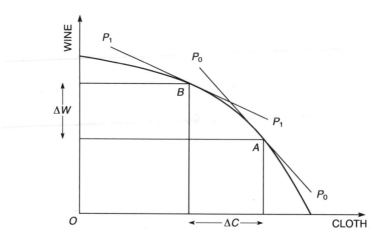

Figure 1.3   *The role of shifting prices*

If the relative price of wine increases to that shown by the slope of the line P_1P_1 then the production mix must move to that shown by point *B*. Production of wine has increased and of cloth has decreased, with factors moving from cloth to wine production, the marginal cost of wine increasing, and the marginal cost of cloth decreasing.

□ Community indifference curves

If we are referring to the demand of only one consumer then we can use indifference curves to illustrate the demand conditions and as a measure of the well-being of that consumer. In international trade however we are concerned with a whole community or nation, and matters become more complicated. As it is not possible to draw any easy analogy in going from one consumer to many, we cannot say that indifference curves can be used to illustrate the demand conditions of a whole nation, let alone the well-being of that nation, in the same way that they can be used for a single consumer, unless some very restrictive assumptions are used. We shall deal with this problem in more depth in Chapter 5, but for the moment we shall summarise the standard results.

Consider the simplest case, that of two consumers, each given an initial endowment of cloth and wine. If the two consumers are free to exchange wine and cloth then they will do so as long as at least one of them can gain from the exchange and the other does not lose. Once neither can gain from any further exchange without the other losing then exchange will cease and they will be at an 'efficient' point. Suppose this efficient point is P_1 in Figure 1.4, where the axes show the total amounts of cloth and wine available to the two individuals. At point P_1 the available amounts of cloth

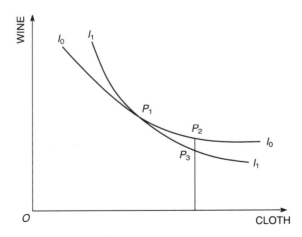

Figure 1.4 *Community indifference curves*

and wine have been distributed in a particular way between the two individuals, giving individual 1 a utility level of u_1, say, and individual 2 a utility level of u_2.

Suppose now that we reduce the amount of wine available in the economy but increase the amount of cloth, and that we choose these two changes so that, after making any exchanges they wish, the two individuals are exactly as well off as they were at point P_1, and let this point be P_2. We may assume that since each individual is indifferent between being at P_1 or at P_2 then the community consisting of those two individuals is also indifferent between being at P_1 or P_2. We may say that P_1 and P_2 are points on the same *community indifference curve*, shown as $I_0 I_0$ in Figure 1.4.

But suppose now that we had taken the same total amount of wine and cloth as those which gave us the efficient point P_1, but gave initially more wine and cloth to individual 1 and therefore less of both to individual 2. We have changed the distribution of income in favour of individual 1, and even after the two individuals have exchanged until they reach an efficient point it is unlikely that that point will yield the same levels of utility to both individuals as they had in our first example. Individual 1 will have more utility, say u_1^* ($> u_1$) and individual 2 will have less, say u_2^* ($< u_2$). In general we cannot claim that the well-being of the community is the same with this new distribution of income as it was with the initial distribution. Thus, point P_1 may be consistent with two different levels of well-being for the community.

Moreover, with our second distribution of income, it is unlikely that the reduction in the initial stock of wine in the economy assumed in obtaining our move from P_1 to P_2 along curve $I_0 I_0$ can be balanced exactly by the same increase in the initial amount of cloth available. Suppose that more cloth is needed to compensate for the loss in wine with our new income distribution. The bundle of goods needed to give both individuals the same level of utility as they enjoy at P_1 may now be that shown by point P_3. As, with our new income distribution, both individuals have exactly the same level of utility at P_1 and P_3, these two points must lie on the same community indifference curve, shown as $I_1 I_1$.

We therefore have the problems that in general any point in our diagram may show different levels of well-being (or welfare) for the community as a whole, and that community indifference curves for different income distributions may intersect one another. These problems can only be resolved by making the assumption that we can judge a given reduction in the utility of one individual to be exactly compensated for by a given increase in the utility of the other (employing a *social welfare function*).

The commonly made assumptions that all consumers have the same preferences and that these preferences obey the mathematical restriction known as *homotheticity* are not sufficient in themselves to resolve the

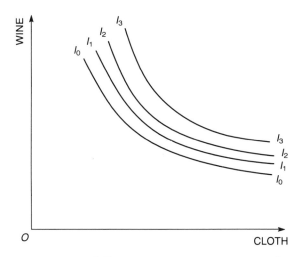

Figure 1.5 *Community indifference curves assuming optimal income redistribution*

problems, nor is the assumption that the distribution of income can in some way be held constant. If, however, we are prepared to assume that redistribution is costless and that any given bundle of goods can be allocated between consumers so that welfare is maximised according to our social welfare function then we derive a set of community indifference curves where no two curves intersect, and the further a curve is from the origin then the higher the level of national welfare it represents. Such a set of indifference curves, derived on the assumption of this optimal redistribution of income, is shown in Figure 1.5.

These assumptions are heroic, and when we come to consider the question of the gains from trade in more depth we shall abandon them. Until then however we shall employ them in order to benefit from the convenience the community indifference curves offer in setting out the various models of international trade we shall develop in the following chapters.

■ 1.4 The gains from trade
□ *The gains from trade restated*

We can now restate the meaning of the gains from trade by combining the supply side of the economy (the production-possibility curve) and the demand side (the community indifference curves). If there is perfect competition then the economy concerned reaches equilibrium under

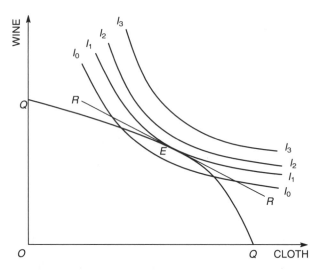

Figure 1.6   *Equilibrium under autarky*

autarky at the point where the production-possibility curve is tangential to a community indifference curve. This point, shown as E in Figure 1.6, is an optimum since the indifference curve I_1 is the highest that can be obtained given the constraint shown by the production-possibility curve. At E the marginal rate of substitution in consumption (the slope of the indifference curve) is equal to the opportunity cost in production (the slope of the production-possibility curve). The price ratio that would be produced by such an equilibrium is shown by the slope of the common tangent RR.

The possibility of trading means that the country can produce and consume at prices that differ from those prevailing in isolation. Suppose that the international terms of trade are given by the price line TT in Figure 1.7, so that cloth is relatively more expensive in the international market than it is in the home market. Domestic producers will take advantage of this fact and move some factors of production from wine to cloth. The reallocation of factors of production will continue until the production point has moved to P, where the price line TT is tangential to the production-possibility curve. This means that the marginal rate of transformation in production equals the international terms of trade. With production at P, cloth can be exported and wine imported in any combination along the price line TT.

The highest possible indifference curve that can be reached given this new, less restricting, constraint is I_3 at point C, where the indifference curve is tangential to the price line. The marginal rate of substitution in consumption is thus also equal to the international terms of trade. Given the production-possibility curve and the international price ratio, point C

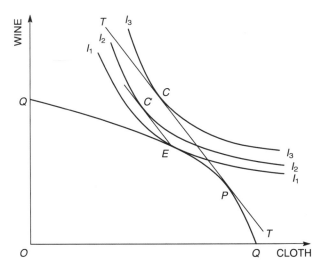

Figure 1.7 *Equilibrium under free trade*

represents the best point the society can achieve, and the move from indifference curve I_1 to indifference curve I_3 may be interpreted as the gain to be obtained from the move to free trade.[4]

It is sometimes useful to think of the gains from trade as consisting of two parts: one depending on the possibility for exchange, the other on the possibility for specialisation in production. If for some reason the country could not change its pattern of production, it would have to continue producing at point E. It could still however gain from trade by exchanging cloth for wine at the international price ratio, its consumption point moving from E to C' on indifference curve I_2 (the price line EC' is parallel to TT). Indifference curve I_2 represents a higher level of welfare than I_1. We refer to this increase in welfare as the *gain from exchange*.

This, however, would not represent an optimal situation, because the marginal rate at which wine can be transformed into cloth by transferring factors of production within the economy differs from the marginal rate at which wine can be traded for cloth in the international market. The economy can make further gains by reducing its production of wine, increasing its production of cloth, and exchanging wine for cloth through trade. It can maximise its gain from such *specialisation in production* by moving to point P.

☐ *The flaw in Ricardo's argument*

It is important to remember that community indifference curves such as the ones in Figure 1.7 can be constructed only if income is redistributed optimally. When moving production from E to P the income distribution will move in favour of the factors of production especially well suited to the production of cloth, the country's export good, while it will move against those factors more suited to the production of wine. The owners of some factors of production will therefore gain by the move to free trade, but others will lose, and the income distribution will change. Only if income is redistributed optimally can we say unambiguously that the society gains from free trade. This was the point that Ricardo and the classical economists overlooked in their argument about the benefits of trade, although they did recognise that trade would change the income distribution. Free trade leads to a potential increase in welfare for everyone (the national income increases), but this increase can only be realised for each individual if income is redistributed appropriately.

This result causes problems for the proponents of economic liberalism. Either they must accept that while free trade is beneficial for the community as a whole some members of the community must lose, or they must accept a policy of redistribution accomplished through intervention.

■ *1.5* Offer curves

Before concluding this chapter, we shall also introduce another standard tool of analysis in international economics, the *offer curve*.

We have seen how, when countries trade with each other, the international terms of trade are established by the interaction of supply and demand in each country. Another way of stating this interaction is by the use of offer curves, first used by Edgeworth and Marshall, and since then often used in international economics, especially for pedagogical purposes. The derivation of a country's offer curve from its production-possibility curve and its community indifference curves is moderately complicated, but offer curves will prove of use when we discuss the theory of tariffs in a later chapter, and so we shall consider one way of deriving them here.

Figure 1.8 shows a production-possibility curve and a set of community indifference curves for a country. Autarkic equilibrium would be at point E. If the country is able to trade at the international price ratio shown by the line T_2 then it will produce at point P_2 and consume at point C_2 on indifference curve I_2. Exports of cloth will be O_2P_2, and imports of wine will be O_2C_2. If the terms of trade were to increase to those shown by the line T_3T_3 then production would shift to P_3, consumption to C_3, with cloth exports becoming O_3P_3 and wine imports changing to O_3C_3, and the country would reach the higher indifference curve I_3.

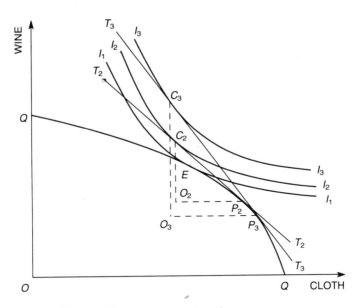

Figure 1.8 *Equilibria under international trade*

Figure 1.9 shows the exports of cloth plotted against the imports of wine at these two terms of trade. At the terms of trade shown by the line OT_2, the country exports OX_2 of cloth (equal to O_2P_2 in Figure 1.8) and imports OM_2 of wine (equal to O_2C_2 in Figure 1.8). At the higher terms of trade shown by the line OT_3, the country exports OX_3 of cloth (equal to O_3P_3) and imports OM_3 of wine (equal to O_3C_3). The set of all such points defines the country's offer curve. The offer curve therefore shows how the country's exports of cloth and imports of wine would change as the price ratio obtainable on the international market changes.

The form of the offer curve depends on the forms of the country's production-possibility curve and community indifference curves. Note that the offer curve drawn in Figure 1.9 starts off with a positive slope as we move from the origin, but becomes negatively sloped if the world price ratio increases sufficiently. Initially, as the country starts trading it is prepared to offer more cloth in exchange for more wine as the relative price of cloth increases. In such cases we would say that the offer curve is *elastic*.

As the volume of trade increases however the country may be prepared to offer less cloth at the margin in exchange for wine imports. If trade continues to increase then the country could become so unwilling to accept any more wine imports that it reduces its cloth exports, even though the terms of trade are becoming more favourable, and the offer curve then

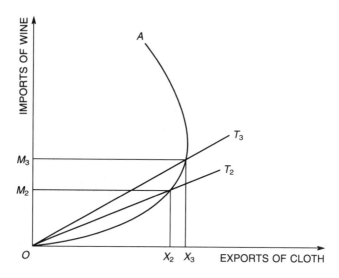

Figure 1.9   *Offer curve for the cloth exporting country*

becomes negatively sloped. The offer curve is usually referred to as being *inelastic* in such cases.

When we derived the offer curve, we argued as though the terms of trade were changing for some exogenous reason, and then derived the shape of the curve. This was a pedagogical device, and must not be misunderstood. The offer curve is a general equilibrium concept. The curve is determined jointly by production and consumption conditions in the country concerned, and we cannot determine the terms of trade until we have the equivalent information for the other country concerned.

We can construct an offer curve for country B by analogous reasoning. We would expect it to have the same general shape as the offer curve for country A, being positively sloped at low volumes of trade, bending away from the exports axis as trade volumes increase, and possibly becoming negatively sloped at high terms of trade. We must remember of course that for country B the export good will be wine.

With that in mind, we might expect the offer curve for country B to look something like the curve OB in Figure 1.10. Curve OA is of course country A's offer curve. The offer curves of the two countries intersect at point E. This point defines the free trade equilibrium for the two countries. Country A will export OC of cloth, which country B is prepared to import in exchange for exporting OW of wine to country A, precisely the amount of wine that A wishes to import. The international terms of trade will be given by the slope of the line OT.

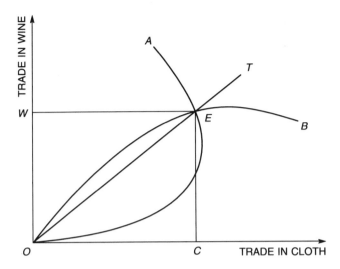

Figure 1.10   *Free trade equilibrium shown with offer curves*

In Figure 1.10 the free trade equilibrium is where country A's offer curve is inelastic but country B's offer curve is elastic. Suppose A were to become more willing to trade at any given terms of trade, perhaps because her production-possibility curve had moved out due an improvement in technology. We would show this by moving A's offer curve outwards. A would find it possible to increase both her exports and her imports, although her terms of trade would deteriorate. If on the other hand B's offer curve were to move outwards then not only would her terms of trade become worse, she would also find that her increased exports of wine would only exchange for a lower volume of cloth imports.

The position of a country facing an elastic offer curve from its trading partner is therefore quite different in some respects to that of a country facing an elastic offer curve when it comes to increasing exports. However, in both the cases discussed an expansion of exports brought about a worsening of the terms of trade.

There is however one particular case where this does not happen, and that is where the country concerned is so small in terms of its partner's market that it can increase its exports and imports without affecting the prices at which it trades. The small country is said to face a *perfectly elastic* offer curve, which must be a straight line through the origin. Such a situation is shown in Figure 1.11. Whether country A's offer curve moves in to or away from the origin, the terms of trade it faces will remain those given by the slope of OB. Of course, if B's offer curve changes then the terms of trade facing A will change. If country A is small then it has to take the international terms of trade as given.

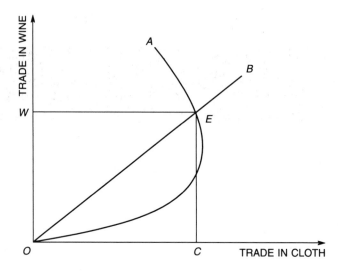

Figure 1.11   *Free trade equilibrium for a small country*

☐ *Notes*

1   David Ricardo (1772–1823) accumulated a fortune during the Napoleonic wars as a member of the London stock exchange. He then retired, turning to theoretical economics, and in 1819 became a Member of Parliament. In 1817 he published his main work, *Principles of Political Economy and Taxation*, which contains the first rigorous exposition of the classical theory of value and distribution; in Chapter 7, 'On Foreign Trade', Ricardo expounds the theory of comparative advantage.

2   Adam Smith (1723–90) was Professor of Moral Philosophy at Glasgow University. The first major figure of classical economics, he introduced the theory of value and taught the blessings of the unhampered market ('the invisible hand'). His major work, *The Wealth of Nations*, was published in 1776.

3   Robert Torrens (1780–1864), an officer in the British Army during the Napoleonic wars, later turned to economics and published a pamphlet in 1815, *Essay on the External Corn Trade*, which contains what seems to be the earliest formulation of the theory of comparative advantage. He also made significant contributions to classical monetary theory and policy. In 1831 he became a Member of Parliament.

4   For a justification of this statement in modern analytical terms, see Grandmont and McFadden (1972), pp. l09ff.

■ *Chapter 2* ■

The Classical Model and the Specific Factors Model

2.1 Introduction	*2.3* The specific factors
2.2 The classical model	model

■ *2.1* Introduction

In this chapter we shall examine the classical model more formally than in Chapter 1, and will use that model to discuss the effects of the move to free trade on real wages in the two countries. We shall then examine the specific factors model, which may be thought of in one way as a logical generalisation of the classical model, certainly in that we may use similar techniques in deriving the production-possibility curve. Although the specific factors model only entered the literature fairly recently, some economists have argued that it is in fact the model used by the classical economists in their discussion of the economic effects of the Corn Laws.

■ *2.2* The classical model

□ *Production possibilities in the classical model*

We shall approach the classical model using a 4-quadrant diagram (which will be used later in deriving the specific factors model). The basic assumptions of the classical model are: (1) labour is the only factor of production, is in fixed total supply in each country, and is perfectly mobile within each country (i.e. between the two industries) but perfectly immobile between countries; (2) the marginal (and average) products of labour are constant in each industry, but these productivities differ between the two countries in at least one of the industries;[1] (3) there is universal perfect competition; (4) there are no impediments to trade such as tariffs and transport costs.

In Figure 2.1, which relates to one of the two countries, the south-west quadrant shows the labour constraint for the economy, the fixed supply of

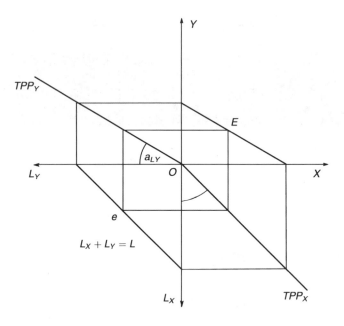

Figure 2.1   *Deriving the classical production-possibility curve*

labour, L, being allocated between the two industries under full employment so that $L_X + L_Y = L$, L_X being employment in the X industry and L_Y employment in the Y industry. This is consistent with assumption (1).

The south-east and north-west quadrants show the total physical product functions for the X and the Y industries (TPP_X and TPP_Y respectively). These functions are consistent with assumption (2): they are straight lines from the origin, their slopes being the (constant) average physical products of labour, a_{LX} and a_{LY} respectively.

By choosing any full employment allocation of labour between the two industries, such as point e, we can then derive the corresponding point on the production-possibility curve for the country, point E in this instance. This will also be a straight line, with slope determined by the ratio of the two marginal product coefficients.

That this is so may be shown by considering the effects of transferring ΔL from the X industry to the Y industry. The reduction in the output of X will be $\Delta X = -a_{LX}\Delta L$, while the increase in Y output will be $\Delta Y = a_{LY}\Delta L$. It follows that the slope of the production-possibility curve (the marginal rate of transformation in production) is

$$MRTP = \frac{\Delta y}{\Delta x} = -\frac{a_{LY}\Delta L}{a_{LX}\Delta L} = -\frac{a_{LY}}{a_{LX}} \qquad (2.1)$$

This is also of course the opportunity cost of Y, and with perfect competition and perfectly mobile labour will also be the ratio of marginal costs. That this is so may be shown as follows: if MC_X is the cost of producing an extra unit of X and w is the money wage then, since this can only be done by employing more labour in the X industry, we must have $MC_X.\Delta X = w.\Delta L_X$; similarly $MC_Y.\Delta Y = w.\Delta L_Y$; since as we move along the production-possibility curve we must have $\Delta L_Y = -\Delta L_X$, it follows that $\Delta Y/\Delta X = -MC_X/MC_Y$.

Note that under autarky relative prices will be determined by the slope of the production-possibility curve (i.e. by the ratio of the marginal costs in the two industries); the nature of tastes is irrelevant to relative commodity prices under autarky, though not of course to outputs. However, tastes are of great importance in the free trade situation, for they will help to determine the terms and the volume of trade.

☐ *Real wages under autarky*

With perfect competition and perfectly mobile labour the money wage rate will be the same in both industries, and labour will be paid the value of its marginal product. It follows that $w = P_X a_{LX} = P_Y a_{LY}$, and that real wages in terms of X and Y are given by $w/P_X = a_{LX}$ and $w/P_Y = a_{LY}$ respectively. Note that we have internal consistency in that under perfect competition firms will produce where price is equal to marginal cost, so that $P_X = MC_X$ and $P_Y = MC_Y$, implying that $P_X/P_Y = MC_X/MC_Y$, while we have shown that $MC_X/MC_Y = a_{LY}/a_{LX}$ and from the above that $P_X/P_Y = a_{LY}/a_{LX}$.

☐ *Free trade with complete specialisation in both countries*

If, as we observed above, relative prices under autarky are determined solely by the relative marginal products of labour, and these are constant by assumption, it follows that there will only be trade if the ratio of the marginal products of labour in the X and Y industries is different between the two countries.[2] Figure 2.2 shows the case where the marginal product of labour in the Y industry is higher in country B than in country A ($b_{LY} > a_{LY}$), as shown by the steeper slope of TPP_Y^B compared to TPP_Y^A, while the marginal product of labour in the X industry is the same in both countries. For simplicity it has been assumed in Figure 2.2 that the two countries have the same fixed labour supply.

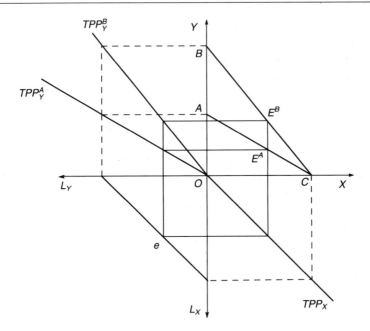

Figure 2.2 *Different technology results in different production-possibility curves*

Note that point e on the labour constraint now gives rise to point A for country A and point B for country B. It is evident that B's production-possibility curve will be steeper than A's, and will lie outside A's at all points except the intersection with the X axis. It follows that the Y good must be relatively cheaper in B under autarky, which is consistent with the assumption that labour is more productive in the Y sector in B than in A.

We may deduce immediately that: (i) since $b_{LY} > a_{LY}$ the real wage in terms of the Y good must be higher in B than in A; (ii) since $b_{LX} = a_{LX}$ the real wage in terms of the X good must be the same in both countries.[3] Note that the tastes in the two countries have no role to play in determining the real wage under autarky.

If the two countries are of 'equal size' (as suggested by Figure 2.2) then the terms of trade under free trade will settle somewhere between the autarky price ratios in the two countries, with A specialising completely in the production of X and B specialising completely in the production of Y.

The complete specialisation follows from the fact that as long as either country is producing both goods the opportunity cost of its export good is constant (determined by the slope of its production-possibility curve). So long as the relative price of its export good in trade is higher than that opportunity cost there will be an incentive to switch resources into the production of that good, and equalisation of the relative price and the opportunity cost can only come about by changes in the relative price (the terms of trade).[4] Either the international terms of trade become equal to the domestic opportunity cost ratio (of which more later), or the country must produce only its export good so that it breaks free of the opportunity cost constraint. In the instance we are considering (countries of the same size) there will be complete specialisation by both countries.

Free trade equilibrium will, as usual, require a common terms of trade and equality of exports and imports for each good; such an outcome is shown in Figure 2.3 (where the difference in slope between the two countries' production-possibility curves is exaggerated for the sake of clarity, and the two countries are no longer assumed to have the same labour supply).

The indifference curves in Figure 2.3 are drawn to reflect the assumption that the two countries have identical and homothetic tastes; this assumption is not crucial to the model. B's production possibility curve is the bold line running from point S_Y^B on the Y axis, while A's production-possibility curve is the flatter line running from point S_X^A on the X axis.

Under free trade the (common) terms of trade will lie somewhere between the slopes of the two production-possibility curves, as shown in Figure 2.3 by the two parallel lines from S_X^A and from S_Y^B. A will specialise in producing the X good, and so will produce at point S_X^A, while B will specialise in producing the Y good, and so will produce at point S_Y^B.

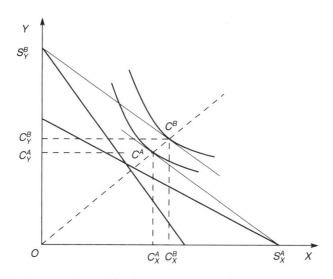

Figure 2.3 *Free trade with both countries specialising completely*

With identical and homothetic tastes and common relative commodity prices the two countries must have their consumption points on the same straight line from the origin (C^A and C^B). A will consume C_X^A of X and C_Y^A of Y, exporting $S_X^A - C_X^A$ of good X and importing C_Y^A of good Y. B will consume C_X^B of X and C_Y^B of Y, exporting $S_Y^B - C_Y^B$ of good Y and importing C_X^B of good X. In the free trade equilibrium we must of course have imports matching exports, i.e. $S_X^A - C_X^A = C_X^B$ and $S_Y^B - C_Y^B = C_Y^A$.

The effect of the move to free trade on real wages

The earlier analysis for country A told us that under autarky the real wage in A in terms of the X good was a_{LX}, while in terms of the Y good it was a_{LY}. By a parallel argument, the real wage in B in terms of the X good was b_{LX} and in terms of the Y good was b_{LY}. Since by assumption $a_{LX} = b_{LX}$ and $a_{LY} < b_{LY}$, it follows that the real wages measured in terms of the X good were the same in both countries under autarky, while real wages measured in terms of the Y good were lower in A than in B. The real wage must therefore have been higher in B than in A under autarky.[5]

As country A is now producing only the X good the wage rate in A, w^A, must be determined only by the marginal product of labour in the X industry there and the price of the X good. Therefore we must have $w^A = P_X a_{LX}$, where P_X is the price of X under free trade. The real wage rate in A in terms of the X good is thus a_{LX}. That is, free trade does not change the real wage rate measured in terms of the export good. This result applies equally to the real wage in B measured in terms of its export good (Y).

However, for both countries the import good must now be relatively cheaper, so if labour in both countries is equally well off in terms of its export good then it must have become better off in terms of its import good. Hence free trade must make labour better off in absolute terms in both countries.

The other obvious question to ask is whether free trade leads to the equalisation of real wage rates between the two countries, or at least to a partial convergence.[6] Since $w^A = P_X . a_{LX}$ and $w^B = P_Y . b_{LY}$ it follows that

$$\frac{w^A}{w^B} = \frac{a_{LX} P_X}{b_{LY} P_y} \tag{2.2}$$

Wages will only be equalised if we get a specific combination of relative marginal productivities in the two different goods in the two countries and the terms of trade (which are determined by demand conditions). We have no reason to expect this to happen in general, and so we must conclude that free trade will not generally equalise real wages between the two countries.

Free trade with incomplete specialisation in the large country

If the two countries are of sufficiently different sizes then trading with the small country will not allow the large country to specialise completely in the production of its export good if the small country is not able to produce and export sufficient of the other good to meet the large country's requirements. In such a case free trade will have no effect on the commodity price ratio in the large country since that must still be tied to the marginal productivities of labour in the two industries in that country; the terms of trade will in fact be the same as the autarky price ratio in the large country. Such a situation is shown in Figure 2.4, where A is the 'large' country.

Country A produces at point S^A on its production-possibility curve and consumes at point C^A, which must be the same consumption point as under autarky. Country B specialises in the production of Y, producing at S_Y^B and consuming at C^B. For equilibrium we must have the same relative price of X (the line between S_Y^B and C^B has the same slope as A's production-possibility curve) and $S_Y^B - C_Y^B = C_Y^A - S_Y^A$, $C_X^B = S_X^A - C_X^A$.

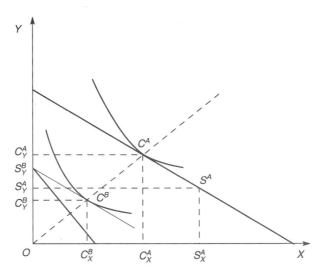

Figure 2.4 *Free trade with incomplete specialisation in the large country*

Since the relative price of X has not changed in A, and A is still producing both goods, the real wage in A cannot change on the move to free trade. However, as before, the real wage in B will stay the same in terms of its export good (Y) and will rise in terms of its import good (X), so that labour in B gains by the move to free trade.

■ 2.3 The specific factors model

The classical model presented above is limited in that it only considers one factor and assumes a fixed-coefficient technology. As we noted earlier, classical economists discussing the economic impact of the Corn Laws did so in terms of a model which envisaged additional factors which were specific to particular sectors. This model was resurrected and put into modern clothing by R.W. Jones in 1971 as a three-factor, two-good, two-country model with neoclassical production functions, now commonly known as the *specific factors model*.[7]

The essence of the model is that one factor, labour, is assumed to be mobile between the two industries within each country, with two other factors each specific to the industry in which they are employed. There are two variants of this: either two individual immobile factors are identified, one, 'capital', used only in the 'manufacturing' sector and the other, 'land', used only in the 'agricultural' sector;[8] or one type of immobile factor is considered, usually named 'capital', which comes in two forms, X-industry-specific capital and Y-industry-specific capital.[9] In both variants it is usual to assume homogeneous factors in fixed supply, constant returns to scale, diminishing marginal productivity, perfectly competitive markets, etc.

The 'labour, land, capital' variant is the extension of the classical Ricardian model, with differences in the productivity of labour in each sector between the two countries arising from differences in their relative endowments of capital and land, but with, of course, diminishing marginal productivity of labour. The 'sector-specific capital' variant of the model can be thought of as a medium-term version of the Heckscher–Ohlin model, which we shall meet in Chapter 3, with capital immobile between the two industries in the medium term but mobile between them in the long term.

☐ *Production possibilities in the specific factors model*

We shall first consider the derivation of the production-possibility curve for one of the countries under the assumptions of the specific factors model, basing our analysis on that used by R.W. Jones, and for clarity we shall work in terms of three factors. We shall identify the agricultural good as X, with land (H) being the factor specific to that industry, and the manufactured good as Y, with capital (K) specific to that sector. Labour (L) is assumed to be employed in both sectors and to be mobile between them.

In Figure 2.5, which obviously bears a close similarity to Figure 2.1, TPP_X and TPP_Y are the total physical product curves for labour in the X and Y industries respectively. The slope of each curve at any point is given by the marginal physical product of labour at the corresponding labour input, the shape of the curves thus reflecting the assumption of diminishing marginal physical product. Each total physical product curve is dependent on the amount of the fixed factor available in that sector. L_X and L_Y are the amounts of labour employed in the production of X and Y respectively, the constraint imposed by the assumption that the supply of labour is fixed at L being shown by the 45° line in the south-west quadrant given by $L_X + L_Y = L$.

We derive the production-possibility curve for this country by varying the amounts of labour employed in X and Y production along the labour constraint line in the south-west quadrant, in each case using the

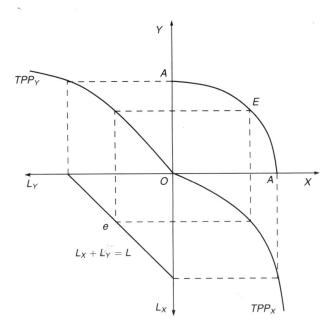

Figure 2.5 *Deriving the production-possibility curve in the specific factors model*

appropriate total physical product curve to determine the outputs of X and Y, and then transferring those outputs to the north-east quadrant. Three such points are shown in Figure 2.5, the two which identify the end points of the production-possibility curve (i.e. all the labour employed in either X or Y), and a third where the available labour is split between the two industries.

The slope of the production-possibility curve at any point is given by the ratio of the marginal physical product of labour in Y (MPL_Y) to the marginal physical product of labour in X (MPL_X). To show this we consider the effects of a transfer of ΔL of labour from the X industry to the Y industry. The increase in Y output will then be $\Delta Y = MPL_Y \Delta L$, while the fall in X output will be $\Delta X = -MPL_X \Delta L$. It follows that

$$\frac{\Delta Y}{\Delta X} = -\frac{MPL_Y \Delta L}{MPL_X \Delta L} = -\frac{MPL_Y}{MPL_X} \tag{2.3}$$

With perfect competition in all markets and mobile labour this will also be equal to the relative price of the X good, since in each industry firms will employ labour to the point where the wage rate is equal to the value of the marginal product of labour, and hence $w = P_X.MPL_X = P_Y.MPL_Y$, so that $P_X/P_Y = MPL_Y/MPL_X$.

Obviously, if both countries in a two-country world had identical endowments of all three factors, identical technologies, and identical and homothetic tastes, autarky prices would be identical and there would be no basis for trade. On the other hand, we know that to allow more than one difference between countries may lead to an indeterminate result. We shall therefore adopt the usual approach of allowing only one difference between the two countries. We shall consider two examples: firstly where there is a difference in the endowment of one of the specific factors; secondly where there is a difference in the endowment of labour.

Two countries differing in their endowments of capital

Let us now assume that our two countries, A and B, differ only in their endowments of capital, with $K^A > K^B$. This implies that the total physical product curve for Y in country A will lie above that in B, while the total physical product curve for X and the labour constraint will be the same in both countries. Figure 2.6 reflects these assumptions.

Note that the maximum X output must be the same in both countries, while the maximum Y output is inevitably greater in A than in B. Moreover, if the same amount of labour is employed in the X industry

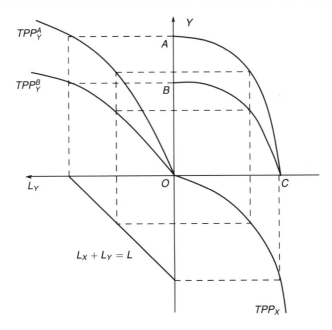

Figure 2.6 *Different capital endowments give different production-possibility curves*

(and hence in the Y industry) in both countries then we may deduce that: (i) the X output will be the same in both A and B; (ii) the Y output in A will be greater than that in B; (iii) the marginal product of labour in the X industry will be the same in both countries, but the marginal product of labour in the Y industry will be greater in A than in B; and hence (iv) the slope of A's production-possibility curve will be greater than that of B's production-possibility curve at the corresponding points.

The last deduction suggests that if we consider points on the two production-possibility curves where they have the same slope then the output of Y will be greater in A than in B and the output of X will be less in A than in B; such a situation is shown in Figure 2.7 by the two tangents of slope θ. The relatively capital-rich country (A) is biased towards the production of the good to which capital is specific (Y).

If we consider the likely autarkic equilibria in A and B under the usual assumption of identical and homothetic tastes in the two countries then it is apparent that country A will have the lower relative price for good Y; that is, $P_X^A/P_Y^A > P_X^B/P_Y^B$.

What we cannot tell from our analysis is whether the autarkic output of X in A is greater or less than in B, and this precludes us from making any unambiguous comparison of factor prices between the two countries under

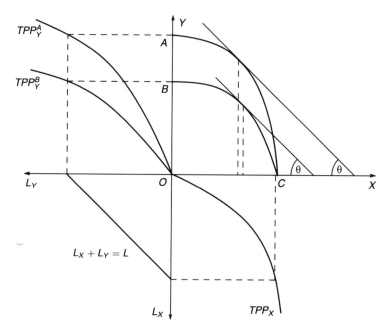

Figure 2.7   *Country A will have the comparative advantage in good Y*

autarky. However, we can be unambiguous about the effects of a move to free trade on factor prices, and on the consequent differences in real factor prices.

☐ *Free trade and factor prices*

As usual, free trade will equalise relative commodity prices in the two countries at some value between the autarky relative prices. In A this will lead to an expansion of Y output and a contraction of X output, with the opposite shifts in the production mix obtaining in B, so that in A there will be a shift of labour from the X sector to the Y sector, while in B there will be a fall in L_Y^B and a rise in L_X^B. We also know from our earlier analysis of the relationship between their production-possibility curves that with the same relative commodity prices in the two countries the quantity of X produced in B must be greater than that produced in A, and therefore that with free trade $L_X^A < L_X^B$ and $L_Y^A > L_Y^B$.

The fall in labour employment in the X industry in A must lead to a decrease in the marginal productivity of land in A, and so the return to land in A, r_H^A, will fall in terms of the X good. Since the X good has become relatively cheaper in A with free trade it follows that r_H^A must also have fallen in terms of the Y good, and so free trade must reduce the real return to land in A.

Conversely, the rise in labour employment in the X industry in B tells us that returns to land in B, r_H^B, must rise in terms of the X good, and since X has now become relatively more expensive in B we know that r_H^B must also have increased in terms of the Y good, so that free trade must increase the real return to land in B. Moreover, since $L_X^A < L_X^B$ and the two countries have the same endowment of land, it follows that the real return to land must be lower in A than in B.

The fall in L_X^A must also lead to an increase in the marginal productivity of labour in the X industry in A, and so to an increase in the real wage measured in terms of the X good, while the corresponding rise in L_Y^A leads to a decrease in the marginal productivity of labour in the Y industry in A, and so to a decrease in the real wage measured in terms of the Y good. Thus we cannot be sure whether the move to free trade makes workers better or worse off in A; workers in A will be more likely to gain the higher the proportion of their incomes they spend on the X good. We may use a similar argument to show that the real wage rate in B will fall in terms of the X good and rise in terms of the Y good, so that again the overall effect of free trade on real wages is ambiguous.

Now consider the real returns to capital in the two countries. The increase in the employment of labour in the Y industry in country A leads to an increase in the marginal productivity of capital, and so to an increase in the return to capital in A in terms of the Y good. Since Y has become relatively more expensive under free trade in A, it must be the case that the return to capital has also increased in terms of the X good, and so we can be clear that real returns to capital have increased overall.

Conversely, the fall in L_Y^B leads to a decrease in the marginal productivity of capital in the Y industry in B, and so to a decrease in the return to capital in terms of the Y good. Since X has become relatively more expensive under free trade in B, it must be the case that the return to capital has also decreased in terms of the X good, and so we can be clear that real returns to capital have fallen overall.

Finally, we have already seen that the real wage rate in A is higher than that in B in terms of the Y good. This implies that the capital–labour ratio in Y production is higher in A than in B, and that in turn implies that the marginal product of capital in the Y sector is lower in A than in B. We may therefore conclude that under free trade the real return to capital is lower in A than in B in terms of both goods.[10]

Many of the results in this section are not surprising. The country which has the larger endowment of capital, the factor specific to the Y industry, has the comparative advantage in the Y good. The move to free trade, with the accompanying changes in relative commodity prices, has an uneven impact on the real returns to factors of production. Labour, being mobile between sectors, tends to lose in terms of one good and to gain in terms of the other, so that its overall position may not be changed significantly. However the two sector-specific factors gain or lose unambiguously; the factor specific to the export sector gains in terms of both goods while the factor specific to the import-competing sector loses in terms of both goods.

Under free trade, with the same relative commodity price in the two countries, the relationship between real returns to factors of production in the two countries is unambiguous. A has the higher endowment of capital, and capital is not free to move from the Y sector, so it is not surprising that the real return to capital will be lower in A. The higher capital endowment in A will also mean a higher employment of labour in the Y sector in A under free trade, and so a lower input of labour into the X sector, and this will necessarily mean that the real return to land is lower in A. On the other hand, the real wage rate will be higher in A, which reflects the fact that labour is free to move between sectors, and has a higher total amount of the specific factors with which to combine in A than in B.

Two countries differing in their endowments of labour

Let us now assume that our two countries, A and B, differ only in their endowments of labour, the mobile factor, with $L^A > L^B$. In terms of the 4-quadrant diagram that we use to derive the production-possibility curve this means that the labour constraint for A, $L_X^A + L_Y^A = L^A$ lies outside the labour constraint for B, $L_X^B + L_Y^B = L^B$. Since the endowments of the specific factors are the same in both countries the total product curves for the two goods will be the same for both countries. Figure 2.8 is consistent with these assumptions.

It is evident that the greater endowment of labour in A allows a greater output of one of the goods for a given output of the other good than in B. This is shown in Figure 2.8, where points β and α_1 correspond to the same X output in both countries, and points β and α_2 to the same Y output in both countries. Country A's production-possibility curve therefore lies outside B's and, unless the rate of decline of the marginal product of labour increases strongly in one or both of the industries, they are likely to be approximately parallel.

We cannot tell *a priori* which country will export which good, or indeed whether there will be trade at all, nor whether A will produce more of both goods than B under autarky or merely more of one good. We must therefore proceed by assuming a particular autarky state.

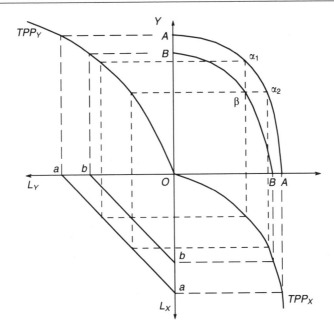

Figure 2.8 *Different production-possibility curves when countries have different labour endowments*

Suppose that X is relatively cheap in country A under autarky, and that A produces more of both goods than country B. We have assumed the same endowments of the specific factors and the same technology in both countries, and this is sufficient to ensure that the input of labour in the production of both goods is higher in A than in B, and thus that the marginal product of labour is lower in both industries in A than in B. Hence we know that the real wage was lower in A than in B under autarky in terms of both goods, and that the real returns to both sector-specific factors were higher in A than in B.

On the other hand, suppose that under autarky the relative price of X was again lower in country A than in country B, but that A produced more X and less Y than B. The higher production of X in A again ensures that more labour will be used in the X industry in A than in B, so that in terms of X the real wage is lower, and the real return to land is higher, in A than in B. Conversely, the lower production of Y in A implies that, in terms of the Y good, the real wage is higher, and the real return to capital lower, in A than in B.

Obviously then in this case we do not know whether labour is better or worse off in country A than in country B; again this depends on the importance of X and Y in the consumption patterns of labour. Further,

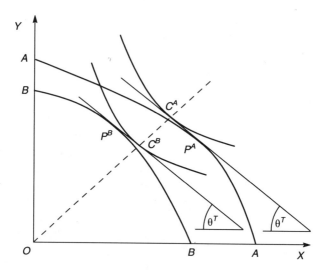

Figure 2.9   *A possible free trade equilibrium*

since land is better off in A than in B in terms of the good that is relatively cheaper in A, we do not know whether returns to land are higher or lower in A than in B in terms of the X good; nor, by the same token, do we know whether returns to capital are lower or higher in A than in B in terms of the X good.

Now suppose that, no matter what the autarkic production mixes, the two countries trade with one another, so that the relative price of X rises in country A and falls in country B, with A switching labour from Y to X production and B making the opposite changes. It is evident that in the free trade equilibrium country A will be producing more X than country B, but again it is not clear whether it will be producing more or less of the Y good. Figure 2.9 shows a free trade case where A is producing less Y (at point P^A) than is B (at P^B) at the commodity price ratio θ^T.

☐ *Free trade and factor prices*

The increase in the production of X in country A under free trade, with the accompanying increase in the use of labour in the X sector there, will lead to an increase in the marginal product of land in A and so to an increase in the real return to land in A measured in terms of the X good. The changes in country B will be in the opposite direction.

As there must be a higher output of X in A than in B under free trade the real return to land in terms of the X good will be higher in A than in B.

Since the Y good becomes relatively cheaper in *A*, and relatively more expensive in *B*, we may conclude that the returns to land in terms of the Y good will also rise in *A* and fall in *B*. Further, since the same relative prices prevail in both countries under free trade, as land in *A* is earning a higher real return in terms of the X good then that must also be the case in terms of the Y good.

The decrease in the production of Y in *A* will lead to a fall in the marginal product of capital in *A*, while the rise in production of Y in *B* will lead to a rise in the marginal product of capital there. Hence we know that the real return to capital measured in terms of the Y good will go down in *A* and up in *B* with free trade. Since the Y good has become cheaper in *A* with trade, and more expensive in *B*, we also know that the real returns to capital have gone down in *A* and up in *B* when measured in terms of the X good. Finally, if *A* produces more of the Y good than *B* under free trade then the real return to capital in *A*, measured in terms of the Y good (and hence in terms of the X good also) will be higher in *A* than in *B*, and vice versa.

The problem of the real return to labour is inevitably more complex (labour being the mobile factor). In *A* the switch of labour from the Y sector to the X sector will lead to an increase in the marginal product of labour in Y and a decrease in its marginal product in X, while in *B* the marginal product of labour will fall in the Y sector and rise in the X sector. These results indicate that the real wage in *A* will rise in terms of the Y good and fall in terms of the X good, with the opposite changes in country *B*. However, the higher X output in country *A* under free trade tells us that the real wage in *A* in terms of the X good (and hence in terms of the Y good) must be lower in that country than in *B*.

Remember that these results are based on the initial assumption that X is relatively cheap in country *A* under autarky. If it were the case that Y was relatively cheap in *A* under autarky then we would find that the results derived for capital would become appropriate for land, and vice versa.

Once again the mobile factor gains in terms of one good and loses in terms of the other in the move from autarky to free trade, so that overall its position may not be very much changed, while the specific factors gain or lose unambiguously in the move, with the factor specific to the export sector gaining and the other immobile factor losing. If we compare real factor rewards between countries under free trade we see that we obtain unambiguous results for wages and for returns to one of the sector-specific factors (the one used in the export sector of the country with the larger labour supply). For the other specific factor we would have an unambiguous result if we knew whether the country with the larger labour supply was producing more of its import-competing good under free trade than was the other country.

□ *Notes*

1   No explicit explanation is given for the existence of these 'technological' differences, but the general view is that Ricardo ascribed them to differences in climate.

2   Note that having the marginal product in one of the industries differ between countries but the other the same will ensure a difference in relative prices under autarky; having both different need not produce a difference in autarkic relative prices.

3   Note that this follows from the particular assumptions made. The original Ricardian model assumed that labour productivities differed between countries in both sectors.

4   When there are increasing costs of production the equalisation of the terms of trade and the opportunity cost ratio comes about through changes in both.

5   Except of course in the extreme case where labour does not consume the Y good!

6   We already know that the real wage was higher in B than in A under autarky and that the move to free trade raises the real wage rate in both countries in terms of a mix of the two goods.

7   Jones (1971).

8   Caves and Jones (1994).

9   See Mayer (1974), Neary (1978) and Neary (1985).

10   Remember that under free trade there is the same commodity price ratio in both countries, so that if the real return to a factor is higher in terms of one good in country B then it must also be higher in terms of the other good.

■ *Chapter 3* ■

The Heckscher–Ohlin Model

■ *3.1* Introduction

In Chapter 2 we discussed the theory of comparative advantage in terms of a one-factor model, where the only factor was labour, and comparative advantage was determined by technological differences, and a three-factor model where labour was the only mobile factor and comparative advantage was determined by differences in the endowment of one of the factors. We saw that in both cases the move to free trade leads to a transfer of the mobile factor from the import-competing sector to the export sector.

The dominant model of comparative advantage in modern economics, the so-called Heckscher–Ohlin model,[1] is a theory of long-term general equilibrium in which the two factors are both mobile between sectors and the cause of trade is different countries having different relative factor endowments. This model gives us some interesting insights into the effects of trade on factor use and factor rewards, not least that the free movement of goods between countries may bring about the equalisation of real payments to factors of production, even though those factors are by assumption unable to move between countries in search of higher real rewards. This does not happen in the classical model unless we get a particular combination of technologies. Nor does it happen in the specific factors model in general, even though we argued in Chapter 2 that the specific factors model in its industry-specific-capital formulation may be thought of as a medium-term version of the Heckscher–Ohlin model.

trade is equivalent to X or Ming factors!

To understand the Heckscher–Ohlin theory of trade we need to introduce additional geometric tools, and this will be our first task in this chapter.

■ 3.2 Factors of production and the production-possibility curve

□ *Linearly homogeneous production functions*

A production function shows the relationship between inputs of factors of production, in the following analysis capital (K) and labour (L), and the output of a good (or goods if we assume joint production). For many reasons it would be advantageous if we could use unspecified production functions. This means that to derive the results we wanted, to prove certain theorems, we would need to assume only that a relationship existed between inputs and outputs; we would not have to assume anything specific about the nature of this relationship.

As a matter of fact, when we come to the effects of technical progress on international trade, we will refer to results that have been obtained using only this weak assumption. But for most of the theorems of trade theory a more specific relationship between inputs and output has to be assumed.

The standard constraint on the production function that we will have to assume is that it is linearly homogeneous or, as it often put, shows constant returns to scale. By this it is meant that the production function is such that if the inputs are all increased by a certain proportion then output is also increased by that same proportion. If, for instance, both labour and capital inputs are increased by 10 per cent then output is also increased by 10 per cent.

This of course means that, as long as the firm cannot affect factor prices, its long-run average cost must be constant (it will cost 10 per cent more to buy the additional inputs). That in turn implies that marginal cost is constant (and equal to average cost).

Constant returns to scale production functions always display positive marginal products of the factors. We shall assume as well that these marginal products are decreasing: that is, as more of one factor is added to a fixed amount of the other factor then the marginal product of the varying factor decreases (and the marginal product of the fixed factor increases).

Constant returns to scale production functions have another property that will make our theorising much more easy. The marginal product of a factor of production depends only on the ratio between the amount of that factor used and the amount of the other factor. That is, if we hold the capital–labour ratio constant (so that we increase or decrease both capital and labour by the same proportion), the marginal product of labour will remain the same, and so will the marginal product of capital. This allows us to state the earlier result in a more simple form: increasing (decreasing) the capital–labour ratio will increase (decrease) the marginal product of labour and decrease (increase) the marginal product of capital.

It also gives us another useful result. The slope of an isoquant is determined by the ratio of the marginal products of the factors of production. Since both these marginal products do not change if we keep capital and labour in the same proportion, their ratio does not change either. This means that all isoquants have the same slope if the capital–labour ratio is the same. This important relationship is illustrated in Figure 3.1.

Along any ray from the origin, such as OR^A, the two factors are combined in the same proportion. Thus Oa_0 of capital divided by Oa'_0 of labour at A_0 equals Oa_1 of capital divided by Oa'_1 of labour at A_1, which also equals Oa_2 of capital divided by Oa'_2 of labour at A_2, and so on. Therefore the marginal productivity of labour is the same along all of OR^A, as is the marginal productivity of capital.

The same holds for OR^B, so the marginal productivity of labour is the same at B_0, B_1 and B_2, and analogously for the marginal productivity of capital. In the same vein, the marginal productivities of the two factors of production are constant along OR^B.

We can now compare the marginal productivity of labour along the isoquant X_0X_0, for instance at the two points A_0 and B_0. The marginal productivity of labour is higher at B_0 than it is at A_0 because the ratio of capital to labour – the capital intensity – is higher at B_0 than at A_0. Each worker has more capital, more machinery, to work with at B_0 than at A_0.

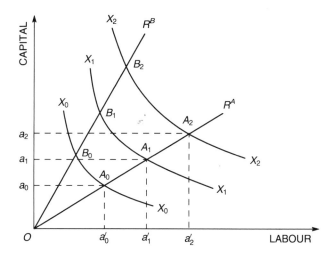

Figure 3.1 *Isoquants with constant returns to scale*

The more capital-intensive the methods of production are, the higher is the marginal productivity of labour. In the same way, the more labour-intensive the methods of production, the higher is the marginal productivity of capital.

One final property of constant returns to scale production functions that is sometimes useful is the 'product exhaustion theorem' (strictly, Euler's Theorem). This says that if each factor is paid an amount equal to the value of its marginal product (as would be the case if factor markets are perfectly competitive) then the revenue raised by selling the output will be just sufficient to pay the factors of production.

But what will determine which methods of production are used? How will labour and capital actually be combined? This cannot be inferred from Figure 3.1. To say something about this we must say something about factor prices.

Competitive factor markets: factor prices and factor intensities

Let us assume that our economy is characterised by perfect competition. In particular, this means that producers buy their factors of production and sell their output in markets where they must take prices as given. We shall start by considering the way in which producers combine factors of production in order to minimise their production costs for a given output (a necessary condition for maximising profits), drawing on the standard result that in order to achieve this the individual producer will combine factors in such a way that the ratio of the marginal products of the factors (the slope of the isoquant) is equal to the ratio of factor prices (the slope of the budget line).

If two goods, X and Y, are produced with different production functions, a possible equilibrium situation is as shown in Figure 3.2. At points R and S the factors of production are allocated so that the quantities specified by the isoquants (X_1 of X and Y_1 of Y) are being produced at the lowest possible cost given the factor prices. In other words, at R and S the two isoquants are tangential to the lowest possible budget line which has a slope equal to the factor price ratio, the line AB. It follows that the ratio of the marginal product of labour to the marginal product of capital is the same for the two products, and that both are equal to the ratio of the wage rate to the return to capital (the negative of the slope of the line AB).

Another possible equilibrium is shown by points R and T, where again the slope of the X isoquant at R is equal to the slope of the Y isoquant at T and both are equal to the given factor price ratio.

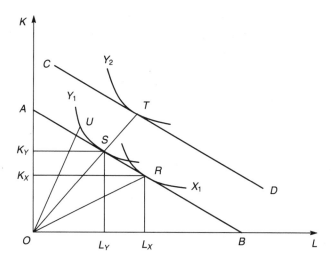

Figure 3.2 *Equilibrium in production under free competition*

An alternative way of deriving this important result is to draw upon another standard result from microeconomics, that a producer facing given factor and product prices will maximise his profits by purchasing factors to the point where the value of the marginal product of each factor (the marginal product times the price of the good) is equal to the price of the factor. Algebraically, using MPL and MPK to show the marginal products of labour and capital respectively, P for prices, w as the wage rate, and r as the return to capital, we have $MPL_Y P_Y = w$ and $MPK_Y P_Y = r$, from which it is easy to show that in order to maximise profits the producer must combine capital and labour so that

$$\frac{MPL_Y P_Y}{MPK_Y P_Y} = \frac{w}{r} \quad \text{or} \quad \frac{MPL_Y}{MPK_Y} = \frac{w}{r}$$

If the producer were producing good Y at a point such as U rather than point S then he would not be maximising profits. At U the marginal product of capital in producing Y is lower than it is at point S, and so the value of the marginal product of capital in Y at point U (the marginal product times the price of Y) is lower than the cost of the unit of capital. Similarly, the value of the marginal product of labour at point U is higher than the cost of that labour. Profits would be increased by employing more labour and less capital, the capital–labour ratio would decrease, and we would move to a point such as S or T.

If for some reason factor prices were to change, factor intensities would also change. Let us assume that the price of labour compared with the price of capital increases. Then more capital-intensive methods of production will be used in both lines of production, as shown in Figure 3.3. Before the price change OA of capital cost the same to purchase as OB of labour, but after the change OA' of capital costs the same as OB' of labour, and OA'' of capital costs the same as OB'' of labour. The two budget lines $A'B'$ and $A''B''$ are parallel, and steeper than the original budget line AB. As labour is now more expensive and capital is cheaper than before, producers of both X and Y will adjust by employing more capital and less labour than before, so that methods of production become more capital-intensive for both goods. If the desired production of X is still X_1 then the capital and labour combination will be at point R', and the higher capital–labour ratio in X is shown by the slope of line OR' being steeper than that of line OR. Similarly, quantity Y_1 of good Y will now be produced at point S', and the slope of the line OS' is steeper than that of line OS.

We may use Figure 3.3 to draw another useful conclusion. At the original factor prices the cost of producing X_1 of X was the same as that of producing Y_1 of Y, as shown by the corresponding isoquants being tangential to the same budget line AB. At the new factor prices the cost of producing X_1 of X is shown by the budget line $A''B''$, while the cost of producing Y_1 of Y is shown by the budget line $A'B'$. As $A'B'$ is nearer to the origin than $A''B''$, the cost of producing Y_1 of Y has fallen relative to that of producing X_1 of X. Alternatively, the cost of producing X_1 of X (at

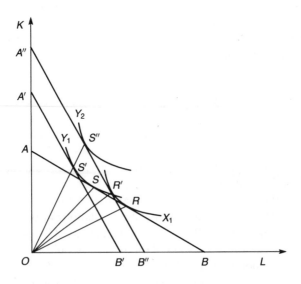

Figure 3.3   *Factor prices, factor intensities and production costs*

point R') is equal to the cost of producing Y_2 of Y (at point S''), and Y_2 of course represents a higher Y output than Y_1. Both are ways of demonstrating the same result, that the fall in the relative price of capital has decreased the average cost of producing Y compared with the average cost of producing X, and Y is of course the capital-intensive good. This result generalises to the statement that, under our assumptions, a decrease in the relative price of a factor decreases the relative average cost of the good which uses that factor more intensively.

These results may usefully be summarised in Figure 3.4. Here the relative average cost of X (AC_X/AC_Y) is measured on the vertical axis above the origin, O, the capital–labour ratios in X and Y production (k/l) on the vertical axis below the origin, and the relative price of labour (w/r) on the horizontal axis. The bottom panel thus shows the relationship between relative factor prices and factor intensities, the upper panel that between relative factor prices and relative average production costs.

We argued earlier that as the relative price of labour increased so producers would substitute capital for labour in both industries. This is shown by the lines OX and OY moving further away from the horizontal axis as w/r increases. We have also assumed that Y is always capital-intensive compared to X, and that is shown by the line OY always being further from the horizontal axis than line OX. Finally, we have just shown that an increase in the relative price of labour leads to an increase in the relative average cost of the labour-intensive good, and this is shown by line OC moving away from the horizontal axis as w/r increases.

Figure 3.4 does not tell us anything new, but it does help us to keep track of the associated changes in our four variables. Suppose the original factor price ratio is that shown by ϕ. Then the capital–labour ratio in X will be ρ_X, and that in Y will be ρ_Y, and as Y is relatively capital-intensive, $\rho_Y > \rho_X$. The relative average cost of producing X is shown by θ. Suppose now that the relative wage rate increases to ϕ'. In both industries producers will substitute capital for labour, the new capital–labour ratio in X being ρ'_X (greater than ρ_X), and that in Y being ρ'_Y (greater than ρ_Y), with Y still relatively capital intensive ($\rho'_Y > \rho'_X$). At the same time, the increase in the relative wage rate from ϕ to ϕ' leads to an increase in the relative average cost of the X good from θ to θ'.

We can extend our results a little further. We have seen that with constant returns to scale average costs are constant for any given ratio of factor prices, and thus know that marginal costs must be equal to those average costs and therefore constant. We also know that in perfect competition producers will produce to the point where marginal cost is equal to the price they receive, and that in the long-run equilibrium there will be no excess profits. This tells us that in such a long-run equilibrium marginal cost = average cost = price, and therefore that we could re-label

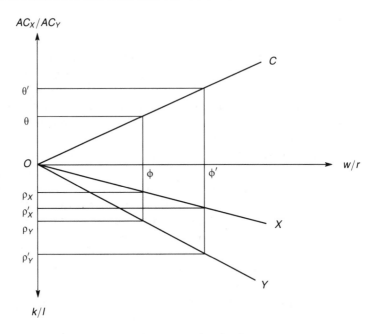

Figure 3.4   *Factor prices, factor intensities and relative costs*

the vertical axis in Figure 3.4 as either MC_X/MC_Y or as P_X/P_Y when we use it to describe such a situation.

Another important point to note is that we have established a set of one-to-one relationships between factor prices, factor intensities and production costs (or relative product prices). We can also use Figure 3.4 to trace the impact of a change in the relative price of good X on relative factor prices and on factor intensities. Suppose that initially the relative price of X was θ, and that for some reason that relative price rose to θ'. Figure 3.4 tells us that the consequence must be that the relative wage rate will increase from ϕ to ϕ', and that the capital–labour ratios will rise in both industries, from ρ_X to ρ'_X in X, and from ρ_Y to ρ'_Y in Y.

The assumption that one good is always labour-intensive and the other always capital-intensive, irrespective of what factor prices are, is essential to establishing these one-to-one relationships. Moreover, as we shall see later, the existence of these relationships allows us to show that, given those extra assumptions which specify the Heckscher–Ohlin model, trade will have some very definite effects on factor prices. We will be able to show that trade will lead either to a complete factor price equalisation (so that the real wage will be the same in both trading countries), or else to a complete specialisation in production. All this will be spelled out carefully in due course, but before that there is some more groundwork to be done.

☐ *Factor reversals*

What if the assumptions just described did not hold? What would happen if the isoquants cut twice? This situation is depicted in Figure 3.5. We can see from Figure 3.5 that the isoquant X_2 cuts the cloth isoquant Y_1 twice. As both these isoquants are each members of families of isoquants, each member having the same shape, we can find another isoquant, such as X_1, which at some point is tangential to the isoquant Y_1. This happens at point R. If the factor price ratio were that represented by the line PP that is tangential to the two isoquants at R then the factor intensity in both lines of production would be that given by the slope of OR.

But what would happen if the factor price ratio were to increase or decrease compared to that shown by PP? Figure 3.6 shows a pair of isoquants, labelled XX and YY, which are again tangential at point R, with common slope ϕ. Suppose that initially the price ratio is ϕ so that the lowest cost point for producing the specified amounts of X or Y is at R. If labour becomes relatively less expensive, as shown by the two lines which have slope ϕ', labour will be substituted for capital in both lines of production, with the least cost production points being R' for X and S' for Y. The capital–labour ratio in the production of the X good is now higher than in the production of the Y good; X is the capital-intensive good for relative wage rates higher than ϕ.

If on the other hand the relative wage rises above ϕ, as shown by the two lines which have slope ϕ'', then capital will be substituted for labour in

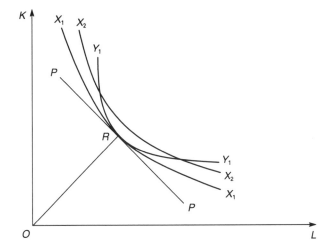

Figure 3.5 *Isoquants cut twice*

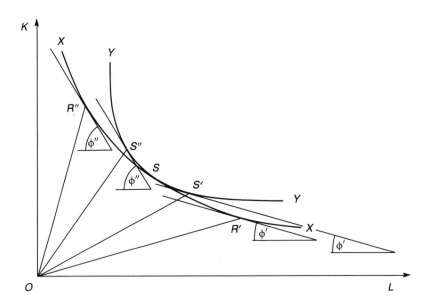

Figure 3.6   *Factor intensity reversals*

both X and Y production, with the least cost production points being R'' for X and S'' for Y. The capital-labour ratio in the production of the Y good is now lower than in the production of the X good; X is the capital-intensive good for relative wage rates higher than ϕ.

From this it follows that we can no longer identify one good as the capital-intensive good and the other as the labour-intensive good. Whether X is the labour-intensive good or the capital-intensive good will depend on the relative price of labour. The relationship between relative factor prices and capital–labour ratios is shown in the bottom panel of Figure 3.7. ϕ is the factor price ratio and ρ the capital–labour ratio at which the *factor intensity reversal* takes place.

It is still however the case that increasing the relative wage rate will increase the relative cost, and hence in a perfectly competitive equilibrium the relative price, of the labour-intensive good. The top panel of Figure 3.7 shows the consequences of this. If we start from a relative wage rate below ϕ, such as ϕ', then increasing the relative wage rate increases the relative cost of X, the labour-intensive good at low relative wage rates. The relative cost of X will continue to rise until the factor price ratio is ϕ. If the relative wage rate increases beyond ϕ, say to ϕ'', then the relative cost of Y, which is now the labour-intensive good, will rise, so that the relative cost of X

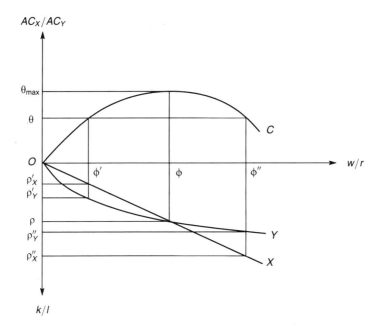

Figure 3.7 *Factor prices and relative costs with a factor reversal*

must fall. We no longer have a one-to-one correspondence between relative factor prices and relative costs (prices); the same average cost ratio can correspond to two different relative wage rates, as is the case with the average cost ratio θ and the factor price ratios ϕ' and ϕ''.

□ *The box diagram*

So far we have not said anything about a country's total factor endowments. The box diagram allows us to study the interrelationships between production functions and the total amounts of factors of production and to derive the conditions for the efficient use of factors.

A box diagram is shown in Figure 3.8. The dimensions of the box measure the endowments of labour and capital in the economy. In Figure 3.8 we are measuring capital along the vertical sides of the box, labour along the horizontal sides. The economy represented therefore has available $O_X U = O_Y V$ of capital and $O_X V = O_Y U$ of labour. The slope of the diagonal $O_X O_Y$ gives the overall factor endowment ratio of the economy.

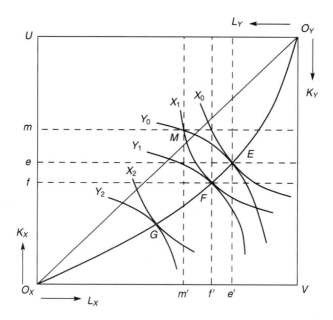

Figure 3.8   *Factor allocation in the box diagram*

Furthermore, we are producing two goods, X and Y, and their production functions are represented by two sets of isoquants. These are of the same kind as those illustrated earlier. In particular, we are still assuming that we have constant returns to scale. The only difference is that we are now measuring inputs into X production from the bottom left-hand corner (O_X) and inputs into Y production from the top right-hand corner (O_Y). The isoquants representing different levels of X output are thus drawn relative to O_X, and those representing Y output relative to O_Y.

Any point in the box, such as M, represents a certain allocation of capital and labour between the two sectors. At M we are using $O_X m$ of capital and $O_X m'$ of labour to produce X_1 units of the X good, and the remainder of the capital (mU) and labour $(m'V)$ to produce Y_0 units of the Y good. This is an application of the assumption that the factors of production are fully employed.

The output combination represented by M is not efficient however. This is shown by the fact that if we reallocate capital and labour so that we move along the isoquant Y_0 then we can obtain more of the X good without foregoing any of the Y good. We can continue to obtain more X without less of Y until we get to point E. If we move beyond E along the Y_0 isoquant then we will start to reduce the output of X. Point E is thus an efficient point – at E we cannot reallocate factors in order to get more of one good without losing some of the other good.

We could of course reallocate labour and capital so that we moved along the isoquant X_1, obtaining more Y without losing any X, and would find that F is also an efficient point. The distinguishing feature of points such as E and F (and G) is that at such points an X isoquant is tangential to a Y isoquant. They have the same slopes at such points, so that the ratio of the marginal product of labour to the marginal product of capital must be the same in both industries at such points. The relative efficiencies of the two factors of production are the same in both industries, and the factors of production are allocated efficiently.

If we combine all the points in the box where an X and a Y isoquant are tangential to each other, we get a curve such as $O_X O_Y$ in Figure 3.8. This curve is called the *contract curve* or the *efficient factor allocation curve*. All the points on the contract curve are efficient in the sense just described: once at such a point we cannot produce more of one good without producing less of the other. Any point off the contract curve may be shown to be inferior to a range of points on the curve by the type of reasoning we have just used. So far, however, we have no way of judging which point on the contract curve is the preferred point. This can only be done once we know something about the demand conditions, which we shall introduce later. The contract curve is derived exclusively from the requirement that we use the available factors efficiently. Most importantly for our purposes, it may be shown that if the factor markets are perfectly competitive then factors of production will be allocated efficiently.

We can make some general observations about the box diagram and the contract curve. Figure 3.9 reproduces the box and the contract curve from Figure 3.8. First, the contract curve lies below the diagonal. The capital–labour ratio in the X industry at any point such as E, shown by the slope of the line $O_X E$, is less than (or equal to, when all factors are employed in the X sector) the capital–labour ratio for the economy, the slope of the line $O_X O_Y$, which in turn is less than (or equal to, when all factors are employed in the Y sector) the capital–labour ratio in the Y-industry, shown by the slope of the line $O_Y E$. This reflects our initial assumption that the X good is labour-intensive, the Y good capital-intensive. The slope of the common tangent to the two isoquants at any point such as E reflects the ratio of the price of labour to the price of capital if factor markets are perfectly competitive.

If initially the economy were at point E in Figure 3.9, and then the demand for the Y good increased, what would we expect to happen to factor intensities and relative factor prices? The increase in demand for Y would increase the relative price of Y, and we would expect the Y industry to expand, bidding factors away from the X industry. An efficient transfer

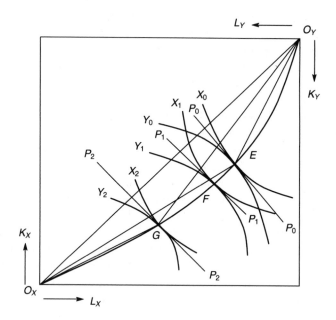

Figure 3.9 *Outputs, factor price ratios and capital–labour ratios in the box diagram*

of factors from X to Y would move the economy along the contract curve from E towards O_X, perhaps to point F. If we compare factor intensities at E and F we observe that the capital–labour ratio has fallen in both industries. How can it be that the capital–labour ratio falls in both sectors while the capital–labour ratio for the economy is unchanged?

The answer to this apparent paradox is that the output mix at F is different from that at E. As the X industry declines it releases a lot of labour relative to the capital released in comparison with the Y industry which wishes to acquire a lot of capital relative to the labour it needs. The only way in which the 'additional' labour (per unit of capital) from the X industry can be absorbed in the economy is for both sectors to become more labour-intensive.

What we have just described is a situation where there is an excess supply of labour (and an excess demand for capital) at the current factor prices. We would expect this to drive down the price of labour while increasing the price of capital. Comparison of points E and F shows that this is just what happens. The common slope of the two isoquants at E, the slope of the line P_0P_0, is greater than the slope of the line P_1P_1 at F. By a set

set of parallel arguments, the capital–labour ratios at point *G* are lower than those at point *F*, and the relative wage rate is also lower at *G* than at *F*. The relatively higher demand for capital by producers in the expanding capital-intensive industry bids up the relative price of capital.

In response to the rise in the relative price of capital, producers in both sectors will of course attempt to economise on the use of this now more expensive factor by substituting labour for capital, so that the capital–labour ratio will fall.

This relationship between an increasing relative price of the capital-intensive good and an increasing relative price of capital, and between the increasing price of capital and the decreasing capital–labour ratio, is just what was predicted when we derived the relationships between those three variables shown in Figure 3.4. We might deduce from this that the introduction of fixed supplies of the two factors does nothing to modify the relationships of Figure 3.4. In fact we would be wrong in doing so, but before we consider why that is so we shall examine the derivation of the production-possibility curve for the economy depicted in the box diagram of Figure 3.9.

The production-possibility curve derived from the box diagram

Figure 3.10 shows a slightly modified box diagram. Inputs into the two goods are still measured in the same way, from O_X and O_Y for *X* and *Y* respectively. However, we are now going to define the bottom right-hand corner of the box, labelled O_P in Figure 3.10, as the origin for two indices of output levels of the two goods, outputs of *X* being indexed on the vertical axis, outputs of *Y* on the horizontal. How can we do this?

We draw upon the fact that, with constant returns to scale production functions, at any given capital–labour ratio the output of a good is directly proportional to the input of either factor. This means that in order to measure the output of a good, all we have to do is to find the point where the appropriate isoquant intersects a ray from the origin with a specified capital–labour ratio, and then measure either the input of labour or the input of capital at that point. The output of the good will then be that factor input multiplied by some constant which depends only on the capital–labour ratio. In the context of the box diagram it is convenient to use the diagonal of the box to define our ray from the origin (since it is a ray from O_X and O_Y).[2]

Consider the *X* isoquant through point *E*. At the point where that isoquant, X_0, cuts the diagonal of the box we know that the output X_0 is

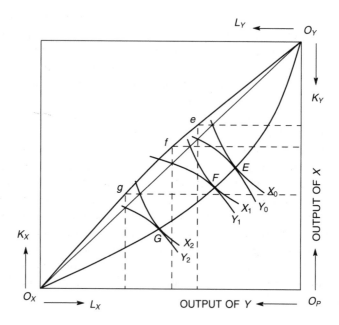

Figure 3.10   *The box diagram and the production-possibility curve*

directly proportional to the input of capital into X production at that point. This input is equal to the vertical distance from the bottom of the box to the horizontal dotted line through point *e*. If we now take the X isoquant through point *F*, X_1, and consider the point where that cuts the diagonal then we know that X_1 is proportional to the input of capital into X production at that point, with that input being the vertical distance from the bottom of the box to the horizontal dotted line through point *f*, and that the factor of proportionality is the same at *e* and at *f*. We can therefore index the output of X by referring to the capital inputs into X production at the points where the X isoquants meet the diagonal of the box.

By a parallel argument, we can index the output of Y by referring to the inputs of labour required to produce specified outputs of Y at the points where the appropriate Y isoquants meet the diagonal of the box.

By drawing the horizontal lines through the points where X isoquants meet the diagonal, the vertical lines through the points where the Y isoquants meet the diagonal, and by then taking the locus of the intersections of the corresponding lines (i.e. those defined by the points on the contract curve), we can obtain a representation of the production-possibility curve, drawn with O_P as its origin. The only difference between this indexed production-possibility curve and the true production-possibility curve is that the scales on the axes have each been changed by multiplication by a constant. Such a transformation will not alter the sign of, or the sign of the change in, the slope of the production-possibility curve.

What we may deduce from the line which runs from O_X through g, f and e to O_Y in Figure 3.10 is that the production-possibility curve is concave as viewed from the origin. That is, with fixed factor endowments and constant returns to scale in production we obtain an increasing opportunity cost production-possibility curve. This may seem surprising. Remember however that the two goods have different efficient factor intensities at any given factor price ratio, so that when one industry expands it must absorb factors in a ratio which is somewhere between its desired factor intensity and that of the contracting industry.

Factor endowments and the range of factor prices

Figure 3.11 reproduces much of Figure 3.4, which showed the relationships between the relative prices of goods, the relative prices of factors, and factor intensities. As before, at any common relative wage rate, w/r, X is the labour-intensive good; as the relative wage rate increases then so do the capital–labour ratios in both X and Y; and as w/r increases so does the relative price of the labour-intensive good.

We now introduce on the k/l axis the overall endowment ratio for the economy, shown as ρ. We observed earlier that the capital–labour ratio in X production will always be less than or equal to the capital–labour endowment ratio. The capital-labour ratio in the X industry will be equal to the economy's endowment ratio when all the capital and all the labour are used in the production of X. In this case we are at the top right-hand corner of the box in Figure 3.9, and the factor price ratio will be the slope of the X isoquant that passes through that corner. This relative factor price is shown in Figure 3.11 as ϕ_{max}.

Similarly, the capital–labour ratio in Y production will always be greater than or equal to the capital–labour endowment ratio. The capital–labour ratio in the Y industry will be equal to the economy's endowment ratio when all the capital and all the labour are used in the production of Y. In this case we are at the bottom left-hand corner of the box in Figure 3.9, and the factor price ratio will be the slope of the Y isoquant that passes through that corner. This relative factor price is shown in Figure 3.11 as ϕ_{min}.

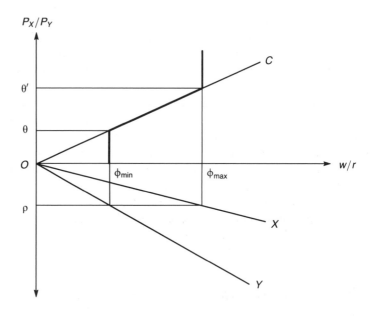

Figure 3.11   *Factor endowments and the range of factor prices*

When the relative wage rate reaches either ϕ_{min} or ϕ_{max} then the economy is completely specialised in the production of either Y or X. These relative factor prices must therefore correspond to particular relative commodity prices, which are of course the slopes of the production-possibility curve where it meets the Y and the X axis respectively. These are shown in Figure 3.11 as θ and θ' respectively.

But we know from our work in Chapter 2 on the classical model that when an economy specialises completely and trades with another country then the relative price of X can move outside the range that would obtain in that country under autarky. If that happens in the Heckscher–Ohlin model, what will happen to relative factor prices?

Once an economy is specialising completely in the production of a good then the price of the other good becomes irrelevant in determining the factor price ratio, since no factors are employed in that sector. The only relationship of relevance is that for the industry where there is still production we should have

$$\frac{MPL.P}{MPK.P} = \frac{w}{r} \quad \text{or} \quad \frac{MPL}{MPK} = \frac{w}{r}$$

so that the actual price of the good still being produced is irrelevant to the factor price ratio. That is, once the relative price of X has fallen below θ, so that only Y is being produced, the relative price of labour will not fall below ϕ_{min}. Similarly, when the relative price of X rises above θ', the relative price of labour cannot rise above ϕ_{max}.

The relationship between relative prices of the goods and the relative prices of the factors must therefore be as shown in Figure 3.11 by the heavier line. It follows that described earlier as long as both goods are being produced, but becomes vertical when there is complete specialisation in one good or the other.

3.3 Comparative advantage in the Heckscher–Ohlin model

The Heckscher–Ohlin theorem states that, within the assumptions of the Heckscher–Ohlin model, the capital-rich country will have the comparative advantage in the capital-intensive good, and the labour-rich country will have the comparative advantage in the labour-intensive good.

The assumptions of the model are that:

(1) there are no transport costs or other impediments to trade;
(2) there is perfect competition in both commodity and factor markets;
(3) all production functions are constant returns to scale;
(4) the production functions are such that the two commodities show different factor intensities at any common factor price ratio;
(5) the production functions differ between commodities, but are the same in both countries;
(6) labour and capital are perfectly mobile between industries within the same country, but perfectly immobile between countries.

The more recent version of the model adds to these the assumption that there are no factor intensity reversals.

The assumptions that the two countries have identical technologies and that perfect competition prevails in both ensure that the relationships between relative factor prices and factor intensities, and between relative factor prices and relative commodity prices, are the same in both countries, subject of course to the constraints imposed by their factor endowments. The assumption that factors are immobile between countries is essential if we are to work within our fixed factor endowment framework.

We have seen that, if there are no factor intensity reversals, there is no ambiguity about which is the labour-intensive good and which the capital-intensive. For convenience we shall assume X is labour-intensive, Y

capital-intensive. There is however some ambiguity about the meaning of the terms 'capital-rich' and 'labour-rich'.

The source of the problem is that two possible interpretations of these terms suggest themselves to economists. The first, and perhaps more 'common-sense', is that one country is 'capital-rich' if it has a greater *physical amount* of capital per unit of labour than has the other. The alternative interpretation is that one country is 'capital-rich' if it has a *lower price for capital under autarky* than has the other. The *caveat* 'under autarky' is of course essential, since as we noted earlier, and shall prove later, free trade will actually equalise factor prices between countries.

To the economist the source of the possible contradiction between the two interpretations of capital-richness are all too obvious. The 'physical' definition of factor abundance is a supply-side definition, whereas the 'factor price' definition takes account of the interaction between the supply of factors and the (derived) demand for those factors.

If we adopt the factor price definition then the Heckscher–Ohlin theorem is little more than a tautology. The one-to-one relationship between factor prices we established earlier assures us that the country in which capital is relatively cheap under autarky must be the country in which the capital-intensive good is relatively cheap under autarky, so that it will have the comparative advantage in that good.

The physical definition causes greater problems. Provided the endowment ratios of the two countries are not too dissimilar (a problem we return to later) then the assumptions we have made, in conjunction with our earlier analysis, do not allow us to say which country will have the lower relative wage rate (and hence the lower relative price of the labour-intensive good) under autarky.

Figure 3.12 shows the case where the physically capital-rich country is also the country where capital is relatively cheap under autarky. The endowment ratios of the two countries are shown as ρ^A and ρ^B respectively, with $\rho^A < \rho^B$ so that B is capital-rich by the physical definition. The relative factor prices under autarky are shown as ϕ^A and ϕ^B. They are shown in Figure 3.12 with $\phi^A < \phi^B$, so that B is also capital-rich by the factor price definition. Note that both factor price ratios lie within the range defined by their respective endowment ratios.

Figure 3.13 however shows the contradictory case. Once again B is capital-rich by the physical definition, but in Figure 3.13 we have $\phi^A > \phi^B$ so that A is capital-rich by the factor price definition. Note again that both factor price ratios lie within the range defined by their respective endowment ratios.

There is therefore nothing in our specification of the relationships between factor prices and factor intensities that allows us to resolve the issue of which definition of factor abundance to use. In order to say

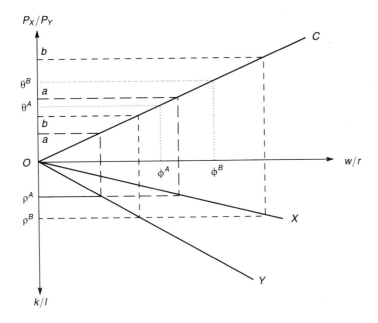

Figure 3.12 *The physically capital-rich country may also be the country where capital is relatively cheap*

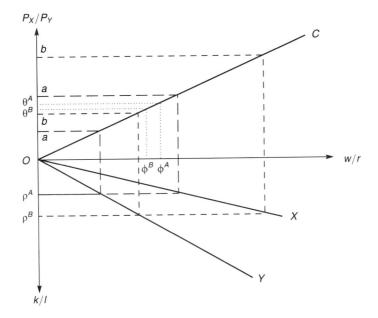

Figure 3.13 *The physically capital-rich country may be the country where capital is relatively expensive*

something specific about this question we must return to the relationship between factor endowments and the production-possibility curves, and between those production possibilities and the tastes of the consumers in the two economies.

Figure 3.14 shows the factor boxes for two economies, with A, the country whose box is marked out by O_Y^A as its top right-hand corner, relatively better endowed with labour. Consider first points E and F. E is on the contract curve for country B, F is on the contract curve for country A. Moreover, E and F are on the same ray from the common X origin, so that the slope of the two isoquants at E must be the same as the slope of the two isoquants at F. Finally, the output of X must be greater than the output of X at E, while a little simple geometry tells us that E is further away from O_Y^B than is F from O_Y^A, so that Y output at E is greater than Y output at F. Given the one-to-one relationship between relative factor prices and relative commodity prices, we now know that the two production-possibility curves will have the same slope (the commodity price ratio) at points where the X output for A is greater than, and the Y output less than, the corresponding outputs for B.

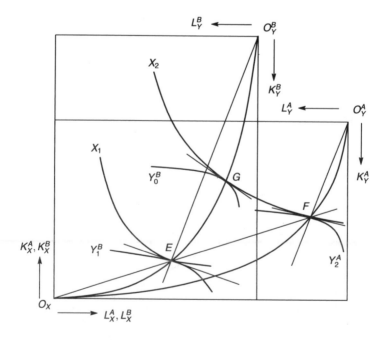

Figure 3.14   *Differences in factor endowments*

Alternatively, we could consider the relationship between points F and G. F is on country A's contract curve, G is on country B's. By construction the X output is the same at both points. We know that the relative price of labour is higher at G than at E, and so higher at G than at F, and hence that the relative price of X at G must be higher than that at F.

Putting these conclusions together tells us that the relative shapes of the two production-possibility curves, and the relative positions of the points corresponding to E, F and G, must be approximately as shown in Figure 3.15. The physically capital-rich country (B) is biased towards the production of the capital-intensive good (Y). That is, at any two points where the two production-possibility curves have the same slope (the same opportunity cost), the ratio of Y production to X production is higher in the physically capital-rich country.

However, as we have noted before, it is always possible for there to be a bias in the tastes of consumers in an economy sufficient to offset any bias in production possibilities. Such a situation is shown in Figure 3.16, where B, the physically capital-rich country, has tastes biased towards consumption of the capital-intensive good, and A, the physically labour-rich country, has tastes biased towards consumption of the labour-intensive good, and the consumption biases are such that under autarky

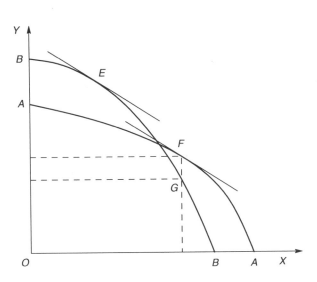

Figure 3.15 *The physically capital-rich country is biased towards producing the capital-intensive good*

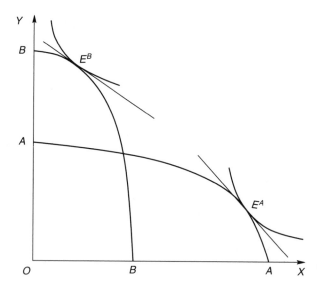

Figure 3.16   *Demand factors offsetting production bias*

the relative price of the capital-intensive good is higher in the physically capital-rich economy. In such a case there is a contradiction between the physical and factor price definitions of factor abundance.

The only way in which we can ensure that the two definitions of factor abundance will always be in agreement is to assume that tastes are identical in the two countries and, to ensure that there are no complications due to the relative physical sizes of the two economies, that tastes are homothetic. The variant of the Heckscher–Ohlin model that makes this an explicit assumption is often referred to as the Heckscher–Ohlin–Samuelson model. From this point we shall assume that tastes are identical and homothetic, so that we can employ the physical definition of factor abundance, knowing that that implies the factor-price definition holds, and therefore that the Heckscher–Ohlin theorem must hold.

Let us emphasise these points again: (1) if we use the factor-price definition then the Heckscher–Ohlin theorem is always true; (2) if we use the physical definition then the Heckscher–Ohlin is only *necessarily* true if we also assume that tastes are identical and homothetic.

Note that if the countries' physical endowment ratios are so far apart that their feasible ranges of relative factor prices do not overlap then the two definitions of factor abundance *must* be equivalent, no matter what the differences in tastes between the two countries.

■ 3.4 Rewards to factors of production

Free trade and factor prices in the Heckscher–Ohlin model

The move to free trade equalises relative commodity prices. As there is a one-to-one relationship between relative commodity prices and relative factor prices, the reduction in the relative price of the capital-intensive good in the labour-rich country which imports it must reduce the relative price of capital in that country; alternatively, we could say that the increase in the relative price of the labour-intensive good which it exports must increase the relative price of labour. By a parallel argument, free trade must increase the relative price of capital in the capital-rich economy.

The economic argument is quite straightforward. Each country exports the good which uses intensively the factor which is relatively cheap in that country under autarky, and imports the good which is intensive in the factor which is relatively expensive. The increased demand for the export good drives up the price of that good, and that price increase has more effect on the factor used intensively therein, with the converse being true for the import good.

The move to free trade must, therefore, change the distribution of income within each economy. The owners of the factor of production used intensively in the export industry will gain relatively by the move to free trade, while owners of the factor of production used intensively in the import-competing industry will lose relatively. This convergence of relative factor prices, and the accompanying changes in the distribution of income, will occur whether or not there is complete specialisation in either or both countries.

We can in fact go a little further than this. We know that a fall in the relative wage rate leads to a fall in the capital–labour ratio in both sectors, and that a fall in the capital–labour ratio results in a fall in the marginal productivity of labour and an increase in the marginal productivity of capital. As the real price of a factor in terms of a good is given by the marginal productivity of the factor in the production of that good, the fall in the relative price of labour must lead to a fall in the real price of labour in terms of either of the goods it produces. We can make a parallel statement for the real payments to capital, and duplicate the argument for the case where the relative wage rate falls.

These arguments imply that the move to free trade will do more than change the relative distribution of income. The capital-rich country exporting capital-intensive goods will experience an increase in the real return to capital and a decrease in the real wage rate. The labour-rich country exporting labour-intensive goods will experience a decrease in the real return to capital and an increase in the real wage rate.

Free trade therefore leads to a convergence of the relative and the real returns to factors of production, given the assumptions of our model. Whether this convergence will result in the equalisation of relative and real returns to factors is the subject of the next section.

Factor price equalisation in the Heckscher–Ohlin model

The weak form of the *factor-price equalisation theorem* states that free trade between two countries in a Heckscher–Ohlin world will equalise *relative* factor prices provided that neither country specialises completely.

The proof of this proposition is trivial given our previous analysis. Figure 3.17 shows the familiar relationships between factor prices, commodity prices and factor intensities. All we need for our present purposes is the top panel of the diagram. Provided that neither country specialises completely, so that the factor-price–commodity-price relationship is as shown by the line OC, a common commodity price ratio due to free trade, say θ^T, must result in a common factor price ratio, in this case ϕ^T.

The box diagram corresponding to this situation is shown in Figure 3.18. With free trade the two economies must be producing at a pair of points such as E^A and E^B, where the common slopes of the isoquants (not shown) at E^A and E^B are identical.

The strong form of the factor-price equalisation theorem states that free trade between two countries in a Heckscher–Ohlin world will equalise *absolute* factor prices provided that neither country specialises completely.

We can only obtain absolute factor-price equalisation if we have relative factor price equalisation. Consider Figure 3.18 again. The capital–labour ratios in X and Y production at E^A and E^B are the same since the two countries share the same technology. As we have constant returns to scale, we also know that the marginal productivity of capital (labour) at E^A in X (Y) production is the same as the marginal productivity of capital (labour) at E^B in X (Y) production. But we also know that the marginal productivity of a factor in the production of a good measures the real reward to that factor in terms of that good.

Hence, the real return to capital in terms of the X (Y) good must be the same in both countries, and the real wage in terms of the X (Y) good must also be the same in both countries. Therefore we must have absolute equalisation of factor prices.

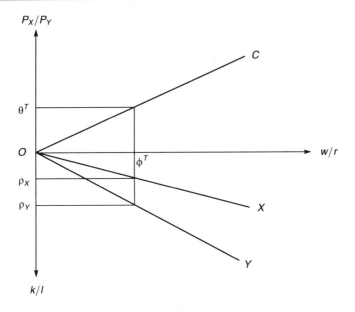

Figure 3.17 *Equalisation of relative factor prices with incomplete specialisation*

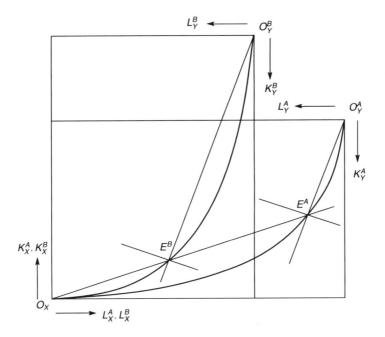

Figure 3.18 *Factor price equalisation with incomplete specialisation*

Equalisation of absolute factor prices is precisely the result we would expect to get if capital and labour were free to move between countries, as well as between industries, in search of the highest real rewards. A basic assumption of the Heckscher–Ohlin model however is that factors are perfectly immobile between countries. We therefore have the interesting result that in a Heckscher–Ohlin world the free movement of goods between countries acts in some sense as a substitute for the free movement of factors between countries.

If there is complete specialisation in one or both countries then there will no longer be equalisation of relative factor prices, and so there cannot be equalisation of absolute factor prices. The reason is that, as we saw earlier, complete specialisation breaks the common one-to-one relationship between relative factor prices and relative commodity prices.

Figure 3.19 shows the case where both countries specialise completely. The range of relative commodity prices for country A under autarky is shown by the gap aa in Figure 3.19, and the range of relative commodity prices for country B by the gap bb. These two ranges do not overlap, so at least one country must specialise completely. In Figure 3.19 both specialise completely, so that the free trade commodity price ratio is θ, which lies

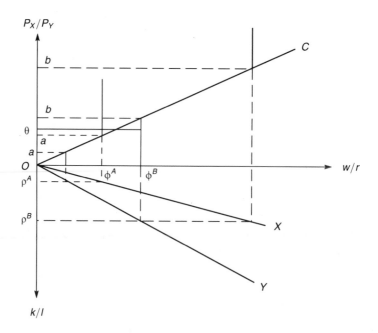

Figure 3.19 *Relative factor prices are not equalised with complete specialisation*

outside both the autarky price ranges. Country A's relative wage rate cannot rise above ϕ^A, while country B's cannot fall below ϕ^B. There cannot, therefore, be relative factor price equalisation, and so there cannot be absolute factor price equalisation.

■ 3.5 Adjustment over time in the Heckscher–Ohlin framework

The Heckscher–Ohlin model concerns itself with comparative advantage and the effects of free trade on welfare and factor rewards in the long run. However, the path by which the economy may move from one long-run equilibrium to another is also of interest. While the economy as a whole may experience welfare gains with each stage of the transition, we know that some groups within the economy will lose and others gain in the long run, and should consider the possibility that some of those who gain in the long run may lose in the short and medium run, and vice versa.

We shall consider first how the economy may gain from the freedom to trade in the short run when no factors are mobile and in the medium term when only some factors (labour in our example) are mobile. We shall simplify the analysis by assuming that we are dealing with a capital-rich country that is small enough not to affect world prices. Extension of this analysis to the case of a large country would mean that we have to consider that a change in the volume of trade will affect world prices. Figure 3.20 illustrates the argument that there are gains to be made from trade whether factors are mobile or not, and that as factors become mobile so those gains will increase.

We shall assume that labour is internally mobile in the medium term but capital internally mobile only in the long term; otherwise we shall maintain all the assumptions of the Heckscher–Ohlin model. This country is assumed to have been in an autarkic state long enough for factors to be allocated efficiently between sectors. The long-run production possibility curve for this country is LL, and A is the autarkic equilibrium point on that curve. When the opportunity to trade is opened for this country it will export Y (the capital-intensive good) and import X.

In the short run factors cannot be moved between industries, so that the production point remains unchanged at point A. However, the opportunity to trade at terms of trade different from the autarky price ratio means that there will still be gains from trade for the community, as shown by the move to the higher indifference curve I_1.

In the medium term it is possible to adjust the production mix by reallocating labour from the import-competing industry to the export

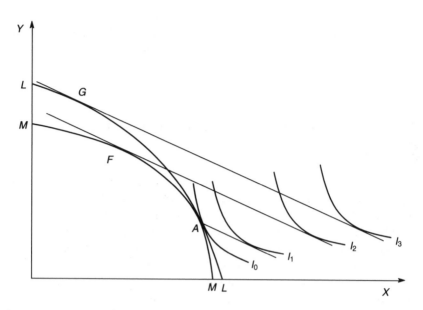

Figure 3.20 *Gains from trade in the short, medium and long run*

industry. As capital cannot be reallocated the production point must move along the medium-run production-possibility curve *MM*, which lies inside *LL* except at point *A*. Trade continues at the same relative prices, and so the production point will move to *F* on *MM*. The gains from trade will be increased by the shift from *X* to *Y* production, shown by the move from indifference curve I_1 to indifference curve I_2 in Figure 3.20.

In the long run, with capital mobile between sectors, the economy will move back to the long run production-possibility curve *LL*, and with the terms of trade unchanged production will occur at point *G*. There is a further gain from trade as a consequence, shown in Figure 3.20 by the move from indifference curve I_2 to indifference curve I_3. At this point, with both factors mobile, the gains from trade predicted by the Heckscher–Ohlin model are fully realised.

In the long-run situation the Heckscher–Ohlin model predicts that the capital owners will gain and workers will lose in the move from autarky to free trade by this capital-rich country. However in the medium-run situation (which could also be analysed using a labour–capital–capital version of the specific factors model), we may show that the owners of capital specific to the export industry gain, that owners of capital specific to the import-competing industry lose, and that the effect on the wage rate is indeterminate. We shall consider this problem in greater detail in Chapter 5.

☐ *Notes*

1 Eli F. Heckscher (1879–1952) was a Swedish economist and economic historian. In 1919 he published in the *Ekonomisk Tidskrift* a paper that contains the core of the Heckscher–Ohlin theory of trade. He is otherwise known primarily for his path-breaking studies on mercantilism and Swedish economic history. Bertil Ohlin (1899–1979), a Swedish economist and politician, was a student of Heckscher. He published his main work, *Interregional and International Trade*, in 1933. He then turned to politics and became the leader of the Swedish Liberal Party.

2 The derivation of the production-possibility curve from the box diagram was originally made in K. M. Savosnick, 'The Box Diagram and the Production-Possibility Curve', *Ekonomisk Tidskrift*, 60, September 1958.

■ *Chapter 4* ■

Technology-Difference Models

■ 4.1 Introduction

We noted in Chapter 2 that one interpretation of the Ricardian model is that its central feature is the presumed difference in technology between the two countries concerned. There is a divergence of opinion among economists on the weight that should be given to technological differences as an explanation of trade flows. At one extreme, some economists are unwilling to accept any model that has technological differences as its central feature. One basis for such an argument is that what we may perceive as a technological difference is in fact due to the omission of a factor of production. So, for instance, the absolute 'technological advantage' of Portugal in Ricardo's model may be a consequence of Portugal being better endowed with a factor we may call 'climate' which is important in the production of both cloth and wine, and its comparative 'technological advantage' due to wine being 'climate-intensive'.

A less extreme position holds that any technological differences can only be short term in nature, with knowledge eventually being dispersed among other countries (subject of course to the time period of any patents held by the innovator). Some economists have produced theories which concentrate on the dispersion process for technological innovation, while others have argued that the basis of much trade is a process of continual innovation by one country which allows it always to stay ahead of its competitors. We shall discuss these models later in this chapter.[1] First we shall consider the role of technology within the framework of the two models we have met already which allow us to look at the interplay between two or more factors – the specific factors and the Heckscher–Ohlin models.

4.2 Technology differences in the specific factors model

We may obtain a simple medium-term technology-difference model considered earlier by assuming that, within the capital–labour version of the specific factors framework of Chapter 2, the two countries are identical in everything but the technology used in the production of one of the goods. That is, countries A and B have the same endowments of both factors, with the same allocation of capital between the two goods, and the same technology for the production of one of the goods (X) but a different technology for the production of the other good (Y). Specifically, we shall assume that country A has a *scale* advantage in the production of Y; if the production function for good Y is $Q_Y = f(k, l)$ in country B then the production function for Y in country A may be written as $Q_Y = \sigma f(k, l)$, where $\sigma > 1$. The 4-quadrant diagram for this model is shown in Figure 4.1. The diagram *looks* very like that presented earlier for the case where there was a difference in capital endowments (Figure 2.2), but there is one particular distinction between the two.

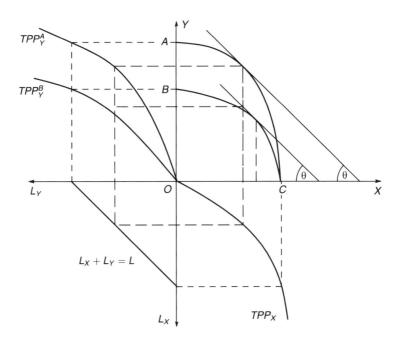

Figure 4.1 *A difference in technology in the Y industry*

Consider Figure 4.1, which shows a pair of total product curves for good Y in countries A and B which could be consistent either with the assumption that there is a greater stock of capital in A or with the assumption that A has a scale advantage in the production of Y. In either case the marginal product of labour in country A must be higher than that in B in any state in which the labour input into Y production is the same; that is, if labour input into Y production is L in both countries then the slope of TPP_Y^A at point a will be greater than that of TPP_Y^B at point b.

However, if the difference in the two total product curves is due to A having a larger capital endowment then the marginal product of capital will be lower in A at point a than in B at point b since more capital is being employed per unit of labour at a than at b. On the other hand, if the two total product curves differ because A has a scale advantage in Y production then the marginal product of capital in Y will be higher at point a than at point b since the same capital and labour inputs are producing a greater amount of Y in country A.

With those important provisos in mind we may note that the two production-possibility curves have the same relative shapes as in the earlier capital-difference case, and that, also as before, at any common commodity price ratio country A will produce more Y and less X than country B. Again, with the assumption of identical and homothetic tastes we can be sure that the Y good will be relatively cheap in A, so that A will have the comparative advantage in the good in which it has the technological advantage. We can also be certain that A will produce more Y than B under autarky, but we cannot be certain which country will produce the greater volume of the X good.

Let us assume that under autarky A produces more X than does B. It follows that labour employment in the X industry will be greater in A than in B, so that the marginal product of labour will be lower, and that of X-specific capital higher, in A than in B; that is, the real wage in terms of X will be lower in A than in B, and the real return to capital in the X sector in terms of X will be higher in A than in B. Since under autarky the X good is relatively expensive in A, the real return to X-specific capital will also be higher in A than in B in terms of Y.

The greater use of labour in the X industry in A means that there will be lower employment of labour in the Y industry in A than in B. We have seen that at the same level of labour use the marginal product of labour is higher in A than in B, so the lower employment of labour in A will reinforce this gap, and we can be sure that the real wage in terms of the Y good will be higher in A than in B. On the other hand, though the marginal product of Y-specific capital is also higher in A than in B at the same level of labour use, the lower actual employment of labour in A will tend to reduce the marginal product of capital in the Y sector there compared to that in B. Therefore we cannot be certain whether the real return to Y-specific capital in terms of the Y good is higher or lower in A than in B; nor then can we say anything definite about the relative real returns to Y-specific capital in terms of the X good.

If under autarky A were producing less of the X good than B then we would conclude: (i) that $L_X^A < L_X^B$; hence, (ii) $MPL_X^A > MPL_X^B$ and $MPK_X^A < MPK_X^B$, so that in terms of the X good the real wage is higher in A than in B and the real return to X-specific capital is lower; (iii) that since Y is relatively cheap in A the real wage in A must also be relatively higher than in B in terms of the Y good; (iv) that for the same reason we cannot say whether the real return to X-specific capital in terms of the Y good is higher or lower in A than in B; (v) that $L_Y^A > L_Y^B$; hence (vi) $MPK_Y^A > MPK_Y^B$ so that the real return to Y-specific capital in terms of the Y good is higher in A than in B; and finally, as X is relatively expensive in A, (vii) that we do not know whether the real return to Y-specific capital in terms of the X good is higher or lower in A than in B.

Following the opening of free trade between the countries, A will switch labour into Y production and B will increase its specialisation in the X good, and with the same relative commodity prices prevailing in both countries we will find that A is producing more Y and less X than B. The real return to X-specific capital in terms of the X good must fall in A and rise in B; since the relative price of X falls in A and rises in B we also know that the owners of X-specific capital in A become worse off, and those in B better off, in terms of the Y good. Finally, we can see that in the free trade equilibrium the real return to X-specific capital will be lower in A than in B in terms of both goods.

The reduction in the employment of labour in the X industry in A will raise the marginal product of labour there, and so the real wage rate in country A in terms of the X good must increase; conversely the real wage rate in B in terms of the X good must fall, and must with free trade be lower in B than in A in terms of the X good. The parallel rise in the use of labour in Y production in A, and fall in that use in B, will lead to a fall in the real wage in terms of Y in country A, and a rise in B. However, since we already know that the real wage is higher in A than in B in terms of the X good under free trade we also know that that is so in terms of the Y good.

Now consider the question of the real returns to Y-specific capital in the two countries. The increase in the employment of labour in the Y sector in A must lead to an increase in the marginal product of capital in Y, and so to an increase in the real return to Y-specific capital in terms of the Y good. Since Y has at the same time become relatively more expensive in A with the move to free trade it follows that the real return to Y-specific capital in A measured in terms of the X good must also have increased.

The reverse changes will occur in B: the real return to Y-specific capital there will fall in terms of both X and Y. Finally, the higher employment of labour in the Y industry in A compared to B, reinforced by the effects of the technology advantage in A, will mean that in the free trade equilibrium the real return to capital employed in the Y sector will be higher in A than in B in terms of both goods.

We see that the returns to the capital which is specific to the sector in which A has the scale advantage rise in A and fall in B in terms of both goods, while the returns to the capital specific to the other sector fall in A and rise in B in terms of both goods. The real wage again shows a less definite pattern, in that in both countries it rises in terms of one good and falls in terms of the other. In the final free trade equilibrium both Y-specific capital and labour earn higher real returns in A, while X-specific capital gets a higher real return in B. The source of the gain to capital in the Y sector in A is obvious, in that it is the specific factor which benefits directly from the technical advantage; because labour in A is mobile between sectors it can also benefit from the technical advantage in the Y sector.

4.3 Technology differences in the Heckscher–Ohlin model

A further extension of the technology-difference problem would be into the two-factor, constant returns to scale framework of the Heckscher–Ohlin model, but still with the scale difference in technology between the two countries in the Y good.[2] This would be appropriate when the diffusion of technological knowledge between countries takes longer than the movement of capital between sectors within a country, as may be the case where patents have a long time span.

Given our assumption of constant returns to scale, the isoquants for Y in countries A and B are geometrically identical in that the same factor-price ratio would result in the same capital–labour ratio in both countries, but with given inputs of capital and labour producing a greater output in A than in B. Such a situation is shown in Figure 4.2, where the isoquant Y_1^B for country B represents the same Y output as the isoquant Y_1^A for country A. By assumption the technology in the X industry is the same in both countries and is labour-intensive compared to Y; X_1 is a typical isoquant for the X industry.

It follows from our assumptions that at any common factor-price ratio the capital–labour ratio will be the same in the Y industry in both

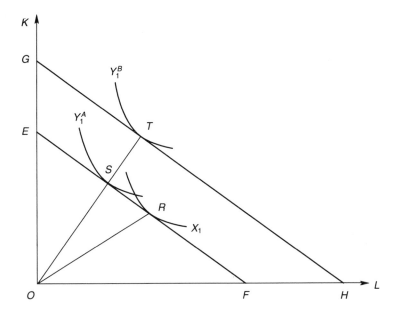

Figure 4.2 *A scale difference in technology in the capital-intensive industry*

countries and in the X industry in both countries. As the two countries also have identical factor boxes, they must also have identical efficient factor allocation curves, as in Figure 4.3, where E is a typical point on that curve. While the X isoquant through point E shows the same output, X_1, for both countries, the Y isoquant shown represents a higher level of output for country A, Y_2^A, than for country B, Y_1^B.

It follows from this that the average cost of Y production at E must be relatively lower for country A than for country B, so that under perfect competition we would expect the relative price of Y to be lower in A than in B. We therefore know that at any common factor price ratio, such as shown by point E in Figure 4.3, there will be the same X output in both countries, a higher Y output in A than in B, and a lower relative price of Y in A than in B. The production-possibility curves for the two countries must therefore have the type of relationship shown in Figure 4.4, where E^A and E^B correspond to point E in Figure 4.3.

Note that now that capital is mobile between the two sectors, A's production-possibility curve must lie completely outside its medium-term curve through E^A, B's must lie outside its medium-term curve through E^B, and A's long-term production-possibility curve must lie outside B's long-run curve. The long-run production-possibility curves for A and B must

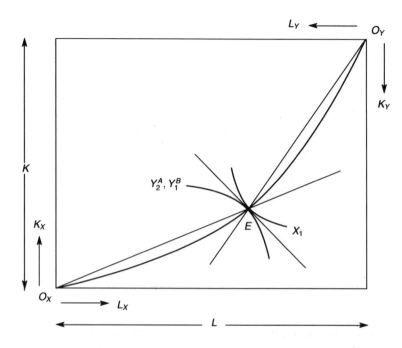

Figure 4.3   *The production boxes for the two countries*

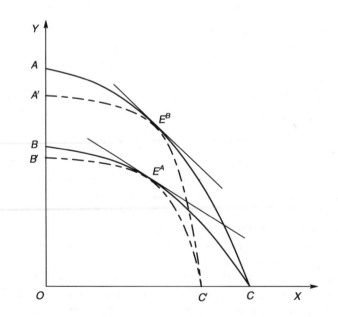

Figure 4.4   *Production-possibility curves in the medium and long term*

again meet on the X axis. Country A, the country with the technological advantage in the production of the Y good, still has production bias in favour of Y in the medium term, and so still has a comparative advantage in that good. The four production-possibility curves are shown in Figure 4.4, where BC is country B's medium-run curve, $B'C'$ its long-run curve, and AC is country A's medium-run curve, $A'C'$ its long-run curve.

Remember that we cannot say whether relative wages will be higher or lower in A than in B under autarky. If relative wages were higher in A than in B then we can say that the capital–labour ratio would be higher in both industries in A than in B. Labour is then better off in terms of both goods in A than in B, capital is worse off in terms of X in A, but may or may not be better off in terms of Y. If relative wages were lower in A than in B then the capital–labour ratio would be lower in both industries in A, so that capital would be better off in terms of both goods in A, labour would be relatively worse off in terms of X in A, but might be better off in terms of Y.

What we can say is that the equalisation of relative commodity prices under free trade, which reduces the relative price of the labour-intensive good in A and increases it in B, will lower the relative wage rate in A and increase it in B, compared to autarky. Moreover, as shown in Figure 4.5, which is drawn to reflect our earlier conclusion that the relative price/cost of X must be higher in A than in B at any common factor-price ratio, the relative wage rate in A will be lower than that in B under free trade – certainly not a case of relative factor-price equalisation. The reduction in the relative wage rate in A will lead to a fall in the capital–labour ratio in both industries in that country. It follows that the move to free trade must unambiguously reduce real wages and increase the real return to capital in country A. A parallel argument shows that the move to free trade must unambiguously increase real wages and decrease the real return to capital in country B.

How do factor rewards in the two countries compare in absolute terms? In terms of the X good it is obvious that labour must be worse off, and capital better off, in A than in B. When we come to the Y good, we know that at any common relative wage rate, and hence common capital–labour ratio, the marginal product of both capital and labour in the Y industry is higher in A than in B. The lower capital–labour ratio in A in the Y good means that capital in A must be better off than in B in terms of Y, and so also in terms of X, but the position of labour is ambiguous. Overall then, we can be sure that free trade benefits capital-owners in country A both compared to autarky and compared to their counterparts in B, and that free trade harms the latter absolutely. We also know that the move from autarky to free trade lowers real wages in A and raises them in B, but we cannot say in which country labour is better off.

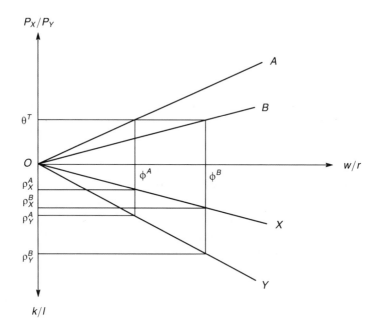

Figure 4.5   *Free trade and factor prices*

■ 4.4 Adjustment to changes in technology

Suppose we have a small country in long-run equilibrium in a Heckscher–
Ohlin world, and that the country is exporting the capital-intensive good,
Y, at the ruling world terms of trade. Suppose now however that the
producers of the import-competing good, X, make a scale advance in
technology of sufficient magnitude to reverse the direction of the country's
trade at the current world prices, even if only labour may be transferred
between sectors in the medium term.

   We may distinguish two possible adjustment paths for this country,
depending on the relative speeds with which capital may be transferred
between the two sectors and the technological knowledge between this
country and the rest of the world. Figure 4.6 is drawn to show the first
adjustment possibility, where the time taken for both labour and capital to
move within our focus economy is less than the time needed for the new
technology to be implemented by the rest of the world.

   The initial production-possibility curve is *AB*, and with the existing
world terms of trade θ the country produces at *r* and consumes where the

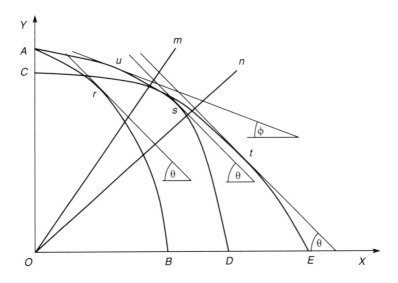

Figure 4.6 *Adjustment following an improvement in technology in the import-competing good*

trade line is tangential to an indifference curve (not shown) on the ray *Om*. In the short term, before there can be any factor movements, the production point will shift to the right. Since a neutral change in technology does not change the relationship between factor prices and factor intensities, this new production point will be on both the new medium and the new long-run production-possibility curves.

In the medium term it is possible to transfer labour but not capital between the two sectors, giving the medium-run production-possibility curve *CD*, which must lie outside the original production point *r*. In the long run, the technological advance in the *X* industry will pivot the production-possibility curve around point *A*, the new long-run curve being shown as *AE* in Figure 4.6.

Both these changes will take place before the rest of the world has adopted the new technology, and so world prices will not change. In the medium term then, the new production point will be at *s* on *CD*, with consumption at the point where the trade line through point *s* meets the ray *Om*. The country has now become an exporter of the labour-intensive good. The country has gained in welfare (consumption must be on a higher indifference curve), labour has moved from the *Y* to the *X* industry, owners of capital in the *X* industry and workers must have gained as a consequence of the technological advance and the labour transfer, but capital owners in the Y industry must have lost through the transfer of labour in terms of the Y good, though they will have an offsetting gain from the fall in price of the X good.

Capital also can be transferred between the two industries before the new technology is acquired by foreign producers of the X good. The country will move out to its long-run production-possibility curve AE, production will move to point t on that curve, and consumption will move to the point where the trade line through t meets the ray Om. The country has transferred capital from Y to X production, expanded its exports of X, and moved to a higher indifference curves by so doing. Workers will gain from the increase in the capital–labour ratio in both industries, but owners of capital already in the X industry will lose while owners of capital that was tied in the Y industry will gain.

However, the new technology will eventually be transferred to producers in the rest of the world. This must reduce the costs of producing X in the rest of the world, and so the relative price of X on the world market will fall. In the period when the rest of the world can transfer labour but not capital into the production of X, this will reduce our focus country's exports of X, and may even result in it becoming an importer of X again. Certainly, once the rest of the world has moved to its new long-run equilibrium, so that we have returned to a state compatible with the Heckscher–Ohlin model, our focus country must again be an exporter of the capital-intensive good, Y, and an importer of X. This equilibrium is shown in Figure 4.6 with new terms of trade ϕ, production at u and consumption where the trade line through u meets ray On.

We would observe a different adjustment path if the new technology were transferred to the rest of the world before capital could be switched between the two industries in our small country. The adoption of the new technology elsewhere would result in a fall in the relative price of X on the world market, though not to ϕ initially (since capital can probably not be transferred between sectors in other countries except in the long run). The focus country would lose its new comparative advantage in the X good, and would become an importer of that good again. Once capital had been transferred within all countries in the world we would again get the long-run equilibrium with terms of trade ϕ and production in the focus country at point u.

▪ 4.5 Imitation-gap theories of trade

The previous analysis made no attempt to elaborate on the causes of technology advance and subsequent international transfer or on the nature of that transfer. An important paper by Posner explicitly considers technological change and transfer as a determinant of trade.[3]

Posner's theory considers technological change as a continuing process, with time lags between the introduction of a new technology for an existing or a new good in one country and the adoption of the technology elsewhere (the *imitation lag*) and between the development of a new good and the emergence of a demand for that good in other countries (the *demand lag*). The essence of the argument is that a continuous process of invention and innovation would give rise to trade, even between countries which are basically similar in their factor endowments and tastes and so would not trade in a static Heckscher–Ohlin world. The introduction of a demand gap means that the model of section 4.4 is not fully appropriate for the Posner model, but the results of that section do give us some insight into the argument, and should be kept in mind in considering the following simplified version of the model.

We start by assuming that there is an innovation in one country which leads to the production of a 'new' good. Posner argues that there will be a time lag before foreign consumers start to buy the new good, even if the 'newness' consists only of the identical good having the same price, though the greater is the difference between the new good and its old substitutes, the longer will be this time lag. Producers in the foreign countries must decide whether to adopt the new technology (do they want to produce the new variety of the good or continue to produce their existing variety?). Should they wish to adopt the new technology, they will be unable to do so for some time period if there is patent protection, and even if not there may be a time lag due to the need to learn the new process, change plant and equipment, etc. Whether the technological innovation will generate trade between two otherwise identical countries will depend on the net effect of the demand and imitation lags.

Suppose, for example, that the demand lag is longer than the imitation lag. In this case the producers in the imitating country would be able to adopt the new technology before the consumers in their domestic market had started to demand the new good, and the technological innovation would not generate trade. This is more likely to be the case if the innovation is fairly simple, or where producers in both countries regularly develop new products and so, given the assumed similarity of tastes, are likely to produce and innovate similar varieties, or where consumers are slow to react to changes in prices and/or changes in the specifications of goods, perhaps because information flows are poor.

We would however usually expect the imitation lag to be longer than the demand lag, and in this case we would expect trade to be generated by innovation. The pattern of trade flows over time will depend on the relative length of these lags. Figure 4.7, which plots against time the trade

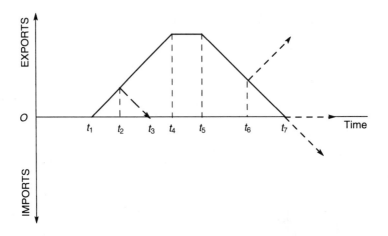

Figure 4.7   *The imitation-gap model*

balance of the country first introducing the innovation, shows various possible outcomes.

In all cases we assume that there is no trade in the good concerned up to time t_1, at which point the innovating country (A) introduces the new good. As consumers in the other country (B) become aware of the good they begin to consume it, and so country A starts to export the good. If the other country were unable to adopt the new technology then country A's exports would continue to increase until they reached a maximum at time t_4, and we could identify the period $t_1 t_4$ as the demand lag – or more strictly as the time needed for all consumers in country B to react to the introduction of the new good.

If producers in country B could adopt the new technology by time t_2 then they could halt A's penetration of their market before it reached its maximum and finally reverse it, with trade ceasing at time t_3. If on the other hand the imitation gap were longer, so that producers in B could not adopt the new technology until time t_5, A's exports to B would continue at their maximum until t_5, and would not be eliminated until t_7.

Figure 4.7 also shows two other possibilities. If producers in A can introduce another innovation at time t_6 then they may be able to resume penetration of B's market, and their exports will expand again. Maintaining a flow of product innovations will allow country A to continue exporting to country B provided the lag between new innovations is shorter than the imitation lag. On the other hand, if producers in A are unable to introduce a new innovation, but the adoption of the new technology in country B stimulates further innovation there, it is possible that B will start to penetrate A's domestic market.

■ 4.6 Product-cycle theories of trade

The theories discussed so far say nothing in explanation of two empirical observations: innovations tend to be concentrated in the richer, more developed countries, and early in the life of a good the production tends to take place in the country making the innovations, although the firm making the innovation may well have the option of producing in another country whose resource endowments are more suited to the production of the good concerned, and production may switch to such countries in the longer term.

The concentration of innovations in the richer countries is not particularly surprising. Although a few inventions may be the consequence of good fortune or individual inspiration, many inventions and most innovations are the outcome of expenditure on research and development (R&D). Why then is R&D expenditure concentrated in some countries rather than others? One possibility is that an environment conducive to R&D may exist in some countries (effective and long-running patents, favourable tax structures, etc.). Another is that as R&D requires specific skills, which are usually education-intensive, and specialist equipment, which is usually capital-intensive, capital-rich countries are more likely to become well-endowed with the factors required for R&D. Finally, it may be easier to introduce new products into a market where consumers have high incomes and a history of adopting new goods. In so far as the developed countries are likely to be relatively well endowed with factors suited to R&D and to have domestic consumers able and willing to purchase new products, we should not be surprised that innovations tend to be concentrated in such countries.

Vernon (1966) and Hirsch (1967) developed theories of trade that attempted to explain the tendency for the production of new goods to be concentrated in the developed countries early in the life of the product, but to move to other economies later on.[4] The basic argument is that the factor requirements for a good will vary over the lifetime of that good, so that we may observe a cycle in the production of a new good. The innovation of a new good is a risky business, and these risks may best be borne by relatively rich firms, particularly if the good in question is one which is of interest to consumers with relatively high incomes. The risks may be reduced by flexibility on the production side, which Hirsch argues will require skilled labour, and by a good flow of information on consumers' responses, which Vernon suggests may be obtained by proximity to the market. All these suggest that in the early, riskier, stage of a product's life-cycle we should expect production to be concentrated in the richer countries.

As the product itself and the manufacturing process become more standardised, and as any patents expire, producers in other countries will seek to enter the market if the pattern of factor prices in their economies is such as to give them a cost advantage over the initial producers. If the production process still requires inputs of highly skilled labour, and the good is still sufficiently costly to restrict its purchase to high-income consumers, we would expect to see such competition arising in other developed countries. It may well be the case that the firm which produced the good initially will itself set up production facilities in other developed countries in order to take advantage of their more favourable factor prices rather than let competitors establish themselves. In either case, we would expect to observe that exports of the good from the originally innovating country will decline.

If the technology for the good becomes completely standardised in a form that can use relatively unskilled labour, and is widely known and freely available, we might expect the location of production to transfer to relatively labour-rich economies. Again, the production might come from newly-established domestic companies in those countries, or it might be a consequence of existing companies transferring operations. Whatever the case may be, we may observe that the country originally producing the good, and even those that started production in the second stage of the product cycle, will experience a decline in their exports, and may even become importers. A good example of the product-cycle model is the radio.

When the radio was invented its market success was uncertain. To begin with, it did not appeal to many customers. Production was small scale, and of a handicraft type that demanded large amounts of skilled labour. The price was high and the good had to be produced close to the market as the commodity was far from perfect. Repairs and improvements of existing radios were necessary to make them work, and a quick feedback from the consumers was important for the producers in order that they could get the essential information required to perfect the product.

After an initial period of trial and error, the radio became an established product suitable for mass production. Demand for the product increased as the networks expanded and the usefulness to the consumers became obvious. Soon it developed into an export item as the innovating firms started to test foreign markets. At the end of the Second World War the radio was a well-established product. In the early stages of its history US producers dominated the international market for radios built with vacuum tubes. Soon, however, Japan took over a large share of this market as the production technique became known. Japan could exploit her low labour costs, and started to expand production and take over a large part of the international market. Then the US industry developed the transistor, and for a number of years the US radio competed successfully with the Japanese products, which continued to be based upon the old technology. Eventually the Japanese learned the transistor technology and again, taking advantage of its low labour costs, started to compete with American producers. Later developments on the part of the US industry with miniaturised transistor technology then allowed the US to regain the technological advantage, but again this knowledge was acquired by the Japanese and they began to dominate the world market again.

Nowadays the Japanese are also innovators in this field, and produce models using the latest technology. Production of less technologically advanced radios has moved to other Asian countries with lower wages, often in factories owned by Japanese firms.

■ 4.7 Increasing returns to scale

Strictly, the discussion of economies of scale should not come under the heading of technological differences, since economies of scale are integral to the production process defined by a given technology. It does however have its basis in technology rather than in factor endowment differences, and provides another explanation of the possibility of trade between countries which are identical in their tastes, their factor endowments and their technologies, so that under constant returns to scale we would not expect them to trade.

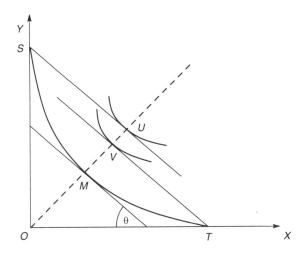

Figure 4.8 *Trade and increasing returns to scale*

If economies of scale are sufficiently strong then the production-possibility curve may bend in towards the origin, as shown in Figure 4.8. Suppose that we have only two countries with the same factor endowments and technologies, so that each country has a production-possibility curve like that in Figure 4.8, and suppose that they have the same tastes, which are such that under autarky they each produce and consume at point M, with a domestic price ratio of θ. If it becomes possible to trade then apparently no trade will take place. However, if there is a disturbance in either country which causes even a momentary divergence between their domestic price ratios then trade will start, and once trade has started it must lead to complete specialisation by both countries. In this very simple example we cannot predict *a priori* which country will produce which good; all we can say is that once a country moves its production towards one of the goods then it will gain a comparative advantage in that good, and its producers will then find it profitable to continue to switch into that good.

In the free trade equilibrium one country will produce at S, the other at T, with the former consuming at U and the other at V. Both countries will gain from specialisation and trade, as shown by their being on higher indifference curves.

It will be apparent that increasing returns to scale do not fit very comfortably into the framework that we have been using so far. Another obvious problem is that increasing returns to scale may be incompatible with perfect competition. It may be better then to consider increasing returns to scale in the context of imperfect competition, and this we shall do in Chapter 8, which deals with some theories of intra-industry trade.

☐ Notes

1 For a survey of the literature see Cheng (1984).
2 See also Chapter 7, which deals with the effect of technological progress on international trade.
3 Posner (1961).
4 Vernon (1966) and Hirsch (1967).

■ *Chapter 5* ■

The Gains from Inter-Industry Trade, the Distribution of Income, and Adjustment

■ 5.1 Introduction

In Chapters 2–4 we have been largely concerned with the positive effects of inter-industry trade – how the move from autarky to free trade will change commodity prices, industry outputs, production costs, factor utilisation, and factor prices. We have however also paid attention to the likely effects on social welfare through our use of community indifference curves. We have also noted the effects of the move to free trade on the distribution of income within a country or, more accurately, on the real returns to factors of production. In this chapter we shall extend our study of both these areas, and also be more specific about how changes in the distribution of income may, or may not, affect our judgement on whether there are 'gains from trade'.

■ 5.2 Gains from inter-industry trade

In our results on the overall gains from inter-industry trade you will have noted two phenomena. The first is that there are gains to be obtained from both the opportunity for consumers to buy goods at a price ratio different from that they face under autarky and the opportunity for producers to transfer resources from the (now) import-competing industry to the export industry.

The second is that the gains from trade are likely to increase as we move through time. The longer the time period that has elapsed since the move to free trade the more mobility we will observe in factors of production, the further away from the origin the production-possibility curve will move, and the higher the community indifference curve that can be attained.

Both these results are in accordance with our intuitive feeling for the way that free trade will generate gains. We would expect the move from autarky to trade to generate gains on both the demand and the supply side, and we would expect these gains to increase as the economy adapts more and more to the change in the policy regime. The results obtained by the use of community indifference curves may not then give us any immediate cause for concern, even though we know that there are major *caveats* to be attached to the construction of such curves.

However, we have also developed a set of results that make it clear that while some members of the community gain from free trade, others will probably lose. In general terms, those factors which are immobile will gain if they are tied in to the export sector, and will lose if they are tied into the import-competing sector. Those factors which are mobile will be in an indeterminate position (like labour in the specific factors model) unless all factors are mobile. When all factors are mobile then the distribution of gains and losses will reflect factor endowments and factor intensities provided that there are no differences in technology. Can we reconcile the claim that the community as a whole benefits while acknowledging that some members within that community will lose?

The construction of non-intersecting community indifference curves

We noted in Chapter 1 that unless we make certain restrictive assumptions we may be unable to construct a set of community indifference curves which (i) do not intersect with one another, and (ii) show higher levels of welfare as we move away from the origin. The first assumption that we make is that all individuals have the same indifference map, and that tastes are *homothetic*. By 'homothetic' we mean that all indifference curves have the same slope where they intersect a straight line drawn from the origin. The economic implication of this is that all goods have unit income elasticity of demand. Homotheticity is a weaker assumption than homogeneity; all homogeneous functions are homothetic, but the reverse is not true.

Figure 5.1 shows another box diagram, but with the axes of the diagram showing quantities of the two goods. The dimensions of the box are determined by the (fixed) amounts of the goods available, and the isoquants we have used so far are replaced by the identical and homothetic

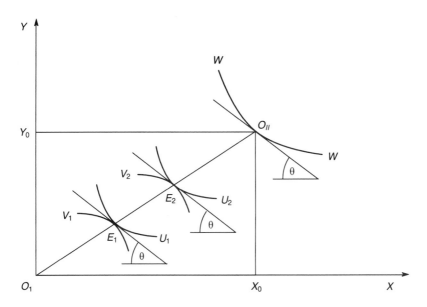

Figure 5.1 *Identical and homothetic tastes and community indifference curves*

indifference curves of two individuals. The efficient allocation curve in the box, defined by the set of points at which indifference curves for the two consumers are tangential, must be the diagonal of the box, with the common slope of each pair of indifference curves therefore the same (θ in Figure 5.1).

For example, if we considered a common slope which was greater than θ then the ray for consumer *I* along which his indifference curves had that slope would be lie above the diagonal of the box. The corresponding ray for consumer *II* would be parallel to the ray for consumer *I* but below the diagonal. The two rays could not intersect to define an equilibrium point.

Now consider point E_1 on the contract curve. Consumer *I* has a utility level, measured from O_I, which is indexed as U_1, and consumer *II* a utility level measured from O_{II}, which is indexed as V_1. This pair of utilities define a level of welfare for the economy which would be given by the quantities of goods X_0 and Y_0, divided between the two consumers in the way shown. We could therefore regard the top right-hand corner of the box, O_{II}, as lying on a community indifference curve representing that level of welfare. As the two consumers each have a marginal rate of substitution in consumption of θ, the marginal rate of substitution for the community, i.e. the slope of the community indifference curve, must also be θ at point O_{II}.

By constructing the set of boxes showing different combinations of X and Y that would allow consumer I to have a utility level of U_1 and consumer II a utility level of V_1, we would trace out a community indifference curve. All points on that community indifference curve would necessarily show the same level of welfare since each consumer has the same utility level.

Now consider point E_2, which is also on the contract curve. Now consumer I has utility level U_2, and consumer II utility level V_2. This pair of utilities also define a level of welfare for the economy which would be given by X_0 and Y_0, but now divided between the two consumers in the way shown by E_2. Once more the top right-hand corner of the box, O_{II}, is lying on a community indifference curve representing that level of welfare. Furthermore, the slope of this new community indifference curve must also be θ at point O_{II}. However it is quite likely that the level of welfare given by the distribution of goods shown by E_2 is different from that given by the distribution of goods shown by E_1.

It should be apparent that the assumption of identical and homothetic tastes is not sufficient to ensure that we can construct community indifference curves that do not intersect. Indeed, all our assumption has done is to ensure that the indifference curve defined by the distribution E_2 lies perfectly on top of the indifference curve defined by E_1, so that we have a pair of curves that intersect everywhere!

What we *have* achieved by making the identical and homothetic tastes assumption is to ensure that the set of curves defined by a box which is larger in both dimensions will always lie further from the origin than the set of curves defined by the box we have just considered. Figure 5.2 demonstrates this. The box from Figure 5.1 is shown with a dotted outline. A new box has been constructed which is greater in both dimensions by the same proportion so that it has the same diagonal as the original box. The set of overlapping community indifference curves defined by that box is labelled as W^*.

The new set of indifference curves must also have slope θ at the point shown by the top right-hand corner of the new box. For every point on the original community indifference curve we can find the larger box which will give a point on the new community indifference curve, and again the new curve must lie outside the original curve at that point and have the same slope. Indeed, the set of community indifference curves will have the same homothetic form as the indifference curves for each consumer.

What we have achieved is not however sufficient for our purposes. We cannot say what welfare level any point on a community indifference curve represents unless we also know the distribution of utilities between the consumers. It is possible that a point on a 'higher' curve represents a lower level of welfare than a point on a 'lower' curve.

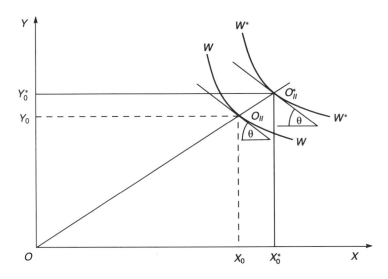

Figure 5.2 *Greater quantities of both goods give a set of 'higher' community indifference curves*

☐ Ordering the indifference curves using a social welfare function

In order to resolve this problem we need a criterion by which we can decide which of the set of overlapping curves passing through any point is the 'best' and which thus ensures that as we move away from the origin we are moving to curves which show a higher level of welfare. The most general way to do this would be to refer to a fully-defined social welfare function which would rank combinations of individual utility levels in terms of the welfare of society. Any such function will allow us to identify the distribution(s) of income within any given box which give the highest level of welfare.

The Pareto welfare judgement states that increasing the welfare of one individual without decreasing the welfare of any other individual constitutes an increase in society's welfare. Any welfare function which is consistent with this will ensure that the community indifference curve chosen as the 'best' from one box will show a higher level of welfare than the 'best' curve defined by a box with proportionately less of both goods. Hence the use of a fully-defined and Pareto-consistent welfare function allows us to obtain our aim of identifying a set of non-intersecting community indifference curves which show higher welfare levels as we move from the origin.

In order to make use of such a set of community indifference curves we then have to assume that some agency, usually taken to be the government, will make those redistributions of income necessary to obtain the highest welfare from any combination of goods, and that it can make those redistributions without using scarce resources and without affecting the operations of the economy in any other way.

A less general alternative often employed is to make the value judgement that any change which gives more of all goods to all consumers and which maintains the same shares in total income for all consumers produces an increase in social welfare. The government then reallocates income after a policy change in order to maintain the initial income distribution. The initial position is assumed to be an efficient position, but we make no judgement about whether the initial income distribution could be improved upon in welfare terms.

Figure 5.3 shows the operation of such a welfare judgement. Suppose that X_0 and Y_0 are the initial quantities of the two goods available, and that their initial distribution is shown by point E. The quantities X_0' and Y_0' have been chosen so that the top right-hand corner of the box they define, O_{II}', lies on the set of community indifference curves shown as WW. How do we identify the point on the contract curve for this new box (its diagonal) that shows the same distribution of income?

We first construct the line connecting the points O_{II} and O_{II}', and then draw from point E the line parallel to this. Where the contract curve for the new box meets this new line, point F, must show the same distribution

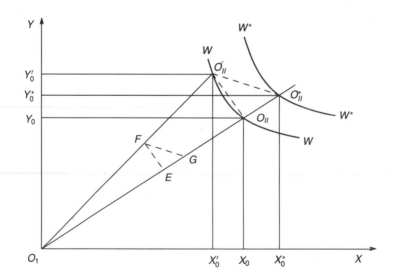

Figure 5.3   *Maintaining the same proportionate shares in national income*

of income as point E (the ratio of $O_I E$ to EO_{II} equals the ratio of $O_I F$ to FO_{II}'). We can now say that point O_{II}' with the distribution shown by point F lies on the same community indifference curve as point O_{II} with the distribution shown by point E. If we do this for all the points on the original set of curves through O_{II} and O_{II}' then we will have reduced the infinite set of curves to one curve.

We can follow a similar procedure to identify the point on the contract curve of the box with dimensions X_0^* and Y_0^* which also has the specified distribution. First we draw the line joining O_{II}' and O_{II}^*, and then draw from point F the line parallel with this. At the point G so defined the proportionate distribution of income is the same as at F, and so the same as at E. We can now construct an unique curve through O_{II}^* which shows a higher level of welfare than the curve through O_{II} while maintaining the same distribution of income.

☐ *Changes in the distribution of income*

In each of the models of inter-industry trade that we have considered, we have commented on the effects of the move from autarky to free trade on the rewards to factors of production. In the specific factors, Heckscher–Ohlin and technology-difference models we have also commented on the change in the distribution of income between the various factors.

The Heckscher–Ohlin model provides what is probably the most widely known result: the move from autarky to free trade will increase the real reward to the factor with which a country is more abundantly endowed, and will reduce the real reward to the other factor.

This is however a *long-run* result. It deals with the situation when both factors of production have had time to move between the two sectors. We should not expect it to hold in the intervening period. We shall consider the changes in the rewards to factors in the course of the adjustment to free trade later in this chapter. First we shall consider a demonstration of the gains from trade that holds 'for all income distributions', so freeing us from the need to make the assumptions that justify the use of community indifference curves.

▮ 5.3 A more general approach to the gains from trade

In two important papers Paul Samuelson[1] developed a general demonstration of the gains from trade using the concepts of the *consumption-possibility curve* and the *utility-possibility frontier*. We shall consider a simplified version of his analysis, using the case of a small country trading at given international prices.

Figure 5.4 shows the production-possibility curve for our small country, *SS*, and the terms of trade line *TT*. Note that we have not introduced community indifference curves to the diagram, nor have we assumed that consumers' tastes are identical and/or homothetic. Under autarky this country can only consume those combinations of X and Y that it can produce from its own resources. We may therefore say that under autarky the curve *SS* is also the country's consumption-possibility curve.

Once the (small) country is free to trade at the given international prices then it may choose to consume at any point on the line *TT*. The country's consumption-possibility curve under free trade is therefore *TT*. Note that, except at point *P*, the country can find a point on *TT* that allows consumption of more of both goods than any combination consumed under autarky. For example, compare points *E* and *F*.

Now consider the box defined by point *E* under autarky. If *E* is a point which satisfies the three Pareto efficiency conditions then the combination of goods shown by *E* must be distributed between our two consumers in such a way that their common marginal rate of substitution in consumption is the same as the slope of the production-possibility curve at *E*, and this defines the individual utility of each consumer.

If we now consider all the possible consumption points on *SS*, and the associated individual utility levels given by the efficient distribution of the quantities between the two consumers, we can plot the pairs of utilities (U_I and U_{II}) to obtain the utility-possibility frontier shown as *AA* in Figure 5.5.

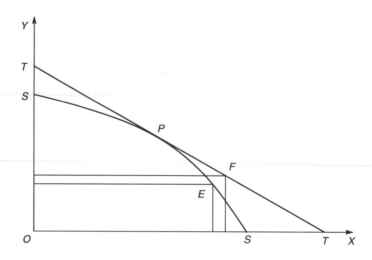

Figure 5.4 *Consumption possibilities for a small country under autarky and free trade*

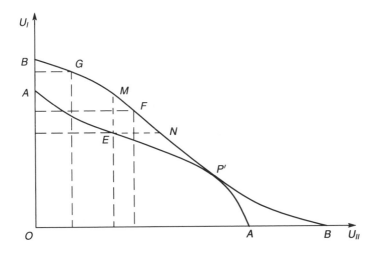

Figure 5.5 *Utility-possibility frontiers for a small country*

This frontier shows the maximum utility that can be given to one individual for specified levels of utility for the other individual under autarky. It will have negative slope (we can only make one individual better off by making the other worse off if we are in a Pareto efficient state), but because utilities are only measured ordinally we cannot say any more about its shape than that.

Now consider the box defined by point *F* on the free trade consumption-possibility curve *TT* in Figure 5.4. As we have more of both goods at *F* than we do at *E* we must be able to allocate them so that we make both individuals better off. If in fact we allocate them efficiently (so that each consumer's marginal rate of substitution is equal to the terms of trade) then we will define a point on the utility-possibility frontier for free trade.

By repeating this process for all the points on *TT* we can obtain that utility-possibility frontier. In the light of our earlier remarks, this utility-possibility frontier for the free trade case, shown as *BB* in Figure 5.5, must lie outside the utility-possibility frontier for autarky, except at the point *P'*, corresponding to *P* in Figure 5.4, where they will touch.

We therefore know that free trade gives the possibility of making both consumers better off than they were in the autarky state. For example, if the autarky point were at *E* on the autarky utility-possibility frontier *AA* in Figure 5.6 then any point on the free trade utility-possibility frontier between *M* and *N*, such as *F*, would make both consumers better off.

However, we also know that the move to free trade will change the distribution of income in the economy. Suppose that the move actually results in point G on the free trade utility-possibility frontier, where consumer I is better off and consumer II is worse off than at E. The Pareto welfare judgement does not allow us to rank these two points. W could assume that the government will redistribute income efficiently between the two consumers in such a way that there is a move along BB from G to a point such as F, and then argue that there has been a gain in welfare.

We could of course assume that the government redistributes income according to a well-defined welfare function, so choosing the optimum point on BB. As point F will be regarded as superior to point E under most welfare judgements, any point on BB which is superior to F according to the welfare function must be superior to E.

If we wish to stay more closely to the Pareto welfare judgement then we could extend that judgement to cases where one person gains but another loses by the use of a *compensation criterion*. The most widely used compensation criterion argues that if we could transfer sufficient utility from the gainer to the loser to make the latter as well off in the new state as he was in the old, and still leave the gainer better off than he was in the old state, then we have an increase in welfare.

The move from G to M in Figure 5.5 would satisfy this criterion, since individual II is as well off at M as at E, and individual I is better off at M than at E. Note that there is no requirement that the compensation *actually* be paid (i.e. no actual redistribution of income), merely that it *could* be paid.

This result is often expressed as our having shown that free trade is better than autarky *for all income distributions*. Strictly we should qualify that statement by pointing out that it assumes we have accepted the Pareto welfare judgement.

■ 5.4 The adjustment problem

As we noted earlier, the move from the autarkic to the free trade position in the Heckscher–Ohlin model is not instantaneous. We shall examine the process of adjustment over time by assuming that we can divide the process of adjustment into three episodes. These are, following the common convention: the short run, in which all factors are immobile; the medium run, in which labour is mobile but capital is not; and the long run, in which both factors are mobile.

We assume for the purposes of this exercise that we are dealing with a small capital-rich country, Y being the capital-intensive good. We make all the other assumptions of the Heckscher–Ohlin model. When the opportunity to trade is opened for this country then it will export Y and import X.

In the long run then, the results of the Heckscher–Ohlin model will hold. Labour and capital will move from the X to the Y industry, the capital–labour ratio will decline in both industries, the real wage will fall, and the real return to capital will rise.

Welfare will increase, but the income distribution will change. If factor owners take a long-term view then we might expect capital owners to favour the move to free trade, and suppliers of labour to oppose it. If however they take a short- or medium-term view then their position may vary according to the industry to which they sell their factors.

We shall consider first how the gains from trade will change as we move from the short run, through the medium run, to the long run.[2] Figure 5.6 shows the changes in the production mix which we would expect to observe in our capital-rich, Y-exporting small economy. We shall assume that autarky has lasted long enough for the economy to be in a Pareto optimal state. Point A is the autarkic equilibrium point

In the short run factors cannot be moved between industries, so that production remains at point A. However, the opportunity to trade at terms of trade different from the autarky price ratio means that there will still be gains from trade for the community, as shown by the move to the higher indifference curve I_1.

Marginal products are unchanged if factors do not move so, for example, labour and capital employed in the Y industry will be as well off in terms of the Y good as under autarky. However, the X good is now

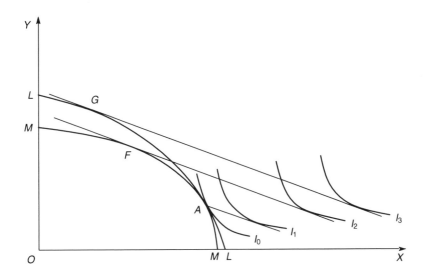

Figure 5.6 *Gains from trade in the short, medium and long run*

relatively cheaper with free trade, so the labour and capital employed in the Y industry must be able to purchase more of the X good, and we may therefore conclude that the owners of both capital and labour employed in Y will gain from free trade in the short term. A parallel argument suggests that the owners of labour and capital employed in the X industry must lose by the move to free trade in the short run.

In the medium term the production mix will change as labour moves from the import-competing industry (X) to the export industry (Y). Trade continues at the same relative prices, and so the gains from trade will be increased by the shift from X to Y production (the move from indifference curve I_1 to indifference curve I_2 in Figure 5.6). In a market economy the rise in the real wage rate in the export industry and the fall in the real wage rate in the import-competing industry will of course produce this reallocation, and the reallocation will bring about equality between the real wage rates in the two industries. Production will therefore move from point A to point B, so that there is increased production of the export good and decreased production of the import-competing good.

With labour mobile between the two sectors, but with two forms of capital, each tied to its own sector, a modification of the specific factors model of Chapter 2, with the capital and land of that model replaced by two forms of sector-specific capital, provides one way of analysing this situation. The results of that model tell us that in the medium term the owners of the form of capital that is specific to the export sector (Y) will gain from the move to free trade while the owners of the capital specific to the import-competing sector will lose, and that the results for labour will be ambiguous.

Figure 5.7 uses a more obviously Heckscher–Ohlin approach, and confirms these results. Autarky production is at point A. In the medium term labour moves from X to Y, but the allocation of capital cannot change. The medium-run allocation point must thus be a point such as B. The capital–labour ratio must fall in the Y sector and increase in the X sector.

Capital owners in the Y sector must gain in terms of the Y good as the marginal product of capital rises there, and in terms of the X good as well since the terms of trade are unchanged. By a parallel argument, capital owners in the X sector must lose in terms of both goods as the marginal product of that capital falls.

The real wage rate will fall in terms of the Y good, but rise in terms of the X good, so that the position of labour is indeed ambiguous. If the owners of factors take a medium-term rather than a long-term view then we may expect some capital owners (those in the Y sector) to be pro-free-trade, and the others to be anti-free-trade. Labour's position will depend on the relative importance of the X and Y goods in labour's consumption.

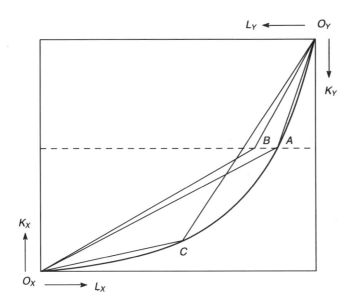

Figure 5.7 *Factor allocation in the short, medium and long run*

In the long run capital will transfer from the import-competing sector, X (where its real return fell with the opening of trade) to the export sector (where its real reward rose with the opening of trade). This must reduce the real return to capital in the export sector and increase the real return to capital in the import-competing sector. The increase in the amount of capital in the export sector must raise the marginal product of labour in that sector, while the decrease in capital in the import-competing sector must reduce the marginal product there, so there will be an incentive for labour as well to move from the import-competing sector to the export sector. The capital-intensive Y sector will not however absorb as much labour per unit of capital as the X sector releases, so the wage rate must fall.

The economy is now operating on its long-run production possibilities curve, LL, in Figure 5.6, and production will shift to point C. As relative prices do not change, the country must be able to move to an even higher indifference curve, I_3. As Y is the capital-intensive good, we know from the Heckscher–Ohlin model that in the long term the real return to *all* capital must be higher after the move to free trade than it was under autarky, while the real wage rate must be lower.

The short-run effect on real returns to capital of the move to free trade is to increase them in the export sector, and decrease them in the import-competing sector. In the medium run, after labour has moved from X to Y, the real return to capital in the export sector increases further, and that in the import-competing sector decreases again. In the long run, with capital able to move from X to Y (with some labour going with it), the return to capital must be the same in both sectors.

☐ *Notes*

1   Samuelson (1939) and (1962).
2   See Neary (1985) for a more detailed analysis of the adjustment problem.

■ *Chapter 6* ■

Empirical Testing of Inter-Industry Trade

■ *6.1* Introduction

The first attempts at testing theories of inter-industry trade were made in 1951 and 1952 by MacDougall[1] who produced results that were interpreted as supporting the Ricardian model's explanation of trade patterns, and by Leontief[2] in 1953, whose results cast doubt upon the Heckscher–Ohlin explanation (the famous 'Leontief Paradox'). Since then there has been considerable work on refining the tests themselves, and on restating the models in ways which make them more suitable for testing. Following Verdoorn's work[3] in 1960 there has been another strand in the empirical analysis – testing theories of intra-industry trade. We shall deal with this in Chapter 9.

We face three major problems in testing all economic theories. The first is that the assumptions of the models may not be consistent with reality. Taking some examples from the Heckscher–Ohlin model, it is possible that neither tastes nor technology are identical between countries, and certainly there are barriers to trade in the form of both transport costs and tariffs and other trade policies. The second problem is that the data available are rarely in the ideal form for carrying out our tests. The third is the possibility that the tests are not methodologically correct, so biasing the results one way or the other.

Two important consequences of these problems are that the results of empirical studies may be challenged, and that results which are inconsistent with the theories can be 'explained away'. On the other hand, those empirical studies that have suggested that theories are incorrect have often stimulated refinements of both the theories themselves and the tests employed, and further empirical work on the extent to which the assumptions made are inconsistent with the real world.

We shall start by considering Leontief's test of the Heckscher–Ohlin model, even though this is reversing the chronological order, since the results of this test have provided a major stimulus to work on what is still the dominant theory of inter-industry trade, and shall discuss some of that later work. We shall then go on to consider tests of the other important group of inter-industry trade models, those that are based on technological differences between countries.

■ 6.2 The Leontief Paradox

Leontief's test of the Heckscher–Ohlin theorem

Leontief argued that the Heckscher–Ohlin theorem predicts that a country will tend to export those commodities which use its abundant factor of production intensively and import those which use its scarce factor intensively. His test was based on the recently constructed input–output table for the United States for 1947.[4] By common consent the United States was the country most abundantly endowed with capital at that time. Therefore, one would have expected the United States to export capital-intensive goods and import labour-intensive ones.

Leontief was unable to obtain direct information on the factor intensity of the actual imports into the United States. However, the Heckscher–Ohlin model predicts that under free trade and with consequent factor-price equalisation, the capital–labour ratio in US import-competing goods should be the same as in its imports, and he could obtain information on the former.

Leontief estimated the consequences for the use of factors of production of the United States decreasing its exports and increasing its import-substitutes by $1 million. He only took two factors explicitly into account, labour and capital. When exports are decreased, both labour and capital are released. When production of import-competing goods is increased, both more labour and capital are needed. According to Leontief's hypothesis, we would expect relatively more capital to be released from the export industries and relatively more labour to be needed by the import-competing industries.

Table 6.1 summarises Leontief's calculations. As we can see, his finding was the reverse of what we would expect. The US export industries used relatively more labour than did its import-competing industries. Hence the United States exports labour-intensive goods and imports capital-intensive goods!

Table 6.1 *Capital and labour needed to reduce exports and increase import-substitutes by $1 million in the United States in 1947*

	Exports	Import-substitutes
Capital ($000 at 1947 prices)	2551	3091
Labour (man years)	182	170
Capital–labour ratio	13.99	18.18

How are we to explain Leontief's paradoxical result – that the most capital-rich of all countries, the United States, was exporting labour-intensive goods in 1947?

Like all empirical findings, Leontief's paradox can be explained in a number of ways. We can in this context only touch on what we regard as some of the main contributions to the heated controversy to which Leontief's findings gave rise.

☐ *Criticisms of the data and the methodology*

In the immediate aftermath of the publication of Leontief's findings, several writers questioned the accuracy and the appropriateness of the data and the nature of the test. Buchanan criticised Leontief's measurement of capital: he argued that Leontief's capital coefficients were 'investment requirement coefficients' which did not take into account the durability of capital.[5] Loeb argued that the differences in capital-intensity between the export sector and the import-competing sector were not statistically significant.[6] Swerling contended that 1947 (the year for which the input–output table was constructed) was an atypical year.[7]

Leontief refined his measurements and tried to answer this and some other criticisms in a paper published in 1956.[8] This paper hardly settled all the points about measurements and the like. This was not to be expected.

☐ *The unbalanced trade problem*

Leamer[9] has argued that the Leontief Paradox is the consequence of an incorrect interpretation of the Heckscher–Ohlin model when trade is not balanced. That is, when a capital-rich country is experiencing unbalanced trade then we cannot conclude from the Heckscher–Ohlin model that its exports will be relatively capital-intensive.

Leamer demonstrated that when a country has a trade surplus (as was the case for the United States in 1947), the appropriate tests are to compare the capital–labour ratio in either the country's *net exports* or its *production* with the capital–labour ratio in the country's *consumption*. When he examined US trade in 1947 he found that, using his tests, there was no evidence of the Leontief Paradox.

☐ *Human capital explanations*

One group of criticisms of Leontief's original work, and one to which he himself leant, focused on the heterogeneity of labour. Labour, it is argued, may be differentiated by its *skill*. One model of the skill element regards it as the outcome of investment in education and training – the creation of *human capital*.

Leontief argued that American labour could not really be compared with labour in other countries, because the productivity of an American worker is substantially higher (three times higher, he suggested) than that of a foreign worker. This would reconcile his findings with the Heckscher–Ohlin theorem.

These are quite strong assumptions to accept. Most economists might acknowledge the superior quality of American labour. Leontief quotes a study by Kravis indicating that wages are higher in US export industries than in its import-competing industries as supporting evidence.[10] This, of course, conflicts with the assumption that labour is a homogeneous factor of production, which would imply the same wage irrespective of occupation. Moreover, it is difficult to see why the United States should possess higher quality labour, but not higher quality capital.[11] Finally, the value of three suggested is entirely *ad hoc*.

There are conceptual problems in dealing with the question of human capital in conjunction with physical capital. One approach has been to aggregate them to form a single input. Kenen tried to estimate the value of human capital involved in US exports and import-competing products.[12] Using a 9 per cent rate of discount, he estimated its value by capitalising the income difference between skilled and unskilled labour. He then added the estimates of human capital to those of physical capital and found, indeed, that the Leontief paradox was reversed. There must however be severe doubts about the validity of this procedure.

The second approach is to treat labour skills/human capital as additional factors of production which are distinct from both physical capital and unskilled labour. Leontief re-estimated his model in 1956, using data for 1951, and disaggregating the labour force into various groups with differing skill-intensities.[13] This work showed that US exports embodied more skilled labour than did its imports, but did not resolve the paradox in that the United States still appeared to importing capital-intensive goods. It has been argued however that the results are consistent with the predictions of a multi-factor Heckscher–Ohlin model on the assumption that the United States is abundant in skilled labour or human capital. Various studies since then have tended to support this analysis.[14]

For example, Keesing[15] showed that there was a rather high correlation between US net exports of various commodities and the amount of skilled labour used in their production, so that the US especially exported goods using a high percentage of skilled labour.

Baldwin[16] analysed United States trade in 1962 in a multi-factor setting. Using costs of education and earnings foregone, he obtained a different measure of human capital. His findings were somewhat ambiguous, to the extent that he found that his measure of human capital was not enough to reverse the paradox except when products using natural resources intensively were excluded. He found that US exports were intensive in their use of labour (which is consistent with the Leontief result) and in highly educated and highly paid labour (particularly that of scientists and engineers).

Stern and Maskus[17] assumed that labour skill was positively correlated with rates of pay, and used a measure based on those as a proxy for human capital. They estimated that US imports were less intensive in their use of human capital than were exports in 1958, but confirmed that the United States was still exporting relatively labour-intensive goods. However, when they considered data for 1972 they found that US exports and imports were roughly equivalent in their intensity of use of human capital, but that the Leontief Paradox had disappeared.

The use of human capital as an explanation of the pattern of US trade is generally regarded as a vindication of the Heckscher–Ohlin model. There seems to be little doubt that the United States exports goods which are intensive in the use of human capital and imports goods which are intensive in 'raw' labour. The general results do not seem to hinge on whether one estimates human capital by discounting wage differentials or by dividing labour into classes of various skills.

In a study of UK trade, Crafts and Thomas[18] conclude that their results are evidence that the (modified) Heckscher–Ohlin model is 'a useful way to examine trade patterns'. Among other results, they found that the United Kingdom has a comparative disadvantage in goods which are intensive in human capital.

☐ *Natural resource explanations*

Another explanation for which Leontief showed a certain understanding is that the only two factors explicitly taken into account in his original analysis are labour and capital. As he notes:

Invisible in all these tables but ever present as a third factor or rather as a whole additional set of factors determining this country's productive capacity and, in particular, its comparative advantage vis-a-vis the rest of the world, are natural resources: agricultural lands, forests, rivers and our rich mineral deposits.[19]

By taking into account this third factor an explanation to the Leontief paradox can be found. It might be the case, for instance, that imports require more capital to labour than exports; it is still, however, possible that imports are intensive in the third factor, say land. If capital and the third factor (land) are substitutes but both are complementary with labour, it might be the case that import-competing goods are capital-intensive in the United States but land-intensive abroad.

Vanek,[20] defining natural resources as products of the extractive industries such as agriculture and mining, found that over the period 1870–1955 the United States became a net importer of goods that were intensive in natural resources. He also found evidence that natural resources and capital were complementary inputs, and argued that the finding that the United States imported capital-intensive goods in fact reflected their imports of goods that were intensive in their use of natural resources.

It is not apparent however that we can treat natural resources as a mobile factor, in which case we should either consider a model with elements of the specific factors model, or exclude resource-based industries when testing the Heckscher–Ohlin theorem. Various studies[21] have shown that if the latter approach is followed then the Leontief Paradox disappears.

□ Demand reversals

One explanation is compatible with the 'weaker' version of the Heckscher–Ohlin theory. We know from Chapter 3 that differential factor endowments establish a bias in each country to the production of the good using its intensive factor. But demand conditions might offset this predisposition. If a capital-rich country, for instance, prefers capital-intensive goods, it may import these and export labour-intensive goods.[22]

A variant on this argument concerns the human capital issue. Morral[23] has argued that in certain high-income countries human capital is both physically abundant but high priced. This is revealed both in the price of equivalent labour being higher in high-income than in low-income countries, and in the ratio of returns to skilled labour to returns to unskilled labour being higher in the former. He has suggested that this may be due to differences in tastes, coining the term *demand reversal* for the phenomenon. Tharakan[24] has suggested that if such demand reversals are permanent then there is the possibility of particular low-income countries specialising in products which are intensive in human but not in physical capital, with such a pattern of trade being consistent with the Heckscher–Ohlin theorem.

☐ *Factor-intensity reversals*

The analytically most interesting explanation is perhaps the one that invokes factor reversals. We have already discussed the theoretical meaning of factor reversals in Chapter 3. Let us now look into the implications of the existence of factor reversals for Leontief's results. Leontief took only one country into account. He only computed factor requirements for marginal changes in the production of US exports and import-competing goods.

Figure 6.1 reproduces the essential elements of Figure 3.7. Country A is the physically capital-rich country. It is also the capital-rich country in factor-price terms, since ϕ^A is greater than ϕ^B. However, it lies on the other side of the factor-intensity reversal to country B. The diagram has been constructed so that the relative price of the X good is higher in A than in B ($\theta^A > \theta^B$), so that country A will export Y and import X. Good Y is however country A's labour-intensive good under autarky ($\rho_Y^A < \rho_X^A$), and will also be so with trade. That is, the capital-rich country will export *its* labour-intensive good.

If we consider the other country then we can identify the problem. The labour-rich country (B) is exporting *its* labour-intensive good, X ($\rho_X^B < \rho_Y^B$). This is the basic problem when the two countries are on opposite sides of a factor-intensity reversal: one exports the good which is intensive in the use of its abundant factor, the other exports the good which is intensive in the use of its scarce factor.

Leontief, however, never brought a second country into the picture. Had he done so and compared, for instance, the factor intensities in US export industries with those of Japan or West Europe, he might well have found that American exports were capital-intensive compared with Japanese or Western European exports. By invoking factor reversals we can thus explain Leontief's puzzling results.[25]

An interesting empirical study of the possibility of factor reversals was made by Minhas.[26] He, together with other economists, derived a new form of production function, what is now called the constant elasticity of substitution (CES) production function.[27] When estimating this production function for different countries Minhas found that factor reversals were

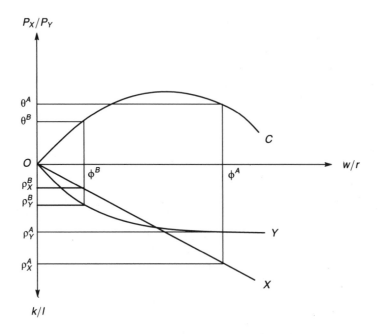

Figure 6.1   *The physically capital-rich country may export its labour-intensive good when there is a factor reversal*

quite common because the elasticity of substitution differs between industries, and that these factor reversals occur in the empirically relevant range of relative-factor prices (i.e. factor-price ratios prevailing in such diverse countries as the United States and India).

This result would tend to reinforce the theoretical possibility of factor reversals as an explanation of the Leontief paradox. Minhas's findings would, alas, also tend to minimise the practical relevance of the factor-price equalisation theorem and the Heckscher–Ohlin theorem about capital-rich countries exporting capital-intensive goods, as both these theorems build on the assumption of a one-to-one correspondence between factor prices and factor intensities.

Minhas's study is, therefore, of considerable empirical relevance. His findings have, however, been criticised on econometric grounds, primarily by Leontief[28], Lary[29] and Hufbauer[30]. They, and others, have suggested that factor-intensity reversals may not be common if we exclude the natural resource-intensive sectors. This has had important implications for factor-based studies of international trade. The tendency has developed for relying on just that methodology that Leontief used: inferring the factor-intensity of a country's imports from the factor-intensity of its import-competing goods.

6.3 Testing models based on technology differences

We shall now consider the other broad group of models of inter-industry trade. These are models which may be categorised as technology-difference and technology-gap models. Such models obviously embody a criticism of the Heckscher–Ohlin model, to which the assumption of a common technology is central.

Labour productivity and comparative advantage

The Ricardian theory of comparative advantage suggests that labour costs will be the determinant of trade: the country with the lower labour cost in the production of a good will be the exporter of that commodity. A pioneering attempt at empirical testing of this theory was made by MacDougall, published in 1951 and 1952.[31] MacDougall used data on 25 products from 1937 to compare labour productivity and exports for the United States and Great Britain. The bilateral trade between them was only a small fraction of their total trade. What MacDougall then tested was whether their relative exports to third countries were connected with their labour productivities.

Wage rates in the manufacturing sector were roughly twice as high in the United States as in Britain. Therefore, MacDougall argued, the United States should be the dominant exporter in markets where her labour productivity was more than twice as high as in Britain. Britain, on the other hand, should be the dominant supplier in any line of production where her labour productivity was more than 50 per cent of the American. Whenever labour productivity in US industry was twice that of its British counterpart, we should expect export shares of the two countries to be roughly equal in third markets.

In most cases the ratio of US to British exports was higher whenever her ratio of labour productivity was higher. However, the dividing line between British and US exports in third markets was not where American productivity was twice as high as in Britain. In these markets Britain had still a comparative advantage (we should remember that the test used figures from 1937). The American industries needed even a larger productivity advantage, roughly 2.4, to be even with the British in third markets. The basic explanation for this phenomenon seems to be in terms of demand factors and political preferences. MacDougall himself suggested that imperial preferences and other tariff advantages that were enjoyed by countries which were close to her politically could be possible explanations for the advantage that Britain at the time enjoyed in her export markets. Other reasons could be that Britain had been the pioneering industrial nation and that her dominance in international finance and her commercial reputation still gave her certain advantages which were difficult to measure but which were still important.

MacDougall's study have been interpreted as giving support to the Ricardian theory of comparative advantage, despite the fact that the results are obviously inconsistent with the simple Ricardian model (which implies complete specialisation in most cases). They have instead been interpreted as supporting the more general 'Ricardian' argument that differences in relative labour productivities are the determinant of comparative advantage. In so far as these differences are due to differences in technology then we do have a test of an alternative to the Heckscher–Ohlin model.

This interpretation was subsequently challenged by Bhagwati,[32] but most economists have largely ignored Bhagwati's criticisms and have accepted MacDougall's results as at least demonstrating a relationship between relative labour productivities and export performance.

It may also be argued that MacDougall's results do not allow us to distinguish between the Heckscher–Ohlin and the Ricardian models. If factor prices are not equalised in the Heckscher–Ohlin model (perhaps because of transport costs or other barriers to trade) then neither will capital–labour ratios. Since the productivity of labour depends on the capital–labour ratio, it would be possible to observe a relationship between trade and labour productivity that is consistent with MacDougall's findings.

Follow-up studies of MacDougall's work have been made by Stern[33] and by Balassa.[34] Stern's study is of special interest. He repeats MacDougall's procedure with data from 1950 instead of from 1937. His general findings confirm the earlier results. But in markets where the higher American labour productivity and the lower British wages offset each other, the British predominance has now diminished so that US producers now have about 80 per cent of the British exports as compared with 40 per cent before. This suggests that Britain is losing some of the 'immaterial' comparative advantages that she enjoyed before and that export shares in these markets will be determined purely on economic grounds.

6.4 Technological-gap and product-cycle models

In Chapter 4 we met Posner's technological-gap theory and Vernon's 'product life-cycle' theory.[35] A distinguishing feature of such models is that technological change is a dynamic phenomenon. They are not however as fully developed as the Heckscher–Ohlin and Ricardian models.

Introducing 'technology' as a separate explanatory variable in empirical studies is not a simple problem. A major problem is that it is difficult to quantify. Moreover, it is likely to be closely related to other variables which would be used , such as the supply of human capital. A final problem is that, as we noted when considering technology-difference models, there are barriers to the free movement of a specific 'piece' of technology between countries (patents, etc.), but these barriers have a limited lifetime.

In a multi-country study, Gruber and Vernon[36] defined technology-intensive industries as those where at least 6 per cent of the total employment consisted of engineers and scientists. They concluded that only for the United States was technology-intensity of unambiguously significant importance. Hirsch,[37] in an attempt to consider both factor proportions and technological theories of trade, found that his measures of physical capital, human capital and technology were mutually correlated. This made it difficult to draw a clear distinction between the importance of these variables in explaining trade patterns.

In 1981, Aquino[38] used the framework of the product life-cycle theory in an examination of how comparative advantage in manufactures shifted from technology-rich to technology-poor countries over time. He measured the technology endowments of countries using past levels of expenditure on research and development. Once again, the strong correlations between his various explanatory variables makes it difficult to interpret his results.

6.5 Econometric studies

More recently, attention has been focused on econometric studies of the importance of various country-specific attributes in explaining the pattern of trade. Typically, such studies are of cross-sectional data from a selection of countries and for a number of commodities. They tend to be eclectic, in that the attributes may be suggested by a range of trade models, rather than being directed at testing a particular model. Many of these studies have already been cited in the discussion on the Leontief Paradox. Some will be mentioned again when we consider tests of models of intra-industry trade in Chapter 9.

Hufbauer[39] is regarded as the pioneer of the cross-section, multi-industry, multi-country approach to the testing of trade theories. He calculated the rank-order correlations between various national attributes (GDP *per capita*, proportion of workers who were skilled, etc.) and attributes of the commodities which were traded (such as capital- and skill-intensities and economies of scale). He concluded from his results that actual trade patterns are not explicable in terms of a single theory.

Researchers since Hufbauer have tended to use multiple regression analysis in cross-sectional studies. Two problems may be identified for almost all such studies. First, as we have already seen, many of the explanatory variables suggested by economic theory are highly correlated with one another, making interpretation of the regression results difficult. Second, such studies are almost invariably static (i.e. the data come from just one time period), whereas some of the explanatory variables used are suggested by dynamic models.

Leamer[40] considered the commodity trade of 12 Atlantic-area countries in 1958. He classified his explanatory variables as 'state of development variables' (GNP and population), 'trade resistance variables' (distance and tariffs) and 'resource variables' (capital-intensity, R&D, education and, as a proxy for industrial sophistication, electricity use). When he used a country's imports as a proportion of its GNP as the dependent variable, he found that the best explanatory variables were the state-of-development variables, with the resistance variables also performing well. However, when he attempted to explain the variation in countries' import–export ratios he found that his resource variables performed better than the others.

Stern and Maskus[41] used various econometric techniques in an analysis of changes in the determinants of the structure of US manufactures trade between 1958 and 1976. They found difficulty in establishing whether the impact of physical capital was positive or negative, but that their technological variables were positively correlated with net exports. Branson and Monoyios[42] obtained the result that both physical and human capital were positively correlated with American net exports.

■ 6.6 Summary and conclusions

There are three main types of theories of inter-industry trade, all of which focus largely on the supply side of the model: Ricardian, Heckscher–Ohlin and technological. The empirical evidence does not suggest a dominance of one set of theories over the others.

As a consequence, many economists are adopting an eclectic approach, classifying goods into three classes which match the three theories. That is:

(a) Ricardo goods, where comparative advantage depends largely on production conditions. These usually include extraction industries (agriculture, mining, etc.) and industries which carry out basic processing of raw materials.
(b) Heckscher–Ohlin goods, which have generally known and relatively stable technologies, with comparative advantage resting largely on factor endowments, and which are not tied down to the availability of specific factors. Textiles are often cited as the typical Heckscher–Ohlin good.
(c) Technological goods, for which the production process is sophisticated and subject to frequent change, with the most recent technology probably specific to certain countries, and with proximity to large high-income markets an important factor. Computers and pharmaceutical products are examples of such goods.

It is then argued that the countries which have, and will keep, the comparative advantage in the last group are the most developed nations. Comparative advantage in the Heckscher–Ohlin goods however may shift around among countries in response to changes in factor prices and factor availabilities, so that the so-called 'foot-loose industries' would come in this group. Comparative advantage in the Ricardian goods may, it has been suggested, lie with the developing countries.

☐ *Notes*

1   MacDougall (1951).
2   Leontief (1953).
3   Verdoorn (1960).
4   Leontief was one of the pioneers of input–output analysis.
5   Buchanan (1955).
6   Loeb (1954).
7   Swerling (1954).
8   Leontief (1956).
9   Leamer (1980)
10 Kravis (1956)
11 Were both labour and capital more efficient in the United States by the same proportion then the model being tested would be more akin to the technology-difference model considered in Chapter 4.
12 Kenen (1965).
13 Leontief (1956).
14 See Tharakan (1985) for a more detailed discussion.

15   Keesing (1966).

16   Baldwin (1971).

17   Stern and Maskus (1981).

18   Crafts and Thomas (1986).

19   Leontief (1953), p. 346.

20   Vanek (1959).

21   For example Baldwin (1971).

22   The argument about demand effects as an explanation of the Leontief paradox was proposed by Valavanis-Vail (1954).

23   Morrall (1972).

24   Tharakan (1994), p.66.

25   This point is made in Jones (1956).

26   Minhas (1963).

27   Arrow, Chenery, Minhas and Solow (1961). The mathematical form of the CES production function allows for the possibility of factor intensity reversals. The Cobb–Douglas production function, dominant then as now in empirical studies, does not. The implication of using the Cobb–Douglas function is that you can never 'observe' factor-intensity reversals since the mathematical form precludes it! The Cobb–Douglas function is in fact a special form of the (more general) CES function.

28   Leontief (1964).

29   Lary (1968).

30   Hufbauer (1970).

31   MacDougall (1951).

32   Bhagwati (1964)

33   Stern (1962).

34   Balassa (1963).

35   Posner (1961) and Vernon (1966).

36   Gruber and Vernon (1970).

37   Hirsch (1974).

38   Aquino (1981).

39   Hufbauer (1970).

40   Leamer (1974).

41   Stern and Maskus (1981). The authors use both standard linear regression methods and probit analysis.

42   Branson and Monoyios (1977).

■ *Chapter 7* ■

Factor Accumulation and Technological Progress in Inter-Industry Trade

■ *7.1* Introduction

In the context of the inter-industry trade models we have met in the earlier chapters, a country grows if its production-possibility curve moves outwards. The obvious sources of such economic growth are an increase in the country's endowment of one (or more) of the factors of production, and an improvement in the technology with which one or both goods are produced. We shall examine both these possibilities later in this chapter, considering in particular the effects on welfare and the rewards to factors of production.

Any form of economic growth will, except in very particular circumstances, have an effect on the growing country's volume of trade. Whether trade will increase or decrease will depend on the form of the shift in the production-possibility curve and the change in the consumption pattern as incomes change. In the case of a large country, a change in the volume of trade will bring about a change in the prices at which trade takes place. This raises the possibility that, for a large trading country, growth could lead to a reduction in welfare – a possibility that does not exist under autarky.

We can discuss these problems in fairly general terms (i.e. without specifying the source of the growth), and that is what we shall do in the next section.

■ 7.2 The effects of growth on trade

We shall start by considering a very simple case which may be used as a bench-mark against which to consider more complex situations – what has been called *neutral growth in trade*.[1] In Figure 7.1 the country's production-possibility curve before growth takes place is QQ, and the country produces at P. It faces given terms of trade, shown by the line UV, and exports a quantity MP of good X and imports MC of good Y, so consuming at C.

Suppose now that the country's production-possibility curve shifts outwards to become Q^*Q^*. The shift shown has a particular form. The new production-possibility curve is tangential to the line U^*V^* (which has the same slope as UV) at P^*, and P^* is on the straight line drawn from the origin through point P. This means that the outputs of the two goods have increased by the same proportion. We would then say that there has been *neutral growth in production*. Note that we could draw an infinite number of production-possibility curves which are tangential to the line U^*V^* at P^*.

Suppose now that the country produces at point P^* and exports M^*P^* of X and imports M^*C^* of Y so that it consumes at point C^*, where C^* is on the straight line drawn from the origin through the original consumption

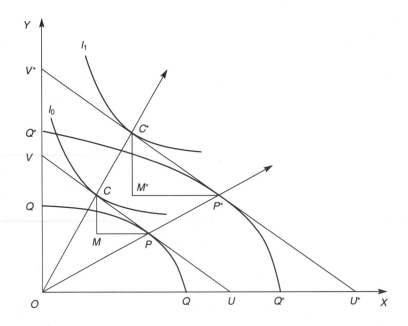

Figure 7.1   *Neutral growth in production and consumption*

point *C*. Consumption of the two goods has therefore increased by the same proportion, and we would say that there has been *neutral growth in consumption*. Moreover, the proportionate increase in consumption of each of the two goods must be exactly the same as the proportionate increase in their outputs (as may be shown by the use of similar triangles).

The consequence of these two neutral growth outcomes is that the exports of *X* and the imports of *Y* have also increased by that same proportion. Furthermore, the proportionate increase in trade (measured in terms of either exports of *X* or imports of *Y*) is exactly the same as the proportionate increase in the value of the country's output at world prices. Again, this may be shown by the use of similar triangles. At the original production point *P* the value of output in terms of the *X* good is given by *OU*. At the new production point P^* the value of output in terms of the *X* good is OU^*. But since *UV* is parallel to U^*V^*, *OPU* and OP^*U^* are similar triangles. It follows that $OQ^*/OQ = OP^*/OP$. But *OCP* and OC^*P^* are also similar triangles, so that $OP^*/OP = C^*P^*/CP$. Finally, *MCP* and $M^*C^*P^*$ are similar triangles, so that $C^*P^*/CP = C^*M^*/CM = M^*P^*/MP$. We have therefore shown that the ratio of the new volume of exports to the original volume (measured by M^*P^*/MP) is equal to the ratio of the new value of output to the original value of output (measured by OU^*/OU). Obviously the same is true of the change in the import volume.

Any outcome in which the proportionate increase in trade is equal to the proportionate increase in output is referred to as *neutral growth in trade*.

Note that whereas neutral growth in production coupled with neutral growth in consumption is sufficient to give neutral growth in trade, it is not necessary. Figure 7.2 shows a case where neutral growth in trade occurs without there being neutral growth in either production or consumption. That is, in Figure 7.2 the ratios C^*M^*/CM, M^*P^*/MP, and OU^*/OU are all the same, even though neither OPP^* nor OCC^* are straight lines.

We can now define four other forms of growth, each of which shows a *bias* when compared with neutral growth. If the proportionate growth in trade is less than the proportionate increase in income then growth is said to have an *anti-trade bias*. In the extreme, where growth results in an absolute decrease in trade, we say that there is an *ultra-anti-trade bias*. If, on the other hand, the proportionate growth in trade is greater than the proportionate growth in income, we have *pro-trade biased* growth. The extreme version of this, *ultra-pro-trade biased* growth, occurs when the increase in trade is greater than the increase in income.

Which form of bias occurs depends on what happens to production and consumption. Suppose, for example, that there is neutral growth in consumption, but that production of the import-competing good increases

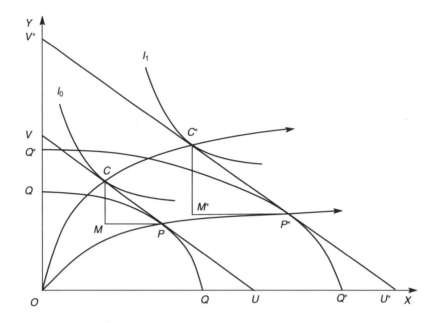

Figure 7.2   *Neutral growth in trade without neutral growth in production and consumption*

by proportionately more than production of the export good. In such a case, illustrated in Figure 7.3, there will be an anti-trade bias in the growth.

Such an example suggests that we may use definitions of bias for growth in production and consumption which parallel those given for bias in trade. For example, growth in production which increases production of the import-competing good by proportionately more than it increases production of the export good (as in the example above) may be defined as having an anti-trade bias. The definitions of bias in the growth of production are illustrated in Figure 7.4, where X is again the export good.

The original production point is at P. If the production point after growth (at constant relative prices) lies to the left of the 'neutral' line but to the right of the vertical line through P then production of the export good has increased, but by proportionately less than has production of the import-competing good. Such an outcome shows an anti-trade bias in production growth. If the new production point lies to the left of the vertical line through P then output of the export good has fallen in absolute terms, and we have ultra-anti-trade bias in the growth of

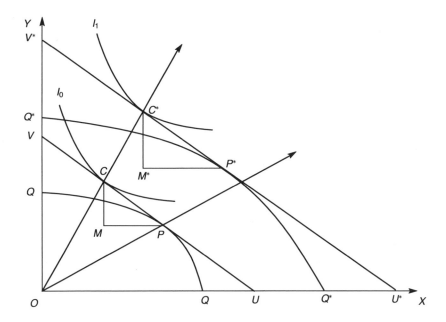

Figure 7.3   *An example of anti-trade biased growth*

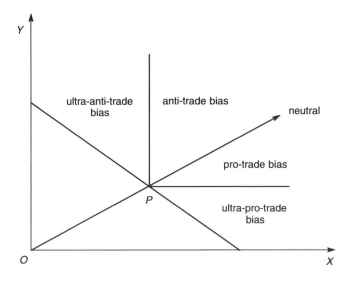

Figure 7.4   *Bias in the growth of production*

production. Similarly, points to the right of the 'neutral' line but above the horizontal line through P show pro-trade bias in production, while points below the horizontal line through P show ultra-pro-trade bias since the output of the import-competing good has decreased in absolute terms.

Figure 7.5 illustrates the possible biases in growth in consumption, and the biases are defined in an analogous manner. For example, post-growth consumption points to the left of the 'neutral' line but to the right of the vertical line through C show pro-trade bias in consumption growth.

Unfortunately, there is no simple set of rules which allows us to combine the biases in the growth of production and consumption to obtain the bias in the growth of trade. Some cases are simple: neutral growth in both consumption and production must give neutral growth in trade but, as Figure 7.2 shows, a pro-trade bias in production can be exactly offset by an anti-trade bias in consumption, so also giving neutral growth in trade. On the other hand, pro-trade growth in consumption (production) coupled with neutral growth in production (consumption) may give either a pro-trade or an ultra-pro-trade bias to growth in trade. Biases may, in other words, offset each other to a greater or lesser extent, or may augment one another.

In our later discussion of the causes of growth we shall concentrate on the production side of the problem. In order to keep the analysis as simple as possible we shall ensure that there is always neutral growth in consumption by making the familiar assumption that the community indifference curves are homothetic.

■ 7.3 Immiserising growth in a large country

Our discussion of the possible effects of growth on the volume of trade has so far been conducted on the assumption that relative prices do not change. If we were dealing with a small country then that would in fact be the case, and growth of any form would lead to an increase in welfare for the growing country. But if the growing country is large then any change in its volume of trade must bring about a change in the terms of trade. If the volume of trade decreases then the terms of trade will move in favour of the growing country (as they do for a large country imposing a tariff), and this will increase the gain in welfare for the growing country. If however growth increases the volume of trade then the terms of trade will move against the growing country, and so reduce the gain in welfare. In the extreme case, the terms of trade could move against the growing country to such an extent that its welfare is actually reduced. This paradox (that

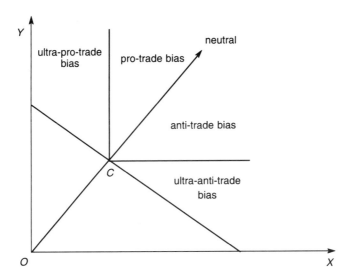

Figure 7.5   *Bias in the growth of consumption*

growth can make a country worse off) has been termed *immiserising growth*.[2] Figure 7.6 gives a graphical illustration of such a situation.

Initially the country's production-possibility curve is QQ, and it terms of trade are given by the slope of line WW. It therefore produces at point P, exports X and imports Y, and consumes at C on indifference curve I_1. Growth then shifts its production-possibility curve out to Q^*Q^*. As it is a large country, the increase in its exports will drive down their price on the world market, while the increase in its demand for the import good will lead to an increase in that price. The country's terms of trade fall to the level shown by the slope of line W^*W^*. At those terms of trade the country produces at P^*, and will consume at C^* on indifference curve I_0. The country has suffered a loss in welfare (the move from I_1 to I_0) despite the outward shift in its production-possibility curve. Its growth has been immiserising.

Note that even anti-trade biased growth will increase the growing country's trade (at constant prices), and so will lead to the terms of trade turning against a large country. Only ultra-anti-trade biased growth leads to a decrease in trade and so to a (welfare-increasing) improvement in its terms of trade. However, even ultra-pro-trade biased growth will not *necessarily* worsen the terms of trade to such an extent that welfare is decreased. The final outcome will also depend on supply and demand

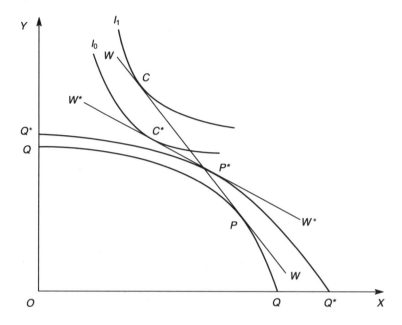

Figure 7.6 *Immiserising growth for a large country*

conditions in the rest of the world; for example, an inelastic demand for its exports, and/or an inelastic supply of its imports will exacerbate the deterioration in its terms of trade.

Finally, we should note that the source of the immiserisation is not that the country has grown, but that it has monopoly/monopsony power on the world market. As we shall see in Chapters 10 and 11, the appropriate way for a country to tackle that problem is to impose the optimum tariff. A large country will always benefit from growth if it adjusts its optimum tariff to conform with the new situation.

7.4 Increases in the endowments of factors of production

One obvious source of growth is an increase in the endowment of one or more of the factors of production. We shall not discuss here how or why that increase has come about, but will instead concentrate on the effects of such an increase on the production-possibility curve and on the rewards to the factors of production. We shall work within the familiar framework of the Heckscher–Ohlin model.

☐ *The Rybczynski Theorem*

We shall start by giving an exposition in geometric terms of the Rybczynski theorem.[3] This theorem states that if the endowment of one of the factors of production increases, the endowment of the other being constant, the output of the good using the accumulating factor intensively will increase and the output of the other good will decrease in absolute terms, provided that commodity and factor prices are kept constant. We shall demonstrate a proof of the theorem for the case where there is an increase in the endowment of labour, using Figure 7.7 as our starting point.

Good X is labour-intensive, and before growth the country's factor endowments, K of capital and L of labour, define the box $O_X U O_Y V$. There is then an increase in the labour endowment of ΔL, giving the new factor box $O_X U O_Y^* V^*$.

Suppose that the pre-growth equilibrium point is E, with outputs X_1 and Y_1, and a factor-price ratio of ϕ. If the factor-price ratio remains the same after the growth has taken place then, since the production technology has not changed for either good, there must be the same capital–labour ratios for the two goods as there were before growth. The corresponding

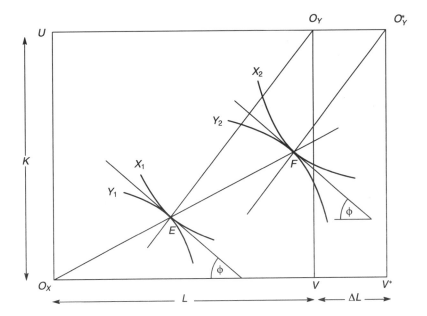

Figure 7.7   *The Rybczynski Theorem: growth in the endowment of labour*

equilibrium point in the post-growth situation must then be F. As the distance O_XF is greater than O_XE, the output of X at F must be higher than it was at point E. Some simple geometry will show that the distance O_Y^*F must be less than O_YE, so that the output of Y at F must be lower than at E. This establishes part of the Rybczynski Theorem: at constant factor prices, the increase in the endowment of labour has increased the production of the labour-intensive good (X) and decreased the production of the capital-intensive good. A parallel argument would establish that an increase in the endowment of capital would increase the production of the capital-intensive good and decrease the production of the labour-intensive good provided that the factor price ratio remained at ϕ.

No particular assumptions were made in choosing point E, so the theorem just established is valid in general. This allows us to identify the relationship between the new (post-growth) production-possibility curve and the original curve following the increase in the labour endowment, as shown in Figure 7.8: to every point on the original curve (such as E) there is a corresponding point (F) on the new curve, showing a higher output of X and a lower output of Y, and where the factor-price ratio is the same for both. However, we can identify one further link between these two points: since there has been no change in technology, the relationship between relative factor prices and relative marginal costs is unchanged. Thus the slope of the new production-possibility curve at F is the same as the slope of the original curve at E. This establishes the final part of the Rybczynski Theorem.

What we have, of course, is either ultra-pro-trade or ultra-anti-trade biased growth in production. If the country is relatively labour-rich, so that X is its export good, then growth in the labour endowment results in ultra-pro-trade biased growth in production. If, on the other hand, it is capital-rich, labour growth leads to an ultra-anti-trade bias in production.

If the growing country is a small country, and the initial free trade equilibrium was at E, then the new free trade equilibrium will be at F. Because the terms of trade are constant, the relative factor prices cannot change either, and so neither can the capital–labour ratios. If they are unchanged then since we have constant returns to scale and perfect competition in the Heckscher–Ohlin model, marginal products are unchanged, and so the real returns to labour and capital are unchanged as well. The only changes produced by this form of growth are in the outputs of the two goods, and in the distribution of factors between the industries.

If the country were a large country however then we would have to consider the effects on prices as well. Suppose first that the country is labour-rich, so that (remembering our assumption that consumption growth is neutral) the country's trade would grow at constant terms of

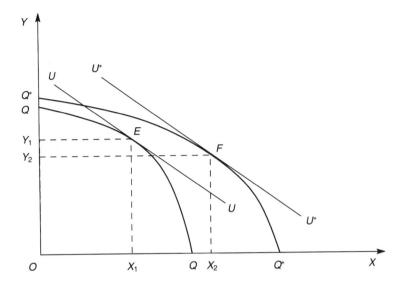

Figure 7.8   *The effect of growth in the endowment of labour on the production-possibility curve*

trade. The ensuing fall in the relative price of X would then result in a smaller transfer of resources from Y to X, so that the production point on the new production-possibility curve would lie closer to the Y axis than point F. This would then imply a lower relative wage rate, leading to lower capital–labour ratios in both sectors, and hence to a lower real wage rate and a higher real return to capital.

   If, on the other hand, the country is capital-rich, there could be ultra-anti-trade biased growth in trade, and so an increase in the relative price of X. The relative and the absolute wage rate would then increase, and the relative and absolute return to capital would decline.

☐ *Balanced growth in labour and capital*

An interesting extension to the Rybczynski Theorem is the case where the labour and the capital endowments grow by the same proportion – what might be referred to as balanced growth. Figure 7.9 shows the two factor boxes for this case. Note that the ratio of the capital and labour endowments is the same before and after growth, so that the boxes have the same diagonal.

   If the original production point was at E then, if there is no change in the relative wage rate, the new production point will be at F. Since the

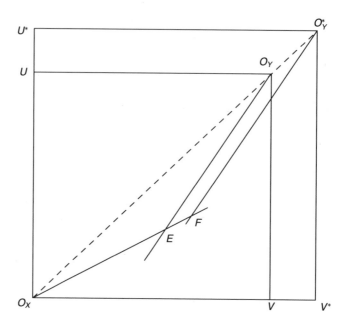

Figure 7.9   *Balanced growth in the endowments of labour and capital*

triangles $O_X O_Y E$ and $O_X O_Y^* F$ are similar, production of Y and production of X must have increased by the same proportion. Moreover, triangles $O_X O_Y U$ and $O_X O_Y^* U^*$ are similar, from which we may deduce that the proportionate increase in the outputs of X and Y must be the same as the proportionate increases in the endowments of capital and labour.

Balanced growth in the endowments of the two factors of production therefore results in neutral (or balanced) growth in production. Moreover, it does so whatever the original production mix. Essentially, we have established that under the Heckscher–Ohlin assumptions the production-possibility curve is linearly homogeneous in terms of the factor endowments.

Constant returns to scale implies that the marginal products of capital and labour are the same in both industries at point F as they were at point E. Therefore the real wage and the real return to capital are the same in terms of both X and Y at the two points.

Unless there is a strong anti-trade bias in consumption growth, balanced growth must lead to growth in the volume of trade at constant prices. For a small country the terms of trade will be unchanged, and so as a consequence will be the real rewards to capital and labour. For a large country however the terms of trade must deteriorate, so reducing the welfare gain from growth, and possibly leading to immiserising growth.

■ 7.5 Technical progress and international trade

We have just dealt with the effects of factor growth on trade. Another important element in modern economic life is technical progress. Innovations of different kinds – technical progress, in short – transformed the agricultural economies of the eighteenth century into the modern industrial economy. The study of the effects of technical progress on international trade needs no justification.

Classical and neoclassical economists showed no great interest in the study of the effects of technical progress. It is significant that many leading classical and neoclassical economists were so preoccupied with one type of factor growth – the increase in population – that they failed completely to grasp the importance of technical progress for economic development.[4]

We shall now study how technical progress affects international trade. To do this it is convenient to illustrate geometrically how technical progress affects the production function and how technical progress can be classified into different subgroups.

☐ *The classification of technical progress*

In order to classify technical progress we use the same type of production function used in earlier parts of the book, i.e. a production function with two inputs, labour and capital. We also assume the production function to be homogeneous of the first degree. Technical progress means that more output can be produced with given amounts of inputs (or that a given output can be produced with less inputs).

In the classification of technical progress we will, in this chapter, follow Hicks's way of classifying technical progress.[5] There technical progress is classified according to the effect it has on the marginal productivities of the factors of production. A neutral innovation is one which increases the marginal productivity of both factors of production in the same proportion. Labour-saving technical progress increases the marginal productivity of capital more than it increases the marginal productivity of labour. Capital-saving innovations increase the marginal productivity of labour more than they increase the marginal productivity of capital.

We will now show how the effects of technical progress can be illustrated in a geometric fashion.[6] The effects of neutral innovations on the production function are illustrated in Figure 7.10. Isoquant Q_1^{old} shows in a familiar way how labour and capital can be combined before the technical progress has taken place to produce 1 unit of the good. If factor prices are as depicted by the iso-cost line *EF*, entrepreneurs will combine factors of production along ray *OR* and produce at point *R*.

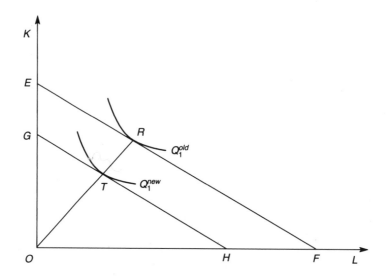

Figure 7.10   *The effects of neutral innovation on the production function*

The isoquant Q_1^{new} depicts the new production function for the good after neutral technical progress has taken place. That the innovation is neutral is shown by the fact that both marginal productivities have increased in the same proportion. If relative factor prices are the same (GH is parallel to EF), the factors of production even after the innovation will be combined in the same ratio as before. This is indicated by the fact that GH is tangential to the new isoquant Q_1^{new} at the point, T, at which this isoquant is cut by the ray OR.

The new isoquant lies below the old one, in the sense that it will be tangential to the lower iso-cost line GH, which shows that less labour and capital are needed to produce 1 unit of the good after the innovation.

Neutral technical progress is a particular (and very simple) form of change in the production function. In general, technical progress can change the production function in any way. The only thing we know is that, in order to qualify as *progress*, the innovation must allow more output to be produced with constant inputs, or the same output with less inputs.

Labour-saving technical progress is illustrated in Figure 7.11. We again start with a pre-improvement isoquant Q_1^{old} and a ruling factor-price ratio shown by the slope of EF. The capital–labour ratio used in production will then be OR. After the innovation we get a new isoquant Q_1^{new}. There has been technical progress (according to our definition) since the new isoquant is tangential to the lower iso-cost line GH. The innovation is also labour-saving – the marginal productivity of capital is higher relative to the

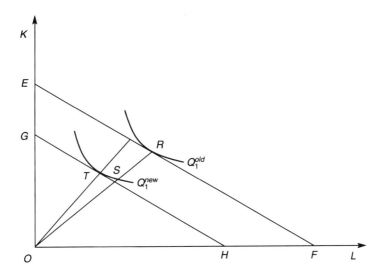

Figure 7.11   *Labour-saving technical progress*

marginal productivity of labour in the new situation. For a given capital–labour ratio, such as that shown by the ray OR, the slope of the isoquant Q_1^{new} (at T) is lower than that of Q_1^{old} (at R). In order to maintain that capital–labour ratio, the relative price of capital would have to increase, since at the old capital–labour ratio capital would be more efficient and its price would be bid up.

It follows that for the same factor-price ratio to prevail in the new situation, the factors of production would have to be used in the ratio OT instead of OS (GH is parallel to EF), and the production method would be more capital-intensive. The relative marginal productivity of capital is higher than before the innovation but the relative price of capital is the same, so producers will find it advantageous to use more capital per unit of labour than before.

In an analogous way, Figure 7.12 demonstrates a change in the isoquants caused by a capital-saving innovation. Here the relative marginal productivity of labour has increased. If the factor-price ratio were to be the same before and after the innovation, we would get a more labour-intensive method of production at T compared with that at R. This is explained by the fact that the relative marginal productivity of labour is higher than before, but the relative price of labour is the same. Hence producers substitute labour for capital and production becomes more labour-intensive.

We have now seen how technical progress can be classified, and we should have an understanding of the meaning of the different kinds of

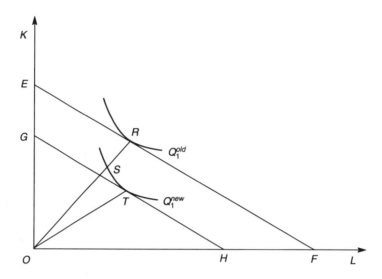

Figure 7.12   *Capital-saving technical progress*

innovations. It is now time to consider the effects of these different types on the production mix, the volume of trade, and the returns to factors of production.

The procedure we shall follow is similar to that we used when proving the Rybczynski Theorem, but with one important difference. Since the cost of producing the good in the innovating industry will have fallen with technical progress, the relationship between the relative prices of factors and of goods must have changed. We need to establish the effects of technical progress on the production mix when the relative prices of X and Y are constant, but we cannot start there. Since we must determine how the innovation affects factor allocation before we can discover how it affects outputs, we must start by considering what happens if relative factor prices remain the same.

Neutral technical progress and the terms of trade

To study the effects of technical progress on trade we will again use the standard trade model, with two countries consuming and producing two goods and using two factors of production. We shall consider only one country explicitly; that is, we assume that the technical progress is specific to one country.

Let us assume that we have a country with two sectors, manufacturing and agriculture. Manufacturing (Y) is capital-intensive and agriculture (X) is labour-intensive, and neutral technical progress takes place in the former. The box diagram for the country is illustrated in Figure 7.13.

We start from an equilibrium situation at E, where isoquants showing outputs X_1 for agriculture and Y_1 for manufacturing are tangential. Relative factor prices are shown by the slope of their common tangent. A neutral innovation takes place in manufacturing, so that the Y production function is now characterised by the isoquant Y_2^*. Since the innovation is neutral, the new equilibrium at the specified factor prices must also be at E, so that the allocation of capital and labour between the two sectors is unchanged. The output of X must be the same before and after the innovation. The output of Y however must be higher after the innovation $(Y_2^* > Y_1)$

We have obtained this result by assuming that relative factor prices are unchanged, but we need to know what the outcome would be if the terms of trade were unchanged. We must therefore deduce what will happen to the relative price of X if the relative wage rate stays the same. To do this, we rely again on our assumption that there is perfect competition, which

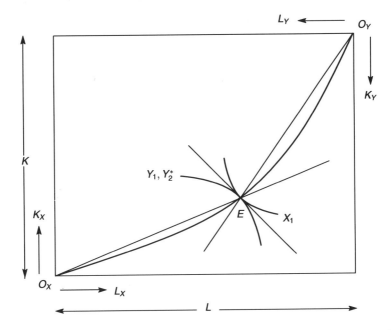

Figure 7.13 *Neutral technical progress in the capital-intensive sector and factor allocation*

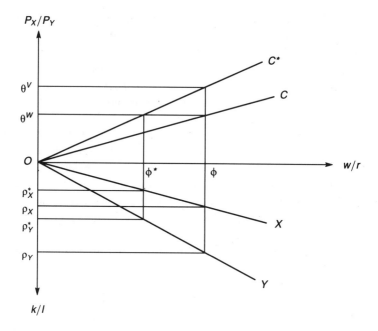

Figure 7.14   *Real returns to factors of production after neutral technical progress in the capital-intensive sector*

implies that in long-run equilibrium the relative price of X will equal the relative average cost of X. The increase in the output of Y for given factor inputs must reduce the average cost of producing Y, and so will increase the relative cost of producing X at any given factor-price ratio. Hence, for a given factor-price ratio the relative price of X must be lower after the innovation. Figure 7.14 illustrates the changes in the relationships between capital–labour ratios and relative factor prices, and between factor prices and the relative prices of the two goods.

The pre-innovation relationship between the relative price of X and the relative wage rate is shown by OC, so that if the relative price of X before the technical progress is shown in Figure 7.14 by θ^W then the relative wage rate will be ϕ. At that relative wage rate the capital–labour ratio will be ρ_X in X and ρ_Y in Y. The neutral technical progress does not change the relationships between the capital–labour ratios and the relative wage rate, but it will cause the line OC to move upwards to OC^*. After the innovation, a relative wage rate of ϕ can only be maintained if the relative price of X increases to θ^V. If, on the other hand, the relative price of X remains at θ^W then the relative wage rate must fall to ϕ^*. The capital–labour ratios will then fall to ρ_X^* in X and ρ_Y^* in Y.

Figure 7.15 shows how these results can be used to determine the changes in the production-possibility curve following the neutral technical innovation in the Y sector. The original production-possibility curve is AB, and with the relative price of X as shown by the slope of line WW (θ^W in Figure 7.14), production will be at E. If there is neutral technical progress in Y and relative factor prices do not change then the production point will move up to point F, which must be on the new production-possibility curve CB. However, the slope of the new production-possibility at F must be greater than the slope of AB at E, as shown by the line VV (which has slope θ^V).

But if the relative price of X stays the same as it was before the innovation then the production point on the new production-possibility curve must be at E* (line W*W* has the same slope as WW). We must conclude therefore that if the relative price of X (the terms of trade) remains constant then the output of the good in which the innovation took place (Y) will increase absolutely, and the output of the other good will decrease absolutely. If Y is the export good then there has been ultra-pro-trade biased growth in production. If Y is the import good then there has been ultra-anti-trade biased growth.

If the innovating country is a small country then point E* will show the new equilibrium. The technical innovation in Y reduces costs, and so the Y

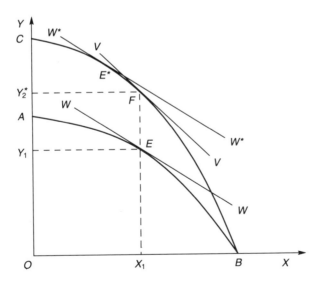

Figure 7.15 *Neutral technical progress in the capital-intensive sector and the production-possibility curve*

industry will expand. In order to do so it must bid factors of production away from X. But Y is capital-intensive, so as it grows it will require relatively more capital per unit of labour than X will release, and this will increase the relative price of capital. Firms in both sectors will then substitute labour for capital, so reducing their capital–labour ratios.

The reduction in the capital–labour ratio in the X sector implies that the marginal product of labour has decreased and that of capital has increased. It follows that, in terms of the X good, the real wage rate has fallen and the real return to capital has risen. Since the price of Y has not changed relative to the price of X, labour must also be worse off, and capital better off, in terms of the Y good. This is an unambiguous result: neutral technical progress in the capital-intensive sector in a small country will reduce the real wage rate and increase the real return to capital.

If we are considering a large country and Y is the export good then (if tastes are homothetic) the volume of trade will increase at constant terms of trade, and the terms of trade will move against the country so that the relative price of Y will fall. The production point will then move down CB from E^* towards the X axis. We cannot tell in general whether the new equilibrium production point will be to the left or to the right of F, and so we cannot say unambiguously how the real returns to factors of production will change compared with their pre-innovation levels.

If, on the other hand, the country is large and Y is the import-competing good then the effect on the volume of trade depends on the balance of the production and consumption effects. The relative price of Y will fall if there is an increase in trade at constant terms of trade, and then the consequences will be the same as though outlined above. It is possible however that there will be ultra-anti-trade bias overall, so that the relative price of Y increases, and the production point moves to the left of E^*. We can then be certain that the output of Y will have increased and the output of X will have decreased compared with the pre-innovation position. This shift in the production point will then magnify the fall in the real wage rate and the rise in the real return to capital measured in terms of the X good. Unfortunately the increase in the relative price of Y means that, although labour must be worse off in terms of the Y good, we cannot say whether capital will gain or lose.

Capital-saving technical progress in the capital-intensive industry

The effects of a capital-saving innovation in manufacturing, the capital-intensive industry, on the allocation of factors at fixed factor prices is shown in Figure 7.16. We start out from an equilibrium at E, where isoquants X_1 and Y_1 shows the outputs of X and Y respectively. Suppose now that the innovation takes place, but that relative factor prices are unchanged (the tangent at the new equilibrium point F has the same slope as the tangent at E). The output of X at F (the isoquant is not shown) must be less than at E, and the output of Y (Y_2^*) must be higher. Capital-saving technical progress in the capital-intensive sector at constant factor prices therefore leads to an increase in the output of the capital-intensive sector and a decrease in the output of the labour-intensive sector. However, we need to know how outputs would change if the relative prices of the two goods were unchanged.

Once again, we must now determine how the relationship between the relative prices of factors and goods changes as a consequence of the innovation. The innovation will reduce the average cost of producing the Y good, so that a given relative wage rate can only be maintained after the innovation if the relative price of X increases. This is shown in Figure 7.17 by the upward shift of OC to OC^*. If the relative wage rate stays at ϕ then the relative cost of producing X, and so the relative price of X, must increase to θ^V. Conversely, if the relative price of X remains at θ^W then the relative wage rate must fall to ϕ^*.

Figure 7.17 also records the changes in the relationship between the relative wage rate and the capital–labour ratio in Y brought about by the

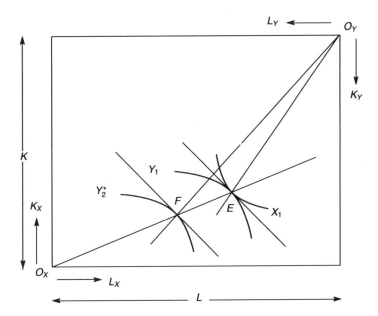

Figure 7.16 *Capital-saving technical progress in the capital-intensive sector and factor allocation*

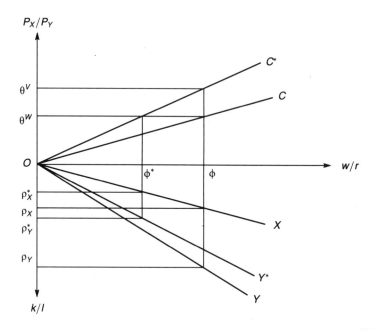

Figure 7.17   *Real returns to factors of production after capital-saving technical progress in the capital-intensive sector*

innovation: at any given relative wage rate the capital–labour ratio in Y is lower.

The effects of the innovation on the production-possibility curve are shown in Figure 7.18. The pre-innovation production point is at E on production-possibility curve AB. The post-innovation point consistent with the same relative wage rate is at F (a higher Y output and a lower X output). The new production-possibility curve CB must however be steeper at F than the old curve at E. It follows that if the relative price of X remains unchanged then the production point would be at E* (on CB but nearer to the Y axis). That is, at constant terms of trade there will be an increase in Y output and a decrease in X output. Once again we have ultra-biased growth: pro-trade if Y is the export good, anti-trade if not.

If the country is small then the production point will in fact remain at E*. Referring to Figure 7.17, we see that the fall in the relative wage rate implied by this will lead to a lower capital–labour ratio in the X sector. It follows that labour must be worse off, and capital better off, in terms of the X good after the innovation. Once again, since the price of Y relative to that of X is unchanged, labour must be worse off in terms of the Y good, and capital better off. Capital-saving technical progress in the capital-

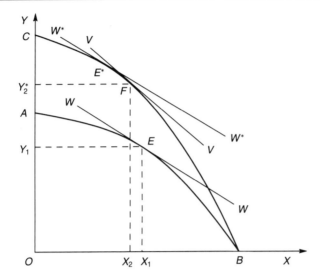

Figure 7.18 *Capital-saving technical progress in the capital-intensive sector and the production-possibility curve*

intensive sector of a small country will reduce the real wage rate and increase the real return to capital.

If the country is large then, once again, the effect of growth on the terms of trade must be taken into account. The problem is complicated by there being two distinct components in the effect of capital-saving technical progress: it both reduces the average cost of producing the Y good and changes the capital–labour ratio in Y production. An innovation which produces a large reduction in average costs but a small change in the capital–labour ratio will have quite different implications for the shape of the production-possibility curve than one which results in a small cost change but a large change in factor intensities. The effects of a given change in the terms of trade on real factor rewards will also be affected by the precise form of the innovation. The number of possible combinations of innovation effects, domestic demand bias, and demand and supply conditions in the rest of the world would require too much time to elaborate, and we shall not pursue the topic any further.

Labour-saving technical progress in the capital-intensive industry

The effects of labour-saving technical progress in manufacturing (Y), the capital-intensive industry, can be illustrated in a manner analogous to that of our previous discussion. In Figure 7.19 we begin with the factor box, and an initial equilibrium at E. If there is labour-saving technical progress in Y and factor prices remain the same then the new equilibrium point will be at F. It is apparent that X output must be higher at F than at E. It is not however clear whether Y output will be higher or lower: a large reduction in cost and a small change in factor intensity in Y will tend to make Y output higher at F; a small cost reduction and a large change in the capital–labour ratio will be more likely to result in a reduction in Y output.

Figure 7.20 shows the direction of the changes in the familiar relationships. The effect of the innovation in reducing the average cost of Y production will move OC up to OC^*. The labour-saving nature of the innovation will move OY down to OY^*. As before, holding the factor price ratio constant (at, say ϕ) implies that the relative price of X must increase (from θ^W to θ^V).

It follows that if the terms of trade remain constant (at θ^W, say) then the relative wage rate must fall (to ϕ^*). If the relative wage rate falls then the capital–labour ratio in the X sector must fall. We cannot however be certain about the movement of the capital–labour ratio in Y: it may fall (as shown in Figure 7.20), but it may rise.

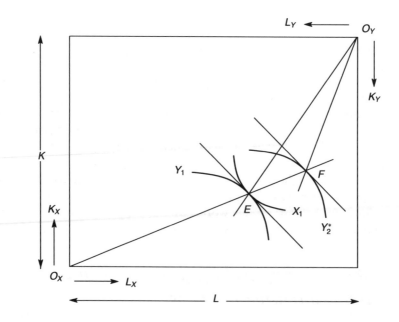

Figure 7.19 *Labour-saving technical progress in the capital-intensive sector*

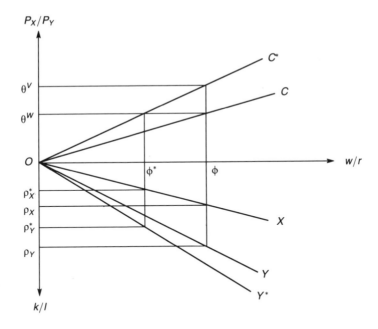

Figure 7.20 *Real returns to factors of production after labour-saving technical progress in the capital-intensive sector*

It is apparent that this example of technological progress will give us few simple answers. We do not know if Y output will fall or rise at constant factor prices. Even assuming constant commodity prices will not resolve the ambiguities: Y output might rise in that case, but we could not be certain whether X output would go up or down.

Figure 7.21 shows one of the many possible outcomes. It assumes that the effect of the labour-saving technical progress in the Y sector at constant factor prices is to increase the output of both goods. It may then the case if the terms of trade do not change that, as in Figure 7.21, the output of X falls, but this is not necessarily the case.

The one thing we can be sure of is that if the country is small, so that the terms of trade do not change, the relative wage rate will fall, and so the capital–labour ratio must fall in the X sector. Since the terms of trade have not changed, this must mean that the real wage will fall and the real return to capital will rise (in terms of either good).

If the country is large then we can obtain no general results. As in the case of capital-saving progress in the Y sector, we shall not discuss this case any further.

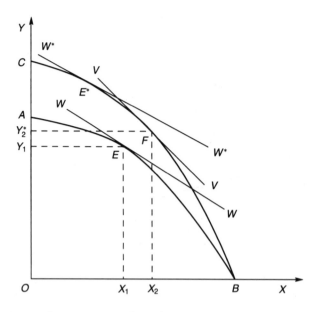

Figure 7.21   *Labour-saving technical progress in the capital-intensive sector and the production-possibility curve*

7.6 Concluding comments on growth and trade

Growth in an open economy will have two major economic effects: on the level of welfare for the economy as a whole, and on the distribution of income between factors of production. Our initial analysis shows that there is an important difference between small and large countries in the effect that growth will have on welfare. For a small country, growth is necessarily welfare-increasing: growth, through shifting the production-possibility curve outwards, allows a country trading at constant prices to reach a higher community indifference curve.

For a large country however, growth need not be welfare-increasing. An expansion in a large country's trade volume will turn the terms of trade against it, and that will reduce the welfare gain. Indeed, in the extreme case the country's welfare may be reduced. On the other hand, growth that reduces a large country's trade volume will turn the terms of trade in its favour, and this will increase the welfare gain.

Such considerations may have influenced those economists who advocate that less-developed countries should plan their development so that growth is concentrated in the import-competing sectors. The argument is however only valid for a country large enough to affect its terms of trade, and very few less-developed countries (LDCs) would fall under that heading. Moreover, if a country can affect its terms of trade then imposing the optimum tariff is the first-best policy. A better guide to development policy is to avoid the introduction of distortions by the use of either domestic or trade policies. We shall return to this problem later when we consider import-substitution and export-promotion policies in Chapter 19.

A further consideration is that economic growth in one country, whether large or small, increases world welfare (the world's production-possibility curve moves outwards). If many small countries pursue the goal of artificially promoting growth in their import-competing sectors then they will reduce this gain in world welfare, and each may become worse off.

The effects of growth on the distribution of income between labour and capital are reasonably clear when growth comes from increases in the endowments of factors, rather less so when growth is the result of technical progress. In the following discussion we shall restrict ourselves to the small country case.

Growth in the endowment of capital in a small open economy increases the real wage rate, but decreases the real return to capital. Conversely, growth in the labour force in the absence of growth in the capital stock will reduce the real wage rate and increase the real return to capital. Balanced growth (equal proportionate increases in both endowments) will leave the real rewards to factors of production unchanged. It should be clear from these results that if both the capital stock and the labour supply increase, but capital (labour) increases faster than labour (capital) then the real wage will rise (fall) and the real return to capital will fall (rise).

The uncertainty about the effect of technical progress on the real rewards to factors comes largely from the wide range of forms which that progress can take. In the formal analysis of this chapter we have focused on technical progress in the capital-intensive sector, but the symmetry of the Heckscher–Ohlin model means that the results for innovations in the labour-intensive sector may be deduced with little difficulty. The summary in Table 7.1 continues to focus on progress in the capital-intensive sector.

As we see, technical progress in the capital-intensive sector almost invariably reduces the real wage rate and increases the real return to capital. Technical progress in the labour-intensive sector will of course tend to increase the real wage and decrease the real return to capital. It may be argued that technical progress is more likely to take place in the capital-intensive sector, in which case the prospect for wage earners may seem bleak.

Table 7.1   *Technical progress in the capital-intensive sector (Y) and real rewards to factors of production*

	Real wage rate	Real return to capital
Capital-saving	Falls in terms of both X and Y	Rises in terms of both X and Y
Neutral	Falls in terms of both X and Y	Rises in terms of both X and Y
Labour-saving	Falls in terms of X Indeterminate in terms of Y	Rises in terms of X Indeterminate in terms of Y

Wicksell pointed to these results in his Lectures, with the famous dictum:

> The capitalist saver is thus, fundamentally, the friend of labour, though the technical innovator is not infrequently its enemy. The great innovations by which industry has from time to time been revolutionised, at first reduced a number of workers to beggary, as experience shows, while causing the profits of the capitalists to soar. There is no need to explain away this circumstance by invoking 'economic friction', and so on, for it is in full accord with a rational and consistent theory. But it is really not capital which should bear the blame; in proportion as accumulation continues, these evils must disappear, interest on capital will fall and wages will rise – unless the labourers on their part simultaneously counteract this result by a large increase in their numbers.[7]

☐ *Notes*

1   The terminology is that suggested by Johnson, which in turn reflects that used by Hicks.

2   The term 'immiserising growth' is due to Bhagwati (1955). The paradox was noted by Edgeworth in 1894 (Edgeworth (1984).

3   Rybczynski (1955).

4   Even a great economist like Knut Wicksell (1851–1926) was a sworn neo-Malthusian at the beginning of this century. No student of his at the University of Lund could get a degree in economics unless he agreed that the population question was the root of all social evil and that no economic progress could be achieved unless birth control were practised and the increase in population curtailed.

5   Hicks (1932). Hicks originally used his classification for discussing the effects of technical progress on the income distribution. It should be observed that Hicks only thought in terms of production functions that are homogeneous of the first degree. See also Johnson (1959).

6   Strictly speaking, the Hicksian classifications are at constant factor inputs. This is not clearly brought out by the geometric illustration, where we also want to illustrate the fact that an innovation means constant production with less inputs. For illustrative reasons, we let the latter fact take precedence over the former. Nothing substantial in the analysis is changed by this because the critical fact to illustrate is the change in relation between marginal productivities caused by the innovation.

7   Wicksell (1908).

■ *Chapter 8* ■

Intra-industry Trade

■ 8.1 Introduction

Intra-industry trade may be broadly defined as the situation where countries simultaneously import and export what are essentially the same products. So, for example, the United Kingdom both exports cars to Sweden and imports them. The European Community imports wheat from the United States and exports wheat to third countries.

Interest in the phenomenon was largely stimulated by work done in the 1960s on the impact of the formation of the EEC on trade flows within the member countries. The original study was that by Verdoorn on the changes in the pattern of trade of the Benelux countries following their union.[1] He found that specialisation and trade between the member countries had taken place within similar product categories rather than between different product categories. Similarly, Balassa,[2] in an analysis of the product composition of trade between each pair of the original EEC members over the periods 1958–63 and 1963–70, found that trade was increasingly an exchange of similar goods. Grubel and Lloyd[3] subsequently estimated that 71 per cent of the increase in trade between the EEC countries from 1959 to 1967 was intra-industry.

There are some very simple explanations of intra-industry trade which can be encompassed within the types of inter-industry trade models we have studied so far. For example, transport costs may make it economic to export a good from France to Germany at the south of their common border, but to import the good from Germany into France in the north, rather than transport the good from south to north within France and vice-versa in Germany. Seasonal differences may also play a part: a southern hemisphere country may import grains from the northern hemisphere before its own harvest, but export them after the harvest.

Such explanations would however cover only a small proportion of the volume of intra-industry trade which economists have claimed to observe.

In searching for more general models of such trade, economists have been led into the field of imperfect competition, developing what are often referred to as the 'new trade theories'.[4] Explanations of intra-industry trade typically involve all or some of product differentiation, economies of scale, monopolistic competition or oligopolistic behaviour, the workings of multinational companies, and so on.

The difficulty created by this is that the range of possible imperfect competition models, and the varying circumstances in which they could be used, creates a very large number of possible models. Compare this with the relatively small number of models we have discussed in the earlier chapters on inter-industry trade.

As a consequence, this chapter will cover only a limited subset of the range of intra-industry trade models that have been suggested in the literature.[5] This chapter will assume that the reader is familiar with those basic theories of imperfect competition which are covered in many microeconomics textbooks.

We shall start by considering a group of models in which there is, once trade is established, competition between a large number of firms based in different countries. We shall then meet some models in which the world market is supplied by a limited number of firms, so that there is oligopolistic behaviour.

8.2 Intra-industry trade when there are many firms

☐ *The neo-Heckscher–Ohlin model*

Although the standard Heckscher–Ohlin model is unable to explain intra-industry trade, not all authors have been willing to abandon it completely. Instead, some have attempted to maintain an explanation of intra-industry trade based on factor endowments by linking product specifications to different combinations of the basic factors, such as capital and labour. Such models may be referred to as neo-Heckscher–Ohlin models. One example of such a model, due to Falvey, is discussed below.[6]

Consider a world in which there are two countries, two homogeneous factors of production and two industries. One factor, labour, is mobile between the two industries, but the other, capital, is industry-specific (a framework similar to the specific factors model discussed in Chapter 2). One industry in each country, say X, produces a homogeneous good, but the other, Y, produces a differentiated product.

The basis of the differentiation in the Y product is its quality, what is usually referred to as *vertical differentiation*. The demand for different qualities is assumed to depend on the consumer's income as well as the prices being charged. Suppose for simplicity that there were only two varieties of good Y, called Y_1 and Y_2, with Y_2 the superior good, and assume that each consumer buys a number of units of one or both of the goods in each time period. At low income levels, consumers, though preferring Y_2, are constrained to spend much of their income on the inferior good, Y_1. However, at higher incomes consumers would consume more of the superior good, and less of the inferior good.

In order to produce a higher quality version of Y a firm must use more capital per unit of labour. In order to simplify the algebra, let us assume that to produce 1 unit of Y, of no matter what quality, requires the use of 1 unit of labour. The quantity of capital required to produce 1 unit of any variety of good Y is ρ, and the higher is ρ, the higher is the quality of the good, so that we may use ρ to index that quality.

The cost of producing 1 unit of good Y of quality ρ in country A will be

$$C_A(\rho) = w_A + \rho r_A \tag{8.1}$$

where w_A and r_A are the wage rate and the reward to the quality-specific capital respectively in country A. Similarly, the cost of producing 1 unit of the same quality Y good in country B will be

$$C_B(\rho) = w_B + \rho r_B \tag{8.2}$$

Suppose that $w_B < w_A$ and $r_B > r_A$, so that we may regard country A as the capital-rich country. There will be some quality of good Y, ρ_1, where the unit cost is the same in both countries. This quality is given by

$$w_A + \rho_1 r_A = w_B + \rho_1 r_B$$

or

$$\rho_1 = \frac{w_A - w_B}{r_B - r_A} \tag{8.3}$$

We may then write the inter-country differences in the unit cost of producing any other quality of good Y, relative to this marginal quality good, as

$$C_B(\rho) - C_A(\rho) = \frac{w_A - w_B}{\rho_1}(\rho - \rho_1) \tag{8.4}$$

Country A will have a comparative advantage in producing a good of quality ρ when the unit cost of producing that variety is lower in A than in B; that is, when $C_A(\rho) < C_B(\rho)$. Since $w_B < w_A$, the first expression in equation (8.4) must be positive; it follows that $C_A(\rho) < C_B(\rho)$ if $\rho_1 < \rho$, and vice-versa.

That is, country A, in which capital is relatively cheap under autarky, has a comparative advantage in producing those qualities which are superior to the marginal quality, and a comparative disadvantage in those goods which are inferior to the marginal quality. Provided that there is a demand for both high quality goods (those where $\rho > \rho_1$) and low quality goods, there will be intra-industry trade in the Y good between the two countries, with the relatively capital-rich country exporting the higher quality varieties of the capital-intensive good. The labour-rich country will export both the labour-intensive good and the lower quality varieties of the capital-intensive good.

Examples of such trade may be found in some parts of the clothing industry, where labour-rich economies have tended to export lower quality goods while importing higher quality versions from the capital-rich countries.

An alternative 'Heckscher–Ohlin' explanation of intra-industry trade that has been suggested extends the basic model to include the human capital embodied in skilled labour. If higher quality versions of a good embody a greater proportion of skilled labour (and so of human capital) then the standard Heckscher–Ohlin prediction would apply: countries that are well endowed with human capital will export goods intensive in that factor.

☐ Neo-Chamberlinian models

The broad group of models which may be classified as 'neo-Chamberlinian' differ from the model described in the previous section in that the goods in question are *horizontally differentiated*. Horizontal differentiation of goods occurs when varieties differ in their *characteristics*; such characteristics may be either 'actual' (the colour of a wine) or 'perceived' (the taste of the wine). That is, while individual consumers may have an unique ranking of different varieties, according to how well the varieties' characteristics match their preferences, there is no ranking that would be agreed by all consumers. It is of course difficult to think of a real commodity where horizontal differentiation exists without vertical differentiation, but for some goods the former may dominate.

Probably the most familiar theory of horizontal differentiation is the 'Lancaster' model. This views goods as bundles of different attributes, with firms producing varieties with different commodity combinations in order to appeal to diverse consumer tastes. However, in the Lancaster model, consumers are assumed to have a preference for one variety. The

Chamberlin model, in contrast, assumes that all consumers have a *preference for variety*; that is, they seek to consume as many varieties as possible.

The version of the group of neo-Chamberlin models that we shall consider is based on that suggested by Krugman.[7] The economy under consideration is assumed to have only one factor of production, labour, which is in fixed supply. There is a large number of firms, each of which produces a different variety of the same good X (each of the *n* firms, or the variety each produces, is indicated by the subscript *i*), and firms are free to enter or leave the industry. There is no limit to the number of varieties that can be produced. Some fixed labour input is required by each firm, but each then produces its chosen variety with the same constant marginal labour requirement; the total labour requirement for firm *i* is thus

$$l_i = \alpha + \beta x_i \tag{8.5}$$

where x_i is the output of variety *i* of good X. Note that average labour requirements fall with increasing output.

Krugman's model assumes that each consumer has the same utility function, in which all varieties enter the utility function *symmetrically*. That is, (i) the consumption of one more unit of any variety gives the same addition to total utility; and (ii) the consumption of more varieties increases total utility. The actual utility function suggested by Krugman (which is not unique in meeting these specifications) is

$$u = \sum_{i=1}^{n} v(c_i) \tag{8.6}$$

where $\partial v(c_i)/\partial c_i > 0$, and the addition of another variety while keeping total consumption the same will increase welfare.

These four assumptions (fixed labour supply, freedom of entry and exit, decreasing average labour requirements and all varieties entering the utility function symmetrically) are sufficient to ensure that no two firms will produce the same variety, and that the number of firms in the economy (and hence the number of varieties) is determinate.

If each firm faces a given wage rate, w, then its total costs are $w(\alpha + \beta x_i)$. If the price of variety *i* is p_i, then the individual firm's profits are

$$\pi_i = p_i x_i - w(\alpha + \beta x_i) \tag{8.7}$$

But if there is free entry into the industry, the long-run equilibrium requires that for each and every firm only normal profits are made, so that in that equilibrium we must have price equal to average cost, i.e.

$$p_i = w\left(\frac{\alpha}{x_i} + \beta\right) \tag{8.8}$$

The symmetry of the model implies that each firm will produce exactly the same output of its chosen variety, with the same average cost, and will sell at the same price. That is, $x_i = x$, $l_i = l$, and $p_i = p$ for all firms.

The number of firms may be determined by the condition that the labour used in the production of all varieties cannot exceed the fixed supply of labour. Each firm uses an amount l of labour, where $l = \alpha + \beta x$. If the total labour supply is L then the number of firms, n, is given by

$$n = \frac{L}{l} = \frac{L}{\alpha + \beta x} \tag{8.9}$$

Each consumer will consume exactly the same amount (c) of each variety, so that his total utility will be

$$u = nv(c) \tag{8.10}$$

It should be evident that the total expenditure on all varieties of the good must be equal to the total payments made to labour.

Now suppose that there is a second economy which is identical to the first in every way. If the two countries are free to trade, and there are no transport costs or other barriers, there will be trade in this differentiated product. A firm in one country which originally produced a variety identical to one produced in the second country will merely change the variety it produces to one which is not produced by any other firm. The firm will do this because its production costs are the same no matter what variety it produces, and it can sell the same volume of its new variety as it did of the old one.

Each variety (some new) will be produced by just one firm, so that each variety will be produced in only one of the countries. The free trade equilibrium will be identical with the autarky equilibria, in that each country will produce n varieties, which will be produced at the same cost and sold at the same price as before. However, each consumer in each country will now consume an amount of $0.5c$ of each of the $2n$ varieties, giving him a utility of

$$u = \sum_{i=1}^{2n} v(0.5c_i) \tag{8.11}$$

which, given the specification of the utility function, must represent an increase in the individual's utility.

There must be a welfare gain for both countries. There are no losses on the production side, since the number of firms in each country will not change. Moreover, the real wage rate remains the same in both countries. The only source of welfare change is on the consumption side and here, as we have seen, all consumers gain because they enjoy a wider variety (although the total volume of their consumption stays the same).

Note that while we can deduce that each country will produce one half of the range of varieties, we cannot say which variety will be produced in each country. The Krugman model is in this sense indeterminate.

The Krugman model outlined above shows that, with decreasing average costs in production and horizontal product differentiation, welfare-increasing intra-industry trade will exist even between identical economies. Similar results have been obtained by other economists.[8]

Venables[9] has analysed a model which augments a Krugman-type model with the production of a homogeneous good produced under constant cost conditions. Various equilibria are possible in such a model, including the case where one country specialises in the production of the differentiated good and the other in the homogeneous good. The Krugman model is in fact a special case of a more general class of models.

Lawrence and Spiller[10] extend the basic model to include two factors of production which are used to make a capital-intensive horizontally differentiated product and a labour-intensive homogeneous product. They also assume that firms entering the differentiated-good sector face an initial capital outlay, and that the two countries have different initial factor endowments. They conclude that the number of varieties produced will rise in the capital-rich country and fall in the other, and that the scale of production of the differentiated good will increase in the former, while the labour-rich country increases production of the homogeneous good. These results are obviously similar to those of the basic Heckscher–Ohlin model and the Falvey model.

Such neo-Chamberlinian models as those described above are of course limited by their own assumptions. The form of utility function assumed rules out the possibility that consumers have some preference over varieties, and implies that there can never be an excess of varieties. Product variety is also completely independent of demand in such models. The assumptions of the Krugman and Venables models also imply that there are no adjustment costs: firms face no costs in changing the variety they produce, and no variety will disappear with the opening of trade.

□ *Neo-Hotelling models*

The class of models grouped under the heading *neo-Hotelling* build upon the approach to consumer behaviour first proposed by Lancaster.[11] Products are horizontally differentiated by the set of characteristics (or attributes) embodied in each variety, and consumers have diverse preferences over different sets of characteristics. Consumers are, however, unable to buy several varieties of a good and 'blend' them in order to obtain a variety which better suits their preferences.

Lancaster suggested a variety of trade models, incorporating his characteristics-based model of product differentiation, which could explain the existence of intra-industry trade. We shall consider only the most simple of these models, and shall then comment briefly on some of the implications of the more sophisticated variants.

The most simple version of a Lancastrian characteristics model assumes that the differentiated good possesses only two characteristics, and that consumers' preferences may be ordered in terms of the ratio of these two characteristics embodied in any variety. One way of representing the range of varieties available is to consider them as spread out along a straight line – the so-called 'spectrum' approach. In Figure 8.1, the line *ab* represents this spectrum. The variety at the *a* end of the line consists only of characteristic *A*; as we move to the right so the ratio of characteristic *B* to characteristic *A* in the variety increases, so that at the other end of the line, point *b*, we have a variety possessing none of characteristic *A*.

Each consumer is assumed to have a most-preferred (ideal) variety, for which he has a maximum willingness to pay. Suppose, for example, that the variety v_0 in Figure 8.1 is the ideal variety for a particular consumer. His demand for that variety will depend on his income and the price of that variety. Taking his income as fixed for the moment, let us represent his demand curve as $D(v_0)$ in Figure 8.2.

The consumer is prepared to buy other varieties, but he will buy less of such varieties at a given price and income level the further the variety is away from his ideal. That is, for any given income, the consumer's demand curve for a less-preferred variety is lower than that for a more-preferred variety. The usual assumption is that there is symmetry, in that the consumer is indifferent between a variety a distance *d* 'above' his ideal specification and one a distance *d* 'below'. In terms of Figure 8.1, the consumer whose ideal variety is v_0 is indifferent between the varieties .

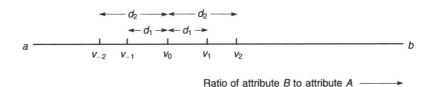

Figure 8.1 *The spectrum of varieties*

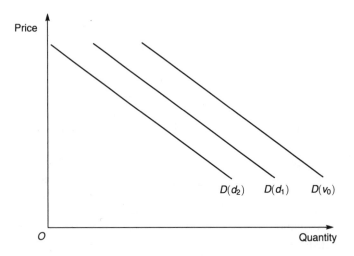

Figure 8.2   *A consumer's demand falls as the distance between a variety and his ideal variety increases*

shown as v_1 and v_{-1}, which are both a distance d_1 from v_0, and his demand for either would be shown by a demand curve such as $D(d_1)$ in Figure 8.2. For varieties still further away from the ideal variety, such as v_2 and v_{-2}, his demand curve will be even lower, at $D(d_2)$.

The consumer's demand for a given variety will also be affected by the existence of other varieties. Suppose our consumer is already buying the non-ideal variety v_1, since his ideal variety is not available. He would be prepared to switch to the variety v_2 if the price of v_2 were sufficiently low. The nearer variety v_2 is to variety v_1, the lower the price difference needed to induce him to switch. That is, the consumer's demand for v_1 would become more own-price elastic.

Preferences for varieties are however assumed to differ between consumers. For simplicity, we shall assume that consumers are evenly distributed along some section of the spectrum of attributes shown in Figure 8.1. We shall also assume that the 'extreme' consumers (those preferring the highest or lowest ratio of attributes) have ideal varieties some way inside the points *a* and *b*, so that they also could in principle obtain varieties with a higher or lower ratio of attributes than their ideal variety.

On the supply side, the Lancaster intra-industry trade model assumes that firms are free to enter or leave the market, and may produce any variety, and that the cost of producing any variety is the same for all varieties. However, we also assume that the production of any one variety is subject to (initially) decreasing average costs. We could assume the total cost curve is linear, as in the Krugman model, or that the average cost curve has the familiar 'U shape'. The number of varieties produced cannot then be infinite, and so some consumers will be unable to buy their most-preferred variety.

Firms entering the market must decide on the variety they are going to produce and the price at which they will sell it. The lower the price that a firm charges, the greater will be its sales; as a firm reduces its price, it will attract buyers whose most-preferred variety is further away from the variety it produces, *ceteris paribus*. If there is too narrow a gap between two adjacent varieties then neither of the firms will be able to sell enough to cover their costs; either one will leave the market completely, or one or both will change the variety being produced. This is sufficient to ensure that no two firms will produce the same variety. If, however, the gap between two adjacent varieties is too large then a new firm will enter to exploit the opportunity to make profits.

This freedom of entry and exit, together with the equal density of preferences and the identity of cost functions, ensures that in the long-run equilibrium the actual varieties produced will be spaced evenly along the spectrum, and that each variety will be produced in the same quantity and will sell at the same price. Each firm will be making 'normal' profits (price will be equal to average cost).[12] Lancaster refers to this situation as *perfect monopolistic competition*.

The version of the Lancaster model we shall discuss assumes that there are two countries which are identical *in every respect*. There are two sectors: 'manufacturing', producing the differentiated good, and 'agriculture', producing a homogeneous good under conditions of constant returns. There is one mobile factor of production (labour), but each sector may have another factor of production which is specific. Demand for the differentiated good is assumed to have an income elasticity greater than one.[13]

Under autarky the equilibrium will be the same in both countries. In particular, the same varieties will be produced in the two countries and in the same quantities, there will be the same agricultural output, and prices and incomes will be the same.

What happens then when these two identical countries are able to trade with one another, and there are no barriers to trade?

Because the countries are identical, the opening of free trade is equivalent to creating one country which is twice the size of either of the original countries, except that factors of production cannot move between countries. In particular, production of the differentiated good must adjust so that once again each variety is produced by only one firm (which must obviously be in only one of the countries), and the varieties evenly spaced along the spectrum. Each variety will be produced in the same volume and sold at the same price. All varieties will however be consumed in both countries.

The symmetry of the model ensures that half the varieties will be produced in one country, and half in the other. Each firm will sell half its output on its domestic market, and will export the other half. That is, half of the consumers in each country will prefer a variety produced in the other country, and half will prefer a domestic variety.

The agricultural good will not be traded. Trade must obviously be balanced, since each country exports the same volume of each of the same number of goods at the same price. Note that, as with the Krugman model, we cannot predict which varieties will be produced in each country.

The total number of varieties produced must be higher than under autarky. To demonstrate this, let us assume first that the number and specifications of varieties stays the same, with half of the firms in each country leaving the market. Each firm could now sell twice the volume of goods that it sold under autarky at the same price. The increase in output would however reduce average costs, and so super-normal profits would be made. New firms would be attracted into the industry, each producing a new variety. The new equilibrium will be established with a higher number of varieties than before, the varieties once again being spaced out evenly along the spectrum.

Provided that the demand for the differentiated good has an income elasticity greater than one and is not perfectly inelastic with respect to price, the total number of firms in the manufacturing sectors in the two countries must be less than under autarky. Each firm will then be producing a greater volume than under autarky, so that average costs (and hence prices) must be lower.

Figure 8.3 illustrates the autarky and trade equilibria for a typical firm in the manufacturing sector. The average cost of production, AC, initially declines as output increases. Under autarky the firm faces demand curve D_1, and will be in long-run equilibrium at point E_1. It will produce a quantity Q_1 which is sold at price P_1. (The marginal revenue and marginal cost curves are not shown, but they also will intersect at quantity Q_1.)

The opening up of trade will increase the number of varieties. The firm in question will probably have to change the specification of its product, but can produce it with the same costs as before, so that AC is unchanged. The increase in the number of potential consumers will tend to shift the demand curve facing this firm upwards, but the increase in the number of varieties will tend to shift it down, and the increased nearness of adjacent varieties will make it more elastic. The new long-run equilibrium will be at a point such as E_2. Output will be higher at Q_2, and average cost will be equal to price at the lower level P_2.

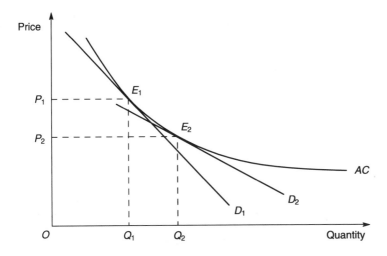

Figure 8.3 *Autarkic and free trade equilibria for a typical firm*

What then will be the welfare effects of the opening of trade? Greenaway has devised a diagrammatic representation of the gain to consumers from an increase in the number of varieties, and the change in the distribution of consumers' surplus.[14] In Figure 8.4, the horizontal axis shows a section of the attributes spectrum. Among the varieties being produced in each country under autarky are A_1 and A_2.

As we have observed, there will be some 'borderline' consumers who will be on the margin between buying one or other of two adjacent varieties. Examples of such consumers in Figure 8.4 are those who ideal varieties are v_1, v_2 or v_3. In the version of the Lancaster model we have considered, such consumers have the conventional downward sloping demand curve for the variety they consume, and will therefore gain consumers' surplus from consuming that variety. The aggregate level of consumers' surplus for the borderline consumers of variety v_1 is shown on the vertical axis as M_A. As we have assumed that consumers are evenly distributed along the spectrum, this level of consumers' surplus must be the same for all borderline consumers.

A consumer whose ideal variety is closer to the variety being produced will consume more of the variety than a borderline consumer and will derive greater consumer surplus. The consumers who enjoy the greatest consumer surplus are those whose ideal variety coincides with one of the varieties actually produced, such as those whose ideal variety is A_1. If we assume that consumers' surplus increases linearly the closer the ideal variety is to the chosen variety then we will obtain the 'saw tooth' function

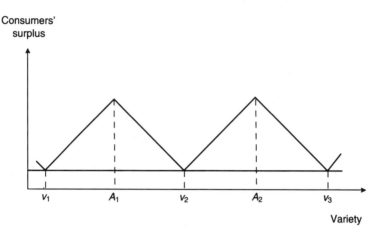

Figure 8.4   *Consumers' surplus under autarky*

in Figure 8.4 (remember that the varieties produced will be spread equi-distantly along the spectrum).

Now suppose that trade is possible. We shall assume for simplicity that the number of varieties available (in both countries) goes up by exactly 50 per cent, and that the distribution of the new varieties along the spectrum is that shown by Figure 8.5. That is, the 'space' occupied by two adjacent varieties under autarky is occupied by three varieties with free trade.

Consider first those borderline consumers whose ideal variety is v_1, and who chose variety A_1 under autarky. They will still be borderline consumers, but they must be better off for two reasons. First, they can now buy variety T_1, and as this is closer to their ideal variety they would increase their consumption even if the price stayed the same. The price of each variety has however fallen (there are fewer firms so average cost is lower), and this will increase consumption and thus consumers' surplus. The new consumers' surplus for such borderline consumers is shown by M_T in Figure 8.5.

On the other hand, there will be some consumers who were borderline under autarky but who can now obtain their ideal variety. Those whose ideal variety is T_2 (v_2 in Figure 8.4) come in this category. These consumers are obviously better off with trade. Moreover, their consumer surplus must be higher than that of the consumers who could buy their ideal variety under autarky, as a consequence of the fall in price.

At the other extreme, some consumers who could buy their ideal variety under autarky cannot now do so. It is impossible to generalise about whether they will gain or lose from the move. They are now buying a variety they regard as 'inferior', which will tend to reduce their consumer

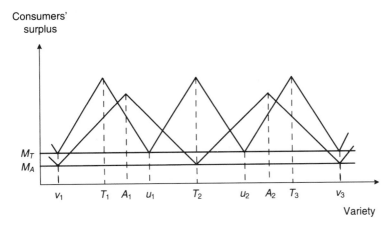

Consumers'
surplus

M_T
M_A

v_1 T_1 A_1 u_1 T_2 u_2 A_2 T_3 v_3

Variety

Figure 8.5   *Changes in consumers' surplus with free trade*

surplus, but they can buy a variety at a lower price, which will increase it. It is however clear that some consumers may become worse off. An obvious example from Figure 8.5 is a consumer whose ideal variety is u_1. Under free trade he is a 'borderline' consumer with consumer's surplus M_T, whereas under autarky he chose variety A_1 and enjoyed a consumer's surplus above M_T.

Although we have taken a very simple example, the general picture is unlikely to change if there is a greater or smaller increase in varieties than 50 per cent. The distributional implications of the move to free trade are therefore quite complex. Many consumers may gain, some considerably, but there are others who may lose.

What Figure 8.5 does suggest is that the aggregate of consumers' surplus over all consumers must increase. The total area under the 'saw teeth' for free trade must be greater than that for autarky.

What about the effect on producers? If we continue to assume that each producer has a linear total cost function, and that the number of varieties increases by 50 per cent, then the analysis is very simple. Figure 8.6 reproduces Figure 8.3, but with the marginal cost curve shown and the producer surplus areas identified. The demand curves are omitted for simplicity but, as in Figure 8.3, the demand curve for the autarky variety would be tangential to the AC curve at E_1, and the demand curve for the free trade variety would be tangential to the AC curve at E_2.

Under autarky the firm will be producing Q_1 and selling it at a price P_1, so the producer surplus would be area A plus area B. With free trade the firm will be producing Q_2 (of a different variety) and selling it at a price P_2, so the producer surplus would be area B plus area C.

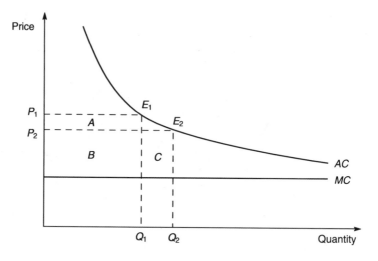

Figure 8.6   *Changes in producers' surplus with free trade*

If the firm's total costs are a linear function of its output, i.e.

$$C = \alpha + \beta Q$$

then its average cost curve is given by

$$AC = \beta + \frac{\alpha}{Q} \tag{8.12}$$

In long-run equilibrium price is equal to average cost, so the firm sells its output Q_1 at price

$$P_1 = \beta + \frac{\alpha}{Q_1} \tag{8.13}$$

and its producer surplus is

$$(P_1 - MC)Q_1 = \left(\beta + \frac{\alpha}{Q_1} - \beta\right)Q_1 = \alpha \tag{8.14}$$

With free trade the firm produces output Q_2 which it sells at price

$$P_2 = \beta + \frac{\alpha}{Q_2} \tag{8.15}$$

and so has producer's surplus

$$(P_2 - MC)Q_2 = \left(\beta + \frac{\alpha}{Q_2} - \beta\right)Q_2 = \alpha \tag{8.16}$$

That is, there is no change in the producer's surplus. Firms neither gain nor lose in such a situation. If the typical firm's costs are not linear then it is possible that producers' surplus may rise or fall.

Note that the demand specification in this model is quite different from that of the Krugman model. The ease with which one variety will be substituted for another decreases as the varieties become further apart. Further, the introduction of a new variety in the Lancaster model drives all the varieties produced closer together, and will mean that on average a consumer has a greater likelihood of obtaining a variety that is closer to his ideal variety. In the Krugman model the introduction of a new variety did not affect the varieties already being produced.

Lancaster considers various alternative specifications of his model. Among his conclusions are:

(1) If there were constant returns to scale in agriculture and *manufacturing* were the inferior good then free trade would lead to one of the countries exporting manufactures and the other exporting the agricultural good; that is, inter-industry rather than intra-industry trade.

(2) If there were diseconomies of scale in agriculture then, whatever the income elasticities of demand for manufactures and the agricultural good, there would be intra-industry trade of the form described earlier.

(3) If the countries were as described in our basic model, except for one country being larger than the other in every respect (k times the number of consumers, k times the number of varieties under autarky, etc.), then the autarkic price of the differentiated good would be lower in the large country, and it would *appear* to have a comparative advantage in that good. With free trade, however, *per capita* incomes and prices would be equalised between the countries, and there would again be intra-industry trade in the manufactured good, but with the number of manufacturing firms in the large country k times the number in the small country. Each firm in the large country would export a proportion $1/(k+1)$ of its output, each firm in the small country a proportion $k/(k+1)$. The increase in *per capita* real income would be larger in the small country – another instance of a small country securing most of the gains from trade.

Finally, Lancaster analyses a 'Heckscher–Ohlin' variant of his model. There are assumed to be two mobile factors, with manufacturing capital-intensive, agriculture labour-intensive. The factor endowments in the countries are not so dissimilar that there would be complete specialisation with free trade. Lancaster argues that the relatively labour-rich country will export both the agricultural good and some varieties of the manufactured product, and will import the other varieties. The labour-rich country will produce fewer varieties of the manufactured product than will the capital-rich country, and will be a net importer of manufactures.

■ 8.3 Oligopolistic models

The models we have discussed so far have assumed that there are many firms in the manufacturing sector in each country – so-called *large number models*. The other broad class of models which we must consider are the *small number* or *oligopolistic* models. The essential distinction between the two is that in the latter we must consider the *strategic interdependence* between firms in the industry. Each firm in the market knows that it is sufficiently large for its decisions to affect the profits of other firms. It must then consider how its competitors are likely to react to its decisions. The view it takes of its competitors' reactions is usually described as its *conjectural variation*.

There is no 'universally preferred' form of oligopolistic model. A major difference between alternative models is the form of conjectural variation assumed to influence a firm's decisions. Many duopoly models (the version of oligopoly with which we shall mostly concern ourselves) make the assumption that the competitors exhibit 'Cournot behaviour'. That is, each firm takes the other's output as given when it makes decisions about its own output; that is, output is the firm's strategic variable.

The attraction of the Cournot assumption is that it yields a determinate solution. In equilibrium, each firm will produce the same output and will charge the same price, so supplying half the market. Its drawbacks are that it ignores strategic interdependence and results in an adjustment to the equilibrium which has been characterised as unrealistic.

□ *The Brander–Krugman model*

We shall consider first a model which explains intra-industry trade in an identical commodity, an early example of which is that developed by Brander and Krugman.[15] The model, which is set in a partial equilibrium framework, assumes two countries which are identical in all respects. For the good in question, the model assumes that there is one producer in each of the countries, each with the same costs of production, that the domestic demand function for the good is the same in both countries, and that both firms display Cournot behaviour.

The common total cost function is assumed to be linear, i.e.

$$C(Q) = F + fQ \tag{8.17}$$

where Q is output, F represents fixed costs, and f the (constant) marginal cost. The demand function in country i ($i = 1$ for the 'home' country, 2 for the 'foreign' country) is

$$P^i = a - b(Q^i + Q_2^i) \tag{8.18}$$

where the superscripts refers to the country in which the good is consumed, and the subscripts to the country in which it is produced.

The revenue earned by the home producer in his own market therefore depends on both his own sales and those of his foreign competitor, and may be written as

$$R_1^1 = [a - b(Q_1^1 + Q_2^1)]Q_1^1$$

while his revenue from sales in the foreign market, for similar reasons, is

$$R_1^2 = [a - b(Q_1^2 + Q_2^2)]Q_1^2$$

His total costs will be

$$C_1 = F + f(Q_1^1 + Q_1^2)$$

so that his profit may be written as

$$\pi_1 = [a - b(Q_1^1 + Q_2^1)]Q_1^1 + [a - b(Q_1^2 + Q_2^2)]Q_1^2 - F - f(Q_1^1 + Q_1^2) \tag{8.19}$$

The profits of the foreign producer may, following the same reasoning, be written as

$$\pi_2 = [a - b(Q_1^1 + Q_2^1)]Q_2^1 + [a - b(Q_1^2 + Q_2^2)]Q_2^2 - F - f(Q_2^1 + Q_2^2) \tag{8.20}$$

The Cournot assumption implies that each of these producers will seek to maximise his profits by choosing his sales to the two markets on the assumption that the sales of the other producer will not change. That is, the home producer will choose as his sales in the two markets the values which satisfy

$$\frac{\partial \pi_1}{\partial Q_1^1} = a - 2bQ_1^1 - bQ_2^1 - f = 0 \tag{8.21}$$

and

$$\frac{\partial \pi_1}{\partial Q_1^2} = a - 2bQ_1^2 - bQ_2^2 - f = 0 \tag{8.22}$$

treating his competitor's sales volumes as constants. Similarly, the foreign producer will set his target sales in the two countries by solving the equations

$$\frac{\partial \pi_2}{\partial Q_2^1} = a - bQ_1^1 - 2bQ_2^1 - f = 0 \tag{8.23}$$

and

$$\frac{\partial \pi_2}{\partial Q_2^2} = a - bQ_1^2 - 2bQ_2^2 - f = 0 \tag{8.24}$$

but with the sales of the first producer assumed to be constant.

The joint equilibrium for the two producers may be obtained by solving the set of four equations ((8.21)–(8.24)). Because we have assumed constant marginal cost, however, we can in this case split the problem into two: we may solve equations (8.21) and (8.23) to obtain the equilibrium sales in the home market, and equations (8.22) and (8.24) to obtain the equilibrium sales in the foreign market. The symmetry we have assumed in this model means that, in the equilibrium, the firms will each produce the same output, and will each sell one half of that output on its domestic market and export the other half.

We may demonstrate the equilibrium, and the path towards that equilibrium, diagrammatically. Solving equation (8.21) for the sales of the home producer in his domestic market gives

$$Q_1^1 = \frac{1}{2}(a - f) - \frac{1}{2}Q_2^1 \tag{8.25}$$

Equation (8.25) defines the home producer's *reaction function* in his domestic market. That is, it specifies the sales in that market that the home producer should choose, in order to maximise profits, for any volume of sales in that market by his foreign competitor.

Similarly, solving (8.23) for the sales of the foreign producer in the home market gives

$$Q_2^1 = \frac{1}{2}(a - f) - \frac{1}{2}Q_1^1 \tag{8.26}$$

which is the reaction function for the foreign producer in the home market.

Figure 8.7 shows these two reaction functions for the home market; R_1 is the reaction function for the home producer, R_2 that of his competitor. The intersection of the two reaction functions determines the equilibrium in the market.

To demonstrate how the equilibrium is obtained, assume that initially the foreign producer attempts to sell a quantity q_1 in the home market. The home producer's reaction curve shows that if faced by foreign sales of q_1 the home producer can maximise his profits in the home market by selling a quantity q_2 (point x on R_1). The foreign producer will react to that by

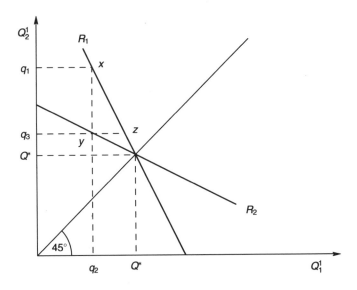

Figure 8.7 *Equilibrium in the home market*

choosing to sell a quantity q_3 in the home market (point y on R_2). The home producer will react in turn (point z on R_1), and so on. The market will converge on the equilibrium shown by the intersection of R_1 and R_2, with both producers selling a quantity Q^* on the home market. A similar analysis may be performed for the foreign market.

This model is of course little different from the standard Cournot duopoly model, the only difference being that the producers are assumed to be based in different countries, so that we observe intra-industry trade. We may however make the model more interesting in an international trade sense by introducing the possibility of transport costs.

☐ *The reciprocal dumping model*

Transport costs may be introduced into a duopoly model by assuming that some proportion of exports is 'absorbed' by charges – the so-called *iceberg* model of transport costs.[16] Formally, we assume that only a proportion g $(0 < g < 1)$ of each unit of exports may be sold in the export market. That is, in order to 1 one unit in the export market a producer must produce and ship $1/g$ units. This increases the marginal cost of production for the export market above that for the home market.

The introduction of transport costs in this manner requires us to modify the profit functions for each of the producers. If we are to continue to take as the decision variables the producer's *sales* to the two markets, the producer's costs must be modified appropriately. For example, the home producer's profits are now

$$\pi_1 = [a - b(Q_1^1 + Q_2^1)]Q_1^1 + [a - b(Q_1^2 + Q_2^2)]Q_1^2 - F - f\left(Q_1^1 + \frac{Q_1^2}{g}\right)$$

(8.27)

A similar modification must of course be made to the foreign producer's profit function.

There will be no change to either producer's reaction function for his own domestic market, since he reacts to what his competitor sells in that market, not to what his competitor produces for that market.

However, each producer's reaction function for his export market must be affected. For example, partially differentiating the home producer's profit function (8.27) with respect to his export sales gives

$$\frac{\partial \pi_1}{\partial Q_1^2} = a - 2bQ_1^2 - bQ_2^2 - \frac{f}{g} = 0$$

(8.28)

so that the home producer's reaction function in the foreign market is now

$$Q_1^2 = \frac{1}{2}\left(a - \frac{f}{g}\right) - \frac{1}{2}Q_2^2$$

(8.29)

The symmetry of the model implies that the foreign producer's reaction function for the home market will now be

$$Q_2^1 = \frac{1}{2}\left(a - \frac{f}{g}\right) - \frac{1}{2}Q_1^1$$

(8.30)

Since g is less than one, f/g must be greater than f, and so the foreign producer's reaction function for the home market must be closer to his quantity axis than before. This is shown in Figure 8.8, where R_2^* is the foreign producer's reaction curve when transport costs are present.

The equilibrium in the home market when there are transport costs is shown by point e^*. Comparing this with the equilibrium when there are no transport costs (point e in Figure 8.8), we see that the foreign producer's exports to the home market are reduced, while the domestic producer's sales on his domestic market are increased. The same must of course be true for the foreign market.

Note that the reduction in the foreign producer's exports to the home market must be greater than the increase in the home producer's sales. It follows that the price in the home market (and of course in the foreign market) must increase, and that the output of both producers will fall.

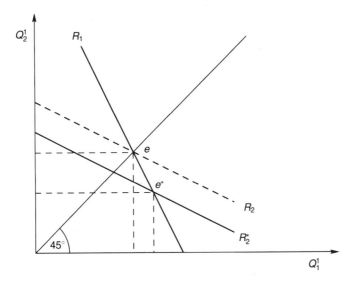

Figure 8.8 *Equilibrium in the home market with transport costs*

Given the symmetry of the situation, so that the same price obtains in the two markets, each producer must be receiving a higher price for sales in his home market than he is from sales in his export market *net of transport costs*. This led Brander and Krugman to describe such intra-industry trade as *reciprocal dumping*.

☐ *Extensions and modifications of the Brander–Krugman model*

The simple alternative to the Cournot behaviour of the Brander–Krugman model is to assume Bertrand behaviour, in which each firm regards price as its strategic variable, and assumes that its competitor's price is given. This also is, of course, a form of zero conjectural variation, and so shares some of the limitations of the Cournot assumption. Whereas in the Cournot version a firm consistently underestimates the quantity response of its rival, in the Bertrand model the firm consistently overestimates that response. In neither case does the firm identify the systematic nature of its error.

As we know from the analysis of duopolies in a closed economy setting, the Cournot and Bertrand models can lead to quite different outcomes.[17] We shall return to this in Chapter 13, where we consider the operation of trade policy in an intra-industry trade context.

It may be argued that models which do not assume zero conjectural variations are more 'realistic' and would give us greater insight into the problems of oligopolistic trade. Certainly, there is a fundamental conflict between assuming on the one hand that producers take such simplistic views of the likely reactions of their rivals while, as we shall do when considering trade policy, assuming that they are sufficiently sophisticated to realise that there are gains to be made from protection.

However, as is usually the case, making the assumptions more realistic greatly increases the complexity of the model. In particular, abandoning the zero conjectural variation assumption (whether Cournot or Bertrand) means that we cannot separate the two markets as we did with the Brander–Krugman model, and so cannot use the simple reaction curve technique.

Vertical differentiation and natural oligopolies

A very different class of models has been developed in a series of papers by Shaked and Sutton.[18] In the simplified version which we shall consider here, the product is vertically differentiated. The development of a higher quality version requires a firm to carry out R&D before it can enter the market. This R&D expenditure is then treated as a fixed cost. Average variable costs may be assumed constant (or even zero in the most simple version), or to increase slowly with improved quality goods.

All consumers are assumed to have the same tastes, so that there is a common ranking of commodities in terms of their perceived quality, but consumers are assumed to have different incomes with higher quality versions being bought by higher-income consumers.

The models operate with a three-stage decision-making process on the part of firms. Each firm decides first on whether to enter a given market. It then decides on the quality of good that it will produce. Finally, it decides on the price at which it will sell that variety. These decisions will depend in part on the number of firms already in the market, and the outcome for the firm in the final equilibrium will depend on the number of firms who enter subsequently.

The equilibrium attained in such models, including the number of firms, is sensitive to the values assumed for the parameters, in particular the range of the distribution of income, the nature of consumer tastes and the relationship between average variable costs and product quality. With a wide distribution of income and variable costs increasing with quality, a large number of firms can co-exist. With a narrow distribution of income and no variation in average variable costs with quality, the market may only support one or two firms. In the latter case a 'natural oligopoly' has arisen.

Figure 8.9 illustrates the nature of the final (Nash) equilibrium when variable costs do not change as quality changes and the other model parameters allow only two firms to operate in the market. $F(v)$ is the cost of the R&D needed to develop a variety of quality v. TR^1 is the total revenue curve for firm 1 which is producing the lower quality variety v_1, and was the first firm to enter the market. TR^2 is the total revenue curve for firm 2, which enters second and produces the higher quality variety v_2.

Firm 1 would obtain zero total revenue if it were to attempt to produce variety v_2, but can obtain revenue if it produces a lower quality. It cannot continue to increase its total revenue by reducing the quality it produces however, since at some point customers will switch to the higher quality variety. Firm 1 is in equilibrium when producing variety v_1 since its marginal revenue from changing the quality of its product (the slope of TR^1) is equal to the marginal cost of changing its variety (the slope of $F(v)$ at v_1).

Firm 2 would obtain zero total revenue if it were to attempt to produce variety v_1, but can obtain revenue if it produces a higher quality. The rate at which it can increase its total revenue by improving the quality it produces must at some point start to decline, since customers will switch to the lower quality good. Firm 2 is in equilibrium when producing quality v_2

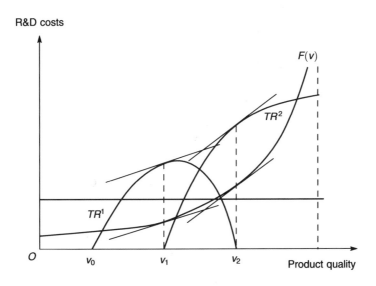

Figure 8.9 *Duopoly equilibrium with a vertically differentiated good*

since its marginal revenue from changing the quality of its product (the slope of TR^2) is equal to the marginal cost of such a change (the slope of $F(v)$ at v_2).

How then would a move from autarky to free trade affect the countries concerned? Consider the case of two identical countries, each of which has two firms producing the differentiated good under autarky. Suppose now that these countries start to trade with one another.

The firm producing the high (low) quality good in one country will now find itself in direct competition with the firm producing the high (low) quality good in the other country. One of each pair of producers will exit the market since neither can make profits with the other present. Free trade will result in there being only one producer of each of the two qualities, each producer supplying both markets. Once again, we cannot predict which of each pair of firms will survive. Consumers will gain in this model from the reduction in price that comes from the expansion of the market facing each surviving firm.

Consumers should also gain in the longer term through the development of higher quality goods. In terms of Figure 8.9, the expansion of the market through trade results in an upward shift in the total revenue curves facing both firms. For any given quality the slope of each total revenue curve must now be steeper, so increasing the return from developing a new higher quality variety. In the new long-term equilibrium both firms will improve the quality of their product.

Whether we shall observe intra-industry trade in such a model depends on which firms exit from the industry. If one firm leaves from each country then there will be intra-industry trade with one country exporting the low quality product, the other exporting the high quality version. But which country will export which good is of course indeterminate. If however both firms in one country exit then we shall observe inter-industry trade.

Abandoning the assumption that the distribution of income is the same in the two countries can however remove this indeterminacy. If one country has a higher average income than the other then the qualities produced under autarky will be higher in the former country. When trade opens, we may find that there will be more varieties produced than in the earlier (equal-income) model. The high-income country will tend to specialise in the higher quality products, and will export some of these, while importing lower quality products from the low-income country. The expansion of the market will, as before, lead to a fall in price, so that the varieties which disappear will be those of lower quality, and probably a general improvement in quality as well.

If we assume that high average incomes are positively correlated with a high endowment of capital relative to labour then we would observe an outcome similar to that of the Falvey–Kierzkowski models, with the capital-rich country exporting the higher quality goods. But note that the way in which quality enters the two groups of models is quite different.

■ 8.4 Conclusions

We have examined a variety of models in which intra-industry trade can arise. These are however only a selection of those which have been developed, and an even smaller subgroup of the wide range of models possible. The models, despite their variety, do have several features in common.

First, while it is possible to deduce that intra-industry trade will emerge, it is often impossible to predict which country will export which good(s). Second, diversity of preferences among consumers, possibly coupled with income differences, plays an important role. Third, similarity of tastes between trading partners may play a major role. Fourth, economies of scale are a frequent element of intra-industry trade models, and may be an important source of gains from trade.

Finally, note that in many of these models the move from autarky to free trade will involve lower adjustment costs than would be the case with inter-industry trade. Although individual firms may leave the market, the market itself is often bigger. Factors of production released by the firms that leave the market will probably be taken up by those that remain, rather than transferring to another sector. This should imply lower costs of retraining skilled labour, modifying capital, and so on. Moreover, factors are more likely to be employed with the same intensity in other firms in the same sector than will be the case when they move between sectors which have differing factor intensities. There may in that case be smaller changes in relative and real rewards to factors in adjustment to intra-industry trade than we would expect in adjustment to inter-industry trade.

□ *Notes*

1 Verdoorn (1960).
2 Balassa (1975), Chapter 3.
3 Grubel and Lloyd (1975).
4 See Krugman (1992) for a discussion of the development of the new trade theory and its implications for trade policy.
5 Those who wish to pursue this subject in more depth should consult a specialised text. Good examples, on which this chapter is largely based, are Greenaway and Milner (1986), and Vousden, (1990), Chapters 5, 6 and 7.
6 See, for example, Falvey (1981) on which the neo-Heckscher–Ohlin model in this chapter is based, and Falvey and Kierzkowski (1987).

7   Krugman (1979).
8   See Dixit and Norman (1980).
9   Venables (1984).
10   Lawrence and Spiller (1986).
11   Lancaster (1980).
12   This is an example of a Nash equilibrium.
13   This is sufficient to ensure that the model yields a unique and stable equilibrium. Lancaster discusses other sets of assumptions that would also give this result.
14   Greenaway (1982).
15   Brander and Krugman (1983).
16   As is done by Brander and Krugman (1983).
17   Eaton and Grossman (1986) demonstrated the effect of assuming Bertrand rather than Cournot behaviour in the Brander–Spencer framework
18   Shaked and Sutton (1984).

■ *Chapter 9* ■

Empirical Work in Intra-Industry Trade

■ *9.1* Introduction

As with inter-industry trade, the main focus of empirical work on intra-industry trade must be on the testing of models and hypotheses, and we shall comment on that in the second part of this chapter. However, before we can undertake any testing, we have to deal with two major problems: how we should *define* an 'industry', and how we should *measure* the extent of trade between such industries.

☐ *Defining an industry*

This problem is sufficiently complex for there to be no agreed single definition. Two main criteria have been used, but neither is dominant, and economists seeking to define an industry for empirical purposes will either follow one of these definitions or will attempt to use both and seek a balance between them.

The first criterion is that two different products are the output of a single industry if it is relatively easy to substitute one for the other in the production process. So, for example, cars, lorries, buses and tractors could all be considered to be outputs of the same industry according to this definition. Closely related to this criterion (though some economists might claim it is a third criterion in its own right) is that the products should use an identical technology intensity. By this criterion, mechanical typewriters and word processors are not products of the same industry, even though the uses to which they will be put by consumers may be quite similar.

The second criterion is that different products are the output of the same industry if the consumers of the product put them to essentially the same use. By this criterion, glass, plastic and cardboard milk containers are the product of the same industry.

It is obvious that there will be some cases where the two criteria are in direct conflict. The choice between them is often determined by the use to which the data generated by the criteria will be put.

☐ *The level of aggregation*

The raw data with which economists studying intra-industry trade will work are drawn from published statistics on trade in various recognised 'categories'. The most commonly used classification is the Standard International Trade Classification (SITC). Products are grouped together under a series of numbers ('digits') in increasing order of disaggregation.[1] There are 10 'Sections' at the one-digit level, 63 two-digit 'Divisions', 233 three-digit 'Groups', 786 four-digit 'Subgroups', and finally 1486 'Items' at the five-digit level.

So, for example, at the one-digit level, 'Chemicals' forms Section 5. This is then split into nine two-digit Divisions, such as 'Chemical Elements and Compounds' (51), 'Mineral tar and crude chemicals from coal, petroleum and natural gas' (52), and so on. Each Division is then further subdivided, so that 512 is the Group of 51 which deals with organic chemicals. Further subdivision gives, for example, Subgroup 5121 as 'hydrocarbons and derivatives'.

The economist has to decide on the appropriate level of disaggregation to use. At one extreme, the use of a very detailed classification might lead us to conclude that there is very little intra-industry trade: if French and Belgian beers are classified as different products then there will be no intra-industry trade in beer between France and Belgium. At the other extreme, working with a very high level of aggregation might suggest that most trade is intra-industry: if we work at the level of 'Chemicals' then a country exporting pharmaceutical products and importing manufactured fertilisers is engaging in intra-industry trade. Such problems have lead some economists to suggest that intra-industry trade is merely a 'statistical artefact'.[2]

☐ *Measuring intra-industry trade*

The first measure of the extent of intra-industry trade was proposed by Balassa in 1966.[3] He proposed that it be measured by the extent to which exports of a given good are offset by imports of an equivalent good. Algebraically, if X_j is the value of the exports of commodity j by a country, and M_j is the value of the 'matching' imports then the Balassa index is

$$A_j = \frac{|X_j - M_j|}{X_j + M_j} \tag{9.1}$$

If there is no intra-industry trade then either there are no exports ($X_j = 0$) or no imports ($M_j = 0$), and so $A_j = 1$. If there is 'perfectly matching' intra-industry trade then $X_j = M_j$ and $A_j = 0$.

The Balassa index has not found much favour. Most studies use the Grubel and Lloyd index[4] which, as we shall see, is a simple modification of the Balassa formula. The basic Grubel–Lloyd index may be written as

$$B_j = \frac{(X_j + M_j) - |X_j - M_j|}{(X_j + M_j)} \tag{9.2}$$

where X_j and M_j have the same meanings as before. This index may be written as a simple transformation of the Balassa index:

$$B_j = 1 - \frac{|X_j - M_j|}{(X_j + M_j)} = 1 - A_j$$

Why then has the Grubel–Lloyd index taken precedence over the Balassa index? The basic answer is that the values taken by the former are intuitively more appealing. The Grubel–Lloyd index has a value of zero when there is no intra-industry trade (either X_j or M_j zero) and a value of one when there is 'perfectly matching' intra-industry trade; that is, it is positively related to the level of intra-industry trade. The Balassa index on the other hand is positively related to the level of inter-industry trade.

Table 9.1 gives a simple example of the calculation of the Grubel–Lloyd index for some hypothetical examples. Two important points to note are that: (1) the index is non-linear – for example, when M_j is increased (X_j is decreased) by a constant amount while holding the other term constant, the index increases by a decreasing amount (decreases by an increasing amount); (2) the index is symmetric in X_j and M_j.

Table 9.1 *Calculating the Grubel–Lloyd index for hypothetical values of Xj and Mj*

X_j	M_j	$|X_j - M_j|$	$(X_j + M_j)$	B_j
4	0	4	4	0.00
4	1	3	5	0.40
4	2	2	6	0.67
4	3	1	7	0.86
4	4	0	8	1.00
3	4	1	7	0.86
2	4	2	6	0.67
1	4	3	5	0.40
0	4	4	4	0.00

☐ *The categorical aggregation problem*

Consider Table 9.2, which records some hypothetical data on imports and exports of two categories of goods (U and V), each disaggregated into two subcategories.[5]

At the most disaggregated level, the level of intra-industry trade in category U_1 is the same as that in V_1, and that in category U_2 is the same as that in V_2. Yet the level of intra-industry trade in the more aggregated category U is lower than that in category V. The reason for this anomaly is that the country concerned is a net importer of both U_1 and U_2, but is a net importer of V_1 and a net exporter of V_2. This is an example of the *categorical aggregation problem*.

The source of the problem is that the Grubel–Lloyd index at any given level of aggregation is a *weighted average* of the indices for the next most disaggregated groups. We may show this formally as follows.

Let j be the aggregated group, so that X_j and M_j are the exports and imports in that group. Suppose that there are n subgroups within j, with the exports and imports in that subgroup being X_{ij} and M_{ij} respectively. Then we may write the Grubel–Lloyd index for the aggregated group j as

$$B_j = \frac{|X_j - M_j|}{(X_j + M_j)} = 1 - \frac{|(X_{1j} - M_{1j}) + (X_{2j} - M_{2j})|}{(X_{1j} + X_{2j}) + (X_{2j} + M_{2j})} \tag{9.3}$$

If $X_{1j} - M_{1j}$ and $X_{2j} - M_{2j}$ have the same sign (i.e. the country is either a net exporter or a net importer in both subcategories) then $|(X_{1j} - M_{1j}) + (X_{2j} - M_{2j})| = |X_{1j} - M_{1j}| + |X_{2j} - M_{2j}|$ and we may write (9.3) as

$$B_j = w_{1j}B_{1j} + w_{2j}B_{2j} \tag{9.4}$$

where

$$B_{ij} = 1 - \frac{|X_{ij} - M_{ij}|}{(X_{ij} + M_{ij})}$$

is the Grubel–Lloyd index for subcategory i, and

$$w_{ij} = \frac{(X_{ij} - M_{ij})}{(X_j + M_j)}$$

is the share of subcategory i trade in category j trade.

If however $X_{1j} - M_{1j}$ and $X_{2j} - M_{2j}$ have the opposite sign (i.e. the country is a net exporter in one subcategory and a net importer in the other) then $|(X_{1j} - M_{1j}) + (X_{2j} - M_{2j})| < |X_{1j} - M_{1j}| + |X_{2j} - M_{2j}|$, and so $B_j > w_{1j}B_{1j} + w_{2j}B_{2j}$.

Table 9.2 *Calculating the Grubel–Lloyd index for different levels of*
aggregation

Category	X_j	M_j	$|X_j - M_j|$	$(X_j + M_j)$	B_j
U	180	310	130	490	0.7347
of which					
U_1	80	160	80	240	0.6667
U_2	100	150	50	250	0.8000
V	230	260	130	490	0.9388
of which					
V_1	80	160	80	240	0.6667
V_2	150	100	50	250	0.8000

Various methods have been suggested for modifying the Grubel–Lloyd index to meet this (and other) problems, but they are beyond the scope of this chapter. Greenaway and Milner[6] discuss this and other problems in greater depth.

9.2 Some estimates of the extent of intra-industry trade

Table 9.3 presents estimates of average levels of intra-industry trade at the one-digit level in the United Kingdom in 1977, calculated from the indices for the three-digit and four-digit classifications. Note that the index of intra-industry trade is always lower at the four-digit level than at the three-digit level (by some 15 per cent on average), and that the level of intra-industry trade is higher in chemicals and manufactures than in the other products.

Table 9.4 shows the (arithmetic) average levels of intra-industry trade at the one-digit level (but calculated at the three-digit level) in the United Kingdom in selected years. Within each of the years reported we may observe the same basic pattern as before – the level of intra-industry trade is higher in Sections 5–8 than in Sections 0–4. On the other hand, the rate of growth in intra-industry trade appears to have been higher in the former categories. However, given our earlier observations about the non-linearity of the Grubel–Lloyd index, we should not give too much weight to this.

Table 9.5 shows the average levels of intra-industry trade at the one-digit level for various developed countries in 1980. Note again the same general pattern of there being more intra-industry trade in the manufactures categories. Also of interest are the comparatively low level

Table 9.3 *Average* levels of intra-industry trade in the United Kingdom in 1977 (Grubel–Lloyd index)*

SITC Section	Third digit	Fourth digit
0 Food and live animals	0.35	0.34
1 Beverages and tobacco	0.35	0.34
2 Crude materials, etc.	0.40	0.29
3 Mineral fuels, etc.	0.58	0.49
4 Animal and vegetable oils, etc.	0.50	0.28
5 Chemicals	0.69	0.67
6 Manufactured goods (classified by material)	0.69	0.58
7 Machinery and transport equipment	0.69	0.57
8 Miscellaneous manufactures	0.80	0.70
Average of 9 sections	0.56	0.47

* Arithmetic averages.
Source: Derived from Greenaway and Milner (1989).

Table 9.4 *Intra-industry trade at the three-digit level in the United Kingdom in selected years*

SITC Section	1964	1970	1977	1980
0 Food and live animals	0.22	0.31	0.35	0.38
1 Beverages and tobacco	0.28	0.27	0.35	0.43
2 Crude materials, etc.	0.19	0.36	0.40	0.34
3 Mineral fuels, etc.	0.35	0.26	0.58	0.59
4 Animal and vegetable oils, etc.	0.29	0.25	0.50	0.48
5 Chemicals	0.56	0.59	0.69	0.69
6 Manufactured goods (classified by material)	0.52	0.56	0.69	0.71
7 Machinery and transport equipment	0.51	0.60	0.69	0.68
8 Miscellaneous manufactures	0.75	0.79	0.80	0.80

of intra-industry trade in Japan, especially in Sections 0–3, and the generally high level of intra-industry trade in the Netherlands.

Finally, Table 9.6 shows the average levels of intra-industry trade between the developed market economies (DMEs), the newly industrialised countries (NICs) and the non-NIC developing countries (LDCs). Intra-industry trade is dominant for all DME trade, but particularly so in trade between the DMEs. It is of lesser but still significant importance for the NICs, but it of relatively minor importance to the LDCs.

Table 9.5   *Intra-industry trade in selected countries in 1980*

Section	USA	Japan	West Germany	Italy	Netherlands	United Kingdom
0	0.31	0.15	0.48	0.32	0.61	0.38
1	0.36	0.06	0.53	0.54	0.68	0.43
2	0.39	0.08	0.38	0.22	0.49	0.34
3	0.23	0.10	0.45	0.24	0.51	0.59
4	0.22	0.63	0.59	0.52	0.52	0.48
5	0.59	0.64	0.66	0.74	0.72	0.69
6	0.59	0.35	0.72	0.57	0.72	0.71
7	0.63	0.31	0.52	0.66	0.70	0.68
8	0.53	0.49	0.69	0.51	0.67	0.80
9	0.40	0.36	0.48	0.43	0.66	0.59

Source to Tables 9.4 and 9.5: Greenaway and Milner (1989).

Table 9.6   *Average levels of intra-industry trade for country types in 1978*

	Total trade	Trade with DMEs only	Trade with all LDCs	Trade with NICs only
DMEs	0.59	0.64	0.21	—
NICs	0.42	0.48	0.38	0.31
LDCs	0.15	0.10	0.22	—

Source: Adapted from Havrylyshyn (1983) by Greenaway and Milner (1989).

9.3 Explaining the level and growth of intra-industry trade

Greenaway and Milner (1989) have surveyed the literature on the testing of hypotheses concerning intra-industry trade (IIT). The hypotheses are either suggested by the various theories of IIT or by more casual empiricism. They suggest that the hypotheses may usefully be grouped under three headings: *country-specific* – variations in intra-industry trade intensity for any given industry will depend on the characteristics of the trading partners; *industry-specific* – variations in intra-industry trade intensity across industries will depend on commodity/industry-specific demand and supply characteristics; and *policy-based* – variations in intra-industry trade intensity are influenced by policy/institutional factors.

The major country-specific hypotheses are that average levels of IIT will be higher: (1) in DMEs rather than in LDCs because of differences in incomes and in economic structure; (2) in 'large' countries than in 'small' ones since the scope for product diversity and economies of scale may be expected to be higher in the former (a 'weak' hypothesis); (3) when there is taste overlap between trading partners, since this may increase the scope for the exchange of differentiated commodities; (4) when trading partners are geographically close, either because proximity means lower transport costs (*ceteris paribus*) or because physical proximity is positively correlated with similarity of cultures and tastes.

Table 9.7 summarises the results of five econometric studies which covered some or all of these hypotheses.[7] There is broad similarity between the studies in their choice of variables to act as proxies for the proposed explanatory variables. The general consistency of the signs of estimated coefficients with those expected, and the significance levels of the coefficients gives very strong support for the country-specific hypotheses. It is reasonable to make the overall conclusion is that there is strong support for the view that there are consistent inter-country variations in average levels of IIT, related to their level of development, market size and physical/cultural proximity.

There are however some *caveats*. First, although differences in *per capita* income seems important, this disappeared in the Balassa study when he considered DMEs and LDCs *separately*. However Loertscher and Wolter, considering intra-OECD trade only, still found *per capita* income differences important. Second, the 'distance' proxies may be capturing influences other than distance (they may be collinear with the taste similarity variable for example). Finally, the dependent variable is IIT's *share in overall trade*, which may explain the occurrence of unexpected signs.

There are five industry-specific hypotheses. IIT will be greater: (1) the greater the potential for attribute or product differentiation; (2) in commodities where there is scope for scale economies; (3) when the market structure tends towards monopolistically competitive conditions; (4) when there is potential for product cycle trade and/or technological differentiation; (5) when there is a higher involvement by trans-national corporations.

Table 9.8 summarises the results of seven econometric studies[8] which covered some or all of these industry-specific hypotheses. A major difficulty in such studies is in obtaining data on variables which are reasonable proxies for the variables which economic theory tells us are probable explanatory variables. That the explanatory powers of the regressions in these studies are low (as measured by their R^2 values) is not surprising, given these difficulties.

Table 9.7 *Evidence on the country-specific hypotheses*

Explanatory variable	Expected sign	Loertscher and Wolter (1980)	Havrylyshyn and Civan (1983)	Tharakan (1984)	Balassa (1986a, 1986b)
Level of development					
1. Average *per capita* income	+	+	+[a]		+[a]
2. *Per capita* income differential	–	–[b]		–	–[a]
Country or market size					
1. Average GDP	+	+	+		+[a]
Taste overlap					
1. Direction of trade or similarity of *per capita* income	+	+[a]		+[a]	
Distance					
1. Distance between trading partners	–	–[b]			–[a]
2. Inverse measure of importance of transport costs	+	–[b]		–[a]	
3. Existence of common border	+	+[b]			+[a]

[a] 1 per cent significance level.
[b] 5 per cent significance level.
Source: Adapted from Greeenaway and Milner (1989).

Table 9.8 Evidence on the industry-specific hypotheses

Explanatory variables	Expected sign	Finger and De Rosa (1979)	Caves (1981)	Lundberg (1982), Culem and Lundberg (1983)	Toh (1982)	Greenaway and Milner (1984)	Balassa (1986b)
Product differentiation							
1. Classification heterogeneity	+		+[b]			+[a]	+[a]
2. Hufbauer index	+	+[b]	+[c]	+[a]	+[a]		
Scale economies							
1. Measure of relative value-added or minimum efficient scale	-/+	-	-			-[b]	[a]
2. Scale factor proxy	+	-		+[c]	+[a]		
Market structure							
1. Concentration ratio	-				-[a]	-[b]	-[a]
2. Extent of entry barriers to foreign firms	-				-[b]		
Technological factors							
1. R & D intensity	+		+	+[c]		+	
2. Rate of product turnover	+	-			+[b]		
Foreign direct investment							
1. Extent of foreign investment	-		-[b]				+[c]
2. Extent of 'intra-firm trade	+		+[b]				

Notes to Table 9.8:
[a] 1 per cent significance level.
[b] 5 per cent significance level.
[c] 10 per cent significance level.
Source: Adapted from Greenaway and Milner (1989).

Consideration of the results of the seven studies suggests some general conclusions. First, the product differentiation variables have the correct sign and are significant over all studies. Second, the technological intensity variables have generally correct signs and are sometimes significant. Third, the scale economy variables are less consistent, reflecting perhaps the difficulties of 'measuring' scale influences. Scale *per se* and IIT may not be continuously related, but there may be industry-specific relationships that are difficult to capture in cross-sectional analysis. Fourth, the market structure and the foreign direct investment effects seem to be consistent – all have the correct sign and are significant. However, not all the studies are looking at the same thing: Greenaway and Milner are examining domestic concentration and IIT, but Toh is considering rivalry between international oligopolists.

Greenaway and Milner conclude that there are some systematic inter-industry characteristics of IIT, and varying degrees of support for the hypotheses, but country characteristics seem more important than industry or product characteristics in 'explaining' IIT. Major *caveats* are that there are problems with omitted variables and measurement error, and that industry classification may not be identical across countries.

Finally, there are two policy-based hypotheses. First, we may hypothesise that IIT will be greater when tariffs and non-tariff barriers are low. However, even the *direction* of the possible effects of trade policy is difficult to assess; certainly we may expect trade barriers *per se* to restrict intra-industry trade, but they will also restrict inter-industry trade, so that the effects on the Grubel–Lloyd index of barriers to trade in *all* goods is indeterminate. The second policy-based hypothesis is that IIT will be greater in the trade of (market) economies subject to some form of economic integration. It will be difficult to interpret a positive result to a test of this hypothesis; it may be that economic integration has an effect because it reduces trade barriers, but it could also be a consequence of the fact that economic integration usually takes place between countries in close proximity to one another (and so probably with overlapping tastes, etc.).

Table 9.9 summarises the results of seven econometric studies[9] which considered these possible effects on IIT. The effect of trade barriers on share of IIT in each industry's gross trade is uncertain. We could perhaps

Table 9.9 *Evidence on the policy-based hypotheses*

	Pagoulatos and Sorenson (1975)	Loertscher and Wolter (1980)	Caves (1981)	Toh (1982)	Bergstrand (1983)	Havrylyshyn and Civan (1983)	Balassa* (1986a)
Trade barriers							
1. Industry average nominal tariffs	−[a]		+	+	−		+[a]
2. Non-tariff barriers	−			−			
Integration effect							
1. Membership of customs union		+[b]				+[a]	

[a] 1 per cent significance level.
[b] 5 per cent significance level.
* The Balassa study gives an insignificant coefficient for EEC membership.
Source: Adapted from Greenaway and Milner (1989).

argue that both trade barrier proxies should have a negative sign – but two of studies cited refute this for industry average nominal tariffs; for non-tariff barriers, although we have the 'correct' sign, it is insignificant. However, we should note that measurement errors are likely to be of major importance. The integration effect dummy is significant, but we cannot be sure that it is not capturing other proximity effects.

Greenaway and Milner conclude that there is no consistent empirical evidence that inter-country or inter-industry variations in IIT are systematically or predominantly 'explained' by policy interventions.

■ *9.4 Conclusions*

The evidence that there is intra-industry trade, and that it forms a significant portion of all trade for developed economies and in manufactured products of various types, seems fairly conclusive. The growing econometric literature on intra-industry trade suggests that it is related to various determining factors, such as country and industry characteristics. There is however much scope for improvement in the indices used to measure intra-industry trade, and the development of models of intra-industry trade which lend themselves more readily to econometric investigation.

□ *Notes*

1 The composition of the product groups in the SITC is governed by considerations of ease of data collection and consistency, so we should not expect such published data to be in a form that is well suited to the needs of economists.
2 For example, Finger (1975) and Lipsey, R.E. (1976).
3 Balassa (1966).
4 Grubel and Lloyd (1975).
5 See Tables 5.5 and 5.2 in Greenaway and Milner (1989) for examples using UK trade data. Much of the discussion of empirical studies of intra-industry trade is based upon this paper.
6 Greenaway and Milner (1989).
7 The studies are by: Loertscher and Wolter (1980), Havrylyshyn and Civan (1983), Tharakan (1984), and Balassa (1986a) and (1986c).
8 The studies are by: Finger and De Rosa. (1979), Caves (1981), Lundberg (1982), Culem and Lundberg (1983), Toh (1982), Greenaway and Milner (1984), and Balassa (1986b).
9 The studies are by: Pagoulatos and Sorensen (1975), Loertscher and Wolter (1980), Caves (1981), Toh (1982), Bergstrand (1983), Havrylyshyn and Civan (1983), and Balassa (1986a).

■ *PART 2* ■

INTERNATIONAL TRADE POLICY

■ *Chapter 10* ■

The Partial Equilibrium Analysis of Trade Policy

■ *10.1* Protectionism

There are many reasons why a country restricts trade, and tariffs have long been used to do this. Classical economics taught, as we have seen, the blessings of free trade. During the eighteenth and at the beginning of the nineteenth century, tariffs were used primarily to raise government revenue. The taxing of imports is probably the easiest existing means by which a government may acquire income. In the 1840s the teaching of the classical economists started to bear fruit in their home country, England. Income taxes were introduced, protection of agriculture was abolished, and the famous Corn Laws were repealed in 1846. Capitalists and workers joined forces against the land-owning class, and the tariffs which helped English agriculture were abolished. England continued its course toward free trade and was, from the 1850s to the First World War, for all practical purposes, a free-trading nation.

Other European countries, especially France and Germany, followed England's path and lowered already low tariffs in the 1860s. The United States alone stood as a fairly protectionist nation, though a trend towards the liberalisation of trade was also predominant. World trade grew at an extremely fast rate during this period.

Soon, however, demands for a more protectionist policy were heard. There were two specific factors in the 1870s which helped protectionism. One was the invasion of the European Continent by cheap grain from the United States and Russia, made possible by railways, steamships and innovations in agriculture. The other was the depression of 1873–79, the longest and deepest period of stagnant trade the world had yet known.

Distressed farmers in Germany and France started to ask for protection. At first Bismarck in Germany did not want to listen to them, but as the need for government income grew, he gave in, and during the 1880s tariffs on iron and food products were introduced. France also revised her trade policy in the 1890s and increased tariffs.

The period between the world wars saw a drastic increase in tariffs and other trade impediments; the 1930s especially was a period when protectionism increased. Since the Second World War the trend, especially among leading industrial nations, has been towards trade liberalisation. Many impediments to trade have been abolished and the average level of tariffs has fallen.

Protectionism is not however dead. The majority of the post-war tariff cuts have been concentrated on trade between developed countries (LDCs), and largely on manufactured goods. Even in that case there are still important non-tariff barriers to trade. The less-developed countries still face barriers to trade with the developed world, often under the guise of 'managed trade', as in textiles and footwear.

The motives of modern governments in restricting imports are various, and will be dealt with in detail in Chapter 15. Possible motives include: a desire to 'protect' the domestic producers of the import-competing good, perhaps for reasons of food or military security, or in response to political pressure; a wish to reduce consumption of the good; in order to reduce imports for balance of payments reasons; and a need to raise revenue.

As we shall see in this chapter and Chapter 11, protection of the domestic market brings benefits to some people, and losses to others. We must be able to identify the gainers and the losers, as well as the overall welfare effects of policies, if we are to explain the persistence of protectionism (as we shall do in Chapter 15).

We shall start by examining the effects of tariffs. Later in the chapter we shall consider various other barriers to trade, and compare trade restrictions with other policies.

■ 10.2 The partial equilibrium model of trade

The basic partial equilibrium analysis of trade policy is in terms of one good being traded between two countries or, what is essentially the same thing, between one country and the rest of the world. We shall use the partial equilibrium concepts of consumer and producer surplus and of the revenue/cost implications for the government's budget in determining the welfare and distributional effects of those policies.

We must make the usual *ceteris paribus* assumption, which implies that we should be wary of applying this methodology to situations where it is inappropriate. Strictly, we can only use partial equilibrium methods when the change in the policy instrument is small and/or when the market concerned is a small part of, or has very weak linkages with, other parts of the economy, and/or where the change in policy we are considering is not part of a larger package of measures.

Despite these strictures, these methods are widely used in situations where they are not strictly appropriate – for example in the analysis of the formation of customs unions (Chapter 16). The reason is that these methods give us useful insights into the effects of policy changes and give us some scope for quantifying those changes in money terms.

☐ *Free trade between two large countries*

We start by considering the more general, and also more difficult, case of trade between two large countries – that is, between two countries who can each affect the price of the good in the other country by changing the volume of their trade. Here we shall concentrate on only one form of trade policy, the tariff. We shall consider the many other forms of policy later in this chapter, using the simpler model of the small country.

We shall assume that we are dealing with a homogeneous good that is produced and consumed in perfectly competitive markets in both countries, and that we can characterise the individual markets by the usual supply and demand functions. As usual, we shall assume for simplicity that there are no transport costs or other impediments to free trade.

If the two countries, A and B, did not trade with one another then the (autarkic) equilibrium prices would be P_A^* and P_B^*, as shown in the two panels of Figure 10.1. Note that the prices are expressed in terms of the appropriate currencies (£ for country A, $ for country B).

In order to determine the direction of trade in the good we need to know the exchange rate between the two currencies. We assume that the good in question is not important enough for changes in the volume of its trade to change the exchange rate. Obviously, there would be a £:$ exchange rate at which the two autarky prices would be the same, so that there would be no trade. An exchange rate below this (i.e. with fewer $ to the £) would make the autarky price in B lower than that in A, and the usual process of arbitrage would lead to the export of the good from B to A. Equally, there are exchange rates high enough to lead to A exporting the good to B. We shall assume the former: that B will export the good to A.

There are various ways in which we can represent the joint equilibrium of the two markets when there is trade between them, and we shall use just two of them (all the others are variants of one or both of these). Firstly, we

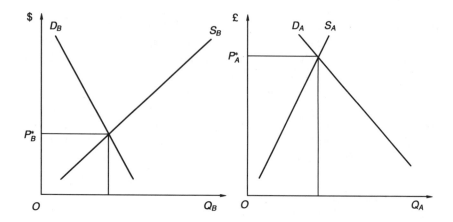

Figure 10.1   *Autarkic equilibrium in A and B*

shall use the 'back-to-back' diagram, as in Figure 10.2. First, we use the exchange rate to convert one currency into the other, so that we can express the prices in the two markets in common terms. It does not matter here whether we choose to work in £ or $, so we will just label the vertical axis as 'Price'. We then rotate the diagram for country B in Figure 10.1 about its price axis, and join it to that for country A. Note that P_B^* is less than P_A^*, so that B will export the good to A.

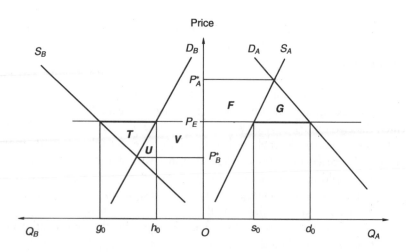

Figure 10.2   *Joint equilibrium in A and B under free trade*

The joint equilibrium of the two markets under free trade must be at a common price where B's desired exports to A (the difference in volume between B's supply of and demand for the good) are equal to A's desired imports (the difference between A's demand for and supply of the good). In Figure 10.2 the free trade equilibrium price is thus P_E, with A's imports, $d_0 - s_0$, from B equal to B's exports to A, $g_0 - h_0$.

We can use the conventional tools of consumer and producer surplus to demonstrate the welfare gains made by both countries from the free trade in this good (remembering the *ceteris paribus* restriction). In the exporting country the increase in price will lead to an expansion of production and an increase in producer surplus equal to areas T plus U plus V. At the same time the price increase will reduce consumption in B and so will cause a loss of consumer surplus of area U plus V.

Free trade therefore leads to a redistribution of welfare from consumers to producers in the exporting country, the transfer being measured by areas U and V. If we make the conventional assumption that a loss of £1 in welfare for any one agent is exactly compensated for by a gain of £1 in welfare for another (i.e. if we cancel out any internal transfers when assessing the impact on the economy) then it is evident that there is a net gain to the exporting country equal to area T.

In the importing country the fall in price leads to a gain in consumer surplus of area F plus area G, and a loss in producer surplus of area F. Again there has been a transfer of welfare, this time of area F from producers to consumers, but a net gain to the importing country equal to area G.

☐ *Tariffs and the large country*

Tariffs may be either *ad valorem* (the tariff is a set proportion of the price of the good at the border) or *specific* (the tariff is specified in money terms per unit), or perhaps a combination of the two. We shall generally assume that we are dealing with an *ad valorem* tariff. The basic effect of any tariff is to drive a wedge between the price of the good within the importing country (P_A) and the price in the rest of the world (P_B). If the tariff is set at a proportion t (or $100t$ per cent) then in equilibrium we must have $P_A = P_B(1 + t)$. The effect of the tariff will usually be to increase the price within the importing country,[1] so stimulating production in the import-competing industry and depressing demand, both of these effects reducing imports.

Suppose now that the government of the importing country (A) decides to restrict trade by imposing a tariff on imports. The immediate effect of the tariff is to increase the price of the good in the importing country, so both decreasing consumption and increasing production, and thus reducing the demand for imports. This reduction in the market for exports by country B will lead to a price reduction in B as producers compete for the reduced overall market for their output. A new equilibrium will be reached when the price in A is above that in B by the amount of the tariff and the reduced volume of imports by A is equal to the reduced volume of exports by B.

Such a 'tariff-ridden' equilibrium is shown in Figure 10.3, where P_E is the original free trade price, P_A is the post-tariff price in A, and P_B is the post-tariff price in B. Production in the importing country has increased from s_0 to s_1, while consumption has fallen from d_0 to d_1, so that imports have been reduced from $d_0 - s_0$ to $d_1 - s_1$.

Meanwhile, production in country B has decreased from g_0 to g_1, while consumption has increased from h_0 to h_1, so that exports have been reduced from $g_0 - h_0$ to $g_1 - h_1$ (which is equal of course to $d_1 - s_1$).

Welfare in the exporting country must have decreased. While consumers there have benefited from the price reduction, gaining consumer surplus of $Y + Z$, producers have lost surplus equal to $V + W + X + Y + Z$, so that there is a net loss overall of $V + W + X$.

The picture for the importing country is not so clear. There is a loss in consumer surplus of $J + K + L + M$, and a gain in producer surplus of J. There is also however an increase in government revenue as a result of the tariff, measured by area L plus area N (the unit tariff in money terms, $P_A - P_B$, times the new volume of imports, $d_1 - s_1$).

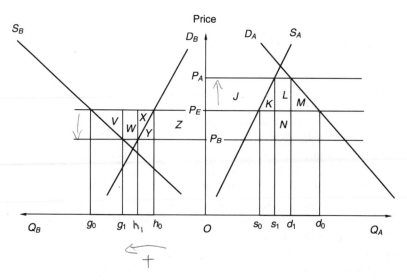

Figure 10.3   *Joint equilibrium in A and B with a tariff*

If we assume that the government uses the tariff revenue to either reduce taxes elsewhere or to pay additional benefits, and that £1 of money so spent is equivalent in welfare terms to £1 more or less in consumer or producer surplus, then the net effect on welfare in the importing country is measured by the sum of the gains in government revenue and producer surplus, less the loss in consumer surplus, i.e. area N less areas K and M. The importing country will therefore make a welfare gain if $N > K + M$, a loss if $N < K + M$.

These three areas are usually identified as follows. K is referred to as the *production loss* due to the tariff, the loss being due to the employment of resources in the additional production of the good which would have been more efficiently used elsewhere. L is known as the *consumption loss*, this loss coming from the diversion of consumers' expenditure from the import good to others they prefer less. These are referred to jointly as the *dead-weight loss* of the tariff. Area N is often referred to as the *terms-of-trade gain* of the tariff; the imposition of the tariff has driven down the price that the importing country must pay, so that it need use less resources in the production of export goods in order to purchase a unit of imports.

We may measure the monetary equivalents of the various losses and gains from the imposition of a tariff by calculating the appropriate areas in Figure 10.2. For example, if we assume that the demand and supply schedules are linear over the relevant range then the three sources of loss or gain for the importing country are given by:

the loss in consumer surplus $= 0.5(d_0 + d_1)(P_A - P_E)$
the gain in producer surplus $= 0.5(s_0 + s_1)(P_A - P_E)$
the gain in tariff revenue $\quad = (d_1 - s_1)(P_A - P_B)$

The two elements of the net welfare change are then:

the dead-weight loss $\quad\quad = 0.5(d_0 - s_0 - d_1 + s_1)(P_A - P_E)$
the terms-of-trade gain $\quad\; = (d_1 - s_1)(P_E - P_B)$

So if a large importing country may gain from the imposition of a tariff, while the exporting country must lose, what will be the effects on the economic efficiency of the world? That the world must lose may also be deduced from Figure 10.3. The only source of benefit is the terms-of-trade gain for country A (the importer), which is measured by area N. But area N must be equal to area W, part of B's welfare loss, since $d_1 - s_1 = g_1 - h_1$. Assuming that an extra £1 of welfare for country A is exactly balanced by £1 of welfare loss for country B, we can offset areas N and W against one another. The world as a whole therefore loses unambiguously, the loss being due to the inefficient use of resources in the presence of the tariff, and measured by the sum of the areas K, M, V and X.

□ *The optimum tariff*

The observation that a large importing country might gain from imposing a tariff, coupled with the obvious result that it must lose from a tariff which eliminates trade, indicates that there must be some tariff which maximises its welfare gain. Such a tariff is known as the *optimum tariff*. We shall meet a more rigorous general-equilibrium analysis of the optimum tariff in Chapter 11, but it is useful to introduce the concept here.

The optimum tariff will be that tariff that maximises the difference between the terms-of-trade gain (area N in Figure 10.3) and the dead-weight loss (area K plus area M). Other things being equal, a small tariff will produce a small terms-of-trade gain per unit of imports, but over a large volume of imports; on the other hand, it will produce a small increase in the price of the good in A and a small reduction in imports, and so a *see 23* small dead-weight loss. We would therefore expect there to be a net gain *on lec notes* from imposing a small tariff.

see 23 Conversely, a high tariff will result in a large terms-of-trade gain per unit but over a small volume of trade, but a large price rise over a large *see 23* reduction in trade and hence a large dead-weight loss, so that we would *on lec notes* expect a high tariff to result in a net loss. Indeed, once we have increased the tariff to the level where there is no trade (the prohibitive tariff), all the gains from trade identified in Figure 10.2 must have disappeared, the importing country is back at its autarky level of welfare, and there must therefore have been a fall in welfare compared to free trade.

The effect of increasing the tariff upon the welfare of the importing country will therefore be as shown in Figure 10.4. Initially welfare

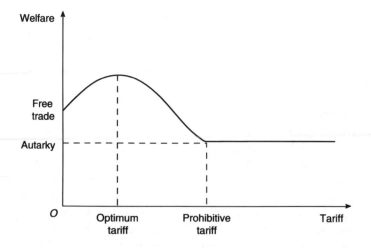

Figure 10.4   *The effects on welfare of increasing the tariff for a large country*

increases as the tariff increases. Welfare reaches its maximum when, by definition, the tariff is set at its optimum level. Further increases in the tariff then reduce welfare, until we reach the prohibitive tariff, which must produce the autarky level of welfare, lower than that from free trade. Increases in the tariff beyond the prohibitive tariff level will not reduce welfare any further.

■ 10.3 Excess demand and supply analysis

The alternative representation of the joint equilibrium of the two markets is by the use of excess (or import) demand and excess (or export) supply curves, as in Figure 10.5. As we know that country A is the importer in our example, we define A's excess demand curve as the horizontal difference between its demand and supply curves, giving us the downward sloping curve ED_A. At prices below P_A^* (not shown in Figure 10.5) there is a positive excess demand: A will be an importer if the price in B's market is less than P_A^*. At prices above P_A^* there is a negative excess demand (i.e. an excess supply), indicating that if the price in B's market were above P_A^* then A would export to B.

We obtain country B's excess supply curve in a similar manner, defining the excess supply as the difference between what would be supplied and what would be consumed in B at any common price. We thus obtain the upward sloping curve ES_B in Figure 10.5. For prices above P_B^* (not shown in Figure 10.5) country B will be an exporter, while for prices below P_B^* it will be an importer.

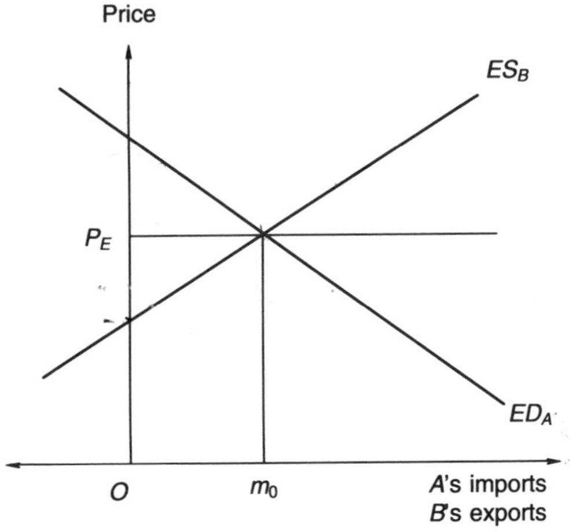

Figure 10.5 *Free trade equilibrium in A and B*

The joint equilibrium of the two markets under free trade is then defined by the intersection of ED_A and ES_B. At price P_E country A's demand for imports is equal to country B's supply of exports at m_0, and by the construction of the two curves we know that $m_0 = d_0 - s_0 = g_0 - h_0$.

We can represent that effects of a tariff by noting that the equilibrium will obtain when the prices P_A and P_B differ by the amount of the tariff and A's imports are equal to B's exports; such a tariff-ridden equilibrium is shown in Figure 10.6. A little basic geometry comparing areas in Figure 10.6 with those in Figure 10.3 shows that the area marked as $K + M$ in Figure 10.6 must be the dead-weight loss for the importing country, that N is the terms-of-trade gain made by country A, that $L + N$ is the tariff revenue for A, that area N plus area $V + X$ is the loss to the exporting country, and that area $K + M$ plus area $V + X$ is the loss in welfare for the world as a whole.

The advantages of this excess demand/excess supply analysis in terms of its simplicity are clear, but inevitably we cannot represent as much as we can using the back-to-back representation. In particular, we cannot identify in Figure 10.6 the actual volumes of supply and demand in the two countries, nor can we identify the actual changes in consumer and producer surplus. The parallels between this situation and that where we use offer curves rather than the full production-possibility curve/indifference map representation are obvious.

We may explain the existence of a welfare-increasing tariff by noting again that a large importing country has monopsony power (it can affect

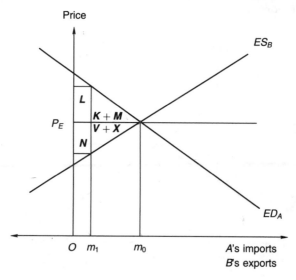

Figure 10.6   *Tariff-ridden equilibrium in A and B*

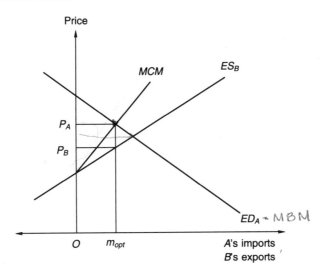

Figure 10.7 *The optimum tariff for a large importing country*

the price at which it buys imports by varying its import volume), so that there is a market imperfection for the importer. The marginal cost to the importing country is greater than the price of those imports.

In Figure 10.7 the supply curve for imports is ES_B, and the marginal cost of imports is shown by MCM. The marginal cost of imports curve shows what the importing country has to forego (in terms of other goods) in order to produce the exports necessary to purchase 1 more unit of imports.

Since the marginal benefit to A's economy from consuming imports is shown by the excess demand curve, ED_A, the volume of imports that will maximise A's welfare is determined by the intersection of that curve with MCM. The optimum tariff is thus that tariff which will bring about that level of imports.

It is important to remember that the conclusion that a tariff reduces the economic well-being of the world as a whole still applies in the case of the optimum tariff. The optimum tariff reduces the welfare of the exporting country to an extent greater than the gains made by the importing country.

■ 10.4 Other distortions to free trade

Although the previous analysis has been conducted in terms of a tariff on imports, which reduces the volume of trade, it would be a mistake to think that policies which increase the volume of trade will increase the welfare of the world as a whole. Provided that there are no distortions elsewhere, free trade is the optimal policy for the world as a whole. We are faced with the apparently paradoxical situation that while free trade may not be Pareto optimal for an individual large country (as shown by the optimal tariff argument), it is Pareto optimal for the world.

☐ *An import tariff in a small country*

As usual, a country is said to be small if it cannot affect the price it pays for its imports or receives for its exports by varying the quantity that it trades. That is, a small importing country faces a perfectly elastic (horizontal) supply curve of imports; a small exporting country faces a perfectly elastic demand curve for its exports. The analysis of trade policy is thus much more simple in the case of the small country as there can be no terms-of-trade effects to complicate the analysis. This implies that any policy imposed by a small country can have no effect on the welfare of its trading partners since, as we saw in the large-country example, these effects can only come about through changes in prices.

Consider first the case of the small importing country imposing a tariff. We shall discuss this problem using Figure 10.8. The importing country's demand and supply curve for the good in question are D_h and S_h respectively. The world price of the good is P_w, and since the country is small it can import any volume at that price, so that the excess supply curve of the rest of the world is the horizontal line ES_w. The price that rules in the importing country's market under free trade must then be P_w. The country will produce s_0 domestically, consume d_0, and import the difference, $d_0 - s_0$.

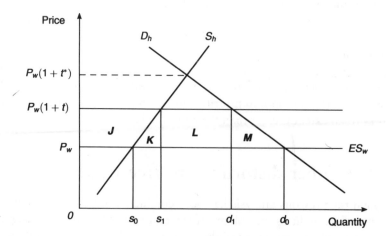

Figure 10.8   *A small importing country imposing a tariff*

Suppose the country then imposes an *ad valorem* tariff, t, on imports. This will drive the domestic price up by the amount of the tariff (tP_w), reducing consumption to d_1, and increasing domestic production to s_1. Imports will fall to $d_1 - s_1$, but this cannot of course affect the price of the good in the world market.

The increase in price and the expansion of output increase domestic producer surplus by the area J. At the same time, the price increase and the cut in consumption reduce consumer surplus by the sum of the areas J, K, L and M. Finally, there will be an increase in government revenue equal to area L.

Once again we may measure the welfare changes due to the tariff by calculating the areas J, K, L and M. This time we will illustrate this by calculating an *ex ante* estimate of the effects; that is, by assuming that we know the proposed tariff and the current volumes of domestic consumption and domestic production, and have estimates of the domestic demand and supply elasticities, thus producing a prediction of the gains and losses from the tariff.

If the pre-tariff consumption and production are d_0 and s_0 respectively, the world price is P_w, and the demand and supply elasticities are ϵ (defined so that $\epsilon > 0$) and η respectively, then: (i) the loss in consumer surplus will be $d_0(1 - 0.5\epsilon t)tP_w$; (ii) the gain in producer surplus will be $s_0(1 + 0.5\eta t)tP_w$; and (iii) the dead-weight loss will be $0.5(\epsilon d_0 + \eta s_0)t^2 P_w$.

There is thus a transfer of welfare (real income) from consumers to producers (area J) and from consumers to taxpayers (area L), but also a further net loss (also borne by consumers) of areas K and M. As there is no terms-of-trade effect, there must be a net loss to the country as a whole. The optimum (welfare-maximising) tariff for a small country is therefore zero. Figure 10.9 is a representation of the effect on the welfare of a small country of increases in its tariff.

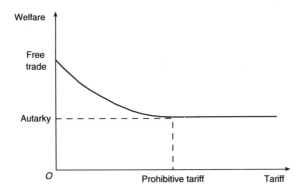

Figure 10.9   *The level of welfare in a small country as its tariff is increased*

☐ *An import subsidy in a small country*

Suppose that, rather than reduce imports by the use of a tariff, the government of the small importing country decides to increase imports by subsidising them, so that the price paid by consumers is driven below the world market price. The operation of such a policy is shown in Figure 10.10. Note that, once again, the price on the world market will be unchanged.

If the subsidy is paid at an *ad valorem* rate of s on the world price then the domestic price will be $P_w(1-s)$. Domestic production will fall to s_1, while consumption increases to d_1. Imports will therefore expand from $d_0 - s_0$ to $d_1 - s_1$.

Consumers will gain from such a policy, the increase in consumer surplus being measured by the sum of areas H, J, K, L and M. Producers will of course lose, the reduction in producer surplus being areas H and J. The cost of the subsidy to taxpayers will be sP_w per unit over the new volume of imports, i.e. the sum of areas J, K, L, M and N. The gain to consumers is less than the sum of the losses to producers and taxpayers, and the net loss to the economy is area J plus area N.

Import expansion by the use of a subsidy will therefore reduce the welfare of a small country, just as restricting imports by the use of a tariff reduces welfare. The best policy on imports for a small country is free trade. As we shall see next, the same is true for the policy on exports for a small country.

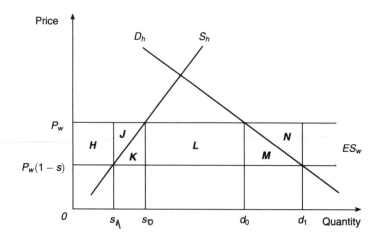

Figure 10.10   *A small importing country imposing a subsidy*

An export subsidy in a small country

We shall consider first the use of an export subsidy. Such a situation is shown in Figure 10.11. Under free trade the price prevailing in the small country will be the world price, P_w. A quantity s_0 will be produced, of which only d_0 will be consumed domestically, the remainder being exported.

If an export subsidy is paid at an *ad valorem* rate of s on the world price P_w then the domestic price will be driven up to $P_w(1+s)$ since domestic producers will be receiving that price inclusive of the subsidy for exports. Consumption will fall to d_1, production will increase to s_1, and so exports will expand from $s_0 - d_0$ to $s_1 - d_1$.

The loss in consumer surplus from the policy will be given by areas J and K, the gain in producer surplus by areas J, K and L, so that gains to producers exceed losses to consumers. However, the subsidy will cost taxpayers an amount equal to the sum of areas K, L and M, so that overall there will be a loss to the economy of area K (a consumption loss) and area M (a production loss). Once again we have a trade policy which is inferior to free trade.

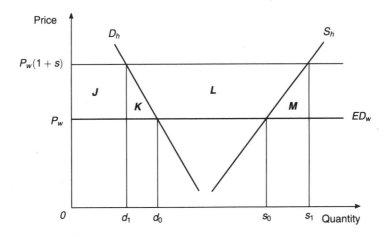

Figure 10.11 *A small exporting country imposing a subsidy*

An export tax in a small country

Alternatively, the government might decide to levy a tax on exports. Such a policy may be discussed in terms of Figure 10.12. We shall assume that a

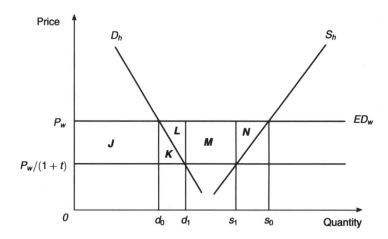

Figure 10.12　*A small exporting country imposing an export tax*

tax is charged on exports at the *ad valorem* rate of t on the world price P_w, so driving the domestic price below the world price by the amount tP_w. Domestic production will fall from s_0 to s_1, domestic consumption will increase from d_0 to d_1, and so exports will fall from $s_0 - d_0$ to $s_1 - d_1$.

The government earns a revenue equal to area M, and consumers experience a gain in welfare of area J plus area K, but the sum of these is exceeded by the loss made by producers, areas J, K, L, M and N. The net loss to the economy compared to free trade is thus area L plus area N.

☐ *Import quotas*

The tariff is a price-based measure; it restricts the volume of imports by increasing the domestic price, so discouraging consumption and encouraging domestic production. Various governments have however devised a whole range of import-restricting polices that do not operate directly through the price mechanism – the so-called *non-tariff barriers* (NTBs) to trade.

One of the most important of such policy instruments is the *quota,* which limits the volume of imports to some specified quantity in a specified time period, that volume being less than the usual volume of trade. The effect of the quota is of course to raise the domestic price since it restricts the supply to the domestic market, and in many ways the welfare effects of a quota are identical to those of a tariff.

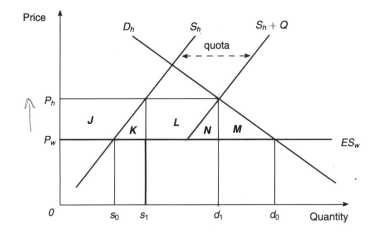

Figure 10.13 *A small exporting country imposing an import quota*

In Figure 10.13 imports under free trade were $d_0 - s_0$, the difference between domestic consumption and production. The government then introduces a quota on imports equal to $d_1 - s_1$. If the price in the importing country is less than the world price P_w then there will be no imports, but as soon as it rises above P_w foreign producers will be willing to supply the market. The aggregate supply curve facing the domestic consumers will thus follow the domestic supply curve (S_h) for prices below P_w, and will follow the world excess supply curve (ES_w) at price P_w until the quota limit is reached; it then follows the line $S_h + Q$ (parallel to S_h) for prices above P_w.

The market in the importing country will then clear at price P_h, and imports will be $d_1 - s_1$, equal to the quota. As with the tariff, there will be a loss in consumer surplus (of areas J, K, L, N and M), and a gain in producer surplus of area J. A tariff which increased the domestic price to P_h (the equivalent tariff) would have the same effects on consumers and producers.

A major difference between the welfare consequences of a tariff and a quota is in what happens to area $L + N$ in Figure 10.13, which would have been the revenue to the government from the equivalent tariff. If imports can be bought at price P_w on the world market but can be sold at price P_h on the domestic market then those with the right to import will be able to make a gain of $P_h - P_w$ per unit over the volume of the quota.

Typically the government will issue licences for the import of various proportions of the quota. If the licences are issued free of charge then the holders of those licences will gain all the rent shown by area $L + N$, and if the licence-holders are domestic agents then this area will be an internal transfer from consumers to others in the economy. If the government sells the licences then part of the rent will accrue to the government; if the licences are sold for the maximum amount possible (area $L + N$) then the revenue from these sales will equal the revenue from the equivalent tariff. In both cases the net loss from the quota will be the same as that from the equivalent tariff (areas K and M).

☐ *Voluntary export restraints*

The 'voluntary' export restriction (VER) is a relatively new but increasingly popular way of restricting imports.[2] The essence of the VER is that the importing country negotiates with its foreign suppliers quantitative restrictions on the amount of exports they will supply to the domestic market. These negotiations may be between governments, or between other bodies, such as associations of manufacturers, acting with government approval.

In many respects the VER has effects similar to those of the quota; if the quota in Figure 10.13 were replaced with a VER of the same quantity then the effects on the price, and hence of production, consumption and imports would be the same. It follows that the effects on consumer and producer surplus would also be unchanged.

The difference between the quota and the VER lies in the likely destination of the rents arising from the quantitative restriction on imports. Each supplier holding part of the overall VER quantity will be able to sell that quantity in the importing country at the domestic price P_h, and so will be able to secure the rent, rather than it going to the domestic importing company. If all the rents from the VER do go to foreign companies then the net loss to the importing country of the VER will be the sum of areas K, L, M and N in Figure 10.13. The revenue that would accrue to the government of the importing country from the equivalent tariff (area $L + N$) will go instead to the overseas suppliers taking part in the VER arrangement.

This ability to earn rents is one of the reasons why foreign suppliers can be persuaded to voluntarily restrict their exports. Since a VER is usually specified in quantity terms (so many units per year, say), foreign suppliers may be able to increase their rents by supplying higher cost items, for example by substituting 'luxury' cars for 'standard' cars.

Another 'carrot' is that foreign suppliers who do not join in the VER scheme at the outset may find it difficult to enter the scheme at a later date, so that those who join early are themselves given a protected position as suppliers to the importing country's market.

This protection may also appeal to foreign suppliers who fear that they may lose their competitive edge in the future, but believe that membership of the VER scheme will ensure that they can continue to supply the importer's market.

There is also, of course, an implicit 'stick' wielded by the government of the importing country, which is that failure to agree to participate in a voluntary scheme to restrict trade may lead to the government imposing other forms of trade restriction, such as a tariff, which will reduce imports to the same level as the VER but will not allow the foreign suppliers to gain the rents from the restriction.

10.5 Tariffs in comparison with quantitative restrictions

While it is reasonably obvious why the exporting countries may agree to join a VER scheme rather than face a tariff or a quota, it is not so clear from a purely economic point of view why the government of the importing country might favour some form of quantitative restriction (a quota or a VER) rather than a tariff.

The previous comparative static analysis demonstrated a formal equivalence between tariffs and quotas in their effects upon consumers, producers and national welfare. There was however the important difference that with a tariff there is a redistribution from consumers to the government (taxpayers), whereas with a quota the redistribution is from consumers to holders of the import licences. On these grounds we would probably rank a tariff as preferable to a quota, since it is likely that the quota will lead to a more unequal distribution of income within the economy.

However, the equivalence between tariffs and quotas breaks down if we consider the consequences of changes in market conditions under the two policy instruments. We shall consider two examples of this here: a change in the world price of the import good, and a shift in the domestic demand curve.

Figure 10.14 shows the case of a fall in the world price of the good, from P_w to P_w^*. With a tariff the fall in the world price will lead to a fall in the domestic price from P_h to P_h^*. Domestic production will therefore fall from s_1 to s_2, and domestic producers will suffer a fall in their profits. At the same time consumers will become better off. Whether the dead-weight loss increases or falls will depend on the elasticities of demand and of domestic supply.

With a quota the fall in the world price has no effect upon the domestic price, so that domestic producers and consumers are not affected. The

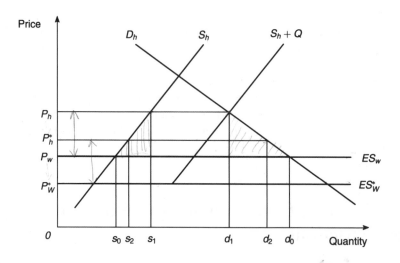

Figure 10.14   *The effects of a fall in the world price under a tariff and a quota*

dead-weight loss must however increase, as must the rents to holders of import licences. Producers will prefer a quota to a tariff in such circumstances, whereas consumers will give them the opposite ranking.

If there were an increase in the world price then these conclusions would be reversed. Producers would prefer the tariff to the quota, consumers the quota to the tariff. If domestic producers regard the likelihoods of a given increase or decrease in the world price to be the same and are neutral in their reaction to variations in their profits then they may be indifferent between a quota and the equivalent tariff. If however they are pessimistic about world price movements and/or are averse to variations in their profits then they will prefer the quota.

Figure 10.15 shows the second example, where the domestic demand curve shifts outwards. If a tariff were being used then the domestic price would be unchanged, and the increase in domestic demand would come solely from an increase in imports, since domestic production would be unaltered.

Under a quota system there could be no increase in imports, the domestic price would rise to P_h^*, and the (smaller) increase in demand would be met by expanding domestic production from s_1 to s_2.

Domestic producers would obviously prefer the quota to its equivalent tariff in these circumstances. Conversely, they would prefer the tariff to the quota if domestic demand were to fall. In this case it is the tariff which assures domestic producers of stable profits, so that if they are risk-averse

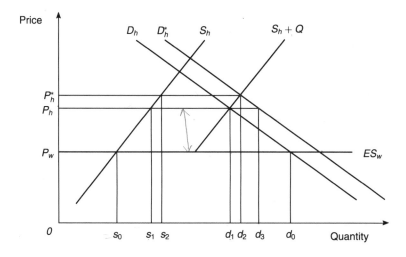

Figure 10.15   *The effects of an increase in domestic demand under a tariff and a quota*

then they may prefer the tariff to the quota. On the other hand, if they are optimistic about increases in demand for their good then they may regard the quota as superior.

Domestic consumers would prefer the tariff to the quota when demand is expanding, and the quota to the tariff when demand is contracting. Finally, we would expect to see little change in the dead-weight loss with a tariff (unless the demand curve is markedly non-linear), whereas with a quota the dead-weight loss would increase in times of expanding demand, decrease when demand contracted.

When we consider the relative effects of tariffs and quotas under these more dynamic situations it is evident that there is no direct equivalence. The analysis does not however make any very clear predictions about which policy will be preferred by producers or consumers. To advance our analysis we must move into the area of political economy, which we do in Chapter 15.

■ 10.6 Trade policy versus non-trade policy ✳

Let us assume that the objective of the government is to give protection to the domestic industry, so increasing domestic production and producer surplus. As we have seen, they can do this by the use of various trade policies, such as tariffs or quotas. However, trade policies are not the only way in which a given domestic production target can be achieved. One alternative would be to subsidise domestic production, while leaving consumers free to buy the good at the world price.

Figure 10.16 (which replicates Figure 10.8) allows us to compare the effects of a tariff and a production subsidy for a small country. Under free trade the domestic price is P_w, consumption is d_0, production s_0, and imports $d_0 - s_0$. We assume that the government's policy target is to increase domestic production to s_1, which it can achieve by setting a tariff of t. Through its effect on the price, the tariff reduces domestic consumption to d_1, and imports to $d_1 - s_1$.

Domestic producers would be induced to supply the same quantity s_1 with a domestic price of P_w if they were paid a production subsidy which would shift the supply curve down to S_h^*. This subsidy would be the same in money terms as the tariff. Since it would leave domestic prices unchanged, consumption would remain at d_0, and imports would fall only to $d_0 - s_1$.

Since there is no change in the price with the production subsidy there will be no change in consumption, and so no change in consumer surplus, so that consumers would prefer the production subsidy to the tariff.

Producers will be receiving the same price (inclusive of the subsidy) for the same quantity as under the tariff, giving them the same gain in surplus (area J), so they will be indifferent between the tariff and the production subsidy on those grounds.

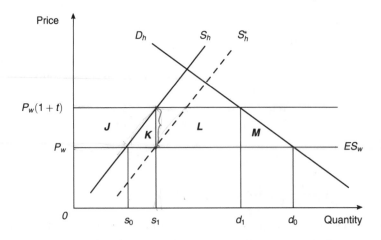

Figure 10.16   *The effects of a tariff and of the equivalent production subsidy*

The cost of the subsidy to the government (taxpayers) will be measured by areas J and K, so that taxpayers will prefer the tariff to the subsidy.

The overall welfare cost of the subsidy is the additional cost to taxpayers less the gain to producers, or area K. This is of course the production loss we identified when discussing the tariff. The production subsidy does not however impose the consumption loss of area M that results from the tariff.

On the standard welfare grounds, a production subsidy is preferable to a tariff if the aim of the government is to achieve a given level of domestic production. The distributional consequences of the production subsidy and the import tariff are however quite different.

This example generalises quite readily to other cases. If the government of a small country wishes to restrict domestic consumption of a good then it could do so with a tariff or with a tax on consumption. The consumption tax would be preferable since there would be no expansion in inefficient domestic production, and so the production loss associated with a tariff would be avoided.

Similarly, a production tax would be preferable to an import subsidy if the aim were to restrict domestic production, a consumption subsidy better than an import subsidy if the intention were to increase domestic consumption, and so on.

The general principle is that when the intention of the government of a small country is to achieve some domestic production or consumption target then a policy directed specifically at that target is preferable on welfare grounds to a trade policy.

Unfortunately, these results do not extend to the case of the large country. The problem is complicated by the fact that any policy which affects the large country's trade must also affect the world price.

For example, consider the case of the production subsidy in comparison with a tariff. The use of a subsidy which results in exactly the same domestic output as the tariff will lead to a world price between the free trade price and the price in the exporting country under the tariff regime. Consumers will not only gain in comparison with the tariff case, they will actually be better off than under free trade. However, there is now an outflow from taxpayers rather than an inflow. Put another way, the consumption loss of the tariff becomes a consumption gain with the production subsidy, but with the subsidy the country loses some of the terms-of-trade gains it made with the tariff.

It is not clear whether the production subsidy will be superior or inferior to the tariff in such circumstances. Certainly however, there will be no production subsidy that can yield a higher level of welfare than the optimum tariff.

What is clear however is that the exporting country will suffer a greater loss under a tariff regime than when the importer subsidies its own producers, since the tariff results in a lower price for exporters than does the subsidy. For the same reason, the loss in welfare for the world as a whole will be lower with the production subsidy than with the tariff.

☐ *Notes*

1   There are some unusual circumstances in which the imposition of a tariff can reduce the domestic price of the imported good – the Metzler Paradox. We shall deal with this in Chapter 11.
2   For a more detailed discussion of voluntary export restraints see Hamilton (1985).

■ *Chapter 11* ■

The General Equilibrium Analysis of Trade Policy

■ *11.1* Introduction

We shall concentrate in this chapter on tariffs, examining them in a general equilibrium framework. We shall not deal explicitly with the other trade policy instruments that we met in Chapter 10. There is however an important result – the Lerner Symmetry Theorem – which allows us to extend the results we shall obtain for tariffs to other price-based instruments. We shall discuss this theorem at the end of the chapter.

■ *11.2* Small and large countries

Once again, it is important whether the importing country is 'small' or 'large'. If the former then the reduction in imports brought about by the tariff will have no effect on the price in the rest of the world, and the domestic price will increase by the full amount of the tariff. If the importing country is large however then the cut in its imports will drive down the price in the rest of the world, and the domestic price will rise by less than the full amount of the tariff. We shall start by considering the case of the small country, the simpler of the two possibilities.

The effects on a small country of imposing an import tariff

The general equilibria of a small country under free trade and with an import tariff are shown in Figure 11.1. With free trade at the world price

WW = world price ratio

DO = domestic price ratio

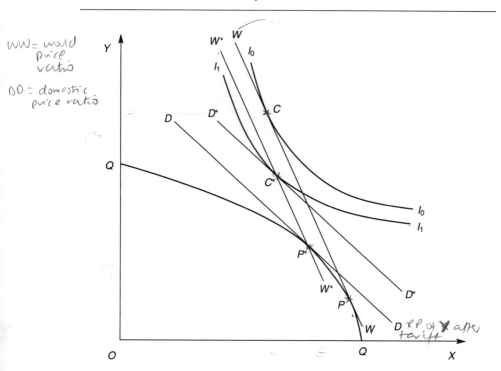

Figure 11.1 *A tariff will reduce the welfare of a small country*

ratio shown by the slope of the line WW, the production mix is that shown by point P, while consumption is at C on indifference curve I_0.

Suppose now that the government imposes a tariff on imports of good Y. The world price of both goods will be unchanged, so that the relative price of Y within the importing country will increase by the amount of the tariff, as shown by the slope of the line DD. That is, if the relative price of Y on the world market is θ then the relative price of Y within the importing country must be $\theta^* = \theta(1 + t)$, where t is the *ad valorem* tariff rate. Producers in the importing country will adapt to these changes in relative prices, the import-competing industry expanding and the export industry contracting, and the new production will be at point P^*.

Trade must however be at the same price ratio as before, so consumption must be at some point along the line W^*W^*, which is parallel to the original trade line WW. Consumers in the importing country also face the new domestic price ratio θ^*, so the consumption point must be on an indifference curve where that curve has slope θ^*. The consumption point must therefore be where the line cuts W^*W^* an indifference curve and that curve has a slope equal to the new domestic price ratio. Provided that X and Y are both 'normal' goods, the only possible consumption point would be C^* on indifference curve I_1 (the tangent to I_1 at C^*, D^*D^*, must of course be parallel to DD).

The 'positive' effects of the tariff are thus to increase production and decrease consumption of the import good, so reducing imports, and to decrease production and exports of the other good.

The tariff has lead to the violation of one of the Pareto optimality conditions that are satisfied under free trade for a small country. The marginal rate at which X can be transformed into Y by shifting resources between the two production sectors (the slope of the production-possibility curve) is no longer equal to the marginal rate at which X can be exchanged for Y on the world market. By reducing domestic production of the import good, using the released resources to produce additional X, and then trading that extra X for Y on the world market, the importing country can increase the amount of Y available for consumption.

If we make the assumptions necessary for the use of the indifference curves as an indicator of welfare, then the fact that the new consumption point must be on a lower indifference curve than the free trade point also shows that the tariff has made the small importing country worse off. This will be the case no matter what the level of the tariff. Note that since the world price is not affected by the tariff, the welfare of the rest of the world will not change. The world as a whole will become worse off as a result of the tariff, but the burden is borne only by the country imposing the tariff.

The effects on a large country of imposing an import tariff

In general the effect on the domestic price ratio in a large country of its imposing a tariff will also be to increase the relative price of the imported good, leading to expansion of the import-competing sector and contraction of the export sector. With a large country however the consequent reduction in its demand for imports will be to drive the world price of that good down, while the reduction in the supply of its exports will push up the world price of that good. The importing country's terms of trade are turned in its favour by the a tariff. If θ_F is the ratio of the price of Y to the price of X on the world market with free trade, θ_T the world price ratio after the imposition of the tariff, and t the tariff rate, then we must have $\theta_T < \theta_F < (1 + t)\theta_T$.

This terms-of-trade effect makes the welfare consequences of a tariff more difficult to predict in the large-country case. The trade-reducing effect of the tariff will reduce welfare (as it does for the small country), but the terms-of-trade effects will increase welfare. If the trade-reduction effect dominates then the overall effect of the tariff is to reduce welfare.

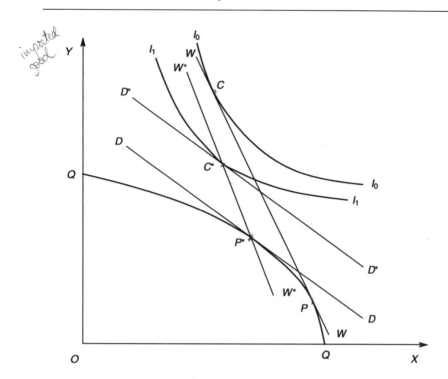

imported good (handwritten annotation)

Figure 11.2   *A tariff that reduces welfare in a large country*

Figure 11.2 illustrates such a case. Free trade production and consumption are at P and C respectively, the terms of trade being shown by the slope of the line WW. Imposition of the tariff increases the domestic terms of trade (the slope of lines DD and D^*D^*) but decreases the world price ratio (the slope of line W^*W^*). The new production point will be P^*, where the production-possibility curve has the same slope as the new domestic terms of trade. Trade will be carried out at the new world terms of trade, so that consumption must take place at some point on the line W^*W^*. That consumption must be consistent with the new domestic terms of trade, so that at the new consumption point, C^*, the indifference curve has the appropriate slope.

As in the small-country case, the tariff has lead to a shift of resources from the export industry to the import-competing industry (from P to P^*) and a reduction in imports. In the example shown in Figure 11.2 the new consumption point is on a lower indifference curve than the free trade point, and the effect of the tariff has been to decrease welfare.

Figure 11.3 illustrates the other possibility. Here the terms-of-trade effect is large and dominates the trade reducing effect of the tariff. Production again moves from P to P^* in response to the increase in the

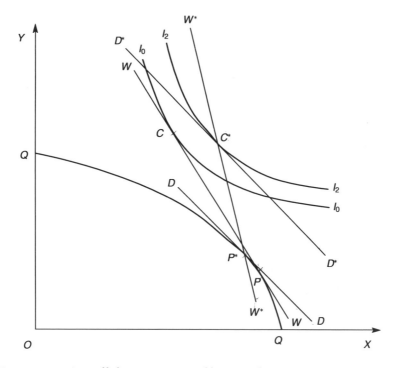

Figure 11.3 *A tariff that increases welfare in a large country*

relative price of X, the import-competing industry expanding and the
export industry contracting. The country then trades along the line W^*W^*
(the new international trade line), and consumption takes place at C^*,
where an indifference curve with slope equal to the new domestic price
ratio meets W^*W^*. In this case C^* is on a higher indifference curve than C,
and the use of the tariff has increased welfare in the country imposing the
tariff.

We may explain the possibility of a welfare-increasing tariff in the large-
country case by reference to the Pareto efficiency conditions. With free
trade and universal perfect competition the conditions for efficient
allocation of goods between consumers and for efficient allocation of
factors between industries are satisfied, since consumers and producers
face common prices. Moreover, the marginal rate at which consumers
substitute good X for good Y (the MRSC) is equal to the marginal rate at
which X can be transformed into Y by reallocating resources within the
economy (the MRTP).

However, because the country is large (i.e. has monopsony power), the
marginal rate at which it can transform X into Y through trade (the
MRTT) is not equal to the *average* rate at which it can transform X into Y

by trading (the *ARTT*), which is of course the terms of trade. If this large country tries to export more X and import more Y then it will push the price of X down and drive the price of Y up, so that the marginal rate at which it can transform X into Y through trade will be lower than the terms of trade. The marginal rate of transformation through reallocating resources domestically is however equal to the terms of trade under free trade. Formally, we have $MRSC = MRTP = ARTT > MRTT$.

The large trading country is therefore not in a Pareto efficient state under free trade. If it reduces its domestic production of its export good (X) by 1 unit in order to produce more Y, and at the same time reduces its exports of X by 1 unit and imports less Y, it will find that the extra domestic production of Y is greater than the loss of Y on the import side. To achieve Pareto efficiency it needs to equate its *MRTP* to the *marginal* rate of transformation through trade.

The imposition of a tariff will increase the domestic price ratio, so decreasing the *MRTP*, and will decrease the terms of trade and so increase the *MRTT*. If the tariff is small then this will bring the *MRTP* and the *MRTT* closer together, and this will increase welfare. If, on the other hand, the tariff is large then the relative positions of the *MRTP* and the *MRTT* may be reversed (i.e. the tariff may lead to *MRTP* < *MRTT*), and if the divergence becomes large enough then welfare may be reduced.

The observation that the welfare for a large country will be increased by a small tariff but decreased by a large tariff implies that there will be some tariff which maximises welfare – the *optimum tariff*. In order to examine this possibility in a general-equilibrium setting we need to introduce a new concept, that of the *trade indifference curve*. The set of trade indifference curves may be used both to derive the offer curve introduced in Chapter 1 and to represent the welfare obtained by the country through various trading positions.

■ 11.3 Offer curves and the optimum tariff

□ *Trade indifference curves*

Each individual trade indifference curve shows those combinations of imports and exports that will result in the same welfare level for the country concerned. We assume that factors of production and goods are allocated in accordance with the Pareto optimality conditions for an autarkic economy. Each trade indifference curve corresponds to one of the community indifference curves, and may be derived from that indifference curve and the production-possibility curve by a geometric technique first used by Meade.[1] The derivation is illustrated using Figure 11.4.

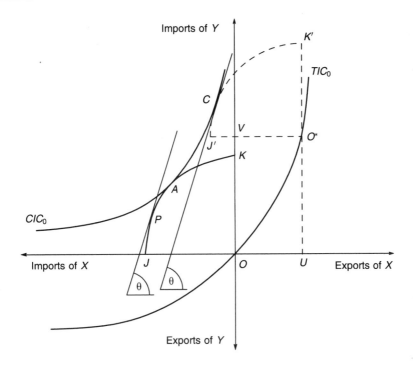

Figure 11.4 *Deriving the basic trade indifference curve*

Figure 11.4 is arranged so that production and consumption of the two goods are shown in the north-west quadrant. The production-possibility curve and the indifference curves are therefore drawn as mirror images in the vertical axis of their usual representation. Point *A* therefore represents the autarkic state, with community indifference curve CIC_0 tangential to the production-possibility curve. We now look for another production point and consumption point that will satisfy the three Pareto optimality conditions while giving the same level of welfare.

Consider point *P* on the production-possibility curve. Production here implies that factors are allocated efficiently, and gives a *MRTP* of θ. We now look for the point on CIC_0 giving the same slope θ; suppose that this point is *C*. The fact that *C* is on a community indifference curve implies that the *MRSC* is the same for all consumers, while by our choice of *C* we have ensured that the *MRTP* is equal to that *MRSC*. The pair of points *P* and *C* therefore satisfy all three Pareto optimality conditions. Moreover, consumption at *C* yields the same welfare as consumption at *A*.

But in order for consumption to be at *C* while production is at *P*, the country must be trading. In this case the country must be exporting a quantity O^*P of good X and importing a quantity O^*C of good Y. In summary, production at point P and consumption at point C will yield the same level of welfare for this country as production and consumption at point A. The country will be indifferent between exporting O^*P of X and importing O^*C of Y and not trading at all.

We may show the export and import volumes involved by production at P and consumption at C by a simple geometric device, also shown in Figure 11.4. The 'block' $O'J'CK'$ is identical with the block defined by the production-possibility curve $(OJAK)$, but has been positioned so that it is tangential to the community indifference curve CIC_0 at point C. Imagine that the original production-possibility curve has been moved, in such a way that it has always been kept tangential to the community indifference curve, until it has reached the position shown by $O'J'CK'$. The horizontal distance moved by the block must then be equal to the horizontal distance between points P and C, and the vertical distance moved must equal the vertical distance between P and C.

These distances are of course the exports of X and imports of Y identified previously. If we concentrate on the bottom right-hand corner of the block, O', we see that the distance OU is the horizontal movement of the block, and so the exports of X, while OV is the vertical movement, and so the imports of Y. Since the country is indifferent between having no trade (shown by point O) and exporting OU while importing OV, points O and O' must lie on the same trade indifference curve.

The production point P and consumption point C are an arbitrary pair of matching points. We could follow the same procedure of choosing some point on the production-possibility curve and then finding the 'matching' point on the community indifference curve CIC_0 to obtain another point on the trade indifference curve. What we are in effect doing is sliding the production-possibility 'block' around the community indifference curve CIC_0, keeping them always tangential, and recording the path traced out by the bottom right-hand corner of the block. That path defines the trade indifference curve TIC_0 corresponding to the community indifference curve CIC_0.

The country is indifferent between all the possible trading mixes defined by TIC_0 (including not trading at all), since all such trading mixes result in the same level of welfare. Note that this level of welfare may be obtained by exporting X and importing Y (as in the original construction), or by importing X and exporting Y.

We may identify two more specific relationships between the community indifference curve CIC_0 and the trade indifference curve TIC_0. Firstly, there is a one-to-one relationship between points on the two curves: if we know the trade mix then we also know the consumption (and production) mix.

Secondly, since the movement in the bottom right-hand corner of the production block comes from the sliding of that block along the community indifference curve, the corner of the block must move in the direction shown by the common tangent of the block and CIC_0. That is, the slope of the trade indifference curve TIC_0 at any point (say O') must be the same as the slope of the community indifference curve at the corresponding point (C) and of the production-possibility curve at its corresponding point (P). The slope of the trade indifference curve is therefore equal to both the $MRSC$ and the $MRTP$.

Figure 11.5 shows the construction of the trade indifference curve corresponding to community indifference curve CIC_1, which is higher than CIC_0 (we shall ignore indifference curves lower than CIC_0). The block $O''J''C''K''$ is again identical to the production-possibility block $OJAK$, but has been moved so that it is tangential to community indifference curve CIC_1 at point C''. The point on the real production-possibility curve which has the same slope as does CIC_1 at C'' is P. Again, we have consumption and production mixes which satisfy the three Pareto efficiency conditions. The exports of X and imports of Y needed for consumption at C'' and

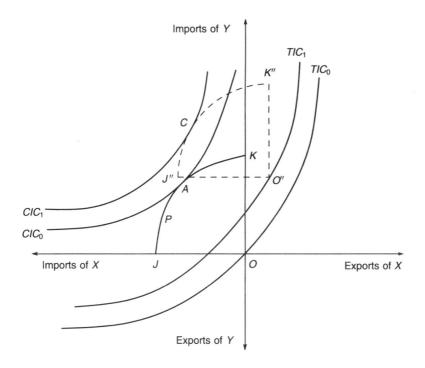

Figure 11.5 *Deriving higher trade indifference curves*

production at P'' to be consistent are shown by the horizontal and vertical distances of O'' from O.

Point O'' therefore defines a trade mix which will give the level of welfare shown by the community indifference curve CIC_1. The curve produced by the bottom right-hand corner of the block $O''J''C''K''$ as it is moved along CIC_1 is the trade indifference curve TIC_1 corresponding to CIC_1. TIC_1 necessarily shows a higher level of welfare than does TIC_0; that is, as we move in a north-west direction so we meet trade indifference curves showing higher levels of welfare.

☐ *Deriving the free-trade offer curve*

Trade indifference curves show combinations of exports and imports that will produce a given level of welfare. However, we are concerned only with those combinations which can be achieved efficiently through trade with the rest of the world. For any given value of the terms of trade and for any tariff there will be a limited number of combinations (usually one) which will maximise the country's welfare.

Let us first consider the free trade case, shown in Figure 11.6. Suppose the terms of trade facing our country are θ, the slope of the line OF. The country can trade any combination of X and Y shown by that line. The highest trade indifference curve it can reach given that constraint is TIC_1, at point L. With terms of trade equal to the slope of OF the country will maximise welfare by exporting OX_1 of X and importing OY_1 of Y.

Consider what point L shows us. Under free trade the domestic price ratio is equal to the world price ratio, with the former determining the $MRSC$ and $MRTP$. The slope of the trade indifference curve is equal to the international price ratio, but is also itself equal to the $MRSC$ and $MRTP$. We therefore have a consistent representation of the free trade position.

If the terms of trade are higher than θ, as is the case for the line OF', the welfare-maximising trade mix will be exports OX_2 of X and imports OY_2 of Y, shown by point M, the more favourable terms of trade allowing the country to reach a higher level of welfare. If the terms of trade were sufficiently low, such as those shown by the line OF^* then the optimal choice under free trade would be for the country to import a quantity OX_3 of X while exporting OY_3 of Y, as shown by point N. There will be no trade if the terms of trade are equal to the slope of TIC_0 as it passes through the origin, since that slope must be equal to the autarky price ratio in our country. All points such as L, M, O and N lie on the country's offer curve.

Note that all trade indifference curves other than TIC_0 pass through the north-west quadrant. A point in that quadrant *could* be obtained by

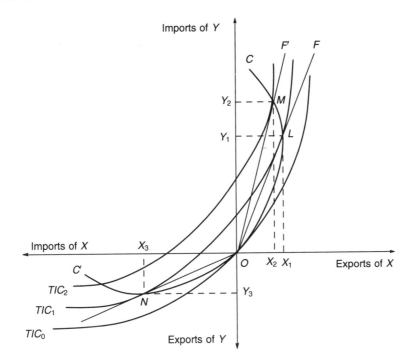

Figure 11.6 *Deriving the free trade offer curve*

importing both X and Y, but importing both goods is not of course a viable option in our simple economy. The offer curve must lie only in the north-east and south-west quadrants, in each quadrant bending away from the export axis and towards the import axis.

We cannot, of course, tell which good a country will export until we also know enough about its trading partner(s) to enable us to determine the pattern of comparative advantage. Once we do know which good each country will export then we need only draw the relevant part of each country's offer curve, giving the simpler representation we used in Chapter 1.

☐ *The tariff-ridden offer curve*

We may also derive the offer curve of a country when it imposes a tariff using the trade indifference curves. The essential difference from what we have just done is that the domestic price ratio will differ from the terms of trade by the amount of the tariff. In Figure 11.7 we show the derivation of a tariff-ridden offer curve on the assumption that our country has the

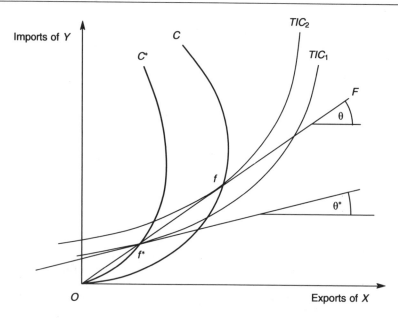

Figure 11.7 *Deriving a tariff-ridden offer curve*

comparative advantage in the X good, so that we concentrate on the north-east quadrant.

Suppose that the terms of trade are θ, so that the country can trade anywhere along the line OF, with f being the free trade equilibrium point. The country has however imposed a tariff on the import good (Y) which reduces the domestic relative price of X to θ^*. Consumers and producers adjust to the domestic price ratio, so that equilibrium with the specified terms of trade and tariff must be at a point where the trade line OF meets a trade indifference curve and that trade indifference curve has slope θ^*. Since the trade indifference curves get steeper as we move in a north-east direction, the tariff-ridden equilibrium point, f^*, must lie nearer to the origin than point f. Moreover, f^* must be on a lower trade indifference curve (TIC_1) than f since f is on the highest attainable trade indifference curve (TIC_2) given the terms of trade are θ.

If we keep the tariff constant (either at a given *ad valorem* rate or as a specific money value) then we can determine the domestic price ratio for any given terms of trade. By repeating the previous procedure for all possible terms of trade we can then map out the tariff-ridden offer curve OC' for the specified tariff.

In general, a tariff-ridden offer curve will still bend in towards the import good axis, and will lie 'inside' the free trade offer curve. In fact, we can show that the offer curve for a given tariff will lie inside the tariff-

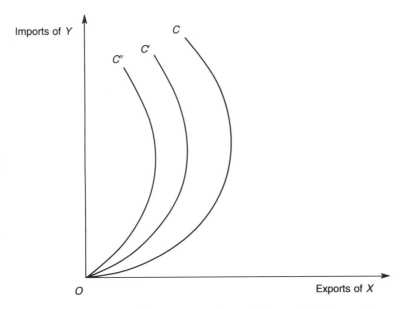

Figure 11.8 *The effects of increases in the tariff on tariff-ridden offer curves*

ridden offer curves given by lower tariffs. This is shown in Figure 11.8, where OC'' is the offer curve for a tariff t_2, OC' is the offer for a tariff t_1, and the tariffs are such that $t_2 > t_1 > 0$.

☐ Tariff-ridden equilibrium

We have already discussed the tariff-ridden equilibrium using the production-possibility curve and the community indifference map. As the trade indifference map and the offer curve for a country are derived directly from these, the representation we get for the tariff-ridden equilibrium must be consistent.

Consider first the small-country case. By definition, A is a small country if it cannot affect world prices by altering its trading position. That implies that country A must face an offer curve (from B) that is a straight line through the origin, as shown by OC_B in Figure 11.9. Such an offer curve is referred to as *perfectly elastic*.

If A imposes a tariff then its offer curve will shift in towards its import axis – from OC_A to OC'_A. The trade equilibrium will thus move from e to e'. The terms of trade faced by A on the world market do not change: in each case they are given by the slope of OC_B. A's imports will fall, from Oy_1 to Oy_2 and its exports will fall (by the same proportion) from Ox_1 to Ox_2.

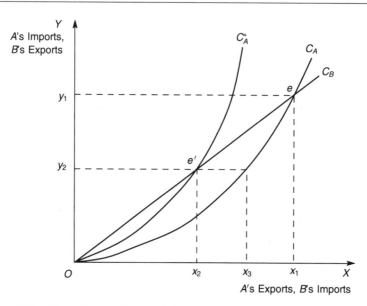

Figure 11.9   *The effects of a tariff for a small country*

In order to purchase Oy_2 of imports, consumers in A must forego Ox_3 of the export good. The domestic price ratio for the imported good, Ox_3/Oy_2, is necessarily greater than it was under free trade; that is, $Ox_3/Oy_2 > Ox_1/Oy_1$.

Figure 11.10 shows the situation when A is a large country: the offer curve it faces bends in the opposite direction to its own. Once again, the imposition of a tariff by A shifts its offer curve will shift in towards its import axis – from OC_A to OC'_A, and the equilibrium will move from e to e'.

The terms of trade faced by A on the world market must change from Oe to Oe'. A's imports will fall, from Oy_1 to Oy_2 and its exports will fall (by the same proportion) from Ox_1 to Ox_2. In order to purchase Oy_2 of imports, consumers in A must forego Ox_3 of the export good. The domestic price ratio for the imported good, Ox_3/Oy_2, is, in the example shown, greater than it was under free trade; that is, $Ox_3/Oy_2 > Ox_1/Oy_1$.

These results are, of course, consistent with our earlier conclusions. The imposition of a tariff by a large country will, it is suggested, improve its terms of trade with the rest of the world, but will increase the domestic relative price of the imported good. This is, in fact, the 'usual' case rather than the necessary one. As we shall see in the final section of this chapter, in some extreme cases the imposition of a tariff may cause the domestic relative price of the imported good to fall – the so-called Metzler effect. In what follows, however, we shall assume that the 'usual' case holds true.

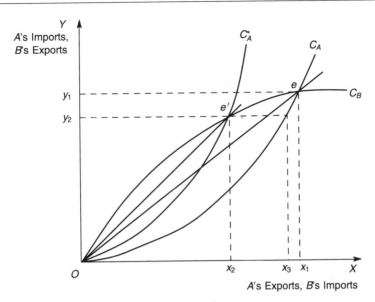

Figure 11.10   *The effects of a tariff for a large country*

☐ *The optimum tariff for a large country*

Suppose that the country imposing a tariff (country A) has the trade
indifference curves shown as A_1 and A_2 in Figure 11.11, with the associated
free trade offer curve shown as OC_A, and that it faces the tariff-free offer
curve from its trading partner shown as OC_B. Free trade equilibrium is
then at point e where OC_A and OC_B intersect.

The way in which we construct free trade offer curves implies that at
point e there is tangency between a country A trade indifference curve (A_1
in Figure 11.11) and the equilibrium terms of trade line and between a
country B trade indifference curve (not shown) and that terms of trade line.
Therefore there must also be tangency between the country A and country
B indifference curves.

The trading possibilities for country A are constrained by country B's
offer curve. A cannot obtain any greater volume of imports of Y in return
for a given volume of exports of X than that shown by OC_B. Therefore,
A's feasible trade combinations must lie on or below B's offer curve.

However, given that constraint, it is obvious from inspection of Figure
11.11 that A_1 is not the highest trade indifference curve that A can attain. A
movement from point e along OC_B towards the origin will bring A onto
higher indifference curves, the highest possible level of welfare being
attained at point m, where A's trade indifference curve A_2 is tangential to
B's offer curve. Further movements along OC_B towards the origin will then

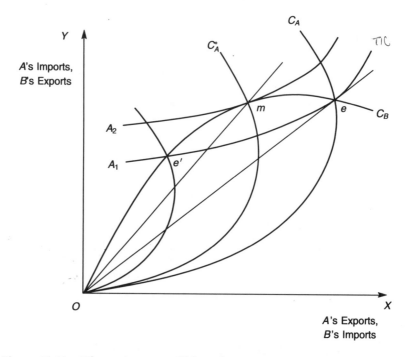

Figure 11.11 *The optimum tariff for a large country*

decrease A's welfare, with point e' showing the same level of welfare as with free trade, and points beyond e' a lower level of welfare than that.

We have seen that the imposition of an import tariff by country A will shift its offer curve in towards the Y axis, and that increasing the tariff increases that shift. A small tariff will result in an intersection between OC_B and A's tariff-ridden offer curve that will lie on a higher trade indifference curve than the free trade equilibrium. Further increases in A's tariff will bring the equilibrium to m, at which point A's welfare is maximised. The tariff which produces an equilibrium at m is the *optimum*, or welfare-maximising, tariff.

An increase in the tariff beyond the optimum tariff then reduces A's welfare, and if the tariff is increased sufficiently then A's welfare will be reduced below the free trade level. If the tariff is continually increased then ultimately A's tariff-ridden offer curve will move so far to the left that it will intersect with B's offer curve only at the origin, and trade will be eliminated. This tariff is known as the *prohibitive* tariff.

We may explain the existence of the (non-zero) optimum tariff for a large country by reference to the Pareto optimality conditions for a trading economy. At the free trade point e three Pareto optimality conditions are satisfied for country A. The marginal rate of substitution in consumption is the same for all consumers, the marginal rate of technical substitution is the same for both industries, and the common $MRSC$ is equal to the marginal rate of transformation in production.

However, the $MRSC$ and the $MRTP$ (shown by the slope of A's trade indifference curve at e) are not equal to the marginal rate of transformation through trade (shown by the slope of B's offer curve at e). As we noted earlier, an inequality between these means that the potential exists for the importing country to make a welfare gain by restricting trade.

At point m all four Pareto optimality conditions are satisfied. The slope of A's trade indifference curve at m (the $MRSC$ and $MRTP$ for A at that point) is equal to the slope of OC_B at m. There are no additional gains to be made by further restricting trade.

In the case of the small country, of course, the marginal rate of transformation through trade must be equal to the average rate of transformation through trade. The optimal tariff for a small country is zero.

Note however that country B must have been made worse off by the use of the optimum (or indeed any) tariff by country A. As we saw when constructing an offer curve, welfare increases the further away from the origin we move along the offer curve. Since the use of a tariff by A shifts the equilibrium point along B's offer curve towards the origin, the tariff imposed by A must reduce the welfare of B. A has gained in welfare by the use of the optimum tariff, but at the expense of B.

What is more, the world as a whole will become worse off as a consequence of A's use of the optimum tariff. We may show this by further reference to Pareto optimality criteria. As we observed above, at the free trade point e a trade indifference curve for A is tangential to a trade indifference curve for B. This implies that the marginal rate of substitution in consumption is the same for consumers in both A and B, so that there are no gains in welfare to be made by reallocation between consumers.

Further, the tangency of the two trade indifference curves also implies that the marginal rate of transformation in production is the same in both countries, so that there are no gains to be made by reallocating production between the two countries. Hence, the world as a whole (taken to be just A and B in this example) must be in a Pareto optimal state under free trade, and any move from free trade will reduce world welfare. This of course means that the loss made by B will exceed the gain made by A, in imposing the tariff.

The fact that country B will lose when A imposes a tariff raises the possibility that B will retaliate by imposing a tariff in its turn in an attempt

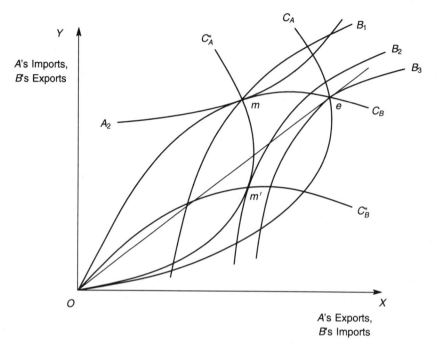

Figure 11.12   *Retaliation by the second country*

to recoup some of that loss. Figure 11.12 shows the situation from B's point of view after A has imposed its tariff (only B's trade indifference curves are shown). It is apparent that B can increase its welfare compared to point m if it shifts its offer curve downwards by imposing a tariff on its imports of X, and that the maximum welfare that B can obtain given that A has already used a tariff is at point m'.

Such a retaliation by country B must of course make A worse off than at m, and may provoke a retaliation from A in return. We may observe successive rounds of retaliation – an example of a *tariff war*. In a notable paper,[2] Johnson showed that, provided that at each stage the country retaliating imposed the optimum tariff given the other country's tariff-ridden offer curve, there would be a policy equilibrium with both countries having a tariff on imports and with some trade. That is, the tariff war would not result in the elimination of trade. One country would inevitably lose, though not necessarily the one suffering the consequences of the first tariff, the other country might gain or lose, and the world as a whole would inevitably be worse off.

Figure 11.13 shows the nature of the policy equilibrium demonstrated by Johnson. At point e^0 there is a country A trade indifference curve (A^0)

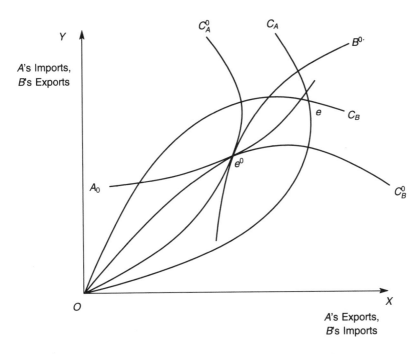

Figure 11.13 *Policy equilibrium as the outcome of a tariff war*

tangential to B's tariff-ridden offer curve (OC_B^0), so that there is no incentive for A to change its tariff. At the same time, there is at z a country B trade indifference curve (B^0) tangential to A's tariff-ridden offer curve (OC_A^0), so that there is no incentive for B to change its tariff either.

11.4 Tariffs and real rewards to factors of production

☐ *When no factors are mobile*

With the exception of the Metzler Paradox situation discussed later in this chapter, the effect of a tariff is to increase the relative price of the imported good. This is essentially the reverse of the move from autarky to free trade discussed earlier. Indeed, the tariff which eliminates trade (the *prohibitive tariff*) returns factor rewards to their autarky levels.

It is instructive to consider the differences in the effects of a tariff in the short, medium and long term, and we shall do so in terms of the Heckscher–Ohlin framework. For simplicity, we shall assume that we are dealing with a small country that produces both goods under free trade. The analyses of the large-country and the complete specialisation cases are simple extensions of this case.

In the short run the increase in the relative price of the imported good effected by the tariff cannot, by definition, bring about any reallocation of capital and labour within the economy. Since the capital–labour ratios are unaltered in both industries, the marginal products of factors must also be unchanged.

It follows that labour and capital employed in the import-competing sector will have the same real income in terms of the import good, and that since the price of the export good has fallen relatively, both factors must be better off in terms of the export good. In the short run then the effect of a tariff is to increase the real income of the factors employed in the import-competing industry.

Using a similar argument, the unchanged capital–labour ratio in the export industry in the short run implies that both the capital and the labour employed there will have the same real return in terms of the export good. The increase in the relative price of the import good then means that both factors will be worse off in terms of that good, so that both the capital and the labour employed in the export industry will suffer a loss in real income.

In the short run, then, the imposition of a tariff shifts real income from those owning factors of production employed in the export industry to those owning factors used in the import-competing industry.

☐ *When only labour is mobile*

In the medium term labour is, we assume, free to move between the two sectors, but capital is still immobile. This situation can be examined in terms of the capital–capital–labour version of the specific factors model.

The increase in the domestic price of the import good will, in the short run, lead to an increase in the money wage in the import-competing industry, while the money wage in the export industry will be unchanged. This implies that in the medium term labour will move from the export sector to the import-competing sector, and will continue to do so until money wages are equalised.

As we saw when we used the specific factors model to analyse the effects of the move from autarky to free trade, the effects of this transfer of labour on the real returns to the factors specific to the two sectors are readily determined. The inflow of labour into the import-competing industry will decrease the capital–labour ratio there, so increasing the marginal product of capital. The real return to capital in the import-competing sector must therefore increase in terms of the import good, and so must also increase in terms of the (now relatively cheaper) export good. This is an increase in the real return to capital in this sector compared to the short-run position, and so a further gain compared to free trade.

Conversely, the outflow of labour from the export sector will lead to a fall in the marginal product of capital there, and so to a fall in the real return to capital in the export sector measured in terms of the export good. As the relative price of the import good has increased, capital specific to the export sector must also become worse off in terms of the import good. Hence, the real return to capital in the export sector must fall. Again, this is a fall compared to the short-run position, exacerbating the loss already produced by the imposition of the tariff.

The position of labour is, however, indeterminate. The fall in the capital–labour ratio in the import-competing industry implies that the real wage measured in terms of the import good must fall compared with free trade. The labour that was employed in the import-competing sector finds some or all of its short-term gains eroded by the influx of labour from the export sector. However, the increase in the capital–labour ratio in the export industry means that the real wage measured in terms of the export good must increase compared with free trade and hence with the short-run position.

The labour that remains employed in the export sector finds some or all of its short-term losses recouped as a result of the outflow of labour to the import-competing sector. Whether, in the medium term, workers are made better or worse off than their free trade state by the imposition of a tariff depends on the importance of exports and imports in their consumption pattern.

In summary, in the medium term the imposition of a tariff increases the real return to capital specific to the import-competing sector, and reduces the real return to capital specific to the export sector. The medium-term effects of the tariff on the mobile factor are indeterminate. Note that these results do not depend on any assumption about the relative capital intensity of the two goods.

When both factors are mobile: the Stolper– Samuelson theorem

When we consider the long-term effects of a tariff, however, we must assume either that the country we are examining is capital-rich and so exports the capital-intensive good, or is labour-rich and exports the labour-intensive good. We shall assume here that we are dealing with a capital-rich country.

The higher return to capital enjoyed in the import-competing sector in the medium term will encourage capital to transfer there from the export sector in the long term. Figure 11.14 shows the usual box diagram, with X the labour-intensive import good and Y the capital-intensive export good. The initial free trade position is shown as point F. The increase in the relative price of the import good leads to the transfer of capital and labour from the export sector to the import-competing sector; the tariff-ridden equilibrium is shown as point T in Figure 11.14. This transfer must result in a higher capital–labour ratio in both sectors.

The increase in the capital–labour ratio in both industries implies that the marginal product of labour has risen in both. This in turn means that the real wage rate must have increased in terms of both goods. Conversely, the increases in the capital–labour ratios mean that the marginal product of capital has fallen in both industries, so that the real return to capital must be lower in terms of both goods. The tariff has lead to a transfer of income from capital owners to workers.

This is a particular example of a famous result in the context of the Heckscher–Ohlin model, known as the Stolper–Samuelson Theorem.[3] The more general version of the theorem may be stated as follows: '[in the long term] the imposition of a tariff will result in an increase in the real returns

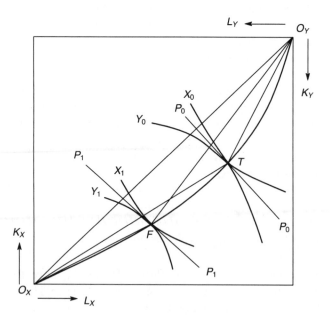

Figure 11.14   *The Stolper–Samuelson Theorem*

to the factor used intensively in the import-competing industry and to a decrease in the real returns to the other factor'.

11.5 Tariffs and real rewards to factors of production over time

The Stolper–Samuelson theorem shows that when all factors are mobile (in the long run) there can be no ambiguity about which factor gains and which loses through the imposition of a tariff. The mobility of capital and labour ensures that there will be no divergence between sectors in either the real return to capital or the real wage rate. Labour will gain and capital will lose if the country is capital-rich, capital will gain and labour will lose if it is labour-rich.

Equally, in the short term, when neither factor is mobile, we can be certain how factor rewards will change. In the medium term, however, when only labour is mobile, we cannot always be sure how the real rewards to factors will change.

The views of the owners of factors of production on the desirability of a tariff will therefore depend on their views of the speed with which factors of production can move between sectors.[4] If all factor owners believe that factors will remain perfectly immobile then those owning capital and labour in the import-competing sector will be in favour of the tariff, those owning factors tied to the export sector will be against it. That is, factors will combine along sectoral lines.

If labour is seen as mobile, while capital is not, the capital owners will again divide along sectoral lines. The position of the workers however less clear. If the import good is sufficiently important in their consumption then they will oppose the tariff. If the export good is sufficiently important then they will favour the tariff.

If all factors of production are perfectly mobile then the owners of factors will split along factor lines. The owners of the factor used intensively in the import-competing sector will favour the tariff, the owners of the other factor will oppose it.

11.6 The Metzler Paradox

The results just referred to for the effects of a tariff on the terms of trade, domestic prices, and real returns to factors are standard. No one seems to doubt that a tariff will improve a country's terms of trade or, in the limiting case, leave them unchanged. The effect on domestic prices is a more disputed question in economic literature. We will, therefore, go on to

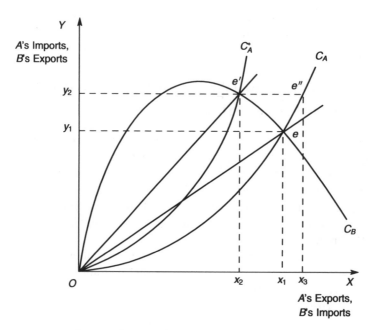

Figure 11.15   *The Metzler Paradox*

relate a case according to which the effect on domestic prices ought to be the opposite of the one just stated.

It is again convenient to use geometry to present the argument. Figure 11.15 illustrates offer curves for countries A and B, denoted by OC_A and OC_B respectively. The difference is now that country B's offer curve is inelastic at the free trade equilibrium point e. Country A has the comparative advantage in the production of good X, and exchanges Ox_1 of X for Oy_1 of Y at the terms of trade Oe. When country A introduces a tariff, its offer curve shifts from OC_A to OC_A^*. The new point of equilibrium is at point e', and Ox_2 of X is traded for Oy_2 of Y. Because of the fact that country B's offer curve is inelastic in the relevant range, a large improvement is produced in the terms of trade of country A. The improvement is, in fact, so large that the country with the tariff receives a larger amount of imports for a smaller amount of exports. The new terms of trade are given by the ray Oe' from the origin.

In the domestic market the relative price of Y will be higher, and domestic consumers will have to pay Ox_3 of X for Oy_2 of Y; thus in the domestic market the relative price of imports has also fallen. This can be seen from the fact that the ratio Ox_3/Oy_2 is smaller than Ox_1/Oy_1, and hence domestic consumers, even when the tariff is included in the domestic price of importables, will get more of the imported good for 1 unit of exportables than they did under free trade. This can also be seen from the fact that the ray from the origin representing the domestic price ratio, Oe'', is to the left of Oe.

If the price of the imported good falls in the domestic market because of the tariff, then the effects on income distribution are the opposite to the ones suggested by the Stolper–Samuelson theorem. As the relative price of imports falls, the relative price of exports rises. This means that production of exportables will be more profitable because of the tariff, and resources will be transferred from the import-competing sector to the export sector. The factor reward of the factor used intensively in the export sector will increase and the income distribution will turn in favour of the country's abundant factor of production, i.e. the one used intensively in the export sector.

This is a quite striking result, first set out in a classic article by Metzler.[5] He admitted that the result to be expected was an increase in the relative price of importables in the domestic market, but he argued that if the following condition were fulfilled, the relative price of imports would instead fall in the domestic market:

$$\eta < 1 - k \tag{11.1}$$

where η is defined as country B's demand elasticity for country A's (the tariff-imposing country's) exports, and $1 - k$ is defined as country A's marginal propensity to consume its export good Metzler's. Condition (11.1) says, in other words, that only if the trading partner's (i.e. the rest of the world's) demand elasticity for the tariff-imposing country's exports is larger than that country's marginal propensity to consume exportables, will the price of the import good increase in the country which has levied the tariff. If the country's marginal propensity to consume its export good is larger than the foreign demand elasticity confronting its exports, the domestic price of imports will instead fall because of the tariff. We observe that the country's marginal propensity to consume its exportables can never be larger than unity. If the foreign demand elasticity (h) is larger than unity, an orthodox result always follows.

It is fairly easy to understand the economics behind Metzler's result. The larger a country's marginal propensity to consume exportables, the larger is the amount of its tariff revenue spent on demanding the good exported by the country. Hence an excess demand for exports may come from this source. If the foreign country's demand elasticity for the first country's exports is low, it means that its demand for this good will fall only slightly, though its relative price increases. Under such circumstances, a tariff could create an excessive demand in the tariff-imposing country's market for its export good – if this happens, the price of imports will fall because of the tariff.

■ *11.7* The Lerner Symmetry Theorem

Lerner showed that in a long-run static equilibrium, an *ad valorem* tax on exports has the same effects as an *ad valorem* tariff on imports set at the same rate.[6] The essence of the argument is that both will have the same effect on the relative price of importables and on the terms of trade.

Suppose that country A imports Y and exports X, and imposes a non-prohibitive export tax at a rate τ on X. The domestic price of the import good, P_Y^A, will continue to be the same as the world price, P_Y^W. The domestic price of the export good, P_X^A, however is now lower than the world price of that good, P_X^W, the relationship being

$$P_X^A = \frac{P_X^W}{(1+\tau)} \tag{11.2}$$

The domestic price ratio in A is then

$$\frac{P_X^A}{P_Y^A} = \frac{P_X^W}{P_X^W(1+\tau)} \tag{11.3}$$

which is exactly the result we would have obtained had an *ad valorem* import tariff at rate τ been imposed on imports of Y. Both the export tax and the import tariff will increase the relative price of the import good in the domestic market and, if the country is large, will reduce the relative price of the import on the world market. Both will reduce the volume of trade. Provided that the revenue from the export tax is spent in the same way as the revenue from the import tariff, the effects of the two policies must be the same.

The symmetry between the export tax and the import tariff also extends to there being an *optimum export tax*, which is identical to the optimum tariff. The optimum tariff exploits the country's monopsony power in the market for the import good; the optimum export tax exploits its equivalent monopoly power in the export good.

There is an equivalent symmetry between a subsidy on imports and a subsidy on exports. Both will reduce the relative price of the import good in the domestic market, and both will increase the volume of imports and exports. If the country is large then both will increase the relative price of the import good on the world market.

Note however that the subsidies must decrease welfare, even for a large country. A large country loses from either subsidy because they turn the terms of trade against it, so that a subsidy can never bring the marginal rate of transformation through trade into equality with the domestic marginal rate of transformation through production.

☐ *Notes*

1 Meade (1952).
2 Johnson (1953).
3 Stolper and Samuelson (1941).
4 For a discussion of the 'adjustment problem', see Neary (1985).
5 Metzler (1949a). The argument was refined somewhat in Metzler (1949b), but the essence of the argument remains unchanged. For a discussion and criticism of Metzler's two articles, see Södersten and Vind (1968), the comments by Jones (1969), and the response by Södersten and Vind (1969).
6 Lerner (1936).

■ *Chapter 12* ■

Trade Policy and Distortions in Domestic Markets

■ 12.1 Introduction

In our analysis of trade policy in Chapters 10 and 11 we learned that when the domestic factor and commodity markets are working under fully competitive conditions then in general the use of trade policy will reduce welfare. The only exception is the use of an appropriate tariff (or export tax) when the country is large enough to affect the prices at which it trades with the rest of the world.

Suppose however that not every domestic market is operating efficiently (so that under autarky the country would not be in a Pareto optimal state). Such *market distortions* exist in many countries, especially perhaps in the less-developed ones. Distortions may occur in commodity markets, and we shall consider as examples the existence of a single domestic producer and the problem of externalities. There could equally be distortions in the factor markets, such as wage differentials between sectors, and we shall examine these also.

The existence of market distortions raises three interesting questions. First, does free trade necessarily lead to an increase in welfare compared to the autarky state? Second, could intervention by the government increase the level of welfare? Third, is the use of trade policy the *best* way in which the government could intervene? As we shall see, the answers to these questions are, in order, no, yes, and no. That is, free trade may reduce welfare if there are domestic market distortions, the government can increase welfare by intervening, and the use of a (single) trade policy instrument is never optimal.

We shall analyse these arguments using a mixture of the partial and general equilibrium approaches met in the preceding chapters. Unless we state otherwise, we shall assume that the country concerned is small, and that all markets other than the one specified are operating under conditions of perfect competition. Note that here we are concerned only with the effects of tariffs compared with free trade on the welfare of a country and with comparing tariffs and other means (subsidies, taxes) available for correcting distortions. We shall not consider the more complex question of the effects of government intervention on such matters as the distribution of income, although application of the principles discussed earlier would allow us to gain some insight.

12.2 Specified production and consumption targets

We shall start by using two extremely simple examples which demonstrate the basic result which, in general, make intervention using trade policy inferior to other forms of 'targeted' intervention. Consider first the problem shown in Figure 12.1.

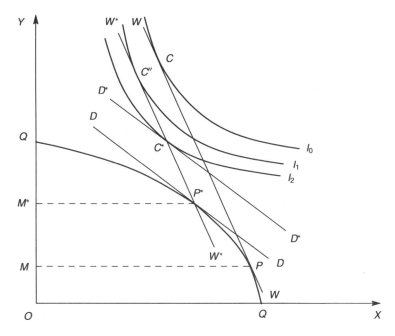

Figure 12.1   *Obtaining a specified output of the import-competing good*

Under free trade, and with all markets perfectly competitive, the output mix is shown by point P, and consumption by point C. Suppose however that the government regards the output of the import-competing good Y as too low at OM (for reasons we shall not explore for the moment), and wishes to change it to that shown by OM^*. To obtain the desired output target the government must change the relative prices faced by domestic producers from those on the world market (shown by the slope of line WW) to those shown by the slope of line DD.

It could do that by imposing the appropriate tariff on imports of Y, in which case consumption would be at point C^*. Welfare would be reduced from the free trade level, as shown by the shift from indifference curve I_0 to indifference curve I_2. It is however easy to identify a superior policy. If the government gives an appropriate subsidy to the production of the import-competing good then it can again change the price ratio to that shown by the slope of DD, and production will be at P^*. Domestic consumers however will still be able to buy at the original world prices, and so will consume where the line W^*W^* (parallel to WW) is tangential to indifference curve I_1, at point C'. The policy of subsiding production of Y is superior to the use of the tariff since it gives the desired production target but a higher level of welfare (I_1 is a higher indifference curve than I_2).

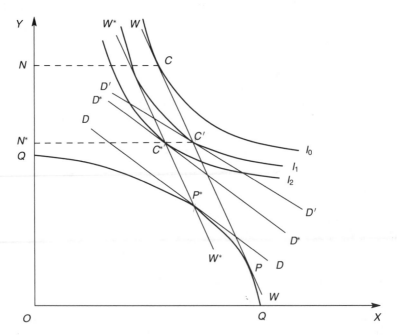

Figure 12.2 *Obtaining a specified consumption of the import-competing good*

Now consider the problem shown in Figure 12.2, where again free trade gives the production mix shown by P and the consumption mix shown by C, but where the government wishes for some reason to reduce the consumption of the import-competing good Y from ON to ON^*.

Once again, a tariff could be used to obtain the desired level of consumption. The appropriate tariff would lead to production at P^* and consumption at C^*. Once again, however, a more efficient policy is easily identified. The target consumption level could also be achieved at point C', where indifference curve I_1 meets the original trade line WW, and since I_1 is a higher indifference curve than I_2, this must be a superior alternative. A policy which would yield this outcome is to impose a tax on the consumption of Y, so changing the relative prices faced by consumers to those shown by the slope of line $D'D'$. Such a policy would not affect the prices faced by domestic producers, and so production would continue at point P.

The common feature of both examples is that the tariff affects both producers and consumers, whereas the target is to affect the decisions of producers in the first example and of consumers in the second. In each case the tariff imposes additional welfare losses by affecting the behaviour of the group that is not targeted. Such secondary effects are known as *by-product distortions*.[1] The use of a tariff introduces a distortion in consumption in the first example, and a distortion in production in the second example, and is therefore a *second-best policy* in each case. The use of a subsidy or tax in the targeted area, the *first-best policy*, avoids these distortions and their associated welfare costs.[2]

12.3 Domestic distortions in commodity markets

☐ *A single domestic producer in a small country*

A single domestic producer would under autarky be a monopolist, and its presence would lead to a Pareto suboptimal outcome: the marginal cost of producing the good would be less than the marginal benefit obtained from the consumption of the good. Under free trade, as we shall see, the presence of a monopoly will only be suboptimal if the country in which it is based is a large country (in our usual sense).

If the single domestic producer is based in a small country then, since the country cannot (by definition) affect world prices, neither can the domestic producer. That is, it is a price-taker on the world market. The consequences will be discussed in terms of Figure 12.3, where the country concerned is an importer of the good. The analysis for the case where the country (and so the domestic producer) exports the good follows essentially the same lines. The domestic producer is assumed to have increasing costs.

The domestic demand curve is shown as D, so that the marginal revenue curve that would face the domestic producer under autarky is MR. The producer's marginal cost curve is MC, so that under autarky the producer would sell a quantity Q_A at price P_A. If the country is an importer of the good under free trade then the world price, P_W, must be less than the autarky price, as shown in Figure 12.3.

Under free trade the price prevailing in the domestic market will be P_W, and that will also be the marginal revenue facing the domestic producer. Domestic production will therefore rise to Q_F, and domestic consumption to C_F, the difference being imported. The domestic firm will lose some of the producer surplus it would have enjoyed under autarky (a loss equal to area *abcd*), but this will be partially offset by a gain equal to area *deh* from its increased production. Domestic consumers will increase their surplus by area *abcd* (due to the fall in price of the quantity they consumed under autarky), plus area *bdf* (due to their increased consumption at the lower

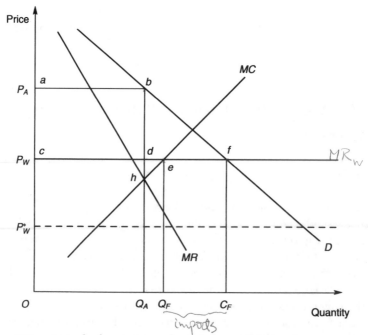

Figure 12.3   *A single domestic producer in a small importing country*

price). There will therefore be a net gain to the country equal to area *deh* plus area *bdf*.

Note that had the world market price been sufficiently low, for example P_W^*, then the output of the domestic producer would have fallen with the move to free trade. The country would however still enjoy a net gain in welfare.

A more interesting problem that may occur when there is a domestic monopoly is the possibility that the autarkic price ratio may suggest that the country would import the 'monopolised' good under free trade, whereas it will in fact export the good. Figure 12.4 may be used to give a partial equilibrium illustration of this problem.

Once again, the domestic price under autarky is P_A, while the world price is P_W. Comparison of the two prices suggests that the country will import the good under free trade, since $P_W < P_A$. However, if we consider Figure 12.4 it is evident that the domestic producer, now constrained to take the world price as given, will choose to produce quantity Q_F, selling C_F on the domestic market and exporting the remainder. Domestic consumers will gain as before following the reduction in the price they pay, and it is possible that in this case the domestic producer will gain as well (area *dfh* may be greater than area *abcd*).

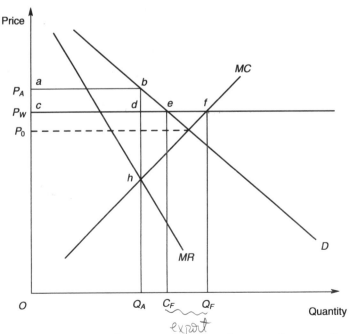

Figure 12.4 *Apparent and true comparative advantage for a small country*

The apparent comparative disadvantage in the monopolised good suggested by comparing the autarky price with the world price has misrepresented the true comparative advantage in that good. The comparison that should be made in order to obtain the true comparative advantage is between the world price and the domestic price that would occur if the domestic producer were to produce the socially optimal output under autarky – price P_O in Figure 12.4.

Fortunately, whether the move to free trade results in imports with either increased or decreased domestic output, or in exports, our conclusion about the welfare effects is the same. In the free trade position the marginal cost of purchasing the imported good and the marginal cost of producing the good domestically are equal, and also equal to the marginal benefit gained from the consumption of the good. There is no policy which can improve on this position. For a small country with a single domestic producer, free trade is the first-best policy.

☐ A single domestic producer in a large country

The analysis for a single domestic producer in a large country is necessarily more complicated, both in terms of the analysis required and the wide range of possible assumptions that could be made. For example, the single domestic producer might be an exporter under free trade, and might then have monopoly power in the world market. That market power might include the ability to separate the two markets (so that exported goods could not be re-imported), and could then practise price discrimination. On the other hand, the good produced by the single domestic producer might be imported. The country in which the single producer is based might also have market power in the other good, whether imported or exported. We shall therefore not attempt any formal analysis of the problem, but will content ourselves with some observations.

It is most probably the case that in a *laissez faire* situation each of the marginal rate of substitution in consumption, the marginal rate of transformation through (domestic) production, and the marginal rate of transformation through trade will be different. It is difficult to predict on *a priori* grounds whether the use of any one policy instrument on its own will increase or decrease welfare. Certainly, it is unlikely that the use of any instrument on its own will maximise welfare, since there are at least two distortions present. The optimal policy mix will probably consist of some policy aimed at correcting the distortion due to the existence of the single domestic producer (perhaps a production subsidy) and an optimal tariff applied to whichever good is imported.

☐ *A negative production externality*

Consider an economy with an agricultural and an industrial sector, and assume that production in the agricultural sector imposes costs on the rest of the economy for which it does not pay – perhaps through the excessive use of fertilisers which pollute the water supply. This implies that the private cost of producing a certain amount of agricultural products is lower than the social cost, because farmers do not include in their calculations the cost of cleansing the water supply (or the costs to others of an uncleansed supply). Then relative prices in the domestic market will not reflect the true (social) marginal cost of transformation in production.

Figure 12.5 illustrates this situation geometrically, in a general equilibrium format. Production of agricultural goods is measured on the vertical axis and production of industrial goods on the horizontal axis. The 'true' production-possibility curve, which reflects the social marginal rate of transformation, is QQ. Because of the distortion caused by the negative externality in agriculture, production and consumption under autarky will be at a point such as A, where the relative price of the industrial good (the slope of the line DD) is higher than the opportunity cost of industrial production (the slope of the line MM). The optimal production and consumption point under autarky would be P, which could be obtained by imposing a tax on agricultural production which exactly reflected the difference between the private and the social cost of agricultural production.

Suppose now that the world terms of trade are given by a price line with slope equal to that of line WW, which lies between the slopes of DD and MM. The country has a comparative advantage in agriculture (at distorted prices), as agricultural products are more expensive on the international market than in the distorted domestic market. With free trade the country will produce at P_F. It will trade according to the international terms of trade, exporting the agricultural product, and will consume at C_F. As C_F is on the indifference curve I_0, a lower level of welfare than that shown by the curve through A (indifference curve I_1), the country will be worse off because it is trading. Free trade has in this case accentuated the impact of the negative externality.

Note that the country's true comparative advantage is determined by comparing the world price ratio with the price ratio that would obtain under autarky if the distortion due to the externality had been eliminated. That is, by a comparison of the slope of WW with the common slope of the production-possibility curve and the indifference curve I_2 at point P.

A return to the autarky state will necessarily be welfare-increasing in such circumstances, and this could be achieved by imposing the prohibitive tariff on imports of the industrial good. The tariff however introduces a

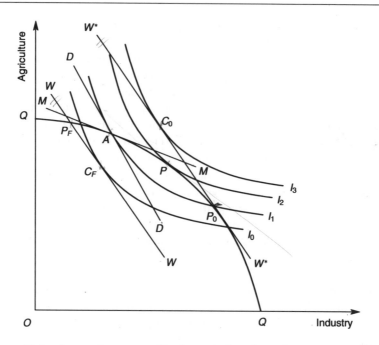

Figure 12.5   *A negative externality in agricultural production: a tariff may increase welfare*

by-product distortion for consumers, because the domestic price will differ from the world market price. This will entail a loss of welfare for consumers. The tariff will lead to an improvement in the allocation of resources, because it will curtail the production of the agricultural good and decrease the cost to society of the water pollution. In the case illustrated in Figure 12.5, gains on the production side are larger than losses on the consumption side, and the tariff leads to an improvement in welfare.

The first-best policy would be to tackle the externality problem directly, perhaps by imposing a tax on the pollution, and following a policy of free trade. This would lead to production at point P_O and consumption at point C_O (line W^*W^* has the same slope as WW), and so to the highest obtainable level of welfare (given that we are considering a small country).

This outcome is, however, not necessarily so, even when the country exports the agricultural good. Figure 12.6 illustrates the opposite possibility. Production and consumption under autarky are at point A, with the domestic price ratio shown by the slope of line DD and the opportunity cost ratio by the slope of MM. The essential difference between the situation shown in Figure 12.6 and that in Figure 12.5 is that the world terms of trade in Figure 12.6 are lower yet cause only a small shift in the production mix (from A to P_F). Trade will again lead to a worsening in resource allocation and a loss on the production side, but the gain on the consumption side in this case outweighs the loss on the production side, so that the country moves to a higher indifference curve than under autarky.

Although the country has once again specialised in the wrong commodity, a tariff on imports of the industrial good would in this case reduce welfare, as it would move the country to a lower indifference curve. The optimal intervention would again be to alleviate the effects of the externality directly (by imposing the appropriate tax). Production under free trade would then be at P_O, consumption at C_O, and welfare would be maximised.

It is not necessarily the case that the country will export the agricultural good. If the relative price of the manufactured good on the world market is sufficiently high then the country will export that good. It would not however export that good (and import the agricultural good) to the appropriate extent. Once again, the first-best policy is to levy the appropriate tax on agricultural production while following a policy of free trade.

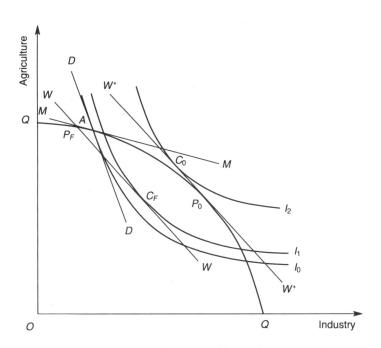

Figure 12.6 *A negative externality: a tariff may decrease welfare*

■ *12.4 Domestic distortions in factor markets*

The number of different forms of distortions in factor markets is extremely large. Just three of the possibilities on the labour market side are that wages are rigid, that there is a wage differential between sectors that is not a consequence of different qualities of labour, and that labour is immobile between sectors. Broadly similar problems may exist in the markets for other factors of production. We cannot analyse all these different problems, and so will concentrate on just one.

It is often argued that industry in less-developed countries (LDCs) has to pay a higher wage than agriculture in order to get labour. For example, it is sometimes asserted that in underdeveloped countries the marginal productivity of labour in agriculture is zero, yet agricultural workers earn a positive wage (perhaps equal to the value of their average product). If this is the case, then there will always be a distortion in factor markets as long as the marginal productivity of labour, and hence the wage, in industry is positive. Whether the marginal productivity in agriculture is in reality zero is a question which we shall not discuss here. We shall simply assume that some such distortion in the factor market exists. This may be a reason why industry in these countries is placed at a disadvantage and why it should be protected. We shall now examine whether protection is an appropriate policy or not for this instance of a factor market distortion.

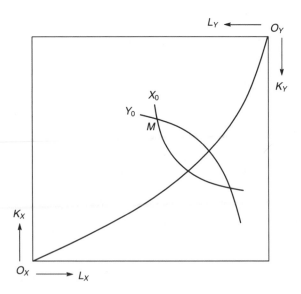

Figure 12.7   *A distortion in the labour market will lead to sub-optimal production*

Figure 12.7 shows the effect on factor allocation of there being a higher wage in the X sector (manufacturing) than in the Y sector (agriculture). The equilibrium allocation of factors of production in such circumstances will be at a point such as *M*, where the slope of the X isoquant (the wage/rental ratio) is higher than that of the Y isoquant. This is obviously an inefficient point. If the wage differential is maintained regardless of the output mix then the effect is to distort the economy's production-possibility curve inwards. Note that the distortion has no effect when the country specialises completely in the production of one of the goods. The effect of such a distortion on production is shown in Figure 12.8, where the production-possibility curve further from the origin is that which would obtain if there were no factor market distortion.

The wage differential between agriculture and industry will also cause the relative marginal cost of production of industry to differ from the opportunity cost of industrial production (the social marginal rate of transformation). To demonstrate this, consider the effects of transferring a small amount of labour and capital from agriculture to industry. If this is done efficiently (given the distortion) then the country will move along the distorted production-possibility curve, and the opportunity cost of the industrial output will be given by the slope of the production-possibility curve (dY/dX). However, the additional cost to industry of employing the additional labour will be higher than the saving in cost to agriculture of releasing it. That is, $MC_X dX > MC_Y dY$, so that $MC_X/MC_Y > dY/dX$. If there is perfect competition in the goods markets, so that price is equal to marginal cost, the relative prices at which goods will be sold will also differ from the opportunity cost of production; that is, $P_X/P_Y > dY/dX$.

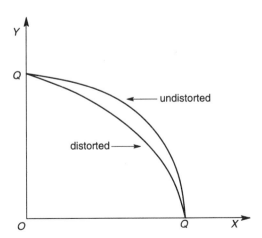

Figure 12.8 *The effect of a labour market distortion on the production-possibility curve*

Figure 12.9 illustrates the effect of a move to free trade when the specified distortion exists in the factor market. The distorted production-possibility curve is, as in Figure 12.8, the one nearer to the origin. Under autarkic conditions the country will produce and consume at a point such as A. The relative price paid by the consumers for the industrial good (the slope of the indifference curve I_1) is greater than the slope of the production-possibility curve.

Suppose now that the country is free to trade at given international prices, shown by the slope of the line WW, so that it will export the agricultural good (Y). The production point will move along the production-possibility curve towards the Y axis, and it is possible that, as in Figure 12.9, the new consumption point, C, will lie on a lower indifference curve (I_0) than the autarky consumption point A. If this is the case then the move to free trade has reduced welfare. It follows that a tariff large enough to prohibit trade would increase welfare (back to the autarky level). The reason for this is that the country is exporting the wrong good. Even with the distortion, the opportunity cost of producing X under autarky (the slope of line DD) is lower than the relative price of X on the world market: the country should be exporting X, not importing it.

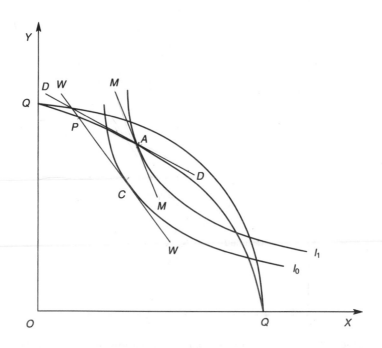

Figure 12.9   *A distortion in the labour market: free trade may reduce welfare*

Note that it is not necessarily the case that free trade reduces welfare. If the relative price of Y on the world market was high, but caused only a minor shift in the production mix towards Y then trade could be welfare increasing, despite the wrong good being exported. If the relative price of X on the world market was higher than the relative price of X under autarky then the country would export X (the right good) and would gain from trade. In none of these cases would a tariff be welfare-increasing. Moreover, as we shall see next, a tariff can never be an optimal solution.

Figure 12.10 may be used to show two policies which will unambiguously increase welfare. As in Figure 12.9, A is the autarky point, and welfare is shown by indifference curve I_1. A possible policy option is to subsidise the production of the industrial good (X). This would bring the production point along the distorted production-possibility curve towards the X axis. A correctly chosen subsidy to industry could take the country's production point to P_2, where the relative marginal cost of production, the social marginal rate of transformation, and the international terms of trade are all equal. Through trade the country could then move to point C_2, which is obviously superior to A.

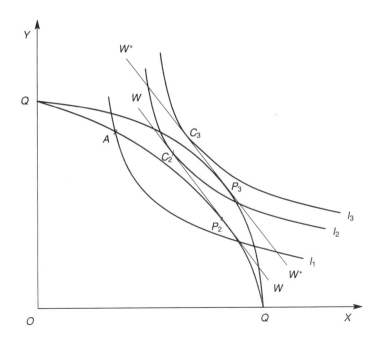

Figure 12.10 *Distortion in the labour market: the optimal policy*

Such a policy of subsidising production of the correct (export) good is better than laissez faire if factor market distortions exist.

A subsidy on production is, however, not the best policy. Since the wage differential will continue, the labour-intensity of production in the industrial sector will continue to be too low (and to be too high in agriculture). That is, a by-product distortion still exists. What is needed is a tax or subsidy on the use of labour. A subsidy to labour in industry could lead to greater employment within industry and to the equalisation in both sectors of the marginal productivity of labour. A tax on the use of labour in agriculture would have the same effect. Only by such a policy could the country reach its undistorted production-possibility curve.

This would mean, in our case, that the country would produce at P_3, and through trade could move to C_3. This point is obviously superior to C_2 and represents the best the country can do, given its factor endowments and technology and the international terms of trade.

Summing up, if distortions in the factor markets exist, protection may give a better result than free trade or a worse result, but it will never be an optimal policy. Subsidies and taxes on production are more efficient means of economic policy, but neither will they be optimal. The best policies are taxes and subsidies on the use of the factors of production. Only these will lead to optimal results.

Note that one cannot, from the simple existence of a wage differential between industry and agriculture, draw the implication that a distortion exists. There may be many rational explanations for such a wage differential. One could be that workers prefer to work in agriculture, where they are therefore willing to accept a lower wage. Another could be that work in industry requires specific training and that the higher wage reflects a return to this investment in human capital. A third reason may be that to work in industry requires a movement for which the former agricultural worker has to be compensated. All these, and several other reasons, are examples of wage differentials with rational economic foundations. Hence no distortions are involved.

One can also, of course, find examples that reflect a true distortion. One could be that labour unions exist in industry but not in agriculture, and that they force the employers in industry to pay a certain minimum wage. Another could be that industrial employers pay 'decent' wages on humanitarian grounds. If this is the case, labour will not be optimally allocated between industries, and total production will be lower than it would otherwise be.

There are also other more intricate factors that could entail distortions. One could be that industry might have to pay a higher wage to get labour because of 'dynamic' reasons. Another may be that industry cannot give employment to the non-adult members of a family the way agriculture can. Hence a higher wage for the head of the household is needed in order to make him move.

■ *12.5* The hierarchy of policies

Corden has suggested that economic theory allows us to place the possible policy responses to any situation into a *hierarchy*. Table 12.1, which is based on a Corden example,[3] reflects the results we have derived in the previous section and elsewhere.

Obviously, such a hierarchy can be extended to include yet other policies. For example, our analysis of trade policy instruments in the preceding chapters suggests that an import quota would rank further down the hierarchy than a tariff on imports, and that a voluntary export restraint would be lower down still.

Table 12.1 *A hierarchy of policies*

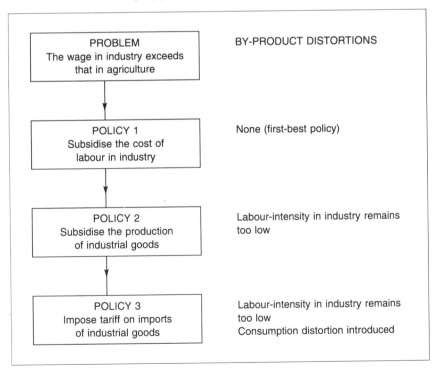

12.6 The infant-industry argument for protection

The oldest existing argument for protection is the *infant-industry argument*. We have left it until the end of our discussion because it is of an essentially different kind to those discussed before. Whereas the domestic distortion arguments are essentially static in nature (there exists some problem) the infant-industry argument is based on dynamic considerations. Nevertheless, as we shall see, although the argument does identify a problem in which a tariff may be welfare-improving, it is once again inferior to some other policy.

The origins of the infant-industry argument are the subject of some dispute. It has been suggested that it was first proposed in 1791 by the then Secretary to the US Treasury, Alexander Hamilton, although some have suggested an even earlier origin. It was certainly contained in a book written in 1841 by the German economist and politician Friedrich List.[4] The core of the argument is the existence of some kind of internal economies. A typical version would be:

(1) A firm (or firms in an industry) cannot compete if it is small; it has to be large before it can harvest all the economies of scale in production and become competitive.
(2) Therefore, it has to be protected for some time, and be permitted to grow, without meeting immediate competition from abroad.
(3) When the firm has become fully developed, the tariff can be dismantled and free trade can be allowed.

The firm (industry) may then be either an exporter (so that the protection has allowed the country to enjoy its 'true' comparative advantage), or it may be competing with imports.

The country List had in mind when he developed the infant-industry argument was Germany of the mid-nineteenth century. Great Britain was then the leading industrial state and German industry had difficulty competing with the older, more established British industry. List was modern in his views in so far as he saw industry as a prerequisite of progress. On this score he had no doubts: 'Manufactories and manufactures are the mothers and children of municipal liberty, of intelligence, of the arts and sciences, of internal and external commerce, of navigation and improvements in transport, of civilisation and political power.'[5]

Free trade was good for Britain, whose position was already established. For young, emerging German industry, however, tariffs were, he argued, necessary. The infant-industry argument soon won acceptance, and even the doyen of classical economics in the 1850s, John Stuart Mill, gave it a niche in his exposition of classical economic theory. List was, in other words, the first successful German economist.

Figure 12.11 is a geometric illustration of the infant-industry argument for protection. To start with, under free trade, the (small) country has production-possibility curve QQ. The international terms of trade are given by the line WW, which is tangential to the production-possibility curve at P_2. The country produces at P_2 and, by exporting good Y and importing good X, moves to C_2 on indifference curve I_2. If nothing changes, the country will continue in this position indefinitely.

The country, in the belief that there are economies in the production of good X that it has not obtained, now decides to protect the X industry. It introduces a tariff (assumed for simplicity to be prohibitive) so that the relative price of X for domestic consumers and producers now becomes equal to the slope of the common tangent (not shown) at A. The country will produce and consume at this point. Protection, as always in the case of a small country, lowers the country's welfare, as seen from the fact that A is on the lower indifference curve I_1.

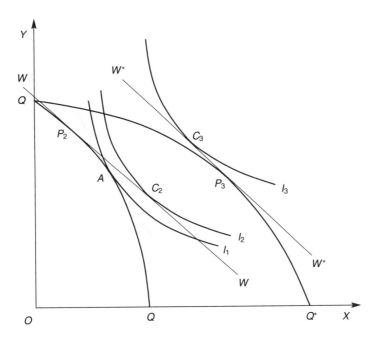

Figure 12.11   *The infant-industry argument for protection*

This is, however, only what happens in the short run. Protection gives rise to an increase in production of industrial goods. Thereby internal economies are reaped, and this will lead to an increase in productive capacity, so that the country's production-possibility curve will shift outwards over time. Ultimately, the country's production-possibility curve will be QQ^*. If the country then starts to trade freely again, at the same international terms of trade as before it introduced protection, the country will produce at P_3. It will now export the X good, and will consume at point C_3 on indifference curve I_3. This represents a higher level of welfare than the original free trade position. By nurturing an infant industry for some time, the country has been able to reach a higher level of welfare than would have been possible if it had been engaged in free trade all the time.

A protectionist policy initially implies a lowering of welfare. In the usual manner a tariff will cause a production and consumption cost. For protection to produce social benefits, the infant industry (or industries) must 'grow up'. They must eventually be able to compete at world market prices (that is, without protection). This requirement has been called 'Mill's test'.[6] Not only, however, do they have to grow up; for a protectionist policy to be profitable, they will also have to be able to pay back the losses due to protection during the infant-industry period.

They must also pass what is sometimes called 'Bastable's test'.[7] This requires that the discounted sum of the future benefits under free trade must be at least as great as the discounted sum of the losses incurred during the protectionist phase. Only then is there a clear-cut case for infant-industry protection.

The outcome of Bastable's test depends on the sequence of events. In the simple example given above it was assumed that the country continued to apply the (prohibitive) tariff until all the internal economies had been obtained, and then moved to free trade. An alternative policy would be to gradually reduce the tariff as the process continued, choosing that level which is just sufficient to encourage the domestic industry to expand in line with its acquisition of the internal economies. Such a policy would lead to a different outcome for Bastable's test. It might, on the grounds of promoting greater efficiency through the threat of competition from imports, be more preferable as well. Indeed, it is not difficult to make the argument that the competition from imports given by a non-prohibitive tariff is more likely to promote the desired gains in efficiency than a prohibitive tariff.

The preceding arguments have been made in terms of a good which the country will ultimately export. However, it is equally applicable to the case where the developed industry remains import-competing. The essence of the argument is that long-term efficiency can be promoted by the short-term use of a tariff. The argument does not depend on whether the industry concerned becomes an exporting industry or remains an import-competing industry.

In either case, it is important to note that both Mill's test and Bastable's test assume that, in the long run, the protection will be removed. In practice this is not always the case. An industry which has become accustomed to privileged access to its domestic market is unlikely to accept the loss of that protection without protest, even if it is competing successfully on world markets. A 'short-run' infant-industry tariff may become a permanent protectionist device.

We now have to look somewhat more closely into the circumstances that could lead to a valid infant-industry type of argument. We did not say *why* the production-possibility curve in Figure 12.11 expanded. One reason could be the existence of internal economies. Let us say that the production function in the industry shows increasing returns to scale. This means that as production expands, the unit cost will fall. Investment will have to take place at some period and production expand until the optimum size is reached. During this time the industry will have to be protected. This, therefore, is the main argument.

In reality this argument is less convincing than it may at first sound. It is not enough to show that present losses have to be incurred if future gains are to be had. This is, in itself, no argument for protection, because if a capital market exists and functions properly, and if domestic producers have a correct view of the profitability of the investment, they will invest in the industry even without a tariff. The existence of internal economies is not, by itself, a sufficient reason for protection. The infant-industry argument has to be built on a more intricate case than this.

It might be the case, for instance, that the capital market does not function properly. This is a common feature in many LDCs. They have small and poorly developed credit markets, and it can be difficult for a single investor to raise the money needed to make the investment, or it could be that investors are not properly informed about the prospects of investment. They might be unduly pessimistic about the future or unwilling to take chances in an unprotected market. The case for infant-industry protection will then be strengthened.

An important reason why the social return of the investment in an infant industry may exceed the private return is connected with education. This phenomenon is usually of special importance for LDCs. One of the results of the investment may be the acquisition of knowledge, for instance in the form of experimenting with a suitable technique of production. Once acquired by one firm, this technique can usually be bought at minimal cost by competing firms. Another factor is that part of the cost of the investment may comprise instructing workers, for instance in the form of on-the-job training. Once the workers have gained these skills they can go to another industry and use them there. These could contribute to the reasons an investment, although socially profitable, may not be undertaken by a private firm in an unprotected market. Protection, therefore, can give the added incentive necessary for undertaking the investment.

We have now shown examples of the economics behind the expansion of the production-possibility curve as illustrated in Figure 12.11. We now have to ask the question: Is a tariff the most suitable policy means for achieving this increase in productive capacity? We have to admit that there are cases in which protection for some time will give better results than free trade. Are there, however, other policy means which would be more efficient than tariffs for promoting the desired increase in productive capacity?

The answer is yes. On a somewhat abstract level we say that an optimum solution implies equality between the foreign rate of transformation (FRT), the domestic rate of transformation in production (DRT), and the domestic rate of transformation in consumption (DRS).[8] From this point of view we can say that if a country has 'monopoly power' in trade, i.e. can influence its own terms of trade, the situation under free trade will be that $DRS = DRT \neq FRT$. Hence there is scope for the optimum tariff. Only that can give $DRS = DRT = FRT$.

In the presence of infant industries, the true domestic rate of transformation in production is not equal to the domestic rate of transformation in consumption. Hence we have a situation where $DRS = FRT \neq DRT$, though a tariff cannot here bring equality between all three rates of transformation. It would give equality between DRT and FRT but inequality with DRS. In this case only a policy combination of taxes and subsidies can produce equality between all three rates of transformation.

This means that tariffs are not the most suitable means of dealing with the problem created by infant industries. It is always possible to reach a better solution by using subsidies, perhaps in combination with taxes.

In the case first discussed, internal economies were present. If the entrepreneurs were not able to reap them because of risk aversion or an imperfect capital market, the state should deal with these imperfections directly. It could, for instance, help the entrepreneurs to acquire correct information or underwrite some of the risks; or it could give loans on favourable conditions. Thereby the private rate of transformation in production can be made to coincide with the true social rate of transformation, and no disturbance on the consumption side will occur. A tariff will always distort consumption by making the domestic price higher than the world price.

Analogous conditions hold if external economies in education exist. If private entrepreneurs are unwilling to undertake some investment because they cannot get profitable returns on their investment in education, the state should subsidise them. This the state can do in the form of starting trade schools or by compensating the entrepreneurs for the cost of on-the-job training. The appropriate policy in this connection is some sort of subsidy or tax concession, not a tariff. Tariffs are only efficient if, for some reason, the country also wants to decrease its dependence on foreign trade.

The infant-industry argument for protection is essentially dynamic.[9] It is an argument for a tariff (or if properly formulated, a subsidy) during a transient period. For some reasons original free trade will not permit a country's true comparative cost situation to develop. Therefore, trade has to be protected for a period of time to enable the country's real pattern of comparative advantage to be established.

Sometimes the existence of external economies (or diseconomies) is given as a reason for infant-industry protection. Such phenomena are, however, distortions in domestic markets, which we discussed earlier.

▌ 12.7 Trade policy for development: some initial comments

We now have met two serious arguments for tariffs. The first was the optimum tariff argument which we met in Chapters 10 and 11. The second, or rather second group of arguments, is that dealt with in this chapter. In a nationalistic world a protectionist policy will always hold appeal. It is quite natural that protectionism has been tried by LDCs as a means of speeding up their economic development. The difficulties involved in fostering economic growth are now well known. Many countries are in desperate situations, and their possibilities of meeting population pressure with increased production are limited. There are cases where the *per capita* income is stagnant or even falling.

Against this background it is easy to understand why protectionism is a tempting alternative. It is usually heavily backed by certain domestic interests: a policy of increasing tariffs is also often easy to implement. Protectionism seems to give a lot of mileage for a little effort.

A protectionist policy also contains very real dangers. It is doubtful, as we have already hinted, whether the optimum tariff argument has much relevance for most underdeveloped countries. A tariff can only increase a country's welfare if the adaptability of supply and demand for the country's exports in the rest of the world is low. This is probably not the case for most of the LDCs. This implies that the value these countries can derive from a tariff must, on this score, be limited. Consequently, the relevance of the optimum tariff argument for LDCs is probably small.

The infant-industry argument may very well be applicable in some instances to underdeveloped countries. Distortions in commodity and factor markets also presumably exist. These could be reasons for using a protectionist policy. In both these cases, however, tariffs are not the optimal means of economic policy. Yet tariffs are often easy to implement, as they are usually easier to use than taxes and subsidies. This argument, incidentally, should not be carried too far. Even most underdeveloped countries have a set of taxes which can be adapted to deal with the distortions.

Protectionism could, however, be a defensible policy under these circumstances, at least as a second-best solution. If tariffs are used to correct distortions and foster development, they should be used with great discrimination and against the background of a carefully worked-out policy. Many LDCs have used tariffs to implement a policy of import-substitution.

The problems connected with different trade strategies such as export-push and import-substitution will be treated in Chapter 19.

☐ *Notes*

1   See Corden (1974) for a fuller discussion of by-product distortions.

2   In the first example, an alternative to the production subsidy on the import-competing good would be a tax on production of the export good, while in the second example an alternative policy would be to subsidise the consumption of the import-competing good. Note that tariffs and taxes generate government revenue, whereas subsidies require government expenditure. This may affect the way in which politicians view the alternative policies.

3   Corden (1974), p. 29.

4   Friedrich List (1789-1846), Professor of Economics at Tübingen University. In 1841 he published his main work, *Das Nationale System der Politischen Oekonomie*, containing his thoughts on the need for a protective tariff for less developed countries.

5   List (1928), p. 230.

6   This title is due to Kemp (1970).

7   See Kemp (1970).

8   For a discussion of these problems, see Bhagwati and Ramaswami (1963).

9   It could also be applicable to a situation with two stationary states of an economy, where in the first state some internal economies were not reaped and the tariff was used to shift the economy over to another stationary state, where these internal economies were then reaped but nothing else happens.

■ *Chapter 13* ■

Trade Policy and Imperfect Competition

■ *13.1* Introduction

In the preceding chapter we took the conventional neoclassical view that market failures reduce economic efficiency and welfare, and considered the use of tariffs as a means of correcting for these distortions. Our general conclusion was that tariffs might still reduce welfare still further, and that even in the cases where tariffs can increase welfare, they are necessarily inferior to other forms of policy intervention. Except in the particular case of the optimal tariff imposed by a large country, the arguments of the last chapter provide no economic justification for the use of tariffs or other trade-distorting measures.

In this chapter we shall review briefly some arguments, advanced in recent years, that have been used to provide some rationalisation of the use of trade-distorting measures. These arguments are largely derived from some of the theories of intra-industry trade discussed in Chapter 8. They take the existence of an imperfectly competitive industry as given, and consider the effects of various policies in that context, an obvious departure from the approach used so far.

We should expect that the conclusions reached will be less clear-cut than those in Chapters 10 and 11, when we assumed that markets were perfectly competitive. As we know from Chapter 8, intra-industry trade is often the outcome of imperfect competition, so that we start from a Pareto suboptimal state. The theory of second best tells us that in such cases the introduction of another distortion may increase or decrease welfare (as we saw in Chapter 12).

The variety of intra-industry trade models, based on differing assumptions, also suggests that any conclusions will be difficult to generalise. What may be true for horizontally differentiated products in a monopolistically competitive model may or may not be true when there is vertical differentiation. The effects of a particular policy in an oligopolistic market may change if we assume Bertrand rather than Cournot behaviour. There is insufficient space to consider all the possibilities, so this chapter is restricted in its coverage, and the analysis is presented in terms of simple models. The subject may be explored in greater depth by referring to the various surveys listed at the end of the chapter.[1]

We shall start by considering the effects of tariffs when there is monopolistic competition, using models involving vertical and then horizontal differentiation. Next we shall examine the role of tariffs when there is a single domestic producer, showing among other things that a tariff may allow an import-competing domestic firm to become an exporter. We shall then consider the use of tariffs to extract rent from a single foreign producer that is using its monopoly power in the domestic market. Finally, we shall consider the role of tariffs in a variety of duopoly models, paying particular attention to what has become known as *strategic trade policy*.

13.2 Trade policy with monopolistic competition

☐ *The Falvey neo-Heckscher–Ohlin model*

The model due to Falvey presented in Chapter 8 assumes that there is vertical product differentiation, and that the basis of that differentiation is the capital intensity of the variety. The model predicts that the relatively capital-rich country (A) will export the higher quality varieties, importing both lower quality varieties of the differentiated good and the other (labour-intensive) product from country B. Using the notation of Chapter 8, the marginal quality under free trade, ρ_1, is given by equation (13.1)

$$\rho_1 = \frac{w_A - w_B}{r_B - r_A} \tag{13.1}$$

Suppose now that country A imposes a tariff on imports of the lower qualities of the differentiated product. Imports of those varieties which are close to the marginal quality may now cease, and may be replaced by domestically-produced varieties. Country A may not however be able to export these newly-produced varieties, since their production cost may still be lower in country B. That is, the imposition of a tariff may mean that there will be some 'middle' range of qualities that is produced in both countries but not traded.

The precise outcome will depend on the effects of the tariff on factor prices in the two countries. Unfortunately, we can make no general statement about the direction of these effects, although it can be shown that under 'reasonable assumptions' the return to the (sector-specific) capital in the labour-rich country will fall while that in the capital-rich country will rise.[2] In order to proceed, we shall make some simplifying assumptions. Let us assume that this is indeed the case, so that, using an asterisk to identify values after the imposition of the tariff, $r_A^* > r_A$, and $r_B^* < r_B$, but that the capital is still relatively cheap in country A ($r_A^* < r_B^*$). Let us also assume that in both countries the industry producing the differentiated product can employ as much labour as it wishes without affecting the wage rate.

The marginal quality of the good that country A exports, ρ_E, will be that for which the prices in the two countries are the same. That is, when

$$w_A + \rho_E r_A^* = w_B + \rho_E r_B^* \tag{13.2}$$

so that the marginal export quality is

$$\rho_E = \frac{w_A - w_B}{r_B^* - r_A^*} \tag{13.3}$$

Since, given our assumptions, $r_B^* - r_A^* > r_B - r_A$, , it follows that $\rho_E < \rho_1$. That is, the marginal quality of A's exports will be higher than before.

The marginal quality of the good that country A imports, ρ_M, will be that for which the price of the domestically-produced good in A is equal to the tariff-inclusive price of imports from B. That is, when

$$w_A + \rho_M r_A^* = (w_B + \rho r_B^*)(1 + t) \tag{13.4}$$

where t is the *ad valorem* tariff. The marginal quality of A's imports is thus

$$\rho_M = \frac{w_A - w_B(1 + t)}{r_B^*(1 + t) - r_A^*} \tag{13.5}$$

The effect of the tariff, *ceteris paribus*, must be to make ρ_M less than ρ_1. However, the changes in r_A and r_B will have the opposite effect, so making the final outcome uncertain. It must however be the case that ρ_M is less than ρ_E, so that there will be a range of non-traded qualities. Country A will produce goods of quality higher than ρ_M, importing those of lower quality, but will export only goods of quality higher than ρ_E.

The welfare effects of the tariff are even less certain. If the return to capital in country B does fall then the cost of A's imports will fall, so that A will enjoy a terms of trade gain. Whether factor owners will gain depends on the effects of the tariff on payments to the factor in question, on the prices of the differentiated good and the homogeneous good, and on the consumption patterns of the factor owners. We cannot give an unambiguous answer without being much more specific in our assumptions. The most interesting conclusion we can draw from this model is that a government may be able to use a tariff to increase the range of varieties produced by its domestic industry.

□ *The Krugman neo-Chamberlinian model*

In the Krugman model discussed in Chapter 8 the good concerned is horizontally differentiated, firms in the industry have identical cost functions, consumers are assumed to have a 'love of variety', and the two countries are assumed to be identical. This ensures that, under free trade, each country will have n firms, each producing the same output, c, with consumers each buying an amount $0.5c$ of each variety (domestically produced and imported). The model does not predict which country will produce a given variety.

The imposition of a tariff by one of the countries will, provided the tariff is not prohibitive, merely induce the typical consumer to reduce the quantity of each imported variety that is consumed, and increase the quantity bought of each domestically-produced variety.[3] The number of varieties produced in each country will not, however, change, and neither will their outputs. Consumers will become worse off in the country imposing the tariff since the increase in the price of the imported varieties moves them away from their utility-maximising position. Since outputs do not change, the welfare effects of the tariff for the country as a whole will depend on the welfare loss for consumers and the revenue raised from the tariff. More specific conclusions could be drawn if the model was more exactly specified, but such conclusions would not, of course, have any general validity.[4]

□ *The Lancaster neo-Hotelling model*

The Lancaster model, discussed in Chapter 8, also assumes that there is horizontal differentiation, but in this case with varieties defined in terms of their characteristics, and with each consumer having a preferred variety. Firms producing the differentiated good are assumed to have identical and decreasing average cost functions. Assuming that the two countries are identical, the model predicts that under free trade each country will produce one half of the available varieties, importing the others, but does not predict which varieties will be imported and which produced domestically.

This indeterminacy in the varieties produced in one country makes it difficult to make general statements about the effects of imposing a tariff. We shall attempt to gain some insight by considering two extreme cases. In the first it is assumed that the varieties produced by one country are perfectly interleaved with those produced by the other (country *A* produces varieties 1, 3, 5, etc., country *B* varieties 2, 4, 6, etc.). The second case assumes that all the varieties at one end of the product spectrum are produced by one of the countries, with the other country producing the remainder.

In the first case, the imposition of a tariff by one country will, by raising the prices of imported varieties, lead some consumers to shift away from each imported variety to the domestic variety on either side. The expansion of production for each domestic firm will however increase its profits, so attracting new producers into the industry until normal profits are restored. The new entrants may be either domestic and foreign, but it is reasonable to assume that the number of domestic firms will increase. Consumers now have more varieties available to them than before, since there are more domestically-produced varieties and the number of imported varieties will not fall (unless the tariff is prohibitive, in which case all imported varieties will disappear from the home market).

The output of the typical domestic firm will depend on whether the initial increase in output due to some consumers switching from imported to domestic goods is greater or less than the reduction due to the increase in the number of domestic firms. If output is greater then costs must be lower and the price of domestically-produced varieties will fall as a consequence of the tariff.

We must also consider the effects of the tariff on foreign producers. Each foreign firm faces a reduction in sales due to the fall in its exports, and this will increase costs and reduce profits below their normal level. Foreign firms will therefore leave the market until normal profits are restored. It is again unclear whether the output of the typical foreign firm will be greater or lower than under free trade, but it is likely that it will be lower. If that is the case then the cost of the imported good at the border of the home country must increase.

The overall welfare effect of the tariff for the home country is indeterminate. There are gains for the consumers of domestically-produced varieties if the price of those varieties falls, and a gain from the tariff revenue. Consumers of imported varieties will lose due to the higher prices they are paying, and the country may lose from a higher real cost of importing those varieties. There is some possibility of a welfare improvement from the imposition of the tariff, since it may reduce the market power of domestic producers (by increasing their numbers) to such an extent that the gains from so doing outweigh losses elsewhere.

In the case where a country produces varieties at one end of the spectrum and imports the others, the scope for substitution between domestic and imported varieties is limited to the two adjacent varieties. The increase, if any, in the number of domestic firms will be minimal, and so therefore will be any effect on the production costs and prices of domestically-produced varieties. Domestic consumers of imported varieties will however be worse off since they will be paying a higher price for, and consuming less of, those varieties. The increase in tariff revenue will probably be less than the loss to the consumers of the foreign varieties, and the cost of imported varieties may rise (for the same reasons as were discussed in the previous case), so that in this case the imposition of a tariff is likely to reduce welfare.

■ *13.3 Tariffs and monopolies*

Protecting a domestic single producer with increasing costs

We saw in Chapter 12 that the first-best policy for a small country with a single domestic producer with increasing costs was free trade. Here we shall consider the effects of the government protecting that single producer.[5] Figure 13.1 reproduces the essential details of Figure 12.3, the world price being P_W, domestic production Q_F, and consumption C_F. We shall assume for the moment that the domestic producer is unable to export the good in question.

If the government introduces a 'low' tariff (less than T_1) then the domestic producer will expand production, while consumption and imports will fall and the government will receive revenue from the tariff. There will be a net welfare loss which is analogous to the loss under perfect competition. The domestic producer is still a price-taker.

When the tariff is set at T_1 then there will be no imports, but the domestic producer is still a price-taker, since any attempt to increase the price above $P_W + T_1$ will induce imports. In the case of a single domestic producer then, the tariff which prohibits imports is not the same as the tariff which brings about the autarky position.

If the tariff is set at a level higher than T_1, say T_2, then the domestic producer is given some market power. It cannot charge a price above $P_W + T_2$, since that would encourage imports, and so for sales up to Q_M its marginal revenue is $P_W + T_2$. If it attempts to produce and sell more than Q_M then it must reduce its price, and its marginal revenue will then be given by the portion of the MR curve to the right of Q_M. The domestic

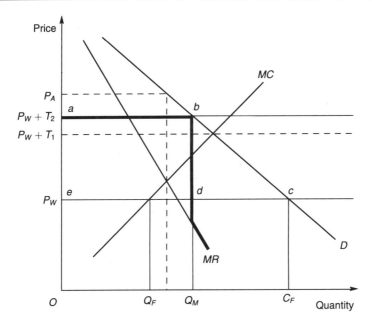

Figure 13.1 *A single domestic producer with a tariff*

producer's marginal revenue curve when the tariff is T_2 is thus that shown by the bold line in Figure 13.1. The profit-maximising output must therefore be Q_M. A reduction in output and sales below Q_M would lose the firm more in revenue than it would save in costs, while an increase beyond Q_M would do the same.

A tariff of T_2 will reduce consumers surplus by the area *abce* and increase the domestic producer's surplus by area *abde*. The net loss in welfare is thus triangle *bcd*. Increasing the tariff beyond T_2 will continue to increase the domestic producer's profits up to the point is reached when the domestic tariff-inclusive price is P_A, at which level of tariff it enjoys the monopoly position that would obtain under autarky. Increasing the tariff beyond this level will not change this state of affairs.

The effect of increasing the tariff is therefore to expand domestic output initially, until it reaches a maximum when the tariff is T_1, and then to reduce it until the autarky position is attained. The higher the tariff, of course, the lower will be consumption.

☐ *Tariffs as a stimulant to exports*

The previous model assumed that the single domestic producer was unable to export the good. We shall now relax that assumption, assuming instead that the good may be either imported or exported at the world price P_W. Figure 13.2 reproduces Figure 13.1, with the exception that the world price lies above the intersection of MC and MR. The domestic producer's marginal revenue cannot now fall below P_W, since it can export as much as it wishes at that price.

Under free trade the country will, as before, consume a quantity C_F, with Q_F being supplied by the domestic producer and the remainder being imported. As in the previous case, a low tariff will reduce domestic consumption and expand domestic production. Increases in the tariff will, again as before, finally give the domestic producer monopoly power, and allow it to increase profits by reducing output. This will be the case for tariffs up to T_M, at which tariff the marginal revenue curve facing the domestic producer is *abcd*. The domestic firm will produce where its marginal cost curve meets this marginal revenue curve. That is, it will produce Q_F , and sell all that production on the home market.

Increasing the tariff above T_M will however now induce the domestic producer to export. Suppose, for example, that the tariff is increased to the level where the domestic price is P_A. The marginal revenue curve facing the domestic producer is now *efgcd*, which intersects the firm's marginal cost curve at *c*. The firm will continue to produce quantity Q_F , but now it will

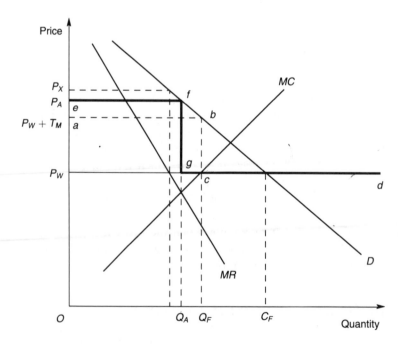

Figure 13.2 *A single domestic producer exporting with the aid of a tariff*

sell only the quantity Q_A on the domestic market, and will export the remainder. Increasing the tariff above this level will cause the domestic firm to produce the same quantity Q_F, but to export a greater proportion. The maximum level of exports, and the maximum profit for the monopolist, will occur when the tariff raises the domestic price to P_X.

The domestic producer is now acting as a price-discriminating monopolist. Some authors have used the term 'dumping' to refer to such a situation, but as we have seen already there are alternative definitions of the term.

☐ 'Snatching' rent from a foreign monopoly

When a foreign firm has monopoly power in the domestic market then it will earn excess profits (rents) in the domestic market, and may return those profits earned to its own country. It may then be in the interest of the home country to seek some way of retaining at least a part of those rents – to 'snatch' them from foreign producer(s). The possibility of such rent-snatching is common to much of the literature on trade policy when there is imperfect competition, and we shall consider it first in a simple model involving a single foreign supplier and no domestic production. Figure 13.3 illustrates such a case.

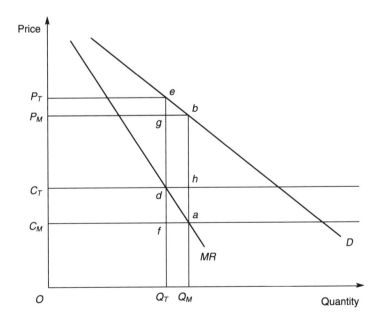

Figure 13.3 *Snatching rent from a foreign monopolist*

The demand curve in the domestic market is D, with derived marginal revenue curve MR. We shall assume that the country is small in relation to the total market faced by the foreign monopolist, so that the cost to the monopolist of shipping an additional unit to the country may be taken to be constant at C_M. The quantity which the monopolist will sell on the domestic market will be Q_M, determined by the intersection of the monopolist's marginal cost of supply curve with the marginal revenue curve MR, and the good will be sold at price P_M. The monopoly then earns profits equal to area $C_M P_M ba$, and sends these home. The average cost of a unit of imports to the home country is thus P_M, not C_M.

Now suppose that the government imposes a tariff. This will increase the cost of imports for the foreign monopoly to, say, C_T, and it will then maximise its profits by selling the lower quantity Q_T at the higher price P_T. Note that if the demand curve is linear, as assumed in Figure 13.3, the price increase will be less than the value of the tariff (indeed, in the linear case $P_T - P_M = 0.5(C_T - C_M)$). The demand curve will have to show a considerable amount of curvature for the increase in price to be greater than the tariff.

There will be a fall in consumers' surplus equal to area $P_M P_T eb$, and a gain in tariff revenue of area $C_M C_T df$. Provided that the price increase is less than the tariff (so that area $C_M C_T\ df$ > area $P_M P_T$), there exists the possibility that the tariff will increase welfare. If this is the case then, since the prohibitive tariff must reduce welfare, there must be some optimal tariff rate that maximises the welfare gain.

The foreign monopoly's profits must have fallen, the decrease being the sum of areas $C_M C_T\ df$ and $fdha$, less area $P_M P_T\ eg$. Note that the tariff has snatched only part of the monopoly's profits.

Finally, the use of a tariff, even an optimal tariff, to secure part of the monopoly's profits must be a less efficient instrument than a tax on those profits. However, if the government feels constrained in its use of profit taxes then a tariff may be a reasonable policy to use.[6]

■ 13.4 Tariffs, subsidies and duopoly

□ *Strategic trade policy in a duopoly setting*

The familiar analysis of duopoly theory tells us that one firm may increase its profits if it can both produce more and convince the other firm that this increased production will be maintained, since by so doing it could induce the other firm to produce less. Such a change is referred to as a *strategic move*.

The problem facing the firm seeking to make such a move is that its threat must be *credible*. That is, the competitor must believe that the increase in output can and will be maintained. Within the standard duopoly framework this may be difficult, being dependent upon such factors as the ability of the firm initiating the change to sustain that change in the face of the reaction of its competitor (which may involve, for example, surviving a competitive war).

The international trade setting of the present problem offers however a different possibility. The government in one country could provide its domestic firm with an export subsidy (which would shift that firm's reaction curve in the other country's market outwards), or a production subsidy (which would shift that firm's reaction curves in both markets outwards). Alternatively, it could impose a tariff on imports from the second country, which would shift the reaction curve for the foreign firm in the domestic market inwards. Such policies will increase the profits of the domestic firm while reducing those of the foreign firm. This is obviously a variant of the rent-snatching we analysed in the previous section, although in this context it is more often referred to as *profit shifting*.

Most importantly, the shift may appear credible to the foreign firm, since it may (reasonably) believe that *A*'s government will persevere with the policy. Such a policy, which makes credible a move that will increase the profitability of the domestic firm, is usually referred to as a *strategic trade policy*. This term should *not* be confused with a policy of support for strategic (i.e. defence oriented) industries, or with a policy of choosing industries to support according to some strategy for promoting a chosen form of industrial structure.

We shall analyse the strategic trade policy argument in terms of variants of the Brander–Spencer model,[7] which may be viewed as a simplified version of the Brander–Krugman model of Chapter 8. As we did then, we shall assume that there are two firms, firm 1 being based in country *A* and firm 2 in country *B*. The firms are small enough for their actions to have a negligible effect on other markets, so that we may use a partial equilibrium framework. We shall assume, as we did in Chapter 8, that the firms display Cournot behaviour: that is, each firm treats its output as its decision variable, and takes its rival's output as given.

We shall consider first the case of a subsidy. In order to simplify the analysis, we assume that the good is not sold in either of the domestic markets, but that the two firms compete only in a third market. This simplifies the analysis of both the impact of a policy intervention on outputs and profits and the welfare effects, since there is no domestic consumption effect to consider. Note that in this case there is no difference between a production subsidy and an export subsidy.

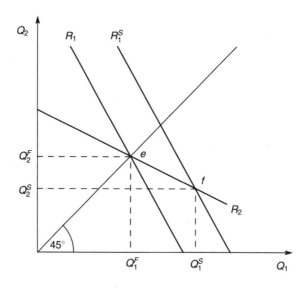

Figure 13.4   *A production subsidy in a simple duopoly model*

Figure 13.4 reproduces the essential elements of Figure 8.7; the basic elements are the same, the only difference being that we are considering only a single third-country market. R_1 shows firm 1's reaction function, and R_2 firm 2's. Both are negatively sloped, since an increase in the output of one firm will reduce the most profitable output for the other firm. As in Chapter 8, we assume that the two firms are identical. Under free trade the Cournot(-Nash) equilibrium will be at e, with each firm supplying 50 per cent of the market $(Q_1^F = Q_2^F)$.

The effect of the subsidy will be to increase the profitability of firm 1 at any given level of output. It is thus profitable for firm 1 to maintain a higher level of output for any given output by firm 2 than it was before. That is, firm 1's reaction curve will shift outwards from R_1 to R_1^S. In the new equilibrium (at point f) the output of A's domestic firm (firm 1) is greater than before (at Q_1^S), and the output of the foreign firm (firm 2) is lower (at Q_2^S).

This will increase the profits of the former and decrease the profits of the latter. Since there is no consumer interest in either country, the welfare effects depend on a comparison of the increase in profits for the domestic firm with the cost of the subsidy, and the expansion in output by the firm ensures that this will be positive. That is, the subsidy raises national welfare in the country providing the subsidy. It must of course reduce welfare in the other country.

When the firms do compete in each other's domestic markets then tariffs offer an alternative method for shifting profits from the foreign firm. As a very simple illustration of this point, let us modify the previous model by assuming that the market in question is in country *A*, and the good is not consumed in country *B*.

If country *A* imposes a tariff on imports then this must reduce firm 2's profitability at any given level of sales in *A*'s market. This will shift firm 2's reaction curve downwards, as shown by the move from R_2 to R_2^T in Figure 13.5.

The new equilibrium will be at point g, with a reduction in firm 2's sales (to Q_2^T) and an increase in firm 1's (to Q_1^T). Once again, profits have been shifted from the foreign to the domestic firm. Note that a tariff will lead to a greater fall in firm 2's output, for any given increase in firm 1's output, than a subsidy.

The models discussed above may be extended, albeit with certain complications, to the case where the two firms compete in each other's domestic markets as well as in the third market. We must of course then distinguish between a production subsidy, which has a direct impact on the domestic market, and an export subsidy, which does not. The basic conclusions, however, stay much the same.

The results of the previous analyses of the effects of a subsidy and a tariff are strongly dependent on the assumption that the firms behave in a

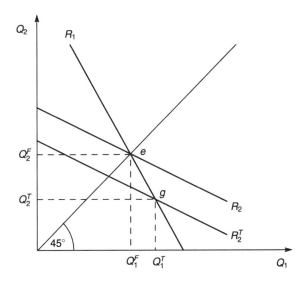

Figure 13.5 *A tariff in a simple duopoly model*

Cournot manner. Alternative conjectures are likely to lead us to different conclusions. For example, Eaton and Grossman[8] have shown that if we assume *Bertrand* behaviour in the case where the two firms sell only on a third market then profits are shifted to the domestic firm by an export tax rather than an export subsidy.

Other economists have objected to the use of either the Cournot or the Bertrand assumption, on the grounds that both implicitly assume that firms do not learn from their mistakes. An alternative assumption is that of *consistent conjectures* – that each firm perceives its rival's reaction curve correctly. Even in this case it has been shown that an appropriate trade subsidy or tax can improve domestic welfare.

☐ *Retaliation*

In Chapters 10 and 11, where we considered the question of the optimum tariff in the inter-industry trade setting, we saw that the possibility of retaliation by the second country had to be taken into account. The same must be true here: for example, in the case where the two firms compete only in a third market, the government in country *B* might respond to the introduction of a subsidy by the *A* government by giving a subsidy to the output of its own domestic producer (firm 2) in an attempt to regain some of the profit shifted by the original subsidy.

Such 'policy wars', which might involve 'subsidy-subsidy' or 'tariff-tariff' retaliation (or even 'subsidy-tariff'), may be analysed by assuming that at each step in the war the retaliating country sets the chosen policy instrument at the level which maximises domestic welfare given the other country's policy. We shall not attempt such an analysis here.[9] A reasonably general conclusion however is that such wars reduce world welfare and the welfare of each country.

Such strategic trade policy results provide a plausible underpinning for the GATT strategy of pursuing multilateral tariff reductions.[10] No individual country will be willing to reduce its own tariff (subsidy, etc.) unilaterally, since that would result in the transfer of profits to foreign firms. It would however be willing to co-operate with other countries in mutual tariff reductions since that would increase the profits of domestic firms.

☐ *Entry deterrence and entry promotion*

Brander and Spencer have argued that where the entry of a (potential) domestic producer is barred by the actions of a foreign firm then it is possible that the use of a tariff will allow the entry of the domestic producer.[11] They consider the case where the domestic market is supplied only by a foreign firm, which knows that the domestic firm, if allowed to enter, will act in the Cournot manner and will treat the foreign firm as a Stackelberg leader. Under certain circumstances the foreign firm may find that it can obtain higher profits if it deters entry.

We know from our earlier analysis that, in such a situation, the government in the home country may snatch rent from the foreign (monopoly) supplier by imposing a tariff. The government in the home country may, however, be able to promote entry by the domestic producer by imposing a yet higher tariff. Brander and Spencer demonstrate that encouraging entry in this way is likely to reduce welfare, since it will reduce both consumers' surplus and tariff revenue, and these losses will only be offset by gains on the production side if the domestic firm's marginal cost is considerably less than the foreign firm's marginal cost.

☐ *Tariffs and export promotion*

Krugman[12] has demonstrated that, under certain assumptions, the protection of a firm's domestic market may increase its exports to other markets. As a simple example of this argument, suppose that the foreign and domestic firms both have decreasing costs, and under free trade supply their own and each other's markets, and also a third country market. Suppose now that the domestic government restricts imports into the domestic market, so allowing the domestic firm to expand production. The domestic firm's average costs will fall as its output increases, while those of the foreign firm will rise, so that the domestic firm's exports to the third country will also increase. The welfare effects for the home country of such a policy are ambiguous: domestic consumers will lose through higher prices since the domestic firm is now a monopoly, but profits will have been shifted from the foreign to the domestic firm, and the domestic firm may earn higher profits from sales on the third-country market.

■ *13.5* Concluding remarks

As the opening discussion suggested, it is often difficult to come to clear general conclusions about the welfare implications of tariffs, subsidies, etc. in an imperfectly competitive situation. Whether a policy intervention brings about an improvement or not will depend, as the theory of second-best suggests, on the particular case that we are considering.

What is true however is that when there is imperfect competition then the use of tariffs, subsidies and other policies *may* be welfare-increasing.

Disquiet has been expressed by many economists that these results may be used to justify the mercantilist instinct that seems to underlie the actions of legislators and negotiators (as we shall discuss at more length in Chapter 17). In any event, it seems a strange reaction for an economist to wish (even implicitly) to ignore or suppress developments in the subject, even if they might lead to policy initiatives to which he/she feels inimical!

☐ *Notes*

1   Much of this chapter follows Vousden, N. (1990), Chapters 6 and 7.
2   See Falvey (1981) for a discussion of this point. Falvey and Kierzkowski (1987) give an explicit general equilibrium formulation of the model.
3   This issue is examined in more detail in Gros (1987).
4   See Harris (1984) for empirical estimates of the cost of protection using a variant of the Krugman model. Vousden (1990) discusses the Harris methodology.
5   An interesting modification to the above analysis is to assume that the monopolist has decreasing average cost. We shall not pursue this topic here, although it is closely connected with the possibility of encouraging entry by a domestic producer in the oligopoly analysis that is undertaken later in the chapter. Vousden (1990) covers the area in some detail.
6   See Katrak (1977) for a discussion of this point.
7   Brander and Spencer (1985).
8   Eaton and Grossman (1986).
9   See Eaton and Grossman (1986) for an example. The assumptions under which such analyses are carried out, in particular the common assumption that the governments too play a Cournot game, have been criticised by, among others, Corden (1990).
10 For an example of such an argument, see Krugman (1992).
11 Brander and Spencer (1985).
12 Krugman (1984).

■ *Chapter 14* ■

Further Topics in Trade Theory and Policy

■ *14.1* Introduction

There are many topics in international trade which are too complicated to consider in detail in a book such as this. On the other hand, it is important that their existence is acknowledged and some attempt made to demonstrate their importance, and that reference be made to sources where they are considered in more detail. This chapter attempts to do that for five such topics: the extension of the standard trade models to include the possibility of non-traded goods; trade in intermediate goods; effective protection and domestic resource cost analyses as a means of quantifying the net effects of policies affecting many sectors of the economy; the particular problems caused by trade in services; and the analysis of policies directed towards stabilising prices.

■ *14.2* Non-traded goods

Many goods are not traded between countries. The most obvious reason for this is that the cost of transporting such a *non-traded* good between countries exceeds the difference in the prices of that good between the countries. High transport costs may make services, particularly those with a low price (e.g. hairdressing, car servicing), even less likely to be traded. Other factors which may lead to a good not being traded include differences in preferred varieties between countries, and additional costs which must be incurred in overcoming social and cultural differences (such in producing a newspaper in another language).

Even when we are dealing with a small open economy, the existence of non-traded goods necessarily complicates the analysis. The reason for this is that the price of a non-traded good is determined by the interaction of domestic supply and demand, whereas the prices of traded goods are set on the world market. That is, the prices of traded goods in a small open economy are exogenously determined, but the prices of non-traded goods are endogenously determined.

This is not to say, of course, that the price of a non-traded good is independent of the world prices of the traded goods, or of the volume of trade. Provided that there is at least one factor of production that is used in both the traded and the non-traded goods sectors then the market for that factor must link the various sectors.

In order to gain a more detailed insight into this problem we shall use an extension of the specific factors model introduced in Chapter 2. We shall assume that we are dealing with a small open economy, in which there are three sectors (producing export, import-competing and non-traded goods), one mobile factor of production (labour) and three other factors of production, each specific to one of the sectors.[1]

The assumption that we are dealing with a small open economy allows an important simplification, one that enables us to work in two dimensions rather than three. The fixed prices of exports and imports allow us to 'merge' them into a single commodity (since 1 unit of the export good may always be exchanged for the same number of units of the import-competing good). We shall call this composite good the *traded good* (X_T). Factors of production transferred from the non-traded sector to the traded sector will be allocated between the production of the export and import-competing goods in a way determined by their (fixed) relative prices. We can thus draw a production-possibility curve for traded and non-traded goods which, if we make the usual assumptions of the specific factors model, will have the familiar shape. The introduction of a set of indifference curves representing consumers' preferences then allows us to derive the equilibrium outputs of traded and non-traded goods. Such an equilibrium is shown in Figure 14.1.

At the equilibrium point, E, a quantity OB of the non-traded good (X_N) is produced and consumed, and a quantity OA of the traded good. What we cannot tell from Figure 14.1 is the division of that quantity of production of the composite traded good between production of the export good and the import-competing good, and equally the division of the consumption of the traded good between exportables and importables. We do know however that, since the total values of production and consumption of the traded goods are the same, the value of exports must be equal to the value of imports.

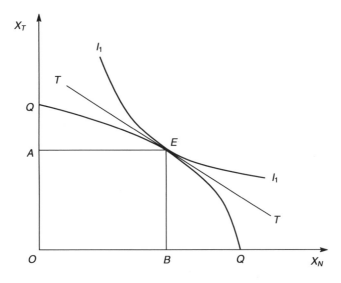

Figure 14.1 *Equilibrium in the production and consumption of traded and non-traded goods*

The slope of the common tangent at point E shows the price of the non-traded good versus the price of whichever of exports and imports is being used as the numeraire. Since the price ratio for exportables and importables is fixed, we can interpret the slope of line TT as the relative price of the non-traded to the traded goods. This relative price is often referred to as the *real exchange rate*.

What now remains is to examine the relationship between the relative price of the non-traded good and the real reward to the only mobile factor in the model (labour). Figure 14.2 shows one way in which we may do this.[2]

Consider first the question of equilibrium in the labour market. As is usual in the specific factors model, we assume that the supply of labour is fixed (at L). The demand for labour comes from producers in the traded and non-traded sectors, and in each case is a function of the wage rate relative to the price of the appropriate good. That is, the demand for labour in the traded goods sector, L_T, may be written as $L_T(w/P_T)$, and the demand for labour in the non-traded goods sector, L_N, as $L_N(w/P_N)$, where w is the wage rate and P_T and P_N are the prices of the traded and non-traded goods respectively.

Since we are dealing with a small open economy, P_T is exogenously determined, and we may without any loss of generality set its value to one. We may then write the relative price of the non-traded good as

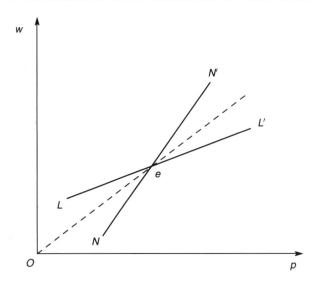

Figure 14.2   *The relative price of the non-traded good and the real wage*

$P_N/P_T = P_N = p$, and thus write the condition that demand equals supply in the labour market as

$$L_T(w) + L_N\left(\frac{w}{p}\right) = L$$

The curve LL' in Figure 14.2 represents this condition. We first show that LL' will be positively sloped, as shown. Suppose that we start from an equilibrium point, such as e. An increase in p (the relative price of the non-traded good) will lead to an excess demand for labour. Equilibrium can only be restored by an increase in the wage rate, so the new equilibrium point must be above and to the right of e. We may also show that the LL' curve must be flatter at e than the ray drawn from the origin through e. To do this, consider the effects of increasing w and p in the same proportion, so that we move up the ray Oe from e. The demand for labour in the non-traded good sector will not change, since w/p is unchanged. However the demand for labour in the traded goods sector must fall since w has risen. We would therefore have unemployed labour, and the wage rate would have to move downwards.

We must now consider equilibrium in the (domestic) market for the non-traded good. The supply of that good, Q_N, will depend on the labour input (the other factor is fixed), and we know that is a function of w/p. That is,

$Q_N = Q_N(w/p)$. The demand for the non-traded good, C_N, will depend on the price of the good and on the real level of income, y, and the real level of income is in turn dependent on the relative price of the non-traded good; that is, $C_N = C_N(p, y(p))$. Equilibrium in the non-traded good market thus requires that

$$Q_N \left(\frac{w}{p} \right) = C_N(p, y(p))$$

The curve NN' in Figure 14.2 shows the combinations of w and p that give equilibrium in the non-traded good market. First, let us show this curve must be upward sloping. Suppose e is the initial equilibrium position. Then an increase in p will lead to an excess supply of the non-traded good. To eliminate this excess supply the wage rate, w, must increase. Hence the new equilibrium point must be above and to the right of e. The NN' curve must however be steeper at e than the ray Oe. Suppose again that, starting from e, we increase w and p in the same proportion, so that we move along the ray Oe. Since w/p has not changed the supply of the non-traded good will not change. But the demand for the non-traded good must fall since its price has risen and real income has fallen. Increasing w and p in the same proportion would thus lead to an excess supply of the non-traded good, and so would put us *above* the NN' line.

The intersection of LL' and NN' defines the joint equilibrium of the labour and non-traded goods markets. As a simple example of the use of this diagram,[3] suppose that there is an increase in the labour supply in our small open economy. This must have the effect of shifting the LL' curve downwards since at given relative commodity prices the labour market can only clear at a lower wage. In the new equilibrium the wage rate and the relative price of the non-traded good will both have fallen. Since the NN' curve is steeper than the ray from the origin, it must be the case that the relative price of the non-traded good will fall by less than the wage rate.

☐ 'Dutch disease'

The existence of a non-traded goods sector in an economy has been advanced as an explanation of the phenomenon known as 'Dutch disease'.[4] A boom in a traded goods sector has, in some instances, led to a decline in other traded goods sectors. If these declining sectors are in manufacturing then there will be 'de-industrialisation'. The examples most commonly cited are those of the Netherlands following its exploitation of its natural gas reserves, and the United Kingdom and Norway after the discovery and development of North Sea oil.

Suppose that, as before, we assume that labour is the only mobile factor in a small open economy, and suppose that one of the traded goods sectors expands. With a given supply of labour, this expansion must increase the wage rate. This in turn must increase production costs in other sectors, both traded and non-traded. The other traded goods sectors however cannot increase prices, since these are determined on the world market, and they must therefore contract. The non-traded goods sectors can, however, pass some of the increase in costs on to the domestic consumers since they do not face competition from imports. The net effect of the boom in one of the traded goods sectors will therefore be to reduce the size of the remaining traded goods sectors, and in particular relative to the non-traded goods sectors.

The boom in one of the sectors has reduced the comparative advantage the country enjoyed in its other export goods, and increased its comparative disadvantage in its import-competing goods. Moreover, what we defined previously as the real exchange rate (the price of non-tradables relative to the price of traded goods) has appreciated.

■ 14.3 Trade in intermediate goods

☐ *Intermediate and final goods*

The production of a *final good* (one which will be purchased by consumers or by other firms) involves in nearly all cases the bringing together of a set of *intermediate goods* (or *manufactured inputs*) to make the final product. For example, the production of a book requires the use of paper, ink and electric power. These intermediate goods are combined using factors of production (labour, capital, etc.) in a *process* which produces the book. Obviously, some goods may be both sold directly to consumers and as intermediate inputs for some other process, as is the case with electric power. As a further complication, in some cases a good may be used in its own production; electric power is an example of this as well.

Empirical studies have shown that a large share of international trade consists of trade in intermediate goods. Much of trade theory, however, has been concerned only with trade in final goods. One reason for the neglect of intermediate goods in trade theory may lie in the great variety of possible models, as suggested in part by the considerations given above. We shall examine, very briefly, two such models in order to obtain some insight into the complications introduced into trade theory by intermediate goods. These models will also serve as an introduction to a technique that is widely used for assessing the effects of protection, the *effective tariff*.

Gross production, net production, and value-added

The total quantity of a good produced by a sector is referred to as its *gross production* or gross output. Some of that output may, however, go to other production sectors as an intermediate input. The *net production* of the good, equal to gross production less that which goes to other sectors, goes to final demand.

The distinction is important on several grounds. For example, if we define welfare in the normal way then it depends on the volumes of goods consumed – that is, on net production. If, on the other hand, we are interested in the level of activity within a sector then we should examine gross production.

The term *value-added* is given to the difference between the price at which a final good is sold and the cost of the intermediate goods used in its production. Suppose, for example, that one copy of a book may be sold by the publishing company for £20, and that the costs of the inputs are £4 for paper, £1 for ink, and £2 for electric power. The value-added in the production and sale of the book is then £$(20 - 4 - 1 - 2)$ = £13. This value-added is the sum available for payments to the factors of production (wages and salaries for the staff in the publishers, royalties to the author, payments for buildings and equipment, etc., with the residual being the profit for the company).

It is important in what follows to keep in mind the distinction between inputs and factors of production. Inputs are goods used in the production of another good. Examples of factors of production are the familiar labour, land and capital. The production process uses those factors of production to combine the inputs into the final product, and in so doing adds value.

Suppose that, following on with the example above, the publisher is able to sell the book for £21 rather than £20. Provided that the total cost of the inputs does not change, the value-added will also increase by £1, so that there is now £14 available for payments to the factors of production. Conversely, suppose that the price of paper increases, so that the cost of paper for one book becomes £5, but the prices of the other inputs and of the book stay the same. If we assume that it is impossible for the publisher to substitute one input for another (which would be reasonable in this example), then value-added will fall by £1, so that the payments to factors of production must also fall by £1.

More formally, suppose that the price of 1 unit of good j is P_j, that the production of that 1 unit requires the use of a_{ij} units of input i, that the price of 1 unit of input i is P_i, and that there are n inputs. Then we may write the value-added for good j, V_j, as

$$V_j = P_j - \sum_{i=1}^{n} a_{ij} P_i \qquad (14.1)$$

Two alternative expressions may be used for value-added. The first works in terms of the cost of input i per unit of good j. This cost, d_{ij}, is given by $a_{ij} P_i$. We may then write the value-added for good j as

$$V_j = P_j - \sum_{i=1}^{n} d_{ij} \qquad (14.2)$$

The second alternative is to work in terms of the cost of input i per £1-worth of good j. This cost share, c_{ij}, is given by $a_{ij} P_i / P_j = d_{ij} / P_j$. We may now write the value-added for good j as

$$V_j = P_j \left(1 - \sum_{i=1}^{n} c_{ij} \right) \qquad (14.3)$$

□ The pattern of trade

When we introduce intermediate goods into the picture then the number of possible patterns of trade increases. For example, suppose that there are four goods, two of which (A and B) are strictly intermediate, and two (X and Y) used only for final consumption. Even in this relatively simple world we can identify many possible trade structures (in addition to autarky): the country may export one, two or three of the four goods, importing the others. What then will determine the pattern of trade?

Suppose that the two final goods each require fixed amounts of the intermediate goods per unit of output (as we shall see, this greatly simplifies the analysis). Let us also assume that each of the four goods is produced using capital and labour, and that there are fixed endowments of the two factors, constant returns to scale, no factor intensity reversals, and perfect competition. Finally, assume that the country is small and is following a policy of free trade, so that we can take the prices of the four goods as given.

We can demonstrate some of the influences on the pattern of trade as follows. Suppose that the world price of 1 unit of intermediate good A is P. There will be some quantity of good B that will also be worth P at its world price, which we may call B^*. Good A (B) will be produced in our small country if, and only if, the cost of the capital and labour used in producing 1 unit of good A (B^* units of good B) is less than or equal to the price, P, at which it can be sold.

We may in the same way identify quantities of X and Y (X^* and Y^* respectively) which also have a value of P on the world market. Final good

X (Y) will be produced if, and only if, the cost of labour and capital used in producing the quantity X* (Y*) is less than or equal to the difference between the price at which it may be sold (P) and the cost of the purchased inputs of A and B. That is, the value-added in producing X* (Y*) must be at least as great as the cost of the factors used. Value-added is relatively simple to deal with in this model, since by assumption both the intermediate input requirements and the prices at which they must be bought are fixed.

Figure 14.3 shows the isoquants for the quantities of the four goods specified above. It assumes that, as is often the case, the intermediate goods are more labour-intensive than the final goods. It must be remembered that the isoquants for the two final goods refer to the value-added in their production. The budget line CC in Figure 14.3 shows those combinations of capital and labour that may bought for a cost of P. Its slope is given by the relative prices of labour and capital, which are assumed for the moment to be known.

In the situation shown, intermediate good A will be produced, since the cost of producing 1 unit of A is equal to the price at which that unit can be sold. Intermediate good B will not however be produced, since the cost of producing quantity B* must be greater than P, but B* units are worth only P at world prices.

Final good Y will also be produced, since the cost of the labour and capital used in the production of Y* is equal to the value-added from its production and sale. Final good X will not however be produced, since the

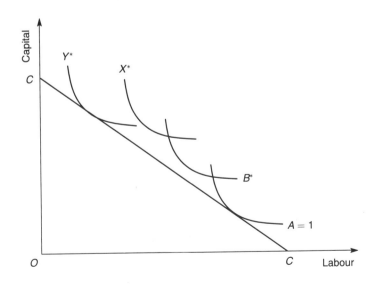

Figure 14.3 *Trade with final and intermediate goods*

value-added in that good will not pay for the required amounts of the factors of production.

Relative factor prices will be determined by the (fixed) supplies of capital and labour and the derived demands for those factors, which in turn will depend upon the demand conditions for the final goods, the world prices of all four goods, and the factor intensities in those goods which are produced. Which goods will be produced will depend on the factor prices and the production functions. Only in the exceptional circumstance that all four isoquants are tangential to the budget line CC will all four goods be produced.

The pattern of trade is still not determinate. It is obvious that some of intermediate good B must be imported since it is required for the production of final good Y. It is also clear that if final good X is to be consumed then it too must be imported. Goods A and Y must be traded, and at least one of them must be exported (to pay for the imports of B and X), but we can determine no more than that without introducing consumer preferences.

Different demand conditions and/or different endowments of capital and labour could lead to different production structures, and hence to different trade patterns.

Intermediate goods and the production-possibility curve

If we are to examine the effects of trade in final and intermediate goods on welfare then we must work in terms of those goods which are consumed, using the familiar devices of the production-possibility curve and the indifference map. The introduction of intermediate goods to the analysis must however complicate the issue, since trade in intermediate goods will change the production-possibility curve. To examine how this occurs, we shall consider a slightly different model.[5]

Suppose that there are two final goods, X and Y, and one intermediate good, A, that is used in the production of Y, but not of X. Let us also work in terms of a specific factors framework, with labour the only mobile factor of production, and some other factor being specific to each of the three sectors. Finally, assume that the quantity of the intermediate good used to produce one unit of good Y may be varied (so that the amount of the intermediate good available does not set an upper limit on the production of Y). We can now derive the production-possibility curve under autarky in a way that broadly follows that of Chapter 2.

In Figure 14.4, the labour constraint line *ab* shows the quantity of labour available for the production of the two final goods given that an amount

L_M of labour has been allocated to production of the intermediate good. The total product curves for the two final goods are TPP_X and TPP_Y, and the associated production-possibility curve is AB.

Suppose now that a greater quantity of labour is allocated to production of the intermediate good. This has two effects: first, the labour constraint line for production of X and Y must shift in towards the origin – to cd, say; second, the total product curve for good Y will shift upwards (to TPP_Y^*) since more of the intermediate good is available. The production-possibility curve corresponding to this new allocation of labour to intermediate good production is CD.

Obviously, we may repeat this procedure for all the possible allocations of labour to the production of the intermediate good, so obtaining a family of such production-possibility curves. The envelope of these curves, shown as QQ in Figure 14.4, which we shall call the production-possibility *frontier*, shows the combinations of outputs of X and Y when labour is allocated optimally between the production of the three goods.

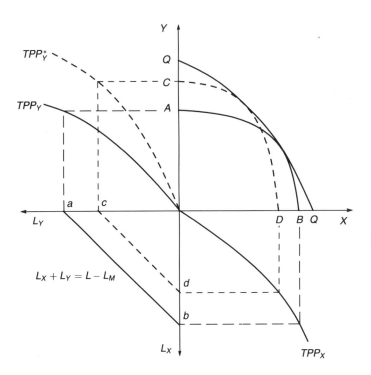

Figure 14.4 *Intermediate goods and the production-possibility curve*

The autarkic equilibrium may be derived in the usual manner, by introducing the indifference map for consumers (which involves only the consumption of the final goods). The point of tangency of the highest attainable indifference curve with the economy's production-possibility frontier will determine the outputs of the final goods, and their relative prices. Once we know this equilibrium, we can determine the allocation of labour between the three sectors by identifying the particular production-possibility curve that is tangential to the frontier at that point, and from that we can determine the wage rate and the rewards to the specific factors.

If the country now moves to free trade, we may see (as we discussed earlier) one of several trade patterns. Any pattern of trade will however cause a shift in the production possibility frontier. For example, suppose that at the given world prices the country exports the final goods X and Y and imports the intermediate good. The availability of the intermediate good through trade will, *ceteris paribus*, allow labour to be switched from producing that good to producing the final goods. At the same time it will allow a higher total product curve for good Y. For example, the labour constraint shown as *ab* in Figure 14.4 may be combined with the total product curve shown as TPP^*_Y. The consequence will be to shift the individual production-possibility curve corresponding to *ab* outwards. It then follows that the production-possibility frontier with free trade will lie outside the frontier for the autarkic state.[6]

The trade pattern assumed in this argument results in the country consuming inside its production-possibility frontier, since both X and Y are exported. A possible free trade equilibrium is shown in Figure 14.5,

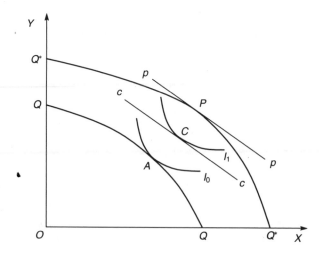

Figure 14.5   *Consumption and production when the intermediate good is imported*

where QQ is the production-possibility frontier under autarky, and Q^*Q^* the frontier with free trade. With given relative prices for X and Y on the world market (shown by the slopes of lines cc and pp), the production point for X and Y will be P, and the consumption point will be C.

We shall not attempt to demonstrate that there are gains from trade, although that will be the case. The possibility of gains from trade is however shown in Figure 14.5. The move to free trade has shifted the production-possibility frontier out sufficiently for the new consumption point (C) to be on a higher community indifference curve than the autarky consumption point (A).

14.4 Effective tariffs, effective protection and domestic resource cost analysis

☐ *Effective tariffs and effective protection*

In the majority of cases a country will impose tariffs on a number of goods, at least some of which will be inputs into other goods. A tariff on an imported final good will, as we know, increase the price of that good. It will therefore also increase the value-added in the production of that good (provided it is produced domestically). On the other hand, a tariff on an imported intermediate good will, by increasing the price of that good, reduce the value-added for any sector which purchases that good as an intermediate input. When tariffs are the only instrument used then the net effect of the set of tariffs on a particular sector is usually referred to as the *effective tariff*, to which we shall turn next. When non-tariff barriers are present then the net effect of all instruments is often referred to as the *effective protection* to the industry or sector concerned.

The effective tariff on good j (strictly on the process which results in good j) is defined as the proportionate difference in the value-added in that process brought about by the imposition of tariffs (or other instruments) on good j and on all goods which are inputs into that good, compared with the value-added at world prices. That is, if V_j^d is the value-added at domestic prices, and V_j^w is the value-added at world prices, the effective tariff is

$$\tau_j = \frac{V_j^d - V_j^w}{V_j^w} \tag{14.4}$$

If we identify domestic and world prices by the superscripts d and w respectively, and assume that there is no possibility of substituting one input for another, we may write the two value-added terms as

$$V_j^d = P_j^d - \sum_i a_{ij} P_i^d \tag{14.5}$$

and

$$V_j^w = P_j^w - \sum_i a_{ij} P_j^w \tag{14.6}$$

Suppose that the divergences between the domestic and world prices are due to the imposition of tariffs, so that $P_j^d = P_j^w(1 + t_j)$ and $P_i^d = P_i^w(1 + t_i)$. Then we may rewrite (14.5) as

$$V_j^d = P_j^w(1 + t_j) - \sum_i a_{ij} P_i^w (1 + t_i) \tag{14.7}$$

Substituting for V_j^d and V_j^w in (14.4) then gives, after a little manipulation,

$$\tau_j = \frac{P_j^w t_j - \sum_i a_{ij} P_i^w t_i}{P_j^w - \sum_i a_{ij} P_i^w} \tag{14.8}$$

Alternatively, we may work in terms of the cost shares (c_{ij}) defined earlier, which after some further manipulation gives as the effective tariff

$$\tau_j = \frac{t_j - \sum_i c_{ij} t_i}{1 - \sum_i c_{ij}} \tag{14.9}$$

A final variation is to define the average tariff on the intermediate inputs for good j, $\bar{t}_j$, as the weighted average of the actual tariffs; i.e.

$$\bar{t}_j = \frac{\sum_i c_{ij} t_i}{\sum_i c_{ij}} \tag{14.10}$$

which allows us to write the effective tariff as

$$\tau_j = \frac{t_j - \bar{t}_j \sum_i c_{ij}}{1 - \sum_i c_{ij}} \tag{14.11}$$

These different formulae for the effective tariff allow us to obtain several interesting results (we shall assume that $\sum c_{ij} < 1$, so that there is positive value-added at world prices). First, if there is a tariff on the output good $(t_j > 0)$ but no tariffs on the inputs then expression (14.9) tells us that the effective tariff on the output is greater than the nominal tariff on the output; i.e. $\tau_j > t_j$. Second, if the tariff on the output good and the tariffs on the input goods are all the same $(t_j = t_i = t)$ then equation (14.9) shows that the effective tariff has the same value; i.e. $\tau_j = t$. Thirdly, if the average tariff on the inputs is sufficiently greater than the tariff on the output then the effective tariff may be negative; that is, domestic production of the output good is effectively taxed.

When instruments other than tariffs are in force (such as voluntary export restraints or VERs) then specifying the effects of protection on value-added is considerably more difficult. The basic concepts are straightforward (such as calculating the tariff-equivalent to a specified VER), but their implementation is often not.

Our discussion of effective protection has excluded the possibility of non-traded intermediate inputs within the economy. If such inputs are present then some modification of the various formulae for the effective tariff is needed. At least three methods for incorporating non-traded inputs have been suggested. One, the 'Corden' method ignores their existence, and calculates the effective tariff in the manner of equation (14.9). The others (due to Balassa and Scott) include the cost of non-traded intermediate inputs in the calculation of value-added, but differ in the assumptions that they make about the likely consequences of a tariff structure for the prices of the non-traded inputs. The Balassa method essentially assumes that the prices of non-traded inputs would be the same whether or not there were tariffs present, whereas the Scott method assumes that their prices will increase by a proportion equal to the average nominal tariff.[7]

Empirical estimates of effective tariffs and protection

There have been many exercises in estimating effective tariffs for many countries. The data requirements are fairly demanding: even in the absence of any distortions other than tariffs, estimates are required of border and domestic prices (or, equivalently, nominal tariffs) for a large number of products, and of the cost-share coefficients. We shall not discuss these problems here.[8]

Table 14.1 gives estimates of effective tariffs for some broad categories of goods for the United Kingdom in 1986. Some points are immediately evident. First, effective tariffs tend to be higher than nominal tariffs for agriculture and manufactures. Second, effective tariffs are negative (although small) for primary activities and for services and distribution. Third, both nominal and effective tariffs tend to be higher as we move from primary goods through intermediate goods and on to finished goods. This latter phenomenon, referred to as *tariff escalation*, is not confined to the United Kingdom.

Table 14.1   *UK nominal and effective tariffs by sector, 1986*

Sector	Nominal tariffs (%)	Effective tariffs (%)
Primary activities	0.1	−2.0
Agriculture, processed foodstuffs, beverages	3.9	8.9
Intermediate goods 1	0.5	0.7
Intermediate goods 2	1.4	2.4
Machinery and transport equipment	1.8	3.0
Finished goods	2.4	4.6
Services and distribution	0.0	−0.5

Source: Ennew, Greenaway and Reed (1990).

☐ *Domestic resource cost analysis*

In Chapter 12 we saw that the presence of distortions in an economy could lead to a situation in which the country's apparent comparative advantage (as shown by relative market prices) gave an incorrect picture of its true comparative advantage. Domestic resource cost (DRC) analysis is an attempt to identify the goods in which a country has a true comparative advantage. It may thus be used as a measure of the costs of using protection to protect a domestic sector and of the welfare losses caused by other distortions, whether due to market structure or government intervention. It has close links with the concept of effective protection which we discussed earlier in this chapter.

Domestic resource cost is usually expressed as the ratio between the cost of domestic resources, valued at their *social opportunity cost*, used to produce 1 unit of the good in question and the value-added in the good calculated at border prices. We may interpret this as showing the cost to the economy at the margin of either saving foreign exchange through import substitution or earning foreign exchange through exporting.

In a small open economy with no taxes, tariffs, etc. and perfectly functioning markets the social opportunity cost of a factor of production would be equal to its market price, and the domestic prices of all goods would be equal to their border prices. In that case the DRC ratio would be. If, in an economy subject to distortions, the DRC ratio is less than one then this is an indication that the economy would benefit from transferring resources into the production of the commodity, since the value of the output, net of the cost of intermediate goods, on the world market is greater than the opportunity cost of the resources used. On the other hand, if the DRC ratio is greater than one then resources would be better employed elsewhere, since the resources used in saving or acquiring $1 of foreign exchange are worth more than $1 in alternative uses. There is obviously a relationship between the effective tariff and the DRC ratio. Indeed, if factor markets were working perfectly then there would be an exact algebraic relationship.[9] Where this is not the case there will be divergences, since market prices for factors will not reflect their opportunity costs (shadow prices).

■ 14.5 Trade in services

□ *The distinction between goods and services*

There are two approaches to distinguishing between goods and services. The first distinguishes between them on the basis of their characteristics.[10] The emphasis in this approach is on the non-storability of services and/or their intangible nature. This suggests that most services must be purchased by customers as they are produced. This in turn implies that if a service is to be consumed then, unless they are already in the same locale, either the consumer must move to be near the supplier or the supplier must move to be near the consumer. These distinctions suggest an obvious means of categorising services as well as differentiating services from goods. A simple example of a service where the consumer usually moves would be a visit to a museum or a theatre. On the other hand, in retail banking the supplier usually moves to the consumer by establishing a branch near him.

The second approach accepts these distinguishing characteristics, but extends it in two important ways.[11] First, it points out that some services do not require the movement of either consumer or supplier. An example of such a service is given by television broadcasts. Secondly, it emphasises the difficulties inherent in separating goods from services in many cases. Many services are 'embodied' in goods, and may form a greater or lesser part of the total value of the good. For example, a compact disc provides a service (the music) but a good (the disc itself) is required for the provision of the service.

It is debatable whether all services, whether embedded in a good or not, are necessarily 'unstorable'. The core of the debate is whether a service is 'consumed' on purchase or at some later date. For example, insurance may be purchased to cover some subsequent period. Some aspects of this service are consumed over the whole period ('peace of mind', for example), others may be consumed under certain circumstances at any time within the period, as when a claim is made.

Classification of services is however a useful device, even if we accept that no classification can ever be perfect. Stern and Hoekman have suggested the following four-way division.[12]

(1) *Separated services* – no movement is required by either the supplier or the consumer.[13]
(2) *Demander-located services* – movement of the supplier only.
(3) *Provider-located services* – movement of the consumer only.
(4) *Footloose or non-separated services* – supplier and consumer both move to another location where some service is provided.

Defining and measuring international trade in services

Defining international trade in goods is relatively straightforward. Goods are for the most part tangible, and we may identify their export or import by recording their movement across the national boundary. It is obviously much more difficult to identify the movement of an intangible service across a boundary. The problem of measurement, even where we can identify the trade, is complicated in some cases by the 'bundling' together of goods and services, as with the warranty on an imported car.

Stern and Hoekman[14] have proposed that we define trade in services as 'occurring when domestic factors receive income from non-residents in exchange for their services'. This is broadly in accord with the definition of services used in balance-of-payments accounts, although much trade which is strictly in the form of services may be subsumed into merchandise trade due to the 'bundling' referred to above.

Comparative advantage and international trade in services

There is no particular reason to look outside the models discussed in Part 1 for explanations of comparative advantage in services. Some services may be intensive in their use of particular factors of production (perhaps labour with particular skills), and so a relative abundance of such factors may determine comparative advantage. Others may require particular technologies which are only in place in certain countries. Yet others may depend on the presence of natural resources (e.g. beaches for tourism). The production of some services is subject to scale economies, while others may be readily differentiated, so that the models of intra-industry trade discussed in Chapter 8 may be appropriate.

There are however two problems that may distort the pattern of trade in services away from that suggested by our familiar trade models. The first is the potential difficulty faced by a consumer in assessing the *quality* of a service. For example, a tourist contemplating taking a holiday in another country may have incomplete information about the standards of hotels, beaches, etc. This uncertainty has provided ample excuse for governments interested in protecting their domestic service industries to discriminate against foreign suppliers, a question we shall return to later.

The second (though often related) problem, of which insurance and international transport provide the clearest examples, is that of enforcement of the conditions inherent in many services. For example, with free trade in services the cheapest source of car insurance for a German driver may be a British company. Should the German driver then have an accident with an Italian driver while in France, and should there be some dispute over settlement of the claims arising from the accident, in which country should the driver take legal action? Unless all the countries concerned have agreed to treat judgements in foreign courts as enforceable in their own courts, there may be considerable difficulties. The prospect of such circumstances may induce the German driver to insure with a German company.

☐ Foreign direct investment and international trade in services

We shall discuss foreign direct investment (FDI) in greater detail in Chapter 22, but the link between FDI and trade in services is of sufficient importance to justify some specific comments here. The importance of suppliers and consumers being geographically close to one another for many services provides an obvious incentive for existing suppliers to locate new operations in the same country as potential consumers.[15] Such relocation may of course be a substitute for trade in services in some instances. In others it may be a complement in that establishment of an agent in the other country may be needed before the service can be provided. The available data suggest that in recent years FDI in services has grown at a faster rate than international trade in services.

Direct investment is not of course the only way in which an established provider of services may extend its operations into another country. Among the various alternatives the most important are probably joint ventures between foreign- and locally-owned firms, licensing and franchise agreements, and management contracts. These provide 'presence in the market' for the foreign firm without it having to establish in the host country.

☐ *National policies and services*

The service sectors are more subject to government intervention than goods-producing industries.[16] In broad terms however the intangibility of services make it much more difficult for governments to apply such measures as tariffs (although a tariff against a car is of course a barrier against the free entry of services embodied in that car).

The basic policy measures that may be taken to protect domestic service sectors concern the 'right of establishment' of a foreign firm and/or its 'right of presence'. Examples of regulation/restrictions which differentiate between foreign and domestic firms are: exclusion from certain types of transaction (e.g. deposit-taking by banks); barring establishment of foreign firms in certain geographic regions; limits on the assets that can be owned by foreign firms; local content and minimum value-added requirements; rules on employment of domestic nationals.

Justification for such discriminatory measures typically consists of an appeal to need for consumer protection (the lack of knowledge problem noted above), the need for national control over some sectors of economy for economic policy reasons, and the familiar infant-industry argument. It seems likely that the real motivation for such policies is the misgivings that many governments have about foreign firms establishing and operating within their economy, which may owe more to political than economic considerations. Establishing 'market presence' via licensing agreements, franchises, sub-contracting arrangements, etc. in theory at least involves little foreign ownership or control over operations.

The particular problems associated with trade and FDI in services have made it difficult to bring services within the GATT framework. This in turn may lead to trade disputes, particularly where a good and service are bundled together. For example, a country exporting a bundled product may claim it is a good, and so entitled to treatment under GATT procedures, while the importing country may claim it is a service, and so outside those procedures. We shall return to these problems in Chapter 17.

■ *14.6 Price stabilisation*

The prices of many commodities, especially agricultural and other primary products, tend to fluctuate over time. This price variability has led governments to introduce policies designed to stabilise prices. Such policies may be intended to secure price stability in the home market, a policy often referred to as *price insulation*, or in the world market. In the latter case governments may collude with one another. We shall leave the question of price stabilisation in the world market to Chapter 18, where we consider international buffer stocks. In this section we shall consider the stabilisation of domestic prices by the use of variable taxes and subsidies on trade. The European Community's Common Agricultural Policy (CAP) has used similar policy instruments to secure stability for some commodities, notably grains.

Stabilising domestic prices by using variable trade taxes and subsidies

To demonstrate the operation of a variable trade tax/subsidy policy we shall use a very simple model, in which a small country has a variable demand for imports/supply of exports of an agricultural good, and faces a variable world price. For simplicity, we shall assume that there are only two domestic situations that can occur: a bad domestic harvest, which results in a high import demand (or a low export supply), and a good domestic harvest, in which case there is a low import demand (or a high export supply). Similarly, we assume that there are only two possible world prices: high and low (corresponding to bad and good harvests in the rest of the world respectively).

Figure 14.6 represents this simple model. The domestic excess demand curve is ED^B when domestic harvests are poor, ES^G when they are good. The world price is P_W^B when world harvests are bad, P_W^G when they are good. Four situations are shown in Figure 14.6, chosen to show the four basic possibilities: *A*, where there is a high world (and so domestic) price but the country has a good harvest and exports; *B*, where there is a high world price and a bad domestic harvest, so that the country imports; *C*, where there is a low world price and a good harvest and the country imports; and *D*, where there is a low world price and a good domestic harvest, and the country exports.

Now suppose that the government of this small country decides to stabilise the domestic price at a *target price* of P^T. In case *A* the free trade price is above the target price, and the country is exporting. The domestic price may be reduced to P^T by imposing an export tax equal to $P^B - P^T$ and so reducing exports to OX. In case *B* the free trade price is above the target price, but the country is importing. The domestic price may be reduced to P^T by subsidising imports by that amount, again equal to $P^B - P^T$, that will increase imports to OM. In cases *C* and *D* the domestic price with free trade is below the target price. In case *C*, where the country is importing, the domestic price may be increased to the target price by using an import tariff of $P^T - P^G$, and so reducing imports to OM. In case *D*, where the country is exporting, an export subsidy equal to $P^T - P^G$ will increase exports to OX, and so drive the domestic price up to P^T.

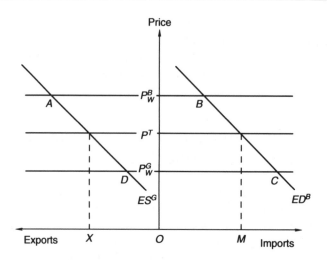

Figure 14.6   *Domestic price stabilisation by a small country*

If the target price is set equal to the average price under free trade then (with linear excess demand/supply curves) the average tax/subsidy will be zero, and the policy will be self-financing: that is, the average revenue/cost of the policy will also be zero.

Since the country is small, changing the quantity imported or exported will have no effect on world prices. However, if the country using the price insulation policy is large then world prices will be affected, and in a way that has an adverse effect on other countries. Figure 14.7 illustrates this possibility.

As before, the country (H) using the variable tax/subsidy policy and the rest of the world are assumed to have either good or bad harvests. ED_H^B is the excess demand curve for H when domestic harvests are poor, ES_H^G its excess supply curve when harvests are good. Similarly, ED_W^B is the excess demand curve for the rest of the world when there is a poor world harvest, ES_W^G the rest of the world's excess supply curve when its harvests are good.

Points A, B, C and D again show the various outcomes under free trade, and the policies chosen by the home country if it wishes to stabilise its domestic price at P^T are also as before. However, the policies used by H now have an effect on the world price. In the situation shown by A the use of an export tax to reduce exports to OX will increase the world price (which is already above its average value). Similarly, the use of an import subsidy in case B will again increase the world price. Conversely, the use of a tariff on imports in case C, and of an export subsidy in case D, will

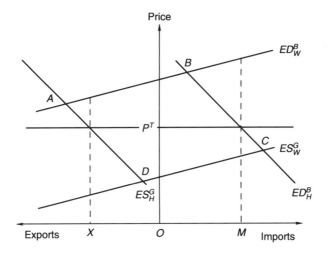

Figure 14.7 *Domestic price stabilisation by a large country*

reduce the world price, which is already below its average level in both cases.

In the large country case, then, stabilisation of the domestic price destabilises the price in the rest of the world. Country *H* is effectively 'exporting' its instability (the effects of its good and bad harvests) to the rest of the world.

An alternative policy for a large country would be the operation of a buffer stock, which would buy the excess supply from the domestic and world markets when the aggregate supply exceeded the aggregate demand at the target price, and conversely sell enough to meet the excess demand when there was a shortfall at the target price. This is essentially the policy operated by the United States in the grains market. Such a policy confers a benefit on the rest of the world, since it stabilises prices there as well as in the domestic market.[17] The operation of a price-stabilising buffer stock is discussed in Chapter 18.

☐ Notes

1 For more detailed treatments of this model, and its extension into a Heckscher–Ohlin framework, see Corden and Neary (1982) and Neary (1985), on which this discussion is based.

2 See Neary (1985).

3 Neary (1985), discusses a more complicated example, that of labour-saving technological progress in the traded goods sector.

4   A detailed discussion of the effects of North Sea oil on the UK economy may be found in Forsyth and Kay (1980).

5   For a general discussion of the construction of the production-possibility curve when there are intermediate goods, see Sanyal and Jones (1982).

6   There may be further outward shifts in the production-possibility frontier if the intermediate good is a differentiated product, since trade may allow domestic producers access to superior varieties of the intermediate good. See Ethier (1982) for such an argument.

7   A comparison of the three methods is given in Schweinberger (1975).

8   There are many sources of information on the problems faced in estimating effective tariffs and on possible remedies. Corden (1971, 1972) contains several papers on various aspects of effective protection.

9   For a more formal discussion of the relationship between the effective tariff and the DRC ratio, see Tower (1992).

10   This approach is due to Hill (1977).

11   See Bhagwati (1987).

12   Stern and Hoekman (1987).

13   The term is due to Sampson and Snape (1985). It is analogous to Bhagwati's 'long-distance' or 'disembodied' services (Bhagwati, 1987).

14   Stern and Hoekman (1987).

15   See Balasubramanyam (1991) for a discussion of this issue and of possible policy responses by governments.

16   See Hindley and Smith (1984).

17   The relative merits of variable trade taxes/subsidies and buffer stock schemes are discussed at more length in Rayner and Reed (1979).

■ *Chapter 15* ■

The Political Economy of Protection

■ *15.1* Introduction

The preceding chapters have suggested guidelines which we might expect to influence policy-makers. First, assuming that markets are competitive, free trade and non-interference in domestic markets is the best policy for a government to follow if it wishes to achieve the highest possible level of potential welfare, except in the special case of the optimum tariff for a large country (and then only in the absence of retaliation).

Second, if the government wishes to achieve some policy objective, such as a given output of a good or the correction of the effects of a domestic distortion, a tariff is always inferior to at least one other policy in that it imposes greater welfare costs (the so-called 'by-product distortions').

Third, if a government is constrained to restrict imports in order to achieve its objectives, a tariff will be superior to a quantitative restriction, and among quantitative restrictions an import quota will generally be superior to a voluntary export restraint (VER).

Fourth, the imposition of, or changes in, a tariff (or any other instrument) must cause a change in the distribution of income; there will be both gainers and losers. In some cases we may be able to predict which groups will gain or lose (as for capital and labour in the Heckscher–Ohlin model), but in others we may be uncertain how the change will affect a given group (as with labour in the specific factors model).

Fifth, who will gain and who will lose, and over what time period, will depend on the speed with which factors of production move within the economy (see the discussion of adjustment within the Heckscher–Ohlin framework in Chapters 3, 5 and 11).

Sixth, changes in trade policy will tend to cause greater adjustments in the employment of factors when trade is predominantly inter-industry than will be the case when trade is intra-industry.

The first two results suggest that a rational government intent on maximising the well-being of their country would pursue a policy of free trade. But even the most casual observer would note that free trade is the exception in the modern world, rather than the rule. It is most unlikely that governments are unaware of the benefits associated with free trade, so (assuming they are not all irrational),[1] why do they choose to pursue trade-restricting policies?

■ 15.2 Political markets

Economists have sought an answer to this question by considering the *political market for protection*. We may trace such modern developments in political economy back to work, starting in the late 1950s, by such political scientists and economists as Becker, Buchanan and Tullock, Downs, Olson and Stigler. In such markets the role of money is taken by the votes cast by the electorate, and the 'goods' are the policies provided.

The demand for policies is assumed to come from members of society, whether as individuals (e.g. consumers) or as organised groups (e.g. firms in a particular sector, labour unions, share owners, etc.). Demand for increased protection (or opposition to its reduction) will come from those who will benefit. In previous chapters we have identified various groups who benefit from protection, in particular producers in the import-competing sectors and owners of factors of production specific to those sectors.

We have also identified those who suffer from protection, in particular consumers of the imported goods, and producers in the export sectors and owners of factors of production specific to those sectors. Such 'countervailing' groups will tend to oppose increased protection.

The supply of policies is assumed to come from elected legislators and heads of state, and/or the bureaucrats who provide advice to politicians and who administer policy once it has been introduced. The politicians are assumed to be motivated by the desire to be elected, or to be re-elected if they are already in office. They will therefore either offer or maintain policies which maximise their chances at the ballot box. How they will behave then depends upon the voting system, their perception of the intensity of preferences of different groups for potential policy changes and their ability to 'deliver' the votes of their members, and on the need to obtain funds for campaigning.

The bureaucrats may have a variety of goals. It is often assumed that the goal of a bureaucracy is to maximise its prestige, perhaps by employing more staff, or emphasising the importance of its role or the complexity of its operations. It has also been suggested that bureaucracies may be responsive to groups other than their political masters. They may for example identify themselves with the interests of the group whose activities they are meant to control (e.g. Departments of Agriculture may be 'captured' by the farm lobby).

Support (demand) for policies may be manifested in various ways. Most models assume that the electorate votes directly for or against a policy proposal at the ballot box (either as part of a general election or in a referendum). At the same time, however, those proposing or opposing a policy change may engage in public campaigns, lobby the decision-makers directly, or 'buy' support for such policies by donations to the campaign funds of political parties.

Offers to supply a given policy may come from political parties (one party may, say, wish to promote the interests of low-income workers), or from other looser groups of politicians (all those, say, who represent farming communities). The usual assumption is that such politicians will provide those policies which maximise their chances of election (or re-election).

☐ *The median voter model*

The policies produced by the 'equilibrium' in the political market will depend to a large extent on the voting procedure in operation. Perhaps the most commonly used model is the *median voter* model, in which the politicians seek to persuade the median voter (the one who turns a minority into a majority) to vote for them. This may be applied to cases where the whole electorate votes on a given issue (as in a national referendum), or to the more general case where politicians stand for constituencies in which they have to secure a majority for election, and their party has to secure a majority of constituencies before it can become the government.

Robert Baldwin[2] has suggested that we need to consider five points when using the median voter model to provide an explanation of the existence of protection in a democracy and of the pressure for increased rather than decreased protection.

First, compensation does not necessarily take place. In that case the producers of import-competing goods (and the owners of factors specific to those goods) will indeed lose from reductions in protection. If they vote in accordance with their own interest, and form a group able to command a stable majority in the parliament, then protectionism will be the favoured policy.

Second, the benefits from tariff reductions may be spread over a large group, so that each member of the group makes a small personal gain. Such groups are usually identified as the households consuming the good concerned, firms in the export industries, and firms using imported goods as inputs into their own products. They may, particularly in the case of households, also be uncertain of the size and timing of their gains (less well informed), and they may be more difficult to organise as a group. Moreover, they may take the view that they will get the benefits of tariff reductions whether or not they take the trouble to vote or lobby for them (tariff reductions are a 'public good', so that there may be 'free riders').

On the other hand, the losers from tariff reductions may be less numerous, such as the owners of firms in the import-competing industry. They may expect to make a greater loss individually, and be more certain of the size and timing of their losses, and so may be easier to organise. Such organisation may be facilitated if the losers are already organised into groups for other reasons (trade associations, labour unions, etc.). Members of such organised groups may be more willing to vote or lobby for increased protection.

Third, the prospective losers from tariff reductions may be better represented in parliament than the prospective gainers by virtue of their geographical distribution across electoral districts. If, for example, there are three equally sized districts, and the prospective losers have a bare majority in two of them and no members in the third, and those elected carry out the wishes of the majority of their own electorate, then the potential losers will have a majority in parliament even though they form only just over 33 per cent of the voters.

Fourth, vote trading ('logrolling') may affect the outcome of majority voting. Consider again the case of three equally sized districts. Import-competing industry *A* is concentrated in district 1, and there is a bare majority in that constituency strongly in favour of protection for industry *A* and weakly against protection for import-competing industry *B* (whose output they may consume). Industry *B* is concentrated in district 2, with a bare majority there strongly in favour of protection for industry *B* and weakly opposed to protection for industry *A*. The export industries are in district 3, where all the voters are strongly against protection for any industry. A proposal that only industry *A* be protected would then lose by a vote of two-to-one, as would a proposal that only industry *B* be protected. However, a proposal that there be protection for both import-competing industries would win by a vote of two-to-one provided that the representatives of districts *A* and *B* can agree that each will vote in favour of the other.

Fifth, tariffs generate revenue for governments, who might have few alternative sources of finance. This is particularly true in less-developed countries (LDCs) with undeveloped or inefficient tax systems, where tariff revenues account for a substantial proportion of government revenues. We might add to this that a production subsidy, a means of giving support to an industry that we have argued is superior to a tariff, must be financed by the government raising revenue elsewhere.

All these considerations, if true, will lead us to expect that in an economy where representatives are elected by majority vote, and a government holds power by having a majority of those elected, the tendency will be for protection to be maintained, and possibly increased.

☐ Lobbying

Another important element in the political market for protection is the extent and the effectiveness of the lobbying activity by pressure groups mentioned above. Finger[3] has argued that the form of government institutions encourages lobbying. The reallocation of income caused by a change in policy may be politically dangerous if carried out openly. The government may react by establishing a bureaucracy (commissions, boards of experts, etc.) with the overt aim of assessing the costs and benefits of any change, but which will in practice slow down change and obfuscate the process. The response from those with an interest in either changing or maintaining the status quo will then be to lobby the bureaucracy with a view to manipulating its procedures.

It has been argued that the rules for tariff negotiations under the GATT provide *prima facie* evidence of the influence of pressure groups. A concession is defined as a reduction in tariffs, these concessions being balanced by cuts in the tariffs of other countries. Yet pure trade theory suggests that tariff reductions benefit the country concerned. The GATT rules do however have an internal logic if we assume that within each country the pressure against tariff cuts from the import-competing sectors must be offset by pressure for trade expansion by the export industries.

Lobbying also may be viewed as an economic activity. The organisation of a lobbying group uses resources, as does the lobbying activity itself[4]. Bruno Frey[5] has devised a model which explains the optimal amount of lobbying by an industry in terms of the relationship between the costs of lobbying and the benefits that may be obtained.

☐ The optimal amount of lobbying

Frey has constructed a simple model which allows us to examine the factors which might determine the optimum amount of lobbying. Let us consider first the benefits which may be obtained from protection by those who form the lobbying group, and let us assume that these benefits may be represented by the addition to producer surplus gained by increasing the tariff from its present level. Suppose that the lobby is organised by the members of a perfectly competitive industry, and that the supply and demand curves for that industry have the usual shapes. Then increasing the tariff will increase the gain in producer surplus, probably at a decreasing rate, until trade is eliminated. Once the prohibitive tariff has been reached then further increases in the tariff can no longer increase the producer surplus.

Curve OBC in Figure 15.1 is drawn to reflect this argument. The horizontal axis shows the increase in the tariff (so that the origin represents the starting tariff) and the vertical axis measures the monetary value of the gains which may be made by the lobbyists. The curve increases until the tariff has increased by t_p, that increase which would result in the prohibitive tariff being reached, and then becomes horizontal.

Lobbying will however also involve costs. These costs will encompass the costs of organising the lobby group, employing professional lobby agents, etc., and also the costs of overcoming opposition to the increase in the tariff. The former may include 'start-up' costs, which are likely to be lower if the members of the lobbying group are already organised for some other purpose, and 'operating' costs, which will be lower if the group is well organised, if free riding is low, if the lobbying is efficient, etc.

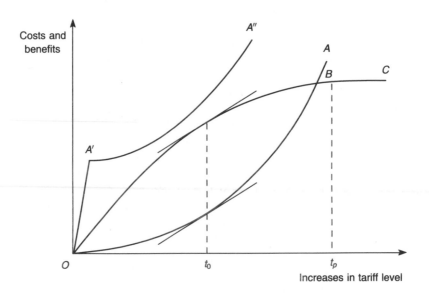

Figure 15.1 *The demand for and supply of tariff protection*

The latter are likely to be lower the less organised are opposing interests (consumers, export interests, foreign competitors, etc.) and the more the society accepts that the group in question should receive protection (as often seems to be the case with farmers and strategically important or prestige industries).

Curve OA in Figure 15.1 represents a cost-of-lobbying curve where there are no start-up costs, and where the marginal cost of lobbying increases at an increasing rate as the sought-after tariff increase becomes larger. OA has been drawn to intersect OBC to the left of B, but this need not be the case.

The optimal amount of lobbying from the point of view of those seeking the increased protection will be that which secures the tariff increase which maximises the net gain from lobbying. This net gain is of course the vertical distance between the benefits curve OBC and the cost curve OA. The optimum tariff increase is shown in Figure 15.1 as t_o, the tariff increase for which the slope of OBC (the marginal benefit from the tariff increase) is equal to the slope of OA (the marginal cost of securing the tariff increase).

If the costs of lobbying are low enough, and increase at a sufficiently low rate, then the optimal rate of lobbying could result in the prohibitive tariff being imposed. This would happen if the cost-of-lobbying curve intersected OBC to the right of B and if the slope of the cost curve at t_p were less than the slope of the OB portion of the benefits curve at t_p.

If the costs of lobbying are sufficiently high, perhaps because of high start-up costs, the optimal amount of lobbying to obtain a tariff increase might be zero. Such a case is shown in Figure 15.1 by the cost-of-lobbying curve $OA'A''$. The costs of lobbying in this case always exceed the benefits obtainable from a tariff increase.

■ 15.3 The choice of protective instrument

The model discussed above considers lobbying where a tariff is the only policy instrument under consideration, and the industry conducting the lobby is competitive. However, lobbying is not confined to seeking tariff protection.[6]

It is arguable that producers may prefer quantitative restrictions to tariff protection, and that governments may not only share that preference, but may also prefer voluntary export restraints to import quotas.

Producers may prefer quotas because they see them as being more 'certain' in their effects; the volume of imports will not increase if the domestic market expands or the world market contracts, or if new foreign producers enter the market. As we saw in Chapter 10, domestic producers in a competitive industry will be better off under these circumstances with a quantitative restriction than with its equivalent tariff. It is also of course the case that domestic producers will suffer more with a quota than a tariff in the alternative circumstances, but it may be that producers take the view that growth is more common than contraction.

Governments may prefer quantitative restrictions because their consequences are less readily apparent to consumers. A tariff of 20 per cent will, in a small country, increase domestic prices by 20 per cent, and few consumers would be unaware of that fact given their familiarity with indirect taxes of many kinds. A quantitative restriction will also, of course, increase prices, but not everyone may be aware of that, and few may be in a position to estimate the extent to which prices have been increased. A government wishing to protect a given industry may well in such circumstances prefer to employ a quantitative restriction rather than a tariff since the consequent adverse reaction by consumers may be less.

Quotas are however technically illegal under GATT rules, so that a government would risk a protest to the GATT from those countries from which it imports if it uses a quota. Voluntary export restraints are not however specifically outlawed by the GATT rules, and they also offer an incentive to (existing) foreign suppliers not to protest by allowing them to capture the rents generated by the restriction, and giving them a guaranteed market over the period of the agreement. Governments are likely therefore to prefer a voluntary export restriction to a quota.

In terms of the earlier analysis, if producers' preferences are for a quantitative restriction rather than its equivalent tariff, the benefits curve will be higher, and probably steeper, than that for the equivalent tariff. The government's preferences will be reflected in the cost-of-lobbying curve. If the government is more concerned with 'hiding' the protection given to domestic producers than it is by foreign reaction, it will be more amenable to lobbying for a quantitative restriction than for a tariff, and so we would expect the cost-of-lobbying curve to be lower for the former. If on the other hand the government is more concerned about foreign reaction then the cost-of-lobbying curve may be higher. In either case, it is probable that the cost of lobbying for a voluntary export restraint will be lower than that for a quota.

Figure 15.2 is a modified version of Figure 15.1. For simplicity we shall assume that the original position is free trade, so that the horizontal axis measures the actual tariff rate. The benefits curve for different tariffs is shown as $OABC$. The benefits curve for a voluntary export restraint is shown as $OA'B'C'$, the VER being converted into its tariff equivalent to facilitate comparison. The positions of the two benefits curves reflect the assumption that a given VER yields greater benefits to producers than its equivalent tariff. In both cases no further benefits can be obtained once

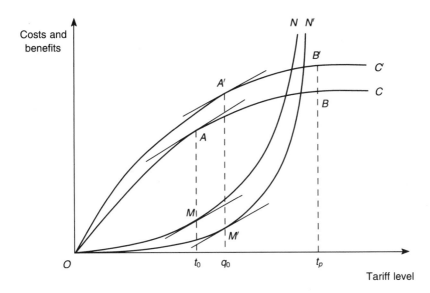

Figure 15.2   *Lobbying for a quantitative restriction compared with lobbying for a tariff*

imports have been eliminated, at tariff t_p or at a zero quantitative restraint (equivalent to a tariff of t_p).

The cost-of-lobbying curve for the tariff option is shown by OMN, and that for the VER by $OM'N'$. The latter curve is the lower of the two, reflecting the assumption that the government will be more willing to accede to a VER than a tariff. If the government is unwilling to reduce imports below some level by either method then both cost curves will approach the vertical at the same tariff (or quota-equivalent) below t_p.

In Figure 15.2 the tariff resulting from an optimum use of lobbying will be t_O, yielding a benefit to the lobbyists of MA. If, as we have assumed, the benefits curve for the VER is steeper than that for the tariff at the equivalent tariff rate, while the cost curve for the VER is flatter than that for the tariff at the equivalent rate, then the quota resulting from the optimum lobbying effort will have a tariff equivalent, q_O, which will be higher than t_O. That is, the outcome of optimal lobbying for a VER is, in the case illustrated, both greater protection and greater benefits for the lobbyists than would be the outcome of optimal lobbying for a tariff.

It is possible that optimal lobbying for a VER would result in lower protection than optimal lobbying for a tariff, but if the VER lobbying results in a lower net benefit than the tariff lobbying, we would expect the producers to lobby for the tariff.

15.4 Tariff lobbying by a single domestic producer

The benefits given by a tariff to firms in imperfectly competitive industries differ from those given to firms in perfectly competitive industries. We shall consider the case of a single domestic producer who may, if the tariff is high enough, be given monopoly power in the domestic market.[7]

In Figure 15.3, the curve $OABA^*CD$ shows the benefits (assumed here to be additional profits) obtained by the single domestic producer from tariff protection. The tariff which will eliminate trade is t_p. For tariffs lower than t_p, the domestic producer will be a price-taker, producing up to the point where his marginal cost is equal to the tariff-inclusive price. Increasing the tariff will increase the domestic producer's profits by increasing the price at which he may sell and increasing his sales volume.

If the tariff is increased above t_p then the domestic producer will be the only supplier to his home market. He will restrict his output in line with the reduction in demand, so increasing his profits, but he is still constrained by the ability of consumers to import at the tariff-inclusive price.

If the tariff is increased to t_m then the single domestic producer will have monopoly power in the home market, and will produce to the point where

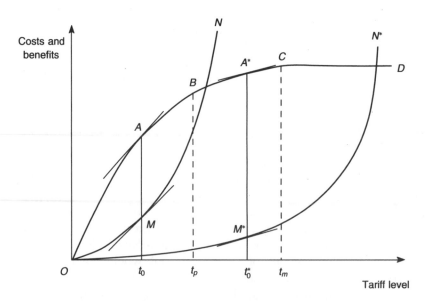

Figure 15.3   *A single domestic producer lobbying for a tariff*

he equates his marginal cost with his marginal revenue. Tariffs above t_m yield no further increases in profits (though they do give additional protection against any reduction in the world price).

Whether the single domestic producer will find it optimal to lobby for tariff protection only (tariffs less than t_p), for trade elimination (tariffs between t_p and t_m) or for monopoly power (tariffs greater than t_m) will depend on the costs of lobbying. If lobbying costs are high (as shown by the curve OMN in Figure 15.3) optimal lobbying may lead to restriction of imports only, the tariff being t_o. If lobbying costs are sufficiently lower than this (as with curve OM^*N^* in Figure 15.3) then optimal lobbying may lead to trade elimination without pure monopoly power, the tariff in the case shown being t_o^*. If the costs of lobbying were particularly low then the single domestic producer might find it optimal to lobby for the monopoly-conferring tariff.

■ 15.5 'Capturing' anti-dumping legislation

Anti-dumping legislation is common, and is sanctioned by Article VI of the GATT, which permits discriminatory action, using a countervailing duty, against goods which are dumped by a particular country.[8] The countervailing duty must not be greater than the 'margin of dumping'.

The procedure for identifying dumping is usually initiated by domestic firms, who claim that the action of the foreign countries is 'damaging' them. The evidence cited may be either that the low-price imports are reducing the domestic companies' sales, or that the imports are reducing their market share, or even that the volume of imports is increasing. It has been suggested that another 'hidden' motive may be that the imports are damaging the ability of domestic producers to maintain a cartel in their home market.

Domestic firms are said to have 'captured' the anti-dumping legislation if they manage to persuade the relevant domestic authority to define the relevant factors affecting the case in a way best suited to their interests.

Table 15.1 shows the number of anti-dumping cases that were initiated by a selection of countries between 1980 and 1986. It is notable that the United States and the European Community[9] are two of those most active in invoking anti-dumping legislation against foreign suppliers and two of those most subject to such action by other countries. The other interesting contrast is between Australia and Canada on the one hand, which have initiated many actions but have been subject to few by other countries, and Japan, which has been the target of many anti-dumping claims but never invoked the legislation itself.

Table 15.1   *Anti-dumping cases brought by and against selected countries between 1980 and 1986*

	Number of cases	
	By	Against
Australia	416	3
Canada	230	35
European Community	280	289
Japan	0	112
United States	350	112
Others	12	737
Totals	1288	1288

Source: Finger and Olechowski (1987), Tables A8.3, A8.4.

A decision has been reached in just over 80 per cent of the 1288 anti-dumping cases initiated in the 1980–86 period. Of those cases some 62 per cent were decided in favour of those bringing the action.

Messerlin[10] provides an interesting analysis of the capture of the European Community's anti-dumping legislation by EC chemical firms who had already been fined by the EC's competition policy authority for operating cartels in polyvinyl chloride (PVC) and low-density polythene (LDeP). The firms alleged that these chemicals had been dumped in the EC market by Czechoslovakia and East Germany (PVC and LDeP), Romania and Hungary (PVC), and Poland and the Soviet Union (LDeP). Note that all these countries were at the time non-market economies in which it is difficult to ascertain a 'home market price'.

Messerlin argues that the firms captured four important components of the anti-dumping legislation. First, they defined the market in which the dumping allegedly occurred (whereas in anti-cartel cases it is the EC authority which does so). Second, they captured the determination of the dumping margin by persuading the anti-dumping authority to take the price in Sweden as the price which would have prevailed in the Eastern European countries had they been market economies. Since the cartels were major exporters to Sweden, Messerlin argues, and probably had greater market power there so that they could charge prices above the EC price, such a comparison must inevitably lead to the conclusion that dumping was occurring!

Third, the EC cartel captured the 'injury test'. They successfully argued that they were suffering injury from the alleged dumping because the shares of the EC market taken by the Eastern European countries had risen, because their prices had been undercut by these imports, and because these increased imports and falling prices were 'causing' losses. These arguments are interesting, because they amount to a claim that a cartel has a right to restrict sales and to raise prices.

Finally, the EC firms captured the duration of the dumping measures in that, although the anti-dumping measures (countervailing duties or agreements to increase prices) lasted only five years, the EC firms used that period to increase their concentration while failing to reduce their excess production capacity.

Messerlin estimated that the anti-dumping measures increased prices in the European Community by between 3 and 11.6 per cent for LDeP and 10 and 14 per cent for PVC. He estimated the annual welfare loss under two assumptions. Had the cartels been able to survive without the anti-dumping measures then the loss might have been between 3.9 and 5.4 million DM for LDeP, and between 31.4 and 43.5 million DM for PVC. But if the cartels had collapsed without the anti-dumping measures then the welfare gain to the European Community could have been between 55.6 and 77 million DM for LDeP and 59.5 and 82.4 million DM in the case of PVC.

▪ *15.6* Rent-seeking

Rent-seeking, first identified by Krueger,[11] refers to an attempt to secure the rents generated by quantitative restrictions. For example, as we have seen, the imposition of an import quota generates rents. If the quota is allocated by means of import licences then each licence carries with it a share of those rents. The import licences then become a valuable asset, and there will be competition to secure a licence.

Such competition will involve activity similar to that of the lobbies described earlier, and that activity will use scarce resources. The resources are being used to secure an asset rather than in the production of a marketable good or service, and so will reduce welfare (the activity shifts the economy's production-possibility curve inwards).

Krueger used the classical model of Chapter 2 to analyse the impact of rent-seeking in a small country specialising in the production of food and importing manufactures. The model is augmented by the inclusion of internal distribution costs, with those working in the distribution sector able to obtain rents from quantitative restrictions on imports by virtue of a system which allocates import licences to distributors.

Krueger specifies the form of rent-seeking activity as competitive, with people continuing to enter the distribution sector until the average wage in distribution (including the rents) is equal to the wage in the food sector.

Krueger demonstrated the following. First, the welfare cost of a quantitative restriction is equal to the welfare cost of its tariff equivalent *plus* the additional cost of rent-seeking activities. It follows that we cannot use the tariff equivalents of two or more quotas to rank those quotas, since the costs of rent-seeking depend on factors other than the equivalent tariff.

Second, while for a tariff or an import quota without rent seeking the dead-weight loss is likely to be lower the less elastic is domestic demand, the dead-weight loss of a quantitative restriction with rent-seeking is likely to be higher.

Third, an import *prohibition* might be preferable to a non-prohibitive quota if there is competition for licences under the quota (since the import prohibition would not allow rent-seeking – although it might encourage smuggling, another form of resource-wasting activity).

Fourth, there may be a lower dead-weight loss from licensing only one importer (creating a monopoly) than if competition for rents is allowed. This will however have important effects on the income distribution. Krueger comments that the government may find itself on the horns of a dilemma over the last result: if it restricts imports and licenses to only one (or a small number of) importers then it will be seen to be favouring the licensees; if it allows competition for import licences then it may produce a more even income distribution and avoid charges of favouritism, but it will increase the cost to the economy of the restrictions.

A secondary effect of (successful) rent-seeking activity may be to weaken peoples' belief in the market system, which may be seen as 'rewarding the rich and well-connected'. This in turn may lead to pressure for more direct government intervention, thereby both reducing economic efficiency and increasing the amount of economic activity devoted to rent-seeking.

Krueger estimated that in 1964 the total amount of rents obtained in India from public investment, imports, other controlled commodities, credit rationing and the railways were about 7.3 per cent of national income, and that in Turkey in 1968 the rents from import licences alone were about 15 per cent of Turkey's GNP.

Rent-seeking is just one form of what Bhagwati[12] has named *directly unproductive profit-seeking* (DUP) *activities*. Bhagwati defines them as being 'ways of making a profit (i.e. income) by undertaking activities that are directly unproductive; that is, they yield pecuniary returns but produce neither goods nor services that enter a conventional utility function directly nor intermediate inputs into such goods and services'. DUP activities include the rent-seeking considered above, as well as the seeking of revenue, tariffs, monopoly power, etc., and the development of such activities as smuggling.

15.7 Empirical work on the political economy of protection

Empirical studies of the political economy of protection fall into three major groups. In the first group are detailed examinations of the voting patterns of elected representatives on trade-related issues, which are then related to variables which may be thought to influence those patterns. In the second group we have statistical estimation of the impact of various economic and political variables on the observed pattern of protection across economic activities within a country. The third approach examines the pattern of negotiations on tariff reductions under the GATT.

One of the most important of the first group is Baldwin's study of the voting patterns of US Congressmen on protection issues.[13] He found that two factors were associated with a tendency for Congressmen to vote in favour of protective measures. The first was a relatively high proportion of import-competing industries in their constituency. Given the large number of Congressmen, this has been interpreted as supporting the 'log-rolling' hypothesis (industry A supports industry B's bid for protection, even if that may harm industry A by raising the prices of some factors and inputs used by A, in return for industry B supporting A's bid for protection).

The second factor was the contribution that the three major trades unions in favour of the measure had made to a Congressman's campaign funds. This is obviously indicative of the ability of organised labour in the United States to obtain protection but, given the previous result, may also be interpreted as suggesting some agreement on objectives between capital and labour, which could be consistent with a specific factors model where both capital and the type of labour employed are relatively immobile.

In a further study,[14] Baldwin analysed the vote on the 1973 US Trade Bill. He concluded that Democrats in both Senate and House of Representatives were significantly more protectionist than were Republicans, and that protectionist trade union contributions were given primarily to those who voted against the Act. Baldwin also found that both the President and Congress are more likely to adopt protectionist legislation just prior to an election.

One of the earliest statistical studies was that by Caves.[15] He tested three models on Canadian nominal and effective protection in 1963. The first was the 'adding-machine' model, where the assumed aim of the policymakers was to maximise the benefit to the greatest possible number of voters. The second was the 'interest group' model, intended to pick up the influence of lobbying activity. The third was the 'national interest' model, where infant industry protection was offered to sectors where it was most likely to be effective, defined by Caves to be industries offering high wages and showing a record of rapid growth and 'balanced development'.

Caves found no evidence for the adding-machine model, and only weak evidence for the national interest model. The interest group model seemed to perform reasonably well, explaining about half the variation in tariff rates between different industries.

Ray used similar methods in a study of US tariffs.[16] He found US tariffs to be positively related to the degree of concentration and the labour-intensity in the industry, and negatively related to the intensity of skilled labour. The positive effect of the degree of concentration is consistent with the lobbying hypothesis, since lobbies should be more easy to organise in a concentrated industry. The role of labour-intensity is consistent with the predictions of the Heckscher–Ohlin model, since unskilled labour is relatively scarce in the United States and so should gain from protection, but also with the voting power of labour, even if unorganised. The negative effect of skilled labour, with which the United States is relatively well-endowed, is also consistent with the Heckscher–Ohlin model, and may also reflect a greater degree of political activity on the part of skilled workers.

Ray also found that non-tariff barriers appeared to complement the tariffs but were relatively more important in industries which were intensive in their use of physical capital and produced non-differentiated goods. It has been suggested that the Unietd States may be so uncompetitive in such industries that, given the low level of tariffs negotiated under the GATT, only non-tariff barriers could offer sufficient protection. There was also evidence that the US used non-tariff barriers in retaliation to their use by other countries.

Ray also analysed protection in seven major competitors to the United States. He found that skilled labour lost from the tariff structures, possibly reflecting the relative importance of skilled labour in those countries' export industries. This might in turn reflect relative abundance of skilled labour in a Heckscher–Ohlin context, or might reflect the importance of skilled labour in manufactured exports (see the discussion of the Neo-Heckscher–Ohlin model in Chapter 8).

Greenaway and Milner have investigated the inter-industry pattern of protection in the United Kingdom.[17] They attempt to explain the target level of protection of each industry, which may take the form of tariff or non-tariff barriers, in terms of a number of industry-specific factors. First they consider factors which make it easier to organise lobbies: the concentration of market power, the degree of unionisation and the geographical concentration. They include also the range of products (a specialised industry can concentrate its lobbying efforts on a narrow range of products), the share of sales going to other industries (who might lobby against protection), and employment in the industry (relating directly to the number of voters).

As possible measures of relative factor intensities they considered the employment-output ratio and relative wage costs, both of which should be related to the labour-intensity of production, and the ratio of unskilled to skilled labour (the United Kingdom may be relatively abundant in skilled labour). Finally, they included as possible measures of adjustment pressures the non-EC import share of the industry, its total export share, and its level of intra-industry trade.

They do not find support for the product and labour market power hypotheses, and only limited support for the geographical and product specialisation hypotheses. They do find strong support for the countervailing power hypothesis. Indeed, they comment, 'this is the only political economy (narrowly-defined) influence on the structure of tariff protection'.

By contrast, there is clear evidence of comparative advantage and adjustment cost influences being relevant. High import share, greater wage cost (labour-intensity) and greater intensity of unskilled labour do appear to increase the pressures for protection and induce higher nominal tariffs. These influences are subject to offsetting pressures however where exports are more important, even if imports and exports are of simultaneous importance to a given industry. The result for the intra-industry variable is consistent with the ease of adjustment hypothesis.

There is some support, therefore, for current political economy and adjustment pressures affecting the structure of (*ex ante*) tariffs bargained for in the future. There is some support, therefore, for the view that adjustment pressures did influence the exceptions from the 'Swiss formula' in the Tokyo Round of GATT negotiations (see Chapter 17). Historical factors do not appear to dominate the current inter-industry pattern of nominal tariff protection in the United Kingdom. The results 'do suggest that there are current "endogenous"/political economy influences on target rates of nominal protection'.

The results for effective tariffs are broadly similar, save that the 'countervailing power' hypothesis appears to hold for nominal tariff but not effective tariff-setting. Greenaway and Milner suggest that 'it is credible that foreign governments will be perceived by UK producers to be more likely to respond to or retaliate against UK nominal tariffs than effective tariffs'.

The United Kingdom like other developed market economies, has placed increased reliance on non-tariff barriers of various forms since the mid-1970s. These have included quotas and subsidies, as well as 'grey area' measures like voluntary export restraints and other source-specific measures. Ideally one would include the tariff equivalent on any non-tariff barrier, then estimate the model for total protection. Information on tariff equivalence is however very scarce. Greenway and Milner did, however, have access to information on the presence or absence of non-tariff barriers. The pattern of results was not inconsistent with the estimates for tariffs. They suggest that 'for this sample, tariff and non-tariff barriers may be complements rather than substitutes'.

Cheh is an early example of the third approach, examining the pattern of negotiations on tariff reductions.[18] He considered the exceptions made by the United States to the universal tariff reductions agreed in the Kennedy Round. Excluding certain strategic goods and those where GATT escape clauses were already in operation (e.g. textiles), he found that the exceptions seemed to be made for industries which were labour intensive (particularly with an unskilled or ageing work force), and/or geographically concentrated and/or slow-growing or declining. He concluded that the exceptions were aimed at avoiding short-term labour adjustment costs.

Riedel repeated Cheh's analysis for West Germany.[19] He found no support for Cheh's conclusions when considering nominal tariffs, but similar results when he considered effective protection, including the effects of non-tariff barriers.

☐ *Notes*

1   But Frey *et al.*, in an survey of economists, found that while 79 per cent of US and 70 per cent of German economists believed that protection decreased welfare, only 47 per cent of Swiss, 44 per cent of Austrian and 27 per cent of French economists shared that view (Frey, Pommerehne, Schneider and Gilbert (1984)).
2   Baldwin (1976).
3   Finger (1981).
4   For further reading on the factors influencing the formation and functions of pressure groups see Olson (1965), Stigler (1974) and Pincus (1975).
5   Frey (1985).
6   See Vousden (1990) for a fuller discussion of the choice between tariffs and quantitative restrictions.
7   Cassing and Hillman (1985) offer an alternative way of examining this problem.
8   See Chapter 17 for the definition and consequences of dumping.
9   The European Community, rather than individual members, is responsible for initiating anti-dumping action, but it is the individual members who are subject to action by other countries. For convenience the European Community members have been grouped together in Table 15.1. West Germany was the subject of over 25 per cent of the anti-dumping actions initiated against European Community members, with Italy, Belgium, France and the United Kingdom accounting for nearly 85 per cent of the remainder.

Spain, not then a member of the European Community, had 47 cases initiated against it in the same period.

10 Messerlin (1990).
11 Krueger (1974).
12 Bhagwati (1982a).
13 Baldwin (1976).
14 Baldwin (1986).
15 Caves (1976).
16 Ray (1981).
17 Greenaway and Milner (1991).
18 Cheh (1974).
19 Riedel (1977).

■ *Chapter 16* ■

The Theory of Customs Unions

■ 16.1 Introduction

One of the major aspects of international trading relations during the post-war period has been the development of regional trade groupings, primarily in the form of customs unions. This development naturally aroused the attention of trade theorists. Standard trade theory had only been concerned with the effects of non-discriminatory tariff changes, the type of tariff theory we have studied in Chapters 10, 11 and 12. But customs unions are by definition discriminatory. They mean a lowering of tariffs within the union and an establishing of a joint outer tariff wall. They combine free trade with protectionism.

This makes customs unions difficult to deal with from a theoretical point of view. We are working in an area covered by *the theory of the second best*. Broadly, this states that when we are dealing with a situation where there are two or more distortions then removing some but not all of the distortions may increase or may decrease welfare.

The formation of a customs union must fall in this class of problems. Suppose that a small country has a tariff on imports of the same good from two other countries (and so two sources of distortion), but that otherwise there is free trade. Were it to eliminate the tariff on imports from both countries then there would be universal free trade, and its welfare would increase – a case of a *first-best* policy change. But by joining one of the other countries in a customs union it will eliminate the tariff on imports from its new partner while retaining a tariff on imports from the third country. Only one of the distortions has been removed, and in general we cannot tell whether this will increase or reduce welfare.

The fallacy that must be avoided is to argue that, since tariffs reduce world welfare, and since the formation of a customs union reduces the number of tariffs in the world, it must be the case that forming a customs union is a move towards free trade and therefore gives an increase in welfare.

We have seen that ordinary tariff theory is quite complicated when general-equilibrium considerations are taken into account. The theory of customs unions is even more complex. For that reason this chapter will, on the whole, deal with the theory of customs unions in a partial equilibrium framework.

To begin with, economists tried to formulate general propositions about the welfare effects of a customs union. The free trade aspects of customs unions were stressed, and the general consensus seemed to be that customs unions would increase welfare. This was disputed on several grounds as the theory developed; economists tended to oscillate between broad generalisations and agnosticism.

There is now a reasonably well-developed body of theory on customs unions. There are still however many issues which have not been resolved. The main results in customs union theory, as it stands today, will now be surveyed, but many of the more sophisticated analyses will not be covered in depth.*

■ *16.2* Trade creation and trade diversion

The pioneering study of the theory of customs unions was made by Jacob Viner (working before the general theory of the second best had been developed).[1] By considering a very simple model, Viner showed that while forming a customs union could have welfare-increasing effects in some circumstances, it could have welfare-reducing effects in others. His work should not be treated as an attempt to provide a general model of a customs union. Its importance lies in the demonstration that a customs union could reduce welfare.

Viner introduced the key concepts of *trade creation* and *trade diversion*. They may be illustrated by Table 16.1, which shows the (constant) production cost of a homogeneous commodity in three countries. Let us disregard transportation cost, mark-ups, etc., so that production cost

Table 16.1   *Production cost of commodity X in three countries*

Country	A	B	C
Production cost	50	40	30

completely determines the supply price of the good, and tariffs are the only source of divergence between price and cost. The model assumes that the countries involved are fully employed both before and after the formation of the customs union. In this sense the analysis is of a neoclassical type. It also assumes that the demand for the good is perfectly price inelastic. This being the case, the analysis focuses on the effects of union on the allocation of resources and the welfare implications of these effects.

First, let us assume that initially A levies a non-discriminatory tariff of 100 per cent. Consumers in A would be faced with a choice between home-produced goods at a price of 50, imports from B at a price of 80, and imports from C at a price of 60. A would then not import the good , and the price in A's home market would be 50.

If A now forms a customs union with B, while maintaining the same 100 per cent tariff on imports from C, consumers in A will face a choice between home-produced goods at a price of 50, imports from B at a price of 40, and imports from C at a price of 60. A would then import the good from B, and the price in A's home market would be 40. Rather than producing the good itself at a cost of 50 in resources, A will now import a unit of the good for exports using resources costing 40, and so will make a welfare gain. This is an example of *trade creation* – the replacing of relatively high-cost domestic production with lower-cost imports from the partner country.

Now let us assume that before the union A levies a tariff of 50 per cent, and that it is non-discriminatory. Then consumers in A would be faced with a choice between home-produced goods at a price of 50, imports from B at a price of 60, and imports from C at a price of 45. A would import the good from the lower-cost source, country C, and the price in A's home market would be 45.

Suppose again that A and B form a customs union. Consumers in A will be faced with the choice of paying 50 for the home-produced good, 40 for imports from B, and 45 for imports from C. A will now import X from B, and the price in A's market will be 40. Imports will be switched from the low-cost supplier, C to the high-cost supplier, B. A now has to use domestic resources to produce exports with a value of 40 in order to import 1 unit from B, whereas before joining the customs union it only had to produce exports with a value of 30 to import 1 unit from C.

This is an example of *trade diversion*. Trade diversion takes place when a country switches its source of imports from a more efficiently-producing country to a less efficiently-producing country because of the customs union. This will lead to a lowering of welfare, as it entails a less efficient allocation of resources.

In this simple Vinerian model trade creation is always welfare-increasing, while trade diversion always leads to a reduction in welfare. Unfortunately, if we relax the assumption that demand is perfectly price inelastic then this simple one-to-one correspondence disappears. Both trade creation and trade diversion arise because formation of the union leads to a fall in the price faced by consumers in A. If demand is not perfectly inelastic then this fall in price will lead to an increase in consumption, and this is a source of welfare gain. Such consumption gains enhance the welfare-increasing effects of trade creation. They will however offset the welfare-reducing effects of trade diversion, and may even result in trade diversion leading to an increase in welfare.[2]

A further complication is that when we allow the possibility of increasing production costs in A and B then it is quite possible for trade creation and trade diversion to occur simultaneously, since A may import from both B and C before the union is formed.

We may demonstrate these effects with the partial equilibrium model shown in Figure 16.1. We concentrate on one good (the *focus good*), and assume that it is produced under increasing cost conditions by the two countries who will form the customs union. These two countries are large with respect to each other, but small with respect to the rest of the world, so that each can export to or import from the rest of the world at a constant world price (P_w).

The home country, A, is an importer of the good before the union is formed, and the future partner country, B, is a net exporter, but with exports which are less than A's imports. Before the customs union is formed, A imposes a non-discriminatory tariff of t on imports, and this tariff is kept as the common external tariff (CET) of the union. We shall consider a simple case where before union B exports only to A, and after union the two countries combined are self-sufficient at a price P_u between P_w and P_{w+t}.

Before the customs union is formed, country B will have a domestic price equal to the world price P_w, producing q_4, consuming q_3, and exporting a quantity $q_4 - q_3$ to A. (In fact, B would be indifferent between exporting these goods to A or some other country since the same price will be received in either case.)

The pre-union price in country A will be P_{w+t}. Consumption will be q_2 and domestic production q_1, so that A imports $q_2 - q_1$. Of these imports, a quantity $q_5 - q_1$ ($= q_4 - q_3$) will be from B, and the remainder $(q_2 - q_5)$ from the rest of the world.

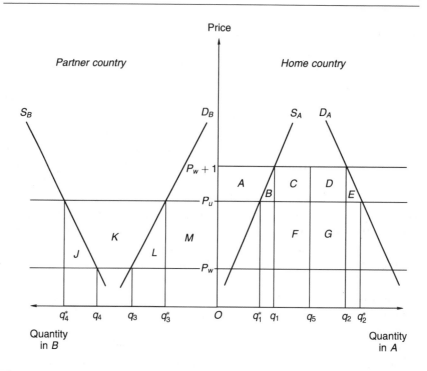

Figure 16.1   *A case with trade diversion and trade creation*

When the customs union is formed there will be no trade with the rest of the world. The minimum tariff-inclusive price at which imports from the rest of the world would be available is P_{w+t}, and union demand can be met wholly from union production at the lower price p_u. The partner country will direct all its exports to the home country. In this market, the partner country's producers will receive a price above the world price and hence will cease supplying the world market.

Formation of the customs union entails adjustments in both member countries. In country A we observe trade creation, trade diversion and an expansion of consumption. The trade creation comes about as an amount $q_1 - q_1^*$ of domestic production is replaced by lower cost imports from B. There is trade diversion as the former low-cost imports from the rest of the world of $q_2 - q_5$ are replaced by more expensive imports from B. Finally, consumption expands by $q_2^* - q_2$ as a consequence of the fall in price.

In the partner country, production expands by $q_4^* - q_4$ and consumption declines by $q_3 - q_3^*$ as a result of the higher price level. The partner country's exports increase from $q_4 - q_3$ to $q_4^* - q_3^*$.

The partner country obtains a net benefit form customs union formation in this case. The producers' surplus gains, shown by the sum of the areas,

K, L and M, outweigh the consumers' surplus losses, shown by areas L and M. The net gain, shown by area K, arises from B's ability to expand its exports and to obtain a higher price for them.

In the home country, the net welfare effect depends on the relative size of the trade creation, trade diversion and consumption effects. The consumers gain is measured by the sum of areas A, B, C, D and E, producers' surplus falls by area A, and tariff revenue by the sum of areas C, D, F and G. The net effect is given by $(B + E) - (F + G)$. Area B represents the Vinerian trade creation effect; area F is a loss on the terms of trade with the partner country; area G is the Vinerian trade diversion loss; and area E is the consumption expansion effect. In terms of this good, country A will lose from the formation of the customs union if the gains from the trade creation and consumption expansion effects are less than the losses from the trade diversion and terms of trade effects.

Other things being equal, the home country is more likely to gain: (a) the nearer the union price is to the world price; (b) the smaller the volume of imports before the union was formed; and (c) the more price responsive are domestic supply and demand.

If country A gains then the customs union as a whole must gain. If country A loses then the union will still gain if B's net gain is greater than country A's net loss. Since the rest of the world is unaffected by the formation of the customs union (the world price does not change), the world as a whole will gain if the union gains, and *vice versa*.

It is not however necessarily the case that the union, and hence the world, will gain. We shall examine the conditions under which the union may be welfare-reducing in the next section, where we also consider the possibility that, whether customs union results in a gain or a loss for country A, there is always a better trade policy that can be pursued.

16.3 A customs union compared with a non-preferential trade policy

Cooper and Massell have argued that there is always a non-preferential tariff policy for country A that is superior to joining a customs union.[3] That is, country A could obtain all the benefits of joining the customs union with country B while avoiding all the losses by imposing the appropriate non-preferential tariff. This is a neat circumvention of the second-best problem.

We may demonstrate the essence of the Cooper and Massell argument in terms of Figure 16.2, which is essentially the same as Figure 16.1. P_u is again the price that would obtain in A and B if they formed a customs union. Country A could however follow another policy that would result in the same price – charging a tariff equal to $P_u - P_w$ on imports from all countries. This non-preferential tariff would therefore give exactly the same gain in consumers' surplus (area $A + B + C + D + E$) and loss in producers' surplus (area A) as the customs union. The old tariff revenue of area $C + D + F + G$ would however be replaced by a new tariff revenue equal to area $U + F + G + V$.

There must be a net welfare gain to country A from this non-preferential tariff reduction, equal to area $B + E + U + V$. This policy brings all the gains that would be given by the customs union (area B and area E) but none of the losses. Country A expands its imports, but continues to import at the world price, so avoiding the trade diversion and terms of trade losses of the customs union.

Note that such a non-preferential tariff reduction by country A does not confer any welfare gains on country B, since B continues to export the same quantity at the ruling world price. It is obvious then that, in this case at least, B would prefer the customs union.

We have taken a particular example of the Cooper and Massell argument, but within the framework used so far it has general validity.

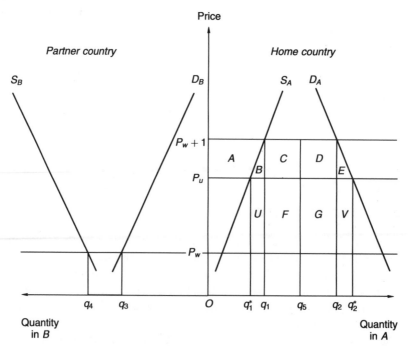

Figure 16.2 *The Cooper and Massell argument*

Cooper and Massell suggest that, analytically, the welfare effects of customs union formation can be split into two components: (a) a non-preferential reduction in the tariff to $P_u - P_w$, and (b) a move from this position to a customs union with the initial tariff as the CET. All the gains from customs union formation come from the first step, and all the losses with the second.

This of course raises the question of why a country such as *A* should choose to join a customs union rather than making the appropriate non-preferential tariff cut. Does a customs union offer some source of gain that will make *A* prefer the union?

◼ *16.4* The export interest

☐ *Customs unions and the export interest*

It might be objected that the preceding analysis is incomplete because it considers the home country only as an importer. For the importer, any trade diversion will involve a terms-of-trade loss, an adverse impact on the welfare of the country. However, this change in the terms of trade was to the benefit of the exporting, partner country. Since each member country in a customs union is likely to have a range of export as well as import goods, the losses through trade diversion on imports might be matched by gains through trade diversion on exports.

If trade diversion losses were mutually offsetting, then – taken over a range of import and export goods – they could be disregarded as netting to zero. This would suggest the basis of an argument in favour of customs union membership rather than unilateral tariff reduction: membership of a customs union presents a means of securing trade creation gains without running into balance-of-payments difficulties. The production gains associated with trade creation arise as resources are reallocated from industries where costs are high at the margin to other industries where costs compare favourably with those of world suppliers.

Remember that we have assumed that resources are fully mobile and that trade is balanced. In practice, however, there may be delays in reallocating resources and increasing exports to match the increased imports from trade creation. Membership of a customs union might then help to balance trade by opening up export markets through trade creation in other countries in the customs union. In a customs union too, exporters can be more confident of continued unrestricted access to markets than in international trade generally: this may make the export adjustment easier than in the case of unilateral tariff reduction.

However, it is not always the case that trade diversion increases welfare in the country which is the exporter within the customs union. Figure 16.3 shows a instance where trade diversion may reduce welfare for both *A* and *B*. The essential difference between the situation shown in Figure 16.3 and that of Figure 16.1 is that here country *B* imports the good (at the world price P_w) before the customs union is established. After customs union formation however, country *B* exports the good to its new partner.

The welfare effects on country *A* are broadly those we have met before. Net welfare is increased by area *B* (the trade creation effect) and area *D* (the consumption effect), but is decreased by area *E* (the trade diversion effect). Forming the customs union will decrease *A*'s welfare if $E > B + D$.

On joining the customs union the price in Country *B* will increase from the world price P_w to the customs union self-sufficiency price P_u. Consumers' surplus in *B* will fall by the sum of the areas *J*, *K*, *L*, *M* and *N*, while producers' surplus will increase by areas *H*, *J* and *K*. The net gain to country *B* is thus $H - (L + M + N)$. A sufficient condition for country *B* to suffer a loss in welfare is that its volume of imports pre-union exceed its volume of exports post-union.

Here then we have a case where both *A* and *B* may lose welfare as a consequence of forming a customs union. It would therefore be unwise to

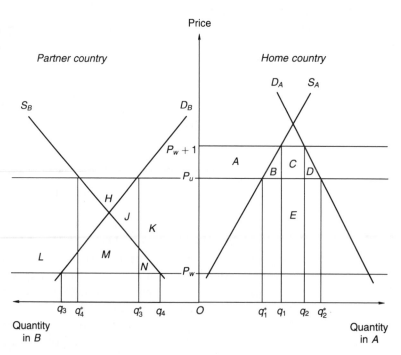

Figure 16.3   *Trade diversion may reduce welfare for both partners*

assume that the effects of trade diversion would, taken over all goods, cancel each other out.

□ *The export interest and third country tariffs*

Paul and Ronald Wonnacott have sought to take further the export argument for customs union membership.[4] The key feature of their argument is that they drop the assumption that the rest of the world does not impose tariffs on imports. The effect of this is that for the two small countries contemplating customs union formation there are two world prices – a price at which they import from the rest of the world and a price at which they can export to them. They are not able to influence either of these prices. Additionally, the Wonnacotts suggest that it may be more realistic to take account of transport costs in trade with the third country. These costs would strengthen the separation of the world export and import prices. Zero transport cost are still assumed on trade between the partner countries on the ground that customs union members are generally geographically close together.

The Wonnacotts point out that in a tariff-ridden world it is most unrealistic to assume that only the customs union member countries have tariffs. Until now we have followed the standard assumption in the literature that the third (non-member) country is so large that it is indifferent to trade with the customs union countries, and since its welfare is unaffected by any such trade there is no economic reason for imposing tariffs. Thus if we are going to resort to the large-country assumption then we must also assume that this country imposes no tariffs.

The Wonnacotts suggest that there may be an alternative assumption implicit in much of the literature which would also suggest a single international price: that 'there are many outside countries operating in a highly-competitive international market place, [so that] the tariffs of each of these countries will fall completely on their own consumers, and will have no effect on international prices at all'. A supporting argument for the Wonnacotts' view that account should be taken of tariffs in the rest of the world is that third countries may be large in relation to the focus good, but not in relation to all other goods. From a tariff-bargaining position, therefore, third countries might impose tariffs on the focus good in order to negotiate tariff concessions from their trading partners.

The chief contribution of the Wonnacotts' analysis is to show that in a tariff-ridden world there are some welfare gains from customs union membership that cannot be secured through unilateral non-preferential tariff reductions. These gains arise where the exporting member of the customs union is a low-cost producer, but prior to customs union formation could not fully exploit its comparative advantage because of the tariffs imposed by other countries.

A simplified version of the Wonnacotts' argument may be illustrated with reference to Figure 16.4. Two world prices are shown: an import price, P_M, and an export price, P_X. The higher price (P_M) is the market price in the third country and is the price which must be paid for imports from that country. Exports to the third country receive a price of only P_X, because they are subject to a tariff of $(P_X - P_M)$.

Before the customs union is formed, country A imposes a non-preferential tariff on imports of $P_A - P_B$, and imports only from country B. The price levels are then P_A in A and P_B in B. Country A produces q_1, consumes q_2 and imports $q_2 - q_1$. Country B produces q_4, exports $q_4 - q_3$ $(= q_2 - q_1)$, and consumes the remainder, q_3.

The formation of the customs union will result in a common price level of P_U, at which price the customs union is exactly self-sufficient. Consumers in country A will secure a gain of $A + B + C + D$ in consumers' surplus, which will exceed the loss of producers' surplus (A) by an amount $B + C + D$. Tariff revenue in country A falls by $C + E$, which means that the net welfare outcome for A is, in general,

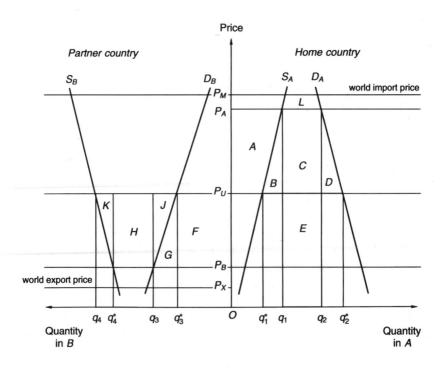

Figure 16.4 *The Wonnacotts' analysis*

indeterminate at $B + D - E$. In country B, producers' surplus rises by $F + G + H + J + K$ and consumers' surplus falls by $F + G$ in consequence of the price rise, leaving a net gain of $H + J + K$. These changes are similar to those we have met before.

For the customs union as a whole, though, the outcome in the case shown *must* be beneficial since the only negative term in country A's welfare change, E, is exactly equal to part of B's welfare gain, H. The net gain for the customs union is $B + D + J + K$.

The Wonnacotts' rebuttal of the Cooper and Massell argument hinges on the presence of third-country tariffs (and/or transport costs) driving a wedge between the price at which the customs union members can buy and the price at which they can sell on the world market. The emphasis is on securing better access to export markets through reciprocal concessions in the home market. Tariffs are not cut unilaterally – even though in some cases this might appear advantageous – because they can be used as bargaining counters to reduce the tariff barriers in export markets. In a customs union, welfare losses on import goods may be accepted in exchange for larger gains on export goods. The new analysis seems to provide a much better insight into tariff negotiations in the real world, and in particular into the process of customs union formation.

Note that the Wonnacotts do not argue that customs union membership will always be welfare-improving in the presence of third-country tariffs, only that a country *may* be able to secure gains on its exports in a customs union which are unobtainable by unilateral tariff action.

16.5 Setting the common external tariff to avoid trade diversion

Kemp and Wan have argued that for any customs union there is a set of CETs that will leave the members as a group *and* the rest of the world at least as well off as they were before the formation of the union.[5] If the union as a whole is better off then it follows that a system of lump-sum transfers between the members will allow each member to be better off. A simple partial equilibrium representation of the Kemp and Wan result is given in Figure 16.5.

In Figure 16.5 the left-hand diagram shows the excess demand curve for country H (ED_H) and the excess supply curve for country P (ES_P), the two countries that will form the union. ES'_P is the excess supply curve for country P in terms of prices in H's market when P's exports are subject to H's (non-preferential) pre-union tariff.

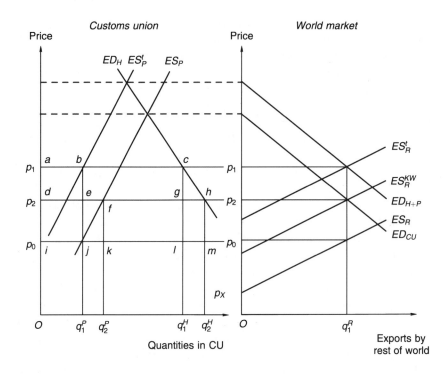

Figure 16.5   *A CET that avoids trade diversion*

In the right-hand diagram ES_R is the excess supply curve for the rest of the world in terms of world prices, and ES_R^t that excess supply curve in terms of H's prices, when the rest-of-the-world exporters are faced by H's pre-union tariff. ED_{H+P} is the net excess demand from H and P before the union is formed (i.e. the horizontal difference between ED_H and ES_P^t).

The pre-union equilibrium is given by the intersection of ED_{H+P} and ES_R^t. The price in H will be P_1, with H importing q_1^H, of which q_1^P will come from P, and q_1^R from the rest of the world. The price in P and the rest of the world will be P_0.

Suppose now that H and P form the customs union, so that the excess supply curve for goods from P to H's market becomes ES_P, and the excess demand from the union facing the rest-of-the-world exporters shifts to ED_{CU}. If the union were to adopt H's initial tariff as its CET then exports by the rest of the world would fall (as shown by the intersection of ED_{CU} and ES_R^t), and there would be trade diversion.

In order to avoid trade diversion the union must impose a CET on imports from the rest of the world that will maintain those imports at their pre-union level, q_1^R. The tariff that will achieve this is that which makes

ES_R^{KW} the rest of the world's tariff-inclusive excess supply curve. The price within the union will now be P_2, with H importing a quantity q_2^H, of which q_2^P comes from P and q_1^R from the rest of the world.

Since the rest of the world is exporting the same quantity as before the union (and is receiving the same price, P_0), its welfare must be unchanged.

Country H will experience a gain in consumers' surplus, but losses in both producers' surplus and tariff revenue. The net change in consumers' and producers' surpluses is shown by area *achd*. The loss in tariff revenue on imports from P is area *abji*. The pre-union tariff revenue on imports from the rest of the world was *bclj*, while the post-union revenue on imports from the rest of the world is *fhmk*. Since, however, area *eglj* = area *fhmk*, it is evident that the net loss in tariff revenue on imports from the rest of the world is equal to area *bcge*. Areas *abed* and *bcge* are transfers from tariff revenue to consumers. The net gain for H is therefore area *chg* less area *deji*; we may interpret the latter area as a terms-of-trade loss for H, its partner being the beneficiary. H may gain or lose from adopting the non-trade-diverting common external tariff.

P must however make a net gain compared with its pre-union position, since it is a net exporter and the price it receives for its exports has increased from P_0 to P_2. The gain for P (the difference between the gains for its producers and the losses for its consumers) is area *dfji*.

It follows that the union as a whole must be better off, since area *deji*, the terms-of-trade loss for H, is part of the net gain made by P. The net gain for the union as a whole is given by area *chg* plus area *efj*.

Kemp and Wan argue that an interesting corollary to the proposition is that it implies that there is an incentive to form and enlarge customs unions until the world is one big customs union – that is, until there is free trade.

16.6 Customs unions when there are economies of scale

Another assumption made in the standard analysis that has frequently been challenged is that of rising marginal costs in the home and partner countries. It has been claimed that some industries are characterised by falling marginal (and, hence, average) costs over a wide range of output, and that some national markets might be too small to absorb the output of a plant of optimum size. Membership of a customs union would offer access to a larger market tariff-free and would enable produces to operate at lower average costs.

Viner qualified his arguments about the effects of customs union formation with reference to economies of scale. He conceded that, in a tariff-ridden world, cost-reduction might be achieved through customs union membership, but suggested that 'It does not seem probable that the prospects of reduction in unit-costs of production as the result of enlargement of the tariff area are ordinarily substantial, even when the individual member countries are quite small in economic size'.[6]

Viner further argued that 'There is a possibility – though not, as is generally taken for granted in the literature, a certainty – that if the unit-cost of production falls as the result of the enlarged protected market consequent upon customs union there will be a gain from customs union for one of the members, for both the members, and/or for the union as a whole, but there is also a possibility – and often a probability – that there will be a loss in each case'.

Corden has investigated the welfare implications of customs union formation in the presence of economies of scale, and the following section draws on his analysis.[7] The assumptions on which the analysis is based are similar to those used earlier in this chapter, but with the following amendments:

(a) there is a single actual or potential producer in each of the union countries, who has a declining average cost curve and who pays constant prices for his factors of production whatever the scale of output (there are thus no factor rents);

(b) the price at which exports from the home and partner country could be sold to the third-country market (export price) is below the price at which third-country imports are available to the home and partner countries (import price) because of: (i) transport costs, and (ii) the third country's tariff;

(c) the average cost curve in each country is assumed to reach its minimum at a level above the export price, so that exporting the product to the third country is ruled out;

(d) pre-customs union, the home and partner countries do not trade with each other because of tariffs and the relatively high production costs.

Consider Figure 16.6 which, in order to simplify the analysis, has been drawn to reflect some specific assumptions. For the producer in the home country to operate profitably, the average cost curve must cut, or at least touch, the effective demand (average revenue) curve facing the producer. Pre-customs union, this curve is given by $TQRVYZ$ since: (a) no market exists for the home product at a price in excess of T, the tariff-inclusive price of third-country supplies; (b) below this price, the entire home market is available to home producer; (c) at price P_m, home producers can capture the partner country market ($q_2 - q_1 = q_3$ at the tariff-inclusive price T); and (d) the third-country market can absorb the entire home production at price P_x. We could construct a similar effective demand

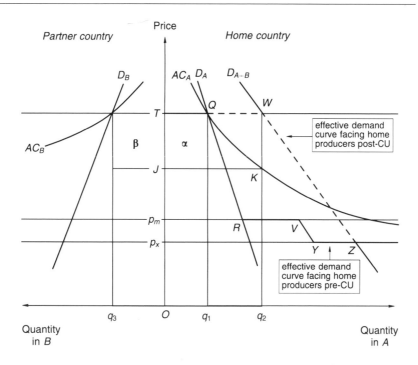

Figure 16.6 *Customs union formation when both countries have decreasing cost industries initially*

curve for the producer in the partner country. As drawn, the producer in each country can break-even whilst supplying all the requirements of his domestic market at price T.

Now consider the welfare effects of forming a customs union between the home and partner countries. These will depend on the pre-customs union production pattern. We will distinguish three cases: where both countries have a producer pre-customs union; where only one country has a producer pre-customs union; and where neither country has a producer pre-customs union. The way in which the costs and benefits of customs union formation are shared will also depend on which country supplies the integrated market after union.

The first case will be discussed using Figure 16.6. Both countries are initially self-sufficient at price T, this price being maintained by the tariff $T - P_m$. Remember that in both countries the price is (by design) just high enough to allow the domestic producers to cover their average costs before the formation of the customs union.

When the customs union is formed, one or other of the firms will leave the market. We shall assume that it is the firm in the partner country which leaves. The customs union maintains a tariff on imports from the rest of the world of $T - P_m$ so that the price within the customs union remains at OT. The firm in the home country will meet the whole of the customs union demand. It will produce q_2, selling q_1 at home as before and exporting $q_2 - q_1$ ($= q_3$) to the partner country. The average cost of production in the home country firm falls from T to J as a result of the expansion in output.

The firm now makes excess profits shown by the area $JTWK$, which is of course equal to area α + area β. There is no change in consumers' surplus in the home country, and there is no tariff revenue in that country either before or after the customs union is formed, so welfare in the home country must have increased by area α + area β. There is no consumers' surplus change in the partner country either (the same price prevails), there was no tariff revenue (no imports) before the customs union and there is none after it is formed, and the firm which has just left the market was making no producer's surplus, so the welfare position in the partner country is unchanged. It follows that the customs union as a whole must gain.

In the second case the partner country has no domestic firm, and imports from the rest of the world at price P_m. The analysis is simplified by assuming that, before the customs union is formed, the partner country levies a tariff of $T - P_m$, so that the domestic price is T. This case is covered by Figure 16.7.

The welfare analysis for the home country is exactly the same as in the previous case. The home country gains area α + area β. The partner country experiences trade diversion however, since the quantity q_3 previously imported from the rest of the world at price P_m is now imported from the partner at price T. There is no change in consumers' surplus in the partner country, since the price faced by those consumers is unchanged. Obviously there can be no producer surplus effects either. The loss to the partner country consists of the increase in the cost of imports, this being measured by the loss in tariff revenue, i.e. area β + area γ. The net welfare gain for the customs union is therefore (area α + area β) − (area β + area γ) = area α − area γ.

It is possible, though unlikely, that after the customs union was formed a new producer could become established in the partner country where previously none existed, and that this producer could capture the whole union market, leading to the closure of the home country producer ('production reversal'). The consequences for the home country would then be similar to those described for the partner country in the first case that is a zero net welfare effect. For the partner country, with its newly established industry, there would be a loss of tariff revenue $(\beta + \gamma)$ previously collected on imports, but a gain for producers of excess profits

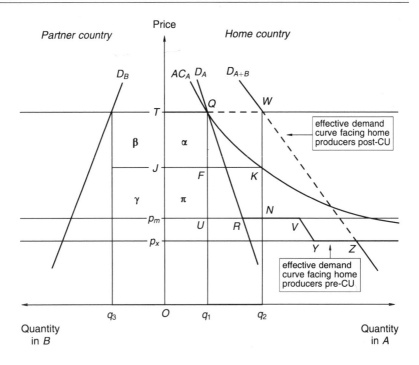

Figure 16.7 *Customs union formation when only one country has a decreasing cost industry initially*

on home sales (β) and on exports to the home country (α). The net welfare effect is thus $(\alpha + \beta) - (\beta + \gamma) = \alpha - \gamma$. The partner would be more likely to gain:

(i) the larger the cost reduction achieved in the customs union market, and
(ii) the larger the share of exports in total production.

In the final case, neither country has a producer pre-customs union, but a producer establishes in one of them (say the home country) post-customs union, protected by a CET of $T - P_m$. This possibility may be analysed in terms of Figure 16.8.

The new firm in the home country will produce q_2, selling q_1 at home and exporting $q_2 - q_1$ to the partner country. The home country loses its former tariff revenue (area α + area π), but gains the excess profits of area α + area β. The home country will therefore make an overall gain if area β > area π, a loss otherwise. The partner country loses its tariff revenue of area β + area γ, and there are no compensating gains since its domestic price is unchanged. The customs union as a whole must lose, the loss being

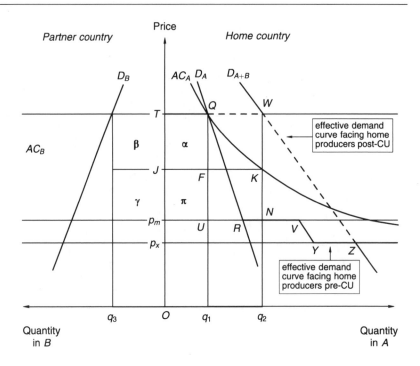

Figure 16.8 *Customs union formation when neither country has a decreasing cost industry initially*

area γ + area π. We may regard the customs union loss (and of course the partner country's loss) as a trade-diversion effect.

The welfare effects in the cases described may be summarised as follows: from the point of view of the union as a whole, the direction of welfare change depends on the change in the number of producers. If there are fewer producers in the union than previously, welfare will increase, if there are more, welfare will decline. If there is a single producer before and after union, the welfare outcome is uncertain: it is more likely to increase: (a) the greater is the cost reduction achieved in the larger market; and (b) the smaller is the trade-diversion effect in the non-producing country.

☐ *Made-to-measure tariffs*

The analysis, following Corden, has thus far assumed that the customs union tariff rate is the same as the pre-customs union national tariff rate. The union producer was thus able to receive excess profits through lowering costs in the larger union market. The customs union authorities might however decide to fix the CET such that the union price just covers the average costs of the producer, so eliminating the rents identified in the earlier analysis (the 'made-to-measure' tariff). In this situation, the benefits of customs union formation would accrue not to the producer in the form of excess profits but to the consumers as an increase in consumers' surplus. Consumption would increase (through trade creation) in countries which had production pre-customs union; but consumption would fall where trade diversion occurred as higher-cost (and higher-priced to consumers) partner supplies displaced low-cost world supplies.

∎ *16.7* Intra-industry trade and customs union formation

As we noted in Chapter 8 on theories of intra-industry trade, a considerable part of the expansion of trade between the original members of the EEC was intra-industry in form. Although there are many models of intra-industry trade, there have been rather few attempts to apply them to the customs union problem. We can however gain some insight into the possibility of trade creation gains from intra-industry trade by considering a simple model based on the Neo-Chamberlinian model of Chapter 8.[8]

Assume that the two (developed) countries that will form the customs union, *H* and *P*, each produce a homogeneous good (food) and a differentiated good (manufactures). Variants of the manufactured good are all equally imperfect substitutes for one another, and are produced under homothetically increasing returns to scale. Both export their own varieties of the manufactured good to each other and to the rest of the world, *W*, which produces only food. Food is produced under constant returns to scale, and is imported by the two developed countries from the rest of the world.

The analysis is simplified by assuming that *H* and *P* have the same tariffs on imports of food and manufactures before forming the customs union, with that tariff becoming the CET. The rest of the world is assumed to impose no restrictions on imports of manufactures.

In such a case the formation of the customs union cannot cause trade diversion, since the customs union countries export only manufactures to each other and do not import manufactures from the rest of the world. There will however be trade creation, yielding gains which parallel those discussed in Chapter 8. Consumers in each country will now have (tariff-free) access to a greater variety of goods, and will gain from consuming that greater variety.

16.8 When will a customs union increase welfare?

Our analysis suggests that if a customs union primarily leads to trade creation, it will lead to an increase in welfare for its members, and that if it primarily gives rise to trade diversion, it may lead to a lowering of that welfare. In the latter case, it will certainly lead to a lowering in the welfare of the third country (the rest of the world). More sophisticated models suggest that there is some ambiguity in these results, but that in general terms trade creation will be superior to trade diversion. Economists have therefore answered the basic question (whether a customs union will increase welfare) by identifying the factors which are likely to promote trade creation rather than trade diversion.

The first group of factors is concerned with the degree of overlap between the bundles of goods which the member countries produce before joining the union. If there is no overlap between these bundles (as might be the case if an agricultural country joined a manufacturing country) then there is no scope for trade creation but a considerable possibility of trade diversion. On the other hand, if there is considerable overlap then there is scope for both inter-industry and intra-industry trade creation. Conversely, the less the overlap between the union members and the rest of the world, the lower will be the scope for trade diversion.

The second group concerns differences in production costs between countries in industries which they have in common. The greater the difference in costs between member countries, the greater will be the gains which can be made from trade creation. On the other hand, the smaller the difference in costs between the lowest-cost union producer and the lowest-cost non-union producer, the lower will be the losses from trade diversion.

The third group are the 'tariff factors'. The higher the tariffs charged before the union on goods in which there will be trade creation, the higher will be the gains. The lower the pre-union tariffs on goods in which there will be trade diversion, and the lower the CET on those goods after union, the lower will be the losses from trade diversion.

It is tempting to suggest a fourth factor: that the more countries there are within the customs union, the more likely it is to be welfare-increasing. The argument used for this factor is that the more countries there are within the union, the more likely it is that the union will include the lowest-cost producer(s) of each good, and so the less likely it is that there will be trade diversion. The argument is not particularly convincing, having something in common with the fallacy we noted at the start of this chapter. We could of course assume that those countries forming the union take care to select partners in such a way as to ensure that the lowest-cost producer is within the union, or at least that there is only a small difference in efficiency between the low-cost union producer and the lowest-cost non-union producer, but that does not have the status of a general principle.

◼ 16.9 Customs unions and the terms of trade

The models discussed in this chapter reflect the dominant tradition of the literature on customs unions in that they have been exclusively 'small-country' models. Neither the individual countries in the customs union nor the union as a whole is able to affect world prices. One important implication is that in most cases the member countries' imports come entirely from the rest of the world before the union is formed, and exclusively from the partner country afterwards.[9] This precludes an important effect that may influence the decision of countries on whether to form or join a customs union: the possibility of making a terms of trade gain on their reduced trade with the rest of the world.

Mundell, in his analysis of the terms of trade effects of customs union formation,[10] notes that 'a [discriminatory] tariff reduction in a member country unambiguously improves the terms of trade of the partner country'. The implications may be summarised as follows.

Suppose that the two countries forming the customs union (H and P) are large with respect to each other and to the rest of the world (W). On forming the customs union, H will discriminate in favour of P in some goods, and this will improve P's terms of trade with both H and W. At the same time, P discriminates in favour of H in other goods, which will improve H's terms of trade with both P and W. The net effect on the terms of trade between the two member countries is indeterminate, but the effect on the terms of trade facing W is unambiguous: the rest of the world must suffer a terms-of-trade loss on its trade with the customs union. That of course means that the customs union as a whole must gain on its (reduced) trade with the rest of the world, but we cannot tell whether both H and P will gain, or whether one will gain and the other lose.

Another possible source of gain arising from the size of the customs union is in the area of international policy-making. A group of countries that are individually unable to exert much influence may be able to do so if they can present a united front to the rest of the world. Membership of a customs union is one way of achieving such a goal. The individual member country may be large enough within the customs union to influence the union's policy stance, and the customs union may be large enough to influence decision-making at the global level.

■ *16.10* Dynamic considerations

It has been argued that there are other important effects of a 'dynamic' kind that are ignored in the standard static models of customs union formation. One such argument is that a customs union will lead to enforced competition and thus increased efficiency, better investment decisions, and so on. This argument was applied to the formation of the original EEC, and was the subject of much debate before Britain joined.[11]

A counter-argument is that greater gains could be made by making non-discriminatory tariff reductions rather than by joining a customs union, and in particular that a policy of free trade would generate greater competitive pressure than would exist within the protected market of a customs union. It is possible however that the greater certainty about future policy coming from membership of a customs union outweighs these disadvantages.

■ *16.11* Other barriers to trade

As we noted earlier, non-tariff barriers are an important impediment to trade. They must therefore be taken into consideration when discussing the effects of customs union. We may conveniently consider them under two headings: those directly affecting trade between the members, and those erected against imports from the rest of the world.

The elimination of non-tariff barriers to trade should be an integral part of the formation of a customs union. Where these barriers are reasonably visible, as would be the case with quotas, then their removal should be straightforward. Others are however more difficult both to identify and to remove, such as differences in safety requirements for motor vehicles, specifications of pharmaceutical products, and so on. Harmonisation of such requirements within the union will remove the barrier to internal trade, but may also be used to create a barrier to imports from the rest of the world.

Non-tariff barriers on imports from outside the union may, if not harmonised, lead to barriers to the free movement of goods within the union. Suppose for example that before union each member country has negotiated its own voluntary export restraint (VER) with an external supplier of a particular good. If these VERs lead to different prices for that good in the members' markets, and they are maintained after the union, then the members face three options. If they do nothing then the VERs in the more restrictive countries will be circumvented by firms or individuals buying the good in the less restricted markets and selling it in the more restricted markets. An alternative is for the countries with the more restrictive VERs to operate border controls on imports of that good from partner countries. The third alternative (preferable in this second-best situation) is for the members of the union to negotiate a common VER with the non-union supplier, as they must do with their CET.

Government policies may also create barriers to the free movement of goods within a customs union. Such policies may consist of giving preference to domestic suppliers in government purchases, of providing subsidies or advantageous taxation allowances to domestic producers, and so on. They may also encompass differences in the way in which, for example, cartels are treated. The recognition of the problems caused may lead to harmonisation of policies, or to the establishment of a common policy (as in the case of the European Communities competition and agricultural policies). This however leads us along the road from the customs union to the common market, which we shall discuss next.

■ 16.12 Higher levels of economic integration

A *common market* may be defined as a customs union which also allows the free movement of factors of production between member countries.[12] Labour would be able to move within the market, while firms could establish in any country within the union, and could obtain finance from the capital market in any member country. The causes of such movements, and the gains from them, would be identical with those discussed in Chapters 21 and 22.

Barriers to the free movement of factors of production may be more complex than those restricting the movement of goods. Some, of course, are simple to identify and to eliminate, such as requirements for work and residence permits for labour and of registration for companies. Others come from differences in such institutional arrangements as state pensions, unemployment benefits, health services and so on, which can usually be resolved by the granting of equivalent rights to nationals of partner countries. A notably difficult issue in EC negotiations has been the recognition by one country of qualifications obtained in another.

Free trade in services within a common market may be difficult to achieve, particularly when it involves the different legal systems likely to operate within the market. An extreme example would be a resident in country *A* who has the misfortune to be in an accident with a motorist from country *B* who has insured himself with a company based in country *C*. If the motorist and/or the insurers deny responsibility, in which country should the country *A* resident pursue his claim?

In practice, it may be difficult to establish a common market without considerable harmonisation of government policies in areas other than those explicitly concerned with the movement of goods and factors of production within the market. We referred to such problems earlier in the context of non-tariff barriers to trade. Maintaining a common market requires that trade is seen by the member countries to be 'fair' as well as 'free'.

The 'highest' form of economic integration is so-called *(complete) economic union*. This involves the complete unification of monetary and fiscal policies, probably with the creation of a common currency. We shall discuss the costs and benefits of establishing a common currency in Chapters 30 and 31. Finally, we should note, though we will not discuss, the argument that economic union may (perhaps should) lead to *political union*.

■ *16.13* Empirical findings

Empirical studies of the effects of customs union formation may be considered under two main headings: those that concentrate on the effects on the level and composition of trade flows, and those that then attempt to estimate the associated welfare effects.[13]

The earliest empirical studies, such as that by the Dutch economist Verdoorn (later used and commentated upon by Scitovsky[14]) suggested that the gains to be obtained from customs union formation were relatively small. Verdoorn, for instance, estimated that trade between the countries of the EEC would increase by 17 per cent. The estimated welfare effect of the prospective union amounted to about one-twentieth of 1 per cent of the sum of the national incomes of the original six countries. Such early studies were, of course, conducted before the EEC had come into being or before the transitional period in which the members adapted to the new state of affairs was completed.

Subsequent studies, with the benefit of data from periods before and after the formation of the EEC, have tended to give rather larger estimates, though with considerable variation between studies. For example, Truman estimated that by 1964, when the reduction of internal tariffs was 60 per cent complete, intra-EEC trade was something like 30 per cent higher than it would have been if the EEC had not been created.[15] Moreover, he found that this increase in the share of consumption held by other EEC producers had been achieved without any net diversion of trade from the rest of the world. The share of imports from non-EEC sources had in fact risen. This external trade creation was explained by Truman as the result of tariff-cutting by former high-tariff countries to the level of the common external tariff being in excess of trade diversion which mainly occurred in the former low-tariff countries.

Williamson and Bottrill lend support to Truman's estimate for trade creation for 1964 and conclude that by 1969 intra-EEC trade was something like 50 per cent higher than it otherwise would have been without the EEC.[16] They attribute most of this increase to trade creation rather than diversion with the harm being done to other countries' exports by diversion being largely offset by positive external trade creation. Nevertheless, the more recent studies still yield estimates of welfare changes that are small.

Hine notes that there is some empirical support for the argument that the member countries that had high tariffs before joining the EEC tended to experience trade creation, while those that had low tariffs suffered mainly trade diversion.[17] He also comments that attempts to identify the 'EEC effect' on a sectoral basis have yielded frequently conflicting results, but that there is some evidence that trade diversion occurred for foodstuffs, chemicals and possibly textiles, and that there was trade creation in the machinery sector.

Finally, studies by Balassa and by Grubel and Lloyd have highlighted the growing importance of intra-industry trade within the EEC.[18] Grubel and Lloyd, for example, estimated that 71 per cent of the increase in trade between the members was intra-industry.

■ *16.14* Summary and conclusions

We finish this chapter by summarising some of the main results of the theory of customs unions. The basic conclusion is that it is impossible to pass any judgement on customs unions in general. Having said this, we find that the basic concepts of the theory are those of trade creation and trade diversion. Trade creation will lead to an improvement of welfare, whereas trade diversion generally leads to a lowering of welfare.

A question that must be asked of all customs unions is why a system of discriminatory tariff reductions (in favour of the partners) has been preferred to non-discriminatory reductions. We have seen that arguments can be made for the customs union in terms of possibly greater stability in the policy environment, possible terms of trade gains, gains from increasing the power of members in the formulation of global trade policy, economies of scale, and perhaps dynamic effects.

A customs union is more likely to lead to an increase in welfare if the union partners are actually competitive but potentially complementary. The larger the cost differentials between the countries of the union in goods they both produce, the larger is the scope for gains. The higher the initial tariffs between the union partners, the greater is the scope for an increase in welfare. The lower the tariffs to the outside world, the smaller are the losses on trade diversion. The larger the part of trade originally covered by trade between the union partners, the greater is the scope for gains from the union.

The empirical evidence on gains from the formation of the European Community is not conclusive. The net gains, if any, seem likely to be small.

☐ *Notes*

*   I am grateful to my colleague, Bob Hine, with whom I have shared the teaching of customs union theory for many years. His survey of the theory, in Greenaway and Winters (1993), both extends and deepens the material presented in this Chapter.

1   Viner (1953).

2   There is some confusion in the literature over the use of the terms 'trade creation' and 'trade diversion'. Some writers use them to refer to the outcomes in which the source of supply shifts, respectively, from high-cost domestic to lower-cost partner sources, and from low-cost non-partner to higher-cost partner sources. Such writers then accept that trade diversion may be welfare-increasing. Others identify trade creation and trade diversion as the supply-side effects of union, which is closer to the original Vinerian approach, so that trade diversion is necessarily welfare-reducing, but add on in each case the *consumption effect*.

3   Cooper and Massell (1965).

4   Wonnacott and Wonnacott (1981).

5   Kemp and Wan (1976). Kemp and Wan cite the proof of the proposition for the standard three-country, two-good case in Vanek (1965).

6   Quoted in Robson (1972).

7   Corden (1972).

8   The model used is a simplified version of that suggested in Ethier and Horn (1984).

9   For a more detailed discussion of this issue see Pomfret (1986), Section 3.

10   Mundell (1964).

11   For an early discussion of the dynamic effects of customs union formation, see Scitovsky (1958).

12   For a discussion of the various forms of economic integration, see El-Agraa (1985).

13   For a discussion of the methodological problems see Mayes (1978). For a survey of studies on the effect on Britain of joining the European Community, see Winters (1987).

14   Scitovsky (1958).

15   Truman (1969).

16   Williamson and Bottrill (1971).

17   Hine (1985).

18   Balassa (1975).

■ *Chapter 17* ■

The General Agreement on Tariffs and Trade

■ *17.1* Introduction

In the period between the First and Second World Wars there was a marked deterioration in international economic relations. In the 1920s an attempt was made to go back to 'normal' conditions. This meant the gold standard, as far as international monetary co-operation is concerned. An attempt was also made to organise world trade on a liberal basis.

This system did not function well. Great Britain, for instance, had difficulties because of an overvalued currency, and(when the depression came at the beginning of the 1930s, the system broke down. Competitive devaluations followed, and trade restrictions were introduced.) Many countries retreated towards an autarkic pattern of production, and trade on a bilateral basis was introduced.

At the end of the Second World War the memory of the inter-war period was still fresh. When the victorious countries (especially Britain and the United States) started to plan for new, more viable relations in the international economy, they were determined to avoid the mistakes of the past. (The Bretton Woods conference (named after the meeting place, Bretton Woods, New Hampshire) held in 1944 was the starting-point for a new order. The world economy was to be organised around three cornerstones: the International Monetary Fund (IMF), the International Trade Organization (ITO), and the International Bank for Reconstruction and Development (IBRD).)

The IMF was designed to take care of short-term problems in connection with international liquidity. It would help to smooth out and to resolve difficulties that the participant countries would have with their balances of payments. The ITO, on the other hand, would deal with the 'real' side of trading relations. It would help to create a liberal system of regulations governing world trade; it would, in the long run, be the vehicle that carried the world toward a system of free trade. The IBRD would help to channel international investments along desired lines. Initially, it was intended to aid in post-war reconstruction. Over time it became the principal agency for helping the less-developed countries (LDCs) to get capital from the more developed, industrial countries.

Attempts at guiding the world economy have met with varying degrees of success. The problems of international liquidity will be discussed in Chapter 31. The debate about trade policy has been, and remains, intense. Protectionist tendencies among the industrial countries have been checked reasonably successfully, although the replacement of tariffs by non-tariff barriers, complaints about the trade-distorting effects of 'domestic' policies, concerns about policies affecting the growing volume and value of trade in services, preferences for developing countries, restrictions on foreign direct investment (FDI), and international recognition of 'intellectual property rights' are on-going problems. The long-running saga of the Uruguay Round of the GATT, which will be discussed later, is the clearest indication that there is still considerable friction between countries over trade issues.

▌ 17.2 The origins, objectives and structure of the GATT

☐ *The International Trade Organization and the GATT*

In 1946, while negotiations on the charter of the ITO were taking place, a group of countries came to a consensus that there was a need for immediate tariff reductions. The United States took an initiative in preparing a document on a general agreement on tariffs and trade. Subsequent deliberations between the group of 23 nations, meeting in Geneva, resulted in a set of mutual tariff reductions which were codified as the GATT. The agreement was intended to be a 'stepping stone' *en route* to the establishment of the ITO, and embodied many of the principles and commitments in the proposed charter.

In the event, the International Trade Organization never came into existence. A conference in Havana in 1947–48 did establish a charter for the ITO (the 'Havana Charter'). However, disagreements between the United States and Britain over the extent of the authority of the proposed ITO over the actions of governments prevented the ratification of the charter; in particular, it was never ratified by the US Senate. No other country would ratify it either, and thus the ITO was never established.

This left the GATT as the framework for trade relations.[1] The GATT Secretariat, with headquarters in Geneva, was a less ambitious organisation than would have been the ITO. It embodied, however, many of the principles that would have formed the basis of the ITO. In particular, the member countries of GATT were to meet in Geneva and negotiate multilaterally (rather than bilaterally) on matters of trade policy. It was also to act as a forum for the settlement of disputes between nations.

The failure to establish the ITO provides an early indication of the influence of the United States in the operation of the post-war international trading system. The structure of the GATT and the timing and progress of negotiations are, as we shall see at various points in this chapter, closely linked to the role of the United States as the dominant trading country and to the domestic political processes governing the ability of the US President to negotiate on trade matters.

Today 100 countries are 'contracting parties' (signatories) to the GATT, accounting for some 80 per cent of world trade. An additional 29 countries have agreed to abide by the GATT rules until such time as they establish their own trade policies.[2] China, Taiwan and the former USSR are not however members.

☐ *The objectives of the GATT*

There seem to have been the three basic objectives behind the establishment of the GATT, all of which may be explained by the desire of the signatories to reverse the move towards protectionism in the 1930s and to prevent such a move being repeated. First, it was to provide a framework for the conduct of trade relations. Second, it was to provide a framework for, and to promote, the progressive elimination of trade barriers. Third, it was to provide a set of rules (codes of conduct) that would inhibit countries from taking unilateral action.

It has been successful in meeting the first two objectives, most notably in securing substantial reductions in tariffs, although it has been claimed, as we shall see later, that the reductions have been concentrated on trade in industrial goods between the developed countries, and there is concern about the proliferation of non-tariff barriers. Its success in dissuading countries from unilateral action has been less clear. The recent actions of the United States in taking unilateral action against countries that, it alleges, are trading 'unfairly' with the United States provide the most obvious example of failure.

☐ *The structure of the GATT*

The Agreement takes the form of 38 'Articles', organised into four 'Parts'.[3] Part I (Articles I and II) deals with the obligations of the contracting parties. Part II (Articles III – XXIII) provides the code for 'fair' trade, such as various technical procedures and conditions under which tariffs may be employed (e.g. anti-dumping, for balance of payments reasons, to safeguard domestic industry). Part III (Articles XXIV–XXXV) details the procedures for the application and amendment of the Agreement. Part IV (an amendment under Part III made in 1965) contains Articles XXXVI–XXXVIII, which deal with the trade of LDCs.

Negotiations under the GATT take the form of 'Rounds', of which the Uruguay Round is the eighth. These negotiations are multilateral in that all contracting parties meet at the same time but, in the early Rounds at least, concessions were agreed on a bilateral basis between major trading partners. The procedures governing the bilateral negotiations, and the manner in which these are transformed into multilateral agreements, are the subject of the basic principles of the GATT.

■ *17.3* **The principles of the GATT**

☐ *Non-Discrimination*

The basic principle of GATT is that of *non-discrimination*, contained in Article I. Contracting parties accept the so-called *most-favoured-nation* (MFN) clause. This means that a country agrees not to give better treatment to any single nation than it gives to all the contracting parties of GATT. The MFN clause rules out any preferential treatment among nations as far as trade policy is concerned, except *vis-à-vis* those not members of the GATT or as allowed under other Articles (e.g. Article XXIV). That is, if any country gives preferential tariff access to any other country (so that the latter becomes the most-favoured nation) then that concession must be extended immediately to all other countries, so that all contracting parties benefit to the same extent. Conversely, if action is taken by one country to protect a domestic industry (say by imposing a quota) then that action must applied to all GATT members.

The MFN principle is essential if bilaterally-negotiated tariff reductions are to be transformed into multilateral reductions. It does not of course apply only in the case of bilateral negotiations. If, as happened in later Rounds, a 'formula' can be agreed for tariff reductions then the MFN clause requires that formula to be applied without discrimination to all contracting parties.

There are however many 'GATT-legal' exceptions to the MFN clause, such as free trade areas, customs unions and other regional groupings, preferences offered to developing countries and to subgroups of those countries, and trade in textiles and clothing.

The MFN clause has played an important part in encouraging countries to negotiate on trade liberalisation. They know that any deal that they negotiate with one country will not be undermined by that country striking a better deal with another, since any subsequent better deal must then be available to them. Confidence is also increased by the requirement that, once agreed on, tariff reductions (or any other changes in trade policy) are *bound*. That is, the contracting parties confirm that they will not change their policy except under such circumstances as are allowed by the GATT procedures. This is an extremely important provision, since it means that member countries cannot increase tariffs selectively.

The non-discrimination principle is also embodied in the *national treatment* clause, which requires that, once they have entered the country, imported goods are subject to the same taxes, regulations, etc. as apply to the equivalent domestic goods.

The presence of the MFN clause owes much to the United States, which has shown an almost fanatical attachment to the principle of most-favoured nation in its trade policy. This goes back to the 1930s when Cordell Hull, Secretary of State in the Roosevelt administration, made it the leading principle in his crusade against the rising tide of protectionism and for a more liberal trade policy. It seemed to be a principle characterised by justice and equality, it harmonised with high-minded American principles, and it gave the American line an air of moral superiority.

☐ *Reciprocity*

Reciprocity has never been formally defined, but has nevertheless been a cornerstone of GATT negotiations. The reciprocity obligation requires that a country receiving a concession from another should offer an 'equivalent' concession in return. In its most simple form reciprocity might involve two countries agreeing tariff reductions on each other's exports that would leave their bilateral balance of trade unchanged.

eg. (Reciprocity also has its roots in US trade policy, particularly in the Reciprocal Trade Agreements Act of 1934 under which Cordell Hull attempted to reverse the damage caused to US trade by foreign retaliation against US tariff increases in 1930) (the Smoot–Hawley Tariff). Hull persuaded the US Congress that he would only be able to persuade foreign governments to reduce their tariffs on US goods if they were offered equivalent access to the US market.)

□ *Transparency*

(Article XI of the GATT forbids the use of direct controls on trade, particularly quantitative restrictions, except under a few designated circumstances) (such as a balance-of-payments crisis, allowed under Article XII).

(The rationale for banning quotas etc. is that a quantitative restriction is a less *transparent* instrument for reducing imports than a tariff.) This has two aspects. First, when facing a tariff, producers exporting to the country concerned have clear information on the barrier they have to surmount in order to sell their goods and services, and may choose the volume they will supply subject to that information. With a quantitative restriction, on the other hand, they face uncertainty about the volume they will be allowed to export and about their net unit revenue. Second, with a tariff the price-increasing effect is immediately apparent to consumers in the importing country, in that a 20 per cent tariff necessarily means that the domestic price is 20 per cent higher than the world price, whatever that may be. The price-raising effect of a quota however may be less apparent unless information about the world price is readily available. As we saw in our consideration of the political economy of protection in Chapter 15, this may reduce the likelihood of consumers lobbying against import restrictions.

□ *The GATT and neo-mercantilism*

It has been argued that the MFN principle and reciprocity have their roots in a neo-mercantilist view of trade. This has been defined by Krugman[4] as reflecting three simple rules: (i) exports are good; (ii) imports are bad; (iii) other things equal, an equal increase in imports and exports is good.

The charge is based upon the formulation, and indeed the wording, of the GATT principles, which refer to a tariff reduction as a concession made to others, and treat such a concession as something for which compensation (a reciprocal concession) is required. This is of course quite at odds with the view of most economists, who would argue that, with a

(5) It provided the means for countries to settle their disputes and avoid unilateral action in the absence of an enforcement machinery.

The GATT 355

few exceptions, the reduction of a tariff benefits the country making the reduction as well as its trading partners. According to this view, tariff reductions should be made voluntarily rather than being an act that requires compensation.

A more pragmatic view is that the principles of the GATT recognise reality. The discussion of the political economy of protection in Chapter 15 suggested that there will be pressure on governments from the import-competing sectors of the economy to give them protection. The reciprocity clause provides a way of mobilising another pressure group, the export sectors of the economy, as a counter-balance to the first.

Moreover, the reciprocity clause may effectively discourage a potential 'free rider' problem in trade liberalisation. That is, certain parties might otherwise seek to benefit from lower tariffs on their exports without offering concessions on their imports. Finally, a comparable concession may reduce the possibility that a tariff-reducing country does not suffer adverse balance-of-payments or terms-of-trade effects, which might inhibit the move towards liberalisation.

The MFN *clause and discrimination against countries*

If the United States, for instance, has a certain tariff structure and applies it equally to all countries, it means that the country does not discriminate between producers, but it does not necessarily follow that the United States does not discriminate between nations. If it has a high tariff on cocoa but a low one on Scottish sweaters, it means that Britain is given better treatment than Ghana. Any change in a tariff structure can also be geared so that it favours some countries over others. It avails the African states little if the United States makes tariff concessions on industrial goods only, if these nations cannot produce and export industrial goods. Thus what is a non-discriminatory policy in principle may become for all practical purposes a policy of discrimination.

It should also be borne in mind that a change in a given nominal tariff rate can differ widely in effects, depending on circumstances. Our earlier discussions have indicated that the effects of a change in tariffs depend on the interplay of all the economic forces in the general equilibrium framework. The lawyer's play of equal treatment can turn out to be something quite different when studied from an economist's point of view.

The principle of MFN treatment is also somewhat peculiar if regarded from a more general, political, point of view. It is a case of extreme nationalism. It lumps all foreigners together in one big pack and contrasts them to the members of one's own nation. The home producer, for some reason, has a moral right to be protected. And all foreigners, regardless of neighbourhood, political ties, common cultural background, etc., should be treated equally, i.e. all foreign producers should have a right to enter the country's home market on the same conditions as all other foreign producers. If anything, the MFN principle seems to build on a combination of extreme and opposing political philosophies.

■ 17.4 Exceptions to the GATT

Since its inception the GATT has allowed various exceptions to its general principles. Some relate to the economic problems faced by signatories, some to particular systems of tariff preferences, others to trade in specific commodities, and yet others to permitted reactions to 'GATT-illegal' actions by other members. As an added twist, successive GATT Rounds have failed to come to terms with the domestic policies of signatories in certain areas, so that they have effectively been put to one side.

They are:

□ *Balance-of-payments problems*

GATT members are allowed to apply quantitative import restrictions in order to deal with severe balance-of-payments problems. The developed countries are subject to Article XII, the LDCs to Article XVIII(B).

Should a developed country seek to use quantitative restrictions under Article XII then it is subject to automatic surveillance by the Contracting Parties. There have been few attempts to use this provision recently, but where it has been used the GATT surveillance has been reasonably effective in encouraging their removal.[5] Quantitative restrictions for balance-of-payments reasons have of course no role under a system of floating exchange rates.

Developing countries have, on the other hand, made extensive use of Article XVIII(B), and have maintained their quantitative restrictions for long periods. GATT surveillance seems to have had little effect on their use of such policies. Although it is evident that many LDCs do have severe and continued balance-of-payments problems, it is difficult to see why a quantitative restriction should be the preferred instrument for restricting imports. One possible argument is that markets are less well developed in many LDCs, so that an import quota may be more easy to administer than a tariff and may have a more certain effect. Nevertheless, the use of quantitative restrictions will cause distortions to the allocation of resources, and will have harmful long-run effects.

(The application of quantitative restrictions under Article XVIII(B) must also impose losses on the country's trading partners, and under that Article they have no right to seek redress.)

(2) ☐ *Regional groupings*

(The major exception to the MFN principle is contained in Article XXIV, which allows for the establishment of free trade areas and customs unions. The major provisos governing such economic integration are that they should not increase tariffs or other barriers to trade with non-members among the GATT countries, and that they should cover (nearly) all trade between the members.)

This exception reflects the importance attached in the immediate post-war period to the reconstruction of the European economies. It is unlikely that such an exception could have been made without the support of the United States, but that country took an active role in promoting European reconstruction (the major example being the Marshall Aid Program and the subsequent Organisation for European Economic Co-operation, OEEC). Economic integration in Western Europe was seen as a means of promoting reconstruction.

The benign view taken of the economic consequences of customs unions reflects the lack of an economic analysis of their consequences. The first attempt at a rigorous analysis, by Jacob Viner, did not appear until 1950 (the theory of customs unions is discussed in Chapter 16).

(Customs unions, and more particularly free trade areas, have proliferated since the inception of the GATT. The three groupings among the developed nations are the European Community, the European Free Trade Area (EFTA) and the recently created free trade area of the United States and Canada. Groupings among the LDCs include the Latin American Free Trade Area, now the Latin American Integration Association (ALADI), the Caribbean Community (CARICOM), the Association of South-East Asian Nations (ASEAN), the West African Economic Community (CEAO), the Mano River Union (MRU), the Economic Community of the West African Sates (ECOWAS), formed by CEAO and MRU members, and the Central African Customs and Economic Union (UDEAC).[6])

(3) ☐ *Tariff preferences*

(Tariff preferences for specified groups of countries are another exception to the MFN principle. Systems of preferences which were in operation before the signing of the GATT were allowed to continue.) The most important at that time was the Commonwealth preference system operated

* in the home market or price below avg. cost in a foreign market.

358   *International Trade Policy*

by the United Kingdom, which was a subject of some dispute between the United Kingdom and the United States, but which is now of little consequence. *As for the new schemes,*

(The GATT has not objected to various preferential arrangements between developed countries and their present or former overseas territories. The most extensive of these is the Lomé Convention, covering trade between the members of the European Community and some of their former colonies.)

(The Generalised System of Preferences (GSP), under which the developed countries may allow concessions on trade restrictions to the LDCs without reciprocity, has also been applied with the approval of the GATT, first under a 10-year exemption to Article I made in 1971, and now under an enabling clause introduced in the Tokyo Round (see later). The GSP is discussed in Chapter 18.

④ □ *Dumping* AD actions governed by the Gatt Art VI and Anti-dumping code.

(Article VI of the GATT allows discriminatory action, through counter-vailing duties, against goods which are being dumped. In order to invoke Article VI the importing country must show that the goods are being sold below their 'normal value', and that they are causing 'material injury' to an established industry or are 'materially retarding' the establishment of a domestic industry. The countervailing duty may not be any greater than the estimated subsidy on the offending goods.

Unfortunately, charges of dumping are difficult to disprove, which has lead to the charge that anti-dumping provisions have been 'captured' by the protectionists.) This is discussed in more detail in Chapter 15.

Anti dumping in Pg 313 last in left notes

⑤ □ *The Multi-Fibre Arrangement*

(Trade in textiles occurs in a very 'managed' market. In the 1950s excess capacity in the textile sectors of many developed countries coincided with an increase in supply from developing countries newly entering the market.) This (lead several countries (notably the United Kingdom) to negotiate VERs with the new suppliers) (particularly Japan, Hong Kong and India).

These bilateral arrangements were superseded in 1961 by a multilateral arrangement, negotiated under the auspices of the GATT, designed (to deal with these 'short-run' problems. The Short Term Arrangement on Cotton Textiles was to 'maintain orderly access' to developed country markets and to avoid 'market disruptions' arising from 'sharp and substantial increase or potential increase in imports of particular products from particular sources'. If this were to occur then the importing country could unilaterally impose import quotas (within specified limits). Such an arrangement is at variance with many GATT principles: it allows unilateral action, specifies quotas rather than tariffs, and is discriminatory.

The Short Term Arrangement lasted only for one year, but was replaced by the Long Term Arrangement Regarding International Trade in Cotton Textiles. This embodied many of the feature of the Short Term Arrangement, and also incorporated further 'management' features, notably control over the growth of imports. This 'exceptional and transitional measure', originally covering the next five years, was renewed in 1967 and again in 1970.

It was replaced by the Multi-Fibre Arrangement (MFA) in 1974. The MFA has 40 signatories (*one* of which is the European Community), and is extended to trade in man-made as well as natural fibres. It covers about 75 per cent of world trade in textiles. The current MFA was scheduled to expire at the end of 1992, but its period has been extended pending the completion of the Uruguay Round. The MFA follows the previous Arrangements in endorsing quantitative import restrictions, and in managing the growth of imports.

The MFA is a major departure from the principles of the GATT. It takes an entire sector out of the GATT arrangements (avoiding the proscriptions on discrimination and on quantitative restrictions). The welfare cost to importing countries is substantial, and is discussed in Chapter 20. The costs to the exporters, largely LDCs, must also be substantial.

6 □ *Agriculture*

The GATT has so far failed to come to grips with the problems posed by agriculture, perhaps the most policy-ridden sector of all. Nearly all developed countries support their agricultural sector in some way. Many policies are overtly trade oriented, with some importing countries using instruments such as tariffs and import quotas, and some exporting countries using export subsidies. Others are domestically oriented, such as production subsidies, but nevertheless have an impact on the volume of trade. However, as Rayner, Ingersent and Hine note,[8] 'Prior to the Uruguay Round, domestic farm programmes were regarded as sacrosanct and agriculture was accorded a "special status" within the GATT with farm trade being given specific exemptions in respect of market access (border protection) and export competition (export subsidies)'.

The wide variety of support mechanisms, and the difficulties inherent in making comparisons between them, has made it difficult to reach international agreement on their moderation. Yet the interaction between the policies pursued by different countries through the international market makes them a source of discord. (The Uruguay Round has been beset with disputes about agricultural policies, most notably between the United States and the European Community.)

☐ *Services*

(Trade in services has largely been ignored in GATT negotiations, but is one of the 'new issues' in the Uruguay Round. It came onto the agenda largely at the behest of the United States, which perceives itself as having a comparative advantage in services) Initially, other developed countries seemed to regard service trade as of minor importance, but have changed their stance in the course of the negotiations, with the European Community in particular becoming more active. (The LDCs have shown little interest, perhaps fearing that negotiations on services will distract attention from areas in which they have more direct concerns.)

▌ 17.5 The GATT Rounds between 1947 and 1961

The GATT started with a round of negotiations, the Geneva Round, in 1947.[9] 23 countries took part. There were 123 agreements, covering just over half of world trade. This first Round was successful in cutting tariffs, largely as the result of the United States, an enthusiast for free trade, being willing to cut its tariffs on imports from Europe while not putting pressure on the European countries to abandon their quantitative restrictions on imports.

Negotiations in this and the succeeding four rounds were on a bilateral 'product-by-product, request-offer' basis. A pair of negotiating countries exchanged two lists, one containing requests that the other country reduce tariffs facing the first country's main exports, the other being a set of offers to bind or reduce tariffs on goods for which the second country was a main supplier to the first.

These lists were also circulated to all other negotiators, who would then be able to take them into account in their own bargaining, and who could join in the negotiations between the original pair of countries if they had a major interest. This procedure did much to transform the results of bilateral negotiations into multilateral liberalisation.

The subsequent four Rounds[10] did not achieve comparable tariff reductions. Among the factors constraining liberalisation were the reduction of the negotiating authority of the US Administration by Congress, the unwillingness of Britain and the Commonwealth countries to reduce preferences, and the creation of the European Community. In addition to these influences, it became increasingly clear that the existing procedures were unlikely to yield major progress in liberalisation, largely as a consequence of the increasing membership.

■ *17.6 The Kennedy Round (1964–67)*

As the European Community developed into a full-scale customs union, the United States began to feel its protectionist slant, particularly in agriculture. Moreover, it seemed likely at that time that the United Kingdom and some other European countries would join the European Community in the near future. As a reaction to this development the Kennedy administration in 1962 introduced a bill aimed at major reciprocal tariff reductions, the so-called Trade Expansion Act put before Congress in that year. From a political point of view, the bill was presented as necessary if the United States was to keep up the Atlantic alliance with Western Europe that had been the cornerstone of American foreign policy. It was also argued that it would improve the US balance of payments, though why joint tariff reductions should improve any particular country's balance of payments was never explained. When American industry showed reluctance to adopt the idea, the Kennedy administration argued that it could now live up to its ideal of competition as the best foundation for a free economy.

The economic content of the Trade Expansion Act was that Congress would grant the Administration the right to make a 50 per cent tariff reduction on all commodities. On top of this came 'the dominant-supplier authority'. This said that on commodity groups in which the United States and the European Community accounted for 80 per cent or more of the trade among non-communist countries, tariffs could be cut by up to 100 per cent. Tariffs could, moreover, be completely eliminated if the US tariff rate were less than 5 per cent, and on tropical products, provided the European Community countries reciprocated. The countries' agricultural policies should also be discussed, as should other non-tariff barriers to trade.

Naturally, the self-interest of the United States was involved. This is perhaps best seen in the dominant-supplier arrangement. Although phrased in a non-discriminatory manner, it was hardly so in spirit, as it would allow the largest tariff cuts to be concentrated on goods that were especially important for trade between the United States and the European Community. The LDCs would be appeased by the fact that unilateral tariff cuts by the industrial countries were foreseen on certain tropical products.

The Trade Expansion Act was adopted by the US Congress in 1962. The enthusiasm of the European countries was less than the Americans had expected, but the negotiations, the Kennedy Round, got under way slowly in 1963.

(A major departure from previous procedures in the Kennedy Round was the use of a formula for cutting tariffs on an across-the-board basis. The formula was the subject of dispute between the United States, which favoured a 'linear cut', and the European Community, which argued for higher reductions in higher tariffs. The source of the disagreement was that the range of tariffs was much lower in the European Community than in the United States. The formula finally agreed was linear, with all tariffs being cut by 35 per cent.)

(Exceptions to the linear formula were however permitted, and these turned out to be of some importance.) Some major primary exporting countries exempted themselves, and negotiated concessions under the traditional reciprocity clause. Developing countries were allowed to opt out from reciprocal concessions, and the majority did so. It has been shown by Finger however that the nine developing countries that did make reciprocal concessions during the Kennedy Round gained significantly higher concessions on their exports to the United States than did the others (an average 33 per cent reduction in tariffs, whereas the others gained only a 5 per cent cut).

(Another feature of the Kennedy Round was the creation of sectoral groups for the discussion of five 'sensitive' sets of products)(aluminium, chemicals, paper and pulp, steel, and textiles and clothing). The establishment of these groups allowed much more scope for lobbying by producer interest groups, constrained the ability of governments to negotiate, and made reciprocity more difficult to achieve (since within each group trade was largely unbalanced). The negotiating group on agriculture faced similar problems.

(The Kennedy Round is also notable as the first instance of considerable difficulties in reaching a final agreement. Negotiations reached a stalemate, and it required the Director General of the GATT and senior politicians (largely from the United States, the United Kingdom and the European Community) to put together a 'crisis' agenda to break the deadlock.)

(The Kennedy Round tariff reductions by developed countries have been estimated as about 36–39 per cent, and affected around 75 per cent (by value) of world trade.) They were however largely (concentrated namely upon the manufactured goods) that were of principal interest to developed countries or on the raw materials that were essential to their industry. However, the cuts in tariffs on raw materials were generally lower than those on final products, and in a wide range of goods the effective rate of protection increased. Relatively low tariff cuts were applied in textiles and clothing, and the developing countries had to accept the continuation of the Long Term Arrangement in return.

Agricultural products were generally excluded from the Kennedy Round because of the conflict of interest between the farm exports of the United States and the drive towards self-sufficiency in farm products in the European Community. Other areas which received relatively little attention were tropical products, domestic subsidies and non-tariff barriers.

■ *17.7 The Tokyo Round (1973–79)*

The economic climate during the Tokyo Round negotiations was far from encouraging. The world was suffering from 'stagflation', non-tariff barriers were proliferating, and trade relations between the United States, the European Community and Japan were strained. Many problems which had been on the agenda for the Kennedy Round, but had not been resolved, notably agriculture and non-tariff barriers, reappeared.

Tariff liberalisation proceeded with relatively little trouble, once a heated debate over the formula to be used has been resolved. As in the Kennedy Round, the main protagonists were the United States and the European Community, the former again arguing for a linear cut, while the European Community sought greater harmonisation of tariffs. After four years agreement was reached on the so-called 'Swiss formula', which had a harmonising element.[11] The agreed formula may be written as

$$t_1 = \frac{ct_0}{c + t_0}$$

where t_0 is the original tariff, and t_1 the final tariff (both in percentage terms). Negotiations resulted in the value of c being set at 16. Application of this formula produced substantial reductions in nominal tariffs, as is shown in Table 17.1. It is worth noting that before the tariffs were reduced there was clear evidence of tariff escalation, and that the tariff cuts increased that escalation.

Once again, the concessions were concentrated in manufactured goods, agricultural commodities being treated differently. Moreover, textiles and clothing, leather, footwear and travel goods received lower tariff cuts, and often none at all. Tropical products did however gain some concessions, many being granted duty-free access. The cuts in tariffs gained by LDCs (for whom tropical products and textiles, footwear, etc. are of considerable interest) were lower than those enjoyed by the industrial countries, being estimated by GATT at about 25 per cent on average.

The Tokyo Round was much concerned with the rules for commercial policy.[12] It set up several study groups. One group, on non-tariff barriers

Acc. to Article XIX it provided an escape clause an country can withdraw concession if unforseen injury occurs to domestic country.

364   *International Trade Policy*

Table 17.1   *Tariff changes in the Tokyo Round*

| | Tariff (%)[1] | | Reduction |
	Pre-Tokyo	Post-Tokyo	(%)
Total industrial products	7.2	4.9	33
Raw materials	0.8	0.4	52
Semi-manufactures	5.8	4.1	30
Finished manufactures	10.3	6.9	33

1 Averages, weighted by MFN imports.
Source: GATT (1979), p.120.

to trade, was split into five subgroups, on technical barriers, quantitative restrictions, subsidies, government procurement and customs matters. Other study groups covered the sectoral approach, tariffs, agriculture (two subgroups), tropical products, and safeguards (i.e. emergency protection). Since such rules are constitutional issues, they must be negotiated multilaterally, and the smaller industrial and the developing countries were more active than in previous Rounds. It is difficult to define, let alone achieve, equality of concessions in such areas, which made it difficult to obtain an overall consensus.

In the event, the negotiations on quantitative restrictions (an extremely sensitive area) were still-born, and little came of the safeguards discussions despite considerable efforts. Discussions on government procurement did produce a new code, and negotiations on liberalisation were conducted on a request-offer basis. However, the available evidence suggests that procurement is still very much biased in favour of domestic suppliers. Agreements were reached in the other groups, but the changes introduced seem to have had little impact.

All in all, the major achievement of the Tokyo Round, the further liberalisation of trade through tariff reductions, must be set off against the failure to resolve various issues. Agricultural problems were not resolved, and continued to be a source of friction in the 1980s and into the Uruguay Round. The failure to resolve the safeguards issue may be seen as one element in the continued growth on non-tariff barriers. Finally, the LDCs remained dissatisfied with their failure to achieve greater concessions.

■ *17.8* The Uruguay Round (1986–)

The period following the Tokyo Round was one of world-wide economic recession and of conflict between the three major trading blocs, the United

States, the European Community and Japan. The US–EC disputes largely centred on agricultural issues (particularly the 'success' of the Community in penetrating markets which the United States had traditionally regarded as its own). At the same time, the United States was attempting to induce the Japanese to open up their domestic market to foreign goods, and to American goods in particular, while the European Community was attempting to limit Japanese export growth.

The GATT Ministerial Meeting in November 1982, the first major attempt to meet the problems left by the Tokyo Round, was largely a failure. Worse, that failure led to a resurgence of protectionism in the United States and the European Community. The US Administration reacted to the failure of the meeting, and protectionist pressure, by considering the initiation of a new Round of negotiations. As Winters notes, 'With a round in progress the Administration can head off some protectionist pressures by claiming that a matter is under negotiation or that to act on it could undermine vital negotiations in some other sector of the talks'.[13] Japan also favoured a new round, preferring multilateral negotiations to the prospect of continued bilateral pressure from the United States and the European Community. The Community's attitude on the other hand was notably lukewarm.

Other countries were also generally in favour of a new round, but were concerned with other issues. The smaller industrial countries wished to curtail the tendency of the 'big three' to ignore GATT principles. The agricultural-exporting nations were concerned about the impact of subsidised US production, and the EC's subsidised exports, on world markets. The developing countries' interests were in securing greater tariff preferences, reducing the impact of VERs in other areas, particularly textiles and clothing, and, again, about agricultural trade.

☐ *United States policy in the 1980s*

By the mid-1980s the United States has lost its comparative advantage in several of its traditional exporting sectors, such as steel and the automobile industry. These sectors already enjoyed considerable protection from imports, and had powerful domestic lobby groups defending their interests.

The traditional policy response in such circumstances is to enlist the support of the export industries by securing greater freedom of access to foreign markets for their products. The export-oriented sectors from which the United States could expect to gain however did not fall within the traditional range of industrial goods, and so the Administration sought to introduce to the agenda for the proposed GATT talks several new items. These 'new issues' included trade-related investment measures or 'TRIMs' (such as local content and minimum export requirements on FDI, which are discussed in Chapter 22), trade aspects of international property rights or 'TRIPs',[14] and trade in services.)

In the late 1980s the United States developed further its policy of using 'muscular liberalism' or 'aggressive unilateralism' in an attempt to force open foreign markets.[15] The argument that countries should not expect to enjoy the benefits of *free* trade if they themselves do not practise *fair* trade has been a recurrent theme in American policy. The Trade Act of 1974 included a provision (*Section 301*) requiring the US Administration to enforce US rights gained in international agreements, and to negotiate with foreign governments on actions taken within their own markets which were seen to be against the interests of US firms. If these negotiations fail then the President has the authority to impose import restrictions on the countries concerned.

If the United States retaliates under Section 301 then it is violating the GATT in several ways. Most importantly, it is discriminating against a country in circumstances which are not allowed under the Agreement, and it is usually imposing a tariff (typically set at 100 per cent) which is above the level at which its tariff will have been bound. Perhaps most importantly, it is failing to honour an agreement that has the force of a treaty in US law.

The United States defends its actions by claiming that it is following a doctrine of 'creative illegality'. That is, it is breaking the letter of the GATT in order to make the provisions of the GATT more effective. Unfortunately, other members of the GATT seem unwilling to accept this argument.

The Omnibus Trade and Competitiveness Act of 1988, which renewed the President's authority to negotiate tariff reductions and so was an important step in promoting a new round of GATT negotiations, also included a revision to Section 301. This revised legislation, commonly referred to as *Super 301, required* the US Trade Representative (USTR) to identify those countries employing practices whose elimination was most likely to increase US exports, and to investigate those practices. Should negotiations to reduce those practices fail then the USTR was to threaten retaliation. In May 1989 Brazil, India and Japan were identified as the first three countries to become the targets for Super 301 negotiations. All three reacted strongly to being labelled as 'unfair traders', and expressed unwillingness to negotiate with the United States while under the threat of retaliation.

American attitudes to trade with Japan, with their threat of unilateral action, pose a major threat to the multilateralism of the GATT procedures.[16] The US stance is exemplified by the Structural Impediments Initiative (SII). The SII was an attempt by the United States to open up trade with Japan by persuading it to abandon what the United States claimed were unfair 'trade' policies. Many of these policies, such as domestic anti-monopoly policies, legislation on workers' rights, and retail distribution systems undoubtedly have an impact on a country's trade balance, but have traditionally been regarded as matters of domestic concern only.

American concern with the EC's agricultural policies, and in particular the export subsidies paid on some grains, and the depressing effect these have on world prices, has more justification. Nevertheless, the United States is not entirely blameless, since its policy of subsidising production has been only partly countered by the retirement of land from production under its Set-Aside legislation.

Punta del Este and the Uruguay Round Agenda

Following US pressure, a Preparatory Committee was established in 1985 to determine the objectives and subject matter for a new round of negotiations, to be launched in September 1986. There was little agreement between the three major parties, and the initiative in the Committee was taken by two groups of smaller countries. The 'G9' group of mid-sized industrial nations proposed broad negotiations, while a group of 10 developing countries ('G10'), led by India and Brazil, proposed a narrower agenda which excluded the 'new issues'. At the time the ensuing conflict over services threatened the whole negotiations.

At the Ministerial meeting at Punta del Este (Uruguay), at which separate committees were set up for agriculture and services, a text broadly reflecting the G9 proposal was adopted. The G10 proposals, and their proposed amendments to the agreed text, were rejected, although they managed to modify the proposals for negotiations over services, which were to be treated in separate but parallel negotiations. The agriculture committee managed to agree on a form of words which would at least bring the United States and the European Community to the negotiating table!

The Uruguay Round agenda is complex. There are 14 negotiating groups on goods and another on services (see Table 17.2). The Declaration also calls for 'balanced concessions . . . within broad trading areas and subjects' in an attempt to avoid 'unwarranted cross-sectoral demands'. As Winters notes, cross-sectoral deals will probably be required, and seeking balance at this level threatens to overload the final agenda. The Declaration continues the earlier tendency to focus on constitutional issues, which, as before, strengthens the role of the smaller and less developed countries.

Table 17.2   *Negotiating groups in the Uruguay Round*

Trade barriers and related matters	Sector-specific
Subsidies and countervailing measures	Agriculture
Non-tariff measures	Natural resource products
Safeguards	Services
Tariffs	Textiles and clothing
Procedures	Tropical Products
	Others
Dispute settlement	
GATT Articles	TRIPs
Functioning of the GATT	TRIMs
Multilateral Trade Negotiations	

Agriculture is given more prominence than in the Kennedy and Tokyo Rounds.[17] This reflects the interests of the United States and the Cairns Group[18] of non-subsidising grain exporters. The Declaration calls for improved market access for exports, for discipline in direct and indirect subsidies, and for the bringing of all measures affecting import access and export competition within GATT rules and disciplines. The attention directed at domestic policies was always likely to cause conflict, particularly with the European Community.

The Declaration also restates the need for non-reciprocal preferences for the LDCs, coupled with exemptions from policy requirements (the so-called 'special and differential treatment' provisions). It does however suggest that the better-off developing nations (by inference the NICs) should 'participate more fully in the framework of rights and obligations under the GATT' (i.e. 'graduate' out of the preference and non-reciprocity arrangements).[19]

☐ The Montreal Impasse and the Geneva Accord

In December 1988 a review of the progress of the Round was undertaken by a meeting of trade ministers in Montreal. Four of the negotiating groups faced serious and possibly inter-related problems. The textiles and clothing and the safeguards groups faced major difficulties, but it was felt that these could be resolved if solutions could be found to the problems facing the agriculture and TRIPs groups.

Unfortunately, a solution to the agricultural group's problems seemed out of reach. The US's stated objective was the abolition of all trade distorting subsidies in agriculture, while the European Community was unwilling to negotiate on the substance of the Common Agricultural Policy (CAP), and seemed more willing to discuss managed rather than free trade in agricultural products. A coalition of six developing countries (the five South American members of the Cairns Group, plus Peru) were blocking an 'agreement to disagree' in the former group in an attempt to force the United States and European Community to come to an agreement on agriculture. The Cairns Group threatened to walk out of all negotiations if a settlement on agriculture were not reached.

The 'Geneva Accord' of April 1989 apparently resolved the conflict between the United States and the European Community in favour of the latter, referring to progressive reduction in trade-distorting support and protection in agriculture rather than their elimination. The Accord however lacked clarity, and the United States was able to reassert its position later on. The US 'position paper' of October 1989 proposed that all NTBs (including agricultural import quotas) should be replaced by tariffs after 10 years ('tariffication' of NTBs), with a preferred 'zero option' that those tariffs should eventually be eliminated. The EC response sought partial tariffication and the right to use import quotas in exceptional circumstances. The failure of the United States and European Community to reach agreement on agricultural policy lead to the suspension of the Round in December 1990 (the intended date for its completion).

The Draft Final Act and the Washington Accord

At the end of 1991 the then Secretary General of the GATT, Arthur Dunkel, tabled a Draft Final Act (often referred to as the Dunkel Text).[20] The agriculture section made provision improved market access through the reduction of specific tariffs and the tariffication of NTBs, cuts in domestic support, and reductions in both export subsidy expenditures and the volume of subsidised exports. The United States and the Cairns Group (excepting Canada) were prepared to accept this, but the EC's response was guarded, largely due to its internal debate over reform of the CAP (the MacSharry Plan). The eventual acceptance by the European Community members of a revised version of the MacSharry Plan, embodying reductions in support prices with accompanying compensation for farmers, raised hopes that the United States would be able to agree to the Dunkel Text.

In November 1992 the United States and the European Community reached a bilateral agreement on agriculture, known as either the

Washington or the Blair House Accord. The European Community agreed to conform to the Dunkel Proposals in many respects, but with important provisos attached to the cuts required in import barriers, domestic support, and export subsidies. However, the Washington Accord has not yet been ratified by either the United States or the European Community, and the French are threatening to veto the acceptance of the Accord in the Council of Ministers.

Agriculture continues to dominate the Uruguay Round. There has been a succession of crises, 'each resolved by finding a form of words which the United States and the European Community could interpret differently'.[21] The Round has continued while postponing a settlement on agriculture, but it seems likely that if a settlement cannot be reached then ultimately the Uruguay Round must fail.

☐ *Other issues*

Negotiations on textiles and clothing have made little more progress. Agreement had been reached in 1989 that the MFA would be gradually phased out, and textiles, etc. brought within the GATT. Unfortunately the United States and Canada chose to press for that agreement to be implemented by first moving to a system of global quotas, which would then be relaxed, whereas the developing countries, with support from the European Community for their own reasons, argued for a relaxation of the existing bilateral quotas. The Draft Final Act records agreement on the phased integration of textiles into the GATT 'on the basis of strengthened rules and disciplines'. Completion of the integration process was scheduled for 1 January 2003, but the failure to bring the Uruguay Round to a conclusion means that the timetable will, at best, be delayed.

Some progress has been made on trade in services, and a framework agreement drawn up. While it is accepted that virtually all traded services would come under the terms of that agreement, there has been slower progress on specific agreements on individual sectors. The Draft Final Act defines the types of service to which an agreement would apply, in terms broad enough to cover such activities as tourism, banking and construction projects, provides for MFN treatment in services (but with allowance for notified exceptions), requires transparency of laws and regulations, and specifies obligations for mutual recognition of qualifications, etc.. The agreement also provides for non-discrimination against foreign service suppliers, for progressive liberalisation of existing laws and regulations, and for consultation and dispute-settlement procedures. There are still, however, doubts about whether some developing countries will agree to a deal on services or not.

TRIPs negotiations have been the subject of no less than five different proposed texts. There is no common accord between the LDCs, particularly on whether TRIP safeguards will increase or decrease the transfer of technology. The Draft Final Act outlines various provisions, including the treatment of nationals of other parties on a basis no worse than that given to domestic nationals, and most favoured nation treatment. Detailed proposals are made for the various areas in which intellectual property rights exist, such as copyright, trademarks, industrial designs, patents, integrated circuits, and 'trade secrets'. Member governments would be obliged to provide procedures and remedies under their domestic law to ensure the protection of foreign holders of rights.

A more pressing issue is the linkage between both trade in services and TRIPs and the unilateralism of US trade policy as embodied in Section 301 and 'Super 301'. The United States wishes to enshrine the principle of retaliation for transgressions in one sector by the use of restrictions in another within the GATT. At present however it is GATT-illegal to retaliate in a goods sector for transgressions in either services or TRIPs because neither is covered by the Agreement, and the LDCs in particular are unwilling to see that situation changed. The United States, on the other hand, feels that if retaliation were restricted to the sector in which the transgression occurred then, as a dominant exporter, it would have very little leverage on the policies of other countries.

The new Secretary General of the GATT, Peter Sutherland, has set a deadline of 15 December 1993 for the completion of the Uruguay Round in an attempt to force a conclusion to negotiations that have gone on for seven years. The deadline reflects the expiry in early 1994 of the 'fast track' negotiating authority given to the US President. The French government however has so far refused to accept that deadline, their main source of concern being the domestic political impact of the agricultural reforms contained in the Washington Accord.

■ *17.9* Unsettled issues and future problems

A system such as the GATT, operating in a dynamic and uncertain world, will never resolve all the issues facing it. Countries will lose their comparative advantage in some of their traditional export sectors, or may experience an increased comparative disadvantage in their import-competing sectors. On the other hand they will experience increased comparative advantage (or decreased disadvantage) in others. There may be many causes for this, the most obvious being technological advances in the production of goods, the effects of factor accumulation at different rates in different countries, and even the effects of a boom or recession in another of their domestic sectors. The effects of such changes, with their consequent impact on sectoral output, employment and profits, will create pressures for protectionism from the declining sectors, which may or may not be counter-balanced by pressures for free trade from the growing sectors. The GATT will always have to be ready to adapt to the changing situations that such movements will bring about.

On the other hand, there are some areas which have been a source of dissension within the GATT almost since its creation. Some have been largely ignored, perhaps from the desire to avoid disrupting progress in other sectors: agriculture, and latterly services, provide good examples of this. Others have become the subject of special treatment, even to the extent of abrogating GATT procedures to allow special arrangements to be made: the Multi-Fibre Arrangement is the pre-eminent example of this. Yet others have come onto the agenda fairly recently, and it would have been unduly optimistic to expect the GATT to have solved all the issues by now.

Despite these criticisms, there seems little doubt that GATT is not just the 'best thing that we have' when it comes to ensuring that the world benefits from free trade. It seems more likely that it may be the only thing we shall ever have, and that we may lose even that if the Uruguay Round does not yield a positive outcome. Many commentators are warning of the possible dangers of either bilateral rather than multilateral agreements , and/or of the possibility that the world will split up into 'trading blocs', possibly centring on North America, an enlarged European Community, and a Japanese-centred Asian bloc. Some of these argue that a continuation of the US policy of 'aggressive unilateralism' will help to bring this about. An opposing school seems to be emerging which takes the view that trading blocs developed along the lines of, say, the Kemp–Wan argument of Chapter 16, may not be as disastrous as the more conventional analysis suggests. However, the probability that trading blocs would in fact develop along such lines seems, given the tendency of governments to follow national self-interest, extremely remote.

The Draft Final Act contains a proposal for a Multinational Trade Organisation (MTO) that would take in the GATT, together with all the amendments made in the completion of the Uruguay Round. The MTO 'would be headed by a Ministerial Conference meeting at least every two years'. There would be a General Council that would oversee the operation of the organisation, and provide a Dispute Settlement Body and a Trade Policy Review Mechanism, and various 'Councils' dealing with broad areas such as goods, services and TRIPs. 'Membership in the MTO would automatically entail taking on all the results of the [Uruguay] Round without exception.'

□ *Notes*

1 An excellent description of the structure, organisation, and operations of the GATT is given by van Meerhaeghe (1992).

2 van Meerhaeghe (1992), p.115.

3 A full list of the articles is given in Greenaway (1983), p. 86.

4 Krugman (1991).

5 See Eglin (1987) for a detailed analysis.

6 See van Meerhaeghe (1992) for details of the memberships and forms of agreement.

7 A particular irony of the MFA is that Italy, a net exporter of textiles, is treated as an importer and so is allowed to restrict access to her domestic market.

8 Rayner, Ingersent and Hine (1993).

9 Winters (1990) analyses the history of the GATT in more depth than is possible here. See also MacBean and Snowden (1981) for discussion of the Rounds up to and including Tokyo, and Winham (1986) for an in-depth consideration of the Tokyo Round.

10 The first four Rounds were at Geneva (1947), Annecy (1949), Torquay (1951), and Geneva (1956). The fifth Round is usually referred to as the 'Dillon Round', and took place in 1960–61.

11 See Ennew, Greenaway and Reed (1992) for a discussion of liberalisation and harmonisation.

12 See Winters (1990) for a more detailed discussion.

13 Winters (1990), p. 1297. This section largely follows his treatment.

14 A word of warning is needed about the abbreviation TRIP. Although the terminology has now settled into the form used in the text, there was a tendency for economists to use the term TRIPs to refer to trade related investment policies (synonymous with what are now called TRIMs)!

15 See Bhagwati (1990) for a biting criticism of US trade policies in the 1980s, and Bhagwati (1992), for an extension of his analysis.

16 See Bhagwati (1990) for a discussion of the view that 'Japan is different'.

17 For a discussion of agricultural problems see Gardner (1991) and Rayner, Ingersent and Hine (1993).

18 Argentina, Australia, Brazil, Canada, Chile, Colombia, Fiji, Hungary, Indonesia, Malaysia, Philippines, New Zealand, Thailand, Uruguay.

19 The 'graduation' issue is discussed in Milner (1991).

20 The press summary issued by GATT for the Draft Final Act is reproduced in *The World Economy*, 16 (1993), pp. 237–59.

21 Winters (1990), p. 1300.

■ *Chapter 18* ■

Trade Policy and the Less-Developed Countries

■ *18.1* Introduction

It is convenient to consider the role played by trade policy in the development of the less-developed countries (LDCs) under two headings, 'external' and 'internal'. By 'internal policies' we mean the use of trade policy by the individual LDC to manipulate its own exports and imports, and this is the subject of Chapter 19. By 'external policies' we mean those policies which require co-operation between LDCs and/or the developed market economies (DMEs), and which are the subject of this chapter.

The problems of the LDCs have now been in the forefront of public discussion for a considerable time, In the years immediately after the Second World War, when the public generally began to realise the importance of the problem, many economists took a sanguine view. Capital accumulation was asserted to be at the root of the problem. If only capital could be inserted into the underdeveloped economies, they would start to grow. After years of dubious development efforts and depressing experiences, one is now less ready to offer panaceas. There are those who argue that the problem of economic development will be with us, not for years, but for decades and perhaps centuries.

We have seen that the representatives of LDCs came to feel frustrated by the work done within the framework of GATT, and that more consideration ought to be given to their specific problems. It was the efforts roused by such feelings that led to the establishment of the United Nations Conference on Trade and Development (UNCTAD).

▇ *18.2* UNCTAD and the world trading system

In 1961 the General Assembly of the United Nations designated the decade of the 1960s as United Nations Development Decade, a period in which 'member states and their peoples will intensify their efforts to mobilise and sustain support for measures required on the part of both developed and developing countries to accelerate progress towards self-sustaining growth'.

Representatives of LDCs soon started to press for a special trade conference within the UN's Economic and Social Council. Despite some opposition their efforts were successful, and in 1964 the first UNCTAD conference was convened in Geneva.

Since that date, a succession of conferences have been held: New Delhi (1968), Santiago (1972), Nairobi (1976), Manila (1979), Belgrade (1983), Geneva (1987); and the most recent (UNCTAD VIII) at Cartagena in 1992. All members of the UN and of its agencies are members. The organisation of the LDCs within UNCTAD is known as the 'Group of 77' (the group now numbers 128 LDCs). Despite wide political, ideological and cultural differences, this group has had some success in co-ordinating the attitudes of LDCs within UNCTAD and so has contributed toward the adoption of a common negotiating stance in other UN bodies.

The work of UNCTAD has spanned the whole field of trade investment and aid; some commentators have suggested that it was as a result of this lack of focus that the first two Conferences achieved very little. In UNCTAD III in Santiago, the area of interest was further extended to cover questions of commodity problems, the transfer of technology and the role of the multinational corporation. The fourth conference concentrated on commodity problems, but UNCTAD V reverted to wide-ranging and inconclusive discussions. UNCTAD VI and VII made no new major initiatives, but confirmed support for programmes approved previously.

The majority of commentators take the view that UNCTAD has done little to achieve either a more efficient use of the world's resources or a more equitable distribution of income.[1] The concern usually expressed is that UNCTAD's proposed changes to the international trading system would result in a reduction in efficiency while effecting little in the way of real resource transfers. In the event, those changes in the trading system which have resulted from UNCTAD proposals have largely been in a much-reduced form. We shall concentrate on two of their 'successes': the Generalised System of Tariff Preferences (GSP); and International Commodity Agreements and Compensatory Finance Schemes.

█ 18.3 The Generalised System of Tariff Preferences

The question of the developed market economies applying reduced (preferential) tariffs on imports of manufactures and semi-manufactures from the LDCs was raised at the first UNCTAD conference, but received little support from the major DMEs.[2] It was raised again at the second conference in 1968, and this time an inter-governmental group was set up to develop a workable scheme. Most developed countries now operate some arrangements for preferential entry of imports of specified goods from the LDCs.

The demands from the LDCs for trade preferences ('differential and more favourable treatment') have grown out of their desire for industrialisation. A policy of import-substitution has not been very successful, for reasons which we will consider in Chapter 19. The idea has gained ground that an 'outward-looking industrialisation' policy is necessary. This means promoting exports, especially exports of industrial products.

Two main arguments have been advanced to support the view that exports of manufactured goods could play a critical role in the economic development of most countries. The first is that, for most countries, industrialisation is the natural means of development. The second is that, in order for the development effort to be successful, the country in question needs to increase its exports, and the type of export that it can most profitably promote is that of industrial goods. But it has proved difficult for most LDCs to gain a foothold in the import markets of the industrial countries. Many believe that tariff preferences could provide the policy means for making such an export expansion possible.

The idea behind tariff preferences was primarily developed by Raul Prebisch, the then Secretary-General of UNCTAD. Prebisch made a distinction between 'conventional' and 'real' reciprocity in trading relations between nations. In this view, conventional reciprocity, when an industrial and an LDC make concessions to each other, leads to the LDC becoming dependent on an archaic trade pattern, where it will go on exporting primary products. Real reciprocity, on the other hand, means that the developed countries grant unilateral tariff reductions to the LDCs.

Thereby the export capacity of the latter countries will grow, their demands for imports from industrial countries will increase, and world trade will expand.

The arguments for tariff preferences proposed at the first UNCTAD conference centred to a large degree around the idea of infant-industry protection (see Chapter 12). Preferences would be granted for a limited time during which infant industries would be able to grow up by having access to large markets.

It should be observed, however, that this argument differs from the ordinary infant-industry argument. In the ordinary (small-country) case the transfers are internal: the consumers in the country in question will have to pay higher prices and subsidise the producers in that country to enable them to learn skills, achieve economies of scale, etc., that will make it possible for them later on to compete at world market prices, and there is no impact on the rest of the world. In the case of a general scheme of tariff preferences the transfers are external and generalised: who will gain and who will lose will depend on the structure of the market.

A model encompassing all the possible combinations of exporters and importers, and of countries that give preferences, countries that receive preferences, and countries that are outside the scheme would be very complex. We shall therefore take as simple a model as possible, and rely on some of the results obtained from the theory of customs unions (Chapter 16) to give us some insight into the consequences of tariff preferences.

Suppose there are four groups of countries: developed countries that are net importers of the good in question, that all charge the same tariff, that will all offer the same tariff preference to the LDCs in the scheme; developed countries that are net exporters and charge no tariff; LDCs that are exporters and are in the scheme; and LDCs that are exporters but not in the scheme. Finally, assume that there is no limit to the volume to which the reduced tariff on imports from the member LDCs applies.

Introduction of the tariff preferences is then akin to the formation of a customs union between the importing developed countries and the LDCs in the scheme (it would be identical if the preference given was the elimination of the tariff). There would then be *trade diversion*; some low-cost exports from the exporting developed countries and non-member LDCs would be displaced by higher-cost exports from the favoured LDCs. The favoured LDCs would gain, the exporting developed countries and the exporting LDCs that were not in the scheme would lose, and the outcome for the importing developed countries would depend on the relative sizes of their consumer gains and producer and taxpayer losses.

In practice, however, most preference schemes apply only to a specified quantity of imports; any imports above that quantity are then subject to the standard tariff. We can make a simple analysis of the effects of such a scheme using Figure 18.1. ES_L is the excess supply curve of the LDCs that will be included in the scheme, and ED_W is the excess demand curve for the importing developed countries that will offer the preferences (less any imports from LDCs not included in the scheme). Before the preference scheme is introduced the favoured LDC exporters sell a quantity X_0 to the DME importers, receiving a price P_L. The same price will be received by the other exporting countries. The price in the importing developed countries, who are assumed to charge the same tariff on imports, is P_W.

Suppose the developed countries now offer to let in a quantity of imports X_1 from the favoured LDCs without charging a tariff, but continue to levy the same tariff on imports above that quota (what is often called a 'tariff-quota' system). The first point to note is that, assuming the quota of tariff-free imports is less than the original import volume, there will be no increase in the total volume of trade, and no effect on the world price. There is no incentive for the favoured LDCs to increase their exports since the price received for the marginal unit is unchanged. There is also no change in the price received by any of the exporting countries or in the price in the importing developed countries. The only effect in this comparative static analysis is that the revenue received by the exporting LDCs in the scheme increases by area J, with an equal reduction in the tariff revenue of the importing developed countries. The tariff preference results only in a transfer of income from the developed countries to the LDCs, and there is no trade diversion.

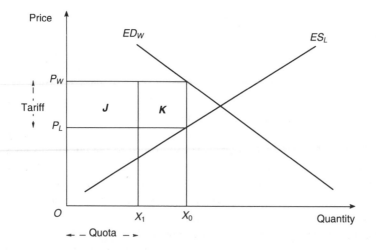

Figure 18.1   *Tariff preferences applied to a specified import volume*

We should note that such a scheme is likely to be costly to administer. Any importing country offering the preferences must 'police' its quota. That is, it must allocate its overall quota among the exporting LDCs within the scheme, and must check that none of them exceed their quota, identify the import volume for each LDC on which the non-preferential tariff is levied, and check that no non-member LDCs obtain unauthorised access to their market without paying the tariff. The favoured exporting countries must in turn allocate their tariff-free quota among their producers and police that allocation.

The dynamic long-term effects of such a scheme will be more complicated. It may be the case that the additional revenue received by the exporters will be used to develop skills, employ more advanced technology, and so on, which will lead to a downward shift in their supply curve and so to an increase in their exports. On the other hand, the additional revenue may be taken up in the form of rents.

More important long-term effects may arise from the coverage of the scheme. As we argued when considering quotas and other quantitative restrictions on imports, such administered schemes may not adjust to changes in the world economy with sufficient speed. In particular, they may make it difficult for LDCs who were not included in the original scheme (perhaps because they were not exporters of the good in question when the scheme was inaugurated) to enter a market in which they have a comparative advantage. At the same time, they may encourage existing members of the scheme to continue to export the good in question, when changing circumstances mean they should be producing some other good.

The quota element of the scheme reduces the benefits to the exporting LDCs in comparison with a simple tariff reduction, which would of course encourage an expansion of exports by the favoured LDCs. However, the quota element does at least reduce the impact of the scheme on non-member countries. With the tariff-quota scheme all the exporting countries continue to receive the same net price at the margin.

Whatever the form of the scheme chosen, an important question will concern the choice of industries that should be given preferences. Presumably, those industries would be chosen in which the LDCs had, or could be expected to have, a comparative advantage. It would be hoped that these would also be the industries in which the industrial countries have substantial tariffs. This would not necessarily be the case, but, if it were, there would perhaps be scope for substantial tariff preferences. There is nothing, however, that says that these industries would also be those that are of an infant-industry type.

Two different principles for granting trade preferences can be imagined. One would be of a fairly non-discriminatory nature, at least as far as the preference-receiving countries are concerned. Broad groups of industries, in which the LDCs would be expected to establish a comparative advantage, would be chosen, and the same preferences, without quota limits, would be granted to all LDCs. This would amount to a general subsidy from the developed countries to industrialisation in the LDCs. However, we should not disregard the political difficulties that such an arrangement could create in the developed countries: industries that are weak and highly protected in these countries are often supported by strong political pressure groups. Such an arrangement would have the advantage of being easy to comprehend and fairly easy to implement, but might reduce world efficiency by introducing trade diversion. Introducing the quota element into the scheme would eliminate the possibility of such trade diversion, but would involve other costs which might be as or more important in reducing world efficiency.

The other principle would be to pick the industries that would be given preferential treatment according to their prospects of becoming infant industries. To pick the right industries to qualify in this respect, to determine the duration of protection, etc., would probably be a most cumbersome undertaking. To this must be added that one cannot be sure that tariffs in industrial countries are so high, and hence a preferential treatment so effective, as to provide enough stimulus for industrialisation in the LDCs. Tariff preferences must then be accompanied by subsidies. We know from tariff theory (Chapter 10) that subsidies are a more efficient policy means than are tariffs. It can then be argued that it would be more efficient to forget about tariff preferences and to concentrate on subsidies altogether if the problem is to promote infant industries.

Even if such an arrangement were to give worthwhile benefits to the LDCs, we must as usual ask whether it is the most efficient means for promoting their industrialisation. Would it not be better if the consumers of the developed countries were taxed and a certain amount of taxes given as aid? From a purely economic point of view, it seems that this would be a more rational policy, as it would avoid the distortion of consumption that a tariff preference might imply. Moreover, it has been argued that the donor countries will view the income transfer to the LDCs as a form of aid, and may therefore reduce their 'pure' aid accordingly. In that case there would be few benefits to the LDCs, obtained at an increased cost in administration, rigidities in the system, etc.

Two arguments have been made against this. First, it can be argued that what the LDCs need is to get some experience of industrialisation, and that this can be facilitated by their having access to the markets of the industrial countries. Second, it may be that the existence of tariff preferences has helped to foster export-promotion rather than import-substitution policies in the LDCs. As we shall argue in Chapter 19, this may be a more substantial source of gains.

From a strictly economic point of view, it is difficult to argue either firmly against or firmly for trade preferences. The question is also sensitive when viewed from a political angle. Some countries tend to view the problem from a primarily protectionist point of view. They do not see anything unnatural in discriminating against foreigners, and some countries may be regarded as more 'foreign' than others. This means that they can use tariff preferences to discriminate against these countries while tying other countries closer to their own sphere of influence by granting them tariff preferences.

Other countries could view the problem from what can be termed a predominantly 'free trade angle'. They could argue that a discriminatory policy would, during a certain period, be used as an instrument for achieving freer trade. But tariff preferences should then be used in as non-discriminatory fashion as possible. Particularly poor or weak countries could be given extra preferential treatment, but otherwise preferences should be granted equally to all underdeveloped countries and should encompass broad commodity groups in which the LDCs could be expected to develop a comparative advantage.

The proposal for a Generalised System of Preferences (GSP) which emerged from the first UNCTAD conference in 1964 was based on the principle that LDCs required preferential tariff treatment without reciprocation on their part, rather than substantial most-favoured-nation (MFN) tariff cuts. Although the latter did not discriminate between the same products exported from different sources, the exports of industrial goods from LDCs faced higher tariffs, on average, than those exported by developed countries. The GSP was also intended to counter the preferential arrangements of the type established between the European Community and non-member European countries as well as a number of LDCs under the Lomé Convention (see Chapter 17).

The GSP system was negotiated at length over the period 1964–71, with the first scheme being implemented by the European Community in 1971, followed closely by Japan. The US scheme did not come into operation until January 1976. These schemes generally provide duty-free entry for most manufactured and semi-manufactured products from a large number of developing countries. However, there are important limitations.

With regard to product coverage, GSP tariff treatment does not extend to agricultural and fishery products. Textile products are excluded outright by the United States and Japan, while the European Community only offers preferential tariff treatment to countries that abide by 'voluntary export restraints'. There are, in addition, limits on the value of imports that can receive GSP tariff treatment and an initial time limit on the scheme of 10 years, insufficient for many developing countries to establish a comparative advantage in a particular line of production.

Estimates of the net benefits of the GSP arrangements vary widely, according to the assumptions made, but they are thought to be small.[3] One reason for this is that the coverage of the GSP is limited to less than 20 per cent of all LDC exports. Secondly, some 80 per cent of imports under the GSP come from seven 'newly industrialised countries' (Brazil, Hong Kong, Israel, Korea, Mexico, Singapore, and Taiwan). Third, many of the goods that are of most interest to the LDCs, such as textiles, are excluded from the GSP as a consequence of their special position in the developed countries.[4] Fourthly, there are various 'escape clauses' in GSP schemes which allow 'donor' countries to withdraw concessions if they experience 'market disruption'.

The idea about tariff preferences met with criticism and resistance at the first UNCTAD conference. One line of argument was that tariffs on most industrial goods were so low in the leading industrial countries that the scope for tariff preferences was limited.[5] Nominal tariff rates were then on average between 10 and 15 per cent. If tariff preferences of 50 per cent were granted, the price advantage of a LDC over competitors from a developed country would be about 5 to 7 per cent. Such a small price advantage, it was argued, would not be decisive. If the LDCs were unable to compete without a trade preference, they would not, under these circumstances, be able to compete with a preference.

This line of argument perhaps sounds plausible; it does, however, have some weaknesses. First, it must be stated that even though average tariff rates are not too high, tariffs on individual products could be substantially higher. Second, it is quite arbitrary to presume that tariff preferences would be limited to, for instance, 50 per cent. A complete preferential treatment of certain sensitive products could perhaps give much higher price advantages than 5 to 7 per cent.

A more important objection is that what really counts is not the nominal tariff rate but the effective rate of protection. Here we must refer the reader to the discussion in Chapter 14. Fairly low nominal rates could conceal much higher effective rates of protection. If that is the case, the question of tariff preferences, it is argued, would have to be viewed in a completely different perspective. Particularly if the import content of domestic production is high, and if there is a variety of tariff rates and many exemptions, protection may be much greater than the tariff rates indicate and may vary widely from industry to industry without any logical pattern.[6]

Most countries have a 'cascading' type of tariff structure, i.e. tariffs on raw materials are lower than tariffs on semi-manufactured goods, which in turn are lower than tariffs on final products. This usually means that the effective rates of protection on final goods are substantially higher than the nominal tariff rates. On most consumer goods of export interest to LDCs, the final tariff rates in the United States, Western Europe and Japan seem to be about 13 to 18 per cent, whereas the effective rates on the same goods seem to be almost double that figure, in the 20 to 30 per cent range.[7] This would indicate that there could conceivably be substantial scope for tariff preferences on these goods.

The various limits on the eligibility of products for GSP treatment clearly restrict its potential benefits. Using 1971 trade flows, Baldwin and Murray have concluded that LDCs stand to gain more from MFN tariff cuts than they would lose from the simultaneous erosion of their GSP preferences.[8] Another study has concluded that as long as processed agricultural goods, and some resource-based traditional manufactures important to the poorer LDCs, are excluded or subject to restricted access, the GSP will have a limited effect in encouraging exports from such sources.[9]

The GSP schemes (in 1980) provided a limited benefit to many of the more advanced developing countries and no benefit to others.[10] However, if the absence of discrimination among the LDCs had been introduced explicitly into the GSP, it was likely that significant improvements could have been made. Generally, these countries were not affected by the value limitations on GSP trade, and they would have benefited particularly from a relaxation in the area of agricultural and fishery products.

Ultimately the strongest argument for tariff preferences will perhaps have to be of a very pragmatic nature. The need for an increase in the rate of economic development in most of the LDCs becomes more pressing each year. It is obviously very difficult to find and implement any policy means that fosters development. Against this background it is natural to see if tariff preferences could not be an efficient means for accelerating development. This could in the end be the strongest reason for trying to work out a scheme for tariff preferences that would prove viable.

18.4 The support and stabilisation of international commodity prices

The agenda for the fourth UNCTAD conference in Nairobi tended to concentrate on the subject of the stabilisation of international commodity prices and the creation of an 'integrated programme for commodities' which would help to improve the terms on which primary commodities are traded (up to that time, to the advantage of developing countries). These objectives can be traced back to earlier UNCTAD conferences. Indeed, the line of argument that the terms of trade between primary products and industrial goods ought to be stabilised and that the purchasing power of a certain amount of primary-product exports should be preserved in terms of imports of industrial goods was eagerly promoted by Prebisch. The wisdom of such a policy and the important questions which it raises will be discussed next.

Exports of primary products are the most important source of earnings of foreign exchange for most LDCs, accounting for 85 to 90 per cent of their export earnings. But prices of primary products both fluctuate widely in the short term and show a tendency to longer-term (secular) movements. This leads to instability in export earnings. The instability gives rise to many problems, including difficulties in planning development, and hampers the development process. If commodity prices could be stabilised, an important obstacle to development could be eliminated. Hence the stabilisation of commodity prices must be given high priority. This is the argument.

Here the ground is slippery and we must tread carefully. It is otherwise easy to perpetuate old dogmas and go on mechanically repeating old half-truths. The traditional view just paraphrased sounds convincing, but we must examine it more carefully. First, we might observe that it is not quite clear what is to be stabilised. Stabilising prices is not the same thing as stabilising earnings, and stabilising export earnings is not necessarily the same thing as stabilising real income.

Second, we must identify the form of price variability we wish to control. It may help to consider price variability as coming in three forms. Long-run variability may arise from long-run shifts in supply and/or demand functions. For example, the demand for a product may decline over time if new substitute products are developed (as with synthetic fibres), or if improvements in technology mean that less of the good is used in making a final product (as with steel in car bodies). The supply of a product may increase because new sources of supply are found (as with the discovery of new oil fields), or because of improved technology (as with many agricultural products). Medium-run variability may occur as a result of variations in demand as the world economy moves through a 'trade cycle'. It might also be caused by variations in supply, perhaps of the 'cobweb theorem' type; such phenomena have been recorded in hog production in the USA and in coffee production in Brazil. Short-term variability seems, on the available evidence, to come mainly from random 'shocks' in the supply of a commodity, such as those caused by variations in weather and the incidence of disease in an agricultural crop.

The distinction is important when we come to discuss policy responses to price variability. Policies which are appropriate for reducing short-term price variability may be inappropriate for medium-term variability. Equally, policies which will control price variability in the medium-term may be incapable of controlling a long-term fall (or rise) in prices due to changing demand or supply conditions.

The terminology of price support and/or stabilisation is rather confusing. The preferred convention is that schemes which take account of the interests of both producers and consumers are called *international commodity agreements* (ICAs), in contrast with the *international cartel*, which considers only the producers' interests. Unfortunately there is a tendency to apply the ICA label to the cartel case as well.[11]

◼ *18.5* Supporting prices in the long run

As we have mentioned already, it has been argued that there ought to be a long-term 'stabilisation' of the terms of trade between LDC primary exports and their principal industrial imports. We shall interpret 'stabilisation' in this context as maintaining the price in the face of a tendency for it to decline, and shall consider policies that might be used for such a purpose. We shall postpone consideration of the question of whether there *is* a long-run tendency for the prices of primary products to decline until Chapter 19.

The argument that the long-run terms of trade *should* be stabilised can claim no foundation in rational economic reasoning. We know from earlier reasoning that international prices must be viewed as endogenous variables in an economic system. Variations in the terms of trade depend in a complex way on changes in production and consumption and on other basic economic variables. An aspiration to control the long-term development of the terms of trade is the same as an aspiration to control all variables in the economic system. To be effective, it would imply perfect economic planning on a world-wide scale. It is difficult to see how anyone who has grasped the core of the problem could support schemes of such an utopian nature.

To claim that a certain amount of primary products *should* have a stable purchasing power over industrial products in the long run is as unrealistic a claim. There is no reason whatsoever to expect such a development to take place, nor is there anything specifically 'just' about it. It is impossible to understand why one should try to keep stable, in the long run, a certain relation between volumes and relative prices given at an arbitrary historical moment.

The most obvious way for a group of producers to manipulate the price of a commodity is for them to form a cartel which will control the quantity sold. The Organisation of Oil Exporting Countries (OPEC) is just such a cartel. We can use the pure theory of monopoly as a way of examining the operations of a cartel, and shall do so in terms of Figure 18.2.

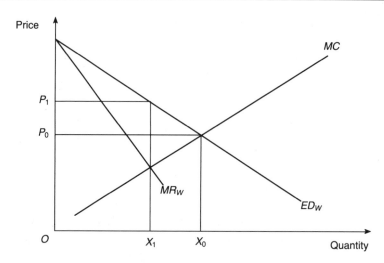

Figure 18.2 *The operation of an export cartel*

ED_W is the demand curve facing the cartel. It is the excess of demand in the rest of the world over the supply coming from countries outside the cartel, who are usually assumed to take the world price as given; such countries are often referred to as the 'competitive fringe'. MR_W is then the marginal revenue curve facing the cartel. MC shows the marginal cost of production by the cartel members, derived by summing their individual marginal cost curves.

The cartel may maximise the total profits earned by its members by restricting output to X_1 and driving the price up to P_1, the familiar outcome in models of pure monopoly. These additional profits are outweighed by the costs to the rest of the world, and the world as a whole loses by an amount equal to the area of the triangle defined by the quantity X_1 and the MC and MR_W curves.

A cartel however differs from the pure monopoly case in that it requires the co-operation of a group of countries. There must be agreement on the total exports of the cartel and on the allocation of those exports between the member countries. That in turn requires policing of the actions of members, since an individual member of a cartel will be able to increase its own profits by exceeding its allocated export quota. The easiest way to police exports would be to monitor imports by the oil-importing countries, but it is unlikely that they will wish to co-operate.

The history of OPEC illustrates these problems. Successive conferences of OPEC members have found it difficult to agree on either their total exports or the allocation of those exports. Some members, notably Iran and Iraq, with large and relatively poor populations have attempted to persuade the more 'oil-rich' countries, particularly Saudi Arabia, to bear most of the brunt of the reductions. Saudi Arabia has become increasingly unwilling to do so, and has used its potential to reduce the world price by increasing its own output as a means of gaining a more even distribution of output and export reductions.

OPEC has also found it increasingly difficult to maintain unity on prices, with members tending to make their own autonomous price changes, or engaging in barter deals in which the price of oil is effectively reduced.

The question of the price that OPEC should set for oil (in order to best serve the ends of its members) has no simple answer. One problem is that setting too high a price will encourage the development of new sources (as in the North Sea) and of ways of economising on the use of oil. Both will tend to shift the demand curve facing the cartel to the left, as shown in Figure 18.3.

Faced with such a situation, the cartel could continue to maximise its profits by reducing output from X_1 to X_2. The cartel price would still however fall (from P_1 to P_2), and profits would necessarily be lower than before the contraction in demand. An alternative response would be to attempt to maintain the price at P_1, but this would require that output be reduced still further (to X_3), and the fall in profits would be greater. Saudi Arabia has expressed particular concern that the high prices sought by some OPEC members will produce just such a reduction in demand.

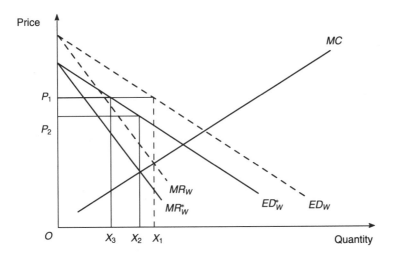

Figure 18.3   *An export cartel when demand is contracting*

There is however an argument that would predict an increase in the price of oil over time, whether there is a cartel or not. It is based on the theory of the optimal extraction of an exhaustible resource over time, which says that the price of the resource should increase over time at a rate equal to the rate of interest. The existence of a cartel will change the path taken by the price, but is not a necessary condition for price to increase.

Finally, we should note that, from the point of world-wide efficiency, the allocation of output quotas among members of a cartel is of importance. The cost of producing a given total output will be minimised if individual quotas are allocated so that the marginal cost of production is the same for all members. An allocation of individual quotas that does not meet this criterion will further increase the cost to the world as a whole of the operation of the cartel.

18.6 Stabilising prices in the medium and short run

We now come to the problem of stabilising prices rather than supporting them. For simplicity, we shall assume we are dealing with a situation where the average price is constant over time, but where prices vary about that average. Before considering policies which will reduce or eliminate such variations in price, we need to consider some more basic issues. Some issues are empirical. Is there (significant) price variability, and if so, what are its causes? Does this result in instability in, for example, foreign exchange earnings or producers' revenues? If so, is there any evidence that such instability has had adverse effects on the countries concerned? If it has not then there may be no justification for introducing a policy to control it.

Other issues are more difficult to answer empirically. Is the stabilisation of prices seen as an end in itself by governments, or is it seen as a means to some other end, such as stabilising foreign exchange earnings or producers' revenues? If the latter, will stabilising prices in fact have such an effect? In either case, we should ask why governments view stabilisation as desirable. Finally, we should ask whether there are market-based mechanisms which should reduce price variability; if there are, and they exist, then we should ask why they are not doing so; if they do not exist, then why?

Empirical evidence on the importance of instability in the prices of primary products has been rather mixed. In 1966 MacBean published an econometric investigation into fluctuations in prices of primary products in the period 1946 to 1958.[12] He found that the LDCs seemed to have only insignificantly greater fluctuations in their export incomes than industrial countries. Three causes that could have been expected to result in instability, the commodity concentration of exports, the proportion of primary goods in total exports, and the geographical concentration of exports, all had little value in explaining the fluctuations that had taken place. An extremely important finding was that the prime causes of the fluctuations in export incomes of LDCs tended to be fluctuations in output, rather than price movements *per se*.

More recent work, by MacBean and Nguyen,[13] suggests that the picture changed somewhat in later time periods. Using a measure of the variability of commodity prices around their trends, they concluded that the prices of primary goods had been at least 50 per cent more variable than the prices of manufactures, and in some cases three times more variable. They also estimated that the export earnings of the LDCs had been approximately twice as variable as those of the developed industrial countries. Bleaney and Greenaway,[14] in a study mainly directed at analysing long-term movements, found a large random component in the relative price of primary commodities.

The 'traditional' explanation for this higher variability in primary product prices emphasises the role of price elasticities of demand and supply. If these are low, as seems to be the case for primary products, then small changes in quantities supplied are translated into large changes in prices. Restrictions on imports of some foodstuffs by the developed countries may further reduce their elasticity of demand for imports.

Another of MacBean's findings in his 1966 study was that the changes in export incomes that had taken place had not led to such adverse effects for the growth of the economies as might have been expected. Built-in stabilisers and high marginal propensities to import seemed to offset fluctuations to a large extent, so that fluctuations in national incomes were not so large as could be expected. Subsequent studies, by Kenen and Voivodas[15] and by Lim[16] produced results which were in broad agreement with those of MacBean. Kenen and Voivodas did, however, find a significant negative correlation between exports and the level of investment during the 1960s.

The question of whether particular groups gain or lose from reducing instability may be examined by using the concept of the attitude to *risk*. We shall explain this briefly in terms of an individual's attitude to uncertainty about their income, although the ideas are readily extended to uncertainty about prices. In broad terms, individuals are *risk-neutral* if they regard a certain income of £100 and an uncertain income with a mean value of £100 as equally acceptable. As a simple example, a risk-neutral individual would be indifferent between being paid £100 and a gamble in which they would be paid £200 if a coin turned up heads and £0 if it turned up tails.

Individuals are *risk-averse* if they are prepared to pay for a greater certainty about the income (or price or whatever) that they will receive by accepting a lower mean income. For example, a risk-averse individual might regard the gamble given above as equivalent to a certain income of £80. The lower the certain income that individuals regard as equivalent to a given gamble, the more risk-averse they are.

Risk-loving individuals would regard a certain income of £100 as inferior to the gamble described. It is commonly argued that many people are risk-loving where small amounts of certain income are involved but risk-averse when the stakes are higher. For example, the same person may be prepared to spend a small amount on a lottery ticket where his expected return is less than the price of the ticket, but will spend a larger amount on fire insurance for his house.

It is arguable that governments (perhaps responding to the views of producers and consumers) are risk-averse when faced with variability in the prices of goods or of foreign currency revenues or payments. For example, variability in the export earnings of an LDC may make it more difficult to plan investment, while variability in the price of an export good may discourage its production if potential producers see it as more risky than some other good. In such cases, a government may be willing to pursue a stabilisation policy even if it reduces the average export revenue (or price).

A major problem in applying this approach lies in deciding on the variable (or variables) we should use in the analysis. If, for example, we are concerned with the gains or losses to producers of price stabilisation, should we work in terms of their revenues or their producers' surplus? For consumers, on the other hand, should we use their expenditure, or should we use consumers' surplus? Some economists, notably Samuelson, have argued strongly that the economic surplus form of analysis is invalid when there is uncertainty about prices. We shall avoid that issue by concentrating on a less contentious variable, export earnings.

Figure 18.4 represents an extremely simple example of the effects of stabilising prices when the price instability is due to variations in supply (the dominant source of price instability).[17] The supply curve[18] for the exporting countries in any one period is either S_1 or S_2, with each having a probability of occurring of 0.5. Note that this is not a systematic variation of S_1, then S_2, then S_1, and so on. D is the demand curve for the importing countries, and is the same in every period.

In periods when supply is low (i.e. the supply curve is S_1), the price will be high (P_1), exports will be low (Q_1), and export revenue will be P_1Q_1. When supply is high (supply curve S_2), the price will be low (P_2), exports will be high (Q_2), and export revenue will be P_2Q_2. Whether revenue is

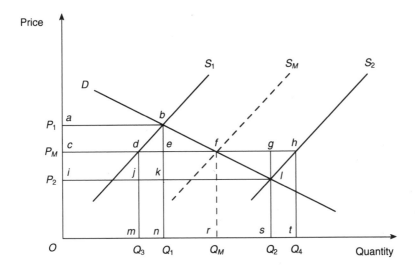

Figure 18.4 *Price stabilisation when supply is unstable*

higher or lower in the low supply case depends on the elasticity of the demand curve. If the demand curve is elastic then $P_1Q_1 < P_2Q_2$; if not, then $P_1Q_1 > P_2Q_2$.

Suppose now that some way is found to stabilise the price at its average level, P_M (obviously $P_M = 0.5P_1 + 0.5P_2$). It should be immediately apparent that stabilising the price will not stabilise the revenue from exports. When the supply curve is S_1, the volume of exports at price P_M will be Q_3, and the export revenue will be P_MQ_3, which is less than P_1Q_1. When the supply curve is S_2, the volume of exports at price P_M will be Q_4, and the export revenue will be P_MQ_4, which is higher than P_2Q_2.

Price stabilisation will increase the average level of export revenues. In Figure 18.4, the loss in revenue due to stabilisation in low supply periods $(P_MQ_3 - P_1Q_1)$ is shown by area *abec* plus area *denm*. The gain in revenue in high supply periods $(P_MQ_4 - P_2Q_2)$ is shown by area *cgli* plus area *ghts*. The average gain in revenue is thus $0.5(cgli + ghts - abec - denm)$. Since area *abec* is equal to area *cekj*, and area *denm* is equal to area *ghts*, there must be a net gain in average export revenue equal to area *eglk*.

However, stabilising prices may *destabilise* export revenues, in the sense of increasing their variability. Suppose the demand curve is elastic, so that before the price is stabilised we have $P_1Q_1 < P_2Q_2$. Stabilising the price has the effect of reducing export earnings in periods when they would have been low, and increasing them when they would have been high. In such a case, extremely risk-averse governments would be unwilling to engage in price stabilisation policies.

Note the difference between the effects of stabilising the price when there is variability in supply, and of stabilising the supply itself. If supply were stabilised at the average of the two supply curves[19] (the supply curve labelled as S_M in Figure 18.4) then export revenue would be constant at $P_M Q_M$, which is the average of $P_M Q_3$ and $P_M Q_4$. Stabilising supply would both increase the average export revenue and eliminate its instability. This is, of course, one more example of the general principle that a policy that deals with the problem at its source (supply variability in this case) is superior to a policy which attempts to deal with the consequences of that problem.

Our final question was concerned with the possible reactions of free markets to price instability. Price variation is a feature in many markets, from those in currencies and other financial assets to those in commodities. In many cases individuals or organisations attempt to profit from the variation in prices by engaging in stock-holding. The basic form of such speculative activity is the purchase of an asset or commodity when its price is low with a view to selling it when its price has risen. Such activity will tend to increase prices in low-price periods and reduce them in high-price periods. For such activity to be profitable however, the costs of storing the commodity and of the capital tied up while it is being stored must not be too high. Typically, we would not expect to observe private stock-holding in the case of perishable goods.

Another possible market-based 'response' to price variability is the establishment of a futures market, which may provide profitable opportunities for speculators (if they can predict price movements successfully), and a means of stabilising future revenues for producers (and of expenditures by consumers). Futures markets, which are not restricted to non-perishable commodities, do exist for some primary products which are exported by the LDCs (such as tin), but it is difficult to know whether they have been used to any great extent by the LDCs.

The existence of futures markets and the extent of private stock-holding may be reduced by the operation of government-backed schemes to stabilise prices. A reduction in the variability of prices will reduce the profitability of speculation in both futures and stock-holding, so that the speculators, who provide the essential liquidity in both activities, will be discouraged.

Both exporting and importing countries may believe that they will gain from a reduction in uncertainty about prices, and so may co-operate in an international commodity agreement. This contrasts with the international cartel form of agreement discussed earlier, where the importing countries would appear to have little to gain.

■ *18.7* International buffer stocks

International co-operation to stabilise commodity prices has often taken the form of an *international buffer stock*. The essence of an international buffer stock is that it controls the world price for the commodity in question by buying and selling the commodity. Obviously, this requires that the buffer stock agency be 'large'. This in turn means that it will usually require the co-operation of several countries, each of whom may be too small to be able to affect world prices.

An international buffer stock in fact requires the holding of two stocks – one of the commodity in question, the other of money. An international buffer stock follows a policy of buying the commodity when its price is low, and selling it when its price is high, as does the private stock-holder. However, the intention of the buffer stock is to stabilise prices rather than to make a profit (it may of course make a profit in the course of its operations, although making a loss seems to be a more common outcome).

The operation of a simple buffer stock can be explained in terms of Figure 18.5 (which shows the relevant features of Figure 18.4). Once again, there is a 50 per cent chance that supply will be S_1, and a 50 per cent chance that it will be S_2 in any period. The demand curve is assumed to be stable, and so the free market price will be either P_1 or P_2.

The target price for the buffer stock is P_M, the average of the two free market prices. If the price is high (at P_1) because of low supplies, the buffer

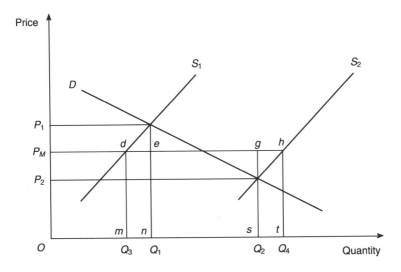

Figure 18.5 *Using a buffer stock to stabilise prices*

stock must sell a quantity $Q_1 - Q_3$ at the target price in order to reduce the market price to P_M. In so doing it increases its stock of money by an amount $P_M(Q_1 - Q_3)$. If, on the other hand, the price is low (at P_2) because of high supplies, the buffer stock must buy a quantity $Q_4 - Q_2$ at the target price in order to drive the market price up to P_M. The cost of those purchases will be $P_M(Q_4 - Q_2)$.

In the simple case shown, the buffer stock will accumulate stocks of neither the commodity nor money. The linearity of the demand and supply functions, and the setting of the target price at the average of the free market prices, ensure that the quantities bought and sold are the same, and since there is a 50 per cent chance of either occurring, the average quantity bought or sold must, in the long run, be zero. By a parallel argument, the average of the expenditures by the buffer stock in buying the commodity in low-price periods and its receipts from selling the commodity in high-price periods must also be zero.

This need not be the outcome if the demand and supply curves are non-linear or if the target price is set incorrectly. In practice, it will be difficult to estimate the form of the demand and supply schedules, and equally difficult to set the correct target price.

In practice, buffer stock schemes operate with a minimum price, and a maximum price, rather than a given target price. The operation of such a scheme is essentially the same as that discussed earlier. The buffer stock buys the commodity if the price looks likely to fall below the minimum (the 'floor' price), and sells it if the price appears to be going above the maximum (the 'ceiling' price). Such schemes reduce the variability of prices rather than eliminating it, but will usually require lower initial stocks of both the commodity and money, and will reduce the frequency with which the buffer stock must intervene in the market.

It may be argued that the most common difficulties experienced in operating international commodity agreements in practice have been caused by attempting to maintain inappropriate prices, coupled with inadequate stocks of the commodity and of money. A common error seems to be setting the target price too high (or trying to maintain a given price in the face of a downward trend). If this is done then the buffer stock will tend to accumulate stocks of the commodity, since it will buy more often, and probably in greater quantities, than it will sell. More importantly, a buffer stock operating with too high a target price will tend to run out of money with which to finance purchases.

The other outcome is of course also possible: if the buffer stock attempts to maintain too low a price then it will tend to run out of the commodity. This may well happen if there is a major cut in output or a significant increase in demand.

18.8 International quota agreements and multilateral contract systems

Two other forms of international commodity agreement (i.e. involving both producers and consumers) are the *international quota agreement* and the *multilateral contract system*. The former seeks to keep prices within an agreed band by the operation of quotas when prices move outside the band. Such agreements specify the ceiling and floor prices, and quotas for either production or exports in the producing countries and for imports in the consuming countries. If the price falls below the specified minimum then the quotas are imposed on the producing countries. If the price moves above the ceiling then the importing countries are allocated a quota of imports.

The multilateral contract system also specifies minimum and maximum prices, accompanied by contracts to buy or sell specified quantities. The producers' contracts to sell are invoked if the market price exceeds the maximum price. The consumers' contracts to buy are invoked either if the price falls to the floor level, or at some price within the price range, depending on the specific agreement.

Both forms of agreement should give some security to both producing and consuming nations but, as we shall see, they have not proved very successful.

18.9 Recent experience with international commodity agreements

The difficulty of setting appropriate maximum and minimum prices in practice should not be underestimated. Prices in world commodity markets may have long-term trends (either up or down), coupled with medium-term cyclical movements and short-term disturbances. Distinguishing the long-term trend from the other phenomena on a continuing basis is extremely difficult, but very important. Buffer stocks, quota agreements and multilateral contract systems may have some success in moderating medium- and short-term changes in price, but should not be used in an attempt to counteract a long-term trend. Continued buying of a commodity in the face of a long-term downward movement in prices, for example, will lead to the accumulation of stocks and a shortage of money, and perhaps to the failure of the scheme.

As with an international cartel, agreement must be made on prices, quotas or contracts (if applicable), and how the burden of running the scheme will be shared among the member countries. In this case, provided that the target price range has been set correctly, the main costs will be for administration, holding stocks, and providing finance. One obvious problem is that there is again a temptation for an individual country to be a 'free rider', staying outside the scheme and so avoiding a contribution to its costs, while still enjoying the benefits of a more stable price.

The history of the operation of international commodity agreements is not encouraging. The first International Wheat Agreement (a multilateral contract system) was signed in 1949, and revised or extended in 1953, 1956, 1959 and 1962. It was replaced with a new agreement, which consisted of the Wheat Trade Convention and the Food Aid Convention, in 1967. The current Wheat Trade Convention, signed in 1971 and renewed regularly, contains no provisions on prices or on rights and obligations. The Food Aid Convention does still provide for annual contributions of various grains by a group of developed and grain exporting nations.

The International Tin Agreement, a mixture of a buffer stock and export controls, was concluded in 1954 but did not become effective until 1956. It was renewed regularly in essentially unchanged form until 1982, when the United States, Bolivia and the USSR withdrew. The Agreement was unable to cope with the major price fluctuations that occurred, particularly in 1976 when prices went above the ceiling. The controlling authority (the Tin Council) ran out of money in 1985, and was formally dissolved in 1990.

The International Coffee Agreement, first established in 1963, employed an export quota system. During the second Agreement (1968) frost damage to the Brazilian crop lead to major price increases and the regulatory mechanism collapsed. After a gap of three years the third Agreement came into force in 1976; the high prices of the late 1970s meant that the export quota provisions were applied only near the end of 1980. The fourth Agreement (1983) is similar to its predecessor; quotas were suspended in 1986 because of high prices, but reintroduced in 1987. There have been considerable and highly discounted sales outside the Agreement. The differences of interest (between large and small producers, and between producers and consumers) make it unlikely that it will be very effective.

The International Cocoa Agreement, involving a buffer stock and export quotas, was signed in 1973 and extended in 1976. The 1981 Agreement was a pure buffer stock system which, despite repeated purchasing, was unable to increase prices. The latest Agreement came into operation at the start of 1987, but buffer stock operations were suspended within 6 months. The economic provisions were suspended in 1990, but the Agreement was extended until September 1992.

The International Natural Rubber Agreement was the first agreement signed under the UNCTAD Integrated Programme (see later), and uses a buffer stock. It managed to keep prices within the specified price range in 1981 and 1982, but then had to adjust the range downwards. The increase in demand in the late 1980s meant that the buffer stock was sold.

The International Sugar Agreement (ISA) has probably the worst record of all. The first Agreement came into force in January 1954, the second in 1959. The economic provisions of the latter were suspended in 1962 following the 1960 Cuba crisis, although the remaining provisions were extended until 1968. The next Agreement, also without economic provisions, was signed in 1968, introduced in 1969, and abandoned in 1973. The next Agreement, again without economic provisions, was agreed in 1977, came into operation in 1978, and ran, with an extension, until the end of 1984 (without the participation of the European Community). It has been argued that it both reduced the export earnings of the developing country compared to a free trade situation and increased the instability of prices. MacBean and Snowden have stated:[20] 'This is one market where free competition would in all likelihood bring the best results in terms of stability, efficiency and equity. The ISAs were palliatives diverting attention from the much greater priority of persuading the rich nations to reduce their protection of beet sugar.'

18.10 The United Nations Integrated Programme for Commodities

It may be argued that if more than one commodity is to be the subject of an international commodity agreement then gains may be made by establishing a common fund to finance buffer stock operations. The basis of the argument is that of 'risk sharing'. Unless commodity prices move perfectly in step with one another, the fund of money that will be needed to finance operations in a combined buffer stock scheme will be lower than the sum of the funds needed to finance individual schemes.

The establishment of such an integrated scheme, involving 18 commodities, was proposed by UNCTAD in the mid-1970s. The proposed scheme involved both price stabilisation through a buffer stock and price enhancement through production controls. The proposal has attracted considerable criticism, both as evidence of a failure to learn from past experience and as involving commodities for which there are already effective price-raising schemes or for which either production control or buffer stock schemes are infeasible.[21] The funding of the scheme (agreed in 1976) appears to be too small for it to have any significant impact.

■ *18.11* Compensatory finance schemes

An interesting multilateral price compensation scheme was proposed at the 1964 UNCTAD conference by James Meade.[22] Let us assume, says Meade, that there are two countries, Ruritania and Urbania, and that Ruritania exports a primary product to Urbania. The two countries now agree on a 'normal' volume traded and a 'standard' price. They then devise a sliding scale whereby if the price falls below the 'standard' price, Urbania pays Ruritania a compensation which equals the shortfall of the 'standard' price on the 'normal' amount traded. Conversely, Ruritania pays Urbania an amount equal to an excess over the 'standard' price times the 'normal' volume if the price is above its normal level.

The main idea behind the Meade proposal is to try to separate the distributional effects of the price mechanism from its allocative effects. When the price of a product falls, this is a signal to producers to produce less and to consumers to consume more. This is the efficiency (or allocative) aspect of the price mechanism, and this we usually do not want to interfere with. But price changes also have distributional implications. When the price falls, producers get hurt, because their incomes fall. So do workers in the LDC; the tax base of the government shrinks; and so on. This can, at least partially, be avoided by a scheme *à la* Meade. It is most natural to think of the scheme as one between governments. If the price falls and the producers in Ruritania get lower incomes, the consumers in Urbania will benefit by lower prices. But they will now have to pay more in taxes, and this increase in taxes will be transferred to the government in Ruritania. The government there can then dispose of this income as it sees fit. It can directly subsidise producers, or it can invest the money for development purposes.

The scheme can easily be extended to a multilateral basis. Then a 'normal' volume of imports is designated for each importing country and a 'normal' volume of exports for each exporting country. A 'standard' price has to be agreed upon. Then if the actual price differs from the 'standard' price, the respective countries will have to pay and receive compensation according to 'normal' volumes.

A difficulty with this scheme, as with others, is that of forecasting the price correctly. If the price is set too high, the scheme amounts to a transfer of resources from the industrial to the primary-producing countries, and vice versa when the price is set too low. One could think of an arrangement whereby initially the price was set too high, but then would be gradually lowered. Then the compensation scheme would also entail an aid arrangement which would help the primary-producing countries to develop other sectors during a transitory period.

The Meade scheme is both simple and elegant, but it has certain drawbacks. An important one is connected with its aggregated nature. If a producer is small and a change in its output does not affect the world price of the goods, it could well be that even though the output of this producer is very low one year, prices would not exceed the 'standard' price. The country would then get no compensation, even though its export proceeds fall considerably. A scheme such as Meade's has difficulties in dealing with fluctuations caused by changes in the supply of single countries. This is a serious deficiency since the primary cause of fluctuations in export earnings seems to be difficulties in controlling supply conditions in the primary-producing countries themselves.

The European Community introduced a scheme broadly similar to the Meade proposal, known as STABEX, under the Lomé Convention of 1975.[23] It covers 52 (originally 46) countries in Africa, the Caribbean and the Pacific for shortfalls in their export earnings in any one year compared with the average value for the preceding four years. STABEX involves 17 agricultural commodities and iron ore, in crude or simply-processed form, which account for about 20 per cent of the export earnings of the countries involved.

For a country to take advantage of the scheme for a particular commodity requires that the commodity account for at least 6.5 per cent of its total merchandise export earnings. If the earnings from exporting the commodity to the European Community fall more than 6.5 per cent below the average earnings for the previous four years then the European Community will make an interest-free loan to the country concerned which is repayable when export earnings recover. The two 6.5 per cent rules are relaxed to 2 per cent for the poorest/landlocked/island states, and the loans become non-repayable grants.

The STABEX scheme has been criticised on various grounds. First, it is discriminatory, in that Lomé Convention countries are favoured at the expense of other LDCs. Second, it covers only a limited range of goods (minerals, which are important to the member countries, are excluded), which discourages diversification into goods not covered by the scheme. Third, it does not apply to exports outside the European Community, so discouraging diversification into other markets. Fourth, it does not apply to semi-processed or processed goods, so discouraging processing in the member countries. Fifth, a 7 per cent proportionate fall in the export revenue from a relatively unimportant good (in export revenue terms) will secure assistance, whereas a 6 per cent fall in a more important good will not. Sixth, the rules are specified in money terms, not in real terms. Finally, the funding has been inadequate: in 1980 and 1981, for example, STABEX had insufficient funds to meet all the claims made following a fall in commodity prices.

The most important scheme so far is the Compensatory Financing Facility (CFF) introduced by the International Monetary Fund in 1963. The CFF was not widely used until 1975, when the IMF relaxed the conditions for access. This scheme allows countries whose export earnings decline to get easier loans than usual. The 'norm' against which current earnings are compared is the average of the earnings in the current year and the two previous years and of forecasts of earnings in the two following years. Countries must also satisfy the IMF that the shortfall was not their fault, that they face a balance-of-payments problem, and that they are willing to co-operate with the IMF in finding a solution to their problem. They must not exceed their borrowing limits.

A study by Finger and de Rosa[24] suggests that the activities of the CFF up to 1977 increased the instability of export earnings as often as they reduced it; subsequent work indicates that there has been no improvement in performance since then.[25] Finger and de Rosa argue that the main reason for the poor performance of the CFF was the bad forecasting of future export earnings.

The CFF became the Compensatory and Contingency Financing Facility (CCFF) in 1988, the new 'contingency' element being intended to provide relief from the effects of external shocks such as increases in oil prices.

■ *18.12* Concluding remarks

We have covered four main areas: preferential tariff arrangements in favour of the LDCs, international cartels intended to increase export earnings, international commodity agreements directed at stabilising commodity prices, and compensatory finance schemes to stabilise export earnings. In all cases the results of our discussion have tended to be on the negative side.

Preferential tariff schemes have some attractions in principle (in encouraging LDCs to be outward-oriented), but may inhibit change and be difficult to administer. Nevertheless, a scheme such as the Generalised System of Preferences may, for the time being, be the most efficient type of trade policy that the developed countries can pursue in favour of the LDCs.

Export cartels may be successful in raising prices in the medium term, but have certain drawbacks. One is that they are usually difficult to enforce for any long period. There is always a temptation for a single producer to break away from the scheme, thereby being able to sell a larger quantity at a good price. Tendencies to overproduction, which usually follow from the price-maintenance policy, can easily cause a breakdown of the system. If the price is maintained at a high level for some time, this can also create difficulties on the demand side. The demand elasticity could be low in the short term, but it could be substantially higher in the long run. A policy of high prices could then mean that demand for the product will not expand as much as it otherwise would. It could also lead to the development of competing products, for instance of a synthetic kind, that can prove very damaging in the long run. Restriction schemes, moreover, easily give rise to a misallocation of resources. They tend to conserve a given production structure both among and within countries, and established but inefficient producers will prevail over new and more efficient ones. Restriction schemes are rarely efficient in the long run. They build on an intrinsic conservatism and will probably eventually prove detrimental to economic growth.

International buffer stocks seem to have had limited success in stabilising commodity prices, and may in any case be directed towards a target which is unimportant or used to seek the wrong target (price enhancement). Instability *per se* need not have disastrous consequences for LDCs. In principle, the governments in the affected countries should be able to plan around trend values for prices and incomes and help to overcome the difficulties of lean years by building up reserves during fat years. Governments of LDCs could for several reasons experience difficulties in doing this. The demand for price stabilisation could be viewed as a demand from weak governments to stronger governments to help solve problems that should primarily concern only the weak governments.

Compensatory finance seems more attractive that a price stabilisation arrangement, but experience to date does not suggest great success. Any scheme of compensatory financing will probably prove unsatisfactory from the point of view of the LDCs. This depends on fluctuations not being their main problem, which instead is a lack of resources. To get some degree of approval, a scheme of compensatory financing has to have some element of aid in it. But to tie aid to fluctuations in export earnings could easily be arbitrary and create a weakness in this type of scheme. Countries that strive successfully to control supply conditions could get the smallest amount of aid. Under such circumstances, resources could easily be transferred to countries where they are least efficiently used.

None of the policies is ideal. For a believer in international competition and division of labour, they have obvious shortcomings. Our discussion has not given too much reason for hope. There are perhaps some gains to be derived for the LDCs from a revision of trade policy in the developed countries. These gains, however, seem to be limited. In the immediate future, export earnings of the LDCs will have to come primarily from exports of primary products. A revision of trade policies, especially of agricultural policies in the developed countries, should be of help to the LDCs, but this help will be limited. Many LDCs will have to try to get their industrialisation under way. Tariff preferences could help in this respect, but how efficient they would prove is an open question. A certain scepticism is probably not unwarranted. Trade policies are not unimportant, but they will have only marginal effects unless supplemented by other means.

☐ *Notes*

1   See, for example, MacBean and Snowden (1981), Chapter 5.
2   Some developed countries had started to operate a preference scheme before then; Australia's scheme was instituted in 1966.
3   See Murray (1977).
4   See Ray (1987) for a discussion of this in the US context.
5   See Patterson (1966).
6   See Little, Scitovsky and Scott (1970).
7   See Balassa (1965).
8   See Baldwin and Murray (1977).
9   See Morton and Tulloch (1977), p. 175.
10   Over three-quarters of the GSP trade can be accounted for by twelve countries: Taiwan, Mexico, Yugoslavia, South Korea, Hong Kong, Brazil, Singapore, India, Peru, Chile, Argentina and Iran. See Baldwin and Murray (1977).
11   See van Meerhaeghe (1992), p.148.
12   MacBean (1966).
13   MacBean and Nguyen (1987).
14   Bleaney and Greenaway (1993).
15   Kenen and Voivodas (1972).
16   Lim (1976).
17   We shall not consider the alternative case where demand instability is the cause of price instability. A discussion of that case (and of the supply instability case) is given in Behrman (1978).
18   An even simpler model would specify perfectly price inelastic supplies. The responsiveness of supply to price in any one period may come from some ability to change output in the short-run, or because there is some domestic demand for the exported product, so that we are really considering excess supply.
19   Consideration of policies which would reduce supply variability are beyond the scope of this book. As an example of such a policy, however, consider the simple 'cobweb' model found in basic microeconomic textbooks. Price variability may arise in such models because producers predict future prices in a naive way (typically, they assume next period's price will be the same as this period's price). A policy of providing producers with better information on which to predict future prices may then reduce supply variability.
20   MacBean and Snowden (1981), p. 121.
21   See MacBean and Snowden (1981), p.124.

22 See Meade (1964).
23 See Hine (1985), pp. 178–81, for a more detailed analysis.
24 Finger and de Rosa (1980).
25 Herrman, Burger and Smit (1980).

■ *Chapter 19* ■

Import-Substitution versus Export-Promotion

■ *19.1* Introduction

Chapter 7 gave us some insights into the effects of economic growth on international trade. The preceding chapters in Part 2 have treated some aspects of the theory of trade policy. It is now opportune to analyse some trade-based strategies for development and survey some experiences that the last few decades have provided.

Economic development is usually viewed as the transformation of a low-income society using traditional technologies and producing mainly primary products into a high-income society using modern technologies to produce both primary products and a variety of industrial goods. The importance attached to *industrialisation* in this definition marks an important distinction between 'development' and 'growth', since the latter might perhaps be achieved by the adoption of more efficient technologies in the existing primary-product sectors.

The desire to industrialise is common to the less-developed countries (LDCs). We may suggest various reasons for this. First, most of the present developed market economies (DMEs) themselves achieved that status through industrialisation, so that it may seem reasonable to assume that following the same route will lead to the same results. Second, primary products may be viewed as an unsatisfactory basis for development, especially if world demand for them is thought to be inelastic. Third, a wider economic base (diversification) may lead to greater stability in national income, foreign exchange earnings, and so on. Fourth, industrialisation may reduce the country's dependence on the rest of the world. Fifth, the speed of technological advances may be higher in industrial processes than in primary products. Sixth, it may be the case that an LDC has (or believes it has) a potential comparative advantage in some industrial activities (the infant-industry argument we met in Chapter 12). Finally, having an industrial sector may be seen as a symbol of independence. Some of these reasons are 'economic' but others, particularly the last, are distinctly 'non-economic'.

For the remainder of this chapter we shall take industrialisation as the goal, and will consider two main sets of policies which may be used to pursue that goal – often identified as *import-substitution* and *export-promotion* policies.

■ *19.2* Export pessimism

In the 1950s many countries (together with economists and international organisations) became 'export pessimistic' – a convenient label for the view that developing countries have only limited potential for obtaining economic growth through the expansion of exports. Many LDCs felt that trade was disadvantageous to them, rather than a possible engine of growth. Arguments for an inward-looking type of industrialisation, for a policy of import-substitution, became prevalent. In the 1960s and 1970s, this export pessimism retreated, and in the 1980s export-promotion became the recommended strategy. In recent years however a new variant of export pessimism has appeared which may promote a shift back to import-substitution policies in the LDCs. We shall explore these 'old' and 'new' forms of export pessimism first, before considering the nature and the consequences of import-substitution and export-promotion policies.

Bhagwati[1] identifies two distinct forms of export pessimism. The first, prevalent during the period from the Second World War to the mid-1960s, has two variants: one usually associated with Prebisch and Singer, the other with Nurkse.

The basic form of the Prebisch–Singer[2] version was that the terms of trade of primary products, then the chief exports of LDCs, had been declining over time and would continue to do so, and that this phenomenon was due to causes which were exogenous to the policies of the LDCs themselves. Bhagwati has characterised the Nurkse[3] version of export pessimism as 'elasticity pessimism'. The central tenet here is that the DMEs would be unable to accommodate LDC exports on sufficient scale as the LDCs accelerated development, and so the relative price of those exports would decline. In both variants the causes of the alleged decline in the terms of trade of the LDCs lie outside their control.

Empirical testing of the hypothesis that the terms of trade of the LDCs are and will continue to be on a downward trend has given only limited support. For example, Spraos[4] concluded that there was a significant downward trend in the ratio of primary-product prices to manufactures prices for the period 1900–1939, but that if post-war data up to 1970 were included then the trend became insignificant. Sapsford,[5] using an extended version of the same data set, concluded that if petroleum products were excluded then there was a downward trend of about 1.3 per cent per annum, but with a substantial upward shift in the data in 1950.

Grilli and Yang,[6] using new data, estimated that the downward trend was about 0.6 per cent per annum, but found no evidence of shifts in the data. Cuddington and Urzula,[7] working with one of the Grilli and Yang series, could find no evidence of a downward trend. Bleaney and Greenaway,[8] taking a more general statistical approach, have concluded that there is a statistically significant downward trend in the ratio of the prices of primary products to those of manufactures of about 0.5 per cent per annum.

Both Grilli and Yang and Bleaney and Greenaway draw a clear distinction between changes in the prices of primary commodities relative to those of manufactures and changes in the terms of trade of LDCs. The latter authors estimate that a 1 per cent fall in the relative price of primary commodities is translated into a 0.3 per cent decline in the terms of trade of non-oil developing countries. They argue that this decline is too slow to warrant policy-makers taking it into consideration as important in determining policy, and that the variability of the price ratio around its long-run trend is the dominant feature, suggesting that 'export instability is a much more serious [policy] issue than terms of trade decline'.

Support for these early versions of export pessimism declined in the 1950s and 1960s. World output grew at an unprecedentedly high rate and, as Table 19.1 shows, world trade grew even faster. Moreover, various countries abandoned the use of import-promoting policies (for reasons we shall discuss later), and were observed to enjoy substantial growth in their exports (this was particularly so for South Korea, Hong Kong, Taiwan and Singapore).

An important aspect of LDC trade during the 1960s was the high rate of growth in their exports of manufactures (at nearly twice the rate of DME incomes). Indeed, LDC exports of manufactures are now of almost equal importance as their other non-fuel exports such as food, minerals and agricultural raw materials. This growth is however dominated by the fast-growing exporting LDCs, which raises the question of whether all or most LDCs could become successful exporters simultaneously.

There are two main arguments as to why they may not be able to do so – the so-called 'new export pessimism'. The first is essentially the Nurkse

Table 19.1 *Post-war annual percentage growth rates of world output and trade*

	World output	World trade
1953–63	4.3	6.1
1963–73	5.1	8.9
1973–83	2.5	2.8

Source: Hufbauer and Schott (1985), Table A-1, p. 97.

hypothesis that the DMEs' markets could not absorb all the increase in exports. Bhagwati has argued that this will not be the case, giving the following reasons.[9] First, it is unlikely that all LDCs would (or could) increase exports to the same extent as the four NICs mentioned above. Second, the share of LDC exports in DME markets is small (about 2 per cent), so that even if the LDCs' exports doubled there should be no worries about the ability of the DMEs to absorb them. Finally, there may be growth in intra-industry trade both between the LDCs and the DMEs and between the LDCs themselves.

The second, and more disturbing, variant of the new export pessimism is that more rapid growth in LDC exports to the DMEs may provoke protectionist reactions. If this protectionist reaction is confined to specific goods that pose a 'threat' to particular sectors within the importing countries then the appropriate response for the exporting country would be to restrict its exports of those goods – a sector-specific policy. If however this protectionist reaction is thought likely to apply to increases in the exports of *any* good by the LDCs to the DMEs then a shift to an overall import-substitution policy would be justified. The important question is whether this generalised pessimism about the protectionist reactions of the DMEs is justified.

Various arguments may be made that the protectionist threat is overstated. Baldwin[10] has argued that protection is in fact less effective than at first sight, since there are many ways in which exporting countries can circumvent it and increase their export earnings – by for example changing the specifications of goods in order to avoid voluntary export restraints. Bhagwati[11] emphasises the role of foreign direct investment in creating political pressures in favour of an open economy. However, the most potent force for resisting increased protectionism must be the GATT, and as we saw in Chapter 17, the current round of multilateral trade negotiations has not yet been concluded successfully.

19.3 Defining import-substitution and export-promotion

The common terminology of 'import-substitution' (IS) and 'export-promotion' (EP) can be misleading. The former may be interpreted correctly as identifying policies that are directed towards the reduction of imports (by for instance tariffs) and their substitution by domestic production. The latter term however does not imply that the policies followed seek to expand exports by the use of, for example, export subsidies. 'Export-promoting' is in fact the term applied to policies that are *neutral* towards trade.

More recently, economists have preferred to use the term 'inward-oriented' to refer to policies which promote domestic production at the expense of imports, and 'outward oriented' to those which do not discriminate against imports (or in favour of exports). However, the use of the IS/EP distinction is now so deeply embedded in the literature that both terminologies must be kept in mind.

The formal distinction between the two forms of policy is usually made in terms of the *effective exchange rates* for imports and exports. The effective exchange rate for imports (EER_M) is the amount of the domestic currency (say, the peso) that would accrue to a domestic firm producing and selling on the domestic market goods that would cost \$1 to import. This would include the value of, for example, any premium due to quantitative restrictions, but less any taxes, say, on inputs. The effective exchange rate for exports (EER_X) is the value in pesos to a domestic firm of producing and exporting goods which are worth \$1 on the world market, including such things as the value of any export subsidies, etc.

If the effective exchange rate for imports is greater than that for exports ($EER_M > EER_X$) then there is an incentive for domestic firms to produce import-competing goods rather than export goods. The net effect of the government's trade policies is thus to stimulate the production of import-competing goods, and those policies would be identified as inward-oriented, or import-substitution policies.

If the two effective exchange rates are the same ($EER_M = EER_X$) then there is no incentive for domestic producers either to switch from producing goods for export to producing goods which will substitute for imports, or vice versa. In that case the practice is to say that the country's policies are outward-oriented or export-promoting.

This of course leaves the case when $EER_M < EER_X$, so that there is an incentive for domestic firms to produce for the export market. Some writers put this in with the $EER_M = EER_X$ case as part of the export-promoting group of strategies; others have proposed that we use the term 'ultra-export-promoting'.

Note that whether a country's policies are categorised as inward- or outward-oriented depends on the balance between the two sets of policy measures affecting both imports and exports. For example, consider a small country where the only policy measure affecting importables is a general nominal tariff of 50 per cent, but where there is also a 50 per cent tax on all exportables. The import tariff will increase the domestic price of importables by 50 per cent over the world price, but the export tax will have an identical effect on the domestic price of exportables. The effective exchange rate for importables will be the same as the effective exchange rate for exportables, and the net effect of the two policy measures will be outward orientation.

■ *19.4* Import-substitution

The background to the import-substitution strategy

The drive for import-substitution in many LDCs has to be explained by reference to economic experiences during the interwar period and the Second World War. The great depression at the beginning of the 1930s hit many LDCs very hard. The dollar price of primary products, on which they were dependent for foreign exchange earnings, fell by 50 per cent from 1929 to 1932, and the value of exports by some 60 per cent. Although prices of industrial products also fell, the LDCs suffered a heavy deterioration in their terms of trade.

Furthermore, they usually had large foreign debts. These had to be serviced in fixed amounts in foreign currency; hence the real burden of debt service increased as prices fell. The inflow of capital to which these countries had become accustomed was also cut off, often in quite an abrupt fashion.

They took the view that they were at the mercy of the major developed, industrial, countries, with the causes of the slump emanating basically from the developed countries themselves. This was exacerbated by the existing institutional arrangements, which prevented the LDCs from pursuing independent economic policies; this is underlined by the fact that practically none of the LDCs had an independent central bank and hence no possibilities existed for applying an independent monetary policy.

It is not surprising that the experiences of the 1930s left deep scars in the memories of the LDCs and made them opt for policies which would free them from the type of economic dependence to which they earlier had been subjected.

Experiences during the Second World War reinforced this view, although their problems were very different from what they had been during the 1930s. During the war the demand for exports from the LDCs increased drastically. Now it was imports that were lacking. They had no difficulty selling their export products at good prices, but they could not import industrial goods, especially capital equipment. This hampered the expansion of industrial capacity in these countries. At the same time, the export boom led to a build-up of foreign reserves, and demand was directed toward domestically-produced goods. This brought with it better use of domestic manufacturing capacity; industrial output increased substantially in many LDCs during the war years, ranging from a 20 per cent increase in India to an almost 50 per cent increase in Mexico.

Hence it is understandable that a large group of LDCs opted for a policy of self-reliance based on import-substitution. By so doing, they showed their distrust for the arguments of gains from trade on which we have placed such stress in this book so far.

☐ *The anatomy of controls on foreign trade*

Controls on foreign trade are at the heart of import-substitution. There exist many types of restrictive measures, differing between countries and usually also over time. It is, however, important to get some grasp over the means used. It is also convenient to characterise a country's control over foreign trade according to the policy instruments used. The economists working on the National Bureau of Economic Research (NBER) studies of import-substitution suggested that a country's protectionist policies could be characterised by various phases with respect to the degree of liberalisation of those policies.[12] There is a logic in the use of restrictive measures that is instructive to study.

Tariffs and surcharges are common protectionist devices. Other instruments are import licenses, of which there can be a large variety, either for users or for wholesalers. They may be obtained by direct permission from some ministry or the central bank, or they may be sold at official auctions; they can be combined with specific import programmes and they might be combined with lists of prohibited import products. Another protectionist measure is the guarantee deposit, which has to be made by the importer for the right to import an item.

Yet other protectionist measures operate through control over foreign exchange transactions. One common form is to control capital movements: for example, foreign firms may be restricted in their right to repatriate dividends and profits. Another is to operate a multiple exchange rate system to encourage some activities while discouraging others. A common practice is to combine a floating exchange rate for capital account transactions with a fixed and overvalued exchange rate for current account transactions. Another is to require importers of 'luxury' goods to buy foreign currency at a disadvantageous rate, while offering an advantageous rate on imports of capital goods and a middle rate for imports of other goods. Domestic exporters, on the other hand, may be allowed to resell part of their foreign earnings at advantageous exchange rates.

Thus the policy instruments are numerous. In order to see how exchange controls work and to understand some of their logic and consistency it is useful to characterise them according to phases following those of the NBER studies.

Phase I is characterised by an imposition of heavy and undifferentiated quantitative controls. Often it entails a sharp intensification of some controls which were operative previously, and may often be a response to hardships brought about by, for example, crop failures, adverse terms of trade, or international depressions.

Phase II is characterised by a continuation of quantitative restrictions. The restrictiveness of the control system tends to become more pronounced. The system also becomes more complex as two new features are added. The first is that the operation of the system becomes more discretionary as *ad hoc* measures increase. The second is that price measures start to be used. Both these phenomena can be regarded as stemming from the fact that the authorities want to streamline the control system and make it more flexible as time goes by.

During Phase I the control system is operated in a rather heavy-handed and undiscriminating fashion. As the authorities perceive special interests and want to increase the effectiveness of the system, rules, regulations and special cases tend to proliferate. Often decision-makers feel that they lose control over the system.

The reasons for manipulating prices are also easy to comprehend. The continuation of quantitative restrictions creates shortages of foreign exchange. To relieve that shortage it is often deemed desirable to induce exporters to export more by the use of export rebates, 'import replenishment' schemes, special credits, and the like. Price incentives are also used on the import side. Tariff increases, surcharges and guarantee deposits are often applied. These measures are aimed both at checking imports and at taxing away the various rents and windfall gains which go together with rationing systems and quantitative restrictions.

The prevalence of various types of controls during Phase II implies that the exchange rate is overvalued. Were it not for the restrictions, the demand for foreign exchange would be much larger than the supply. Phase

III therefore starts with a change of the exchange rate, i.e. a devaluation. Connected with the devaluation is a loosening of trade controls.

Phases I and II can be of long duration. Usually Phase III is of shorter duration. It can either be a tidying-up operation to take care of previous distortions on the way to a more liberal trade regime; or it can be a period of abortive attempts at liberalisation which after some time will be deemed futile, and the country in question will then slide back to Phase II again. There are, however, also instances when Phase III has lasted for several years as the economy has taken considerable time to adjust its relative price structure to the new, more liberal, trade regime. In general Phase III has the character of a disequilibrium period of adjustment.

Phrase IV starts when foreign exchange earnings grow at a reasonably rapid rate so that the liberal measures of Phase III can be sustained. If the supply of foreign exchange matches the demand, there is no need to restrict trade further. It is true that quantitative restrictions may still apply but they are of a reasonably non-distortionary kind. Thus premia that might exist on import licenses do not increase. Phase IV continues as long as the controls of trade are unchanged or diminishing.

Phase V is characterised by full liberalisation of the trade and foreign currency regimes, with the currency fully convertible. Hence Phase V is not a continuation of the previous regimes but an alternative to the first four phases dealt with above.

Naturally, the characterisation of regimes into phases contains moments of arbitrariness. Moreover, countries do not progress in a consistent manner from one phase to another: as we shall see below, they may regress to an earlier phase. Nevertheless, it may still be useful. Countries in Phases I and II are in a very different position than those in Phases IV and V. Phase III is also interesting as an interregnum between regimes of strict controls and those characterised by liberal trade policies.

We shall now consider briefly the experience of four countries since the Second World War – India, Korea, Chile and Brazil. The Indian experience is the best documented of the four, and will be dealt with at some length; it offers some insight into the long-run problems caused by a maintained import-substituting regime. Korea provides an example of the costs and benefits of switching from an inward to an outward oriented strategy. Chile is an exemplar of how a successful trade liberalisation programme can be scuppered by an inappropriate macroeconomic policy. Brazil is an instance of a country which has switched from an outward-oriented stance back to an inward-oriented one.

Table 19.2 shows the average annual growth rates for the value and volume of Indian exports over the specified time periods, and estimates of the ratio of the effective exchange rates for imports (EER_M) and for exports (EER_X) for years at the end of those periods. The broad picture is

Table 19.2   *Annual average percentage growth rates for India's exports and estimated effective exchange rate ratios*

Period	Value of exports	Volume of exports	EER_M/EER_X
1951/52–1955/56	−6.8	5.4	1.27 (1955)
1956/57–1960/61	0.9	−0.2	1.17 (1960)
1961/62–1965/66	4.2	3.7	1.20 (1965)
1966/67–1970/71	7.1	4.9	1.24 (1970)
1971/72–1975/76	21.0	6.3	1.20 (1975)
1976/77–1980/81	5.4	5.2	1.21 (1980)
1981/82–1987/88	8.2	2.2	1.16 (1985)

Source: Balasubramanyam and Basu (1990), Tables 11.1 and 11.2.

of a decline in value (though not in volume) of exports over the period of the first five-year plan (1951–56), stagnation during the second five-year plan (1956–61), and of steady growth in both value and volume since then (with a dramatic increase in export value in the early and mid-1970s). Throughout the whole period however the EER_M/EER_X ratio remained above one, indicating a continued bias in favour of production for the domestic market rather than for exports.

India[13] entered its first five-year plan in 1951 with large currency reserves that had been accumulated during the Second World War. An investment boom in the mid-1950s led to large increases in imports and a deterioration in her balance of payments. Restrictive measures of the Phase I type were applied in the second five-year plan (1956–61), and from then on India has tended to follow an inward-looking development strategy centred on import-substitution as a means of stimulating industrialisation. India's share of world exports fell from 2.5 per cent in 1947 to 1.4 per cent at the end of 1956. A particular feature of this decline is that Indian exports fell relative to those of her competitors because of increasing price uncompetitiveness, rather than being subjected to a 'Prebisch' effect. The decline in export performance did not however bring about a change in policy during the period of the second plan – India remained inward oriented, intent on attaining the objective of 'self-reliance'.

The third five-year plan (1962–66) introduced a range of export promotion measures, including export subsidisation policies and *import entitlement schemes*. The latter scheme had as a main feature the entitlement of exporters to licences for imports equal to twice the import content of their exports. It was extremely complex in its operations, and will not be analysed here.[14]

The rupee was devalued in 1966 following pressure from the consortium giving aid to India. At the same time the import entitlement scheme and some export subsidies were removed, tariffs were reduced on some imported goods, and duties were imposed on exports of some goods where India was thought to face an inelastic demand on the world market. Export incentives were however re-introduced within a couple of months. The import entitlement scheme was replaced by an import replenishment scheme, which allowed exporters licences to import only up to the actual import content of their exports, and cash subsidies on exports were introduced.

India's exports grew strongly in the following years, especially in the period from 1972 to 1977. Moreover, much of this growth was in 'non-traditional' products such as engineering goods and clothing. Econometric analysis by Bhagwati and Srinavasan[15] suggests that India's export-promotion measures contributed to the growth in exports, but that other (and fortuitous) factors were also important. Moreover, as Balasubramanyam and Basu have noted:

> India's export incentive schemes . . . appear to have been not only expensive relative to what they have achieved but many of the schemes also appear to lack any sort of economic rationale . . . [Neoclassical economists] would argue that the root cause of India's export problem is the indiscriminate import-substitution policy the country has pursued. Symptomatic of the problem are the existence of highly profitable domestic markets, lack of imported inputs, high costs of production, the high capital intensity of exports and poor quality of products exported – all of which have constrained exports . . . the import-substituting industrialisation policies have imparted a bias against exports.[16]

From the end of the Korean war in 1953 up to 1961 South Korea was in Phase II, with multiple and badly overvalued (though frequently devalued) exchange rates, import-licensing, and high tariffs on some goods. Two attempts at liberalising her trade policies were made in the early 1960s. The first proved abortive, but the second, in 1964–55, was more successful. The major change was the devaluation of the currency and an increase in the rate of interest to stimulate domestic savings (abandoned in favour of a low interest rate regime in 1971). Other changes introduced were export-promotion schemes, an attempted (but slow) reduction of import controls, and the encouragement of foreign capital inflows.

Starting in the late 1960s, but effectively from 1973, Korea sought to promote the growth of the so-called 'heavy and chemical (HC) industries', such as petrochemicals, machinery, electrical and electronic products, and transport equipment. Nam[17] has argued that a number of external and internal obstacles made this policy very costly for the economy. The former included the various increases in oil prices, delays in adjustment in the industrialised countries, rising protectionism, and recession in the world economy. He places more emphasis however on the internal factors, in particular too rapid an investment in industries in which Korea did not have a comparative advantage due to a lack of adequate technological base and a shortage of skills.

For a variety of reasons, the Korean economy began to stagnate, while also showing signs of structural imbalance, such as business failures, an underdeveloped financial sector, and insufficient development of small- and medium-sized firms (despite continued protection of domestic markets). The government's reaction was to reduce its role in the economy, particularly in financial and investment matters, and to adopt a policy aimed at reducing import controls, particularly on commodities with a high level of protection or with a monopolistic structure in the domestic market.

Chile[18] provides an example of a country in which a determined programme of trade liberalisation yielded dramatic gains, but where the gains were largely lost by an inappropriate exchange rate policy. Chile was hit hard by the 1930s depression and applied restrictive trade policies from then up to the mid-1950s. Several attempts at devaluation were made and 'stabilisation programmes' were launched in connection with them, but all were of short duration. The currency was overvalued most of the time, and there was high inflation and heavy use of quantitative restrictions.

The change in regime in 1973 brought about a major switch in economic policy. In the next four years all import quotas were removed and the average tariff was cut from 90 per cent to 27 per cent, and by June 1979 the tariff was 10 per cent on all imports except cars. This trade liberalisation policy was accompanied by anti-inflationary policies. Inflation came down from over 500 per cent in 1973 to about 30 per cent in 1978. Trade increased dramatically, and Chile began to export products which it had never exported in any great volume before.

Unfortunately, in 1978 the Chilean government abandoned its policy of devaluing the peso in step with inflation in order to maintain competitiveness in world markets, and adopted instead a policy of phased devaluations in an attempt to control inflation. The effect of this policy was to overvalue the peso and stop the expansion of the 'new' exports. By 1981–82 this, coupled with the fall in the price of copper as the world economy slowed down and the onset of the debt crisis, forced Chile into a severe recession. This in turn led to a move towards a rather more protectionist regime, with tariffs increasing to 20 per cent. As Congdon notes: 'The lesson was that, in future liberalisation attempts, exchange-rate policies and anti-inflation programmes should be better designed so that they did not lead to overvalued exchange rates and loss of export competitiveness . . . It became World Bank orthodoxy that trade liberalisation must also be accompanied by a competitive exchange rate.'[19]

From the early 1950s up to 1963 Brazil was in Phase II, interspersed with brief lapses into Phase III.[20] Brazil undertook a devaluation and a stabilisation programme in 1964. Several years of adjustment of a Phase III type followed, but in 1968 quantitative restrictions of the Phase IV kind were established and from then on to the mid-1970s Brazil had an exchange regime which became increasingly liberal, with several years of rapid growth in both imports and exports. In the mid-1970s however, Brazil moved back to an import-substitution policy under the influence of civil servants who argued that the increasing imports showed that there were market opportunities that could (and should) be exploited by domestic producers. Despite occasional pronouncements to the contrary, Brazil has remained highly protectionist since then.

☐ *Income distribution and savings*

The most important aim of import-substitution is to promote domestic industry at the expense of foreign industry. As most LDCs are unable to affect world prices for the majority of their exports, the possibility of terms-of-trade gains is remote. LDCs will not gain much on this score and foreign exporters will not be harmed much by import-substitution.

Domestic price levels will, however, usually be heavily influenced by import-substitution. Prices of industrial goods will go up. This will have important effects on the income distribution within the country. Primarily it is the domestic income distribution that will be affected by import-substitution, not the world income distribution.

Import-substitution aims to protect the domestic manufacturing sector. But gains in this sector impose losses on other sectors. The effect of import-substitution is basically to shift domestic income distribution in favour of entrepreneurs and workers within industry at the expense of farmers. As farmers are often among the poorest groups in a country, the effect of import-substitution will be to increase income inequality. In Pakistan, for instance, farm incomes have been estimated to be 11–13 per cent lower because of import-substitution than they would have been otherwise. When import-substitution was at its height in Argentina in 1947–55, the distortion of prices it brought about was equivalent to a tax of 30–40 per cent of incomes in the agricultural sector.[21]

Attempts to change the income distribution in favour of the industrial sector were often quite deliberate. Increased savings were needed to increase investment and spur the development effort. As the entrepreneurs in the industrial sector were regarded as having a large propensity to invest, it was deemed favourable to shift the income distribution in their favour. This argument has some merit. At the same time, it should be pointed out that high prices might lead not only to high profits but also to high costs. Moreover, there are alternative ways of providing savings for a developing economy. One major alternative is to encourage household saving. This presupposes a well-functioning credit market with the power to inspire confidence and to create safe financial instruments that households can acquire.

Most countries seem to have relied on the first method. In Pakistan and Brazil, for instance, industrial investments were almost completely generated out of profits. Very high rates of protection were used to secure high profits for the domestic industry. Mexico on the other hand is an example of a country pursuing an import-substitution policy where household savings did play an important role for the financing of industry. The country used a policy of comparatively high interest rates to stimulate household savings; as the rate of inflation was low, this meant that the rates were also positive and quite high in real terms. To guarantee stability, some bonds were even denoted in US dollars. This was contrary to the experience of Brazil, where the rate of inflation was high and where, furthermore, usury laws did not permit interest rates to rise above a certain level. This implied that interest rates in real terms were negative for long periods of time. The Mexican policy was successful: around 5 per cent of household incomes were channelled to industrial investments.[22] In Brazil, on the other hand, household savings played a negligible role in industrial investments.

Policies which encourage domestic savings have some distinct advantages. First, they can be pursued without relying on a very uneven income distribution. It is enough to count on the positive time preference that many households have, even though their average income might be quite low. Second, domestic prices need not be as distorted *vis-á-vis* world market prices, for the degree of protection can be lower when excessive profits are no longer needed to fund investments in the industrial sector. Mexico was not the only country that successfully stimulated household savings and channelled them into investments for industrial expansion. Taiwan applied the same type of policy in the 1950s and South Korea followed suit in the mid-1960s.

We must conclude that a policy of import-substitution creates problems from the point of view of economic justice. It tends to discriminate against agriculture and thus sharpen the inequality of an already very uneven income distribution. It also tends to restrict the market for industrial goods because large groups of workers, especially small farmers and farm workers, are too poor to be able to buy industrial products.

☐ *Discrimination against agriculture*

Import-substitution policies intended to promote industrialisation in LDCs will, as we have argued, discriminate against agriculture. As a poor country develops, one would expect demand for food to grow. Increases in *per capita* consumption of food, however, have been extremely slow or non-existent in most LDCs since the mid-1930s. Low growth of production contributed to this, and this in turn was caused to a large extent by the discrimination implicit in the policy of import-substitution.

The high degree of protection offered to industry turned the terms of trade and the income distribution against agriculture. Controls on imports and an overvaluation of the currency, usually associated with import-substitution, made matters worse. Returns to agriculture became depressed and an air of export pessimism prevailed. The best illustration of this is Argentina. Argentina had held a very strong position in the world market in the early 1930s in many important agricultural commodities. This position was much eroded thirty years later. From the early 1930s to the early 1960s, her share in world exports decreased drastically for a long list of important commodities: fresh meat from 40 to 18 per cent, wheat from 23 to 6 per cent, maize from 64 to 17 per cent, and linseed from 79 to less than 7 per cent.[23] Brazil and India had much the same experience with their major export crops, coffee and tea.

Export pessimism certainly seems justified against the background of figures such as these. However, this pessimism was to a large extent policy-induced. It was created by the LDCs themselves in their efforts to foster domestic industry at the expense of the traditional agricultural exports. High degrees of protection, amounting to heavy taxation of agriculture, combined with an overvaluation of the domestic currency, served to depress economic conditions in agriculture while at the same time making imported goods look cheaper than they really were.

Mexico, with a much milder form of protection of domestic industry and less discrimination against agriculture, fared better. Here consumption of agricultural goods increased by almost 50 per cent *per capita*: from 36 dollars *per capita* in the mid-1930s to 50 dollars *per capita* thirty years later. During the same period, production increased by more than 50 per cent and exports of agricultural products went up substantially.

In recent years a re-evaluation of the importance of agriculture as a source of export earnings has also taken place in some countries. A case in point is Argentina. The country has a very strong comparative advantage in agriculture. By lowering discrimination against the agricultural sector, the country was able to take advantage of the booming demand conditions in world agricultural markets in the early 1970s. Her exports of agricultural products, around $1500 million in the 1960s, more than doubled during the agricultural boom that occurred in the early 1970s. Argentina adopted a major trade liberalisation programme in 1978, influenced by Chile's example. Unfortunately, it also introduced a macroeconomic policy similar to Chile's, and its liberalisation programme was abandoned in 1983, with quantitative restrictions being re-imposed on imports.[24]

South Korea is an interesting case for study, in that she combined agricultural support policies with an export-promoting strategy. During the 1950s agricultural growth was satisfactory, and in the 1960s it increased sharply on average. However, poor harvests had very negative effects on the economy: 1961 was a year of bad harvest, and that year South Korea devalued her currency. The devaluation failed as prices increased sharply in connection with the poor harvest. Later on, the export-push strategy became more successful and export earnings increased. The country became less dependent on the short-term fortunes of the agricultural sector, and in times of bad harvests food could be imported to supplement domestic supplies.

India, on the other hand, has a relatively weak agricultural base. The country has hardly been able to increase agricultural production in any decisive way, with import-substitution policies contributing to the problem. Developments in recent years have been somewhat uneven, but the country remains quite heavily dependent on imports of agricultural goods.

Choice of technology and effects on employment

One of the primary aims of a policy of import-substitution is to create employment in the industrial sector. Even here, import-substitution has not been too successful. Perhaps the most pressing social problem in the less-developed world today is the influx of migrants to the cities. Industrial employment has not increased fast enough to absorb the increase in urban population. Besides, the policy of import-substitution might be seen as a major factor in creating this disequilibrium situation, which in turn is a source of constant social and economic tensions.

In most of the LDCs the rate of growth of industrial employment is quite low. Some countries, like Mexico and Taiwan, had an annual increase in their industrial labour force of around 5 per cent yearly from 1950 to 1960, as did Pakistan, which had a very small industrial base to start from. Other major countries, such as India, Brazil and Argentina, had much lower growth rates of industrial employment: in India and Argentina the rate was less than 2 per cent, and in Brazil it was 2.6 per cent. As the increase in urban population was much faster in these countries, unemployment increased. Some of the reasons for the increase in unemployment were intimately linked to the process of import-substitution.

The influx of people to the cities created a demand for investment. The investment needed was of an 'unproductive' kind, especially in infrastructure like roads, drainage, transportation, schools and housing. This type of investment can be viewed as 'capital-widening' of a kind. When referring to them as 'unproductive', it is not to be inferred that they were not needed or that they did not improve the standard of life for city-dwellers. However, had migration to the cities been slower and had more of the would-be city-dwellers stayed in agricultural areas, the same infrastructure could have been provided at lower cost.

Import-substitution discriminated against agriculture and favoured industry. It led to stagnation and impoverishment in rural areas. This, in turn, led to migration to the cities, necessitating the 'unproductive' type of investments we have referred to above. When judging aggregate investment figures one should therefore keep in mind that they might overstate the efficiency of investment. Had export-promoting policies instead been applied, such policies could have led to larger growth of employment from a given amount of investment.

Another consequence of import-substitution is the capital-deepening it induces. The protection given to industry stimulates investment in industry. It is quite clear that most countries pursuing import-substitution policies opted for investments which were far too capital-intensive according to the existing factor-price ratios, had these been allowed to reflect true social costs. Why firms in these countries opted for a capital-intensive type of technique is a complex issue; there is little doubt, however, that a policy of import-substitution favoured this choice of technique.

We have already pointed out that import-substitution forced most countries to import the capital goods needed to speed up the process of industrialisation. Most of the imported capital equipment tended to be highly capital-intensive. This was to a degree not the fault of the importing countries themselves but of the fact that this equipment had been constructed for a completely different set of factor prices than the ones prevailing in the LDCs. Administrators and politicians in LDCs often failed to grasp the significance of this point; they insisted on importing the most advanced machinery available, instead of importing machinery which, though it did not necessarily embody the most modern technology, was less capital-intensive. This led to waste of resources, especially through underutilisation of the cheap labour available.

There were also other factors which worked in the same direction. Prices of imported capital goods were often kept artificially low by means of low, or no, tariffs and an overvaluation of the domestic currency. Furthermore, interest rates were often kept low, even to the extent of making real interest rates negative. This naturally led to capital-rationing, which usually benefited larger firms at the expense of small businesses. Very liberal depreciation allowances lowered the relative price of capital even more and encouraged investment.

Another reason firms in these countries might have chosen to overcapitalise had to do with discrimination. Machines do not talk back and they never strike, at least not to get higher wages. For entrepreneurs, used to reaping easy profits behind high walls of protection, it might have been tempting to substitute machines for labour. This could also be a rational policy, because wages in the industrial sector in several countries seemed to be affected more by profits than by supply and demand conditions in the local labour markets. In order to counteract the influence of unions, which fought militantly for the interests of small groups of elite workers, entrepreneurs might have deliberately tried to minimise the wage bill, even though that implied using capital-intensive methods of production.

One of the striking facts about industry in the LDCs is its low capacity utilisation. It is well known that urban unemployment rates are high in these countries. The unemployment rate of machinery is also very high. Reliable figures are not easy to come by in this area, but it is quite clear from the ones that exist and from available experience that capacity utilisation is much lower in LDCs than it is in developed industrial countries.

In Argentina, for instance, the capacity utilisation of industry in the mid-1960s was estimated to be around 65 per cent. In India, taking capacity utilisation on a two-shift basis as a measuring-rod, most industries worked at less than 50 per cent of their capacity.[25] Figures naturally differed from industry to industry but it seems certain that most LDCs used their industrial capacity far less intensively than did the industrial, developed countries. By way of comparison, in 1964 capacity utilisation in US manufacturing was estimated to be close to 90 per cent, and average capacity utilisation in Western European industry was around 95 per cent.

Contributing to this low capacity utilisation is the fact that shift work seems to be rare in LDCs. With labour being cheap and machinery expensive one would think that the developing countries would use their machinery intensively, with shift work. This is not the case. Again, strictly comparable data do not exist to any great extent, but estimates for Mexico and the United States in the 1960s showed that shift work was more common in the United States than in Mexico: the shift coefficient for Mexico was 1.07, while it was between 1.2 and 1.3 in the United States.[26]

We have pointed to several mechanisms that all worked to create too much capital for industry which was then not used in an effective fashion.

Import-substitution fostered these mechanisms and hence led to over-capitalisation of industry and under-utilisation of existing capacity. It also probably fostered attitudes on the part of domestic producers not conducive to expansion and growth.

Import-substitution meant protection for domestic industry behind high tariff walls. It implied a policy of high profits. With foreign competition gone, high and easily- reaped profits tended to create lax attitudes on the part of domestic producers. They could get by even if they let costs rise and even if they did not use capacity very efficiently. High profits encouraged waste, in terms of unused capacity, and made life easy for the domestic producers.

19.5 Import-substitution versus export-promotion

Import-substitution policies may be considered to be technically successful if they result in a reduction of imports and an expansion of domestic production. This is however a narrow view: the important questions are whether they are economically successful in promoting growth and/or development, and whether they are more or less successful than export-promotion policies. We shall discuss the results of some empirical work on the latter questions later in the chapter. First, we shall give a brief consideration to the technical success of import-substitution policies, and to their possible consequences.

It is informative to split the process of import-substitution into two stages. The first stage involves the substitution of imports of non-durable consumer goods such as textiles by domestic production. The second stage consists of the replacement of imported consumer-durables.

The first stage is usually relatively simple to achieve. Non-durable consumer goods can often be produced by simple technologies which are intensive in their use of labour (particularly in unskilled labour). They may also lend themselves to small-scale production and local distribution, and may require few intermediate inputs. Moreover, there may already be a substantial domestic market for such goods.

The second stage is usually more difficult. Consumer-durables tend to require more sophisticated technologies, higher labour skills, and intermediate inputs. Unless the appropriate domestic industries can also be established, there will be an increased demand for imports of these intermediate inputs, and of capital goods. Import-substitution offers no easy road to self-reliance.

In some countries, such Brazil, Mexico and India, which started early on the road to import-substitution, the share of consumers' goods which were imported was already low at the beginning of the 1950s. By the end of the 1960s these countries imported practically no consumers' goods whatsoever. In other countries, like Pakistan and the Philippines, where import-substitution came later, imports of consumers goods fell drastically during the 1950s and 1960s. Over this period, import-substitution seems to have been successful in several countries to the extent that it has decreased the ratio of imports to the gross domestic product (GDP), but in others the reverse seems to be the case. Table 19.3 gives an illustration of this.

In countries like Argentina, Brazil and Mexico the ratio of imports to total production fell. In other countries, like the Philippines and Taiwan, which also practised a policy of import-substitution, the ratio went up. In interpreting figures like those given in Table 19.3 one has to be careful. Some countries might have a higher 'natural' marginal propensity to import than others. It is likely that small countries like Taiwan and the Philippines have a higher propensity to import as they grow than larger countries like Brazil, Mexico and India. The figures in Table 19.3 should also be judged against what would have been the case had some kind of policy other than import-substitution been attempted. Obviously, such comparisons are difficult to make. Estimates demonstrate, however, that for Mexico – to take an example – imports would have been 22 per cent higher in 1960 than they were had the same proportions of consumption, intermediate and capital goods been imported in 1960 as in 1950.

When it comes to economic growth, countries like those mentioned in Table 19.3 varied in their performance. Looking at the growth rate of GDP at constant prices, Taiwan had the highest rate, growing at over 8 per cent annually from the beginning of the 1950s to the end of the 1960s. Mexico, Brazil and the Philippines showed growth rates of 5–6 per cent, while

Table 19.3 *Imports as a percentage of GDP at current prices*

Country	1950–2	1957–9	1964–6
Argentina	9	11	7
Brazil	12	10	8
Mexico	12	11	8
India	8	7	7
Pakistan	8	7	10
Philippines	14	13	19
Taiwan	13	14	19

Source: Little, Scitovsky and Scott (1970), p. 63.

India, Pakistan and Argentina grew at 3–4 per cent. As population grew rapidly during this period, figures for *per capita* growth rates are substantially lower, being 2–3 per cent for countries like Brazil and Mexico and 1–2 per cent for countries like Argentina, India and Pakistan.

Industrial production grew faster than GDP in most countries but not so much faster as to make industry the dominant sector. Only in countries such as Argentina, Brazil and Mexico was the share of manufacturing industry as high as 25–30 per cent of GDP toward the end of the 1960s; in countries like India and Pakistan it was 10–15 per cent. After two decades of promoting industry through import-substitution, agriculture and services were still by far the most important sectors of the economy.

In recent years, attention has been focused on the 'side-effects' of the import-substitution strategy, many of which are seen (from the neoclassical viewpoint) as being negative. The first, and most general, is that an import-substitution strategy involves the deliberate distortion of markets which, as we have seen, generally reduces welfare. Moreover, the policies used (usually restrictions on imports) are generally inferior as a means of achieving a given production target. Secondly, protection of domestic industry insulates it from markets elsewhere. This is likely to reduce the incentive to adopt new technologies and encourage inefficient practices, and will also provide incentives for rent-seeking. These in turn may make it difficult to abandon the import-substitution strategy at a later date. Finally, an import-substitution strategy involves higher administrative costs (in administering quotas, import licences, etc.) than the alternative of export-promotion, and is often associated with overvalued exchange rates and their associated exchange controls, which are also both economically inefficient and costly to administer.

In the early 1960s some countries, such as India and many Latin American countries, continued to pursue the import-substitution option into its more difficult second stage. Others, having completed the 'easy' first stage of import-substitution, switched to a policy of encouraging industrial exports; the Republic of Korea, Singapore and Taiwan are the exemplars of this switch.

The arguments in favour of an export-promotion strategy are, in large part, those used against import-substitution. That is, an outward-oriented approach does not reduce static efficiency and welfare by introducing distortions, and leaves domestic industry open to competition from foreign producers in both domestic and export markets, which brings dynamic benefits. The opportunities for rent-seeking are reduced, as are administration costs.

A more complicated argument concerns the vulnerability of outward- and inward-oriented economies to cope with 'shocks', such as those coming from the price of oil. It may be argued that an outward-oriented economy, because of its greater degree of specialisation, is likely to suffer both more shocks and more extreme shocks. The counter-argument is that, because of the greater flexibility engendered in such countries by their openness to foreign competition, they are more able to cope with such shocks. Certainly, the 'newly industrialising countries' (NICs), such as the Republic of Korea, Singapore, Taiwan and Hong Kong, seem to have adjusted more successfully to the effects of oil price increases than many of the more inward-oriented economies.

Structural adjustment loans and 'conditionality'

In 1980 the World Bank instituted a programme of structural adjustment loans (SALs), in which lending to LDCs was linked formally to the implementation of policy reforms. In contrast to the traditional nature of World Bank loans, SALs are not tied to specific projects. They are medium-term loans which are conditional on the implementation of reforms to the supply side of the economy.

The IMF stabilisation programme also involves conditionality, although here the policy reforms required are directed at short-term demand management and macroeconomic stabilisation. The World Bank makes the existence of an IMF stabilisation programme a prerequisite for making an SAL.

The two programmes were otherwise intended to be independent of one another, but in practice there has been interaction, and sometimes conflict, between the two. This is not surprising when we consider the experience of countries such as Argentina and Chile, where a trade-liberalisation programme failed because of an inappropriate macroeconomic strategy.

Economists generally agree on the desired end results of policy adjustment under an SAL. The main elements are a combination of the partial or total elimination of quantitative controls on imports, the rationalisation of tariff structures (possibly with some new tariffs being introduced in place of quantitative restrictions), followed by a reduction in tariff levels, and export promotion.

There is as yet less agreement on the sequence in which the various reforms should be introduced. For example, reducing tariffs on intermediate goods while leaving those on final goods unchanged would increase the effective protection given to domestic industry and would result in import-substitution rather than export-promotion, whereas the reverse would occur if tariffs on final goods were reduced by more than those on intermediate products. One suggestion is that the *range* of import tariffs on all goods should be reduced, even if that means that some tariffs must be increased. As we know from our analysis of effective protection, if all goods face the same nominal tariff rate then the effective tariffs on the protected sectors are equal to that same rate. This would avoid discrimination between the various import-competing industries, but would still leave the problem of discrimination in favour of import-competing goods and against exports. Protection of imports may also, as we have seen result in an overvalued exchange rate, which also discriminates against the export sectors. It may be necessary to remedy that discrimination by directly promoting exports.

The introduction of the SAL programme has stimulated research into the problems of transition from an inward-oriented regime to an outward-oriented one. This topic had largely been ignored, so that there were few guidelines for negotiations between the World Bank and governments, and in practice a variety of different paths to liberalisation have been followed. A further practical issue, the subject of some research effort at the moment, is in determining the extent to which governments that have agreed to the reform programme specified for an SAL actually implement that programme.

☐ *Empirical evidence*

Empirical evidence on trade orientation and development is not easily summarised, due to differences in approach in interpretations of a given data set, and so on.[27] It is convenient to divide it into three classes: those that examine the relationship between trade strategy and development using a simple (single) criterion of trade strategy; those that attempt the same using more sophisticated (multiple) criteria; and those that examine the relationship between export growth and the growth of output; the case for outward-oriented trade policies is often predicated on the alleged growth-enhancing properties of exports.

In the simple two-sector trade model 'trade strategy' is readily identified. In practice the identification of trade strategy is far more complicated. This is so for several reasons. First, 'export' and 'import' sectors are not always readily identifiable (as we saw when we considered intra-industry trade in Chapter 8). Second, even when the output of particular sectors can be reasonably clearly labelled 'exportable' or 'importable', the sectors may very well be multi-product, and different instruments of protection may apply to each. Third, it is common in LDCs to find instruments of import-protection simultaneously co-existing with instruments of export-promotion; that is, a given set of policy interventions which *systematically* promotes import-substitution or export-promotion may not be in force. Fourth, the actual and intended effects of policy intervention may be quite different; that is, particular interventions may have unintended consequences. Finally, trade strategy may be time-inconsistent, its emphasis altering through time. Of course this need not be the case. There are many examples of economies which have followed a particular strategy for a very long period, import-substitution in India for instance. However, strategy may change. Many of the NICs which are described as following export-promoting strategies began with import-substitution regimes. The difficulties this creates for the analyst are twofold. On the one hand, deciding which strategy is currently operative; on the other identifying causality between trade strategy and subsequent economic performance.

When confronted with these complications, analysts have reacted in one of two ways, either by attempting to use a summary index of trade strategy, or by relying upon multiple criteria. As in all branches of applied economics, both involve compromises.

Multiple criteria studies endeavour to categorise trade strategy by reference to a number of different criteria. One can think of this approach (loosely) as focusing on policy inputs. We shall consider a recent study, by Greenaway and Nam,[28] as an example of this approach. Greenaway and Nam used information on effective rates of protection, reliance on direct controls, export incentives and exchange rate misalignment, to classify 41 LDCs into four categories, namely strongly outward-oriented, moderately outward-oriented, moderately inward-oriented and strongly inward-oriented. The basis of the classification was as follows:

strong outward-orientation (SOO) – either a complete absence of trade controls, or a situation where any import barriers were offset by export incentives;

moderate outward-orientation (MOO) – limited use of direct controls, relatively low import barriers, and some provision of incentives to export, with overall incentives tending towards neutrality or a slight bias towards production for the home market;

moderately inward-orientation (MIO) – an overall incentive structure distinctly favouring production for the domestic market with a clear anti-export bias, relatively high rates of effective protection, widespread use of direct controls and an overvalued exchange rate;

strong inward-orientation (SIO) – very high rates of effective protection, pervasive use of direct controls, strong disincentives to the export sector, and significant overvaluation of the exchange rate.

The four-way classification is to some degree judgmental, although really only likely to be an issue in separating the MIO and MOO sets. In the case of the SOO and SIO sets, all the indicators pointed in the same direction. Be that as it may, the principal results are summarised in Table 19.4. These results are discussed in detail in Greenaway and Nam and will only be summarised briefly.

Table 19.4   *Trade orientation and various economic indicators*

	Annual average percentage growth in							
	Real GDP		Real GDP per capita		Manufacturing value-added		Manufactured exports	
Development strategy	1963 –73	1973 –85	1963 –73	1973 –85	1963 –73	1973 –85	1965 –73	1973 –85
SOO	9.5	7.7	6.9	5.9	15.6	10.0	14.8	14.2
MOO	7.6	4.3	4.9	1.7	9.4	4.0	16.1	14.5
MIO	6.8	4.7	3.9	1.8	9.6	5.1	10.3	8.5
SIO	4.1	2.5	1.6	–0.1	5.3	3.1	5.7	3.7

Source: Derived from Greenaway and Nam (1988)

Table 19.4 suggests that growth rates in both real GDP and real GDP *per capita* have been higher in the outward-oriented countries than in the rest. Similarly, manufacturing value-added and exports appear to have grown more quickly in the outward-oriented economies between 1963 and 1985. The differences are most marked between the SOO and SIO groups, and often less clearly defined as between the MIO and SIO groups.

These results are suggestive rather than conclusive. They do suggest, however, that outward-orientation has been more conducive to growth and exporting than inward-orientation. The results have been criticised by, among other, Singer.[29] He argues that the findings are misleading on two counts. First, because the SOO group contains only three countries, Korea, Singapore and Hong Kong, the last two of which are city states and should be excluded. Thus the sample only really contains one SOO country. Second, it is claimed that *per capita* income levels fall as we move from the SOO to the SIO countries. Thus, all the results tell us is that the poorer countries find it more difficult to grow.

The first of these criticisms is at best misplaced, at worst disingenuous. If we are to claim that city states are in some sense special (and, if anything, one could readily make a case to the effect that they have special *dis*advantages), we might just as well begin singling out island economies, or landlocked economies, or small economies or continental economies, or whatever.

The second criticism is potentially more valid, on the grounds that poorer countries are more susceptible to terms-of-trade shocks than richer countries with more diversified economies. It worth noting, however, that, as Singer himself points out, Korea was one of the poorest countries in the world in the mid-1960s.

Several analysts have worked with single indicators of trade strategy. These attempt to summarise the relative price effects of the incentive structure in a single index or measure. We shall consider the measure of the bias in a trade regime proposed by Krueger:[30]

$$B = \frac{\sum_{i=1}^{t} w_i r_{mi}}{\sum_{j=1}^{s} w_j r_{xj}}$$

where r is the ratio of the domestic to the international price, m and x refer to importables and exportables respectively, and the ws are weights. Thus B measures the distortion of domestic prices relative to world prices in importables, compared to that in exportables. A value of 1 represents neutrality. Note that, of course, such a value could arise from a free-trade regime, or from a policy-ridden regime where incentives to produce in the import-substitute sector are exactly offset by incentives to produce in the export sector. An index in excess of unity indicates inward-orientation; an index of less than unity indicates outward-orientation. This is an approach in the same spirit as the effective exchange rates for importables and exportables discussed earlier.

The single indicators are in principle amenable to less ambiguous calibration than multiple criteria. In principle they should also be easier to work with. Inevitably there are measurement problems, for instance with the aggregation of individual subgroups within the tradable goods sectors. Aggregation difficulties arise not only through problems in assigning weights to individual groups, but also as a result of the fact that imports and exports may be recorded simultaneously in a given industry. Nevertheless, both of the single indicators discussed have been used.

Bias coefficients and the ratio of the effective exchange rates for importables and exportables were estimated in the Krueger study (as one element in a more comprehensive analysis of trade strategy for some inward-oriented developing countries). Estimates for five of the countries concerned are reported in Table 19.5.

Several points are worthy of note. First, both measures exceed unity for Brazil, Chile, the Philippines and Turkey, suggesting that relative prices favour production for the import-substituting rather than the export sector. Second, for one country, Korea, both indices are less than unity, implying that relative prices favour production for the export sector. Third, for Turkey, and for Brazil and Chile in the late 1950s, the indices are sufficiently high to imply strong inward-orientation. Finally, it is notable that for the 'inward-oriented' cases, the indices decline through time. The timing of the observations coincides with the aftermath of

Table 19.5   *Estimates of bias and of the ratio of effective exchange rates for five LDCs*

Country	Year	Bias Index	EER_M/EER_X
Brazil	1957	2.45	1.28
	1961	1.79	1.64
	1964	1.41	1.00
Chile	1956	3.69	1.21
	1959	1.94	1.18
	1965	1.95	1.18
Philippines	1960–2	2.01	1.64
	1970	1.37	1.37
South Korea	1961	0.67	0.68
	1964	0.78	0.78
Turkey	1958–59	6.31	1.87
	1970	3.01	1.63

Source: Krueger (1978), Tables 6.2 and 6.3

exchange rate devaluation, indicating, as *a priori* theorising suggests, that devaluation reduces anti-export bias (*ceteris paribus*). This particular study is not directly comparable to those discussed above and below, since it does not attempt to correlate bias *per se* with economic performance. Rather it uses information on bias, along with other information, including effective exchange rates, to evaluate the impact of liberalisation packages.

As noted earlier, the question of the relationship between exports and economic growth is much narrower than that discussed above. This relative narrowness should in principle make the analysis easier, but there is sufficient evidence of disagreement on both methodology and results to disprove this contention.

Analysts divide between measuring economic growth in terms of the change in either GNP or GDP, or in GNP or GDP *per capita*, adjusted by an appropriate price index, or that growth expressed as some percentage of a chosen base level. The most obvious measure of export growth is the actual change in value of exports from time period to time period, although not all writers agree. The choice of additional variables for inclusion in estimated multivariate relationships is broad, encompassing such items as the growth in the labour force, growth in domestic and/or foreign investment, the trade or current account balance and foreign aid.

Ideally, all applied economists would work with data for a large group of countries gathered over as long a time period as is consistent with the assumption of structural/ institutional stability, and carry out a joint cross-section/time-series analysis. In practice, the difficulty of obtaining data and/or concern with the quality of those data often leads to either a cross-sectional study over one or two time periods for a 'large' group of countries or to a set of time series analyses for a smaller group of countries. Cross-sectional studies appear the most common, in many cases with the data for each country averaged over some time period. A major argument for the use of cross-sectional analysis is that we may reasonably assume that external influences, for example the general state of the world economy, are common to all countries and may therefore be excluded from the analysis, which is generally not possible with a time series approach. The obvious counter-argument is that it is only with time series data that we can obtain evidence of the direction of causality. Moreover, cross-sectional studies presume a similarity of structure across developing countries.

The majority of those studies conducted between 1977 and 1989 find evidence of a strong association between exports or export growth and economic growth; several find evidence of a difference in the effect of exports on economic growth between countries above and below some critical level of some variable, a 'threshold effect'.

Jung and Marshall[31] attempted to answer the question of causality by employing the test put forward by Granger.[32] Working with time-series data on output and export growth rates over a minimum of 15 observations from 37 countries, they conclude that 'The time series results . . . provide evidence in favour of export promotion [as a means of promoting faster economic growth] in only 4 instances . . . At the very least, it suggests that the statistical evidence in favour of export promotion is not as unanimous as was previously thought' (p.11).

Should we then regard the evidence as an indication that outward-orientation should be recommended as a prescription for economic development? The evidence in favour of linking outward-orientation to growth is supportive, if not conclusive. However, evidence linking inward orientation and economic growth is seriously wanting.

19.6 Concluding remarks on development strategies

The 'old orthodoxy' of the 1950s prescribed a policy of import-substitution in LDCs, and in general that policy was adopted. A major reason for recommending the import-substitution route to development was 'export pessimism', but in the event the world economy grew strongly over the following decades. The 'new orthodoxy' prescribes instead an outward-oriented policy of trade liberalisation. Proponents of the new orthodoxy argue that the weight of the available evidence favours the argument that outward-orientation leads to faster development, and that (since it is essentially neutral) it avoids introducing the distortions and other sources of inefficiency in the domestic economy that follow from inward-orientation. The debate has not however been won, in the sense that there is still a group of economists and governments who favour the inward-orientation approach. They both cast doubt on the evidence used to support the new orthodoxy and use the arguments we identified earlier as the 'new export pessimism'. The reader should also beware that this is an area that is ideologically charged and that the positions taken can be influenced by value judgements.

We should also be careful not to regard strategies of export-promotion and import-substitution as mutually exclusive. In fact, countries which have at later periods in their history gone for export-promotion policies have started by applying import-competing policies for considerable amounts of time.

A common trait in export-promotion strategies is that they are market oriented. Reliance will be placed on pricing incentives rather than on quantitative controls. We have also seen that an outward-looking strategy has to be accompanied by realistic exchange rates, such as those prevailing in the NBER's Phases IV and V, which were the phases of liberalised exchange regimes. The essence of the export-promotion strategy is that it is geared to the international market. Import-substitution works under an umbrella of controls. Buyers and sellers will be oriented toward the domestic market. The outcome of economic activities will be greatly determined by government decisions.

No politician or civil servant thinks, however, that he can control international markets. Exporters will be in a strong position. They will be the ones who have the information about foreign markets, and government officials will tend to accept the statements of exporters most of the time. For example, if exporters claim that they need to import intermediate input because eventual domestic substitutes would be inferior, these claims will generally have to be accepted as the alternative might be export failure.

In general, protectionist policies might create large windfall gains for importers and those domestic producers who can benefit from such policies. It is much more difficult to create artificial gains under an export-promotion strategy. Here the successful firms are usually those which can succeed in the international market-place. Thereby they will achieve a strength of their own that is not directly related to government policy. This will give a pluralistic tinge to society, as the business sector will become an independent source of power.

It is a fact that economies of scale can be reaped more effectively in the context of export-promoting policies. The argument carries special weight for small countries. It should be noted, however, that markets in most LDCs are small in economic terms, even though the population may be large, as the purchasing power of the large majority of the population is minimal. To take an example, markets in India are usually smaller than in South Korea, and comparisons of industry-specific output levels show that they are typically much larger in South Korea. Export-promotion strategies are aimed at realising economies of scale by making it possible to establish plants of optimal size in an industry. On the contrary, import-substitution often discourages output expansion in existing lines of production. Import-substitution policies are often motivated by a wish for self-reliance. Countries pushing such policies want to cut themselves off from the vagaries of international markets. Although this wish is understandable, import-substitution strategies often seem to be counter-productive.

An export-promotion strategy places emphasis on activities geared toward earning foreign exchange. Exports will become the leading growth sector. When export industries slow down their rate of growth, so does the rest of the economy. Demand for foreign exchange will be adapted to the supply of foreign exchange. Moreover, an export-oriented strategy implies that a realistic exchange rate has to be kept. If domestic inflation occurs, the exchange rate will usually be devalued rather quickly. Reliance on exports usually leads to a rather comfortable balance-of-payments position. Hence temporary shortfalls in export earnings can often be handled in a smooth manner.

Economies which rely upon import-substitution are generally plagued by a shortage of foreign exchange. The lack of external reserves can have very negative effects on the rate of development. Disruptions in exchange earnings will have an immediate impact on development efforts, leading at the micro level to partly finished projects standing idle, and at the macro level to ineffectiveness in planning and difficulties in carrying out desired programmes. Experience has tended to confirm the above arguments and to cast further doubts on the possibility of increased self-reliance through import-substitution. It seems that the group of countries that were hardest hit by the drastic increase in oil prices that occurred in 1973 were poor countries that had relied on inward-looking strategies, countries like India, Pakistan, Bangladesh, Sri Lanka, and many of the sub-Saharan countries. The export-oriented economies of the Far East seem to have fared less badly. Although their terms of trade also deteriorated drastically, they seem nevertheless to have shown a greater flexibility in adjusting to the shock.

The countries relying on import-substitution strategies had very low reserves of foreign currencies. They had to cut back their imports immediately. The impact on production, for instance because of reduced fertiliser supplies, was sharp and immediate. Countries that had relied upon promotion of exports were better able to adjust to the new circumstances. They had a better foreign exchange situation to start with, their knowledge of international markets was better, and they could push their exports further to offset at least partially the adverse terms of trade.

The upshot is, ironically, that the countries which had tried to sever themselves from the vagaries of the international markets were in the end most dependent on these markets. Countries opting for a policy of export-promotion had provided themselves with a certain cushion in the form of knowledge of foreign markets and a greater degree of flexibility in dealing with changing the economic fortunes.

Sometimes it has been asserted that export-promoting strategies are dependent on 'strong' governments. Countries like Brazil and South Korea have also had strong governments in the form of dictatorships with strong ties to the military. They have been able to control undue increases in wages and to promote export-expansion in a systematic way. However, other countries, like Turkey in the 1950s, Ghana up to 1966, and Egypt during the 1950s and 1960s have also represented 'strong' governments in the sense that they were able to impose the economic policies that they deemed desirable. It is true that Brazil and South Korea have not always been democracies and that in political terms economic development might have implied a high price as far as human and political liberties are concerned. A 'strong' government is no prerequisite for economic development; nor is it a guarantee for strategies of export-promotion.

The views on inward- versus outward-looking policies of development differ. The mainstream of academic researchers seem to favour export-promoting strategies. They argue for policies to enhance each country's particular advantages relative to world economic conditions. By disregarding world market prices countries pursuing import-substitution have not taken the opportunity to import goods cheaply, and instead have produced them domestically at higher costs; by the same token, they have also abstained from taking advantage of existing export opportunities. Proponents of this argument maintain that behind high walls of protection such countries have created economic distortions leading to several of the problems touched on in this chapter.

Another line of argument reaches different conclusions: import-substitution is the best policy available for the LDCs. The advocates of this line are primarily spokesmen – often in a policy-making capacity – of the LDCs themselves. They point to the fact that the protectionist agricultural policies of the LDCs, and the selective protectionist policies of the developed countries (which discriminate against labour-intensive, low-technology exports), have left little scope for outward-looking policies on the part of the LDCs. Furthermore, they emphasise industrialisation as the major avenue for development. Hence they claim that import-substitution is the superior development strategy for the LDCs. Some radical exponents of this line are critical of import-substitution policies as actually carried out even though they favour them in general. They tend to stress that more direct attacks on uneven income distribution and mass unemployment should accompany any inward-looking development strategy.

The question of inward- versus outward-looking development strategies is one of heated controversy filled with poignant political overtones. We shall have to be satisfied with having surveyed some of the main approaches which have so far been put forward.

☐ *Notes*

1   Bhagwati (1990).
2   Prebisch (1950), (1959) and (1984); Singer (1950).
3   Nurkse (1962).
4   Spraos (1980).
5   Sapsford (1985).
6   Grilli and Yang (1988).
7   Cuddington and Urzula (1989).
8   Bleaney and Greenaway (1993).
9   Bhagwati, (1990) p. 15.
10 Baldwin (1985).
11 Bhagwati (1982b).
12 The NBER studies are summarised in two volumes: Bhagwati (1978) and Krueger (1978).
13 See Balasubramanyam and Basu (1990).
14 Bhagwati and Srinavasan (1975).
15 Bhagwati and Srinavasan (1975).
16 Balasubramanyam and Basu (1990), p. 230.
17 Based on Nam (1990).
18 See Congdon (1990), on which this is based, for a fuller account.
19 Congdon (1990), p. 241.
20 Congdon (1990).
21 Little, Scitovsky and Scott (1970), pp. 41ff.
22 Other aspects of Mexico's policies in the period up to 1983 are not so encouraging. See Congdon (1990) for a discussion of the Mexican experience.
23 See Diaz-Alejandro (1970) Chapter 6, Table 33.
24 Congdon (1990) pp. 241–4.
25 Little, Scitovsky and Scott (1990), pp. 93 ff.
26 Little, Scitovsky and Scott (1990), pp. 94 ff.
27 For a more detailed discussion of the empirical evidence, see Greenaway and Reed (1990).
28 Greenaway and Nam (1988).

29　Singer (1988).
30　Krueger (1978).
31　Jung and Marshall (1985).
32　Granger (1969).

■ *Chapter 20* ■

Empirical Studies of Trade Policy

■ *20.1* Introduction

It is convenient to divide the empirical studies of trade policy into three groups. First, there is work directed towards measurement, covering such problems as obtaining accurate estimates of nominal tariffs, calculating effective tariffs and domestic resource costs (discussed in Chapter 14), and estimating the *tariff-equivalents* of quotas. Second, there are attempts to estimate the costs and benefits associated with the imposition (or removal) of barriers to trade, which will be the subject matter of this chapter. Finally, there are studies which attempt to explain the pattern of protection, which were considered in Chapter 15.

Within the studies which estimate the costs/benefits of changes in trade policy we may identify two other groupings. First, some work is sector-specific and often country-specific, but other studies consider a wide range of sectors, and may cover a number of countries, perhaps even working at the global level. Second, although the early studies, and many later ones, use a partial equilibrium approach, the (relatively) recently developed computable general equilibrium (CGE) modelling approach has been widely applied to trade policy.

In this chapter we shall consider some selected studies which both illustrate the different approaches and give us some idea of the magnitude of the costs arising from barriers to trade.[1] First, however, we shall consider the methodology of the partial and general equilibrium approaches, and discuss some of the problems inherent in both approaches.

▌ 20.2 Estimating the costs of tariff protection using the partial equilibrium approach

The use of partial equilibrium methods in estimating the costs of protection is subject to the familiar caveats. In particular, the sector being considered should not have important linkages with other sectors of the economy or, if it has, the tariff change being considered should be small. If we are considering the effects of tariff elimination then the latter is less likely to be true. Equally, partial equilibrium analysis is not really applicable when we are considering the effects of simultaneous changes in many tariffs (as might be the case when countries form a free trade area or customs union). Nevertheless, for many years the partial equilibrium approach was widely employed for the lack of better alternatives. It is only with the recent developments in computable general equilibrium modelling that economists have been able to overcome these problems. These caveats apply equally of course to empirical studies which employ a partial equilibrium framework for the analysis of any other form of trade restriction.

Finally, it should be noted that the various formulae given below will provide a good indication of the various gains and losses only if there are no other distortions which affect the market in question.

☐ *The small-country case*

The welfare effects of tariff imposition by a small country were discussed in Chapter 10, using Figure 10.8 (the essential elements of which are reproduced here as Figure 20.1). In order to calculate the various gains and losses we need to know the domestic price with the tariff, $P_d = P_w(1 + t)$, the world price, P_w, domestic production and consumption when there is no tariff, s_0 and d_0, and domestic production and consumption when the tariff is in place, s_1 and d_1.

The various gains and losses from the removal of the tariff are given in Table 20.1 in terms of the prices and volumes shown in Figure 20.1.

Typically we have to consider the effects of the removal of a tariff that is already in place, and shall be able to observe P_d, s_1 and d_1. We may be able to observe the world price directly (strictly, the *c.i.f.* price of imported goods at the point of entry[2]). If not, we may be able to obtain information on the tariff levied on imports, and so may deduce the world price as $P_w = P_d/(1 + t)$.[3]

The volumes of domestic production and consumption under free trade will have to be estimated. If we have estimates of the price-response coefficients (slopes) of the domestic supply and demand curves (assumed to

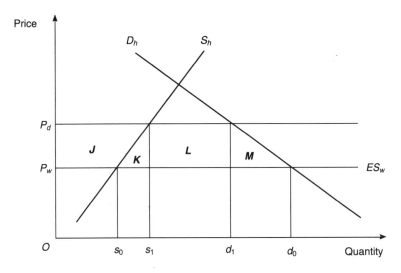

Figure 20.1 *A small importing country removing a tariff*

Table 20.1 *The gains and losses for a small country removing a tariff*

Consumer surplus gain (areas J, K, L and M)	$\frac{1}{2}(d_0 + d_1)(P_d - P_w)$
Producer surplus loss (area J)	$\frac{1}{2}(s_0 + s_1)(P_d - P_w)$
Tariff revenue loss (area L)	$(d_1 - s_1)t$
Dead-weight gain (areas K and M)	$\frac{1}{2}(s_1 - s_0) + (d_0 - d_1)\}(P_d - P_w)$

be linear for this example) and the domestic (tariff-inclusive) and world prices then we may estimate these volumes as:

$$s_0 = s_1 - \alpha(P_d - P_w) = s_1 - \alpha P_d \left(\frac{t}{1+t}\right) \tag{20.1}$$

$$d_0 = d_1 + \beta(P_d - P_w) = d_1 + \beta P_d \left(\frac{t}{1+t}\right) \tag{20.2}$$

where α and β are the price-response coefficients of the supply and demand curve respectively (both defined to be positive). Alternatively, if we have estimates of the elasticities of domestic supply and demand (η and ε respectively, with ε again defined to be positive), we may write these as:

$$s_0 = s_1 \left[1 - \eta \left(\frac{1 - P_w}{P_d} \right) \right] = s_1 \left(1 - \frac{\eta t}{1 + t} \right) \tag{20.3}$$

$$d_0 = d_1 \left[1 - \varepsilon \left(\frac{1 - P_w}{P_d} \right) \right] = d_1 \left(1 + \frac{\varepsilon t}{1 + t} \right) \tag{20.4}$$

Substitution from the appropriate formulae into the expressions given in Table 20.1 then yields estimates of the gains and losses from tariff removal. The modification of the results given above for the case where a tariff is reduced rather than eliminated is straightforward.

☐ *The large-country case*

The calculation of the welfare effects of tariff elimination (or reduction) when we are dealing with a large country is necessarily more complicated, since we have to take into account the effect on the world price as well. It is convenient to start with the excess supply and demand configuration shown in Figure 20.2, since this involves only two price-response coefficients and is sufficient for the calculation of the net welfare gains for both the importing and the exporting countries. Figure 20.2 reproduces Figure 10.6, and the reader should refer back to that section of the book for an explanation of the meaning of the various areas identified in the diagram.

We should be able to obtain data on the tariff-inclusive price in the importing country (P_A) and on the volume of trade (m_1). Let us assume for simplicity that we also know the price in the exporting country (P_B), and also that we have estimates of the price-response coefficients for the export supply and import demand curves, θ and ϕ respectively (both defined to be positive). The (estimated) equilibrium price under free trade will then be given by

$$P_E = \frac{\theta P_A + \phi P_B}{\theta + \phi} \tag{20.5}$$

and the trade volume by

$$m_0 = m_1 + \frac{\theta \phi}{\theta + \phi} (P_A - P_B) \tag{20.6}$$

The estimated net benefits and gains for the importing and exporting countries may then be obtained by substituting for these values in the formulae given in Table 20.2.

If we wish to decompose these welfare changes to obtain the effects on producers and consumers in the importing country then we need estimates

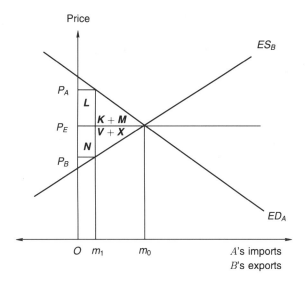

Figure 20.2 *Net gains and losses to both countries from the elimination of a tariff*

of the production and consumption levels in the tariff-ridden case and of the individual price-response coefficients for supply and demand. Given these we may use the formulae of Table 20.1, remembering to replace P_W by P_E.

Table 20.2 *Net gains and losses for the importing and exporting countries in the large-country case*

Importing country

(1) Dead-weight gain (area $K + M$) $\frac{1}{2}(m_0 - m_1)(P_A - P_E)$

(2) Terms-of-trade loss (area N) $m_1(P_E - P_B)$

(3) Net gain for importing country $(1) - (2)$

Exporting country

(4) Dead-weight gain (area $V + X$) $\frac{1}{2}(m_0 - m_1)(P_E - P_B)$

(5) Terms-of-trade gain (area N) $m_1(P_E - P_B)$

(6) Net gain for exporting country $(4) + (5)$

World

(7) Net gain (area $K + M + V + X$) $(1) + (4)$

20.3 Estimating the costs of a quantitative restriction on imports using the partial equilibrium approach

The first problem that we face when estimating the costs of a quantitative restriction on imports, such as a quota or a voluntary export restriction (VER), is in measuring the effect of the quantitative restriction on the domestic price.[4] If we are fortunate then we can observe both the domestic and the world price (P_d and P_w respectively), and can calculate the *tariff-equivalent* of the quantitative restriction as

$$\hat{t} = \frac{P_d - P_w}{P_w} \tag{20.7}$$

We may then use this tariff-equivalent in the appropriate formulae to estimate the effects on producers and consumers.

The second problem we face is in determining how much of the rent created by a quota or VER goes to the government of the importing country, how much is secured by domestic residents, and how much accrues to foreign residents. As we argued in Chapter 10, a VER is much more likely to allow foreign suppliers to acquire these rents than is an import quota. Any proportion of the rent which remains in the importing country should be offset against the difference between consumer losses and producer gains in calculating the net loss to the country of the quantitative restriction. Any rent which goes to foreign suppliers must not, of course, be offset in that way.

An alternative procedure for estimating the extent to which foreign suppliers raise their prices when a VER is in operation is possible in certain circumstances. In some cases, where the national VER quantity is allocated to individual producers by the issue of export licences, a market has developed in those licences. The price paid for an export licence (the *quota premium*) should indicate the *minimum* amount of rent which the purchaser expects to gain from possession of the licence. The more competitive the market, the more likely it is that the quota premium will reflect the actual rent which the most competitive producers expect to gain.

As an example, suppose that licences are issued for an export quantity of Q per licence, and that a producer pays a premium Z for such a licence. The producer will expect to earn a rent at least equal to Z on his exports, which implies that he expects to sell his exports for a premium of Z/Q per unit. We may then take Z/Q as an estimate of the minimum price-raising effect of the VER. We may also calculate from this the implied rent for all exporters holding licences, which in turn is an indication of the amount of rent transferred from consumers in the importing country to producers in the exporting country.

■ *20.4 Computable general equilibrium analyses*

The essential feature of a computable general equilibrium model is that it *is* concerned with general equilibrium. The particular form employed is that of the Walrasian general equilibrium, as formalised by economists such as Arrow and Debreu.[5] It must therefore be consistent with the assumptions that characterise a general equilibrium model, and in particular that all markets clear (so that there is no unemployment, etc.). As we know, such models can only give us the relative prices of goods and factors, although they do give actual outputs, factor utilisations, etc.

It is surprisingly difficult to obtain formal algebraic solutions for outputs, factor inputs, etc. in even the most simple general equilibrium model. For example, even in a simple two-factor, two-good model with Cobb–Douglas production functions it is impossible to obtain an explicit expression for the production-possibility curve.[6] We must instead use a computer to solve for numerical outcomes to such a model.

It will be evident therefore that the solution of a general equilibrium model involving, as many do, a large number of final and intermediate traded goods, non-traded goods, perhaps several factors of production, and possibly more than one country, deriving even a numerical solution may be extremely difficult. In fact, the development of numerical algorithms that can find solutions to such models, even where relatively simple functional forms are assumed for production functions, indifference maps, etc., has occurred only in the last 15 years or so.[7] Since the introduction of these algorithms there has been however an explosion in the amount of work done with computable (or 'applied') general equilibrium models.

Constructing and solving an 'applied' CGE model (that is, one which is to be used for the analysis of a real problem) requires two interrelated inputs. These are the specification of the model and the construction of an appropriate data set. We shall start by considering the problems of model specification.[8] Figure 20.3 shows a flowchart of the general procedure.

□ *Specifying the model and the functional forms*

The first step in specifying a CGE model is to identify the problem(s) to which you are seeking an answer, and then to choose a model structure

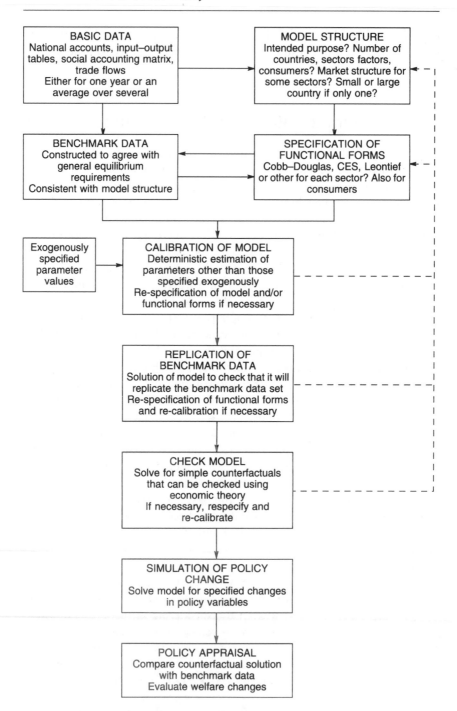

Figure 20.3   *A flowchart for constructing and running a CGE model*

that will allow you to derive that answer. Some authors have argued that having to specify the model structure is an excellent discipline, in that it focuses the researcher's mind on the essentials of the problem!

The first stage of the specification will be the choice of the numbers and natures of countries, sectors, factors and consumers that are required. Suppose, for example, you are concerned primarily with the effect of a change in the tariff on imported agricultural goods. In many cases it may be reasonable to regard the country as small, so that the prices of traded gods are exogenously determined. The rest of the world need not then be considered explicitly. It may also be sufficient, so long as there are no significant linkages between agriculture and some other sector of the economy, to consider just two sectors, agriculture and 'the rest'. You must then decide how many factors of production you wish to consider. The particular nature of agriculture might suggest that you consider three factors, labour as the mobile factor, and land and capital as sector-specific factors. Finally, how many classes of 'typical' consumers should you specify?

If you have no compelling evidence that there are differences in tastes between consumers (say between land-owners, capital-owners and workers, or between identifiable high- and low-income groups) then it may be sufficient to specify just one typical consumer to represent all (which implicitly assumes that consumers have identical and homothetic preferences). If this is not a reasonable assumption then you must specify different groups as appropriate.

On the other hand, Brown and Whalley, in a study of the likely effects of tariff cutting proposals in the Tokyo Round,[9] considered it necessary to specify four trading blocs (the United States, Japan, the European Community(9) and the rest of the world) and 39 product groups.

In principle, the numbers of countries, sectors, factors and consumers is limited only by the computing power available. However, experience has shown that there are advantages to being 'parsimonious' in the model specification, if only because the difficulty of interpreting results (and of finding and correcting errors) increases at an increasing rate as the model becomes more complex.

The second stage of the specification of the model is concerned with the market structures that will be assumed. For example, it may be assumed that all markets are competitive, with homogeneous goods. It is more common, in practice, to assume that otherwise identical goods are in fact differentiated according to their country of origin – the so-called *Armington Assumption*.

Closely linked with the above, and also with the *parameterisation* of the model (of which more later), is the choice of functional forms for the production functions, consumers' preference functions and so on. The most commonly used assumption is that production and preferences may be represented by *constant elasticity of substitution* (CES) functions,[10] although Leontief functions may be used when intermediate goods are to be considered. The CES formulation may also be used to specify the substitution between (differentiated) domestic and imported goods.

Finally, the model must be *closed*. That is, sufficient equations must be specified to allow determination of all the flows within the model and all relative prices. A common way of closing a CGE model (the 'macro closure') is to assume that savings are determined through consumers' preferences (in the same way as expenditure on any good), and that investment is equal to savings. The drawback to this assumption is obvious – there is no room for the separate determination of investment expenditures by firms. All closure rules have some problem inherent in them, and it has been argued that the form of closure specified will have a significant effect on the output of the model. This is perhaps one of the major weaknesses of the CGE approach.

☐ *The 'benchmark' data set*

When applying CGE techniques to 'real' problems the researcher must construct a 'benchmark' data set for use in parameterising the model. This data set, while based on the data for the economy or economies concerned, must be consistent with the assumptions underlying general equilibrium models. In particular, it must be consistent with the assumptions of a static competitive equilibrium, with all markets cleared (no unemployment, etc.), with trade balanced, and so on.[11]

The likelihood that any real set of data will meet these conditions is virtually zero. It follows that the data must be adjusted ('massaged') so that they are consistent with these assumptions. The problems are exacerbated by the fact that it may be difficult to obtain all the data from one source, so that inconsistencies are more than likely and must be corrected. Such an undertaking is not trivial – in some cases the construction of this data set has taken up to 18 months! This may explain why a number of CGE studies have used the same benchmark data.

Typically, published data record flows in value terms and separate data on prices and quantities are not available. In this case it has become the convention to employ the *Harberger Assumption*, where the price of each commodity is set equal to one, implying a quantity equal in numerical size to the recorded flow. Since the CGE model is solved for relative, not absolute, prices this causes no difficulties.

Calibration of the model and replication of the benchmark data

The parameters of the chosen model structure are then estimated in conjunction with the benchmark data. Where possible the researcher will use estimates of the parameters of the model (such as demand elasticities for some goods) obtained from other sources. The remaining parameters are then chosen so that they are consistent with the benchmark data. Typically the parameters are determined exactly: that is, the researcher manipulates the equations of the model so that the parameters are written as functions of the data and solves those equations to obtain the parameter values. This procedure is known as *calibration*.

Note the difference in approach between the *calibration* of a CGE model and the more familiar *estimation* of parameters using econometric methods. The CGE modeller has a strictly limited set of data, and the procedure adopted does not allow him to estimate standard errors. The calibration procedure is deterministic, not econometric.

The researcher will, of course, examine the estimated parameters to see that they are consistent with the values that would be suggested by economic theory and by judgement. If this is not the case then the specification of the model will be modified until this has been achieved. It is for this reason that the specification of the model cannot in general be considered as a separate exercise from the construction of the benchmark data.

Finally, the calibrated CGE model will be solved to check that it will reproduce the benchmark data – the replication procedure. Should it not do so then the researcher will respecify the model and re-estimate the parameters until it does.

Using the CGE model to investigate the effects of policy changes

Once the CGE model has been constructed and calibrated it may be used to investigate the effects of changes in existing policy instruments, or of the introduction of new ones. The policy changes are introduced into the model (for example a new tariff may be specified) and the model is solved for the various flows and relative prices. The output of this simulation – usually referred to as a *counterfactual* experiment – is then compared with the benchmark data, and changes noted.

The use of simple counterfactuals gives the researcher another chance to check the model. If the outcomes are inconsistent with those suggested by the 'accepted wisdom' then the researcher will return to the model specification and examine it for errors, which will then be corrected. This use of simple experiments is of great importance, although the intended purpose of constructing the model will probably be to examine the effects of complex policy changes (such as the elimination of all tariffs). When many policy instruments are changed at the same time it can be extremely difficult to disentangle their effects. Since the 'accepted wisdom', or 'intuition', is not always adequate for the task of considering many simultaneous policy changes, and since a CGE simulation may throw up surprising results as a consequence of the interactions between many changes, it is important that the researcher knows that the model does at least handle simple changes correctly.

☐ *Some of the pros and cons of CGE modelling*

The main weaknesses of the CGE approach should be apparent from the preceding discussion. Perhaps the most important are that there are problems (and considerable work) in obtaining a consistent data set, that parameters are estimated deterministically rather than econometrically, and that the output of the model may be partially determined by the particular closure rule used.

The advantages are thought by many (though not all) economists to outweigh these weaknesses. The most obvious advantage of the CGE approach must be that it *is* general equilibrium in form. It allows us to consider more than one policy change at the same time, and does not restrict those policy changes to be marginal. It also allows us to consider the *distributional* impact of policy changes. That is, we may gain insight into the effects of policy changes on the distribution of income between workers and the owners of capital and/or land, or between different groups of workers. Similarly, CGE modelling allows us to consider the effects of policy on the distribution of employment and output between sectors, on the volume of trade and possibly its distribution between countries, on government revenue and expenditure, and so on. Finally, a well-constructed CGE model ensures that these changes are *micro-consistent* – that is, that changes in one part of the economy are consistent with changes elsewhere.

■ *20.5 Some analyses of the costs of protection*

There have been numerous studies of the costs of protection, both by tariffs and by quantitative restrictions, using either partial equilibrium or

CGE methods. We do not have the space to consider more than a few of these. We shall consider two examples: first, two studies of the effects of the protection of a sector (textiles), one using a partial equilibrium approach and focusing on one country, the other taking a general equilibrium approach in a global setting; and second, a general equilibrium analysis of the effects of Tokyo Round reductions in tariffs.[12]

Sectoral protection – the Multi-Fibre Arrangement

A brief history of the Multi-Fibre Arrangement (MFA) and a description of its provisions are given in Chapter 17. The essence of the MFA is that participating exporting countries 'voluntarily restrain' their exports to the designated importing countries. In addition, tariffs may be levied by the importing countries.

An example of the application of the partial equilibrium approach to the effects with one country (the United Kingdom) of protection in this sector is given by Greenaway.[13] In an attempt to estimate the price-raising effect of VERs within the UK economy, Greenaway focuses on Hong Kong, which is both a major exporter of textiles (with nearly 45 per cent of UK imports) and a country in which there is a well-established market in export licences.

The weighted average of the *c.i.f.* prices of textiles imports into the United Kingdom in 1982 was estimated to be £2.67 per unit.[14] Calculation of the average quota premium per unit of textile exports in Hong Kong indicated that the minimum rent obtainable was £0.34, suggesting that the average *c.i.f.* price per unit would be £2.33 if the restraint were not in place. In addition, the United Kingdom imposed a tariff on these textiles that averaged 17 per cent. The combined effect of the VER and the tariff is thus to increase the average price of these textiles within the United Kingdom to about £3.12 – an increase of almost 34 per cent above the unrestrained *c.i.f.* price.

Greenaway took an existing estimate for the elasticity of demand for textiles, equal to 1.086, in order to estimate the expansion of consumption that would follow from the elimination of all trade restrictions.[15] Estimates of the domestic supply elasticity in the UK textile industry were not available, so values of 1 and 2 were taken as probable outer limits to the likely value. The results presented in Table 20.3 and subsequently are for a supply elasticity of 1.

Greenaway's estimates of the various costs and transfers resulting from the restriction of textile imports are reported in Table 20.4. The largest

Table 20.3   *Estimated changes in consumption, domestic production, and imports following liberalisation of trade in textiles in the United Kingdom, 1982*

	Base level*	Change*
Consumption	204166	56259
Domestic production	62119	−15762
Imports	142047	72021

* Thousand units
Source: Greenaway (1985), Table 4.6.

item is the total loss to consumers, some £170 million in that one year. Of that loss, about £49 million went to UK import-competing producers in additional profits and £53 million as tariff revenue (both internal transfers), and over £59 million was transferred to foreign suppliers.[16] The total loss to the UK economy, calculated as the difference between the loss to consumers and the internal transfers to UK producers and taxpayers, was thus estimated to be some £68 million in 1982. Had the same level of protection been afforded to UK producers by a tariff alone then the cost to the UK economy would have been the sum of the consumption and production distortion losses, just over £9 million. The additional loss due to the use of VERs rather than tariffs (the transfers to foreign suppliers) thus dominates the efficiency losses due to protection.

However, as we noted earlier, the costs of restricting trade continue from year to year. In order to estimate the total costs from retaining the tariff and the VER on UK textile imports we should calculate their present value. On the assumption that clothing protection would have remained in

Table 20.4   *Estimated costs of protection of clothing in the United Kingdom, 1982 (£m)*

Total loss to UK consumers	170.4
Increase in profits for UK producers	49.1
Tariff revenue	53.0
Transfers to foreign suppliers	59.2
Total loss to UK economy	68.4
Loss due to consumption distortion	7.1
Loss due to production distortion	2.0

Source: Greenaway (1985), Table 4.7.

place permanently, and that the discount rate was 5 per cent per annum, Greenaway estimated the present value of consumer losses from protection as £3410 million, and the present value of the net loss to the UK economy as £1370 million.

Such gains and losses usually appear to be a low proportion of the national income (usually well less than 1 per cent), and so it is tempting to disregard them as insignificant. An alternative way of considering the results is to calculate the cost of 'saving a job' in the import-competing industry. The average annual earnings of male textile workers in 1982 were £5920, those of female workers £3620. Greenaway estimated that the annual cost to the UK economy of saving a job was between £4500 and £8500 (depending on whether the supply elasticity is 2 or 1 respectively). The cost to consumers of saving each job is nearly three times as great.

In a CGE analysis of the third MFA, Trela and Whalley[17] considered three major developed importing countries (the United States, Canada and the European Community) and 34 supplying developing countries. The model specified 14 textile and apparel product categories and one other 'composite' good. The benchmark data set was based on 1986.

Trela and Whalley considered the effects of two different liberalisations: the removal of all bilateral MFA quotas and tariffs, and removing the bilateral quotas but not the tariffs. They used as their measure of the welfare effects the Hicksian equivalent variation. Their results are summarised in Table 20.5

The net gain for the exporting developing countries from the removal of both tariffs and quotas suggest that the gains from improved access to the developed countries' markets exceed the losses from the foregone rent transfers under the VERs. The developed importing countries all make gains from this complete liberalisation. When there is partial liberalisation,

Table 20.5 *Estimated welfare effects of liberalisation of the MFA for the United States, Canada, the European Community and the developing countries ($billion, 1986)*

	Removal of tariffs and quotas	Removal of quotas only
United States	12.309	15.038
Canada	0.831	0.928
European Community	2.215	3.039
All developing countries	8.078	2.934

Source: Derived from Trela and Whalley (1990), Tables 3 and 4.

with tariffs maintained, the gains to the developing countries are lower but those to the developed countries higher than when there is full liberalisation. These results reflect the balance between elimination of the rent transfers due to the VERs and the terms-of-trade effect enjoyed by the (large) importing countries through the retention of their tariffs. Trela and Whalley suggest that their results indicate that the tariffs levied by the large importing countries are below their optimum tariffs.

☐ *Multilateral liberalisation – the Tokyo Round*

Brown and Whalley employed a CGE model to analyse the effects of the 'Swiss formula' for tariff reductions that was used in the Tokyo Round and alternatively of complete liberalisation.[18] Their model specified four trading blocs (the United States, Japan, the European Community – then consisting of 9 members – and the rest of the world), and 34 product groups. The products were taken to be differentiated and it was assumed that each was produced in only one of the trading blocs. The model was calibrated on a 1973 benchmark data set.

The results of the Brown and Whalley analysis are summarised in Table 20.6. The gains from tariff reduction via the Swiss formula were rather small. The distribution of the gains was interesting, since it appeared that while the developed countries would gain (especially the European Community), the rest of the world would lose. Brown and Whalley ascribed this effect to the exclusion of agricultural products from the Tokyo Round tariff reductions and the fact that raw materials, which are largely exported by the developing countries, already faced a low tariff.

Table 20.6   *Welfare gains from the Tokyo Round tariff reductions and from complete liberalisation by the developed countries ($US billion, 1973)*

	Tokyo Round reductions (Swiss formula)	Complete liberalisation by developed countries
European Community	1.45	8.08
United States	0.79	2.32
Japan	0.49	−0.15
Rest of World	−1.75	9.28

Source: Adapted from Brown and Whalley (1980).

The gains from full liberalisation, even without the participation of the less-developed countries (LDCs), are substantially larger. This reflects the importance of non-tariff barriers to trade.

It has been argued that the perfectly competitive structure assumed in many CGE models leads them to understate the gains from the reduction of trade barriers. For example, Cox and Harris[19] and subsequently Brown and Stern,[20] have shown that the inclusion of imperfectly competitive sectors within a CGE framework leads to a substantial increase in the estimated welfare gains for Canada of the US–Canadian free trade agreement. Even then the estimated gains for Canada are of the order of 1 per cent of GDP. The results obtained appear, moreover, to be quite sensitive to the assumptions made about the form of imperfect competition.

■ 20.6 Comments and conclusions

The methodological problems that must be faced in attempting to evaluate the costs of trade restrictions are far from trivial, particularly when non-tariff barriers are involved and when there is imperfect competition in some sectors. The estimated gains from the reduction of trade restrictions are not particularly high when compared with GDP although, as we saw in the Greenaway study, the costs of preserving a job in an import-competing industry may be high relative to the wage paid. Nevertheless, it may be argued that it is only by demonstrating that there are gains to be made from reducing trade barriers that economists can persuade policy-makers to pursue liberalisation.

If this is to be done then the CGE approach must provide the better methodology in the long run. There is however much to be done in improving CGE modelling. The development of the modelling of imperfect competition and the generation (and maintenance) of up-to-date benchmark data sets may provide the greatest gains.

□ *Notes*

1   For a considerably more detailed study of empirical work on trade barriers see Milner (1985).
2   The '*c.i.f.* price' of an imported good is equal to the price of the good when it leaves the exporting country plus the costs of 'carriage, insurance and freight'.
3   Care must be taken when working with published tariff rates ('*ex ante* tariffs'). The average of the tariffs actually charged ('*ex post* tariffs') may differ from the published rates for many reasons, such as preferences given to imports from various countries. In calculating the welfare costs of a tariff it

may be more appropriate to use the average tariff rate. The published rate may however be the best indicator of the marginal cost of imports to a consumer. In any event, the average *c.i.f.* price of imports may well differ from the implied price of imports derived from the domestic price and whichever tariff rate is used. Which approach is preferred is a matter of judgement.

4   The problems may be even worse when dealing with other forms of non-tariff barrier. See Milner (1985), for a more detailed discussion of this point, and of other areas of concern, such as the possibility of *tariff-redundancy*.

5   Arrow and Debreu (1954).

6   See Dinwiddy and Teal (1988) for an explanation of the problems and for the computer codings that are needed to derive a numerical solution for even the most simple models.

7   See Shoven and Whalley (1992) for a discussion of the computational problems involved in solving computable general equilibrium models.

8   The discussion will assume that we are interested in questions of trade policy, where CGE modelling has been extensively employed. However the CGE approach has also been used with great effect in studies in the fields of fiscal policy, economic development, agricultural policy and environmental issues.

9   Brown and Whalley (1980).

10   We met the CES function in Chapter 6 when discussing Minhas's work on factor-intensity reversals. The formula for the two-factor CES production function is

$$Q = A\left[\alpha K^{-\rho} + (1 - \alpha)L^{-\rho}\right]^{-1/\rho}$$

where K and L are the factor inputs. The function may be extended without difficulty to allow for more than two inputs, and may be used as a preference function with appropriate modifications. The CES function is linearly homogeneous (so that it implies constant returns to scale when used as a production function, and unit income elasticity of demand for every good when used as a preference function). The parameter α determines the capital–labour ratio, in that at any given relative wage rate the K/L ratio will be higher if α is higher. The elasticity of substitution, σ, is given by $\sigma = 1/(1 + \rho)$. The parameter ρ determines the curvature of the isoquant. As $\rho \to -1$ the isoquant tends to a straight line, implying that the two factors are perfect substitutes. When $\rho = 0$ the CES function becomes the Cobb–Douglas function, with the elasticity of substitution equal to 1. As ρ becomes increasingly positive so the curvature of the isoquant increases, and the two factors become worse and worse substitutes for each other.

11   Data sources may consist of published national accounts, input–output tables and so on. If the researcher is lucky he may have access to a *social accounting matrix* for the economy, which records flows between different sectors in value terms.

12   For a more detailed survey see Milner (1985).

13   Greenaway (1985).

14   Greenaway considers only imports coming under three of the MFA categories – woven trousers, woven and knitted blouses, and woven shirts. These are among the most restricted categories of imports.

15   The estimate was taken from Deaton (1975).

16   Note that producers within the European Community and the European Free Trade Area, and in other countries that export to the United Kingdom without being constrained under the MFA, benefit from the higher price in the United Kingdom. This is of course a form of trade diversion.

17   Trela and Whalley (1990).

18   Brown and Whalley (1980).

19   Cox and Harris (1992).

20   Brown and Stern (1989).

■ *Chapter 21* ■

International Factor Movements

■ *21.1* Introduction

The models of trade we have considered so far have had in common the assumption that factors of production cannot move between countries. This is of course a simplification, intended to codify the observation that while factors of production do move internationally, they do so less freely than do goods and services. In this chapter we shall consider some of the causes and consequences of international movements of labour (migration) and capital (foreign investment) when there are no market imperfections. In Chapter 22 we shall consider the role of foreign investment when imperfections in markets lead to the establishment of multinational enterprises.

■ *21.2* International factor movements in a Heckscher–Ohlin setting

When we considered the Heckscher–Ohlin model we saw that, provided neither of the two countries specialised completely (and there were no factor-intensity reversals), free trade in the two goods equalised factor prices. That is, of course, exactly what we would expect to happen if factors of production were free to move between countries, rather than being perfectly immobile as specified by the model. The free movement of goods acts as a substitute for the free movement of labour and capital within the Heckscher–Ohlin model.

A consequence of factor-price equalisation brought about by free trade (in this model) is that the world is moved out to its production-possibility curve. That is, with free trade the world can produce the same quantities of the two goods as it would were it a single economy with the same total endowments of labour and capital.

Provided that we maintain the assumption that the two countries have identical and homothetic tastes, we may show that perfect mobility of the two factors of production will also move the world onto its production-possibility curve even if there is no trade in the goods produced.

Figure 21.1 shows the factor boxes for the two countries, A and B. Country A's box has O_X^A as its X-origin and Z as its Y-origin, while country B has Z as its X-origin and O_Y^B as its Y-origin. $O_X^A U O_Y^B V$ is therefore the factor box for the world as a whole.

Since A is the physically capital-rich country, the real wage rate must be higher, and the real return to capital lower, in A than in B under autarky, so that the capital–labour ratios will be higher in A than in B in the two sectors. Points a and b show two possible autarkic equilibrium points for A and B respectively.

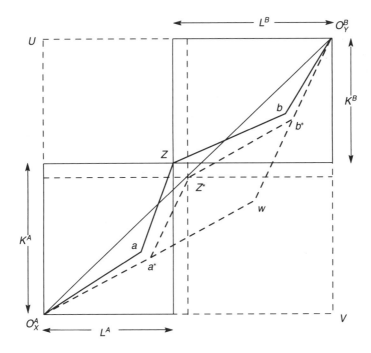

Figure 21.1 *International factor mobility will put the world on its production-possibility frontier*

Now suppose that capital and labour become free to move between the two countries, but that goods cannot be traded. The higher real wage in A will attract labour from B, while the higher real return to capital in B will attract capital from A. The shifting of factors of production will of course lead to changes in the production-possibility curves for the two countries.

Since the two countries have identical and homothetic tastes, the differentials in factor rewards will only be eliminated when the two production-possibility curves have the same slope along a ray drawn from the origin. This in turn requires that the countries have the same capital–labour *endowment* ratio. That is, the new factor boxes for A and B must have the same diagonal as does the 'world' factor box, that is, $O_X^A O_Y^B$. The new equilibrium must therefore be at a point such as Z^*, so that A's box is defined by the corners O_X^A and Z^*, and B's by the corners Z^* and O_Y^B.

With factor rewards equalised, the capital-labour ratio in each sector must be the same in A and B, so that the two countries will be in equilibrium at points such as a^* and b^* respectively. If the world were one country with the factor endowments shown by the box $O_X^A U O_Y^B V$, and if the relative wage rate were the same as that in the two countries in their new equilibrium, the world equilibrium point would be w. Since $a^*Z^*b^*w$ is a parallelogram, and there are constant returns to scale, the world output of X (Y) at w is equal to the sum of A's output of X (Y) at a^* and B's output of X (Y) at b^*. Point w must of course define a point on the world's production-possibility curve.

Although this analysis gives us some insight into the effects of factor movements, we cannot be precise about the new equilibrium. In particular, the relative speed with which capital and labour move will determine the position of point Z^* in Figure 21.1. Moreover, as is usual in such models, the supply of labour and capital is perfectly inelastic with respect to the factor rewards. In order to examine the problem further we will now switch to partial equilibrium analyses of the causes and effects of the migration of labour and then of the transfer of capital.

■ 21.3 The migration of labour

□ *Positive effects*

Labour is generally assumed to be less mobile internationally than capital. However even in relatively recent times the migration of labour has been a major factor in the world economy. In some instances the migration may be regarded as being permanent, as in the emigration of Europeans to North America and Australasia, and the more recent immigration to Europe of peoples from the Caribbean, Africa and Asia. At the other extreme, some migration is essentially temporary, as the case with Turkish 'guest-workers' in Germany and Mexican agricultural workers in California, where there may be a steady turnover of migrants within a fairly stable total.

The motivation for such migration is necessarily complex, depending not only on differences in wage rates (net of income taxes, etc.) but also on differences in the cost of living, the level of public benefits such as health care, education, etc., the perceived ease of integration into the new society, and so on. We shall concentrate on the wage rate effect, either ignoring the other effects or incorporating them into the supply curve for migrant labour.

In Figure 21.2, D_A and S_A represent the demand for, and supply of, a particular type of labour (say, unskilled workers) in country A; D_B and S_B have similar meanings for country B. Wages are assumed to be on a common real scale. Country B is the high-wage country when migration is impossible. The higher wage in B may be the result of, say, trade barriers stopping the equalisation of the prices of goods.

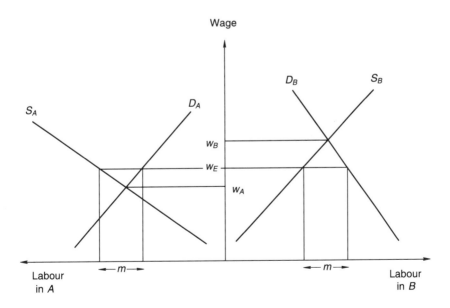

Figure 21.2 *The positive effects of labour migration*

Suppose now that migration becomes possible, and that there are no barriers to migration, whether cultural (such as language differences) or due to policy differences (such as levels of health care). Labour will move from A to B until the wage is equalised; that is, an amount m of labour will migrate, resulting in the common real wage w_E.

☐ *Welfare effects*

It is evident that the gainers from this migration will be the migrants themselves who are receiving a higher wage for working in B, the workers remaining in A who get a higher wage through the reduction in competition for work in A, and the employers in B, whose profits are increased by the expansion of their workforce and the reduction in the wage in B. The losers are the employers in A, who are now paying higher wages for a reduced workforce, and the workers in B, who face a lower wage.

We may use the standard consumer and producer surplus analysis to analyse the welfare effects of the migration, but we must do so with care. The migrants earn their higher incomes in country B, and it is possible that none of their income returns to country A (they may of course send remittances back to A). This is quite different to the examples of trade in goods that we considered previously using similar diagrams; in those cases the revenue earned by sales in overseas markets *is* returned to the exporting country.

In order to identify the country-specific welfare effects accurately we must distinguish between the supply curve of the migrant workers and the supply curve of those who remain in country A. This is done in Figure 21.3, where R_A is the supply curve of those workers who remain in A. The supply curve for the migrants is not shown, but is of course given by the horizontal difference between S_A and R_A.

The gain to workers *native* to A (both those remaining in A and the migrants) is measured by areas a, b, c and d. Of this, the gain to those workers remaining in A is area d, so the gain to the migrant workers must be areas a, b and c. If the migrants make no remittances to country A (as we shall assume), then this gain is enjoyed in country B.

The other gains and losses are more straightforward. The loss to employers in A is shown by areas b, c and d. Country A must therefore lose from the migration by an amount $b + c$.

The gain to employers in B is shown by areas j and k, and the loss to workers native to B is area j. The net gain to country B is thus $j + k$ for the employers, less j for the original B workforce, plus $a + b + c$ for the migrant workers, giving a net gain of $k + a + b + c$.

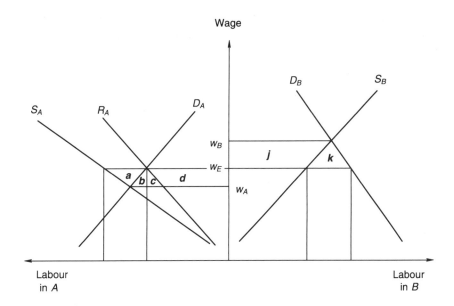

Figure 21.3 *The welfare effects of labour migration*

Our analysis suggests therefore that migration results in a welfare loss from the source country (*A* in our example) and a welfare gain for the host country. The world as a whole must of course gain from the more efficient use of resources, the net gain in our example being *k* + *a*.

☐ *Some policy implications of migration*

The losses suffered by the source country suggest that there might be a policy response to limit emigration. Moreover, the losses identified above may well understate the full cost to the source country, so increasing the pressure for restrictive policies.

Emigrants tend not to be drawn randomly from the workforce in the source country. Various studies have suggested that they tend to earn somewhere around the average income or more, to be younger, to be more 'motivated' than the average, to be better trained, and so on. The loss of such people will therefore tend to reduce the quality of the workforce remaining in the source country below its original average, and will also have effects on such matters as public finance.

A specific instance of this which has concerned governments in both developed and developing countries relates to the human capital embodied in those emigrating, particularly when that human capital is the consequence of inputs financed by the state. Some economists[1] have proposed a 'brain-drain' tax on emigrants, based on the cost of state-financed inputs.

Policy responses to migration in the host countries have been rather mixed. For obvious reasons, employers have tended to lobby against restrictions on immigration while organised labour has tended to lobby for them. Governments have tended to be discriminatory in their policies, favouring moderate restrictions on immigrants with skills which are seen to be in short supply but stricter controls elsewhere. Concerns about difficulties in integrating immigrants into society, increased costs in providing state-financed goods and services, and so on, all of course play their part.

◼ *21.4* Foreign portfolio investment

In the nineteenth and early twentieth centuries, imports of capital played an important role in the development of many countries. For the lending countries, of which Britain was the dominant member, exports of capital were an important outlet for savings, which helped to smooth out business cycles and led to, if not a more rapid, at least a more stable pattern of economic growth. During this period little attempt was made by the creditor countries to exercise control over the debtors; that is, *portfolio* investment was the dominant form.

In Chapter 22 we shall consider foreign direct investment (FDI), which is largely concerned with control (through the creation and operation of subsidiary companies in other countries), and has been the dominant form of foreign investment since the late 1950s. In Part 3 we shall examine the significance of capital movements for balance-of-payments purposes. In this chapter we shall deal only with portfolio investments.

By 'portfolio investment' is meant an investment in a foreign country where the investing party does not seek control over the investment. A portfolio investment typically takes the form of the purchase of equity or government debt in a foreign stock market, or loans made to a foreign company. The question of control is central. Obviously the purchase of bonds issued by a company, which gives no voting rights, or of government debt, and making loans to a foreign company do not give control. The purchase of shares, with their associated voting rights, will give control provided a high enough proportion is acquired. While a majority shareholding is obviously sufficient to give control, effective control may be exercised with a lower proportion than that. In official statistics the borderline between portfolio investment and direct investment varies between countries: in US statistics, for example, foreign investment is classified as portfolio only if the shareholding is less than 10 per cent of the issued stock, but in other countries the borderline is set at around 25 per cent.

Positive and welfare effects of portfolio investment

We may obtain some insight into portfolio investment and its consequences when there are no market imperfections by using Figure 21.4. Initially country A has a fixed stock of capital of O_AC, while B's stock is O_BC. Each country has a perfectly inelastic supply of labour. MPK_A relates the marginal product of capital in A (and hence the real return to capital in A) to its capital stock, with MPK_B having a similar meaning. In the absence of capital mobility the real return to capital will be r_A in A and r_B in B.

If it becomes possible to move capital between the countries then capital will flow from A to B, the movement continuing until the real returns to capital are equalised in the two countries. The equilibrium will be established at E, the intersection of MPK_A and MPK_B.

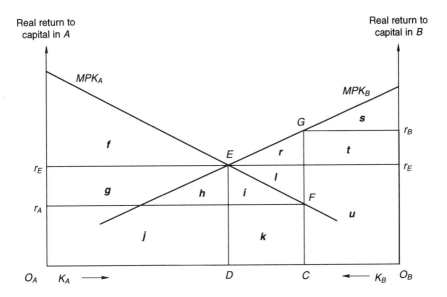

Figure 21.4 *The effects of portfolio investment*

The world as a whole will gain from the change since the transfer of capital from A to B will, until the new equilibrium is reached, increase output in B by more than it reduces output in A. We can demonstrate this gain more formally, and also identify the changes in the distribution of income between capital and labour as follows.

Consider first country A in its initial position when its capital stock is O_AC. The value of output in A is given by the area under MPK_A: that is, area $f+g+h+i+j+k$. As there are no market imperfections, capital will receive a total income equal to areas j and k, and labour will receive the remainder of the value of output, area $f+g+h+i$.

The outflow of capital raises the return to that capital which remains in A to r_E, with the value of output falling to $f+g+h+j$. Total payments to the capital remaining in A will be $g+h+j$, and labour will now receive f. However, the owners of the capital which has been invested in country B will also be earning a return of r_E per unit, so that there will be a flow of income from B to A of $k+i+l$. The total income of capital owners in A will thus be $(g+h+j) + (k+i+l)$.

The welfare effects of this foreign investment are then readily identified. Workers in A lose $g+h+i$, capital-owners gain $g+h+i+l$, and the net gain to country A is area l. We may conclude that the country making the foreign investment gains by so doing.

Note the contrast between the net gain of a country that 'exports' capital and the net loss of a country that 'exports' labour. The essential difference between the two cases is that we assumed that the migrants will both earn and spend their income in the host country, whereas foreign investment generates income for the capital-owners in the source country.

The welfare effects for the host country may be derived using the same procedure. The value of output in the home country increases from $s+t+u$ to $s+t+u+k+i+l+r$, but $k+l+r$ must be paid to capital-owners in A, leaving a net gain of r. This net gain is composed of a loss to capital owners in B of t, and a gain to workers in B of $t+r$.

The world, as we noted earlier, makes a gain from the more efficient use of capital, the gain being $l+r$.

☐ *Policy implications: the transfer problem*

The observation that both countries gain from foreign portfolio investment might suggest that, although different groups may lobby for or against the free movement of capital, there is no national interest that would lead governments to restrict inflows or outflows of capital for portfolio investment (as opposed to *direct* investment, which we deal with later). However, this is not necessarily the case. The *transfer problem* may directly affect the national interest of the countries concerned.

If a country lends $100 million to another country, it means that the lending country puts resources to the value of $100 million at the disposal of the borrowing country. The lending country will have to free resources valued at $100 million in order to export them to the borrowing country, which will import goods for $100 million more. To be successful, any long-term capital movement will have to be accompanied by a transfer of resources of equal size.

The governments of the lending and borrowing countries may however be unwilling to accept the adjustments to their economies which this requires. Since these may involve some or all of exchange-rate adjustment, inflation, terms-of-trade changes and so on, it is in practice more likely that there will be some policy response. Such a response could be to limit international borrowing or lending (perhaps by discriminating against them through the tax system, or even by banning them). The other possibility (and arguably the more probable reaction) is for governments to use macroeconomic policies.

■ *21.5* Summary and conclusions

In a world in which there are no market imperfections, the movement of labour and capital between countries in response to differences in rewards to those factors increases the efficiency with which the world uses them.

There are however both gainers and losers as a result of the redistribution brought about by such factor movements. In the case of labour migration, the gainers are the migrants, the workers remaining in the source country, and the employers in the host country. Employers in the source country and workers in the host country lose. When we consider foreign investment, the gainers and losers switch: capital-owners in the source country gain (whether they have invested in the other country or not), as do workers in the host country, while capital-owners in the host country and workers in the source country both lose.

This apparent symmetry between migration and foreign investment breaks down however when we consider the distribution of gains and losses between the countries. If there are no remittances by the migrant workers to their home country, so that they spend all their income in the host country, the host country will gain from migration but the source country will lose. With foreign investment on the other hand, the income earned by capital exported to the host country will be remitted to the owners of that capital in the source country, and both countries will gain.

There are two other problems which we must consider when discussing foreign investment. The first is the transfer problem. The second is that much foreign investment is concerned with the establishment of control over foreign enterprises. This direct foreign investment raises a complex set of issues which we shall deal with in Chapter 22.

☐ *Note*

1   See, for example, Bhagwati (1979).

■ *Chapter 22* ■

Direct Investments and the Multinational Enterprise

■ *22.1* Introduction

Foreign direct investment (FDI) is increasing in importance in the world economy. They have always attracted a good deal of attention and given rise to heated controversy. This, perhaps, is not astonishing in a world of nationalism. The Marxists saw them in the beginning of the twentieth century as the natural consequence of a maturing capitalism: the logical fruits of an ever-hardening competition, the last manifestations of a doomed system before its collapse. During recent years they have attracted renewed interest both in underdeveloped and developed countries. Resolutions at UNCTAD conferences have increasingly reflected a growing suspicion of foreign direct investment.

As already stated in Chapter 21, the main distinction between direct and portfolio investments is that in the former the investor retains control over the invested capital. Direct investments and management go together. With portfolio investments, no such control is exercised. Here the investor lends the capital in order to get a return on it, but has no control over the use of that capital.

The balance between portfolio and direct investments has changed markedly since the First World War. Until then the largest part of foreign investment consisted of portfolio investment. Great Britain provided more than 50 per cent of the total international capital outstanding in 1914, and about 90 per cent of this was of a portfolio type. The other two major lending countries, France and Germany, were also primarily engaged in

467

portfolio investments. The major recipients of foreign capital were other developed countries – Europe, the United States, Canada and Australasia accounted for over 50 per cent of the outstanding debt in 1913–14, and Latin America for over 40 per cent of the remainder. During a period when exchange risks were negligible and the political situation from this angle was stable, international investments were primarily governed by interest-rate differentials. Young expanding economies, which offered high returns on capital invested, could borrow money from the major lending countries. Interestingly, the United States already differed in this respect. American investors seem to have been of a more dynamic type, not content merely to reap a fairly small interest-rate differential. Even before the First World War a dominant share of US capital exports consisted of direct investments.

Between the two World Wars the flow of international investment decreased, with portfolio investment declining to about three-quarters of that reduced total, and the United States emerging as a major foreign lender, primarily in direct investment.

From the ending of the Second World War to the late 1950s, the role of private portfolio investments was negligible. The most important capital flows were official gifts and loans, followed by direct investments. The United States, with consistently large surpluses on its current account, was the major contributor to all forms of capital flows in the 1940s. In the following period however the United States started to run a deficit due to increased military expenditure abroad and the greater competitiveness of European countries.

From the late 1950s foreign investment started to increase: in real terms the total foreign investment in 1956–61 was over 50 per cent higher than in 1951–55. Some two-thirds of that investment came from the United States (with the encouragement of favourable tax regulations), with a large proportion being direct investment.

During the 1960s some governments started to feel disquiet about the level of FDI in their economies, and through the 1970s there was in general less FDI than before (though Britain, with its oil surpluses, became a large net investor again). At the same time, the flow of FDI into the United States started to increase, encouraged by a weaker dollar post-1973 and restrictive US trade policies (the annual average for 1974–78 was over four time that for 1970–72). The 1970s also saw the start of major private international lending to the less-developed countries (LDCs), with portfolio and direct forms being of approximately equal importance.

There were three major elements in international capital flows in the 1980s. First, there was a continued increase in FDI in the United States. Second, Japan became a major source of FDI, principally to the United States but also to the European Community, while at the same time pursuing policies to restrict FDI in Japan. Finally, portfolio lending to the LDCs, which had continued at a high level, faced a crisis in 1982–83 as a consequence of the inability of many borrowing countries to meet interest and repayment obligations.

We shall consider the debt crisis in Chapter 31. For the remainder of this chapter we shall concentrate on foreign direct investment, the consequent growth in multinational enterprises, and the policy responses that has called forth.

22.2 Direct investments and multinational enterprises

As we have emphasised before, the distinguishing feature of FDI is the exercise of control over decision-making in an enterprise located in one country by investors located in another. Although such investments may be made by individuals or partnerships, most FDI is undertaken by enterprises, and the larger part of that by multinational enterprises (MNEs).[1]

Multinational enterprises are essentially those that own or control production facilities in more than one country, Obviously, a MNE could not come into existence without there having been FDI in the first place. However, their importance nowadays is as major providers of FDI, often using capital which has been raised in the capital markets of the country in which they are investing rather than in the capital market of their home country.

The power (and the need) to exercise control over operations tells us that more is involved in FDI than the mere flow of capital. FDI occurs because the investing enterprise has some advantage, perhaps in technology or management, which it wishes to exploit in foreign markets, or perhaps some disadvantage that it wishes to eliminate. Direct investment is typically industry-specific. Industry-specific investments take two important forms: horizontal and vertical integration. Large corporations wish to integrate horizontally by opening new subsidiaries in various parts of the world. This is often done in a predatory way: one or several existing, competing firms in the host country are simply bought up by a large international rival. In the process, competition is often reduced.

Vertical integration is also a strong motive for direct investment. For instance, there are only a few companies that refine and fabricate copper. It is not surprising that they have sought control over copper mines by vertically integrating backwards in the production process. One obvious reason for vertical integration is a desire to reduce risk.

The investment *per se* may, in the extreme, be seen as a way of facilitating the exploitation of this advantage rather than as an end in itself: capital, it is argued, is only the complementary factor in a direct investment. The central element of FDI is that it consists of a package of capital, knowledge, skills, etc. This of course suggests an explanation of why the majority of FDI is industry-specific, and suggests that we should look for explanations of FDI in the characteristics of those industries.

The immediate problem however is to explain why foreign direct investment occurs (or why MNEs exist) in the first place. There are obvious alternatives to foreign investment. Why does the enterprise possessing the advantages cited above elect to operate in a foreign country rather than expand production at home and increase its exports? Why does it not license foreign firms to produce the goods in question? The simple answer of course is that FDI must be more profitable than the alternatives. That however just begs the basic question: *why* is it more profitable?

☐ *The theory of direct investments*

In a perfectly functioning Heckscher–Ohlin world with incomplete specialisation and no factor-intensity reversals there would be few incentives for international factor movements, since free trade would equalise relative factor prices. We saw in Chapter 21 that failure of factor prices to equalise could provide an incentive for migration and international portfolio investments. The same explanation may be used for some FDI: for example, MNEs may establish foreign subsidiaries to take advantage of lower labour costs in other countries. A more common cause of differences in factor prices that may generate FDI is that the assumption of identical production functions (technologies) central to the Heckscher–Ohlin model is not met. The differences in production functions may be due to 'pure' technical knowledge, but may also be attributable to differences in management skills, or to what has been called a 'difference in atmosphere' between countries. An often-cited example of the latter is the claim that workers in Germany produce more on identical machinery than do workers in Britain.

The other assumption of the Heckscher–Ohlin model that is violated in practice is that there is universal perfect competition. As we saw in Chapter 8, imperfect competition may generate trade flows even if there are no factor-intensity, technology or taste differences between countries. It may also be an explanation of FDI.

We shall now consider some theoretical explanations of FDI, before moving on to consider the welfare and policy implications of the phenomenon.

☐ *The product-cycle hypothesis*

In his work on the 'product-cycle' hypothesis (see Chapter 4) Vernon has emphasised that a firm tends to become multinational at a certain stage in its growth.[2] In the early stages of the product cycle, initial expansion into overseas markets is by means of exports. Because countries are at different stages of economic development, separated by a 'technology gap', new markets are available to receive new products through the *demonstration effect* of richer countries. Prior to the standardisation of the production process, the firm requires close contacts with both its product market and its suppliers.

However, once the product has evolved in a standard form and competing products have been developed, the firm may decide to look overseas for the lower-cost locations and new markets. It is not only that factor inputs may be less expensive abroad but that considerable scale economies from longer production runs may be obtained through the allocation of component production and assembly to different plants. On the demand side, new markets can be established by price reductions, or more typically by the firm operating in an oligopolistic market situation by means of product differentiation.

The product-cycle hypothesis is useful on several counts. It offers an explanation of the concentration of innovations in developed countries, and an integrated theory of trade and FDI. It also provides an explanation of the rapid growth in exports of manufactured goods by the newly industrialised countries. It therefore offers a useful point of departure for a study of the causes of international investment.

☐ *Market imperfections and FDI*

The product-cycle hypothesis does not resolve the question of why MNEs elect to use FDI rather than to license their technology to foreign firms. This issue has been examined by reference to the theory of the firm, notably by Hymer, Kindleberger and Caves.[3]

Such explanations focus on the advantages which some firms enjoy and on which they may be able to obtain rents in foreign markets. Such advantages include access to patented and generally unavailable technology, team-specific management skills, plant economies of scale, special marketing skills, possession of a brand name, and so on.[4] The potential gains from these advantages must of course outweigh the disadvantages of establishing and operating in a foreign country, such as communication difficulties and ignorance of institutions, customs and tastes, before the firm will invest abroad.

FDI allows the firm to exploit its advantages to the full, so that it can capture all the rents given by that control. The licence fee which foreign companies would be prepared to pay might, on the other hand, be lower than those rents. Selling the technology to a foreign enterprise, another possible alternative, may also yield a return which is lower than the (discounted sum of) rents from FDI. In both cases this may be due to foreign enterprises perceiving possible inefficiencies in their management of these advantages, perhaps because they are inexperienced in the operation of the new technology. Management and technology are often complementary. A further concern to the original enterprise may be that lack of direct control will increase the likelihood of the leaking of the technology to competitors.

Caves argues that such phenomena are due to market failures associated with *arm's-length* transactions in intangible assets. Such assets, especially technical knowledge, are public goods, in the sense that their use does not diminish their stock. They may also be replicated at a marginal cost which is low compared to the average cost of producing them in the first place. Second, the potential purchaser will wish to obtain all the information on using the asset before purchase, whereas the prospective seller knows that if all that information is revealed before the sale then the sale may not be completed. Thirdly, as we suggested earlier, there are uncertainty problems in that neither the buyer nor the seller can be completely sure how the asset will perform when managed by the buyer. Finally, the potential seller may not be able to 'disentangle' particular assets from the rest of his operations.

Hymer's analysis views the firm that undertakes FDI as an oligopolist (or perhaps a monopolist) in the goods market which either invests in existing foreign firms in order to control them and so suppress competition and preserve its rents, or establishes a subsidiary in a new market so as to pre-empt the possibility that a rival firm will do so. The latter strategy, termed 'defensive investment', may explain some part of FDI. Examples that have been proposed include Ford and General Motors, each of whom is alleged to have established plants in LDCs in order to keep the other out.

Another explanation of FDI and the role of the MNE that emphasises market imperfections, but this time for intermediate inputs and technology, is due to Buckley and Casson.[5] These markets are imperfect because they are difficult to organise and involve considerable uncertainty.

Faced with imperfect external markets, firms may choose to *internalise* by using backward and forward integration. A particular example is in the development of new processes and products, where there are time-lags, uncertainty, and high investment expenditures, and where success may depend on co-ordination, rapid exchange of information and detailed planning. Internalisation may increase the efficiency with which all of these are done. When internalisation (to the firm) involves operations across national boundaries then there must necessarily be FDI, and a multinational is created.

☐ *'Management' as a factor of production*

We may formalise some of the preceding discussion by including 'management' as a separate factor of production. Consider the following production function:

$$Q = f(L, K, M)$$

where Q denotes the output produced, L and K labour and capital, and M managerial skills or organisational technique. The difference between this formulation of the production function and that used in earlier parts of the book is that we now take management or organisation explicitly into account as an argument in the production function. This is explained by the fact that we now regard management as one of the essential variables needed to explain the phenomenon we are studying.

Speaking in terms of factor endowments, we could say that the United States has a large amount of M compared with other countries. This leads to the marginal product of managerial skills, $\partial Q / \partial M$, being lower in the United States than in other countries. The United States, therefore, ought to export products which are intensive in the use of managerial skills. This might also be the case. However, we are not now primarily interested in explaining trade but in explaining factor movements. We can say that we live in a world where factors of production are at least partially mobile. Some factors, however, are more mobile than others.

The least mobile factor is labour. For legal, institutional and sociological reasons such a small part of the labour force is mobile that we can presume labour to be, for all practical purposes, immobile. Capital is more mobile than labour, but the conditions of supply of capital are not so different between countries as to make capital movements all that important. Furthermore, capital is a joint factor of production often paired with management. The most mobile factor of production is management.

Executives can fairly easily move between countries. The sociological milieu of executives in developed industrial countries is not all that different; to be a director of an oil company or a computer corporation in New York, Paris, London or Frankfurt does involve certain differences in the way of life, but the similarities in general cultural outlook, family life, and, above all, in general working conditions are also great. It might even be argued that making an executive career in an international corporation today implies a willingness to spend one's life in different parts of the world. This is also true, though to a somewhat lesser degree, for the interchange between industrial countries and the LDC entrepreneurs.

If other countries are relatively deficient in these management skills then any given combination of capital and labour will produce a lower output in those countries than in the United States. If we were to define production functions solely in terms of capital and labour then we would have an apparent technological difference between the United States and the rest of the world. As we saw in Chapter 4, free trade will not equalise rewards to labour and capital when there is a difference in technology. In this case, we would expect the real rewards to be higher in the United States.

If the American firms can establish control over foreign firms in the same industry (by FDI) and export their management skills then they will enjoy an advantage over those foreign firms still owned domestically. They will be able to produce a greater output for given inputs of capital and labour, and will be buying those factors at lower cost than they could do in the American market. The profits that can be obtained by producing in the foreign market will be higher than those which could be obtained by producing in the United States and exporting.

■ 22.3 Barriers to trade and FDI

Transport costs offer one explanation of FDI, as indeed they do for multi-plant operations for a firm within a national market. If transport costs are sufficiently high then they may make the expansion of production in domestic plants and the export of that increased production less profitable than production within the putative importing country. This may be the case even if production in the foreign subsidiary firm is at a higher cost than that in the domestic plants.

Transport costs however are part of the 'nature of things'. In particular, we do not usually think of them as being a policy instrument which the government may use to restrict access to markets.[6] The same is not of course true of such barriers to trade as tariffs, import quotas and so on. The imposition of such import restrictions may have as a consequence an increase in FDI inflows; it is open to debate whether increasing such inflows is a possible explanation for the use of protection.

Import barriers have several effects which may be an encouragement to FDI. First, they raise the price of the good within the protected market, so providing increased profits to those firms who produce within the protected market. This provides an obvious incentive for a foreign firm to enter the protected market, by establishing a new subsidiary, by buying control of an existing firm, or by entering into a partnership agreement with an existing firm. Second, import barriers reduce the exports of firms in other countries, who may be induced to invest in the protected country in order to maintain their market share (another example of 'defensive investment'). It has been argued that the investment by Japanese motor manufacturers in both the United States and in Britain in the 1980s, either in the creation of subsidiary companies or through partnerships with existing domestic producers, is an example of this.

There are however reasons for believing that in some cases the effect of imposing import restrictions will be to reduce FDI. Corden[7] cites three such reasons. First, if protection is given to industries producing intermediate products to such an extent that the effective protection for those producing final products is reduced then this will discourage FDI in the latter. Second, some imports are complementary to some FDI; restricting such imports will then reduce FDI. Third, protection of some import-competing sectors will enable them to bid factors of production away from other sectors, and the reduction in their profitability will tend to reduce flows of FDI into the latter sectors.

■ 22.4 Dunning's 'eclectic theory'

It should be apparent from the preceding discussion that there are several explanations for FDI, that many start from similar premisses, and that none offers a complete explanation. Dunning has suggested an eclectic theory of FDI, often referred to as the *OLI paradigm*, that attempts to integrate these explanations.[8]

The *O*, *L* and *I* in the paradigm refer to three groups of conditions that determine whether a firm, industry or company will be a source or a host of FDI (or neither, of course). These groups are *Ownership* advantages, *Locational* considerations, and *Internalisation* gains.

Ownership advantages are advantages which are specific to the firm. It may enjoy such advantages over domestic as well as foreign competitors, so that expansion in the domestic market may be an alternative strategy. We have discussed some of them above, for example advantages in technology and in management and organisational skills. Others often cited are size and diversification, access to or control over raw materials, the ability to call on the political support of their government, access to finance on favourable terms, perhaps in foreign as well as domestic markets, and the ease with which the firm can shift production between countries. There is of course an element of feedback here: the fact that an enterprise is multinational may increase some of its ownership advantages, which in turn may allow it to expand its multinational activities.

Locational considerations encompass such things as transport costs facing both finished products and raw materials, import restrictions, the ease with which the firm can operate in another country, the profitability with which the ownership advantages may be combined with factor endowments in other countries, the tax policies in both source and host countries, and political stability in the host country.

Internalisation gains concern those factors which make it more profitable to carry out transactions within the firm than to rely on external markets. As we saw earlier, such gains arise from avoiding market imperfections (uncertainty, economies of scale, problems of control, the undesirability of providing full information to a prospective purchaser, and so on). The existence of internalisation gains obviously depends to some extent on the existence of ownership advantages.

The essential element in the eclectic theory is that all three types of condition must be met before there will be foreign direct investment. That is, all three conditions are necessary, but no one is sufficient. Suppose for example that a firm has an ownership advantage. If locational considerations indicate that production within a foreign market would be more profitable than producing at home and exporting, but there are no internalisation advantages (the product could be made by a foreign firm with equal efficiency and without jeopardising the home firm's ownership advantages), then the most profitable course for the home firm would be to license its ownership advantage to the foreign firm.

If, on the other hand, there were internalisation gains but no locational advantage to be gained by operating in another country then the firm would choose to expand production in its home market and export to the foreign market.

■ 22.5 Some other considerations

Many of the explanations of flows of FDI and the existence of multinationals we have discussed contain elements that would also be used to explain why particular industries might be imperfectly competitive. We should not be surprised therefore to observe that those industries in which we observe multinational enterprises are often characterised by oligopolistic or monopolistically-competitive structures, multi-plant operations and so on. This should not however lead us to conclude that an imperfectly competitive market structure is a *cause* of FDI.

As we noted earlier, some FDI is financed by borrowing on the capital markets of the host country. One explanation for this (other than possible differentials in interest rates) is that it is a form of hedging against risk. The risk concerned is that of *expropriation* of the foreign subsidiary by the government of the host country. If the FDI which established that subsidiary had been borrowed in the home country then the parent firm would find itself with liabilities unmatched by the foreign assets. If, on the other hand, the borrowing had been from citizens of the host country then the parent company can argue that its creditors should seek compensation from their own government.

■ 22.6 Empirical studies of FDI

Empirical studies in this area are severely hampered by two factors. The first is the relative scarcity of detailed data on FDI flows. Empirical studies tend to use instead such variables as the stock of FDI or the share of foreign-owned companies in output. The second problem is that there are major difficulties in measuring many of the variables which are suggested by the various theories. Reasonable proxy variables may be obtained for some of the ownership advantages (for example, we may attempt to measure the level of technology by consideration of past expenditure on R&D), but others, particularly the internalisation gains, are extremely difficult to proxy.

The study most often cited is that by Caves on the shares of subsidiaries of US firms in the outputs of Canadian and British industries.[9] Caves concluded that these shares had significant positive relationships with a set of factors that may be taken to reflect ownership advantages, such as the level of multi-plant production in the United States, research expenditure and advertising intensity. He also found that differences in wages (a locational factor) explained some of the share of US-owned firms in Britain. He found however little support for the role of internalisation or for firm size.

Wolf, in a study of US industry, looked at three ways of expansion: diversification in the US market, expansion of US production coupled with exporting, and FDI.[10] He used as his explanatory variables the size of the firm and the importance of technology (measured by the proportion of engineers and scientists in the workforce). He found that diversification in the US market was more dependent on size than on technology, while the other two options were explained better by the technology variables, but that the larger a firm was for a given level of technology then the more likely it was to choose FDI rather than the 'production for export' option.

22.7 Taxation and the transfer pricing problem

Taxation policies in source and host countries will affect the flow of FDI. Differences in such policies between countries may also encourage multinational enterprises to engage in (unproductive) activities designed to maximise their post-tax profits on a global (rather than country) basis. We shall discuss this latter problem – *transfer pricing* – at the end of this section.[11]

Other things being equal, comparatively high rates of tax on profits will encourage firms to look outside their home country for a base for some or all of their operations in which they will pay lower taxes. Special provisions in policy on profits earned externally, such as those allowing firms to defer tax payments until the profits were repatriated, will offer further encouragement.

Similarly, a country with comparatively low profit taxes will tend to attract FDI inflows. Such a policy may be designed to obtain just such a result, and may be reinforced by other incentives, such as allowing a foreign firm some period in which it does not pay profit taxes (a 'tax holiday') or generous allowances for writing-off investments against taxes.

Taxation policies may also have an effect on flows of goods between the various establishments making up a multinational, and perhaps also on the prices at which those goods are transferred between one establishment and another. As a simple example, suppose that a multinational has a plant in a low-tax country (country A) which makes an intermediate product (say, car engines), and that these engines are then transported to a plant in a high-tax country (country B) where the final product is manufactured. As Table 22.1 shows, the MNE can increase its profits by increasing the 'price' at which the engines are 'sold' to the plant in the high-tax country.

The 'price' at which car engines are sold by the establishment in A to that in B is an 'accounting price' or 'transfer price', set internally by the multinational. By increasing the price from £500 to £900 the multinational can generate a larger proportion of its profit in the low-tax country, and can increase its total post-tax profit.

There are obviously practical limits to the extent to which these transfer prices can be manipulated. In the extreme, it would presumably be unwise for the MNE to arrange to make a zero profit in country B as this would provoke some reaction from the tax authorities in B. On a more realistic level, the MNE in the above example would take care not to charge a transfer price which was very different from the price at which a car engine would be sold on the open market. On the other hand, the ingenuity of

Table 22.1 *An example of transfer pricing*

	Pricing policy 1	Pricing policy 2
Price at which engine is sold (£)	500	900
Volume of sales (thousand)	20	20
Revenue of engine plant (£ million)	10	18
Production costs in country A (£ million)	6	6
Pre-tax profit in country A (£ million)	4	12
Tax rate in country A (%)	25	25
Post-tax profit in country A (£ million)	3	9
Revenue from car sales in country B (£ million)	80	80
Costs of engines from country A (£ million)	10	18
Other production costs in country B (£ million)	40	40
Pre-tax profit in country B (£ million)	30	22
Tax rate in country B (%)	50	50
Post-tax profit in country B (£ million)	15	11
Total pre-tax profit to MNE (£ million)	34	34
Total post-tax profit to MNE (£ million)	18	20

accountants in devising ways of exploiting loopholes in the tax laws of different countries should not be underestimated.

Inputs of capital equipment and technology transferred from the parent company can also be priced internally in such a manner that the real rate of profit is reduced. The extent to which transfer pricing can be used would appear to depend critically on the degree to which goods and services are traded within the firm rather than on the open market, at 'arm's length', to use Lall's apt phrase.[12] Consequently, considerable scope for transfer pricing exists within the large foreign-owned enterprises which are vertically integrated with the parent company and which are typical of such industries as motor vehicles, chemicals and electrical engineering.

Lall has put forward two forms of explanation for the use of transfer prices. First, there is the kind of transfer pricing which seeks to maximise the present value of total multinational profits in a world characterised by different rates of taxes, tariffs, subsidies, and by multiple exchange rates. However, there is also the need to protect the future level of profits against possible changes in price controls, taxation and, indeed, governments. The role of the multinationals in exacerbating the economic difficulties that confronted the Allende government in Chile between 1970 and 1973 is a case in point.[13]

Quantitative evidence on the actual importance of transfer pricing is limited. It is naturally difficult to assess the extent to which the internal flow of goods and factors are over or under valued. However, Kopitz argues in a survey of the evidence[14] that the hypothesis that transfer pricing is stimulated by tax-rate differentials is not supported. The main incentive for transfer pricing seems to be other policies pursued by host governments, such as ceilings on profit repatriation. There is no doubt that within the context of the LDC, whose economy is heavily dependent on a small number of foreign-owned corporations, particularly of the vertically integrated variety, there is ample scope for the use of transfer pricing.

The cases referred to above will perhaps suffice to illustrate the principle that national economic policy will encounter difficulties in a world where economic integration becomes increasingly important but where the national state is still the dominant political entity. Direct investments certainly give very tangible advantages to firms in the investing countries, but they also lead to policy complications for governments of these countries.

There may of course be competition between potential host countries to set tax rates or offer concessions in order to attract FDI (we shall consider the nature of the gains to host countries later in the chapter). For example, in the 1970s Britain, Belgium and Spain tried to outbid one another in an attempt to persuade Ford to build a proposed new engine plant within their frontiers. The outcome was that Britain, the eventual 'winner', probably paid Ford substantially more than would have been necessary (and which might have been zero) had there been no such competition.

As an example of the possible impact of differences in tax rates on the profits declared by multinationals in different countries, consider the data in Table 22.2. This shows the declared earnings on US direct investments abroad before and after a change in US tax laws, paying particular attention to the role of Switzerland. It illustrates the possible role of taxes which are relatively low on the international scale in attracting FDI, and of concessions in tax laws in encouraging it.

Switzerland had exceptionally low taxes and favourable treatment of foreign firms in the 1950s. (This seems still to be so even if a certain harmonisation of tax regulations has taken place.) This led to many American firms routing their sales from all over the world through sales offices located in Switzerland. This also led to exceptionally high earnings on investments in Switzerland.

In 1962, the United States changed its tax laws. Earlier, taxes on earnings from subsidiaries abroad were deferred until they were repatriated. In 1962 this provision was changed so that earnings on holding companies and so-called 'tax haven operations' became taxable

Table 22.2   *Earnings on US direct investments abroad* (percentage of book value at the beginning of year)*

	1958	1962	1966
MANUFACTURING			
Europe	16	12	11
EEC	17	14	11
Switzerland	36	11	15
TRADE AND OTHER[†]			
EEC	20	18	6
Switzerland	42	40	16

* After foreign taxes.
[†] All direct investments other than mining and smelting, manufacturing, and petroleum.
Source: US Department of Commerce, *Survey of Current Business*, various issues

when earned. This had an immediate effect on the location of service and sales offices: in 1961–62, 40 per cent of these were located in Switzerland; in 1963 this figure fell to 10 per cent.

This is an example of how the source country can try to counteract the undesirable effects of FDI by changes in its legislation. The possibilities for such countervailing measures, however, are limited. Several countries, especially well-developed ones with big taxes and highly developed social services, could find their tax base shrinking as a result of direct investments. Their possibilities of implementing economic policies could also become circumscribed by the operations of multinational firms.

More recently, California and some other American states introduced so-called 'unitary taxation' of the profits of multinationals in an attempt to overcome the transfer pricing problem. The essence of the unitary tax system is that the tax authorities are not prepared to accept a multinational's declaration of where its profits were earned. Rather, they assume that the multinational has earned profits within the state which are in proportion to some other indicator of the relative importance of its activities within the state, such as the proportion of its total assets or of its total labour costs.

It may be argued that, in order to avoid double taxation, the MNE will declare as profits within the state that which the tax authorities consider correct. That is, there is no point in declaring that 40 per cent of profits were earned in the state, and paying tax on the remaining 60 per cent elsewhere, when the state is going to assume that 75 per cent of profits were earned within its boundaries and levy their tax on that basis. What may happen in practice is that the multinationals affected by this policy will use resources in lobbying for a change in the tax laws. In extreme cases MNEs may even elect to leave the state by disinvesting there and reinvesting elsewhere, so reducing the state's tax revenue.

With the increasing internationalisation of firms, the possibility of any single country pursuing its own independent economic policy becomes circumscribed. Corporations could gather in one country to work out pricing and market arrangements for another country. As long as there is no international legislation concerning taxes, restrictive business practices, etc., any single country will have difficulties in efficiently implementing its own laws.

■ 22.8 FDI and the balance of payments

Our analysis of the transfer problem in Chapter 21 would lead us to expect that an FDI, financed by borrowing on the domestic capital market, would lead to a worsening in the balance of payments of the source country and an improvement in that of the host country. The extent depends on several factors, primarily on the interrelations between the source and the host, as expressed in the marginal propensities to import. For a typical American direct investment, a study by the Brookings Institution yields the figures given in Table 22.3. These figures suggest that the link between the investing and the host country is rather weak and that the direct effects on the two countries' balances of payments are small. Such conditions create a strong immediate negative effect on the investing country's balance of payments, and *vice versa* for the host country.

The time perspective plays an important role for the balance of payments of both countries. If the investment in the example given in Table 22.3 was one injection, it would take six years for it to pay off, in the sense that the balance of payments of the investing country would again be positive. If the direct investment, instead, consisted of a steady flow of

Table 22.3   *Balance-of-payments effects of a direct investment*

Balance of payments improving		*Balance of payments worsening*	
Export stimulus	10.6	Capital	100.0
Remitted dividends	8.1	Import stimulus	6.5
Royalties and fees	2.3	Loss of exports	None

$100 million per year, it would take eleven years to reach equilibrium; if the flow of direct investment increased by 22 per cent per year, it would never pay off.

Against this background it is easy to understand that a large and growing volume of direct investments could be problematic from the standpoint of the investing country's balance of payments. Part of the fairly large and persistent deficit that the United States had during the 1960s can also be explained by the outflow of long-term capital.

In the long run, direct investments ought to have a positive effect on the investing country's balance of payments (and a negative effect on the host's). This is especially the case if the flow of direct investments is steady or decreasing. We can see this effect today on investments from the United States and some other developed countries in their dealings with several LDCs. If the flow sharply increases, there could be marked adverse effects on the balance of payments. Direct investments undoubtedly strained the United States' external position in the late 1950s and 1960s.

A further consideration is that, as we noted earlier, investment in another country may be funded by borrowing on the capital market in the host country, or indeed in some other country. The initial capital outflow does not in that case occur, but at the same time some proportion of the foreign profits will go to the lenders, so that part of the future inflow will not appear in the balance of payments.

Multinationals may also affect a country's balance of payments by their direct control over imports and exports. It is not clear whether MNEs tend to encourage or discourage trade flows. It is certainly true that a large proportion of trade flows take place 'within' multinationals (for example Ford (UK) is a major exporter and importer of motor vehicles and of their components), but this may reflect the characteristics of the industries in which they occur rather than of their being MNEs *per se*. We might expect however that multinationals' subsidiaries will import capital equipment from their home country, particularly if that equipment embodies the advanced technology which may have encouraged the MNE to establish the subsidiary in the first place.

■ 22.9 Some other effects

□ *In the source country*

Most of the debate about the merits and demerits of direct investments has treated the effects on the host country; we return to that shortly. Much less attention has been paid to the problems that could arise for the authorities in the investing country. We will touch briefly on some of them.

The welfare analysis of the effects of a foreign *portfolio* investment outflow considered in Chapter 21 is not strictly applicable to the foreign *direct* investment problem, since the former was assumed to take place in the context of perfectly functioning markets, whereas the latter is a response to market imperfections. Nevertheless, it does offer us some useful insights into the problem. If the alternative to the FDI is direct investment in the source country then the choice of foreign investment will reduce the welfare of workers in the source country compared to what it would have been. The other losers in the source country are of course the taxpayers, since profits earned there will be lower than if the direct investment had been domestic.

The investing enterprise will obviously gain, and that gain will probably exceed the losses made by the workers and the taxpayers. If the MNE and its 'owners' are based in the source country, so that it is appropriate to include them in the welfare calculation for the source country, then we may argue that the welfare of the source country has increased. Unfortunately, it is not always clear that the owners are based within any one country, and the calculation of gains and losses will be complicated accordingly.

Another possible cost to the source country is that investors may lobby the government in order, for example, to secure foreign policies which will ensure the safety of their foreign investments. This uses resources in the lobbying activity and may produce distortions in foreign policy.

☐ *In the host country*

The problems created for the host country by direct investments have aroused by far the most intense feelings and discussion. There are many reasons for this, the most important perhaps being those concerned with the questions of control, technology transfer and exploitation, all of which we shall cover later in this section.

Again, we start by considering the static welfare gains by referring to the analysis of Chapter 21. That analysis suggested that workers in the host country will gain, that capital-owners there will lose, and that the gains made by the former will exceed the losses made by the latter. We should include in this analysis, as we did with the source country, the effects on taxpayers. The revenue from the taxation of the profits of foreign-owned companies is obviously a source of gain. A government which considers that FDI brings a welfare gain may adjust its tax policies to encourage FDI, even at the cost of a reduction in its tax revenue, and may subsidise it. A government which takes the opposite view may use tax policies to discourage FDI. The matter is complicated by our analysis of transfer pricing, which indicates another way in which the government can affect its tax revenue by changing its tax rate.

We have already discussed balance-of-payments considerations in general terms, but a related criticism has been levelled at multinationals. That is that they give preference to firms in their home country or abroad (perhaps other subsidiaries of the parent corporation to which the firm in question belongs). If this is the case then the multinational imposes costs on the host country over and above those of an identical but independent firm. This of course begs the question of whether an independent firm would have established in the host country in the first place.

☐ *Control*

An essential aspect of the critique raised against direct investments has been that of *control*. We have already noted that this is an integral part of FDI, distinguishing it from other forms of capital movements. To the host country this means that part of its industry will be controlled by foreigners. Many host countries find this difficult to accept; it has led to counter-measures in many countries.

One obvious aspect of control is that the multinationals may require their subsidiaries to operate policies which are inefficient and/or cause distortions in national markets. Examples of such policies are restrictions on exports, perhaps to avoid competition with other subsidiaries in other countries, and on R&D within the subsidiary. In the latter case, the host countries are deprived of the important stimulus given by research in these industries. Concern over this motivated demands for a Code of Conduct for the transfer of technology at the fourth conference of UNCTAD in 1976.

The fear is that R&D in subsidiary companies is suppressed, so that research becomes concentrated in the home country. The home country started with a comparative advantage in the production of goods which are intensive in research and innovating capacity. By the cumulative effects related to direct investments, this comparative advantage tends to become even more pronounced, and the host countries tend to sink into a position of 'second-rate' economic powers.

Because they are international, multinationals can often circumvent national domestic policies. The example most often cited is their ability to avoid restrictions on credit or on foreign exchange transactions by transferring money internally. In an extreme case a multinational may even be able to make a government policy inoperable, as when Ford (UK) refused to adhere to the British government's pay policy, and the government was unable to enforce compliance.

A multinational may, of course, lobby the government of the host country to persuade it to pursue policies favourable to the MNE's interests. Their ability to transfer operations, in whole or in part, to other countries is a powerful argument in such activities. Part of this lobbying (or pressurising) of the host government may take the form of successful lobbying of the source country government to exert pressure, as was the case with International Telephone and Telegraph in Chile under the Allende government.

☐ *External benefits of FDI to the host country*

It is often argued that multinationals confer benefits on the host country, such as training the local labour in more sophisticated techniques or demonstrating the gains that may be made by different management practices. Such benefits can be labelled as 'external' if they are costless to those learning them and become available and usable in the rest of the economy. If the workers pay for their training (by accepting a wage that is below that which they could earn elsewhere) then the externality is reduced, and may be eliminated. If the skills learned are inapplicable elsewhere in the economy (perhaps because they can only be used with specific equipment which is not available outside the MNE), then there is no external benefit.

It is widely believed that expenditures on R&D have important external effects. In the process of developing a certain product or improving production techniques, scientists and technicians are stimulated; new applications valuable outside the immediate project will be discovered; encouragement for, and incentives to, research in universities and other organisations outside the industry will be provided; and so on. A rational attitude geared toward experimenting will be fostered, competent scientists will be trained, etc., and all this will have positive effects on the whole intellectual climate of the country.

If foreign firms via direct investments take over control of important parts of a country's industry, they may tend to shift research to their home country. This could be entirely rational from the point of view of the international firm, which is simply taking advantage of the economies of scale connected with the research activity. It can even be argued that this behaviour is rational from the world's standpoint, because it maximises world income. It still can have very detrimental effects on the host country, which is deprived of research activities that are perhaps comparatively inefficient but which, to the country itself, can be of great importance. It may even be the case that would-be researchers will emigrate in order to train, and possibly work, in the source country.

The question of external gains has been the subject of various empirical studies, particularly of LDCs. Some of these suggest that the capital-intensive nature of much of the technology exported limits the scope for external gains. There is a tendency for the MNEs in LDCs to become part of a distinct industrial sector with limited linkages to domestic firms, resulting in a so-called 'dualistic economy'. The external effects of FDI in other developed economies are, on the other hand, more likely to be beneficial, though even here there are *caveats* about the tendency to import higher management rather than train local employees, and the apparent suppression of R&D activity mentioned above.

☐ *Direct investments and exploitation*

Direct investments have in the Marxian tradition played a double role, and in both roles they have important political implications. In the first variant, direct investments are necessary to postpone the collapse of the capitalist system, and in the second and milder variant they are merely one of many forms of capitalist oppression.[15]

The essence of the first (and earlier) line of thought is that capitalism needs new markets to survive The inner forces of capitalism, primarily the relentless pursuit and application of new innovations, make it expand to new territories to find new markets and new consumers to postpone the collapse that history, according to Marx, has in store for it. The drive to technical progress also makes capitalists look for cheaper sources of raw materials in distant countries. Imperialism is simply the logical consequence of the economic forces inherent in the capitalist system of production.

This strong version of the Marxian theory of direct investments, which argues the necessity of these investments for the survival of the capitalist system, can hardly be sustained in the light of the development of the capitalist system. That capitalist countries derive profits from their direct investments abroad is one thing; it is quite another to argue that the industrial, capitalist nations are so dependent on the territories they in some sense dominate via direct investments that their economies would break down without them. It is hardly correct to argue that the developed market economies are so dependent on their direct investments (or their trade with third countries in general, for that matter) that their economic systems could not be sustained without them. A certain lowering of US economic welfare would follow if, to take a drastic example, all US foreign investments were nationalised overnight by the countries in question and no compensation paid. But there is no doubt that the effect of such an action would imply marginal changes in the American economy rather than a collapse of its capitalist system.

Capitalism's powers of survival should not be underestimated However, this does not deny that part of international politics can be explained in economic terms, even in fairly crude terms like 'search for profits'. The second tenet of Marxist theory, which relates to the need for raw materials, has to a limited extent been vindicated.

This is not primarily due to the strength of Marxist methodology. However, the assumptions underlying the Marxist analysis, with its emphasis on conflict between various factors of production, on the importance of power relationships and of the natural interest on the part of the producers to try to limit competition and control markets, would seem to be more realistic than the often simple-minded, harmony-geared assumptions of neoclassical economics.

It is not difficult to find examples of varying degrees of economic exploitation. If one country has a strong economic influence over another, and couples that with an allegiance with certain ruling forces of the host country and maintains a close military co-operation with those forces, the host country could be in a difficult position. Then it can certainly be maintained that both political and economic exploitation occur.

An attempt to deal with a situation such as that just sketched would, however, quickly take us beyond the scope of the present work. Suffice it to say that, in general, we expect direct investments to benefit both the investing and the host country, for reasons set out earlier in this chapter. Nevertheless, the multinational corporation remains a topic of considerable controversy There is no doubt that the large multinational firm, through its dominance of local markets and R&D and its ability to shift taxable income, can have substantial negative effects on the host country.

■ 22.10 Policy responses in host countries

Policy responses to FDI are far from uniform. Some countries, perceiving the costs as outweighing the benefits, have sought to restrict FDI and/or the operations of multinationals, by various means. Others, as in the case of Britain's encouragement of Ford's establishment of a new engine plant, have encouraged FDI. We shall discuss examples of both responses, starting with those intended to restrict and/or control FDI.

The problem of foreign control of domestic industry has probably been most acute in Canada. Here nearly 60 per cent of the total capital in manufacturing is controlled by foreigners (over 80 per cent by Americans). Efforts have been made from time to time to increase Canada's control over FDI. In 1963, for instance, a new tax law was introduced requiring firms of less than 25 per cent Canadian ownership and with less than 25 per cent Canadian representation on the board of directors to be taxed at a somewhat higher rate than Canadian corporations.[16] Further legislation in 1973 required that all new FDI be required to obtain government approval. This policy was however gradually reversed in the 1980s, this more open view culminating in the United States–Canada free trade pact of 1987.

Some developing countries, such as Mexico, require 50 per cent of ownership and directorship to be in domestic hands. Although wholly foreign-owned investment is permitted in the export processing sector, all foreign investment is screened, as is also the case in India, by a Foreign Investment Commission, which lays down criteria (often statutory) for the investment. These requirements usually relate to such matters as the sector and location of the investment, the extent of local participation, the transfer of technology, and disclosure of company information. A number of LDCs have also attempted to increase their control of foreign investments by means of equity participation and joint ventures. The latter can be viewed not only as a means of control over foreign investment but as a training ground for local entrepreneurs, managers and technicians.[17]

We now turn to policies intended to attract FDI. The first possibility, which we discussed earlier, is that protection could induce MNEs to establish within the protective wall. We argued then that there are theoretical reasons to suspect that trade barriers will reduce FDI rather than increase it. On a more applied note, Bhagwati[18] has argued that, if we make appropriate adjustments for such variables as economic size, political attitudes, and political stability, the magnitude of FDI inflows into LDCs will be higher for those pursuing an export-promoting strategy than for those following the import-substitution approach. The rationalisation is that MNEs regard the incentives provided by tariffs and quotas as artificial and limited in scope, compared with those offered by low wages in the export-promoting countries. Bhagwati adds that the effectiveness of FDI in promoting economic growth is also higher in the export-promoting countries.

☐ *'Unbundling the package'*

FDI is, as we have seen, a bundle of capital, technology and management skills (the *unambiguous package*) which involves control. It may also, it is argued, be a relatively expensive way of obtaining foreign capital and technology. This offers an explanation of the increasing preference of LDCs for joint ventures between locally-owned and foreign firms (the *ambiguous package*) or for technology-licensing agreements with little or no foreign capital involvement (the *unpackaged* or *unbundling* alternative).[19]

Despite the reluctance of firms to sell or rent their know-how, for reasons which we discussed earlier, licensing arrangements for the sale of technology do exist, for example in India, Brazil and South Korea. This may reflect the ability of the host country government to restrict or deny access for FDI, forcing foreign firms to choose licensing as the second-best alternative (although some, of course, may choose not to license either). Licensing may also be a consequence of the foreign firm having a shortage of managerial skills and/or a lack of knowledge of the host country market, or of a belief that a joint venture will reduce the risks of expropriation.

A final possibility is that foreign firms enter into licensing agreements for technologies which are likely to be overtaken by new developments (in order to maximise their gains during the remaining economic life of the old technology), or for technologies which are relatively unsophisticated. In this case we may presume that licensing is an inefficient way of transferring the most recent technology. The counter-argument, of course, is that the unsophisticated technology may be better suited to the factor endowments of the host country.

The question of course is how these preferred alternatives compare to the unambiguous package. Do they transfer (appropriate) technology and its associated knowledge relatively efficiently, and are they relatively inexpensive? It has been argued that licensing and joint ventures may not be cheaper than the unambiguous package. Joint ventures do not necessarily reduce the outflow of profits to the foreign firm, since there are several ways in which that firm can increase its net profits, such as charging higher royalties and technical fees than they would to wholly-owned subsidiaries, and by using transfer pricing.

The possibility of transfer pricing does not of course exists when there is a licensing arrangement (though royalties, etc. may still be high). If, however, the locally-owned firm has to raise capital on foreign markets then it is possible that it will pay a higher rate of interest than that on foreign capital provided under the FDI alternative.

☐ *Export-processing zones*

Export-processing zones[20] (EPZs) are designated areas within the host country, intended to attract investment, largely from foreign firms, by offering favoured treatment. The privileges offered typically include the absence of import controls (so that, for example, tariffs are not levied on imported intermediate goods provided that the finished products are re-exported). Other privileges may include exemption from domestic taxation and industrial regulations, and the provision of infrastructure.

Export-processing zones have become a favoured option of many LDCs. Establishment of an EPZ requires substantial public investment by the host country, so it is important to enquire whether they yield a net welfare gain, and whether there are better alternatives.

Warr[21] argues that economic activity within EPZs has been typified by labour-intensive industries (such as electronics assembly and garment manufacture), with a high rate of turnover of firms. That is, EPZs tend to attract 'footloose' firms, which will move readily from the current EPZ base, perhaps to another, in response to changing conditions. Since many countries now have EPZs, there is considerable competition between them to attract foreign firms.

The objectives cited by host-country governments when establishing export processing zones usually fall under three headings: increasing foreign exchange earnings, increasing employment, and encouraging the transfer of technology and management skills. Warr argues that the EPZs have contributed to the attainment of the first two objectives, but that the sought-after technology transfer has not in general occurred. He concludes that the benefits from EPZs are limited and that they are certainly not 'engines of development'. He argues that where they have been successful, greater success could have been achieved by a liberalisation of the domestic economy rather than by the establishment of a liberalised zone within the economy.

☐ *Trade-related investment measures*

As we have noted before, governments may compete to attract FDI by multinationals through offering different policy packages. Part of such packages may consist of requirements that the MNE's subsidiary contracts to export some specified proportion of its output, and/or purchase a specified proportion of inputs in the host economy, and/or employ some proportion of its management domestically. In many cases, of course, such requirements are disincentives, which the MNE will trade-off against the incentives in the package in making its decision on location of a subsidiary. Such requirements are known generally as *trade-related investment measures*, or TRIMs.

Greenaway[22] makes the point that TRIMs have to be considered in conjunction with FDI and the incentives given to multinationals to invest in the country concerned. Any welfare analysis of TRIMs must therefore be conducted in a second-best context, and while that makes the analysis complicated, it does raise the possibility that some TRIMs are welfare-increasing. What is left unanswered at the moment is whether there are feasible policy alternatives which are better than TRIMs. That is, are there policies which will remove the distortions associated with FDI without introducing the by-product distortions normally associated with policies which are not targeted at the source of the distortion?

■ 22.11 Summary and conclusions

The main determinant of foreign direct investment is superior technology or skill. The typical agent undertaking FDI is the large multinational firm which wants to retain control over its investment abroad. Such a firm usually possesses superior technology or management and will naturally seek to increase profits by expanding its horizons and investing abroad.

FDI primarily take place under imperfect market conditions. Among developed countries it is often a two-sided affair, even if it is natural that the United States, as the leading industrial country, is also the largest direct investor.

The principal advantage of FDIs is that they raise world output by moving managerial skills and capital from regions where these factors are plentiful, and thus earn a low return, to regions where they are scarce, and thus earn a high return. Normally, direct investments will benefit both the investing country and the host country.

The immediate impact on the investing country's balance of payments can often be adverse, even though the transfer mechanism usually works smoothly. The investing country could have difficulties in controlling domestically located firms operating in international markets. National economic policies could be difficult to implement, and attempts at economic planning could be thwarted.

For the host country, the immediate impact of a direct investment will usually be an improvement in the balance of payments. In the long run, the effects could be negative. From a 'real' point of view, the effects are beneficial as long as the positive effects on the country's economic growth are larger than the negative ones on the balance of payments.

There are some effects of a secondary or external kind that could be detrimental to the host country. The most important are that direct investments could stifle scientific R&D work in the host country and that the multinational corporation could transfer a substantial part of the gains of the investment away from the host country.

Direct investments could conceivably lead to exploitation, primarily of LDCs. The meaning of the 'exploitation', however, has to be well defined and the circumstances carefully scrutinised before any such charge can be meaningfully levelled against the multinational corporations.

☐ *Notes*

1   Also referred to as multinational firms (MNFs), multinational companies (MNCs) or transnational enterprises.

2   Vernon (1966) and (1971 and 1977).

3   Hymer (1976).
    Kindleberger (1969).
    Caves (1982).

4   This discussion, and that later in the chapter of technological transfer, are based on Balasubramanyam (1985).

5   Buckley and Casson (1976).

6   This is not always the case. The infamous 'American Bottoms' legislation, which required imports into the United States to be landed from American ships, had the effect of increasing the costs of exporting to the United States and so protected the American market.

7   Corden (1974).

8   Dunning (1977).

9   Caves (1974).

10 Wolf (1977).

11 A warning! Do not confuse the *transfer problem* discussed in Chapter 21, which is essentially a balance-of-payments problem, with *transfer pricing*, which concerns an MNE's reactions to differential taxes.

12 Lall (1973).

13 de Vylder (1974).

14 Kopitz (1976).

15 For a neo-Marxian treatment of direct investments and imperialism see Baran (1957), Baran and Sweezey (1966), Mandel (1968), and Magdoff (1969). An interesting interpretation of the Marxist view of foreign investment is Cohen (1973).

16 Safarian (1966).

17 Morton and Tulloch (1977), p. 228.

18 Bhagwati (1978).

19 This discussion is based upon Balasubramanyam (1985). The terminology is due to Vernon (1971).

20 For a full discussion of export processing zones, see Warr (1990), on which this brief discussion is based.

21 Warr (1990).

22 Greenaway (1991).

■ *PART 3* ■

INTERNATIONAL MACROECONOMICS

■ *Chapter 23* ■

The Balance of Payments

■ *23.1* Introduction

The balance-of-payments accounts are an integral part of the national income accounts for an open economy. They record (in principle) all transactions between 'residents' of the country concerned and those of other countries, where 'residents' are broadly interpreted as all individuals, businesses, and governments and their agencies; international organisations are also classified as 'foreign' residents for this purpose.

The balance-of-payments accounts however serve another purpose. The balance of a country's foreign transactions, and the accompanying issues of the exchange rate and reserves (whether of gold or of foreign currencies) has long been a focus of interest for policy-makers. The way in which policy-makers view these foreign transactions, and the policies they have adopted, have of course varied over time. There is a distinct contrast, for example, between the mercantilist view that foreign trade should be managed so as to accumulate gold specie through running a surplus, and the view taken in the decades after the Second World War that governments should seek to maintain balance-of-payments 'equilibrium'. There are equally important distinctions between the various exchange-rate regimes that have been employed, from the various gold standards to the floating exchange rates of the 1930s and the recent period, and the pegged exchange-rate system devised at Bretton Woods and used until the early 1970s.

Whatever the objectives of policy-makers however, and regardless of the institutional arrangements, the state of the balance of payments (or of some subset of its components) plays an essential role in providing information to both governments and private individuals and firms. The traditional question asked is whether the balance of payments is in equilibrium, since that may provoke government action and/or lead to changes in exchange rates. As we shall see, however, there have been, and continue to be, disagreements about what is meant by 'equilibrium' and 'disequilibrium' in the balance of payments. To explore this issue we shall have to define carefully the meaning of the balance of payments and see in what sense there will be balance and in what way deficits and surpluses can exist. This chapter is devoted to these problems.

■ 23.2 The balance of payments: book-keeping

The balance of payments is essentially an application of double-entry book-keeping, since it records both transactions and the money flows associated with those transactions. If we do this in a proper way debits and credits will always be equal, so that in an accounting sense the balance of payments will always be in balance. An accounting balance is however not synonymous with equilibrium. An overall balance, with inflows of foreign currency equalling outflows, may conceal imbalances within it that will lead to changes. In such a case we do not have an equilibrium in any meaningful sense. A major task will be to look into this apparent paradox and understand in what way the balance of payments can be in disequilibrium and in what sense it will always be in equilibrium.

It is important to keep in mind that a balance-of-payments account records *flows* between countries over a specified period of time (usually a year for the full accounts, but often less for some components of the accounts). Some items in the balance of payments are readily identified as flows, such as exports. Other items however are flows arising from changes in stocks, and the appropriate handling of these is often a source of confusion. We shall return to this point in more detail when we consider the capital account.

It is also important to note that, although they have their roots in double-entry accounting, balance-of-payments accounts are rarely presented in that form. In basic terms, the accounts usually gather together the transactions that give rise to the balancing monetary flows under what are considered to be appropriate headings (e.g. exports), and record them first. The net values of the monetary flows (again perhaps grouped under various headings) are then entered in the same column, with their sign reversed. We thus have an account in a single column, which must sum to zero.

Traditionally there are two basic elements in a perfectly compiled set of balance-of-payments accounts: the current account and the capital account. Each of these is usually subdivided, the former into visible and invisible trade and unrequited transfers, the latter into long-term and short-term private transactions and changes in official reserves. The essential difference between the two is that capital account transactions necessarily involve domestic residents either acquiring or surrendering claims on foreign residents, whereas current account transactions do not. In practice there is a third element, the 'balancing item' or 'errors and omissions', which reflects our inability to record all international transactions accurately. We shall consider each of these in turn by reference to a fictional country, and then build up the full set of accounts.

It should be noted that there are some international transactions that do not fall readily into one or other of the categories described in what follows, and therefore some differences between the ways in which accounts are presented by various countries. We shall follow the conventions used in IMF statistics and by the majority of countries.

☐ *The current account*

The current account records exports and imports of goods and services and unilateral transfers. Exports, whether of goods or services, are by convention entered as positive items in the account. Imports accordingly are entered as negative items. Exports are normally calculated *f.o.b.* (free on board), i.e. costs for transportation, insurance, etc., are not included, whereas imports are normally calculated *c.i.f.* (cost, insurance, freight), i.e. transportation, insurance costs, etc., are included.

In many cases the payment for exports and imports will result in the transfer of money between the trading countries. For example, a UK firm importing a good from the United States may settle its debt by instructing its UK bank to make a payment to the US account of the US exporter. This is not necessarily the case however. If the UK firm holds a bank account in the United States then it may make payment to the US exporter from that account. In the former case the financial side of the transaction will appear in the UK balance-of-payments account as part of the net change in UK foreign-currency reserves. In the latter it will appear as part of the capital account, since the UK firm has reduced its claims on the US bank.

Balance-of-payments accounts usually differentiate between trade in goods and trade in services. The balance of exports and imports of the former is referred to in the UK accounts as *the balance of visible trade*; in other countries it may be referred to as *the balance of merchandise trade*, or simply as *the balance of trade*. The net balance of exports and imports of services is called *the balance of invisible trade* in the UK statistics.

Invisible trade is a much more heterogeneous category than is visible trade. It is often useful for economic purposes to distinguish between factor and non-factor services. Trade in the latter, of which shipping, banking and insurance services, and payments by residents as tourists abroad are usually the most important, is in economic terms little different from trade in goods. That is, exports and imports of such services are flows of outputs whose values will be determined by the same variables that would affect the demand and supply for goods. Factor services, which consist in the main of interest, profits and dividends, are on the other hand payments for inputs. Exports and imports of such services will depend in large part on the accumulated stock of past investment in and borrowing from foreign residents.

Unilateral transfers, or 'unrequited receipts', are receipts which the residents of a country receive 'for free', without having to make any present or future payments in return. Receipts from abroad are entered as positive items, payments abroad as negative items. This kind of receipt usually takes one of two forms. The first, often referred to as private unrequited transfers, is gifts which domestic residents receive from foreign residents, most notably when migrant workers send money back to relatives living in the country in question. The United States, many northern European countries and the Arab Gulf states are major sources of such remittances, while many Caribbean, Mediterranean and Muslim non-oil exporting states are recipients. The second, official unrequited transfers, is the payment of 'pure' aid (as opposed to 'tied' aid) by governments in developed countries (perhaps via an international agency) to government in less-developed countries (LDCs). Historically, a third form of unilateral transfer has been important, reparation payments. Typically such payments occurred when a country came out of a war morally and physically superior, and was in a position to make the foreign country (its former enemy) pay indemnities. Such payments played an important part after the First World War (and led to academic interest in the so-called transfer problem discussed in Chapter 21) but have since fallen into relative obscurity.

The net value of the balances of visible trade and of invisible trade and of unilateral transfers defines *the balance on current account*. Table 23.1 shows the various components of the current accounts of the United States, Japan, West Germany and the United Kingdom in 1989.

☐ *The capital account*

The capital account records all international transactions that involve a resident of the country concerned changing either his assets with or his liabilities to a resident of another country. As we noted earlier, transactions in the capital account reflect a change in a stock – either assets or liabilities.

It is often useful to make distinctions between various forms of capital account transactions. The basic distinctions are between private and

Table 23.1 *Current account summaries for four countries, 1989*
($US billion)

	United States	Japan	West Germany	United Kingdom
A: Merchandise exports	360.46	269.59	324.48	151.31
B: Merchandise imports	−475.33	−192.74	−247.77	−189.26
C: Visible trade balance (A + B)	−114.87	76.85	76.71	−37.96
D: Exports of services	242.71	143.91	98.31	172.01
E: Imports of services	−223.14	−159.53	−101.13	−157.79
F: Invisible trade balance (D + E)	19.57	−15.62	−2.82	14.22
G: Private unrequited transfers (net)	−1.33	−0.99	−6.17	−0.49
H: Official unrequited transfers (net)	−13.43	−3.30	−12.24	−6.93
I: Current account balance (C + F + G + H)	−110.06	56.94	55.48	−31.16

Source: Based on Table 2.3 in Pilbeam (1992), which is derived from International Monetary Fund, *Balance of Payments Yearbook* (Washington, DC: IMF, 1990)

official transactions, between portfolio and direct investment, and by the term of the investment (i.e. short or long term). The distinction between private and official transactions is fairly transparent, and need not concern us too much, except for noting that the bulk of foreign investment is private.

Direct investment is the act of purchasing an asset and at the same time acquiring control of it (other than the ability to re-sell it). The acquisition of a firm resident in one country by a firm resident in another is an example of such a transaction, as is the transfer of funds from the 'parent' company in order that the 'subsidiary' company may itself acquire assets in its own country. Such business transactions form the major part of private direct investment in other countries, multinational corporations being especially important. There are of course some examples of such transactions by individuals, the most obvious being the purchase of a 'second home' in another country.

Portfolio investment by contrast is the acquisition of an asset that does *not* give the purchaser control. An obvious example is the purchase of shares in a foreign company or of bonds issued by a foreign government.

Loans made to foreign firms or governments come into the same broad category. Such portfolio investment is often also distinguished by the period of the loan (short, medium or long are conventional distinctions, although in many cases only the short and long categories are used). the distinction between short-term and long-term investment is often confusing, but usually relates to the specification of the asset rather than to the length of time for which it is held. For example, a firm or individual that holds a bank account in another country and increases its balance in that account will be engaging in short-term investment, even if its intention is to keep that money in that account for many years. On the other hand, an individual buying a long-term government bond in another country will be making a long-term investment, even if that bond has only one month to go before maturity. Portfolio investments may also be identified as either private or official, according to the sector from which they originate.

The purchase of an asset in another country, whether it is direct or portfolio investment, would appear as a negative item in the capital account for the purchasing firm's country , and as a positive item in the capital account for the other country. That capital outflows appear as a negative item in a country's balance of payments, and capital inflows as positive items, often causes confusion. One way of avoiding this is to consider the direction in which the payment would go (if made directly). The purchase of a foreign asset would then involve the transfer of money to the foreign country, as would the purchase of an (imported) good, and so must appear as a negative item in the balance of payments of the purchaser's country (and as a positive item in the accounts of the seller's country).

The net value of the balances of direct and portfolio investment defines *the balance on capital account*. Table 23.2 shows the various components of the capital accounts of the United States, Japan, West Germany and the United Kingdom in 1989. Official long-term transactions are subsumed in 'Other long-term capital'.

The remaining items in the balance of payments

The balance-of-payments accounts are completed by the entry of: other minor items that can be identified but do not fall comfortably into one of the standard categories; errors and omissions, which reflect transactions that have not been recorded for various reasons and so cannot be entered under a standard heading, but which we know must appear since the full balance-of-payments account must sum to zero; and changes in official

Table 23.2 *Capital account summaries for four countries, 1989 ($US billion)*

	United States	Japan	West Germany	United Kingdom
J: Direct investment (net)	40.50	−45.22	−6.99	0.23
K: Portfolio investment (net)	44.79	−32.53	−4.38	−43.17
L: Other long-term capital (net)	2.64	−15.86	−0.28	−1.76
M: Long-term capital balance (J + K + L)	87.93	−93.61	−11.65	−34.98
N: Short-term capital balance (net)	16.32	45.86	−56.75	27.53

Source: Based on Table 2.3 in Pilbeam (1992).

reserves and in official liabilities that are part of the reserves of other countries.

Errors and omissions (or the balancing item) reflect the difficulties involved in recording accurately, if at all, a wide variety of transactions that occur within a given period (usually 12 months). In some cases there is such a large number of transactions that a sample is taken rather than recording each transaction, with the inevitable errors that occur when samples are used. In others problems may arise when one or other of the parts of a transaction takes more than one year: for example with a large export contract covering several years some payment may be received by the exporter before any deliveries are made, but the last payment will not be made until the contract has been completed. Dishonesty may also play a part, as when goods are smuggled, in which case the merchandise side of the transaction is unreported although payment will be made somehow and will be reflected somewhere in the accounts. Similarly, the desire to avoid taxes may lead to under-reporting of some items in order to reduce tax liabilities.

Finally, there are changes in the reserves of the country whose balance of payments we are considering, and changes in that part of the reserves of other countries that is held in the country concerned. Reserves are held in three forms: in foreign currency, usually but not always the US dollar, as gold, and as Special Deposit Receipts (SDRs) borrowed from the IMF. Note that reserves do not have to be held within the country. Indeed most countries hold a proportion of their reserves in accounts with foreign central banks.

Table 23.3   *Balance-of-payments summaries for four countries, 1989 ($US billion)*

	United States	Japan	West Germany	United Kingdom
I: Current account balance	−110.06	56.94	55.48	−31.16
M: Long-term capital balance	87.93	−93.61	−11.65	−34.98
N: Short-term capital balance	16.32	45.86	−56.75	27.53
O: Other recorded items	1.55	−0.01	0.12	−0.54
P: Net errors and omissions	22.60	−21.95	2.33	24.55
R: Exceptional financing	—	—	—	−1.94
S: Liabilities constituting other authorities' reserves	8.48	—	13.43	7.19
T: Total change in reserves	−26.81	12.77	−2.95	9.34

Source: Based on Table 2.3 in Pilbeam (1992).

The changes in the country's reserves must of course reflect the net value of all the other recorded items in the balance of payments. These changes will of course be recorded accurately, and it is the discrepancy between the changes in reserves and the net value of the other recorded items that allows us to identify the errors and omissions.

Table 23.3 records the full balances of payments for the United States, Japan, West Germany and the United Kingdom in 1989. The balances on current account and on the long- and short-term capital accounts are taken from Tables 23.1 and 23.2.

 ## 23.3 Balance of payments: surpluses and deficits

The terms 'balance-of-payments deficit' and 'balance-of-payments surplus' are familiar to the most casual student of economic affairs. They carry with them the suggestion that something is amiss with the national economy, so that some change may be expected in the near future, which the government may seek to combat or to facilitate, or may leave to take its own course. The terms also often convey some implicit judgement, usually to the effect that a country with a balance-of-payments deficit is in some sense in trouble, while one with a surplus is 'strong'. As we shall see in this section, it may be difficult to pin down what we mean by a deficit or a surplus on the balance of payments. In later chapters we shall discuss what the likely consequences of a deficit or surplus may be, and how governments may react to them and why they might choose to do so.

☐ *Autonomous and accommodating items*

Economists have often found it useful to distinguish between *autonomous* and *accommodating* items in the balance of payments. Transactions are said to be autonomous if their value is determined independently of the balance of payments. Accommodating items on the other hand are determined by the net consequences of the autonomous items. An alternative nomenclature is that items are 'above the line' (autonomous) or 'below the line' (accommodating). Obviously the sum of the accommodating and autonomous items must be zero, since all entries in the balance-of-payments accounts must come under one of the two headings.

Whether the balance of payments is in surplus or deficit then depends on the balance of the autonomous items. The balance of payments is said to be in surplus if autonomous receipts are greater than autonomous payments, and in deficit if autonomous receipts are less than autonomous payments.

Unfortunately, the distinction between autonomous and accommodating items is not as straightforward as it may seem. Essentially the distinction lies in the motives underlying a transaction, which are almost impossible to determine. We cannot attach the labels to particular groups of items in the balance-of-payments accounts without giving the matter some thought. For example, a short-term capital movement could be a reaction to a difference in interest rates between two countries. If those interest rates are largely determined by influences other than the balance of payments then such a transaction should be labelled as autonomous. But other short-term capital movements may occur as part of the financing of a transaction that is itself autonomous (say, the export of some good), and as such should be classified as accommodating.

There is nevertheless a great temptation to assign the labels 'autonomous' and 'accommodating' to groups of items in the balance of payments. That is, to assume that the great majority of trade in goods and of long-term capital movements are autonomous, and that most short-term capital movements are accommodating, so that we shall not go far wrong by assigning those labels to the various components of the balance-of-payments accounts.

Whether that is a reasonable approximation to the truth may depend in part on the policy regime that is in operation. For example, what is an autonomous item under a system of fixed exchange rates and limited capital mobility may not be autonomous when exchange rates are floating and capital may move freely between countries. We shall discuss various policy regimes in more detail in subsequent chapters; here we shall content ourselves with some general observations.

In the 1950s and 1960s there were good reasons for defining trade in goods and services and long-term investment as autonomous items, and all short-term capital movements as accommodating. As we shall see when we consider exchange-rate systems in more detail in Chapters 28 and 29, under the Bretton Woods system the need to keep the exchange rate within the prescribed deviation from its par value required that the government operate in the foreign exchange market, so that changes in the official reserves essentially accommodated surpluses and deficits elsewhere in the balance of payments. At the same time, the limited variability in the exchange rate and the relatively low mobility of capital in that period meant that trade in goods and services and long-term investment were largely determined by macroeconomic variables other than the balance of payments.

In the current system however, the exchange-rate system is one of 'managed flexibility', with the official reserves used to smooth exchange-rate fluctuations rather than to maintain the rate within a given band, and capital is much more mobile. A case can be made for regarding capital movements as autonomous under this system (determined by investment opportunities, savings rates, etc.). Movements in capital then determine the exchange rate which in turn determines the current account balance, so that trade in goods and services is the accommodating item.

☐ *Deficit and surplus in the current account*

Despite the caveats just made, the conventional focus is on three main imbalances that may occur within the balance of payments. The first is the current account and/or the trade account. These are published on a monthly basis by most countries, and so provide regular information for policy-makers and economists. As we shall argue later, there is no particular economic significance to be attached to a surplus or deficit in either account, other than that a surplus indicates that our clams on foreigners have increased while a deficit shows the reverse. It does however provide information on changes in the economy, since visible and invisible trade react quickly to changes in other economic variables, such as relative rates of inflation and of growth. The state of the current account (or the trade balance) may also have an effect on confidence in the foreign exchange markets, which may in turn have a 'knock-on' effect on the economy.

☐ *The basic balance*

The *basic balance* was regarded in the 1950s and 1960s as the best indicator of the economy's position *vis-à-vis* other countries. It is defined as the sum of the current account balance and the net balance on long-term capital, which were then seen as the most stable elements in the balance of payments, and so placed 'above the line'. A worsening of the basic balance (an increase in a deficit or a reduction in a surplus, or even a move from surplus to deficit) was seen as indicating a deterioration in the (relative) state of the economy.

The balance of payments however merely records accumulated transactions within a specified period, and so is a static representation of part of a dynamic system. A deficit on the basic balance could come about in various ways, which are not mutually equivalent. For example, suppose that the basic balance is in deficit because a current account deficit is accompanied by a deficit on the long-term capital account. The long-term capital outflow will, in the future, generate profits, dividends and interest payments, which will improve the current account and so, *ceteris paribus*, will reduce or perhaps reverse the deficit. On the other hand, a basic balance surplus consisting of a deficit on current account that is more than covered by long-term borrowing from abroad may lead to problems in the future when profits, dividends, etc. are paid to the foreign investors.

☐ *The official settlements concept*

An alternative approach is to consider whether the net monetary transfer that has been made by the monetary authorities is positive or negative – the so-called *settlements concept*. If the net transfer is negative (i.e. there is an outflow) then the balance of payments is said to be in deficit, but if there is an inflow then it is in surplus. The basic premise is that the monetary authorities are the ultimate financiers of any deficit in the balance of payments (or the recipients of any surplus). These official settlements are thus seen as the accommodating item, all others being autonomous.

The monetary authorities may finance a deficit by depleting their reserves of foreign currencies, by borrowing from the IMF, or by borrowing from foreign monetary authorities. The latter source is of particular importance when other monetary authorities hold the domestic currency as part of their own reserves. A country whose currency is used as a reserve currency (such as the United States) may be able to run a deficit in its balance of payments without either depleting its own reserves or borrowing from the IMF since the foreign authorities may be prepared to purchase that currency and add it to their own reserves. The settlements approach is more relevant under a system of pegged exchange rates than when exchange rates are floating.

■ 23.4 The external wealth account

We have noted at several points in the preceding discussion that the capital account transactions recorded in the balance of payments reflect changes in the foreign assets held by the country (i.e. claims on foreigners) and of domestic assets held by foreign investors (liabilities to foreigners). The external wealth accounts of a country show the stocks of these assets and liabilities, recorded at one point in time (usually the end of the calendar year). Not all countries compile such accounts.

Since changes in the stocks of assets and liabilities reflect capital flows it is convenient to categorise them in the same way. That is, we may draw distinctions between official and private assets and liabilities, between long-term and short-term, and between portfolio assets and real assets. The net value of a country's assets and liabilities constitutes its *balance of indebtedness*. That is, if its assets exceed its liabilities then it is a net creditor, but if its liabilities exceed its assets then it is a net debtor. We shall return to this question when we consider the international debt problem in Chapter 31.

Compilation of an external wealth account is even more difficult than recording international transactions correctly. Particular problems are caused by valuing real assets (such as the value of a firm) and by the need to revalue them each year. If assets and liabilities are not revalued then changes in them will reflect the flows recorded in the balance of payments.

■ 23.5 Summary and conclusions

The balance-of-payments accounts are constructed on a double-entry basis, so that the balance of payments as a whole must balance. Nevertheless we can identify various imbalances within the accounts that are of use to the economic analyst and the policy-maker, although they must be interpreted with care. In particular, individual consideration should be given to the current account and long-term capital account balances, the states of which have important implications for the consequences of an overall surplus or deficit.

■ *Chapter 24* ■

The Market for Foreign Exchange

■ 24.1 Introduction

In this chapter we shall study the market (or rather markets) for foreign exchange. We shall use a very simple model to analyse some of the factors that determine the demand for and supply of foreign exchange, one in which we shall ignore the role that may be played by assets and concentrate on that played by trade in goods and services. We shall consider an assets-based model of exchange rate determination in Chapter 26. We shall also demonstrate in this chapter how the market for foreign exchange is cleared under a system of flexible exchange rates.

One of the distinguishing features of international trade is the involvement of foreign currencies. If a seller in New York sells goods to a buyer in California, he is paid in US dollars. Despite the considerable regional distance between buyer and seller, they use the same currency. If a buyer in Belgium buys goods from a seller in Holland, the problem of foreign exchange occurs, because the buyer wants to pay in Belgian francs and the seller wants to receive his payment in Dutch guilders. The Belgian importer must then purchase guilders, which he will probably do through his bank. The bank in turn will purchase guilders in the foreign-exchange market.

Under a pegged exchange rate regime the Belgian importer will have a reasonably good idea of the exchange rate he will face since it is maintained within a (relatively) narrow band by the operations of the monetary authorities. Under a completely flexible exchange-rate regime the importer will generally be much less certain about the rate that he must pay. In such circumstances he may, if he knows sufficiently well in advance that he will be importing the goods from the Netherlands, choose to engage in certain operations on the *forward exchange market* in order to reduce his uncertainty. We shall consider operations on the forward exchange market later in this chapter. For the moment we shall concentrate on the *spot market* for foreign exchange.

In most of this chapter we shall assume that exchange rates are perfectly flexible: that is, they are determined by the interaction of supply and demand, without any official operations by the monetary authorities that are intended to control the exchange rate. This is of course only an approximation to the current system, in which the monetary authorities intervene in the foreign-exchange market in order to smooth out short-term fluctuations ('managed' or 'dirty' floating). It is even further removed from the Bretton Woods system, in which the monetary authorities were obliged to intervene in the foreign-exchange market in order to maintain the exchange rate within a defined range around its par value. Nevertheless, as we know from our analysis of government intervention in international trade, a clear understanding of the operations of a perfectly functioning market is an essential prerequisite to understanding the nature and costs of government intervention.

24.2 Institutional aspects of foreign-exchange markets[1]

☐ *Defining the foreign exchange rate*

A foreign exchange rate is simply the price of one currency in terms of another. Since there is an essential symmetry between the two currencies, the exchange rate may be defined in one of two ways: as the amount of the foreign currency that may be bought for 1 unit of the domestic currency, or as the cost in domestic currency of purchasing 1 unit of the foreign currency. The practice in the United Kingdom, and in many other countries, is to use the former, so that the sterling–dollar exchange rate may be quoted in the United Kingdom as £1 = $1.60, but in the United States the same rate would be $1 = £0.625. The practice in the economic literature however is to use the latter definition.

One exchange rate is obviously just the reciprocal of the other. However, care must be taken to identify which exchange-rate definition is being used, particularly when discussing changes in the rate. The formal terminology is that the pound *depreciates* (appreciates) against the dollar if £1 exchanges for *fewer* (more) dollars than before. If, for example, the exchange rate changes from £1 = \$1.60 to £1 = \$1.52 then the pound has depreciated against the dollar by (0.08/1.60) = 5 per cent. Conversely, of course, the dollar has appreciated against the pound. Confusion may however arise in using the terms 'falling' and 'rising' as synonyms for 'depreciating' and 'appreciating'. In the example given, the pound has fallen against the dollar. If we are using the common economic definition of the exchange rate, which would be that originally £0.625 = \$1 but subsequently £0.658 = \$1, then the unwary may be led into thinking that the pound has 'risen'.

Finally, it should be noted that two foreign exchange rates are usually quoted by dealers: the rate at which the foreign currency is offered for sale (the *bid* price), and the (lower) rate at which the foreign currency will be purchased (the *ask* price). The difference between the two, the *spread*, is the gross profit margin of the dealer.

☐ *The structure of the foreign-exchange market*

The major participants in the foreign-exchange markets are commercial banks, foreign-exchange brokers and other authorised dealers, and the monetary authorities. It is important to recognise that, although the participants themselves may be based within individual countries, and countries may have their own trading centres, the market itself is world-wide. The trading centres are in close and continuous contact with one another, and participants will deal in more than one market.

The speed with which information is exchanged between markets provides the opportunity for quick and efficient *arbitrage* between foreign exchange centres and between currencies. The former means that the difference between, say, the sterling-dollar exchange rates quoted in New York and London will reflect only the cost of making transactions in the two centres. If the gap were larger than that then a profit could be made by purchasing sterling for dollars in the centre in which sterling was cheapest (cost less dollars per pound) and selling sterling for dollars in the other centre, so making a profit. Such transactions would drive up the dollar price of the pound in the cheaper centre and reduce it in the other. The latter means that the rates of exchange between each of three currencies must be consistent. That is, ignoring transactions costs, if the sterling–dollar exchange rate is £1 = \$1.5, and the sterling–yen rate is £1 = ¥165 then the dollar-yen rate must be \$1 = ¥(165/1.5) = ¥110.

24.3 A simple model of a spot exchange market

We shall start by treating the problem of the determination of the spot foreign exchange rate in the simplest possible manner, since we are interested in the question from the point of view of economic theory. The model we shall use here assumes that the demand for and supply of foreign exchange arise from international trade in goods and services, and utilises the excess demand/excess supply framework introduced in Chapter 10. For simplicity we shall assume that we can aggregate the goods exported by each country, so that we only have to deal with country A's exportables and importables (= country B's importables and exportables respectively) We shall consider the determination of the exchange rate from A's point of view. Country A's demand for foreign exchange will be derived from its demand for its importables, while its supply of foreign exchange will come from its supply of its exportables.

☐ *The demand for foreign exchange*

Figure 24.1(a) shows the excess (import) demand schedule of country A for its importables. This demand curve is naturally expressed in terms of A's currency, which we shall call the dollar. Figure 24.1(b) shows the excess (export) supply curve of country B for the same aggregate good, but expressed in terms of B's currency, which we shall call the pound.

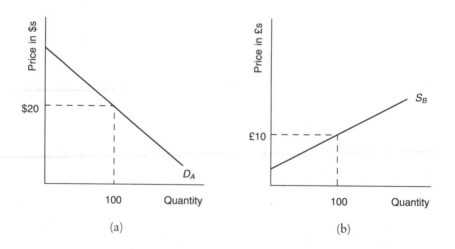

Figure 24.1 *Import demand and export supply for A's importables*

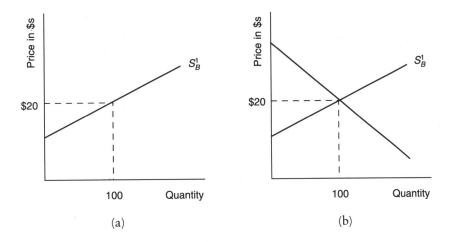

Figure 24.2 *Deriving the $ price for A's importables when £1 = $2*

Suppose for the moment that the exchange rate is determined exogenously to this market, and is known to be £1 = $2. Then we may translate B's export supply curve into $ terms through that exchange rate. For example, if B is prepared to export 100 units at a price of £10 then it will be prepared to export that 100 units at a price of $20. B's $-denominated export supply curve is shown as S_B^1 in Figure 24.2(a). We may then superimpose B's $-denominated export supply curve on A's import demand curve to determine the market clearing ($) price and quantity in A. This is done in Figure 24.2(b).

The market will therefore clear at a price of $20 with imports of 100 units. A will therefore purchase imports worth $2000, and since the exchange rate is £1 = $2 it therefore requires £1000 in B's currency to pay for those imports.

Suppose now that the exchange rate is £1 = $1.5 (the $ has appreciated against the £). Obviously this will have no effect on A's import demand curve, since that is denominated in terms of the $. Nor will it affect B's £-denominated export supply curve, since B exporters will still be prepared to export 100 units if they receive a price of £10 per unit. It will however change B's $-denominated export supply curve, since in order for B exporters to receive £10 a unit the price paid by A's consumers need only now be $15. B's $-denominated supply curve must shift downwards. This new export supply curve (S_B^2) and the consequent market equilibrium are shown in Figures 24.3(a) and 24.3(b) respectively.

The effects of an appreciation of A's currency on the $ price and on the volume of its importables are readily apparent. The $ price must fall, but it will not fall by the full extent of the appreciation (unless B's export supply curve is perfectly elastic) since a lower price will lead to an increase in its demand for imports. In the example shown in Figure 24.3 the price in A has fallen to $17, and the quantity imported has increased to 120 units. In this example the $ value of A's imports has increased from $2000 to $(17 \times 120) = 2040. It need not however always be the case that an appreciation of A's currency will lead to an increase in the value of its imports expressed in terms of that currency. We shall deal with this problem more formally later in this chapter.

What we are interested in however is A's demand for country B's currency, the £. A is now importing a greater volume from B, and B will only supply a greater volume of exports at a higher price in terms of its own currency. It follows that A's demand for £s *must* have increased as a consequence of its exchange rate appreciating. In the example we are considering the £ value of A's imports at the new exchange rate of £1 = $1.5 is £(2040/1.5) = £1360.

If we repeat this exercise for various exchange rates then we may derive A's demand for £s as a function of its exchange rate. Such a demand curve for foreign currency is shown in Figure 24.4; note that even if the underlying demand and supply curves for the good are linear, the demand curve for the foreign currency will in general be non-linear. The importing country's demand curve is drawn in Figure 24.4 with the negative slope

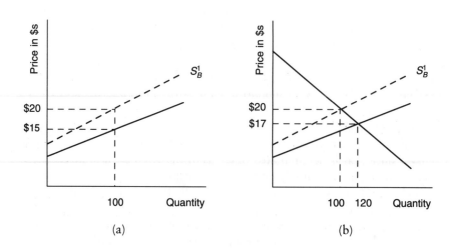

Figure 24.3 *The effects of an appreciation of A's currency on its import volume*

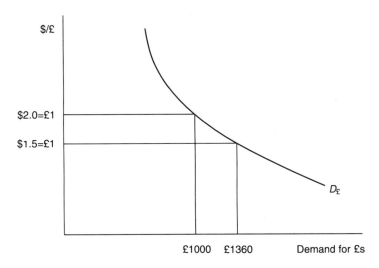

Figure 24.4 *The importing country's demand schedule for the foreign currency*

that we associate with demand curves. This is because the exchange rate on the vertical axis is expressed in terms of the domestic currency cost of 1 unit of foreign currency. Had we expressed the exchange rate in terms of the amount of foreign currency that could be purchased with 1 unit of the domestic currency then the demand curve would have a positive slope. This, of course, is why economists prefer to work with the former definition!

The demand for foreign currency is of course a derived demand. The position and shape (elasticity) of the demand curve for foreign currency will depend on the positions and elasticities of the underlying import demand and export supply curves. We shall now derive the relationship between the slope of the demand schedule for foreign currency and the elasticities of foreign supply (η_m) and domestic demand (ε_m).

Let the price of imports in A be $\$p_m$ and the price in B be $\pounds\pi_m$, and the exchange rate $\$r = \pounds 1$ (the number of units of A's currency required to buy 1 unit of B's currency). It follows that $p_m = r\pi_m$. We shall also use the notation $\hat{z}$ to represent the proportionate change in z; i.e. $\hat{z} = dz/z$, and so $dz = z\hat{z}$. This gives us a convenient framework for dealing with elasticities. The foreign elasticity of supply of the imports is defined in terms of their £ price, so that if M is the volume of imports we have

$$\eta_m = \frac{\hat{M}}{\hat{\pi}_m} \tag{24.1}$$

Country A's elasticities of demand for its imports (ε_m) is of course defined in terms of its own currency, the \$. However since $p_m = r\pi_m$ we may write

$$\hat{P}_m = \frac{dP_m}{P_m} = \frac{\pi_m dr + r d\pi_m}{r\pi_m} = \hat{r} + \hat{\pi}_m \qquad (24.2)$$

and so A's elasticity of demand for its imports is

$$\varepsilon_m = -\frac{\hat{M}}{\hat{P}_m} = -\frac{\hat{M}}{\hat{r} + \hat{\pi}_m} \qquad (24.3)$$

Note that the demand elasticity is defined to be positive.

Now the value of A's imports in terms of the foreign currency is $D_\pounds = M\pi_m$. If we totally differentiate this we obtain:

$$dD_\pounds = Md\pi_m + \pi_m dM \qquad (24.4)$$

which we may rewrite as

$$dD_\pounds = M\pi_m \hat{\pi}_m + \pi_m M\hat{M} \qquad (24.5)$$

We may solve equations (24.1) and (24.3) for $\hat{\pi}_m$ and $\hat{M}$, to obtain

$$\hat{\pi}_m = -\left(\frac{\varepsilon_m}{\varepsilon_m + \eta_m}\right)\hat{r} \qquad (24.6)$$

$$\hat{M} = -\left(\frac{\varepsilon_m \eta_m}{\varepsilon_m + \eta_m}\right)\hat{r} \qquad (24.7)$$

Note that (24.6) confirms that a depreciation of the \$ (an increase in r) will reduce the £ price of A's imports, and (24.7) that a depreciation reduces the volume of imports. Substituting for these in (24.5) gives

$$dD_\pounds = -M\pi_m \hat{r}\left(\frac{\varepsilon_m(1 + \eta_m)}{\varepsilon_m + \eta_m}\right) \qquad (24.8)$$

which must be negative. That is, a depreciation of the domestic currency will always reduce the demand for the foreign currency: the demand curve in Figure 24.4 must indeed be negatively sloped.

Differentiating the term in parentheses in (24.8) with respect to ε_m shows that, *ceteris paribus*, the more elastic is the domestic demand for imports, the greater will be the fall in its demand for foreign currency for a given depreciation of its own currency. Differentiating the same term with respect to η_m does not give such a straightforward result. If A's import demand is elastic then, *ceteris paribus*, the more elastic is B's export supply then the greater will be the effect of a depreciation on A's demand for foreign currency, but if A's import demand is inelastic then the reverse is true.

As we know the effect of the elasticity for imports on the demand for foreign exchange, it is interesting to decide what we may deduce about that elasticity from general considerations. Two factors are important. The first is the question of the elasticity of demand for importables (imported goods). If a country imports necessities and raw materials, we may expect the elasticity of demand for imports to be low and the quantity imported to be insensitive to price changes. If, on the other hand, the country imports luxury goods and goods for which suitable substitutes exist, demand elasticities for imports might be high. Whether or not the country has a domestic import-competing industry is the second extremely important factor. If the country has many well-developed import-competing industries, the elasticity of demand for imports most certainly is high. This is due to the fact that if the price rises, import-competing industries will come in and take a larger share of the market, and imports will fall; if the price falls, it will be the other way around. What of course we do know is that the elasticity of (excess) demand for imports must, if there is an import-competing industry, be greater than the elasticity of demand for the good itself.

Time is another factor to take into account. In the short run it may be difficult to react to price changes by reallocating factors of production. In the short run, therefore, elasticity of demand for imports may not be very high. In the long run, however, it is much more probable that the production pattern will alter according to price changes, and the demand for imports will therefore be more elastic.

If we take into account different types of countries, we find that their demand for imports differs. Most well-developed, industrial countries produce and import to a large extent the same type of goods; in other words, these countries have large and well-developed import-competing industries. For these countries, the demand for imports it often very elastic. Less-developed, agricultural countries often have small, poorly developed import-competing sectors. They import necessities and the industrial goods needed for their development programmes. Their demand for imports is on the whole very inelastic.

We shall find later that the question of elasticity of demand for imports has important implications for economic policy. But for the time being, we shall concentrate on the question of the supply of foreign exchange.

☐ *The supply of foreign exchange*

Country *A*'s supply of foreign currency comes from its receipts for its exports. We may derive the relationship between *A*'s exchange rate and its foreign currency receipts in a way that closely parallels the derivation of its demand for foreign currency.

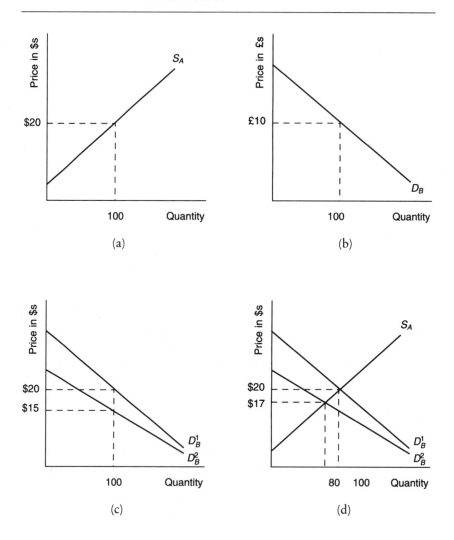

Figure 24.5   *The supply of foreign exchange*

Figure 24.5(a) shows the export supply curve for country *A*, defined in terms of its own currency, the $, while Figure 24.5(b) shows *B*'s demand curve for *A*'s exportables, defined in terms of *B*'s currency, the £. Neither of these curves will be affected by a change in the exchange rate since both are defined in terms of their respective domestic currency.

In Figure 24.5(c), country *B*'s $-denominated demand curve when the exchange rate is $2 = £1 is shown by D_B^1; for example, if *B* will import 100 units at a domestic price of £10 then, at an exchange rate of $2 = £1, *A* will be able to sell 100 units of exports to B at a price of $20. The market clearing price and quantity for A's exportables at this exchange rate is determined by the intersection of B's $-denominated demand curve with A's export supply curve, shown in Figure 24.5(d) by the intersection of D_B^1; and S_A (a price of $20 and an export volume for A of 100).

Suppose again that A's exchange rate appreciates to £1 = $1.5. Then in order to export 100 units to B country A must be prepared to accept a price of $15. That is, B's $-denominated demand curve will shift downwards, as shown by D_B^2 in Figure 24.5(c). Introducing D_B^2 into Figure 24.5(d) shows that the effect of the appreciation of A's exchange rate will be to reduce its exports and the $ price it receives for them. It must therefore follow that the $ value of A's exports will fall – in the example shown from $2000 to $(17 × 80) = $1360. In the case shown the £ value of A's exports also decreases, from £1000 to £(1360/1.5) ≈ £907. The supply curve for £s might then look something like $S_£$ in Figure 24.6, which has the 'normal' positive slope.

It does not follow however that the £ value of its exports *must* fall. Since each $ now buys more £s than before the appreciation, it is quite possible that a reduced $ value of exports will translate into an increased £ value of exports. For instance, supply and demand curves of different slopes might have yielded an original price of $20 and a quantity of 100, but a post-appreciation price of $18 and a quantity of 90. The $ value of A's exports would still have fallen (to $1620), but the £ value of those exports would have risen to £(1620/1.5) = £1080. In such a case the supply curve for £s would have a negative slope, as shown by $S_£$ in Figure 24.7.

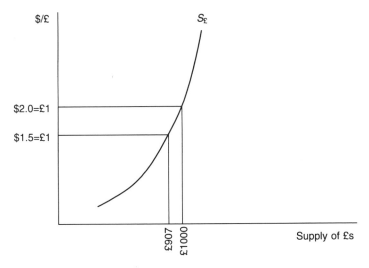

Figure 24.6 *A 'normally sloped' supply curve for the foreign currency*

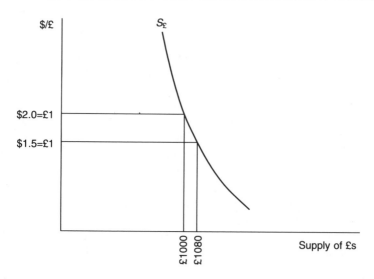

Figure 24.7 *A 'backward sloping' supply curve for the foreign currency*

The factors determining the position and elasticity of the supply curve for foreign currency are of course basically the same as those determining the position and elasticity of the demand curve for foreign currency: the demand and supply elasticities of the goods in question. The difference of course is that now we must consider the elasticities of A's export supply curve and B's import demand curve. The added complication when considering the supply of foreign currency is that the exchange rate enters the problem in a way that may transform the decrease in the value of exports in terms of the domestic currency into an increase in terms of the foreign currency.

We may derive the relationship between the slope of A's supply curve for foreign currency and the elasticities of its export supply curve and B's import demand curve in a way that parallels our earlier analysis of A's demand for foreign currency. If X is A's export volume and π_x their foreign currency price then the value of A's exports (its supply of foreign currency) is $S_£ = X\pi_x$. If we totally differentiate this we obtain:

$$dS_£ = Xd\pi_x + \pi_x dX \tag{24.9}$$

which may be rewritten as

$$dS_£ = X\pi_x \hat{\pi}_x + \pi_x X\hat{X} \tag{24.10}$$

We may write A's export supply elasticity (η_x) and B's import demand elasticity (ε_x) as

$$\eta_x = \frac{\hat{X}}{\hat{P}_x} = \frac{\hat{X}}{\hat{r} + \hat{\pi}_x} \tag{24.11}$$

$$\varepsilon_x = -\frac{\hat{X}}{\hat{\pi}_x} \tag{24.12}$$

Solving (24.11) and (24.12) for $\hat{\pi}_x$ and $\hat{X}$ gives

$$\hat{\pi}_x = -\left(\frac{\eta_x}{\varepsilon_x + \eta_x}\right)\hat{r} \tag{24.13}$$

$$\hat{X} = \left(\frac{\varepsilon_x \eta_x}{\varepsilon_x + \eta_x}\right)\hat{r} \tag{24.14}$$

which we may substitute in (24.10) to obtain

$$dS_{£} = X\pi_x\left(\frac{\eta_x(\varepsilon_x - 1)}{\varepsilon_x + \eta_x}\right)\hat{r} \tag{24.15}$$

The sign of this expression obviously depends on the size of B's elasticity of demand for A's exports. If B's demand is elastic ($\varepsilon_x > 1$) then the expression in (24.15) is positive, so that a depreciation of A's currency (an increase in r) will increase A's supply of £s. In this case the supply curve for foreign currency is positively sloped, as in Figure 24.6. If on the other hand B's import demand is inelastic ($\varepsilon_x < 1$) then A's supply curve for foreign currency is negatively sloped.

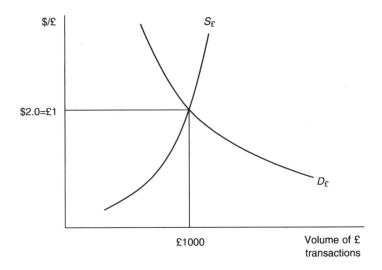

Figure 24.8 *Equilibrium in the foreign exchange market*

For the moment we shall assume that the supply curve for the foreign currency is positively sloped, as in Figure 24.6. The equilibrium exchange rate is then determined by the intersection of the supply and demand curves. This equilibrium is shown in Figure 24.8, and in our example occurs when the exchange rate is £1 = $2 with a volume of foreign exchange transactions of £1000 (= $2,000). The exchange rate will, in this case, be stable. That is, a temporary disturbance which puts the exchange rate up will cause an excess supply of £s, which will in turn lead to a fall in the exchange rate and a move back towards the initial equilibrium. This is not however necessarily the case, and it is to this that we shall turn next.

▌ 24.4 Stability in a floating exchange-rate market

We know from the microeconomic analysis of market stability that a market will be unstable if the supply curve is negatively sloped and is flatter than the demand curve. That is, an excess supply will lead to a price fall that will increase the excess supply, and so on. It has been argued that this is a real possibility in foreign-exchange markets. We shall consider it in more detail by combining our earlier results on the relationships between the slopes of the demand and supply curves for the foreign currency and the elasticities of demand and supply for exports and imports.

A floating exchange rate will be stable if an appreciation of the domestic currency leads to an excess demand for the foreign currency (an excess supply of the domestic currency), since that will leads to a subsequent depreciation. An appreciation leads to an excess demand for the foreign currency if it moves the balance of trade from equilibrium into deficit.

Using our earlier notation, we may write the balance of trade as $B = X\pi_x - M\pi_m$. If we totally differentiate this we obtain:

$$dB = Xd\pi_x + \pi_x dX - Md\pi_m - \pi_m dM \tag{24.16}$$

We have already derived expressions for $Xd\pi_x + \pi_x dX$ and $Md\pi_m + \pi_m dM$ in equations (24.15) and (24.8). Substituting these in (24.16) gives

$$dB = X\pi_x \left(\frac{\eta_x(\varepsilon_x - 1)}{\varepsilon_x + \eta_x} \right) \hat{r} + M\pi_m \left(\frac{\varepsilon_m(1 + \eta_m)}{\varepsilon_m + \eta_m} \right) \hat{r} \tag{24.17}$$

If we start from an initial equilibrium position then $X\pi_x = M\pi_m$, and appreciating the currency ($\hat{r} < 0$) will worsen the trade balance ($dB < 0$) if and only if

$$\frac{\eta_x(\varepsilon_x - 1)}{\varepsilon_x + \eta_x} + \frac{\varepsilon_m(1 + \eta_m)}{\varepsilon_m + \eta_m} > 0 \tag{24.18}$$

This result is usually referred to as the (full) *Marshall–Lerner Condition*. We shall meet it again when we discuss the effects of devaluing a pegged exchange rate on the balance of trade. Essentially it tells us that it does not matter if an appreciation increases the supply of foreign exchange provided that it increases the demand for foreign exchange by a greater amount. In other words, it does not matter if the supply curve for foreign currency is negatively sloped, provided it is steeper than the demand curve for foreign currency.

There are two simple versions of the Marshall–Lerner Condition that are worth noting. The first, a traditional simplification, assumes that the two supply elasticities are infinite. We may show that if we let $\eta_m \to \infty$ and $\eta_x \to \infty$, then (24.18) reduces to

$$\varepsilon_x + \varepsilon_m > 1 \tag{24.19}$$

That is, if either the domestic demand for imports or the foreign country's demand for the home country's exports is elastic then the foreign-exchange market *must* be stable. But the market will still be stable when both demands are inelastic provided that the sum of their elasticities is greater than one. The inequality given in (24.19) is often identified as the (simplified) version of the Marshall–Lerner Condition.

This case (perfectly elastic supply for exports and imports) must not be confused with the 'small-country case'. In the latter the appropriate assumption is that the foreign elasticity of demand and the foreign elasticity of supply are both infinite. Taking the limit of the left-hand side of (24.13) as $\varepsilon_x \to \infty$ and $\eta_m \to \infty$, we have as our condition

$$\eta_x + \varepsilon_m > 0 \tag{24.20}$$

This must always be satisfied. That is, a small country must always be able to improve its balance on current account by devaluing. More importantly, for a small country the flexible exchange rate is always stable.

Which simplified version of the Marshall–Lerner Condition is appropriate? Trade theorists have a natural affinity for the small-country case, but it must be remembered that we are not dealing here with trade in just one good, but with a country's total trade. Even small countries (in GDP terms) may be large traders in particular goods, and so a change in their total trade flows may have an effect on foreign currency prices. This may then make the traditional small-country assumption unrealistic when we are considering foreign-exchange markets.

This does not of course explain why the assumption of perfectly elastic supply of exports and imports, and particularly the former, should be thought more realistic. The argument sometimes used is that this assumption is appropriate for a developed manufacturing country that exports only a small proportion of its manufactures output. In this case the country may be able to expand its exports at constant cost.

24.5 Government intervention in the foreign-exchange market: fixing the exchange rate

To say that the foreign-exchange market is stable does not of course imply that the exchange rate does not change over time. Typically exchange rates in a free market will change as economic conditions change. However, for reasons that we shall explore later, governments are rarely willing to allow complete freedom of movement in exchange rates, and so intervene in the market. Under the current 'dirty floating' system governments intervene in order to smooth out fluctuations in the exchange rate. Under the Bretton Woods scheme governments were required to intervene to maintain the exchange rate between their currency and the US $ within a specified band – what is often referred to as a *pegged exchange-rate system*. Under the EC exchange-rate system members are required to maintain a maximum gap between their currency and those of other members (considerably widened following the problems of mid-1993).

The principles of intervention in foreign-exchange markets are broadly similar to those we discussed in Chapter 18 when considering the use of a buffer stock to stabilise commodity prices. That is, if there is an excess supply at the target price then the government (or its agency) should buy

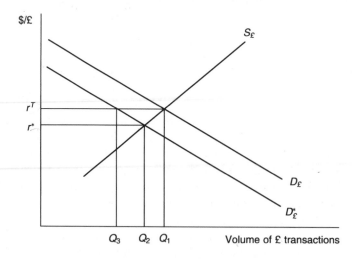

Figure 24.9   *Offsetting the effect of a decrease in demand for the foreign currency*

that excess supply on the market, while if there is an excess demand the government should sell. Figure 24.9 shows an example of the most simple form of intervention.

In this example there is a target exchange rate r^T. If the demand for foreign currency is $D_£$ and the supply is $S_£$ then there is no need for intervention. Suppose however that the demand for foreign currency falls to $D_£^*$, so that in a free market the exchange rate would shift to r^*. In order to bring the exchange rate back to the target rate r^T the government must purchase a quantity of the foreign currency equal to $Q_1 - Q_3$ at the target rate of exchange. That is, it must add to its reserves of the foreign currency.

24.6 An example of adjustment in the foreign-exchange market

Suppose now that country A's demand for importables falls, perhaps because the government in A has imposed a tariff on importables, and that there are no changes in any other elements in the balance of payments. The effect in the foreign-exchange market must be to shift A's demand curve inwards since the $ value of imports must fall and thus at any given exchange rate the £ value of imports must fall. As we can see from Figure 24.10, where $D_£^t$ is the new demand curve for £s, A's exchange rate must

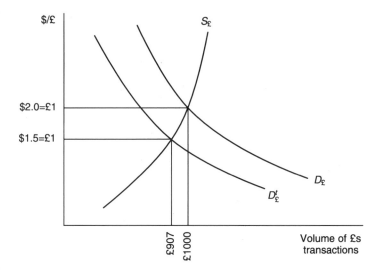

Figure 24.10 *Adjustment of the exchange rate to A imposing a tariff*

then appreciate; that is the foreign currency fetches a lower $ price than before.

The change in the exchange rate must of course bring about adjustments in the markets for the exportables and importables. The appreciation in the $ must again shift B's $-denominated supply curve (for A's importables) downwards, as we saw in Figure 24.3(b). This will, *ceteris paribus*, reduce the price of importables in A, but not by as much as they were increased by the initial imposition of the tariff, and will increase the volume of imports as well (but not to as much as they were before the tariff was imposed).

At the same time B's demand curve for A's exportables must shift downwards, as we saw in Figure 24.5(b), which will reduce both the volume and the $ price of A's exportables. These shifts in the goods markets will of course result in further shifts in the supply and demand curves for foreign exchange, and so further repercussions in the goods markets, and so on.

When all markets finally settle down into a new general equilibrium we should observe that the exchange rate has appreciated, though by less than the initial appreciation due to the tariff, and that the volume and value of trade are less than before.

The effects on the volume of trade etc. are consistent with the general equilibrium effects of a tariff that were discussed in Chapter 11. Note however that the effects differ from those obtained when we considered the partial equilibrium analysis of the effects of a tariff in Chapter 10. In that chapter we were considering the effects of the imposition of a tariff on one of a number of imported goods, so that we could make the usual *ceteris paribus* assumption. In particular, that meant that the imposition of a tariff would have no effect on the exchange rate, and therefore that there would be no 'feed-back' effects on the market for the import good we were considering.

In the case we have just considered, however, we assumed that country A placed a tariff on *all* its importables (or on its only import). In that case there must be a foreign exchange effect, and so the $-denominated supply curve for A's imports must shift. Figure 24.11 illustrates the difference between the partial equilibrium analysis when there is no exchange rate feed-back and the case where there is only one imported good and thus an exchange-rate effect.

Initially the exchange rate is £1 = r_1, so that B's $-denominated supply curve is $S_B(r_1)$. A now imposes a tariff on the import good. If the exchange rate remains unchanged then the tariff-ridden equilibrium would be where imports are M_1, the price in A is P_A^1, and the price received by B is P_B^1. In the final equilibrium, A's currency must have appreciated as a consequence of the imposition of the tariff. B's $-denominated supply curve would now

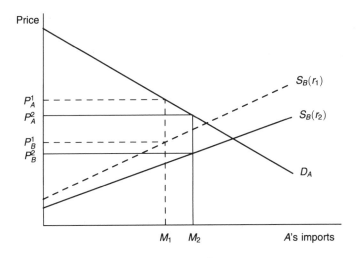

Figure 24.11 *The effects of a tariff when there is an exchange-rate effect*

be lower than it was before, at $S_B(r_2)$. The final equilibrium would then be where imports are M_2, the price in A is P_A^2, and the price received by B is P_B^2.

■ 24.7 The forward-exchange market

The foreign-exchange market we have so far dealt with is the spot market. In a spot transaction the seller of exchange has to deliver the foreign exchange he has sold 'on the spot' (usually within two days). Likewise, a buyer of exchange will immediately receive the foreign exchange he has bought. There is also another important market for foreign exchange, the forward market. In the forward market, when the contract is signed, the seller agrees to sell a certain amount of foreign exchange to be delivered at a future date at a price agreed upon in advance. Analogously, a buyer agrees to buy a certain amount of foreign exchange at a future date and at a predetermined price. The most common forward contracts are for 1 month (30 days), 3 months (90 days), 6 months (180 days), 9 months (270 days) and 1 year (360 days).

The basic questions we must answer are why anyone should wish to agree a contract to buy or sell foreign exchange at some future time, and how the spot and forward markets are linked. The answers to these questions are of course interwoven with each other. The linkages between the spot and forward exchange rates come from the actions of three groups of economic agents who use the markets: arbitrageurs, hedgers and speculators. We shall deal with each of these in turn. It should be noted however that an given individual or company may at different times take on the role of any of these agents.

Interest rate arbitrage and 'covered interest parity'

Let us assume that the spot exchange rate is $2 for £1. This rate must be the same both in London and New York (except for any transactions costs), because if the exchange rate were 2:1 in London but 1.90:1 in New York, it would pay to take dollars from New York to London and sell them there – the arbitrage between centres referred to earlier. The forward rate in either market may however differ from the spot rate.

Let us continue to assume that the spot rate is $2 for £1. If the forward rate is higher than the spot rate, for instance $2.03, we say that there is a *premium* on sterling. The premium is usually expressed as a percentage of the spot rate. We denote the spot rate as r_s and the forward rate r_f. We then get

$$\frac{r_f - r_s}{r_s} = \text{premium on £ (if } r_f > r_s)$$

so that in our example the premium on the pound is 1.5 per cent. Analogously, we say that the pound sterling is at a *discount* if the spot rate is higher than the forward rate. This is the case if, for instance, the spot rate is $2.00 for £1 and the forward rate is $1.96 for £1. We get

$$\frac{r_s - r_f}{r_s} = \text{discount on £ (if } r_s > r_f)$$

giving a discount on the pound of 2 per cent.

If the interest rates in the two countries differ, this gives rise to an interest arbitrage and a difference in spot and forward rates. Let us assume that the short-term interest rate in New York is 5 per cent per annum while it is 10 per cent per annum in London. So $100 in New York will yield an interest of $5 per year or $1.25 per 3 months. In London £100 will yield an interest of £10 per year or £2.50 per 3 months.

Suppose now that the 3-month forward rate in London is the same as the spot rate (i.e. there is no premium or discount), both being £1 = $2. Arbitrageurs would be able to make a (risk-free) profit by borrowing in New York and lending in London for 3 months, while taking out a 3-month forward contract in transfer their future funds back to New York.

This is an example of *covered* interest rate arbitrage. If the forward contract is not taken out, so that the arbitrageurs will have to convert their funds at the going spot rate at the end of the 3-month period, then the operation is *uncovered*.

The mechanics of the covered arbitrage would be as follows:

(1) The arbitrageur borrows funds, say $100 000, in New York for 3 months at the US rate of interest (5 per cent p.a.). In 3 months' time therefore the arbitrageur must repay that $100 000 plus $1 250 interest, or $101 250.
(2) The arbitrageur buys pounds at the current spot rate, and invests that £50 000 in London at the UK rate of interest (10 per cent p.a.) for 3 months. In 3 months' time the arbitrageur will receive the £50 000 plus £1 250 interest, or £51 250.
(3) At the same time the arbitrageur takes out a forward contract to sell £51 250 at the quoted forward exchange rate, which is £1 = $2. He knows therefore that in 3 months' time he will be able to exchange the £51 250 for $102 500.
(4) At the end of the 3 months therefore the arbitrageur will complete his transactions by taking the repayment of his lending in London, completing his forward exchange contract, and repaying his borrowing in New York. He will have made a profit of 102500 − 101250 = 1250.

Such arbitrage would lead to an excess supply of forward pounds, and depress the forward rate. Arbitrage opportunities will exist whenever the difference in interest rates between two centres exceeds the premium/discount of the forward exchange rate. Formally, there will be no opportunity for arbitrage if

$$r_f = \left(\frac{1 + i_a}{1 + i_b}\right) r_s \qquad (24.21)$$

where i_a is the interest rate in London and i_b is the interest rate in New York, defined for the same time period as the forward exchange rate.

This is the basic formulation of the 'theory of interest parity'. In reality, however, we find that the premium or discount often differs from the interest rate differential. There are several reasons for this. Depending upon his subjective risk and liquidity considerations, an arbitrageur might not find it optimal to equalise objective return on his investments in two countries. For this reason alone the premium or discount might not equal the interest rate differential. Interest arbitrage, however, is not the only factor influencing the forward rate.

□ *Hedging*

Another important factor is hedging or covering There is often a time difference between the signing of a contract and the delivery of the goods. An exporter, for instance, may have signed a contract to deliver goods 3 months' hence. He knows that he will then receive, say, $1000. He may, however, fear that the exchange rate will change in the meantime. Hoping to avert a risk, he wants to know the exact sum he will receive. He is thus able to cover himself against risks by hedging. He sells $1000 forward at the going forward rate for the pound sterling. He receives no money and delivers none when he enters this contract, but 3 months' hence, when he receives payment, he delivers the money that he has sold forward and he knows now what he will receive then. Whatever the possible changes in exchange rates during the 3 months, they are of no consequence to him.

Likewise, any importer who enters a contract in the present, and knows that he will have to pay for his goods in the future, can cover himself against any exchange risks by buying forward. If the contract period is limited, 3 months for example, he knows exactly what the price of the goods will be in his own currency when delivered to him, and he can avoid any risks connected with fluctuations in the exchange rate.

Such hedging activity is not of course costless. There are, for example, various transactions costs involved in taking out a forward exchange contract. Exporters and importers will engage in hedging if they consider the costs of so doing are less than those associated with taking the exchange rate risk of not hedging, and that will depend on how risk-averse they are.

Hedging will give rise to a supply of and a demand for forward exchange. What the supply of and demand for forward exchange from this source will be depends on several factors. The volume of trade is important, and so is the risk-aversion of exporters and importers. Hedging may cause the premium or discount on foreign exchange to differ from the interest rate differential.

Hedging is important, especially in a market with flexible exchange rates, as it permits exporters and importers to protect themselves against risks connected with exchange-rate fluctuations, thus enabling them to concentrate on their pure trading functions. It should, however, be observed that the forward market is a short-run market, in which the contract period is usually 3 months. Longer contract periods exist, but these markets are not very well developed, and the upper limit for the contract period is 1 year. For many contracts the period between ordering and payment is longer. In these cases hedging does not function efficiently, and risks connected with fluctuations in exchange rates can hardly be avoided.

☐ *Speculation*

Speculation is a third source for the supply of and the demand for forward exchange. We assume that the speculation is about the development of the future spot rate and that the speculation exclusively takes place in the forward market. The speculator who expects the spot rate to increase in the future buys forward in order to sell spot when he receives his delivery of the currency that he has bought forward. On the contrary, however, a speculator who expects the spot rate to fall sells forward with the intention of buying spot when he needs currency for delivery. The speculator hopes to make a profit by taking on the exchange-rate risk. This is in contrast with the arbitrageur, who is seeking a risk-free profit on interest rate differentials, and the hedger, who is avoiding risk.

We have seen that there is a close link between spot and forward rates through interest arbitrage. If speculators expect the spot rate to increase, they will buy forward, putting pressure on the forward rate, so that it, also, increases. Conversely, if they expect the spot rate to fall, they will sell forward and force the forward rate down. Therefore, speculation tends to make the spot and forward rates move together.

Under a system of flexible exchange rates there are many factors which influence movements in the exchange rates. The most important factors are connected with the supply of and demand for imports and exports. An important question is whether speculation is stabilising or destabilising, i.e. whether it tends to smooth out fluctuations in the exchange rate caused by trade or make them larger than they would otherwise be.

Speculation is a very important phenomenon in connection with a system of flexible exchange rates. It could, conceivably, be of critical importance for the efficient functioning of a system of flexible exchange rates, and could be a source of problems in a pegged exchange rate system. We return to this question in Chapter 30 when discussing the relative merits of different exchange rate systems.

■ 24.8 Comments and conclusions

We have discussed the structure and operation of the spot and the forward exchange markets, and have seen that arbitrage (in various forms) has a major role to play in ensuring that exchange rates do not differ between different centres and that forward and spot exchange rates are mutually dependent. We have also discussed the determination of spot exchange rates within a very simple floating exchange-rate model, one that involves only trade in goods and services. As we shall see later such trade is not the only, and may not be the most important, determinant of the exchange rate. We also considered a very simple example of government intervention in the foreign-exchange market with the intention of maintaining the exchange rate at a given level. We shall return to this topic in Chapter 30, where we shall consider the relative merits of floating and pegged exchange-rate systems. In that chapter we shall also return to the question of speculation, and in particular whether speculation stabilises or destabilises the exchange rate.

☐ *Note*

1   A more detailed discussion is given in Pilbeam (1992), Chapter 1.

■ *Chapter 25* ■

○ Foreign Trade and National Income

One of Keynes's main contributions to economic theory was to describe how equilibrium in national income is created. As most students are familiar with the determination of national income in a closed economy, we will directly treat the case of an open economy. As with the closed economy model, a central assumption is that prices do not change. This is a reasonable assumption if there are unemployed resources, particularly in the short run. We shall also assume that the exchange rate is fixed, so that there is no balance-of-payments adjustment via exchange-rate changes.

■ 25.1 The import function

For the moment we shall assume that there is no taxation or government expenditure, so that we may concentrate on the role of exports and imports. Consumers can either spend their incomes on consumption goods or they can save them, and we assume that aggregate consumption (C) and (hence) aggregate savings (S) are increasing functions of the national income (Y). The consumption function is thus written as

$$C = C(Y) \text{ with } dC/dY > 0 \qquad (25.1)$$

and the savings function as

$$S = S(Y) \text{ with } dS/dY > 0 \qquad (25.2)$$

The derivatives dC/dY and dS/dY are referred to as the *marginal propensity to consume* (c) and the *marginal propensity to save* (s) respectively. Since $C + S = Y$, it follows that $c + s = 1$, and hence that $c < 1$ and $s < 1$.

In an open economy part of consumers' aggregate demand will be for imported goods, and we assume that this import demand can also be expressed as an increasing function of national income. We write the import function as

$$M = M(Y) \text{ with } dM/dY > 0 \tag{25.3}$$

Since aggregate demand consists of demand for domestically-produced goods (C_d) and for imports, it follows that we may write the marginal propensity to consume as the sum of the *marginal propensity to consume domestically-produced goods* $(c_d = dC_d/dY)$ and the *marginal propensity to consume imports* $(m = dM/dY)$.

For convenience we shall assume that the consumption, savings and import functions are linear, so that each of the marginal propensities we have identified is independent of the level of income. A linear import function is shown in Figure 25.1.

Figure 25.1 shows that even at zero national income, something would be imported (by exporting part of the country's capital stock or by borrowing abroad). As the national income increases, so do imports. A country's average propensity to import is defined as the total imports divided by the total national income, i.e. M/Y. The average propensity to import varies greatly between countries. The United States, a large country well endowed with resources, has a relatively low dependence on foreign trade. Its average propensity to import is currently around 10 per cent, about the same value as in the early nineteenth century. However, at the end of that century it had fallen to 7 per cent, after the First World War it was 5 per cent, and it reached a low of approximately 3 per cent in the early 1960s. Another large country, the Soviet Union, also has a very low average propensity to import, between 0.02 and 0.03. India, which in

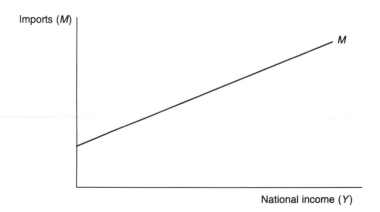

Figure 25.1   *A linear import function*

national income terms is not a large country, had a low average propensity to import for much of the period after the second World War. This low propensity to import seems to have been the result of an economic policy directed towards autarky, a conclusion that is supported by the increase in its average propensity to import to approximately 11.5% in 1993 following a period of trade liberalisation.

Smaller countries are usually more dependent on foreign trade and have a larger average propensity to import. Great Britain, for instance, has an average propensity to import of about 0.2 and Holland one of 0.5.

The marginal propensity to import measures how much of an increase in the national income is spent on imports. If imports increase by 10 when the national income increases by 100, the marginal propensity to import will be 0.1. If the marginal propensity to import is divided by the average propensity to import, we deduce the income elasticity of demand for imports. Expressed in algebraic terms this becomes $e_m = (dM/dY)/(M/Y)$. The income elasticity of imports is defined under the assumption that all other things are equal, for instance that there are no changes in prices. If the demand for imports increases by 5 per cent when the income increases by 10 per cent, the income elasticity of imports equals 0.5. If a country's average and marginal propensities to import are equal, its income elasticity of demand for imports is 1. This implies that as the country's income increases, a constant proportion of the increasing income is spent on imports, and the share of its national product which is traded is constant. If the marginal propensity to import is larger than its average propensity, this tends to increase the country's dependence on foreign trade, and if the opposite is the case, its foreign trade quota will fall.

This way of defining the propensities to import and the import elasticity should not lure the reader into thinking that these concepts are constants that do not change. A country's marginal propensity to import, for instance, is influenced by many economic factors and usually changes from year to year.

25.2 The determination of national income in a small open economy

The condition for national income equilibrium in a small open economy

We will now show how the national income is determined in an open economy. The difference between a closed and an open economy is that in the latter we have the possibility of foreign trade, i.e. of exports and imports. In an open economy we can write the national income identity as

$$Y = C_d + I_d + X \qquad (25.4)$$

where the left-hand side of the expression shows the total domestic supply (Y) and the right-hand side shows the three ways total output can be used, i.e. as consumption of domestically-produced goods (C_d), domestic investment (I_d), or exports (X). An alternative way of writing this, which allows us to identify the balance of trade directly, is to use the relationship between total consumption, consumption of domestically-produced goods and imports ($C = C_d + M$) and thus obtain

$$Y = C + I_d + (X - M) \qquad (25.5)$$

We shall make the familiar assumption that domestic investment is independent of the level of national income, or that it is *autonomous*. We shall also for the moment assume that exports are independent of the national income of the country we are considering (although, since they are the imports of other countries, they will be dependent on the national incomes of those countries). This assumption implies that we are dealing with a small economy: that is, changes in national income in this economy do not have any appreciable effect on the national income of other economies. We shall relax this assumption in the next section.

In a closed economy we know that for national income to be in equilibrium planned investment has to equal planned savings. This is often expressed as the requirement that the *injections* into national income (the autonomous expenditures, planned investment in this simple case) must be equal to the *leakages* from national income (planned savings). In an open economy exactly the same condition applies, but we have two injections (domestic investment and exports) and two leakages (savings and imports). The equilibrium condition may thus be written as

$$I_d = X = S + M \qquad (25.6)$$

We may rewrite (25.6) as

$$S - I_d = X - M \qquad (25.7)$$

which tells us that, in equilibrium, the difference between savings and domestic investment must be equal to the balance of trade. This allows us to employ a simple graphical technique to show the relationship between the equilibrium level of national income and the balance of trade, as in Figure 25.2.

The slope of the $S - I_d$ schedule is equal to the marginal propensity to save, while the slope of the $X - M$ schedule is given by the negative of the

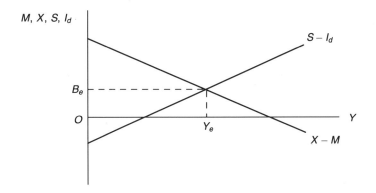

Figure 25.2   *National income and the balance of trade*

marginal propensity to import. The intersection of the two schedules determines the equilibrium level of national income, Y_e, and the corresponding balance of trade, B_e. In the example shown the country has a surplus in its balance of trade.

In Chapter 23 we saw that a country with a surplus on its current account is necessarily increasing its claims on foreigners (or reducing its liabilities to them). That is, it is investing abroad. Equally, a country with a deficit on its current account is increasing its (net) liabilities to foreigners. Ignoring for the moment the other items in the current account, this suggests that we may write

$$X - M = I_f \qquad\qquad (25.8)$$

where I_f is net foreign investment. We may then rewrite the national income equilibrium condition as

$$S = I = I_d + I_f \qquad\qquad (25.9)$$

That is, savings must be equal to total investment (I), which is in turn equal to the sum of domestic investment and foreign investment.

☐ National income multipliers in a small open economy

Totally differentiating equation (25.5) gives

$$dY = dC + dI_d + (dX - dM) \qquad\qquad (25.10)$$

Using the definitions of the marginal propensities to consume and to import we may write this as

$$dY = \frac{dC}{dY}dY + dI_d + (dX - \frac{dM}{dY}dY) = (c - m)dY + dI_d + dX \,(25.11)$$

We may then rearrange this expression to obtain

$$dY = \frac{1}{1 - c + m}(dI_d + dX) \tag{25.12}$$

The term $1/(1 - c + m)$ in (25.12) is the *multiplier* for a small open economy with no government intervention. It is more usual to use the fact that the marginal propensity to save, s, may be expressed as 1-c to write this multiplier as

$$k = \frac{1}{s + m} \tag{25.13}$$

Since $s + m = 1 - c_d$, and so is less than one, it follows that the multiplier is greater than one. That is, an increase in one or both of domestic investment and exports will lead to a greater increase in national income.

The multiplier in a small open economy works in much the same way as the multiplier in the familiar closed economy model. An increase in autonomous expenditure gives rise to an increase in income for those employed in the export and/or capital goods industries. They, in turn, spend more of their increased incomes. How much more they spend on domestic goods depends on two leakages: how much they save and how much they spend on imports. The savings do not create any new incomes. An increase in import spending does not create new incomes in the country itself, only in those foreign countries with which the first country trades.

It is now easy to see that the larger the marginal propensities to save and import, the smaller will be the value of the multiplier. If the marginal propensity to save is 0.2 and if the marginal propensity to import is 0.3, the value of the multiplier will be $1/(0.2 + 0.3) = 2$, i.e. an autonomous increase in exports of 100 will lead to an increase in the national income of 200.

Although a given change in domestic investment or in exports would have the same effect on the national income, they have different implications for the balance of trade. Figure 25.3 shows the effects of an increase in domestic investment of dI_d. The increase in domestic investment shifts the savings–investment schedule downwards, from $S - I_d$ to $S - (I_d + dI_d)$. National income then increases by $dI_d/(s + m)$. This increase in national income must in turn lead to an increase in imports of m times the increase in national income: that is, imports increase by $m.dI_d/(2 + m)$. In the example shown in Figure 25.3 this reduces the surplus on the balance of trade. Had the balance of trade been in deficit then the deficit would have been increased by that amount. Note

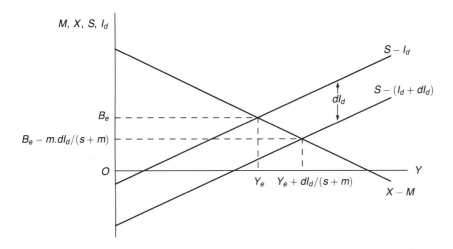

Figure 25.3 *The effects of an increase in domestic investment on national income and the balance of trade*

that the change in the balance of trade is less than the initial change in domestic investment: some of the increased national income will be spent on consuming domestic goods, and some will be saved.

Suppose now that exports had increased by dX, due perhaps to an increase in domestic investment in another country. This has an immediate effect on the balance of trade, increasing the surplus if there is one, or reducing the deficit. The increase in exports must however lead to an increase in national income of $dX/(s+m)$, and some of this will spill over into an increase in imports of $m.dX/(s+m)$. Figure 25.4 shows this for the case where there is an initial balance of trade surplus.

The final change in the balance of trade is

$$dB = dX - \frac{m}{s+m}dX = \frac{s}{s+m}dX \qquad (25.14)$$

This is an interesting result. First, it tells us that the initial improvement in the balance of trade due to the increase in exports is offset by a subsequent increase in imports. Second, the offsetting increase in imports must be less than the initial increase in exports, so that there will still be a net improvement in the balance of trade. The national income adjustment mechanism thus has a limited effect in maintaining equilibrium in the balance of trade. That is, if a country starts with a zero trade balance and then experiences an increase in exports, the final outcome will be a balance of trade surplus. If balance of trade equilibrium is to be restored then some other mechanism must come into play. This may be 'automatic', perhaps

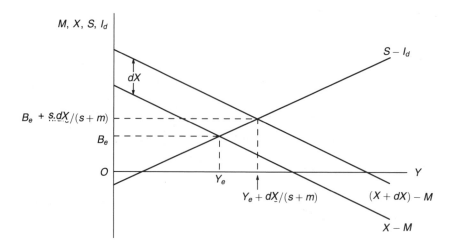

Figure 25.4   *The effects of an increase in exports on national income and the balance of trade*

through changes in domestic and/or foreign prices or the exchange rate, or may result from government action.

Introducing government expenditure and taxation

As we know from the closed economy model, the government can affect the level of national income by changing its expenditure and its taxation. Since imports are dependent on national income, the government can also use such fiscal policy to affect the balance of trade. The government may be introduced into the model in various ways. We shall use a relatively simple formulation, with government expenditure (G) assumed to be determined independently of national income and to be made only on domestically-produced goods, and the only form of taxation being a simple proportional income tax: that is

$$T = tY \text{ with } t < 1 \tag{25.15}$$

Expenditure on domestic and imported goods and services by consumers is now defined in terms of the disposable (post-tax) national income, $(1 - t)Y$, as are savings. The definitions of the various marginal propensities are changed accordingly. Assuming that all functions are linear, the consumption, import and savings functions may be written as:

$$C = C_a + c(1 - t)Y \tag{25.16}$$

$$M = M_a + m(1 - t)Y \tag{25.17}$$

and

$$S = S_a + s(1 - t)Y \tag{25.18}$$

where C_a, M_a and S_a are the 'autonomous' elements of consumption and import expenditure, and $c + s = 1$.

The condition for national income equilibrium ('injections = leakages') must now be written as

$$I_d + X + G = S + M + T \tag{25.19}$$

Substituting for S, M and T from the preceding equations and totally differentiating (while assuming that the tax rate is fixed) then gives

$$dI_d + dX + dG = s(1 - t)dY + m(1 - t)dY + tdY \tag{25.20}$$

With some algebraic manipulation this may be written as

$$dY = \frac{1}{(s + m)(1 - t) + t}(dI_d + dX + dG) \tag{25.21}$$

so that the multiplier is now

$$k = \frac{1}{(s + m)(1 - t) + t} \tag{25.22}$$

Note that increasing the rate of tax leads to a decrease in the multiplier.

We may modify the previous diagrams to incorporate the role of the government by redefining the $S - Id$ schedule to include government expenditure and taxation. The slope of the resultant $(S - I_d) + (T - G)$ schedule is now $s(1 - t) + t = s + (1 - s)t$. The $X - M$ schedule has slope $-m(1 - t)$. Figure 25.5 shows the modified diagram, in this case drawn so that at the equilibrium national income, Y_e, the country has a balance of trade deficit of B_e.

The government has two fiscal policy instruments that it may use to reduce the balance of trade deficit shown in Figure 25.5: it may reduce its expenditure, and it may increase the tax rate. Figure 25.6 shows the effects of reducing government expenditure. The initial equilibrium (at income level Y_e and balance of trade deficit of B_e) is given by the intersection of $X - M$ with $(S - I_d) + (T - G)$. Reducing government expenditure shifts the $(S - I_d) + (T - G)$ schedule upwards, and so the trade account can be brought into balance by reducing government expenditure to G^*. This has been achieved by reducing national income from Y_e to Y_e^*.

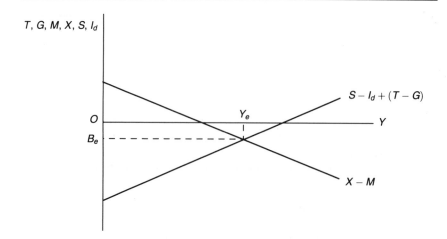

Figure 25.5　*Including the government in the small open economy model*

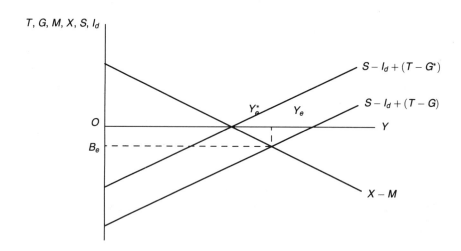

Figure 25.6　*The effects of reducing government expenditure*

The second option, increasing the tax rate, is rather more complicated, since it affects both schedules. The diagrammatic analysis is shown in Figure 25.7, where once again the initial equilibrium national income is Y_e and there is a balance of trade deficit of B_e. First, increasing the tax rate will change the slope of the $(S - I_d) + (T - G)$ schedule, both through its direct effect on the T element and because it reduces the marginal propensity to save from pre-tax income. The new schedule is shown in Figure 25.7 as $(S^* - I_d) + (T^* - G)$.

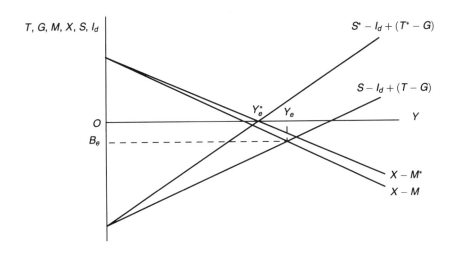

Figure 25.7 *The effects of increasing the tax rate*

Second, increasing the tax rate will reduce the slope of the $X - M$ schedule since it will reduce the marginal propensity to import out of pre-tax income. The new schedule is shown as $X - M^*$ in Figure 25.7. The tax rate has been set to bring about balance in the trade account, and has resulted in a reduction in national income to Y_e^* (which will not in general be the same value as the national income given by the expenditure reduction in the earlier example).

25.3 The determination of national income in a large open economy

In some cases the assumption that we can ignore the effects of a change in imports on the national income of other countries is obviously invalid, the United States being the obvious example. An increase in US national income, and hence of its imports, will have a substantial effect on the exports of its trading partners, and hence on their national incomes. The increase in their incomes will however then increase their imports, some of which will be supplied by the United States, and US national income will then rise again. This linkage between countries is known as the *repercussion effect*. In order to analyse the determination of national income in such a large economy we must take these repercussion effects into account, which means that we must consider how national income equilibrium may be obtained *simultaneously* in all the countries concerned.

We shall do this in the context of a two-country world, the countries being A and B. We shall simplify matters by ignoring the role of governments and by assuming that the consumption and import schedules are linear. The link between the two countries is that A's imports are B's exports, and *vice versa*. Using subscripts to identify the two countries, we may write their national income identities as

$$Y_i = C_i + I_i + X_i - M_i \text{ for } i = A, B \tag{25.23}$$

and their consumption and import schedules as

$$C_i = \bar{C}_i + c_i Y_i \text{ for } i = A, B \tag{25.24}$$

and

$$M_i = \bar{M}_i + m_i Y_i \text{ for } i = A, B \tag{25.25}$$

where $\bar{C}_i$ and $\bar{M}_i$ are the autonomous elements of consumption and imports for country j.

Remembering that $X_A = M_B$ we may substitute from (25.24) and (25.25) into (25.23) to obtain the following relationship for country A:

$$Y_A = C_A + I_A + M_B - M_A$$
$$= \bar{C}_A + c_A Y_A + I_A + \bar{M}_B + m_B Y_B - \bar{M}_A - m_A Y_A$$

which may be rearranged to give

$$Y_A = \frac{1}{1 - c_A + m_A}(\bar{C}_A + I_A + \bar{M}_B - \bar{M}_A) + \frac{m_B}{1 - c_A + m_A} Y_B$$

or, since $s_A = 1 - c_A$,

$$Y_A = \frac{1}{s_A + m_A}(\bar{C}_A + I_A + \bar{M}_B - \bar{M}_A) + \frac{m_B}{s_A + m_A} Y_B \tag{25.26}$$

Similarly we may obtain for country B the relationship

$$Y_B = \frac{1}{s_B + m_B}(\bar{C}_B + I_B + \bar{M}_A - \bar{M}_B) + \frac{m_A}{s_B + m_B} Y_A \tag{25.27}$$

The interdependence of the national incomes of the two countries is thus quite clear.

We may show the interaction between the two diagrammatically. In Figure 25.8 the line labelled AA represents the relationship between A's national income and B's national income given by equation (25.26). The intercept on the Y_A axis is given by the first term on the right-hand side of

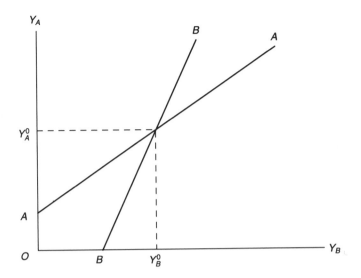

Figure 25.8 *Simultaneous national income equilibrium for two large countries*

(25.26), and the slope by the coefficient of Y_B in that equation, which must be positive. Line BB represents the relationship in equation (25.27). The first term in (25.27) specifies the intercept of BB with the Y_B axis, and the slope is given by the inverse of the coefficient on Y_A. It is reasonably easy to show that BB must be steeper than AA, so that the two lines will intersect at positive national incomes in both countries.

We may also use this diagrammatic technique to examine the effects of an increase in autonomous expenditure in one of the countries, as in Figure 25.9. Suppose that there is an increase in domestic investment in A. This will shift the AA line upwards, to $A'A'$, and the equilibrium national incomes will increase in both countries, from Y_A^0 to Y_A^1 in A and from Y_B^0 to Y_B^1 in B. The increase in national income will be larger in A since it gains from both the direct effect of the increase in domestic investment and from the feedback effect from the subsequent increase in B's national income, whereas B gains only from the indirect effect via A's increased imports.

The multipliers for a change in autonomous expenditure in country A on the national incomes of A and B may be obtained by solving equations (25.26) and (25.27) for Y_A and Y_B. Letting $\bar{C}_A + I_A - \bar{M}_A = \bar{Z}_A$ and $\bar{C}_B + I_B - \bar{M}_B = \bar{Z}_B$, we may write Y_A as

$$Y_A = \cfrac{1}{s_A + \cfrac{m_A s_B}{s_B + m_B}} (\bar{Z}_A + \bar{M}_B) + \cfrac{1}{s_A + \cfrac{s_B(s_A + m_A)}{m_B}} (\bar{Z}_B + \bar{M}_A) \quad (25.28)$$

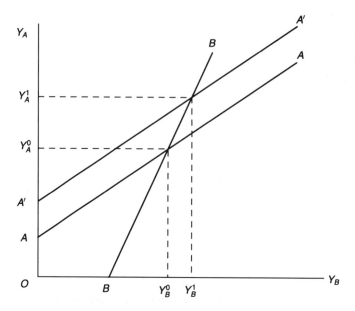

Figure 25.9   *The effects on national incomes of an increase in autonomous expenditure for two large countries*

The multiplier for A's national income for an increase in autonomous expenditure in A or for an increase in the autonomous component of B's imports (A's exports) is thus

$$k_A = \frac{1}{s_A + \dfrac{m_A s_B}{s_B + m_B}} \tag{25.29}$$

which is necessarily greater than would be the case if A were a small country with the same marginal propensities to save and to import. The repercussion effect increases the impact of a change in autonomous expenditure in A because some of the income that 'leaks abroad' through A's imports is returned through an increase in its exports. The multiplier for A's national income for an increase in autonomous expenditure in B or for an increase in A's autonomous imports is

$$k_A^* = \frac{1}{s_A + \dfrac{s_B(s_A + m_A)}{m_B}} \tag{25.30}$$

This is smaller than k_A, reflecting the fact that increases in autonomous expenditure in B or in A's autonomous imports have no direct effect on A's income.

25.4 The international transmission of disturbances

The preceding analyses of the link between national income and the balance of trade suggests that it provides a mechanism for the transmission of disturbances between countries. In the small-country case a country will be affected by changes in its trading partners that alter the demand for its exports, but will not transmit its own disturbances to its trading partners. In the large-country case a country may both 'export' its own disturbances and 'import' those from other countries. However, as we shall see, this transmission effect depends on the maintenance of a fixed exchange-rate regime. We shall examine this case now, using some empirical evidence, and then consider the consequences of a floating exchange-rate regime.

Transmission under fixed exchange rates: some empirical evidence

The theoretical argument for the transmission of an economic disturbance, or of a policy change, from one country to another has been outlined in the preceding sections. The degree to which a country will react to a given change in another country will depend on its size, its 'openness' (how important trade is relative to its national income) and to the multiplier (which depends on its marginal propensity to save and the marginal tax rate as well as its marginal propensity to import). The propensity for a country to transmit its own disturbances or policy changes depends on its size relative to other countries as well as its openness and its multiplier.

In 1979 the OECD published the results of some simulation work using the LINK model, which brought together models of 23 OECD members and 8 non-OECD 'regions', linking those models through a world trade model. The economic theory underlying the project is essentially that described earlier. Among their results are estimates of national income multipliers (including repercussion effects) and of the capacities of countries to affect the economies of others by a fiscal expansion equal to 1 per cent of the country's GNP. We shall concentrate on the results for a small group of 'large' countries: the United States, Japan, France, West Germany and the United Kingdom.

The United States is very large (with a GNP not much less than the sum of the GNPs of the other four countries) and has a relatively large domestic multiplier of 1.47. The OECD estimates suggested that a fiscal expansion in the United States would, despite the United States' relatively low marginal propensity to import, lead to a significant worsening of its balance of trade, and through that would raise the GNPs of the OECD countries as a whole by about 0.74 per cent.

Japan, which is large (its GNP then was about 45 per cent of US GNP), also has a low marginal propensity to import but a multiplier of about 1.26. An expansion in Japan has an expansionary effect on the OECD which is markedly less than that of the Unied States, reflecting both its smaller size and its lower multiplier, of some 0.21 per cent.

West Germany, with a GNP about two-thirds of Japan's, is much more open and, partly because of that, has a lower multiplier. Its openness means however that, despite its smaller size and lower multiplier, the effects of an expansion in Germany has a rather greater effect on the GNP of the OECD (0.23 per cent) than is the case with Japan.

France, smaller still in terms of its GNP but with a similar degree of openness, will have a slightly lower effect on the rest of the OECD. The United Kingdom, yet smaller but more open, has a relatively small impact on other OECD members.

☐ *Transmission under floating exchange rates*

If the exchange rate is perfectly flexible (i.e. there is no government intervention) then in the context of our present simple model, it will adjust to maintain balance of trade equilibrium (see the discussion in Chapter 24). This has important implications for the multiplier, the transmission of disturbances between countries, and for government policy.

Suppose for example that there is an autonomous increase in domestic investment in a small country of dI_d , which therefore shifts the $S - I_d$ schedule downwards. The increase in national income will lead to an increase in imports, and so a deficit on the balance of trade (the country will originally have been in balance on its trade account). This deficit will however cause a depreciation of the exchange rate, which will increase exports and export revenue and decrease imports and the import bill (the Marshall–Lerner condition must be satisfied for a small country). This will shift the $X - M$ schedule upwards until it intersects the new $S - I_d$ schedule at a zero trade balance.

This is shown in Figure 25.10. The initial equilibrium is at Y_e^0, given by the intersection of $S - I_d$ and $X - M$. The increase in domestic investment then shifts the savings-investment schedule down to $S - (I_d + dI_d)$. If exchange rates were fixed then the new equilibrium would be at an income of Y_e^1, and there would be a balance of trade deficit. However, with floating exchange rates imports fall and exports increase, and the new equilibrium is found at Y_e^2, with a zero balance of trade. Under floating exchange rates the $X - M$ schedule is entirely passive: it shifts to that

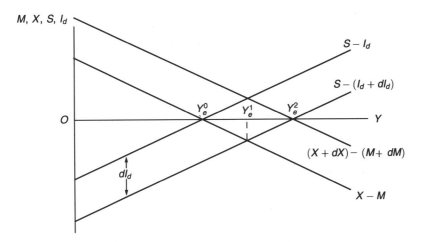

Figure 25.10 *The effect of an increase in investment when the exchange rate is floating*

extent necessary to bring about national income equilibrium and a zero trade balance.

What is also apparent from Figure 25.10 is that the increase in national income brought about by an increase in domestic investment is greater under floating exchange rates than under fixed exchange rates. That is, the multiplier is larger. In fact, we may show that the multiplier for a small open economy with a floating exchange rate is the same as that for a closed economy.

We have argued that the exchange rate will adjust until there is a zero trade balance. It follows therefore that in the final equilibrium, since we started from balanced trade, we must have an increase in exports that is equal to the net increase in imports (the initial increase in imports less any reduction due to the exchange rate adjustment). That is, we must have $dX = dM$. But we also know from equation (25.10) that

$$dY = dC + dI_d + (dX - dM)$$

and substituting $dX = dM$ in this gives

$$dY = dC + dI_d = cdY + dI_d$$

so that

$$dY = \frac{1}{1 - c} dI_d$$

and the multiplier is $1/(1 - c)$ or $1/s$. This is of course the closed economy multiplier. We may conclude that a system of floating exchange rates reproduces the effects of a closed economy when there is a change in domestic autonomous expenditure.

Floating exchange rates also modify the effects of changes in other economies on the economy we are considering. Suppose that there is an expansion in another country that leads to an increase in exports of our country. This may lead initially to an increase in national income and so to an increase in imports, which will partially offset the increased exports (see section 25.2). However, the net trade surplus will now lead to an appreciation of the exchange rate, which will both reduce exports and further increase imports. The appreciation will continue until trade is balanced. Since the schedule has not moved, the final equilibrium must be at the same level of national income as the original equilibrium. Floating exchange rates effectively insulate the economy against external disturbances.

These results suggest one reason why a government may prefer to let its exchange rate float rather than pegging it against other currencies. There are however other aspects to the choice of exchange rate regime, and we shall examine the question in more detail in Chapter 30, after we have discussed other theories of exchange-rate determination.

25.5 An initial look at internal and external balance

We have seen that when exchange rates are fixed it is possible that there may be an internal equilibrium, i.e. that the national income may be in equilibrium, but that there is no external equilibrium, i.e. that there is no equilibrium in the balance of trade (or the balance of payments if we assume the other elements in the balance of payments do not change).

First we must understand clearly what is meant by 'equilibrium' in the national income. In a closed economy the condition for national income equilibrium is that planned saving (*ex ante* savings) equal planned investment (*ex ante* investment). This being the case, consumers will be able to carry out their plans to consume and save and producers will be able to fulfil their plans regarding production of consumer and investment goods. Production of consumer goods will equal their consumption, and savings and investment will be equal. Then there will be no change in the national income from its given equilibrium value.

In an open economy the equilibrium condition has to be reformulated so that it takes into account the possibility of a country not having to rely only on domestic savings, since foreigners may provide part of the total savings by their exporting capital. In the same way, a country may invest both at home and abroad by exporting capital.

It is often said that the two main aims of a country's economic policy are to maintain full employment and an external balance. We shall return to the question of the aims and means in economic policy later. For the time being, we must only observe that equilibrium in a country's national income, according to the Keynesian definition just given, does not necessarily imply that the economy is fully employed. This definition says only that total planned demand equals total planned production. This equilibrium need not be at the full employment level of national income.

We must also be careful in the way we use the terms inflationary and deflationary pressure. By inflationary pressure in the economy, we mean simply that planned total demand for domestic goods is larger than planned total production of those goods. This does not necessarily imply rising prices, but it will, in many instances, lead to a rising price level. By deflationary pressure in the economy, we mean, analogously, that total production is larger than total demand.

Let us first assume that during the previous period of time a country achieved internal balance at a full-employment level and that the balance of payments was in equilibrium. We now get an increase in total demand. There can be many causes for such an increase. Perhaps consumers wish to save less and consume more from a given income. Or it can be a change in a policy variable, for instance a decrease in interest rates, which encourages investment. Whatever the reason, there will be an inflationary pressure in the economy. In the open economy, such pressure may lead to rising prices or to a deficit in the balance of payments; it can, of course, lead to both. Consumers will consume more than before, and producers will continue to invest as much as they used to. As the economy, however, is already at full employment, there is no possibility of increasing domestic production in the short run. Exports will not change, but imports will increase to satisfy the increase in demand for consumer goods. At the end of the period, the country will find that it has a deficit in its balance of payments and that, in fact, a part of its domestic investment has been financed out of capital imports.

It is of no consequence for this process how the internal production pattern has been influenced – how the composition of goods has been affected. It may be that exports and home production of investment goods remain unchanged, but that imports increase. Or perhaps production of exports falls, and factors of production from this sector are drawn into domestic sectors to meet the increase in demand for consumer goods. Whichever way the production pattern changes under inflationary pressure, the main thing for us to observe is the fact that domestic investment is larger than domestic savings and that imports are larger than exports.

It is important to realise that an increase in the national income, generated on the demand side in the way just described, often leads to a deficit in the balance of payments. Inflationary pressure within the economy does not necessarily lead to rising prices but instead gives rise to a deficit in the balance of payments, which has to be covered by an unforeseen accommodating inflow of capital. This accommodating capital inflow can then be seen as a warning signal. This case is a classic example taken from Keynesian analysis. The policy implications in this case are also quite clear, but we shall return to a fuller discussion of these in Chapters 28 and 29.

Let us now assume instead that, starting from an equilibrium with full employment, a decrease in exports occurs. This produces a contractionary effect on the national income which, through the multiplier effect, will be larger than the original decrease in exports. Imports will also fall as national income falls, but the decrease in imports will be smaller than the decrease in exports, so the country will simultaneously fall into a situation of unemployment and a deficit in balance of payments.

This is a tricky situation to escape from. An inflationary policy can return the country to full employment but only at the cost of a deterioration in the deficit in the balance of payments. A simple Keynesian policy, which works by deflating or inflating the national income, cannot alone cope with this situation. (This problem will be discussed at length in Chapters 28 and 29.)

A simpler situation is one in which, again starting from equilibrium with full employment, the country receives an autonomous upward impetus in its savings schedule. As the consumers wish to save more and consume less, deflationary pressure on national income is evolved. Income falls, resulting in some unemployment. As national income falls, so does the demand for imports, but there is no reason to expect a change in exports. Demand for exports depends primarily on incomes abroad, and these, at least to start with, have not changed. At the same time, exporters at home will be, if anything, in a better competitive position than before, as unemployment will create a downward pressure on wages, so that exporters obtain their factors of production more cheaply than previously. The country, therefore, will have a surplus in its balance of payments and be put into a situation where unemployment is combined with a favourable balance of payments.

This situation is comparatively simple to deal with. An inflationary policy will lead the country back toward equilibrium in national income at the full-employment level. This will lead to an increase in demand for imports at an unchanged level of exports, but as the country has a surplus in its balance of payments, there may be little cause for concern.

We have now set out several cases of how changes in the national income affect the balance of payments. There is an intimate connection between income changes and the balance of payments, and any change in the national income will have some effect on it. To sum up, we can say that in general an inflationary change in national income arising from a domestic source will have a negative effect on the balance of payments, and a similar deflationary change in national income will have a favourable effect on the balance of payments. If however the source of the inflationary or deflationary pressure lies in the trade sector then we observe a different pattern of responses. An autonomous decrease in exports will have both a deflationary effect on the national income and lead to a deficit in the balance of payments. Analogously, a shift in consumption away from imports to domestically produced goods will have both an inflationary effect on the national income and lead to a surplus in the balance of payments.

The policy implications of income and balance-of-payments changes will be discussed more fully in Chapter 29, where we will deal with the question of how to achieve both internal and external equilibrium.

■ *Chapter 26* ■

The Capital Account

■ 26.1 Introduction

So far we have concentrated either on the current account in the balance of payments, or on one of its major components, the balance of trade. If there were no capital flows then a theory of the current account would be a theory of the balance of payments. There have been periods in which there has been little capital mobility, though for different reasons. There was no international capital market to speak of in the 1930s, for example, since the volatility of exchange rates dominated any feasible differences in interest rates between countries. When the Bretton Woods system was agreed it was decided to create an international institution (the World Bank) that would facilitate international capital movements, since it was believed that the private capital market would not re-emerge. Moreover, in the immediate post-war period many countries imposed controls on capital movements. This lack of capital mobility may explain why little attention was given to modelling international capital flows in that period, and why the models developed thereafter were initially very simple.

However the international market in private capital did indeed re-emerge. The most casual examination of recent balance-of-payments accounts shows that capital movements through private markets are the dominant item. A theory of the modern balance of payments must therefore embody a theory of international capital movements, and this has led to a greater concentration on developing theories of capital movements in recent years.

We shall distinguish three such theories. They have in common an emphasis on the role of interest rate differentials between countries in explaining capital movements, but differ in other important respects. The oldest is a *flow theory*, in which a given interest rate differential will, if maintained and if nothing else changes, result in a continuous flow of capital from one country to the other. The second is a *stock theory*, in which a change in the interest rate differential will lead to an adjustment in portfolios of assets; that differential will, if maintained and *ceteris paribus*, lead to a flow of capital as a new stock equilibrium is established, but not to a continuous flow of capital. The third, the *monetary approach*, argues that we must explain the balance of payments as a whole, rather than attempting to construct separate models of its components, and concentrates on the factors that may cause a change in foreign currency reserves (and so in the money supply).

We shall discuss each of these in turn in this chapter, but will postpone discussion of the policy implications of the different approaches until Chapters 27 and 28.

■ 26.2 A flow theory of capital movements

The origins of flow theories may be traced back to the experience of the gold standard, when an increase in the domestic interest rate was seen to stimulate an inflow of gold.[1] The modern flow theory argues that in a two-country world, other things being equal (including the exchange rate), we may write the change in country A's stock of foreign liabilities (i.e. liabilities to country B) as

$$\dot{F}_A = I_A + f_A(r_A, r_B) \tag{26.1}$$

where F_A is the stock of liabilities, $\dot{F}_A$ is the change in that stock (i.e. a capital flow), r_A and r_B are the interest rates in countries A and B respectively, and I_A is that component of the capital flow that is independent of interest rates. It is assumed that $\partial f_A/\partial r_A > 0$ and $\partial f_A/\partial r_B < 0$. That is, an increase in the domestic interest rate relative to the foreign interest rate or a decrease in the foreign interest rate relative to the domestic one, will increase an inflow of foreign capital or decrease an outflow. A linear representation of the flow model for country A is shown in Figure 26.1.

The line f_A is drawn on the assumption of a given interest rate in country B. If the interest rate in country A is r_1 then there will be an inflow of capital (an increase in A's foreign liabilities) of f_1. If the interest rate in A is reduced to r_2 then there will be a capital outflow (a decrease in A's foreign liabilities) equal to f_2. An increase in B's interest rate will shift the schedule upwards, say to f_A^*. In that event the original country A interest rate r_1 will lead to a capital outflow of f_3.

Note that at the original country B interest rate, which defines the capital movement schedule as f_A, an interest rate of r_1 in country A will lead to a *continual* inflow of f_1 per period.

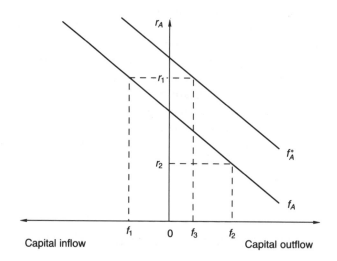

Figure 26.1   *A flow model of international capital movements*

■ 26.3 A stock theory of the capital account

Stock theories of international capital movements are based on *portfolio theory* – that is, the theory of how rational individuals would distribute their wealth between different assets in order to maximise their utility. Central to this theory is the recognition that the return to an asset is subject to risk, and that asset holders will be influenced by both the *expected return* to an asset and the *uncertainty of the actual return*. We shall not study such theories in detail, our prime concern being to demonstrate that they have very different implications for macroeconomic policy.[2]

A simple way of analysing the choice of the portfolio mix is the so-called 'mean–variance' approach. The expected return to an asset is defined as the statistical expectation of the actual return. That is, if the return is y and the distribution function of the return is $g(y)$ then the expected return μ is defined by

$$\mu = E[y] = \int_{-\infty}^{\infty} y g(y) dy \qquad (26.2)$$

The riskiness of the yield is measured by its variance, σ_y^2, which is defined by

$$\sigma^2 = \int_{-\infty}^{\infty} (y - \mu)^2 g(y) \, dy \qquad (26.3)$$

with the obvious interpretation that the higher is the variance of the yield, the more risky is the asset. Money has zero return and hence no yield risk (zero yield variance).

Suppose now that two assets are available, money and an interest-bearing bond costing £1, with expected return μ_1, and variance σ_1^2. An individual with a given amount of wealth, W, may distribute it between money and the asset, say with a proportion π held in the asset and the remainder in money. The expected return from this portfolio is then

$$\mu(\pi) = \pi W \mu_1 + (1 - \pi) W 0 = \pi W \mu_1 \tag{26.4}$$

and the variance of that return (its riskiness) is

$$\sigma^2(\pi) = \pi^2 W^2 \sigma_1^2 + (1 - \pi)^2 W^2 0 = \pi^2 W^2 \sigma_1^2 \tag{26.5}$$

It is apparent from equation (26.4) that the greater the proportion of the investor's wealth that is held in the interest-bearing asset, the higher is his expected return. Equation (26.5) however shows that the riskiness of his return also increases as he holds more of his wealth in the asset rather than as money.

The set of expected returns and their associated variances is shown by the portfolio-possibility curve ON in Figure 26.2. If the investor holds all his wealth in money ($\pi = 0$) then he earns no return, with no risk, and so will be at point O. If he holds all his wealth in the asset ($\pi = 1$) then he will be at point N. If he holds half his wealth in money and half in the asset then he will be at point H.

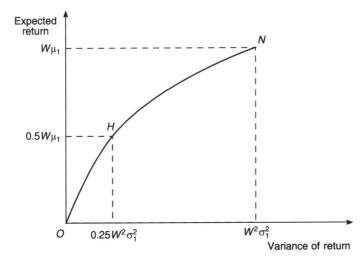

Figure 26.2 *Possible combinations of expected return and riskiness*

In order to determine which combination of the two assets an investor will choose to hold we must introduce his preferences, which we do in terms of an indifference map. Each curve in that map shows those combinations of expected yield and yield variance between which the investor is indifferent.

We usually assume that investors are risk-averse yield-maximisers: that is, if given the choice between two assets with the same expected yield then they will choose the asset with the lower risk (lower yield variance), and with a choice between two assets with the same risk they will choose the one with the higher expected yield. If such is the case then the investor's indifference curves must be positively sloped since a higher yield will trade-off against a higher variance. A pair of such indifference curve is shown in Figure 26.3. The investor's welfare increases as he moves from T_0 to T_1.

Combining the portfolio-possibility curve with the investor's indifference map then allows us to determine his preferred portfolio. Figure 26.4 shows the possibility curve, ON, and the indifference curve, T_M, that is tangential to ON at point M. T_M is the highest indifference curve that the investor can achieve given the characteristics of the asset (which specify ON). The investor will choose to put a proportion p_M of his wealth in the interest-bearing asset.

Figure 26.4 also shows the effect on the portfolio of a reduction in the expected yield of the interest-bearing asset (but without a change in the variance of that yield). What we know must happen is that the portfolio-possibility curve will move down, from ON to ON^*. What is less evident is whether the proportion of the investor's wealth held in the interest-bearing asset will increase or decrease. As it happens, we may show that, under a

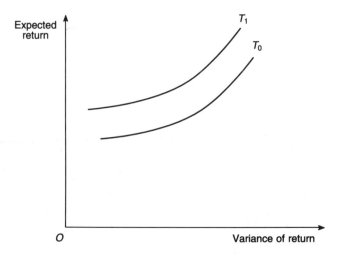

Figure 26.3   *Risk-averse preferences*

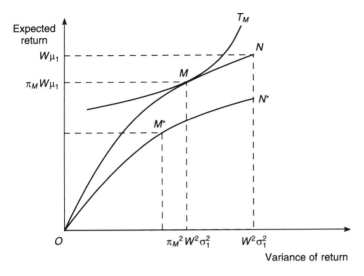

Figure 26.4 *The optimum portfolio*

reasonably common assumption, it must decrease (as at point M^* – the appropriate indifference curve is not shown).[3]

What we have just described is a particular case, since one of the assets (money) has a zero yield and is risk-free. The general case involves many assets, all of which (except money) offer a yield and varying degrees of risk. In such a case the rational investor will *spread his risk* by holding a range of assets. We shall not go into the general case in detail, but we can illustrate the basic principle of risk spreading (or *portfolio diversification*) by considering a very simple case.

Suppose that two interest-bearing assets are available, each with the same expected yield ($\mu_1 = \mu_2 = \mu$) but with different yield variances. Assume that asset 1 is less risky than asset 2: i.e. $\sigma_1^2 < \sigma_2^2$, and that the correlation between the yields offered by the two assets is ρ. Let the proportion of his wealth that an investor holds in asset 1 be π, and for simplicity assume that his total wealth is 1. Since the two assets have the same expected yield, the investor will enjoy that expected yield no matter what the value of π:

$$E[\mu(\pi)] = E[\pi\mu_1 + (1-\pi)\mu_2] = \pi\mu + (1-\pi)\mu = \mu \qquad (26.6)$$

The variability of his total yield however will vary with π and with the correlation between the two individual yields. Applying the standard expectations results gives:

$$\sigma^2(\pi) = \pi^2\sigma_1^2 + (1-\pi)^2\sigma_2^2 + 2\pi(1-\pi)\rho\sigma_1\sigma_2 \qquad (26.7)$$

This is a complicated expression, but we may gain some insight by considering a few special cases.

First, suppose that $\rho = 0$, so that (26.7) reduces to

$$\sigma^2(\pi) = \pi^2 \sigma_1^2 + (1 - \pi)^2 \sigma_2^2 \qquad (26.8)$$

In this case $\sigma^2(\pi)$ must always be less than $\sigma_1{}^2$ (the variance of the less-risky asset) since

$$\sigma_1^2 - \sigma^2(\pi) = (1 - \pi^2)\sigma_1^2 + (1 - \pi)^2 \sigma_2^2$$

and this must be greater than zero since π is less than one. That is, if the yields of the two assets are uncorrelated then any combination of the two assets gives a lower risk than the least-risky single asset.

Second, inspection of (26.7) shows that if ρ is negative then $\sigma(\pi)$ must be lower than when $\rho = 0$. That is, if the yields are negatively correlated then the gain from diversifying the portfolio is even greater. Indeed, in the (extremely unlikely) case where there is perfect negative correlation ($\rho = -1$), the investor can eliminate his risk entirely by setting $\pi = \sigma_2/(\sigma_1 + \sigma_2)$. In this case he would prefer to hold this combination of assets rather than money, since money has zero yield.

Third, (26.7) shows that if ρ is positive then the gain in risk reduction from diversification is reduced. We may show that the investor will choose to put all his wealth into the lower-risk asset if the correlation between the yields of the two assets is greater than $2\sigma_1/\sigma_2$.[4] This is only possible if the variance of the higher-risk asset is at least four times that of the lower-risk asset.

These results may be extended to cases where there are more than two assets. In general an investor will diversify his portfolio over some of the available assets. This conclusion is not significantly modified if we allow the expected yields on assets to vary – the general result is essentially a combination of the analysis of the money and risky asset choice considered earlier and the problem considered above.

There are five general propositions in portfolio analysis, simple examples of which we have just deduced. First, investors will diversify across assets, including money. Second, an increase in the expected yield of an asset will, *ceteris paribus*, increase the stock of that asset held by investors, while an increase in its riskiness (yield variance) will, *ceteris paribus*, have the opposite effect. Third, the less correlated are the yields of different assets the greater are the gains to be made from holding a mix of assets. Fourth, an increase in wealth will lead to an increase in the stock of all assets held by an investor, although the composition may change. Fifth, an appropriate combination of two assets may, depending on the correlation between their yields among other things be superior to a third (have the same yield but smaller variance, or same variance but greater yield), in which case the third asset will not appear in the portfolio.

These results have important implications for the analysis of the capital account. In general, we might expect that there will be a lower correlation between the yields of country *A* assets and country *B* assets than between the yields of assets within any one country. This suggests that we might expect investors to hold assets from both countries. Changes in yields in one country will then lead to an adjustment of portfolios in both countries, so that foreign assets and liabilities will change. In an international setting however there may be another source of risk, that the exchange rate will change. We shall discuss first the case where there is no exchange-rate risk, since this is a simple application of the models just discussed.

☐ *A stock model with fixed exchange rates*

If the exchange rate is fixed (or is pegged with no possibility of a change in the par value) the only sources of risk are in the yields of assets. In such circumstances, what will be the effect of a general increase in interest rates in country *B*?

Suppose that investors in both countries are initially in equilibrium, holding portfolios of assets from both *A* and *B* (e.g. bonds issued by the governments in both countries). Assuming that the investors do not think the riskiness of country *B* bonds has increased, they will adjust their portfolios, reducing their holdings of money and of country *A* bonds and increasing their holdings of country *B* bonds. The price of country *A* bonds will fall, so increasing their yields and increasing the incentive to purchase them, while the price of country *B* bonds will rise, with the opposite effect. In the final equilibrium however investors will hold a higher proportion of their wealth in country *B* bonds than before, and a lower proportion in country *A* bonds.

The increase in *B*'s interest rate has led to a change in the pattern of asset-holding. Thus there will be a 'once-and-for-all' capital flow from *A* to *B*. The capital flow may be spread out over time, since adjustment in portfolios need not of course be instantaneous, but once the adjustment is completed the capital flow will cease.

☐ *A stock model with floating exchange rates*

Under floating exchange rates an additional element of uncertainty is introduced. To gain some insight into the consequences of this we shall use another very simple model. Suppose that there are two assets, one issued by *A*'s government and denominated in *A*'s currency (the £), the other issued by B's government and denominated in B's currency (the $). Suppose also that the interest rates on these bonds are known and fixed (their variances are both zero), so that investors face no uncertainty about yields in the currency in which the bond in denominated. The only risk facing a country A investor considering holding some of his wealth in country B bonds is thus that the exchange rate will change, so that he is uncertain how many £s he will receive for the given $ yield on a country B bond. We shall again assume, for simplicity, that the investor's wealth is equal to £1.

Suppose the country A investor puts a proportion π of his wealth into country B bonds at the prevailing exchange rate of £e = $1, thus buying B bonds to the value of (π /e). By the end of the year those bonds will be worth $(\pi /e)(1 + y_B)$, where y_B is the yield on the bonds. He now sells the bonds and converts their $ value into £s at the new exchange rate of £$e - \Delta e = 1$(if $\Delta e > 0$ then the £ has appreciated against the $). Their £ value is now $(\pi/e)(1 + yB)(e - \Delta e)$. His return on that part of his portfolio will this be

$$\pounds\left(\frac{\pi}{e}(1 + y_B)(e - \Delta e) - \pi\right)\right) = \pounds\pi\left(y_B - \frac{\Delta e}{e} - y_B\frac{\Delta e}{e}\right)$$

$$\cong \pounds\pi\left(y_B - \frac{\Delta e}{e}\right) \qquad (26.9)$$

provided that Δe is not large. Writing $\Delta e/e$ as $\hat{e}$, and assuming that the yield on country A bonds is y_A, we may write the investor's total yield as

$$y = (1 - \pi)y_A + \pi(y_B - \hat{e}) \qquad (26.10)$$

Remembering that we assumed y_A and y_B are known and fixed, we may write the mean and the variance of this yield as

$$E[y(\pi)] = (1 - \pi)y_A + \pi(y_B - E[\hat{e}]) \qquad (26.11)$$

$$\sigma_y^2(\pi) = \pi^2 E[(\hat{e} - E[\hat{e}])^2] \qquad (26.12)$$

where $E[(\hat{e} - E[\hat{e}])^2$ is the variance of the rate of appreciation/depreciation of the £.

Suppose that the investor expects that the value of the exchange rate will not change ($E[\hat{e}] = 0$), but accepts that there is some risk that it may ($E[(\hat{e} - E[\hat{e}])^2] > 0$). Provided that the yield on country B bonds is higher than that on country A bonds, he may be prepared to accept the increased variability in his yield in return for a higher expected yield, and hold some of his wealth in the foreign asset. Even if the investor expects the £ to appreciate ($\Delta e > 0$), he may be prepared to hold some foreign assets provided that there is a sufficient difference in yield. If on the other hand he expects the pound to depreciate ($\Delta e < 0$) then he may be prepared to accept a lower yield on the foreign asset, since he expects to make a gain on his foreign exchange transactions. Of course, if he is able to use a forward exchange market he can remove the risk, but at the cost of the premium he must pay.

☐ *Stock models versus flow models*

Note the difference between the outcomes of an increase in the interest rate in country A in either of the above stock models and in the earlier flow model. In the latter a maintained increase in A's interest rate will lead to a continuing flow of investment from B to A. If the interest rate is subsequently returned to its original level then the flow of investment ceases, and foreign assets and liabilities remain at their new level.

In the stock model an increase in the interest rate in A leads to a flow of investment until the desired portfolio adjustments have been made, and the investment flow then ceases. If the interest rate is now returned to its previous level then the process will be put into reverse, and the investors in both countries return to their previous portfolio holdings. The only way in which a country can bring about a sustained capital inflow is to continually increase its interest rate differential.

The underlying reason for the difference between the two models is that in the stock models we have discussed domestic and foreign bonds are not perfect substitutes for one another. Under fixed exchange rates a difference in interest rates can be maintained so long as the two bonds differ in their riskiness. If they did not, and if capital were perfectly free to move between countries, then a small difference in yields would induce investors to switch completely into the higher yield bond. In the floating exchange rate case, on the other hand, a yield differential may be maintained between bonds that are identical in their yields and riskiness (in terms of the currencies in which they are issued) so long as the exchange rate is thought likely to vary.

■ 26.4 The monetary approach

In the preceding sections we considered two theories of capital movements that, coupled with a theory of the current account, would allow us construct a theory of the balance of payments. The monetary approach on the other hand argues that the balance of payments is essentially a monetary phenomenon, and must be viewed in its entirety.[5] It stresses that the money supply and demand are strong forces in determining a country's external position, as indicated by the change in the country's foreign currency reserves. The basic conclusion of the monetary approach is that, starting from an initial equilibrium position, an increase in the demand for money (or an increase in its supply) will lead to a balance-of-payments surplus (or *vice versa*). Disequilibrium in the money market is thus reflected in disequilibrium in the balance of payments.

We shall consider a simple small-country version of the monetary model that highlights its essential features. Discussion of the implications of the monetary approach for macroeconomic policy will be postponed until Chapter 28.

The monetary model is based on three key assumptions: that there is *a stable money demand function*; that prices are flexible and markets operate perfectly, so that there is always full employment and thus *a given level of output*; and that there is *purchasing power parity* (PPP).

1) A simple money demand equation may be written as

$$L = kPY \qquad\qquad (26.13)$$

where L is the demand for nominal money balances, P is the domestic price level, Y is real national income, and k shows the effect of an increase in money income (PY) on the demand for money. The function is assumed to be stable, so that k is a constant. A rise in real national income will increase the transactions demand for money, and so increase L. An increase in the price level will reduce real money balances (L/P) and, since it is assumed that there is a constant demand for real money balances (*ceteris paribus*), will lead to an offsetting increase in the demand for nominal money balances.

Assume for the moment that the money supply is fixed at M_1, and that the money market clears. Then we may use the money demand equation to derive the aggregate demand schedule for the economy. Setting $L = M_1$ in (26.13) and rearranging gives

$$Y = \left(\frac{M_1}{k}\right)\frac{1}{P} \qquad\qquad (26.14)$$

The aggregate demand schedule for a money supply of M_1 is shown by the curve $AD(M_1)$ in Figure 26.5. An increase in the money supply from M_1 to M_2 would lead to an increase in real money balances, and so would shift the aggregate demand schedule out, say to $AD(M_2)$.

The assumption that prices are flexible and markets operate perfectly means that there is always full employment, and that an increase in prices results in an immediate increase in wages. Output is constant (by assumption) so that the aggregate supply schedule is vertical. The aggregate supply schedule for a given labour supply and technology is shown as AS_1 in Figure 26.5.

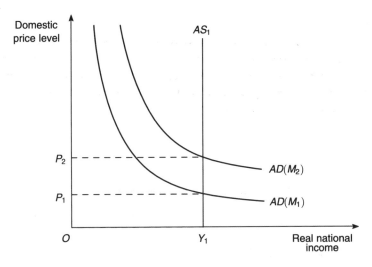

Figure 26.5   *The aggregate demand and supply schedules in the monetary model*

Other things being equal, a money supply of M_1, and so an aggregate demand schedule $AD(M_1)$, means that with an aggregate supply of AS_1 the goods markets will clear at price level P_1. If on the other hand the money supply is M_2, so that the demand schedule is $AD(M_2)$, the price level must rise to P_2.

In its simplest form the *purchasing power parity* assumption is that the exchange rate, e, adjusts to the ratio of the domestic price level, P, and the price level in the rest of the world, P_w. That is

$$e = \frac{P}{P_w} \text{ or } P = eP_w \qquad (26.15)$$

where e is the price in domestic currency of one unit of foreign currency. The price levels are assumed to be defined over the same basket of goods, and the purchasing power parity theory may then be justified by assuming that arbitrage will equalise the prices of goods between countries.

If we take the price level in the rest of the world as given then the relationship between the exchange rate and the domestic price level will be as shown by the line *PPP* in Figure 26.6. *PPP* has a slope of P_w. A domestic price level of P_1 and a foreign price level of P_w are consistent with an exchange rate of e_1. An increase in the domestic price level from P_1 to P_2 would lead domestic consumers to switch from buying domestic goods to buying their foreign equivalents, and foreign consumers likewise. The resulting excess demand for the foreign currency must then drive up its price: the exchange rate will depreciate from e_1 to e_2.

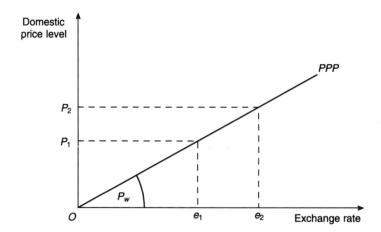

Figure 26.6   *The purchasing power parity schedule*

To complete the model we specify the domestic money supply, which also allows us to identify the balance of payments position of the economy. The money supply, M, is assumed to depend on the supply of 'high-powered' money, H, as specified in equation (26.16):

$$M = mH \tag{26.16}$$

where m is the 'money multiplier'.[6] The supply of high-powered money has two components, currency and central bank deposits held by the clearing banks, and the reserves of foreign currency. Writing these as D and R respectively we may substitute for H in (26.16) to give

$$M = m(D + R) \tag{26.17}$$

The schedule M in Figure 26.7 shows the relationship between the money supply and the level of foreign exchange reserves implied by equation (26.17).

It follows that, assuming m is constant, we may write the change in the money supply as:

$$dM = m(dD + dR) \tag{26.18}$$

which we may rearrange to give:

$$dR = \frac{1}{m}dM - dD \tag{26.19}$$

But if the money market clears then the change in the supply of money must be taken up by a change in the demand for money. From equation (26.13) we know that

$$dL = k(PdY + YdP) \tag{26.20}$$

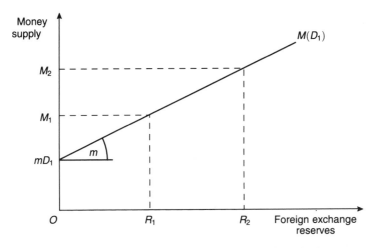

Figure 26.7 *The money supply and the level of foreign exchange reserves*

so that, assuming there was equilibrium initially, and setting $dM = dL$, we must have

$$dR = \frac{k}{m}(PdY + YdP) - dD \qquad (26.21)$$

That is, changes in the foreign exchange reserves (which are of course the complement to the net change in the current and capital accounts) may be the consequence of changes in national income, the price level or the domestic component of high-powered money. If, as we have done so far, we assume that national income is constant because the economy is operating at full employment then $dY = 0$. If we also assume that the exchange rate is fixed and that the foreign price level is given then the purchasing power parity assumption ensures that $dP = 0$. It follows that the only source of a change in the foreign exchange reserves (i.e. a balance of payments deficit or surplus) is a change in the domestic component of the money supply.

Figure 26.8 shows the general equilibrium in the monetary model of the balance of payments with a given world price level. In panel (a) there is equilibrium in the money market, with a domestic money supply of M_1. This is consistent with the real income, Y_1, and the price level, P_1, determined by the intersection of the aggregate demand and supply schedules, $AD(M_1)$ and AS_1 respectively, as shown in panel (b). Panel (c) uses the purchasing power parity relationship to show that the price level is consistent with the exchange rate and the world price level, so that there will be no changes in the reserves, and hence no change in the money supply function in panel (a).[7]

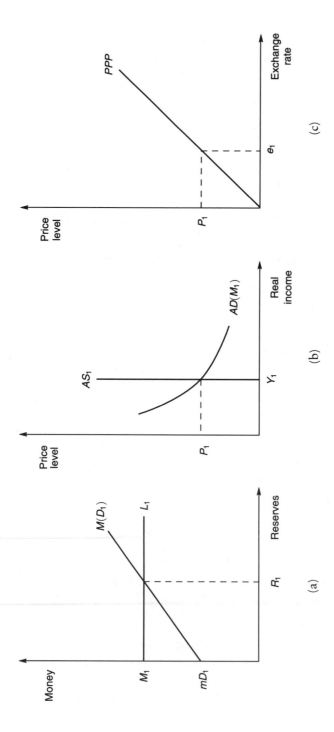

Figure 26.8   *General equilibrium in the monetary approach*

At first sight it may seem that the monetarist approach to the balance of payments is in conflict with the 'orthodox' approach. This will indeed be the case if real income, the price level and the interest rate are exogenous to the model, as we would then have two conflicting explanations of the balance-of-payments position. If on the other hand they are endogenous then one must construct a general equilibrium model in which they are jointly determined, and such a model may make use of relationships found in both approaches.

■ 26.5 Summary and conclusions

We first considered two alternative approaches to the capital account of the balance of payments, the flow theory and the stock theory. Both have been used in conjunction with the orthodox theory of the current account to give a full theory of the balance of payments. We might suspect that the differences in the two capital account theories will lead to different prescriptions for balance of payments policy, and we shall discuss whether this is so in Chapters 27 and 28. We then looked at a simple version of the monetary approach to the balance of payments, in which it is argued that the net change in the current account plus the capital account, as shown by the change in the reserves of foreign currency, is a monetary phenomenon. This raises again the question of whether there will be a difference in policy prescriptions between this model and the orthodox models. We shall examine this question in Chapters 28 and 29 as well.

□ *Notes*

1   See Artis and Lewis (1991), Chapter 2.
2   For a full account of a portfolio balance model involving domestic money, domestic bonds, and foreign bonds see Pilbeam (1992), Chapter 8.
3   The proof of this is as follows. The investor's utility function may be written as $U = U(\mu(\pi), \sigma^2(\pi))$, with $\partial U/\partial \mu(\pi) > 0$ and $\partial U/\partial \sigma^2(\pi) < 0$. To maximise his utility we find must find π such that

$$\frac{dU}{d\pi} = \frac{\partial U}{\partial \mu(\pi)} \frac{\partial \mu(\pi)}{d\pi} + \frac{\partial U}{\partial \sigma^2(\pi)} \frac{\partial \sigma^2(\pi)}{d\pi} = 0$$

But from equations (26.4) and (26.5) we know that and $\partial \mu(\pi)/\partial \pi = W\mu_1$ and $\partial \sigma^2(\pi)/\partial \pi = 2\pi W^2 \sigma_1^2$. Substituting these into the first-order condition and manipulating gives

$$\pi = \frac{\mu_1}{W\sigma_1^2} \left[\frac{\partial U/\partial \mu(\pi)}{-2\partial U/\partial \sigma^2(\pi)} \right]$$

which must be positive. The term in square brackets is the inverse of the (Arrow–Pratt) coefficient of relative risk aversion. If, as is often done, we assume that this is constant, it is evident that π is an increasing function of μ_1, and a decreasing function of σ_1^2. Note that assuming constant relative risk aversion is a sufficient condition for a decrease in expected yield to decrease π, but is not necessary.

4   The value of π that minimises (26.7) is

$$\pi_M = \frac{\sigma_2^2 - \frac{1}{2}\rho\sigma_1\sigma_2}{\sigma_1^2 + \sigma_2{}^2 - \rho\sigma_1\sigma_2}$$

However, π_M cannot be greater than one. Setting $\pi_M = 1$ and solving for ρ gives $\rho = 2\sigma_1/\sigma_2$. The full minimisation condition is thus

$$\pi_M = \frac{\sigma_2^2 - \frac{1}{2}\rho\sigma_1\sigma_2}{\sigma_1^2 + \sigma_2^2 - \rho\sigma_1\sigma_2} \text{ for } \rho < 2\frac{\sigma_1}{\sigma_2}$$

$$= 1 \text{ for } \rho \geq 2\frac{\sigma_1}{\sigma_2}$$

5   The seminal work on the monetarist approach is Frenkel and Johnson (1976), and especially the papers by Frenkel, Johnson and Mussa.

6   For a discussion of this see Greenaway and Shaw (1986), Chapters 6 and 15.

7   In the original version(s) of the monetary model a fourth relationship was developed, between the price level and the balance of payments (or change in reserves). This schedule was known as the 'hoarding' schedule, but the term is rarely used now.

8   A formal reconciliation of the orthodox and monetary approaches is by Frenkel, Gylfason, and Helliwell (1980). An earlier synthesis is given by Kouri and Porter (1974).

■ *Chapter 27* ■

The Determination of a Floating Exchange Rate

■ *27.1* Introduction

There is an extensive literature on the factors determining the level of a floating exchange rate, and in particular its behaviour over time. In this chapter we shall discuss a selection of the models that have been proposed.[1] We may identify the two extremes as the 'Keynesian' models where prices and wages are assumed fixed, and 'monetary' models in which they are assumed to be perfectly flexible, and some form of *purchasing power parity* is assumed to hold. Within both these broad groups we find considerable differences, in particular in the treatment of international capital flows. We shall consider simple versions of these in turn.

Finally, we shall examine the Dornbusch 'sticky price' model, which may be regarded as an intermediate model, with asset prices adjusting immediately but goods prices more slowly. This model is important in that it offers an explanation of why the exchange rate may differ in the short run from its long-run equilibrium value as a consequence of the actions of rational economic agents acting on perfect information, rather than as the result of speculative activity and/or imperfect information.

27.2 A fixed price model with perfectly immobile capital

If there is no movement of capital between countries then the exchange rate is determined solely by the current account. This is of course essentially the model we discussed in section 24.3. We saw then that the Marshall–Lerner Condition has to be satisfied if a floating exchange rate is to be stable. However, exchange rates are determined in the short run, and it is arguable that short-run elasticities are likely to be so low that the Marshall–Lerner Condition is unlikely to be satisfied. If that is the case then a depreciation (appreciation) of the exchange rate will lead to a deterioration (improvement) of the current account and so to further depreciation (appreciation). This short-run effect (often called the 'J curve') is discussed at more length in Chapter 29.

One way in which we may rescue the current-account model is to assume that the Marshall–Lerner Condition will be satisfied in the long run, and that there are 'well-informed' speculators in the foreign exchange market who know this. Suppose now that there is a 'one-off' shock that causes the exchange rate to depreciate. The speculators will know that in the long run the exchange rate will return to its (previous) equilibrium level, and so will be prepared to purchase the depreciating currency now and to hold it for resale when the exchange rate subsequently appreciates. If the speculators are well-informed, so that in the long run their holdings of particular currencies do not change, and if there are enough of them to affect the exchange rate, then their activities will stabilise the market.

We saw in section 25.4 that floating exchange rates insulate the domestic economy from changes in income elsewhere. With fixed prices and no capital mobility, the level of real income and the exchange rate are jointly determined by equilibrium in the goods market and in the balance of payments.[2] This is shown in Figure 27.1.

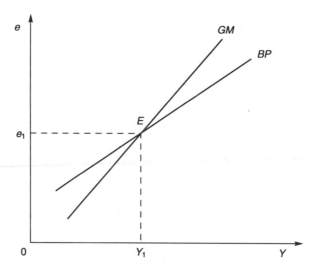

Figure 27.1 *Joint determination of real income and the exchange rate*

The curve GM shows the combinations of real income (Y) and the exchange rate (e) that give equilibrium in the goods market. The exchange rate is defined in terms of the cost of 1 unit of foreign currency. GM must have a positive slope. Starting from an equilibrium position, an increase in output, and so in real income, will lead to an excess supply of goods, since some of the increased income will be spent on imports. In order to eliminate that excess supply the country must increase its exports and/or reduce its imports, and that requires that its exchange rate depreciates. The BP curve shows the combinations of real income and the exchange rate that give equilibrium in the balance of payments. BP must also be positively sloped. An increase in real income leads to a deficit in the balance of payments, and this must be offset by a depreciation of the exchange rate.

Provided that the marginal propensity to save and/or the marginal tax rate are positive, the BP curve must however be flatter than the GM curve. An increase in income will in this case lead to an excess supply in the goods market that is larger than the deficit in the balance of payments. It follows that the depreciation of the exchange rate needed to restore equilibrium in the goods market must be greater than that needed to restore balance-of-payments equilibrium.

The general equilibrium of the economy is then at point E, the intersection of GM and BP. A floating exchange rate will always bring about this equilibrium.

This simple model may be used to give some insight into the effects of government policy on the exchange rate when there is no capital mobility. Suppose that the government attempts to expand the economy, by either fiscal or monetary means. This will shift the GM line to the right. The economy must however remain in balance-of-payments equilibrium, and so the new equilibrium must still be on BP. Since GM is steeper than BP, the exchange rate must depreciate.

■ 27.3 A fixed price model with capital mobility

If there is international capital mobility, so that we must also consider the capital account in the balance of payments, then the effect of the domestic interest rate must be brought into the analysis. We may do this by extending the familiar closed economy IS–LM model into what is often referred to as the IS–LM–BP or *Mundell–Fleming* model.[3] We shall first derive the IS and LM schedules for an open economy, and shall then discuss the derivation of the BP (balance of payments) schedule under different assumptions about the degree of capital mobility.

☐ *The IS schedule for a small open economy*

We shall start with the *IS* schedule, which shows those combinations of real income and the real rate of interest that give equilibrium in the goods market. Foreign incomes and interest rates are assumed to be given. For simplicity we shall assume that the government's tax revenue is independent of the level of national income. The condition for equilibrium in the goods markets for an open economy is, as before, that the injections into the income stream should be equal to the leakages from it. This condition is given in equation (27.1), which is identical with equation (25.19) except that G now represents the government budget deficit (expenditure less tax revenue).

$$I + G + X = S + M \qquad (27.1)$$

As in Chapter 25 we assume that savings (S) and imports (M) are increasing functions of real income (Y) but are independent of the rate of interest (r). The relationship between $S + M$ and Y is shown in the south-east quadrant of Figure 27.2. Investment on the other hand is assumed to be a decreasing function of the rate of interest but independent of real income. Exports and the government deficit are assumed to be independent of both r and Y. The relationship between $I + G + X$ and r is shown in the

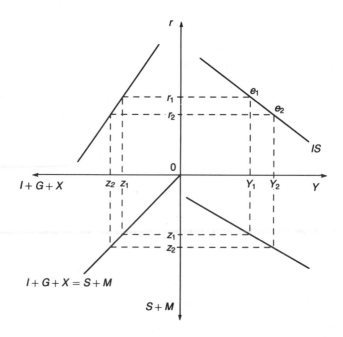

Figure 27.2   *Deriving the IS schedule for an open economy*

north-west quadrant of Figure 27.2. The 45° line in the south-west quadrant represents the equilibrium condition shown in equation (27.1).

We may now derive the *IS* schedule, which will be drawn in the north-east quadrant. A rate of interest of r_1 gives rise to a level of injections z_1. For the goods market to be in equilibrium these injections must be matched by an equal volume of leakages, which requires that the level of income be Y_1. Point e_1 must therefore lie on the *IS* schedule. A lower rate of interest, r_2, leads to greater investment and so to an increased level of injections z_2. For equilibrium we must therefore have a higher level of leakages, and so a higher income, Y_2. Point e_2, which is also on the *IS* schedule, must therefore be below and to the right of e_1. That is, the *IS* schedule has its familiar negative slope.

As in the closed-economy model, the *IS* schedule will be shifted to the right by an increase in the government budget deficit, by an autonomous increase in investment, and by an autonomous fall in savings. In the open economy it will also move to the right if there is an increase in exports or an autonomous fall in imports, or if the exchange rate depreciates and so stimulates such changes.

□ *The LM schedule for a small open economy*

We may derive the *LM* schedule, which shows the combinations of real income and the real rate of interest that give equilibrium in the money market, in a similar manner. We shall use the simple Keynesian specification that money is demanded for either transactions or speculative purposes. The transactions demand, L_1, is assumed to be an increasing function of real income, while the speculative demand, L_2, is a decreasing function of the real rate of interest. These relationships are shown in the south-east and north-west quadrants respectively of Figure 27.3.

The supply of money, M_s, is assumed to be determined exogenously. For equilibrium in the money market this given money supply must be held either for transactions or for speculative purposes. That is

$$L_1 + L_2 = M_s \tag{27.2}$$

Equation (27.2) is represented in Figure 27.3 in the south-west quadrant.

We may now derive the *LM* curve, which will be drawn in the north-east quadrant. If real income is Y_1 then the transactions demand for money is t_1. Equilibrium in the money market requires that the rest of the money supply, $s_1 = Ms - t_1$, must be held for speculative purposes, and that in turn requires that the real interest rate be r_1. Point e_1 is thus on the *LM* curve. A lower level of income, Y_2, implies a lower transactions demand,

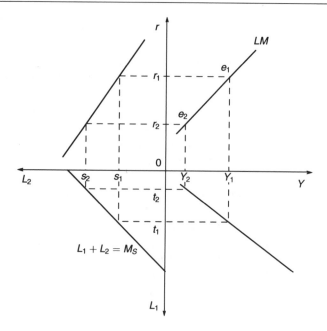

Figure 27.3   *Deriving the LM schedule for an open economy*

t_2, and so a higher speculative demand, s_2, is required for money market equilibrium, which in turn requires a lower interest rate, r_2. The new equilibrium point, e_2, is thus below and to the left of e_1. The *LM* schedule has the familiar positive slope.

An increase in the money supply will shift outwards the line in the south-west quadrant showing the equilibrium condition, and so will shift the *LM* schedule to the right.

☐ *The BP schedule for a small open economy*

The *BP* schedule shows those combinations of real income and the real interest rate that give equilibrium in the balance of payments *for a given exchange rate*. We shall construct the schedule from the Keynesian model of the current account of Chapter 25 and the flow theory model of the capital account discussed in Chapter 26.

Under the assumptions of the Keynesian model imports, M, are an increasing function of income, and exports, X, are exogenously determined. It follows that the current-account balance, $X - M$, is a decreasing function of income. This relationship is shown in the south-east quadrant of Figure 27.4. Note that the level of income giving balance in the current account is Y_0. An income higher than this, say Y_1, will lead to a current-account deficit, while a lower income, such as Y_2, will result in a current-account surplus.

The flow model of the capital account states that the flow of capital is an increasing function of the domestic interest rate and a decreasing function of the foreign interest rate. Taking the foreign interest rate as given, this gives us the relationship between the domestic interest rate and the net inflow of capital shown in the north-west quadrant of Figure 27.4. Note that the rate of interest giving balance in the capital account is r_0 (which in the absence of any exchange-rate risk would be the foreign interest rate). A higher interest rate, such as r_1, will lead to a surplus on the capital account (a net inflow), and a lower rate of interest, say r_2, will lead to a capital-account surplus (a net outflow).

Balance-of-payments equilibrium requires that any deficit on the current account be matched by an equal surplus on the capital account, and *vice versa*. This relationship is shown by the 45° line in the south-west quadrant, which must obviously pass through the point defined by a zero balance on both current and capital accounts.

We may now derive the *BP* schedule in the north-east quadrant. It must pass through the point defined by an income Y_0 and a domestic interest rate r_0. A higher income, Y_1, leads to a current-account deficit of c_1, which must be offset by an equal capital-account surplus of k_1. That is, balance-

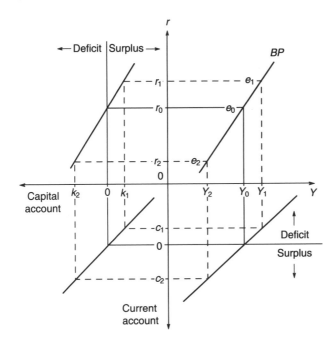

Figure 27.4   *The BP schedule for a small open economy*

of-payments equilibrium requires a domestic interest rate, r_1, that must be higher than r_0. The *BP* schedule must be positively sloped. This may be confirmed by considering the case where a low level of income, Y_2, leads to a current-account surplus of c_2. To maintain overall equilibrium there must be a corresponding capital outflow, and this requires that the interest rate be lower than r_0, at r_2.

The *BP* schedule may be steeper or flatter than the *LM* schedule. Their relative slopes depend on the parameters of the functions underlying them. The parameter that is of particular interest in the present context is the degree of capital mobility. The case we have just considered reflects *limited* mobility of capital between countries. The more highly mobile is capital (i.e. the more sensitive it is to differences in interest rates), the less would be the slope of the capital-account schedule in the north-east quadrant of Figure 27.4, and the flatter would be the *BP* schedule. In the limiting case where capital is *perfectly* mobile (which requires that domestic and foreign assets be seen as perfect substitutes), the *BP* schedule would be horizontal. At the other extreme, where capital is perfectly immobile, the *BP* schedule would be vertical, since changes in the domestic interest rate could have no direct effect on the balance of payments.

Remember that we derived the *BP* schedule on the assumption that the exchange rate was given. What will happen if the exchange rate depreciates from its original value? Assuming that the Marshall–Lerner Condition is satisfied, or that we have the well-informed speculators of Section 27.2, depreciation of the exchange rate will lead to current-account equilibrium at a higher level of income than before. That is, the current-account schedule in the south-east quadrant of Figure 27.4 will move to the right. The capital-account schedule will not however be affected The consequence is that the *BP* schedule will move to the right: at a given interest rate (and so a given state of the capital account) balance-of-payments equilibrium may be obtained with a higher level of real income than before.

Equilibrium in the Mundell–Fleming model with floating exchange rates

All that remains is to place the three schedules on the same diagram, as in Figure 27.5 (in which the *BP* schedule has been drawn as steeper than the *LM* schedule). The model will be in a general equilibrium at a point such as *E*, at which all three schedules intersect.

With a floating exchange rate this must always be the case. The reason is that the exchange rate will adjust so that the *BP* schedule passes through the intersection of the *IS* and *LM* schedules.

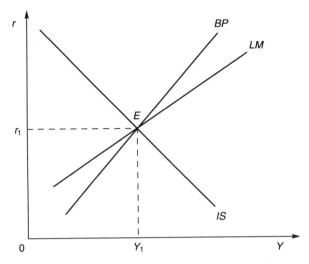

Figure 27.5 *Equilibrium in the Mundell–Fleming model*

Monetary and fiscal expansion in the Mundell–Fleming model

We shall discuss the use of monetary and fiscal policy to obtain specified policy goals in Chapters 28 and 29. For the moment however it is interesting to compare the effects of monetary and fiscal expansion in the Mundell–Fleming model under the two extreme assumptions about capital mobility: that it cannot move at all, and that it is perfectly mobile.

Figure 27.6 shows the effects of a monetary expansion – a shift in the LM schedule to the right. Panel (a) shows the case when capital cannot move between countries (the BP schedule is vertical), while panel (b) shows the case of perfectly mobile capital (the BP schedule is horizontal). In both cases the original LM curve is shown as LM_1, and the initial equilibrium is at E_1, with output Y_1 and interest rate r_1.

When there is a monetary expansion and capital is completely immobile, the initial effect is to shift the LM schedule to LM_2. If exchange rates could not change then the new (short-run) equilibrium would be given by the intersection of LM_2 with IS_1, and there would be a balance-of-payments deficit. With a floating exchange rate however the exchange rate will depreciate. This will shift both the IS and the BP schedules to the right. The LM schedule must remain at LM_2 however,[4] and so the final equilibrium must be at a point such as E_2, where the new IS and BP

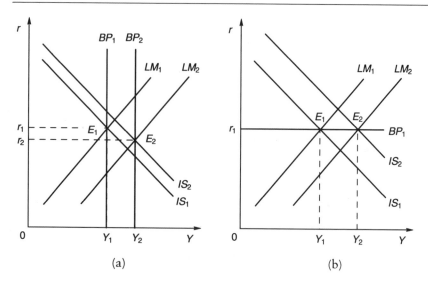

Figure 27.6   *Monetary expansion in the Mundell–Fleming model*

schedules (IS_2 and BP_2) intersect with LM_2. The interest rate must fall (as a consequence of the monetary expansion), though not by as much as it would in the short run under a fixed exchange rate. The level of output must rise, and will increase by more in the long run with a floating exchange rate than it would in the short run with a fixed exchange rate.

If capital is perfectly mobile, however, the rate of interest must be the same in the initial and final equilibria. The monetary expansion initially shifts the LM schedule to LM_2, which will lead to a deficit in the balance of payments and a fall in interest rates. The balance-of-payments deficit leads to a depreciation, which in turn shifts the IS schedule to the right. At the same time however the fall in the interest rate leads to an outflow of capital. In the final equilibrium the IS schedule must have shifted sufficiently to the right for it to intersect the new LM schedule at the original rate of interest. The country will have a current-account surplus balanced by a capital outflow.

Figure 27.7 shows the effects of a fiscal expansion, which will shift the IS schedule to the right. Panel (a) again shows the case when capital cannot move between countries, and panel (b) shows the case of perfectly mobile capital. The original LM curve is LM_1, and the initial equilibrium is at E_1, with output Y_1 and interest rate r_1.

Consider first the case when capital is perfectly immobile (the BP schedule is vertical). The initial fiscal expansion shifts the IS schedule to the right, to IS_2. The short-run equilibrium would be at the intersection of IS_2 and LM_1, which implies a balance-of-payments deficit. The currency

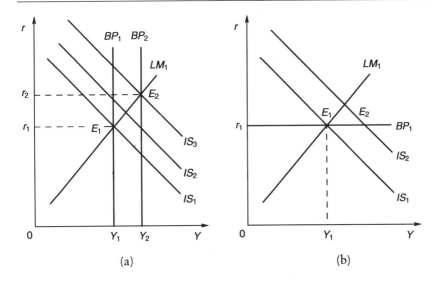

Figure 27.7 *Fiscal expansion in the Mundell–Fleming model*

would therefore depreciate, which will shift the *IS* curve further to the right as well as shifting the *BP* schedule in that direction. The final equilibrium will be at a point such as E_2, with a higher income than before and a higher rate of interest (since the money supply is unchanged while the demand for money has increased with the increased income).

When capital is perfectly mobile, however, a fiscal expansion can have no long-run effect. The initial shift to the right in the *IS* schedule implies a temporary equilibrium at the intersection of IS_2 and LM_1. There will be an increase in the inflow of capital that will outweigh the effects of the fiscal expansion on the current-account balance, and this will lead to appreciation of the exchange rate, and a shift to the left of the *IS* schedule. Since neither the *LM* nor the *BP* schedule will move following a fiscal expansion, the initial and final equilibria must be the same. The *IS* schedule will shift back to IS_1, and the fiscal expansion will have been ineffective.

■ 27.4 Purchasing Power Parity

Purchasing power parity (PPP) has been used both as a model of exchange-rate determination in its own right, and as a central element in monetarist models of exchange rate determination. The theory of purchasing power parity was formalised in the 1920s by Gustav Cassell,[5] although its roots go back much further. It relies upon the assumption of perfect arbitrage between markets under conditions of perfect competition and no barriers to trade. Such perfect arbitrage will then ensure that the price of a specific good will, when converted through the exchange rate, be the same in each of two countries. This unexceptionable proposition is often referred to as the *Law of One Price* (LOOP).

☐ Absolute and relative PPP

The proponents of PPP then extend this argument to all goods. In its strictest form (*Absolute PPP*) the theory argues that the Law of One Price holds for all goods, and that those prices and the exchange rate will adjust so that the price of a given *bundle* of goods will be the same in both countries. This obviously requires that the (relative) prices of all goods be flexible. Formally, if the price of the specified bundle of goods is P_A in country A and P_B in country B then those prices and the exchange rate, e, must satisfy

$$P_A = eP_B \qquad (27.3)$$

where e is the number of units of A's currency required to purchase 1 unit of B's currency. Obviously we can then write the exchange rate as

$$e = \frac{P_A}{P_B} \qquad (27.4)$$

The implication of the absolute PPP theory is that an increase of x per cent in the price of the bundle of goods in country A relative to the price of the same bundle in country B will lead to an x per cent depreciation in A's exchange rate.

A looser version of the theory is known as *Relative* PPP. Taking logarithms of equation (27.4) and totally differentiating gives

$$\hat{e} = \hat{P}_A - \hat{P}_B \qquad (27.5)$$

where as before $\hat{e} = de/e$, etc. That is, the proportionate change in the exchange rate is equal to the difference in the rates of inflation in A and B. If, for example, there is 6 per cent inflation in A and 2 per cent inflation in B then A's exchange rate will depreciate by 4 per cent.

☐ Criticisms of PPP

Criticisms of the two PPP theories may be grouped under three main headings.[6] The first is that the assumptions underlying the Law of One Price do not hold. We shall not pursue here the question of whether prices are perfectly flexible, since that assumption is central to the monetarist approach that we are discussing. It is however important to note that the proponents of the monetary approach defend it as a long-run proposition, accepting that it may take some time for prices to adjust fully. That is, PPP is expected to hold in the long run. As we shall see, the possibility that the prices of goods adjust more slowly than the prices of financial assets is central to Dornbusch's 'sticky price' model of exchange rates, which may be viewed as adding a short-term dimension to the monetarist models.

However, even when prices are flexible, the existence of transport and transactions costs, tariffs and other barriers to trade, and of imperfectly competitive firms able to discriminate between markets, will all lead to a breakdown of the absolute version of PPP. It might be expected that relative PPP will be less affected, but in general it too cannot hold under such circumstances.

A second basic problem is that of defining the common bundle of goods. Even if the Law of One Price does hold, changing the composition of the bundle may change the exchange rate predicted by either version of PPP. If the trading countries have similar tastes then this problem may not be of major importance, provided that those tastes do not change markedly over the time period being considered. If tastes do change over time then the relative version of PPP, interpreted as predicting the change in the exchange rate between two consecutive time periods, would be more appropriate.

Finally, even if the Law of One Price holds for traded goods, the presence of non-traded goods (to which it will not in general apply) leads to various problems. At the most basic level, it results in conflict over whether we should define PPP in terms of traded goods alone or in terms of all goods. Using the former makes sense when we are concerned only with the exchange rate, but makes it more difficult to include PPP in models in which we are concerned with the effects of inflation and in the allocative effects of exchange rate changes. On the other hand, PPP is less likely to hold if non-traded goods are included.

At a more sophisticated level, it has been argued that: (i) productivity tends to be higher in developed countries; (ii) consumers in developed countries spend a higher proportion of their income on traded goods; and (iii) productivity grows more quickly in the manufactured goods sectors than in services (which correspond roughly to traded and non-traded goods). Following from these, it has been argued that the inclusion of both traded and non-traded goods will lead to biases in the calculation of PPP-based exchange rates.[7]

□ *Empirical tests of the PPP hypotheses*

The preceding discussion suggests that neither version of PPP can be expected to hold exactly. However, as we have already noted, the assumption of PPP is central to many models. It therefore becomes a question of whether PPP (in one form or the other) provides a good model of exchange rates, or a good element in such a model. Empirical studies of PPP may be grouped under three broad headings. First, those that essentially ask whether the Law of One Price is obeyed, and in so doing whether it is possible to construct prices indices which would do so; second, those that attempt to estimate generalised forms of equations (27.4) and (27.5) and test whether the parameters are significantly different from those predicted by PPP;[8] and finally those that ask whether PPP provides efficient forecasts of exchange rate movements over time.

Studies using the first approach generally conclude that the Law of One Price does not hold, and in particular that changes in exchange rates result in changes in relative prices, so that it is apparently impossible to construct prices indices for which the Law of One Price will hold.[9] Regression-based studies tend to suggest that neither PPP hypothesis is acceptable in the short term, but that (as we might expect) they may do better in the longer term.[10] The time-series studies are based on more sophisticated models that embody interest rates and rational expectations as well as price levels, and examine whether markets are efficient. So far the evidence from such models is inconclusive, with some authors finding support for PPP, but others rejecting it.[11]

The empirical evidence is therefore rather mixed, but on balance tends to come down against PPP, except perhaps in the long run. We may therefore feel that we must look at models that embody one or other of the PPP hypotheses with some scepticism. On the other hand it is difficult to accept the extreme view that exchange rates are independent of prices. It may be that PPP embodies an important element of exchange-rate determination that, when embodied in a more general model, allows that model to perform well. We shall return to this question later, once we have considered a monetarist and a 'mixed' model.

■ 27.5 A flexible price monetary model

Monetary models of the determination of a floating exchange rate emphasise the role of the demand for and supply of money.[12] They commonly assume that there is a stable money demand function in each economy, and that PPP holds in the long run. The assumption of flexible prices implies, as usual, that there will be full employment. The more simple models, such as the one we shall consider here, assume that there is perfect capital mobility, with a single domestic and a single foreign bond, and that these are perfect substitutes for one another. (More sophisticated models also allow for imperfect substitutability among a range of assets.) Finally, monetary models emphasise the role of expectations.

The money market is specified by assuming a stable demand function that relates the real demand for money to the level of output, Y, and the nominal domestic rate of interest, r, with the partial derivatives having the usual signs. Assuming that the money supply is exogenous and that the money market clears gives (as in the LM formulation used earlier) gives

$$\frac{M}{P} = f(Y, r), \quad \text{with} \quad \frac{\partial f}{\partial Y} > 0, \frac{\partial f}{\partial r} < 0 \tag{27.6}$$

where M is the nominal money stock and P the price level. A typical formulation of this relationship for a two-country world is[13]

$$\ln(M_A) - \ln(P_A) = \eta \ln(Y_A) - \sigma r_A \tag{27.7}$$

$$\ln(M_B) - \ln(P_B) = \eta \ln(Y_B) - \sigma r_B \quad \text{with} \quad \eta > 0, \sigma > 0 \tag{27.8}$$

where $\ln(x)$ is the natural logarithm of x, and A and B are the two countries. Note that, for simplicity, the parameters of the income and interest rate variables are assumed to be the same in both countries.

The absolute version of purchasing power parity is assumed to hold, so that

$$\ln(e) = \ln(P_A) - \ln(P_B) \tag{27.9}$$

where e is the exchange rate, expressed as the number of units of A's currency (the £) per unit of B's currency (the $).

Country A and country B bonds are assumed to be perfect substitutes for one another, so that investors are concerned only with their rates of interest and the future exchange rate. Consider an investor resident in A, choosing between investing £1 in A-bonds or in B-bonds over one time period. If he invests in the former then he will obtain the interest on that bond plus his initial outlay at the end of the period; that is, £$(1 + r_A)$. If he invests in the latter then he buys a bond to the value of $$(1/e)$, and at the end of the period will obtain $$(1/e)(1 + r_B)$. However he must then convert these $s into his own currency at the going spot rate. Suppose that the spot exchange rate at that time has depreciated by $\hat{e}$ (so that the new exchange rate is £$e(1+\hat{e}) = 1). Assuming that both the rate of interest in B and the depreciation in the exchange rate are small, the £ value of his transaction will be approximately £$(1 + \hat{e} + r_B)$.[14] The investor would then be indifferent between A-bonds and B-bonds if

$$(1 + \hat{e} + r_B) = 1 + r_A$$

that is, if

$$\hat{e} + r_B = r_A \tag{27.10}$$

However, when the original decision is made the investor does not know what the future exchange rate will be. In order to make his choice he must instead decide what he *expects* the spot rate to be at the end of the period.

We must therefore replace $\hat{e}$ in equation (27.10) by $E[\hat{e}]$, the investor's *expectation* of the future spot exchange rate at the time when his decision is made. We then obtain, after a little manipulation,

$$r_A - r_B = E[\hat{e}] \tag{27.11}$$

This result is known as the *uncovered interest rate parity* condition. It asserts that if the £/$ exchange rate is expected to depreciate ($E[\hat{e}] > 0$) then the interest rate in A must exceed the interest rate in B by the expected rate of that depreciation. Conversely, if the £ is expected to appreciate against the $($E[\hat{e}] < 0$) then the interest rate in B must exceed that in A by the expected rate of appreciation.

Finally, we must specify how expectations of the exchange rate are formed. Of the various alternatives, three have been used frequently. *Rational* expectations, which assumes that economic agents make the best possible use of the available information; *regressive* expectations, which assumes that the agents have an estimate of the long-run value of the variable in question, and expect the actual value to approach that long-run value over time; and *perfect foresight*, which states that the expected value will in fact be the true value. For the moment however we shall consider some reasonably general implications of the model.

Equations (27.7) and (27.8) may be rearranged to give

$$\ln(P_A) = \ln(M_A) - \eta \ln(Y_A) + \sigma r_A \tag{27.12}$$

$$\ln(P_B) = \ln(M_B) - \eta \ln(Y_B) + \sigma r_B \tag{27.13}$$

and subtracting one from the other then gives

$$\ln(P_A) - \ln(P_B) = \ln(M_A) - \ln(M_B) - \eta(\ln(Y_A) - \ln(Y_B)) \\ + \sigma(r_A - r_B)$$

Equation (27.9) however states that, $\ln(P_A) - \ln(P_B) = \ln(e)$ so that we may write the exchange rate in terms of the nominal money supplies, full-employment outputs and nominal interest rates as

$$\ln(e) = \ln(M_A) - \ln(M_B) - \eta(\ln(Y_A) - \ln(Y_B)) \\ + \sigma(r_A - r_B) \tag{27.14}$$

It is evident from equation (27.14) that an expansion in the domestic money supply (an increase in M_A) must lead to an increase in e: that is, to a depreciation of A's currency. Indeed, (27.14) suggests that an x per cent increase in the domestic money supply will lead to an x per cent depreciation in the exchange rate. This is in agreement with the result obtained earlier for the Mundell–Fleming model with perfect capital mobility.

The effect on the exchange rate of changes in real domestic output, Y_A, is however the reverse of that given by the Mundell–Fleming model. That is, in the monetary model an increase in real domestic output leads to an appreciation of the exchange rate. The reason for the difference is that the monetarist model assumes flexible prices and hence full employment, whereas the Mundell–Fleming model assumes fixed prices with unemployed resources. An increase in real output in the monetarist model can only come from an increase in the supply side of the economy, whereas in the fixed-price model it can come from the demand side.

We face a similar problem when we consider the effect of an increase in the domestic rate of interest on the exchange rate. In the monetary model this leads to a depreciation of the exchange rate. In the Mundell–Fleming model, by contrast, an increase in the domestic interest rate would lead to an inflow of capital and so to appreciation. To see why this is so, recall that the uncovered interest parity condition given in equation (27.11) was that $r_A - r_B = E[\hat{e}]$. Substituting this in equation (27.14) gives

$$\ln(e) = \ln(M_A) - \ln(M_B) - \eta(\ln(Y_A) - \ln(Y_B)) + \sigma E[\hat{e}] \qquad (27.15)$$

That is, an increase in the expected rate of depreciation will lead to a depreciation in the current spot exchange rate. The logic of this effect is quite straightforward: if investors expect their domestic currency to depreciate more quickly in the future then they have an incentive to move into foreign assets now, and by so doing they will cause a depreciation of the current spot exchange rate. A high current domestic interest rate is a sign of a weak currency in the monetary model.

An alternative approach to the role played by expectations in such a model is to use the PPP relationship of equation (27.9): $\ln(e) = \ln(P_A) - \ln(P_B)$, which on total differentiation gives the familiar result that

$$\hat{e} = \hat{P}_A - \hat{P}_B \qquad (27.16)$$

That is, the rate of depreciation of the currency is determined by the difference in the rates of increase of the two price levels. Suppose that investors form rational expectations (i.e. are aware of this relationship) and have expectations of the future rates of inflation of the two currencies, $E[\hat{P}_A]$ and $E[\hat{P}_B]$. Their expectation of the change in the exchange rate would then be given by

$$E[\hat{e}] = E[\hat{P}_A] - E[\hat{P}_B] \qquad (27.17)$$

and substitution in (27.15) would give

$$\ln(e) = \ln(M_A) - \ln(M_B) - \eta(\ln(Y_A) - \ln(Y_B))$$
$$+ \sigma(E[\hat{P}_A] - E[\hat{P}_B]) \qquad (27.18)$$

That is, if investors expect that the future rate of inflation will be higher in A than in B then they will move out of A's currency, and so will cause the spot exchange rate to depreciate.

■ 27.6 The Dornbusch 'sticky price' model

Flexible-price monetary models such as the one discussed above are essentially long-run models, and do not claim to offer an explanation of the short-term behaviour of exchange rates. It has been observed that in practice the exchange rate deviates from its PPP value by a considerable margin and for long periods. Moreover, it has been observed that the exchange rate may 'overshoot' in a move from one equilibrium to another: that is, if the new equilibrium rate were, say, lower than the existing rate, the actual exchange rate might drop below the new equilibrium and then approach it from there. In a famous paper Rudiger Dornbusch[15] proposed a monetary exchange rate model that could explain both phenomena.

What gives the Dornbusch model the ability to do this are two key assumptions: that goods prices and wages adjust slowly to changes in excess demand/supply (with PPP holding only in the long run), and that capital markets are efficient, being in continuous equilibrium with the rate of interest adjusting immediately. The model is often referred to as a 'sticky price' model in recognition of the role played by the slow adjustment of goods prices and wages. For simplicity we shall deal with a 'small-country' version of the model, so that the foreign (country B) variables may be taken as exogenously determined, and assume that outputs are fixed at their full-employment levels.

☐ *Equilibrium in the money market*

Certain elements of the model are taken from the flexible-price model. Thus the asset market is in equilibrium, with money supply equal to money demand, and money demand a function of income and the rate of interest. We therefore have equation (27.19), which repeats equation (27.7) from the flexible-price model

$$\ln(M_A) - \ln(P_A) = \eta \ln(Y_A) - \sigma r_A \quad \text{with } \eta > 0, \sigma > 0 \qquad (27.19)$$

Domestic and foreign bonds are assumed to be perfect substitutes, so the uncovered interest rate parity condition holds. Equation (27.20) repeats equation (27.11).

$$r_A - r_B = E[\hat{e}] \tag{27.20}$$

Purchasing power parity is assumed to determine the long-run equilibrium exchange rate, $\bar{e}$, from the long-run domestic price levels, $\bar{P}_A$ and $\bar{P}_B$: equation (27.21) is thus a modification of equation (27.9).

$$\ln(\bar{e}) = \ln(\bar{P}_A) - \ln(\bar{P}_B) \tag{27.21}$$

If PPP holds only in the long run, the model must specify how expectations of the rate of changes in the spot rate will be formed. Dornbusch assumes they are formed *regressively*: that is,

$$E[\hat{e}] = \theta(\ln(\bar{e}) - \ln(e)) \tag{27.22}$$

where e is the current spot rate and $\theta(>0)$ determines the speed of adjustment to the long-run equilibrium value $\bar{e}$.

Substituting from equations (27.20) and (27.22) into (27.19), and rearranging gives the relationship between the exchange rate and the domestic price level that must be satisfied if the money market in country A is to be in equilibrium:

$$\ln(e) = \ln(\bar{e}) - \frac{1}{\sigma\theta}(\ln(P_A) - \ln(M_A) + \eta \ln(Y_A) - \sigma r_B) \tag{27.23}$$

The money supply, M_A, output, Y_A, and foreign interest rate, r_B, are all exogenous, and the long-run exchange rate, $\bar{e}$, is determined by the long-run price levels, so (27.23) represents the short-term relationship between the exchange rate and price level.

Equation (27.23) shows that, in order to maintain money market equilibrium in the short run, a decrease in the domestic price level must lead to an increase in the exchange rate (a depreciation). The argument in support of this result is that if the price level falls then the transactions demand for money falls too, so that a fall in the interest rate is required in order to induce the public to continue to hold the available money stock. But a fall in the interest rate will only persuade investors to hold domestic bonds if they believe that the domestic currency will appreciate in the future, which requires that they believe the current exchange rate is above its equilibrium level. Curve MM in Figure 27.8 illustrates the money-market equilibrium condition (note that Figure 27.8 is drawn in terms of the actual values of the price level and the exchange rate, not in terms of their logarithms).

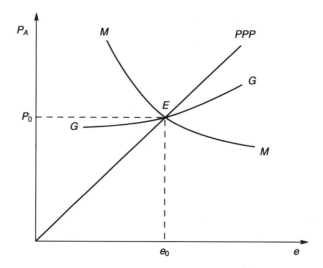

Figure 27.8   *Long-run equilibrium in the Dornbusch model*

☐ *Equilibrium in the goods market*

Aggregate demand in the goods market (D_A) is assumed to depend positively on the real exchange rate (eP_B/P_A) and domestic output, and negatively on the nominal rate of interest. The effects of foreign income (assumed fixed at its full-employment level) and of other exogenous variables are subsumed in a constant. The usual specification of aggregate demand is again in natural logarithms (except for the interest rate), as shown in equation (27.24)

$$\ln(D_A) = \alpha + \beta(\ln(e) + \ln(P_B) - \ln(P_A)) + \phi\ln(Y_A) - \gamma r_A \quad (27.24)$$

where the parameters α, β, ϕ and γ are all positive. Prices are assumed to adjust to the excess of demand over output according to

$$\hat{P}_A = \pi(\ln(D_A) - \ln(Y_A)) \quad (27.25)$$

where the adjustment parameter π is positive but less than one. Prices are therefore 'sticky' in that they do not adjust immediately to clear the goods market. Substituting for aggregate demand from equation (27.24) into (27.25) and rearranging gives

$$\hat{P}_A = \pi(\alpha + \beta(\ln(e) + \ln(P_B) - \ln(P_A)) \\ + (\phi - 1)\ln(Y_A) - \gamma r_A) \quad (27.26)$$

Equation (27.26) still involves the domestic interest rate, r_A. However, we know that the interest rate changes instantaneously to keep the money market in continuous equilibrium, so that we may use equation (27.19) to derive the following expression for the domestic interest rate:

$$r_A = \frac{1}{\sigma} \left(\eta \ln(Y_A) - \ln(M_A) + \ln(P_A) \right)$$

Substituting for r_A in (27.26) then gives, after some manipulation,

$$\hat{P}_A = \pi \left(\alpha + \beta \ln(e) + \beta \ln(P_B) - \left(\beta + \frac{\gamma}{\sigma} \right) \ln(P_A) \right.$$

$$\left. + \left(\phi - 1 - \frac{\gamma\eta}{\sigma} \right) \ln(Y_A) + \frac{\gamma}{\sigma} \ln(M_A) \right)$$

The goods market will be in equilibrium when aggregate demand equals aggregate supply: that is, when $\hat{P}_A = 0$. Setting the right-hand side of the preceding equation equal to 0 and rearranging gives

$$\ln(P_A) = \frac{1}{\beta + \mu} \left(\alpha + \beta \ln(e) + \beta \ln(P_B) \right.$$

$$\left. + (\phi - 1 - \mu\eta) \ln(Y_A) + \mu \ln(M_A) \right) \tag{27.27}$$

where $\mu = \gamma/\sigma$.

The condition for equilibrium in the goods market given in (27.27) implies that the exchange rate and the domestic price level are positively related. A depreciation (increase) in the exchange rate leads to an increased demand for exports, which must be offset by an increase in the price level to reduce domestic demand. The increase in prices will increase the demand for money, which in turn must be offset by an increase in interest rates. The interest rate increase then further reduces aggregate demand. The combinations of $\ln(P_A)$ and $\ln(e)$ that give equilibrium in the goods market are shown by the line GG in Figure 27.8. Note that at points above and to the left of GG there must be an excess supply in the market, while at points below and to the right of GG there must be excess demand.

☐ Long-run equilibrium

The intersection of MM and GG determines the joint short-term equilibrium in the money and the goods markets. We are interested however in comparing long-run equilibria, and in how the model behaves in the transition from one long-run equilibrium to another.

In a long-run equilibrium the purchasing power condition is satisfied. That is, the long-run equilibrium exchange rate $(\bar{e})$ is determined by the long-run domestic price levels. Rearranging equation (27.21) gives

$$\ln(\bar{P}_A) = \ln(\bar{e}) + \ln(\bar{P}_B)$$

which may be represented in Figure 27.8 by the line PPP.[16] Long-run equilibrium requires both that GG and MM be satisfied (short-run equilibrium) and that purchasing power parity be satisfied. Point E in Figure 27.8 is thus a long-run equilibrium since it lies on GG, MM, and PPP. The price level and the exchange rate are at their long-run equilibrium values, P_0 and e_0 respectively.

In order to determine the short-run behaviour of the model it is necessary to know whether GG is flatter than PPP (as shown in Figure 27.8) or not. From equation (27.27) the slope of GG is

$$\frac{\partial \ln(P_A)}{\partial \ln(e)} = \frac{\beta}{\beta + \mu}$$

whereas the purchasing power parity equation indicates that

$$\frac{\partial \ln(_A)}{\partial \ln(\bar{e})} = 1$$

Since $\mu > 0$, it follows that GG must be flatter then PPP.

Monetary expansion and exchange-rate overshooting

Suppose that the economy is initially in long-run equilibrium, and that the authorities then expand the money supply unexpectedly, so shifting the money-market function MM to the right. This is shown in Figure 27.9, where the initial equilibrium is at the intersection of M_0M_0, G_0G_0, and PPP, with domestic price level P_0 and exchange rate e_0. (The MM and GG curves have been drawn as straight lines for convenience.)

In the long run, an x per cent increase in the money supply, shifting the money-market equilibrium schedule from M_0M_0 to M_1M_1, will increase the domestic price level by the same proportion. Increasing the money supply cannot however have any long-run effect on the balance of payments, so the original purchasing-power-parity exchange rate must hold in the long-run: the PPP line in Figure 27.9 does not change. The long-run equilibrium must therefore be where the new money-market equilibrium schedule intersects the PPP line, so that the long-run price

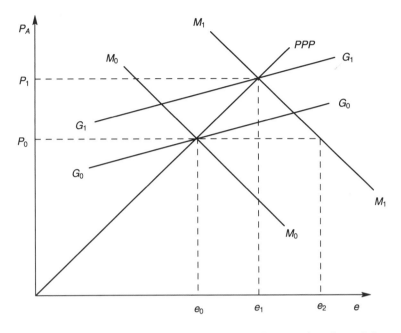

Figure 27.9 *Unexpected monetary expansion in the Dornbusch model*

level will be P_1, and the long-run exchange rate will be e_1. The goods-market equilibrium schedule must shift to $G_1 G_1$.

The interesting question however is what happens during the adjustment to the new long-run equilibrium. The model assumes that investors know what the long-run equilibrium will be, and that they expect the exchange rate to adjust to its new equilibrium over time. The domestic price level will not change initially (the 'sticky price' assumption), but the asset market clears immediately. The effect of the increase in the money supply is that the exchange rate 'jumps' to e_2, which is determined by the new money-market equilibrium schedule and the original price level. This is an example of the phenomenon usually referred to as *exchange-rate overshooting*. The exchange rate jumps beyond its appropriate long-run value.

Why should this happen? The expansion of the money supply can only be absorbed in the short run by a fall in the interest rate, since output is fixed and the domestic price level does not change instantaneously. But the fall in the domestic interest rate would lead investors to move out of the domestic currency unless there was an immediate depreciation of the currency sufficient to offset the interest-rate differential. The exchange rate must therefore depreciate beyond its long-run equilibrium value in order to induce investors to hold domestic bonds in the short run, since only then will they expect the future appreciation that will make them indifferent between domestic and foreign bonds (the uncovered interest parity condition is assumed to hold at all times).

As time progresses the price level will start to adjust to the change in the situation. The lower domestic interest rate will encourage increased expenditure, while the undervalued currency (relative to its PPP value) will lead to an expansion of exports and a decrease in imports. The goods market equilibrium schedule will gradually shift upwards, until it passes through the intersection of M_1M_1 and *PPP*, and the new long-run equilibrium is attained.

Note that exchange-rate overshooting occurs even though investors are rational, and even though they accept that the increase in the money supply will be permanent, so that they know with confidence what the final equilibrium will be. The stickiness of prices in the goods market, coupled with the instantaneous adjustment of the asset market, leads to an immediate exchange-rate shift that is greater than the known long-run movement that will finally result in equilibrium. The Dornbusch model thus provides an explanation of the observed volatility of exchange rates that does not rely on imperfect information, or on a lack of belief in the monetary authority's control over the money supply.

■ 27.7 Empirical evidence on monetary models

In general the various models we have discussed have not performed well empirically (and neither have those we have not discussed).[17] There have been various empirical studies comparing different exchange-rate models, with no clear evidence favouring one over the others. Indeed, in many cases the estimated parameters are either insignificant or, worse, have the wrong signs. Exchange-rate models have fared little better in tests of their forecasting capability, a common conclusion being that they perform worse than a simple random-walk model. Finally, tests on market efficiency (essentially tests of the uncovered interest rate parity hypothesis) tend to reject it.

The foreign exchange market is undoubtedly extremely complex, and the theories of exchange-rate determination are increasing in complexity as well, and it is necessarily extremely difficult to formulate econometric models that reflect these complexities. One possible explanation for the poor performance of exchange-rate models is our present inability to model expectations with any great confidence. It is evident that there is great scope for work in this area.

■ 27.8 Summary and conclusions

The models of exchange-rate determination discussed in this chapter all have major flaws. The fixed-price models are either restricted to a situation where capital is completely immobile or take the naive view that domestic and foreign assets are perfect substitutes and that a maintained interest rate differential will result in a continual flow of capital.

The monetary models take a more sophisticated view of capital movements, but all make the PPP hypothesis a central part. Since the empirical evidence does not favour PPP, this must cast some doubts on such models. This is compounded by the central role played by expectations in such models, given that there is some doubt about how to model them.

Of perhaps more concern is that the various models can offer quite different predictions of the outcome of monetary and fiscal expansions on the exchange rate. We shall return to this when discussing government policy in Chapter 28.

☐ *Notes*

1 For a detailed discussion of this area see Llewellyn and Milner (1990), especially the chapters by Dornbusch, Beenstock and MacDonald, and Pilbeam (1992), especially Chapters 6–9.

2 The analysis is based on that introduced in Mundell (1961a).

3 See Mundell (1962) and (1963), and Fleming (1962).

4 We are following the original specification of the model, which assumes that the domestic price level is fixed. A less restricted model would take account of the fact that a change in the exchange rate will change the prices of importables, and so would affect the price level. A depreciation, for example, raises the domestic price level. In such a case it would no longer be valid to assume that the *LM* schedule does not move. A depreciation of the exchange rate would in fact move the *LM* schedule to the left. The original amendment to the Mundell–Fleming model to allow for such effects is in Branson and Buiter (1983).

5 Cassell (1928).

6 For a more detailed discussion of the criticisms of PPP, and of the empirical work that will be discussed later, see MacDonald (1990). For greater detail see MacDonald (1988).

7 See Balassa (1964), in which it is argued that productivity differentials will lead to developed countries having apparently overvalued exchange rates. See also Samuelson (1964). The arguments in these two papers are often grouped together as the 'Balassa–Samuelson thesis'.

8 Equation (27.4) suggests that if we regress the logarithm of the exchange rate on the logarithm of the ratio of the two prices indices then the coefficient

is +1. Testing whether the estimated coefficient is significantly different from this is thus a test of the absolute PPP hypothesis. Equation (27.5) suggests that the regression should be of the change in the logarithm of the exchange rate on the change in the logarithm of the ratio of the price indices, and that if relative PPP holds then the slope coefficient should be +1.

9   See for example Isard (1977), and Kravis and Lipsey (1978).

10 For a recent study of PPP in the short and long run, see Manzur (1990).

11 For example, MacDonald (1985) concludes that the market is efficient, while Frankel and Froot (1985) come to the opposite conclusion.

12 The flexible price monetary model was developed in: Frenkel (1976), Mussa (1976), and Bilson, (1978).

13 The specific algebraic model used here follows that in Chapter 7 of Pilbeam (1992).

14 $(1 + \hat{e})(1 + r_B) \approx 1 + \hat{e} + r_B$ if $\hat{e}$ and r_B are small.

15 Dornbusch (1976).

16 The PPP function has unit elasticity, which implies that it is a straight line drawn from the origin in a graph of the *real* values of the domestic price level and the exchange rate.

17 For a more detailed discussion of empirical results, see MacDonald (1990) and Pilbeam (1992), Chapter 9.

■ *Chapter 28* ■

Macroeconomic Policy with Floating Exchange Rates

■ 28.1 Introduction

The Bretton Woods system, under which currencies were pegged against the US dollar, and so effectively against gold, started to disintegrate in 1967 (see Chapter 31 for a more detailed discussion). The developed market economies, led by the United Kingdom and followed soon afterwards by Switzerland and then Japan, began to adopt floating exchange rates in the early 1970s. Although such regimes were not 'legitimised' by amendments to the IMF Articles until 1978, most developed countries have operated a floating exchange-rate system since the mid-1970s.

Strictly speaking, national monetary authorities have continued to 'manage' their exchange rates, rather than let them be determined purely by market forces – what is often referred to as 'dirty' floating. This management has usually taken the form of intervention into the market in order to smooth out short-term fluctuations in the exchange rate, while supposedly allowing the market to determine the long-run equilibrium exchange rate. If intervention in the foreign exchange is restricted to such smoothing operations, with no attempt to influence the mean rate, than we would not expect there to be any long-run changes in the foreign exchange reserves. In practice there seems little doubt that governments have not resisted the temptation to extend management into the longer term.

In this chapter we shall confine the discussion to the problems of macroeconomic policy-making under freely floating exchange rates. In Chapter 29 we consider policy when exchange rates are pegged. In so far as governments do intervene in the foreign exchange markets then some elements of the discussion of that chapter will be relevant here. The focus of attention in both chapters is on the problems of formulating macroeconomic policies in order to obtain a specified target or targets.

The discussion will therefore be restricted to the Mundell–Fleming model with fixed prices but under varying assumptions about capital mobility, and the simple monetarist flexible-price model discussed in Chapter 27.

∎ 28.2 The policy environment and policy targets

☐ *The environment*

The environment in which policy must be made, and so the choice of appropriate policy instruments, will, for simplicity, be assumed to depend on two conditions. First, it is determined by the degree of price flexibility. We shall consider the two polar cases, a fixed-price (Keynesian) economy, in which resources may be unemployed, and a flexible-price economy where all markets clear. The second determining factor is the nature of the international capital market. At the two extremes, capital may be perfectly immobile or perfectly mobile, and as we saw in Chapter 27, the effects of both monetary and fiscal policy may vary markedly between these two cases. If capital is mobile, whether perfectly or not, then we might also consider the differences in policy suggested by the flow and the stock models of international capital movements.

☐ *Policy targets*

In all but the most laissez-faire cases, governments set themselves 'policy targets', often stated explicitly in election manifestos or in subsequent policy pronouncements. We shall focus here on familiar macroeconomic targets: in an economy with fixed prices and/or imperfectly functioning markets the dominant *internal* target is usually taken to be obtaining as high a level of employment as is consistent with an acceptable level of inflation. In a economy with flexible prices and perfectly functioning markets (and so by assumption full employment) the internal target is generally the avoidance of inflation. To these is often added some control over the interest rate, perhaps with a view to attaining some desired rate of growth, although perfect capital mobility will, under the assumptions of a flow model, preclude this.

In principle there is no *external* problem under a system of freely-floating exchange rates. That is, the government does not have to take explicit account of the balance of payments when formulating policy, since with a floating exchange rate the balance of payments must always be in equilibrium. This contrasts markedly with the situation under pegged exchange rates, where it is possible to run a deficit or surplus on the balance of payments (though not indefinitely), so that policy-makers must take the country's external position into account.

In practice, however, policy-makers may not be indifferent to the structure of the balance of payments. For example, they may regard an overall balance made up of individual balances on the current and the long-term capital account as preferable to an overall balance consisting of a deficit on current account financed by an inflow of foreign capital, or *vice versa*.

It is unlikely that we shall be able to give unambiguous answers to even the most simple policy questions. Nevertheless, commentators on economic policy-making almost invariably do make unambiguous prescriptions. That they do so will usually reflect their belief that one model of the range that we shall discuss best reflects reality. The moral is that one should seek out the assumptions on which the recommendations are based. Often one must infer them from the policy prescriptions.

■ 28.3 The Mundell–Fleming Model

The Mundell–Fleming model, outlined in Chapter 27, provides the most simple environment in which to discuss macroeconomic policy when prices are fixed. It allows us to consider the relative effectiveness of monetary and fiscal policy under varying degrees of capital mobility, but is of course based on the flow model of international capital movements. We shall assume initially that there is just one policy target, 'full employment with acceptable inflation', identified here with a target level of income, Y_f. We shall start by considering the effectiveness of monetary policy under three different levels of capital mobility, and then repeat that exercise for fiscal policy.

☐ *Monetary policy and capital mobility*

We discussed the effects of a monetary expansion (and by implication a contraction) under the assumptions of perfectly immobile and perfectly mobile capital in Chapter 27. We shall repeat them briefly here, before considering the more interesting (and arguably more realistic) case of imperfectly mobile capital. In order to simplify the exposition we shall assume that initially there is current-account balance and so no net inflow or outflow of capital.[1]

With perfectly immobile capital (a vertical *BP* schedule) a monetary expansion, which shifts the *LM* schedule to the right, leads to an incipient balance-of-payments deficit and so to a depreciation of the exchange rate. This in turn leads to both the *IS* and *BP* schedules shifting to the right, and a new equilibrium is obtained at a higher level of income. The policy problem lies in choosing the appropriate monetary expansion, since the subsequent shifts in the *IS* and *BP* schedules amplify the initial effect. The 'side effects' of the monetary expansion are a fall in the rate of interest and a depreciation in the exchange rate.

When capital is perfectly mobile (the *BP* schedule is horizontal) then the shift to the right in the *LM* schedule results in a capital outflow, and so a depreciation of the exchange rate and thus an equivalent shift in the *IS* schedule. The appropriate monetary expansion is that which shifts the *LM* curve to the extent that it intersects with the *BP* schedule at the target level of income. There are no subsequent effects that will amplify or diminish the effects of the initial expansion. The side effects of the monetary expansion in this case are a depreciation of the exchange rate, and a current account surplus with a matching capital outflow. The rate of interest must be the same in both equilibria.

Figure 28.1 shows the intermediate case, where there is limited capital mobility. The *BP* schedule has a positive slope, since an increase in income, which leads to a current-account deficit, may be offset by an increase in the domestic rate of interest, which results in a capital-account surplus.

A monetary expansion must lead initially to a fall in the rate of interest and to an increase in income. Both contribute to a deficit in the balance of

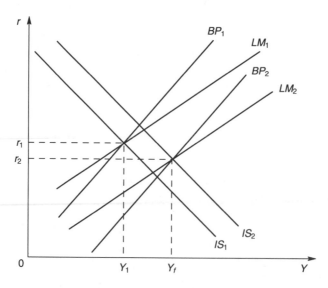

Figure 28.1 *Monetary policy in the Mundell–Fleming model with limited capital mobility*

payments, and so to a depreciation of the exchange rate. This in turn results in an improvement in the current account, shifting the *IS* schedule to the right, and in a rightward shift of the *BP* schedule. The movement in the *IS* schedule amplifies the effect of the initial monetary expansion on income, while at the same time partially offsetting the initial fall in the rate of interest.

In the final equilibrium, shown by the intersection of LM_2, IS_2, and BP_2, income is higher than before the monetary expansion, and the domestic rate of interest is lower.[2] Since the latter must lead to an outflow of capital, it follows that the exchange rate must have depreciated to such an extent that it outweighs the effect of the income increase, and produces a current-account surplus. Note that the more mobile is capital (the flatter the *BP* schedule), the greater will be the effect of a given monetary expansion on the level of income, and the smaller will be its effect on the rate of interest. This is consistent with our earlier analysis of the two extreme cases. However, in all cases the effect of a monetary expansion is to increase the level of income.

☐ *Fiscal policy and capital mobility*

We saw in Chapter 27 that whereas a fiscal expansion is effective in increasing income when there is no capital mobility, it is totally ineffective when capital is perfectly mobile. Indeed, in the former case the initial effect of the fiscal expansion is amplified by the consequent depreciation of the currency and the improvement in the current account that brings about. In the latter case the inflow of capital brought about by the short-term increase in the domestic interest rate leads to an appreciation of the exchange rate, and so to a worsening of the current account that exactly offsets the initial expansionary effect. The contrast between these two extreme cases suggests that in the intermediate case the *degree* of capital mobility will play a crucial part in determining the effects of a fiscal expansion.

Figure 28.2 is drawn on the assumption that capital is sufficiently immobile for the *BP* schedule to be steeper than the *LM* schedule. The initial equilibrium is again at the intersection of LM_1, IS_1, and BP_1, giving an equilibrium income of Y_1, and the target level of income is Y_f.

A fiscal expansion will shift the *IS* schedule to the right, say to IS_2. If nothing else changed then there would be an increase in income coupled with a rise in the rate of interest. In the case shown in Figure 28.2, the net effect must be a balance-of-payments deficit, shown by the intersection of IS_2 and LM_1 being to the *right* of BP_1. This must always be the case if the *BP* schedule is steeper than *LM*. The exchange rate must therefore

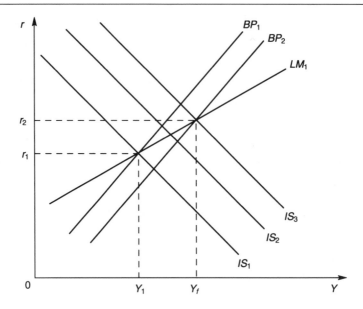

Figure 28.2 *Fiscal policy in the Mundell–Fleming model with limited capital mobility – Case 1*

depreciate, which shifts the *IS* schedule yet further to the right and the *BP* schedule in the same direction. Given that the government chooses the appropriate fiscal expansion, the new equilibrium will be at the target income Y_f, determined by the intersection of IS_3, BP_2, and LM_1. Both income and the domestic rate of interest have increased, and the depreciation in the exchange rate has amplified the income effect of the initial fiscal expansion. There is a deficit on the current account, balanced by an inflow of capital.

Figure 28.3 shows the other possibility – that capital is sufficiently for the *BP* schedule to be flatter than *LM*. As before, the fiscal expansion shifts the *IS* schedule to the right, to IS_2. The increase in income worsens the current account position, but the increase in the rate of interest leads to a capital inflow. In this case the net effect, should nothing else change, is an improvement in the balance of payments, indicated by the fact that the intersection of IS_2 and LM_1 is to the *left* of BP_1 (which must always be the case when *BP* is flatter than *LM*).

It follows that the exchange rate will appreciate. Appreciation of the exchange rate must shift the *IS* curve to the left, so that in the new equilibrium it will lie somewhere between IS_1 and IS_2. The appreciation will also shift the *BP* schedule to the left. With an appropriate choice of the initial fiscal expansion the government can secure a new equilibrium at the target level of income, Y_f. Note that in this case the final effect on income

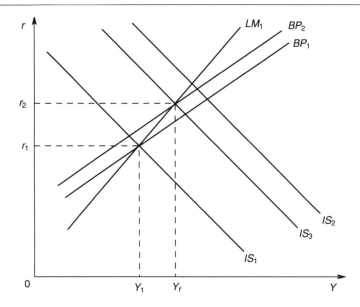

Figure 28.3 *Fiscal policy in the Mundell–Fleming model with limited capital mobility – Case 2*

is less than the initial effect: if capital is sufficiently mobile then the effect of a fiscal expansion is dampened. The rate of interest, however, is still higher than in the initial equilibrium: there is, as in the previous case, a capital inflow, balanced by a current-account deficit.

The effects of a fiscal expansion depend, therefore, on the degree of capital mobility to a more marked extent than is the case with a monetary expansion. In the latter case the effect of the initial expansion is usually amplified by subsequent shifts in the *IS* schedule; even in the 'worst' case, when capital is perfectly mobile, there is no dampening of the initial impact. With a fiscal expansion however the initial impact may be amplified or diminished, depending on the degree of capital mobility, and is in fact nullified when capital is perfectly mobile. A similar indeterminacy obtains when we consider the effects of an expansion on the exchange rate. A monetary expansion always leads to a depreciation of the exchange rate, but a fiscal expansion may lead to depreciation or appreciation, depending on the degree of capital mobility

Finally, it is important to note the different effects of monetary and fiscal expansion on the interest rate, and hence on the composition of the balance of payments (assuming as before that we start from a position of balance on both the current and the capital accounts). Monetary expansion always leads to a fall in the domestic interest rate, and hence to a capital outflow, which must be balanced by a surplus on the current account.

Fiscal expansion on the other hand always leads to an increase in the domestic interest rate, so that in the final equilibrium there must be a capital inflow, balanced by a deficit on the current account.

Combining monetary and fiscal policy when there are two policy targets

In the preceding analysis we assumed that the government had only one policy objective, represented by the target level of income Y_f. It is however quite possible that the government is also concerned with the domestic rate of interest, perhaps because it takes a view on the desirable level of investment, or perhaps because it is concerned with the composition of the balance of payments. At the most basic level the government may prefer that the interest rate rise as the economy moves towards the target income, in which case it will choose to use a fiscal rather than a monetary expansion. Should it want the rate of interest to fall then it will opt for a monetary expansion. At a more sophisticated level, the government may choose to specify a target level of the rate of interest as well as a target level of income.

An important principle in policy-making, due to Tinbergen,[3] states that in order to achieve *n* policy targets it is necessary to have *n* independent policy instruments. In the case we are considering, the two targets are the level of income, Y_f, and the desired rate of interest, r_t. The policy instruments are monetary policy and fiscal policy. The two instruments are independent since they have different effects on the income/interest rate mix. Monetary expansion lowers the rate of interest while expanding income, fiscal policy increases the rate of interest while increasing income.

Figure 28.4 illustrates an example of the use of both monetary and fiscal policy to attain the twin targets Y_f and r_t, starting from an initial position in which income, Y_1, is below the target income, while the rate of interest, r_1, is above its target value. We may simplify the analysis by remembering that fiscal expansion and contraction do not shift the LM schedule.

We know that a monetary expansion will both increase income and reduce the rate of interest. Suppose that the money supply is increased to the level that is consistent with both targets, shown by the schedule LM_2 passing through the point defined by Y_f and r_t. From our earlier analysis, we know that the monetary expansion will lead to a shift to the right of the IS schedule. It is however most unlikely that the new IS will also pass through the point defined by Y_f and r_t.

Suppose instead that the IS schedule shifts out to IS_2. At the new equilibrium, given by the intersection of LM_2 and IS_2 (and BP_2), both income and the rate of interest are above their target levels. A fiscal

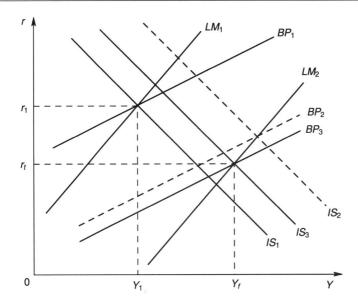

Figure 28.4 *Using monetary and fiscal policy to attain two policy targets*

contraction will however reduce both income and the rate of interest. The target values may now be obtained by a fiscal contraction that moves the *IS* schedule to IS_3.

Had the shift in the *IS* schedule following the monetary expansion not been so marked, so that IS_2 intersected LM_2 to the south-west of the target point, both income and the rate of interest would be below their desired levels. The appropriate fiscal policy in that case would be an expansion.

We have analysed this problem as though the government seeks out the desired values of its targets in a step-by-step manner. This need not of course be the case. If the effects of monetary and fiscal policy are known with certainty then it is in principle possible to obtain the policy target in one step by choosing the appropriate combination of monetary and fiscal policy. Nevertheless, various commentators have argued that policy-makers do in fact tend to seek their objectives by changing policies sequentially rather than simultaneously.

A corollary to the Tinbergen principle is that it is in general impossible to attain two targets by the use of one instrument (as we saw above). It has been argued that policy-makers may well restrict themselves to an insufficient range of policy instruments, and that this may explain the tendency for what have been called 'stop–go' policy changes. Figure 28.5 may be used to illustrate this phenomenon. Suppose that the government is unwilling to use monetary policy, and generally regards full employment at Y_f as its policy target, although it has a view on the level of the domestic

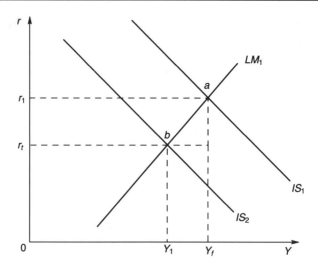

Figure 28.5   *Pursuing two targets with one instrument: 'stop–go' policy*

interest rate, r_t, that is required for long-term growth in the economy. An appropriate fiscal policy will put the IS schedule at IS_1, so that it intersects with the (fixed) LM_1 schedule at point *a*, so attaining the target income. (The BP schedules are omitted in order to simplify the diagram.)

The rate of interest at *a* is however above its desired value. If the government becomes concerned about the effects of this high rate of interest then it may elect to pursue a contractionary fiscal policy in order to reduce the interest rate. The target rate, r_t, may be attained by a fiscal contraction that shifts the IS schedule to IS_2, resulting in equilibrium at point *b*. At this point however income is below the target value. If at some point the government decides that it must once again pursue full employment then it must once again use fiscal expansion in order to go back to point *a*.

■ 28.4 The monetary approach

In discussing this approach we shall use the simple monetarist model developed in section 26.4. The key assumptions of the model are a stable money demand function, flexible prices and perfect markets (and hence full employment), and purchasing power parity (PPP). The money supply is assumed to depend on the supply of high-powered money, which in turn consists of currency and central bank deposits held by the commercial banks, and the foreign currency reserves. Figure 28.6, which reproduces Figure 26.8, shows general equilibrium in the monetary model.

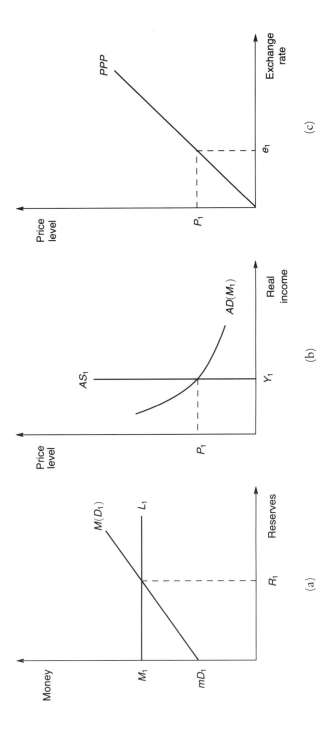

Figure 28.6   *General equilibrium in the monetary approach*

Within the context of the monetary model there can be no balance-of-payments problem when exchange rates are free to move, nor can there be involuntary unemployment. Most of the policy problems underlying the discussion in Section 28.3 are therefore assumed away! We shall focus on the effects on the domestic economy and the exchange rate of two changes in the economy: first, a change in the money supply, and second an increase in real income due to an increase in output.

An expansion in the money supply under floating exchange rates

Suppose that the authorities increase the domestic element of the money supply from D_1 to D_2. This is shown in Panel (a) of Figure 28.7 by the upward shift in the money supply schedule from $M(D_1)$ to $M(D_2)$. Initially, since the price level has not changed, this increase in the money supply leads to domestic residents having excess real money balances. They will therefore increase their demand for goods, which will shift the aggregate demand schedule in panel (b) to the right. This will have two effects: an increase in imports, and an increase in the domestic price level. The former will lead to a depreciation of the exchange rate, and the latter to a reduction in real money balances.

The final equilibrium will be obtained when the money demand has increased sufficiently for the money market to be cleared (the intersection of L_2 with $M(D_2)$ in panel (a)), with a price level, P_2, that is consistent both with equilibrium in the goods market (the intersection of $AD(M_2)$ and AS_1 in panel (b)) and with the PPP exchange rate (e_2 in panel (c)).

Consideration of the algebraic formulation of the model given in section 26.4 shows that in the long run the effects of an x per cent increase in the money supply are an x per cent increase in the domestic price level and an x per cent depreciation of the exchange rate.

Two conclusions are worth noting. First, that there is no change in the foreign exchange reserves, and so no subsequent changes in the money supply. Second, there is no 'balance-of-payments problem'. That is, the authorities are assumed to be content to let the exchange rate adjust to the expansion of the money supply.

An increase in aggregate supply under floating exchange rates

The increase in aggregate supply, and hence in real income, is shown in panel (b) of Figure 28.8 by the shift of the AS schedule from AS_1 to AS_2. At

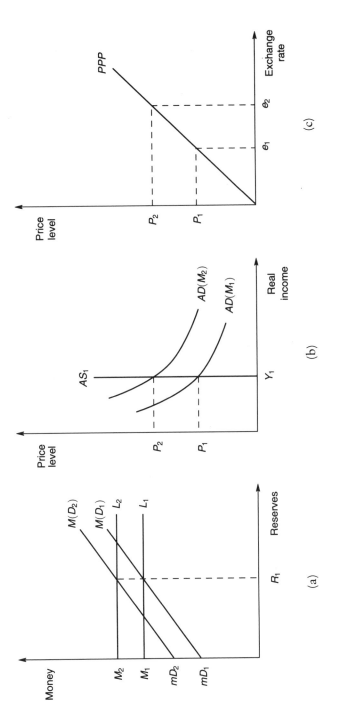

Figure 28.7 *An increase in money supply in the monetary approach*

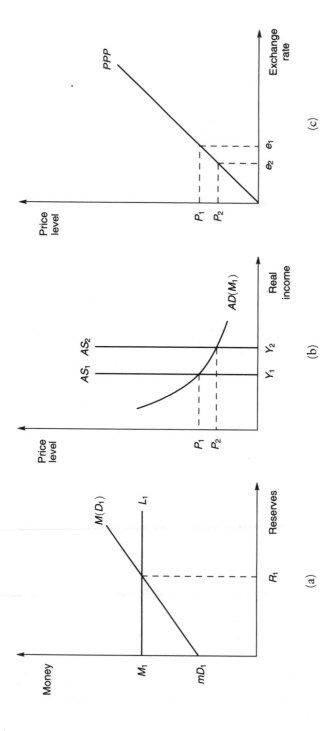

Figure 28.8 *An increase in aggregate supply in the monetary approach*

the current price level, P_1, there is an excess supply of goods and an increase in the transactions demand for money.

The excess supply in the goods market will lead to a fall in the price level, which will both moderate the transactions demand for money and lead to an appreciation in the exchange rate as imports fall and exports rise. Since the money supply has not changed, equilibrium can only be restored when the price level has fallen by enough to exactly counteract the effects of the increased income on the money demand. It follows from this that the aggregate demand schedule cannot have changed. The final equilibrium is achieved at a price level P_2 and with an (appreciated) exchange rate e (panel (c)).

■ 28.5 Summary and conclusions

We have given most attention to the Mundell–Fleming fixed price model in our discussion of macroeconomic policy-making under floating exchange rates. This is largely because the range of policy problems is much more extensive than under the flexible-price monetary model. Nevertheless, it is possible to amend the Mundell–Fleming model to allow for price flexibility, so broadening its relevance, and to modify the flexible-price assumption of the monetary model, say by using the Dornbusch 'sticky price' variation. We chosen not to pursue these possibilities, which fall more within the province of texts on macroeconomic policy and international finance.

Our concern is more with the environment within which policy-making takes place, and in particular the influence of the exchange-rate system and the degree of capital mobility. We move in Chapter 29 to considering macroeconomic policy under a pegged exchange-rate system. As we shall see, some of the conclusions we have reached in this chapter do not hold under pegged exchange rates. This then raises the question of whether one exchange-rate system is better than the other, and if so, under what circumstances. We shall attempt to shed some light on this question, which has been the subject of considerable debate, in Chapter 30.

☐ *Notes*

1 The main body of the text will therefore refer, for example, to 'a deficit on the current account'. This is a convenient shorthand for 'an increased deficit or a reduced surplus on the current account'.

2 If there were some increase in the price level then the *LM* schedule would shift some of the way back towards its initial position, so reducing the expansionary effect of the original increase in the money supply.

3   Tinbergen (1952). Viewed algebraically, the Tinbergen principle is equivalent to saying that n independent equations are needed in order to solve for n variables. In the policy context the variables are the values of the policy instruments, and the equations specify the relationships between the policy instruments and the targets.

■ *Chapter 29* ■

Macroeconomic Policy with Fixed and Pegged Exchange Rates

■ 29.1 Introduction

The distinction between fixed and pegged exchange rates is often rather blurred, sometimes by design. The essential distinction between the two is that a fixed exchange rate is just that: *fixed*. The epitome of the fixed exchange rate system was the *gold standard* (strictly the *gold currency standard*), in which the exchange rate between two currencies was determined by the relative weight in gold of the main coin of the realm.[1] That is, if the weight in gold of a sovereign was four times that of a US dollar coin then the exchange rate was £1 = \$4.[2]

A pegged exchange rate on the other hand is maintained by the actions of the monetary authorities, as discussed in Chapter 24. The value at which the exchange rate is pegged (the par value) is therefore a policy variable: it may be changed.

There is thus both a clear difference between the two systems and a common element. Under a fixed exchange-rate system, such as the gold standard, adjustment to balance-of-payments surpluses or deficits cannot come about through changes in the exchange rate. Adjustment must either come about 'automatically' through the workings of the economic system or be brought about by the government, perhaps reinforcing the automatic mechanism. A pegged exchange-rate system may, so long as the exchange rate is not changed, and is not expected to change,[3] be expected to display the same characteristics. However, there is another option open to the government: it may appreciate or depreciate (devalue) the currency.

613

The other side of the coin is that under a pegged exchange-rate system a country may run a surplus or deficit on the balance of payments for some length of time. To do so, it may have to follow policies which thwart the automatic adjustment mechanism (if it exists and operates efficiently), but it can be done. The state of the balance of payments therefore becomes a policy target: a government may choose to pursue a 'neutral' policy (no change in the reserves), but it may also elect to run at a deficit or a surplus. Moreover, a government faced with a balance-of-payments deficit (or surplus) need not use changes in the exchange rate to correct the problem. It may choose to leave the exchange rate unchanged and deal with the balance-of-payments problem by the use of monetary or fiscal policy.

Policy-making under a pegged exchange-rate system is therefore more complicated than under a floating system. There is necessarily an additional policy target, maintaining a given state of the balance of payments, and also an additional policy instrument, changing the par value of the currency. However, in practice, the original (Bretton Woods) IMF system, of which pegged exchange rates were an integral part, required that governments only changed the par value of their currency in the event of serious structural problems. Moreover, for various reasons governments were unwilling to alter the par value of their currency (and in particular to devalue it) even when it was clear that there were such problems: maintaining the exchange rate was often seen by governments as a matter of national pride, and perhaps as an indicator of good macroeconomic management. More jaundiced observers suggested that maintaining the existing exchange rate became a totem rather than a rational objective.

The pegged exchange-rate system also contains a major asymmetry. The pressure on a country with a persistent balance-of-payments deficit to devalue its currency is much greater than the pressure on a country with a persistent surplus to appreciate. The immediate reason for the difference is that maintaining the par value against a deficit requires continual buying of the domestic currency, thus depleting the reserves. Since foreign exchange reserves are necessarily limited, the ability of a government to withstand downward pressure on its currency is also limited. This is not to say that maintaining an undervalued currency is beneficial to a country in the long run, merely that the immediate pressure on a surplus country is much less than that on a deficit country.

The asymmetry has led to concentration on the effectiveness of policies aimed at correcting a balance-of-payments deficit, so that much of the work on the effects of changes in the par value of a currency is written in terms of a devaluation. We shall follow the same convention.

We shall start by giving a quick overview of the gold standard, arguing that adjustment was to a great extent automatic, working through changes in the money supply. We shall then examine in more detail the effects of devaluation on the balance of payments, using the simplifying assumption that capital is immobile. We then move on to consider the operations of monetary, fiscal and exchange rate policies under a pegged exchange-rate regime. As we shall see, the relative effectiveness of monetary and fiscal policy is very much dependent on whether capital is internationally mobile or not (as is the case with floating exchange rates). Finally, we shall examine the implications of the monetary approach when exchange rates are pegged.

■ 29.2 The gold standard

The gold standard emerged slowly during the nineteenth century. It became more widely established about 1870, and was full fledged during the forty years from the beginning of the 1870s to the outbreak of the First World War in 1914. The leading countries tried to revive the gold standard in the 1920s. Britain, for instance, went back to the gold standard in 1925, and other countries followed. The system collapsed with the Great Depression in the beginning of the 1930s.

The main objective of economic policy under the gold standard was to keep the balance of payments in equilibrium, so that here was no change in the reserves of gold and foreign currency. The main instrument for this was monetary policy, so that the dominant authority handling economic policy in those days was the central bank.

Under the gold standard a British sovereign (£1) contained 113.0016 grains of pure gold. The US dollar coin contained 23.22 grains. Both currencies were tied to gold, in that both central banks had a commitment to buy or sell gold at the fixed rate implied by the gold content of the coins. This implied that £1 was worth US$4.87. The dollar rate could fluctuate between an upper 'gold point' of 4.90 and a lower 'gold point' of 4.84, these limits being set by the cost of shipping gold between London and New York (3 cents per sovereign).

Suppose that the United States had a deficit in its balance of payments. The demand for foreign exchange in the United States (the £) would then be larger than the supply of foreign exchange, and so the price of foreign exchange would start to rise. It could not rise to more than 4.90, since if US importers found they had to pay more than $4.90 to buy £1 on the foreign exchange market they could buy gold to the value of £1 from the Federal Reserve Bank in New York for $4.87, ship it to the United Kingdom at a cost of 3 cents, and sell it to the Bank of England for a £1 note, which they could then use to pay for their imports. No matter how long the US deficit persisted, US importers knew that they would never have to pay more than $4.90 for £1.

The 'standard' explanation of the effects of a US deficit under the gold standard are as follows. The US authorities would be faced with a fall in their foreign exchange reserves, and possibly an outflow of gold. This would reduce the money supply (for the reasons discussed in Chapter 28), unless the monetary authorities took steps to counteract the effect of a fall in reserves by increasing the other components of 'high-powered' money – a policy known as *sterilisation*. If the money supply did fall then this would lead to a fall in the general price level, so that US goods would become more competitive, so increasing exports and reducing imports. This process would continue until the deficit was eliminated.

On the other hand, a balance-of-payments surplus would lead to an increase in foreign exchange reserves, or even an inflow of gold. This, unless offset by the central bank, would lead to an increase in the price level and a loss of competitiveness, so that exports would fall and imports rise, and again there would be a return to balance-of-payments equilibrium.

Any change in the foreign exchange reserves of one country is necessarily mirrored in an opposite change in the reserves of its trading partners. If the country with a balance-of-payments disequilibrium is small then the effects on its trading partners will be negligible. If, on the other hand it is large, then the change in the foreign-exchange reserves of its trading partners will produce adjustment in their economies that will reinforce the adjustment in its own economy.

This adjustment mechanism was *automatic*, provided that the central bank did not completely sterilise the effects of the change in reserves on the money supply, and would be successful provided that the change in the price level did in fact bring about the appropriate adjustment in the balance of payments. Whether the latter happens or not is closely related to two questions: whether a change in the exchange rate will in fact shift the balance of trade in the right direction (essentially the Marshall–Lerner Condition discussed earlier), and whether capital is internationally immobile or not.

From the latter half of the nineteenth century at least, there was considerable mobility of capital between countries. The response of central banks to an outflow of gold then tended to be to increase interest rates in an attempt to attract an inflow of capital, which if successful would counteract the fall in the money supply. The increase in interest rates would reinforce the contraction in the deficit economy and so the adjustment process. Such a policy is not of course 'automatic'.

The attempt to return to the gold standard in the mid-1920s proved to be a failure.[4] Various reasons have been proposed, among them that a fall in the money supply and higher interest rates did not result in a fall in prices but rather in a fall in employment (particularly true for the United

Kingdom), and that the monetary authorities in the United States (which had a substantial balance-of-payments surplus) sterilised the inflow in order to avoid inflationary pressures. Whatever the cause(s), the adjustment mechanism did not work during this period.

■ 29.3 Devaluation: the elasticities approach

We now turn to the problems of macroeconomic policy when exchange rates are pegged. What we are describing is essentially the Bretton Woods system that operated from the end of the Second World War until its gradual disintegration in the early 1970s. Currencies had a par value against the US dollar, and the monetary authorities in each country were required to maintain their exchange rate within a prescribed range around that par value. The US authorities were committed to transactions with other monetary authorities, buying and selling gold at specified prices, so that other currencies were ultimately convertible into gold. (The system has for that reason been referred to as a gold *exchange* standard.)

The mechanisms by which one currency may be pegged to another were described in Chapter 24. In what follows we shall ignore the possible influence on the balance of payments of changes in the exchange rate within this band, on the not-unreasonable assumption that the permissible range of exchange rates was too narrow for this effect to be important. In this and the following section we shall consider approaches to the question of how changes in the par value, and in particular devaluation,[5] might affect the balance of payments when capital is immobile, so that changes in the balance on current account (which we shall continue to take as determined by the balance of trade) are reflected in changes in the balance of payments. We shall then discuss how macroeconomic policy will operate in such situations.

Devaluing the exchange rate changes the prices of domestically-produced traded goods relative to the prices of the same goods produced in other countries. That is, it reduces the relative prices of the devaluing country's exports and of its import-competing goods. This will, in time, increase the volume of exports and decrease the volume of imports. As we saw in Chapter 24, however, it does not necessarily follow that this will improve the balance of the devaluing country's foreign exchange earnings and foreign exchange payments. Whether it does so depends on the elasticities of supply and demand in the trading countries. The caveat 'in time' is also of some importance: economists are familiar with the proposition that elasticities are lower in the short run than in the long run.

It is tempting to borrow the analysis of the stability of a floating exchange rate from Chapter 24 and apply it directly to the question of whether devaluation improves the current account, and indeed this is what is often done. The reasoning is obvious: a floating exchange-rate market is stable only if a depreciation improves the balance of trade, and that is the question we are considering here.

The problem however is that the Marshall–Lerner Condition derived in Chapter 24 is based on the analysis of marginal changes, and uses *point* elasticities. A devaluation on the other hand is usually very much non-marginal: for example, the UK devaluation of 1967 was 14 per cent. This poses two problems. The first is that point elasticities are no longer appropriate: it is not too difficult to construct examples in which the (appropriate) Marshall–Lerner Condition is not satisfied yet a non-marginal devaluation will nonetheless improve the balance of trade, and *vice versa*. The second is that the income effects of a non-marginal devaluation are not negligible, so that the demand and supply curves underlying the derivation of the Marshall–Lerner Condition cannot be assumed to be fixed.

The Marshall–Lerner Condition may however be rescued provided that we remember that the elasticities are *arc* rather than *point* elasticities, and provided that we assume that the government neutralises the income effects of the devaluation. With those qualifications, the Marshall–Lerner Condition derived in Chapter 24 still holds. That is, for a country facing given import prices and able to expand exports at constant cost, a devaluation will improve the balance of trade if

$$\varepsilon_x + \varepsilon_m > 1 \tag{29.1}$$

where e_x is the foreign elasticity of demand for the devaluing country's exports and e_m is its elasticity of demand for imports (see equation 24.19).

In the general case the condition is

$$\frac{\eta_x(\varepsilon_x - 1)}{\varepsilon_x + \eta_x} + \frac{\varepsilon_m(1 + \eta_m)}{\varepsilon_m + \eta_m} \tag{29.2}$$

where η_x is the foreign elasticity of supply for the devaluing country's imports and η_x is the devaluing country's elasticity of supply for its exports (see equation 24.18).

As we noted above, there is a general consensus that both demand and supply elasticities will be greater in the long run than in the short run: that is, traded volumes will take some time to adjust to their new equilibrium levels. This raises the possibility that the Marshall–Lerner Condition may be satisfied in the long run but not in the short run. If that is the case then devaluation will initially make a balance-of-payments deficit worse. If this does happen then we have what is known as the 'J-curve effect', which is illustrated in Figure 29.1. If of course the Marshall–Lerner Condition is not

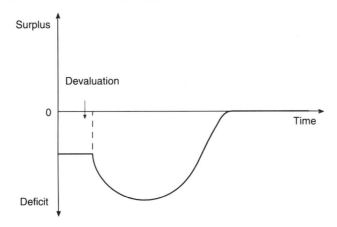

Figure 29.1 *The 'J-curve effect'*

satisfied in the long run either then the curve in Figure 29.1 will flatten out at a deficit greater than that before the devaluation.

The 'elasticities' approach just outlined does not deal explicitly with what is often thought to be the strongest argument against devaluation, that it will probably lead to an increase in the general price level. It will of course do this whether or not it improves the balance of payments.

The inflationary impact of a devaluation may come through various channels. The most obvious is that it increases the domestic prices of imports. If these are final goods then there is an immediate impact on the price level. If they are intermediate goods then the increase in their prices will push up the production costs of those goods in which they are used. The prices of domestically-produced goods may also rise even if they do not use imported intermediate goods: this will almost certainly be the case if they are close substitutes for imports, but may come about through a reduction in the degree of competition within the economy. Finally, the domestic prices of exportables may rise, since exporters may not reduce the foreign currency prices of their goods by the extent of the devaluation, and may be unwilling to sell on the domestic market at lower prices than they receive for exports. Devaluation may have a second-stage inflationary impact if the increase in the price level leads to increased wage demands, and if domestic firms are more willing to give increases because of the reduction in competitive pressure from imports.

The consequence of such inflation will be that it erodes the impact of the devaluation. As we have argued earlier, the correct measure of changes in a country's international competitiveness is the real exchange rate, not the nominal exchange rate. A 10 per cent nominal devaluation followed by a 6 per cent inflation implies that the real exchange rate has only been devalued by 4 per cent.

■ 29.4 Devaluation: the absorption approach

The absorption approach was developed in a famous paper by Sidney Alexander, published in 1952.[6] It is in part a reaction against the restrictive assumptions underlying the elasticities approach, and emphasises the macroeconomic (income) effects of a devaluation.

Using the analysis of Chapter 24, and including the government's budget deficit (i.e. government expenditure less tax revenue) as G, the national income equation for an open economy is

$$Y = C + I_d + G + X - M \qquad (29.3)$$

We may rearrange this equation to express the current-account surplus in terms of the other variables as

$$X - M = Y - (C + I_d + G) \qquad (29.4)$$

The terms in parentheses, which are the components of expenditure, are defined to be the *absorption* of the economy, usually denoted as A, so that, writing B for the current-account surplus, (29.4) becomes

$$B = Y - A \qquad (29.5)$$

which is the basic relationship in the absorption approach. Equation (29.5) states that if domestic output exceeds domestic absorption then there must be a surplus on the current account, whereas a current-account deficit implies that absorption exceeds output. It follows that the current-account balance will be improved only if we can increase output relative to absorption. Formally,

$$dB = dY - dA \qquad (29.6)$$

It is often useful to classify balance-of-payments policy instruments according to whether their initial impact is on output or on absorption. In order to change absorption without changing output, a policy must lead to the replacement of foreign goods by domestic goods, or *vice versa*. Such policies, of which devaluation and the imposition of import restrictions are examples, are referred to as *expenditure-switching* policies. Policies that affect both output and absorption directly are known as *expenditure-reducing* policies; fiscal and monetary policies are the prime examples. Note that the distinction is made on the basis of the initial impact of a policy. As we shall now see, taking devaluation as an example, ultimately all policies will affect both absorption and output.

Some of the components of absorption will be affected directly by changes in income, so that if a devaluation affects Y then it must also affect A. We shall define the marginal propensity to absorb as a, and shall assume that $0 < a < 1$.[7] There will however be some components of absorption that will be affected directly by a devaluation, rather than through the change in income. Writing these as D gives

$$dA = adY + dD \tag{29.7}$$

Combining (29.6) and (29.7) gives, after rearrangement,

$$dB = (1 - a)dY - dD \tag{29.8}$$

Equation (29.8) suggests that there are three factors which affect the impact of a devaluation on the balance on current account – the value of the marginal propensity to absorb (a), the effect of devaluation on output (dY), and the effect of devaluation on direct absorption (dD). These factors may in turn be affected by the extent to which there are unemployed resources in the economy. We shall consider the two extreme cases, where there is sufficient unemployment for output to be expanded without prices increasing, and where there is full employment, and so output cannot be increased.

Normally we would expect the marginal propensity to absorb to be less than unity, since its major determinants are the marginal propensity to consume and the marginal tax rate(s). A policy that increased output (without decreasing direct absorption) would then lead to an improvement in the current-account balance. Alexander and others have however suggested that the marginal propensity to absorb might exceed unity if a devaluation leads to an increase in investment. We shall ignore this possibility in what follows, and assume that $a < 1$.

☐ *The effects of devaluation on national income*

There are two main ways in which a devaluation may affect the level of national income.[8] First, it will tend to increase the production of exports and of import-competing goods. If there are unemployed resources then the devaluation will increase the level of national income directly, as we argued in Chapter 25. It will therefore, *ceteris paribus*, lead to an improvement in the balance on current account. If there is full employment however then national income cannot increase, and prices may rise, so reducing the effectiveness of the devaluation. If there is a non-traded goods sector then there may be yet other effects, to which we shall return later in this section.

The second impact of a devaluation on national income comes through its effect on the *terms of trade*. It is often argued that devaluation will lead to a deterioration in the terms of trade. Typically, imports are diversified over products, and it is likely that the foreign-currency prices paid by the devaluing country will not change by very much. Exports on the other hand tend to be concentrated in fewer products, and exporters are likely to reduce their foreign currency prices in order to expand their sales. The devaluing country therefore has to export a greater volume in order to import the same volume as before, and this will reduce national income. If absorption did not change then the terms-of-trade effect would lead to a worsening of the current account. Absorption will of course change as income changes, but if the marginal propensity to absorb is less than unity then the net consequence of the terms-of-trade effect must still be to increase the balance-of-payments deficit.

The effects of devaluation on direct absorption

There are various ways in which a devaluation might be expected to change direct absorption. The first is through its effects on the *income distribution*. As we have seen, devaluation may increase the domestic price level. If there is unemployment then wage levels may not rise in step with the increase in prices, and so income will be redistributed from wage-earners to profit-earners. If wage earners have a higher marginal propensity to consume than profit-earners then this will lead to a reduction in absorption. Certainly those on fixed incomes will suffer a fall in their real income, and since there is evidence that the majority of those on fixed incomes have low incomes and a high marginal propensity to consume, this also will reduce absorption. These effects may be reinforced if the income tax system is progressive, since if inflation does result in increases in money income then some income-earners will move into higher tax brackets and so experience a reduction in their post-tax real income.

Income redistribution between different production sectors of the economy may also play a role. Not all sectors will use imported intermediate goods, and so will not suffer the same rise in costs as those that do. Moreover, sectors may differ in their ability to increase their prices, depending on whether they face competition from imports, have market power, and so on. Devaluation will therefore tend to increase the profitability of some sectors, but reduce it in others. The effect of devaluation here is not easily determined, since it depends on how the marginal propensity to absorb varies across sectors.

Another influence on direct absorption may come through the *real-balance effect*. A simple version of this is based on the assumption that the amount of money that people wish to hold is constant in real terms – if prices double then the quantity of money they wish to hold also doubles.

An increase in the price level following devaluation necessarily reduces the real value of the existing money balances, and so people increase their rate of savings until they have restored their desired real balances. This reduces absorption over the adjustment period, but not of course in the long term.

The real-balance effect will have a further effect on absorption if people hold assets. A reduction in their real balances may then induce them to sell assets in an attempt to replenish their money stocks. If there are no capital movements between countries then this must have the effect of reducing asset prices and increasing the rate of interest. This in turn will affect consumption and investment, and so reduce absorption.

It should be stressed that the real-balance effect is based on the assumption that the money supply remains constant. If the central bank were to increase the money supply in step with the increase in prices, perhaps in an attempt to maintain the existing rate of interest, then the real-balance effect will not come into play.

Another short-term change in direct absorption may come through the *money-illusion effect*. There are various arguments that fall under this heading, all assuming that consumers do not make a rational judgement about relative changes in the price level and in their money income, and so act as though their real income is unchanged when in fact it has fallen, or as though it has fallen by more than it has. Money illusion may therefore reduce or increase consumption, depending on the form it takes. Insofar as money illusion is based on imperfect information, increased uncertainty, and so on, it will be a short-term effect.

☐ Devaluation and non-traded goods

In Chapter 14 we constructed a simple model for a small open economy in which there was a sector producing a non-traded good, and discussed the role of the relative price of the non-traded good in securing a general equilibrium. In the barter economy described in Chapter 14 a country cannot run a balance-of-payments deficit, but in practice it may do so, by running down its reserves or perhaps, if a developing country, because it is receiving foreign aid.

Suppose that the economy is running a deficit, and decides to remedy it by devaluing its currency. The immediate effects of the devaluation will be to raise the price of traded goods relative to non-traded goods and to reduce absorption. The former effect will encourage the movement of resources from the non-traded to the traded goods sectors. At the same time, it will encourage consumers to switch from traded to non-traded goods. The immediate consequences of the devaluation are thus an excess demand for non-traded goods, which obviously cannot be met by increasing imports, and an excess supply of traded goods, which will be exported so that the current account will improve. Subsequent price adjustments as the non-traded goods sector moves back to equilibrium will tend to offset the immediate effects, but will not reverse them. The devaluation improves the trading position of the economy by leading to a transfer of resources from non-traded to traded goods.

■ 29.5 Internal and external balance

Combining exchange-rate adjustments and fiscal policy

As we noted earlier, under a system of pegged exchange rates the balance of payments becomes a policy target – what is often referred to as the *external balance* target. On the other hand, the exchange rate, or more exactly the real exchange rate, is available as a policy instrument. During the operation of the Bretton Woods system, governments were usually also committed to maintaining *internal balance*, usually defined as the highest level of employment consistent with stable prices (or with an acceptable level of inflation).[9]

As we argued in Chapter 28, to attain two targets simultaneously requires the use of two independent instruments. We shall discuss the problems of internal and external balance when the two instruments are the exchange rate and fiscal policy. We shall use a diagrammatic technique developed (independently) by Swan and Salter,[10] and shown in Figure 29.2. We shall assume that the Marshall–Lerner Condition is satisfied, and that capital is perfectly immobile.

The vertical axis shows the real exchange rate, defined as the amount of domestic currency required to buy 1 unit of the foreign currency, so that a depreciation is a movement away from the origin. The horizontal axis shows domestic absorption, which we shall assume is to be controlled by the use of fiscal policy.

Curve *IB* shows those combinations of the real exchange rate and domestic absorption that give internal balance. We must first show that *IB* must have a negative slope. Suppose that we are initially in internal balance, so that we are on *IB*. If there a depreciation of the exchange rate then the balance of payments will move into surplus, and thus there will be inflationary pressure. In order to counteract this there must be a reduction in absorption (through a fiscal contraction in our example). That is, the new equilibrium position must lie above and to the left of the original point. The *IB* schedule must therefore be negatively sloped. It follows from

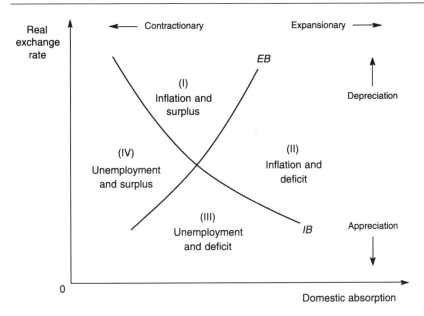

Figure 29.2 *The Salter–Swan diagram*

this argument that points above and to the right of the *IB* schedule must show an inflationary situation, while points below and to the left show a state of unemployment.

The *EB* schedule shows all those combinations of the real exchange rate and absorption that will give external balance, and must be positively sloped. To see that this is so, suppose again that we are initially on the *EB* schedule, and that the exchange rate depreciates. This will lead to a surplus on the balance of payments, and in order to restore equilibrium there must therefore be an increase in domestic absorption. The new equilibrium point must lie above and to the right of the original point. It must also be the case that points above and to the left of *EB* show a surplus on the balance of payments, points below and to the right a deficit.

The intersection of the *IB* and *EB* schedules defines the desired policy goal of internal and external balance. The two schedules define four 'zones', characterised by the following types of imbalances:

Zone I: balance-of-payments surplus and inflationary pressure
Zone II: balance-of-payments deficit and inflationary pressure
Zone III: balance-of-payments deficit and unemployment
Zone IV: balance-of-payments surplus and unemployment.

We may now use the Salter–Swan diagram to investigate how the two policy instruments should be combined in order to achieve simultaneous internal and external balance. We shall do so, using Figure 29.3, by considering two situations, both in zone III and so with the same form of policy disequilibrium, but which nevertheless require different policy mixes.

Consider first point *a*, which lies below and to the left of the intersection of *IB* and *EB*. The appropriate policy here is to depreciate the currency and to increase domestic absorption (use an expansionary fiscal policy), which will move the economy up and to the right. An appropriate mix of depreciation and expansion will produce simultaneous internal and external balance. This result is intuitively appealing, since we know that depreciation will solve the balance-of-payments problem, and an expansionary fiscal policy will solve the unemployment problem.

The procedure needed to obtain both internal and external balance may however be less intuitively appealing in the case of point *b*. Here we once again have a deficit and unemployment, but in order to obtain both policy objectives we need to move up and to the left. That is, we need to depreciate the exchange rate while following a contractionary fiscal policy.

The reason for this apparent anomaly is of course that both policies affect both target variables. Depreciation for example both improves the balance of payments and causes inflationary pressure. If we start from point *b* and continually depreciate the currency we shall eventually move from zone III to zone II: that is, we shall reach internal balance before we reach external balance. It is to counteract the inflationary effects of the

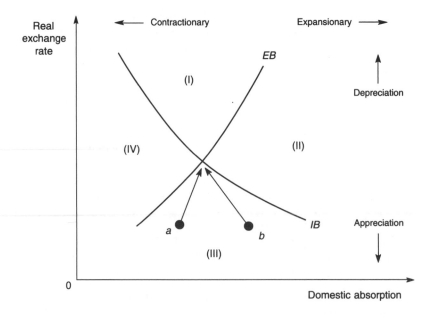

Figure 29.3   *Mixing policies to obtain the policy goal*

depreciation that we must employ a contractionary fiscal policy. When we started from point *a* on the other hand, depreciating the currency alone would have brought about external balance while still leaving some unemployment in the economy, and so an expansionary fiscal policy was needed to reinforce the inflationary effects of the depreciation.

The 'piecemeal' approach and the assignment problem

As was suggested in Chapter 28, policy-makers may follow a 'piecemeal' approach to policy-making, adjusting policy in order to attain one policy target, and then switching attention to the next policy target, and so on. If they combine this approach with the use of just one policy instrument to obtain each target then, even if they use the same number of instruments, they may move away from rather than towards the ultimate goal of simultaneously attaining their targets. This possibility is known as the *assignment problem.*

If the two instruments are the exchange rate and fiscal policy, the 'intuitive' assignment is to use the exchange rate to achieve external balance, and fiscal policy to achieve internal balance. Whether this is in fact the *correct* assignment (i.e. the one which will bring about the joint policy equilibrium under a piecemeal approach) depends on the relative impact of the two instruments on the two targets.

Panel (a) in Figure 29.4 shows the case where the assignment of the exchange rate to the external balance is the correct choice. Suppose we start from point *c*, where there is a deficit and unemployment, and decide first to obtain external balance. The appropriate depreciation of the currency will move us vertically upwards until we reach the *EB* schedule. We now have external balance, but there is still unemployment. A fiscal expansion will now move us to the right until we reach the *IB* schedule, where we have internal balance, but at the expense of a deficit. A further depreciation moves us vertically upwards to the *EB* schedule again, but now there is inflationary pressure, and we must use a fiscal contraction to get back to the *IB* schedule, and so on. Repeated use of the two instruments will eventually bring us to the intersection of *EB* and *IB*. The piecemeal policy process will be convergent in this case.

Panel (b) of Figure 29.4 shows the case where the assignment of the exchange rate instrument to the external balance target is incorrect. Staring from point *c*, depreciating to achieve external balance, then using an expansionary fiscal policy to obtain internal balance, and so on, will in this case lead to a cyclical movement away from the intersection of *IB* and *EB*. The piecemeal process will not result in a joint policy equilibrium.

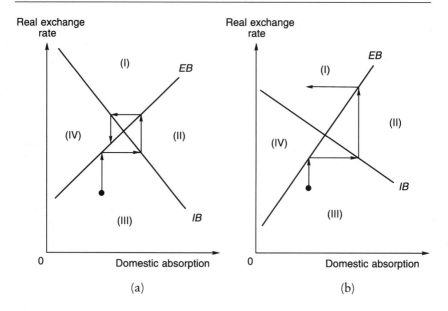

Figure 29.4 *The assignment problem with exchange rate and fiscal policies*

The difference in the two cases is in the relative slopes of the *IB* and *EB* schedules (there is an obvious similarity to the familiar cobweb theorem). In the first case the exchange rate exercises a relatively greater effect on external balance than on internal balance. That is, it would take a greater change in fiscal policy to offset the effects of a depreciation on the external balance than it would to offset its effects on the internal balance. The *EB* schedule is steeper than the *IB* schedule. In the second case the exchange rate exercises a relatively greater effect on the internal balance, so the *IB* schedule is the steeper. In this case the correct assignment is to use the exchange rate to achieve internal balance, and fiscal policy to control the external balance.

The case shown in panel (b) should not be dismissed as a 'economic curiosity'. There was a serious debate in the 1960s over the appropriate assignment of instruments to targets when a group of economists claimed that the empirical evidence showed that changing the exchange rate had little effect on the balance of payments but a marked effect on unemployment and inflation.

☐ Combining monetary and fiscal policy

Governments were usually unwilling to use exchange-rate changes as a policy instrument under the pegged exchange-rate system, not least because the IMF procedures required that a currency only be devalued if there was a 'fundamental imbalance' in the balance of payments. In order to achieve both internal and external balance it was necessary therefore to use another policy instrument – monetary policy.

Figure 29.5 shows the internal- and external-balance schedules when the two instruments are monetary policy (on the vertical axis) and fiscal policy (on the horizontal axis). Note that in this case both the *IB* and the *EB* schedule are negatively sloped. Starting from a position of balance, a fiscal expansion will lead to both a deficit and to inflationary pressure, which must be counteracted by a monetary contraction. In drawing the case shown in Figure 29.5 it has been assumed that monetary policy has a relatively greater effect on the external balance, so that the *EB* schedule is flatter than the *IB* schedule. This however is not necessarily the case.

Note how the four zones have 'moved' compared with the previous example. Points above the external-balance schedule now show a deficit in the balance of payments.

Suppose that the economy is at point *c*, where there is both inflation and a deficit. The appropriate 'one-step' policy in this case is a mix of monetary and fiscal contraction, which will move the economy to the intersection of *IB* and *EB*. It should be evident however that were the starting point to the left of the intersection of *IB* and *EB* then the appropriate policy mix would be a fiscal expansion coupled with a monetary contraction.

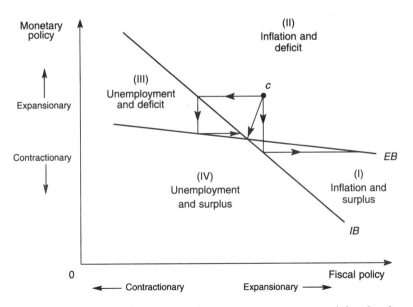

Figure 29.5 *Internal and external balance using monetary and fiscal policy*

Figure 29.5 may also be used to emphasise the importance of correctly assigning instruments to targets if policy is likely to be conducted on a 'piecemeal' basis. In the case shown, using fiscal policy to bring about internal balance, and monetary policy to obtain external balance, will lead to convergence on the policy goal of simultaneous balance. The alternative assignment would lead to divergence. It is therefore important to know which of monetary and fiscal policy has relatively more effect on the balance of payments. To emphasise this point in the context of these two instruments, note that in many countries monetary and fiscal policy are under the control of separate institutions (the central bank and the ministry of finance), and that in some (notably Germany) the central bank is not subject to direct government control.

29.6 Pegged exchange rates with capital mobility

Although the analyses of the previous sections give some useful insights into the problems of internal and external balance, they suffer from the drawback that capital is assumed to be completely immobile. Although that was a reasonable simplification when the theories were developed, it is much less so today. In order to introduce the possibility of capital mobility we must return to the *IS–LM–BP* framework of the Mundell–Fleming model, or to the analysis of the monetary approach.

☐ *The Mundell–Fleming model*

The basic elements of the Mundell–Fleming model, the *IS*, *LM*, and *BP* schedules, are derived in exactly the same way as in the floating exchange-rate case. The essential difference now is that the *BP* schedule does not move automatically. As long as the exchange rate remains the same, the *BP* schedule cannot move. It is therefore possible for the government to pursue policies that result in balance-of-payments disequilibrium. Figure 29.6 shows just such a case. The intersection of the *IS* and *LM* schedules determines the internal equilibrium of the economy, with an interest rate of r_1 and national income equal to Y_1. Since this intersection is above and to the left of the *BP* schedule, it follows that the economy is running a balance-of-payments surplus.

If the government wishes to obtain both internal and external balance then it has three basic options. First, it could appreciate the exchange rate, thus shifting the *BP* schedule so that it passes through the intersection of the *IS* and *LM* schedules. Second, it could pursue an expansionary

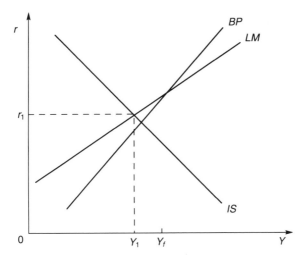

Figure 29.6   *A surplus in the balance of payments in the Mundell–Fleming model*

monetary policy, and shift the *LM* schedule to the right until it passes through the intersection of *IS* and *BP*. Third, it could use an expansionary fiscal policy to shift *IS* to the right until it passes though the intersection of *LM* and *BP*. The three policy options would each, of course, give different outcomes for income and the interest rate, and one or another might be infeasible given the output constraint, but in general all are possible. In practice, as we argued above, policy-makers may be unwilling to alter the exchange rate, and so we will restrict our analysis from now on to the use of fiscal and monetary policy.

☐ *Monetary policy and sterilisation*

Before we go on to analyse the policy problems in more detail, we have to consider another difference between the use of the Mundell–Fleming model under a pegged exchange rate and its use under floating exchange rates. With a pegged exchange rate the government may operate a balance-of-payments deficit (surplus), but only by decreasing (increasing) the reserves of foreign currency. That is, if there is a deficit on the balance of payments then there will be an excess supply of the domestic currency on the exchange markets. In order to maintain the par value the government must then buy the domestic currency, and so will deplete the reserves. The foreign currency reserves are however part of the monetary base of the economy, so that the reduction in the reserves would reduce the money supply, and shift the *LM* schedule to the left.

It is therefore important that we specify how the government reacts to this effect. It may choose to counteract the fall in the money supply caused by the fall in reserves by an off-setting monetary expansion. In such a case we say that the government has *sterilised* the effects of its intervention in the foreign exchange markets. At the other extreme, the government could allow the full effect of the fall in the reserves to be transmitted to the money supply – a policy of *non-sterilisation*. It may of course choose to offset some of the effect, so partially sterilising its intervention in support of the currency.

The difference between sterilisation and non-sterilisation is shown in Figure 29.7. Initially, the economy is in internal and external balance at the intersection of LM_1, IS and BP, with income equal to Y_1 and an interest rate of r_1.

Suppose now that the government expands the money supply, so shifting the LM schedule out to LM_2. The immediate effect is to increase income to Y_2, reduce the interest rate to r_2, and put the balance of payments into deficit. The balance-of-payments deficit will lead to an excess supply of the domestic currency on the foreign exchange markets, and the government will be forced to intervene, running down its reserves as it buys up that excess supply. If the government does not sterilise the effects of its intervention on the foreign-exchange markets then the money supply will fall, and the LM schedule will move back towards LM_1, so that the interest rate will rise and income will fall. If, on the other hand, the government completely sterilises its intervention then the LM schedule will remain at

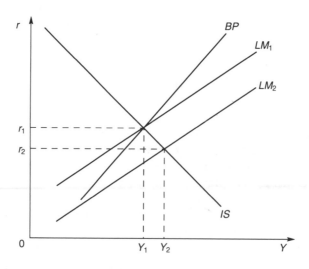

Figure 29.7   *Sterilised and unsterilised intervention in the foreign-exchange market*

LM_2. This is not, however, a viable long-term situation! Maintaining the LM schedule at LM_2 means that there will be a continued balance-of-payments deficit, and so a continued depletion of the reserves. Ultimately the government must either reduce the money supply, returning to the original position, or use fiscal policy to deal with the balance-of-payments deficit, or devalue the currency. Which option it chooses will depend on its other policy objectives.

We shall discuss fiscal policy on the assumption that the government does not sterilise its effects. A fiscal expansion will shift the IS schedule to the right, and so will lead to an expansion in output and to an increase in the rate of interest. The effects of the expansion on the balance of payments are indeterminate, since the increase in incomes will drive the current account into deficit, while the increase in interest rates will result in a capital-account surplus. Since the government does not sterilise its effects on the balance of payments, there will be a shift in the LM schedule that will either reinforce or partially counteract the effects of the change in fiscal policy.

Figure 29.8 gives an example of the use of fiscal and monetary policy to obtain the objective of full employment (shown by an income of Y_f) while maintaining balance-of-payments equilibrium. We shall assume that an expansionary fiscal policy worsens the balance of payments. The initial equilibrium is at the intersection of LM_1, IS_1 and BP, with income Y_1 and interest rate r_1. There is balance-of-payments equilibrium (since the economy is on BP), but income is below the target level.

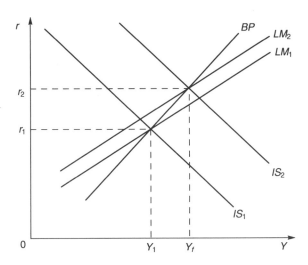

Figure 29.8 *Internal and external balance in the Mundell–Fleming model*

The appropriate policy mix here is a fiscal expansion, shifting the *IS* schedule to IS_2, coupled with a monetary contraction that moves the *LM* schedule to LM_2, so that they intersect on the *BP* schedule at the point where income is at its target level, Y_f.

Note that if the government chooses to specify its target in terms of the level of income then it cannot control the rate of interest. It could of course choose to target the rate of interest, but then it would not be able to choose the level of income. If it wanted to pursue target levels of income and the rate of interest while maintaining balance-of-payments equilibrium then it would have to change the exchange rate, or introduce some other policy instrument that would be distinct from either monetary or fiscal policy, such as an import tariff. The instruments–targets rule still applies. If the government sets three targets (income, the interest rate, and the balance of payments) then it must use three instruments.

The example discussed above assumed that there was limited capital mobility, in contrast to the zero capital mobility assumed previously. To complete the story, we should also consider what would happen if capital were perfectly mobile. We shall do this in terms of Figure 29.9, where, reflecting the assumption of perfect mobility, the *BP* schedule is horizontal.

Once again, the initial equilibrium is at the intersection of LM_1, IS_1 and *BP*, with income Y_1 and interest rate r_1. Consider first the use of an expansionary monetary policy that shifts the *LM* schedule out to LM_2. This will exert downward pressure on the domestic interest rate, and so will trigger an outflow of capital. Since capital is perfectly mobile, the government cannot pursue a sterilisation policy. It must intervene in the foreign-exchange markets to maintain the par value of the currency, and will in fact continue to do so until the *LM* schedule has moved back to LM_1. In other words, monetary policy is completely ineffective when the exchange rate is pegged (and maintained its par value) and capital is perfectly mobile.

Now consider a fiscal expansion that shifts the *IS* schedule out to IS_2. This will put upward pressure on the domestic interest rate, and so there will be a capital inflow. The government will have to purchase foreign currency in order to stop the domestic currency appreciating. Once again it cannot sterilise its foreign exchange interventions, as capital will continue to flow in so long as any interest rate differential is maintained. The *LM* schedule must therefore move out, and will continue to do so until it intersects IS_2 on the *BP* schedule. Fiscal policy is effective with a pegged exchange rate and perfect capital mobility.

These results are of course completely different to those we obtained in Chapter 28. With a floating exchange rate and perfect capital mobility, monetary policy is effective but fiscal policy is not. This is one of the most famous results in this area.

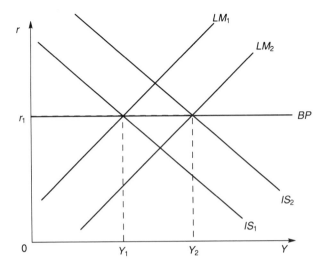

Figure 29.9 *Monetary and fiscal policy when there is perfect capital mobility*

29.7 Pegged exchange rates and the monetary approach

We shall use the same model as before, the only differences being that the exchange rate is assumed to be pegged, and the government is assumed not to sterilise the effects of any intervention in the foreign exchange market. We start by examining the monetarist view of the effects of a devaluation.

☐ *Devaluation under the monetary approach*

Figure 29.10 is based on Figure 28.6. In panel (a), the initial equilibrium has the reserves at R_1, the domestic money base at D_1, and the money market in equilibrium with M_1 being demanded and supplied. At the same time, aggregate demand is equal to aggregate supply at real income Y_1 and price level P_1, as shown in panel (b). The equilibrium exchange rate, as determined by purchasing power parity (PPP) in panel (c) is e_1.

Suppose now that the domestic currency is devalued, so that the exchange rate becomes e_2. Domestic goods are now more competitive, so that there is an increased demand for the domestic currency from both domestic and foreign consumers. The demand for money, therefore increases, to L_2 (panel (a)). The balance-of-payments surplus however puts pressure on the domestic currency to appreciate, and to counter this the

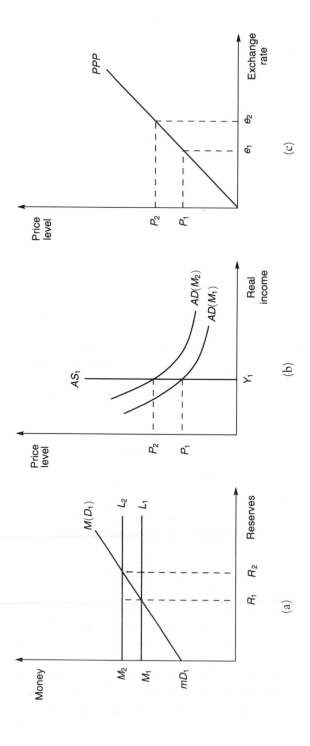

Figure 29.10   *Devaluation under the monetary approach*

domestic authorities have to purchase the foreign currency, so increasing the reserves and expanding the domestic money supply. This in turn increases domestic demand, and so pushes up the price level. Equilibrium will be restored when the price level has risen to P_2 (its PPP level) and the money supply and demand are equal at M_2.

The central message of the monetary approach is that any improvement in the balance of payments brought about by a devaluation must be transitory. As we noted earlier, the monetarist view is that a disequilibrium in the balance of payments can only occur through a disequilibrium in the money market. Once money market equilibrium has been restored then the balance of payments must be returned to equilibrium.

An expansion in the money supply under the monetary approach

Figure 29.11 starts with the same equilibrium as in Figure 29.10. Suppose now that the monetary authorities expand the domestic element of the money base, so shifting the money supply function in panel (a) up to $M(D_2)$.

Domestic residents now have excess real money balances, and will attempt to reduce them by increasing their expenditure on goods, so that the aggregate demand schedule moves up to $AD(M_2)$ (panel (b)). This will drive the domestic price level up to P_2, which will reduce the country's competitiveness on the world market. The monetary authorities will be forced to purchase the domestic currency in order to prevent a depreciation, and this will diminish the foreign-exchange reserves, and so the money supply. In the final equilibrium the exchange rate must return to its PPP value, which requires that the price level return to P_1. For this to happen, the aggregate demand schedule must return to $AD(M_1)$, which requires that the money supply also return to its original level. The fall in the reserves will produce a fall in the money supply (a movement along $M(D_2)$) that exactly offsets the effect of the initial expansion. Once again, the effect is temporary.

An increase in income under the monetary approach

We shall discuss the effects of an increase in income (an expansion in aggregate supply) in terms of Figure 29.12, in which the initial equilibrium is as before. The increase in income is shown by the shift in the aggregate supply schedule in panel (b) from AS_1 to AS_2.

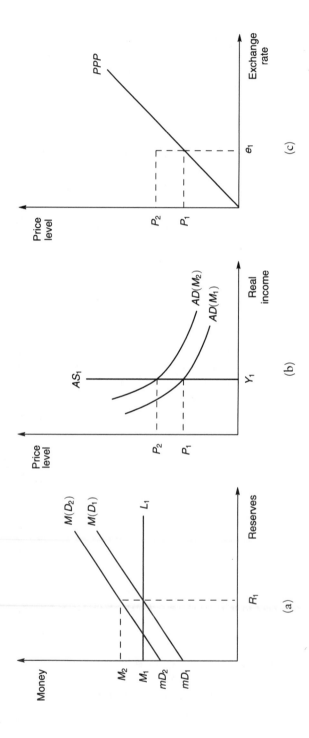

Figure 29.11   A money supply expansion under the monetary approach

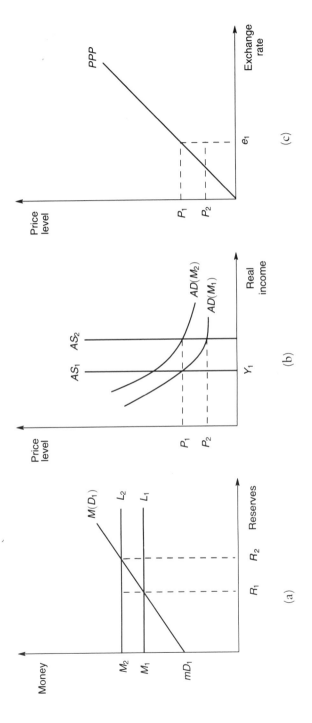

Figure 29.12 *An increase in income under the monetary approach*

The increased income will lead to increased demand for real money balances, shown by the money demand schedule in panel (a) moving up to L_2, and so to a fall in expenditure. This, coupled with the increase in aggregate supply, will drive the price level down to P_2. The increased competitiveness of domestic goods following the fall in prices will put pressure on the domestic currency to appreciate, forcing the domestic monetary authorities to purchase the foreign currency. This will increase the reserves, so that the money supply will increase. There will now be excess money balances, which consumers will reduce by increasing their expenditure on goods, so shifting the aggregate demand schedule upwards, and leading to an increase in the price level.

Once again, equilibrium will be restored when domestic prices have returned to their PPP level. This requires that the aggregate demand schedule move sufficiently to restore equilibrium at the original price level (to $AD(M_2)$ in panel (b)), and that the increase in the reserves is just sufficient to expand the money supply to the level consistent with that price level and the new demand for real money balances.

In this instance, as in the case of a devaluation and an expansion in the money supply, the dominant force is PPP. Given the foreign price level and the requirement to maintain the same exchange rate, the new equilibrium has to result in the same domestic price level as before. The difference in this case is that there has been a real change in the economy.

■ 29.8 Summary and conclusions

Under a fixed exchange-rate system (e.g. the gold currency standard), there are forces leading to an automatic adjustment to balance-of-payments equilibrium. Under a pegged exchange-rate system we would, so long as there is no change in the par value, expect the same mechanisms to operate. In both cases the authorities may take action to reinforce the automatic mechanisms.

Under a pegged exchange-rate system, however, the par value of the currency is a policy variable, and the balance of payments is a policy target. Policy-makers may elect to maintain a deficit or surplus on the balance of payments, although their ability to maintain a deficit is limited by the size of their foreign-currency reserves.

We have considered three policy instruments that governments may use in order to achieve equilibrium in the balance of payments: changing the par value, fiscal policy, and monetary policy. Whether devaluation will improve the balance of payments was shown to depend on a variety of factors. We have considered two approaches, the elasticities approach (the Marshall–Lerner Condition), and the absorption approach, and suggested that the latter is more satisfactory in that it takes the income effects of a non-marginal change in the exchange rate into account.

The effects of all policies depend very much on three factors: whether there are unemployed resources, whether the authorities sterilise the effects of their operations on the foreign exchange markets, and the extent to which capital is mobile between countries. We have examined the consequences of different degrees of capital mobility and of price flexibility at some length in the context of the Mundell–Fleming model, while using the monetary model to give another viewpoint on the effectiveness of policy when there is full employment.

We also showed that the result from Chapter 28 about the relative effectiveness of fiscal and monetary policy when there is perfect capital mobility obtained for the floating exchange rate case is reversed under pegged exchange rates.

Finally, we have extended the instruments–targets analysis of Chapter 28 on macroeconomic policy under floating exchange rates to the pegged rate system. In particular we have discussed how exchange rate and fiscal policy may be combined to give external and internal balance, and have then repeated that exercise for the use of fiscal and monetary policy (on the assumption that the government may be unwilling to change the par value of its currency). We modified that analysis for the possible use of piecemeal policy, and showed the importance of the correct assignment of instruments to targets.

☐ *Notes*

1   See Artis and Lewis (1991), Chapter 2, for a discussion of the gold standard in its various guises.

2   This is of course a simplification. In some countries lower denomination coins were silver, and it was possible for two exchange rates to exist: that defined by gold coins and that defined by silver coins (see Artis and Lewis (1991)). We shall ignore the problems introduced by this *bi-metallic* standard.

3   If there is a widespread expectation that the exchange rate will change then speculative pressure may force that change.

4   In the intervening period currencies were not convertible into gold, and a floating exchange rate system operated. The gold standard was however seen as the 'normal' system, and countries were anxious to return to that system. There was however a shortage of gold in relation to the prevailing price levels, and so a return to the full gold standard was deemed impossible. The solution adopted was that countries should withdraw gold from circulation, and that smaller countries should hold their reserves in 'gold-convertible' currencies, such as the US dollar and the pound sterling, rather than in gold itself. This meant that, so long as the countries with gold-convertible currencies were willing to convert their currencies into gold at a fixed price,

the other countries could always obtain gold if required. This system is known as a *gold exchange standard*. There was however an important difference between this new regime and the old gold standard. Experience showed that the convertibility of a currency into gold could be abandoned. The pound in particular was considered to be overvalued (it had returned to its pre-war rate), and this lead to a sustained fall in the UK gold reserves. The gold exchange system finally collapsed under the strains imposed by the Great Depression.

5   The Bretton Woods system put more pressure on deficit countries to devalue their currency than it did on surplus countries to appreciate. We shall discuss this problem at more length in Chapter 31.

6   Alexander (1952).

7   The conventional Keynesian model would assume that investment and government expenditure are independent of income, so that the marginal propensity to absorb would reflect the joint effect of the marginal tax rate and the marginal propensity to consume. In the model discussed in Chapter 25, where there is a constant marginal tax rate t, and a marginal propensity to consume out of post-tax income of c, the marginal propensity to absorb would be given by $a = c(1 - t) - t$.

8   A third effect was suggested by Machlup (1955). He argued that a devaluation may allow the removal of restrictions on trade, which will lead to more efficient resource use and so to a higher national income.

9   The internal/external balance problem was first explored in detail in Meade (1951).

10   Salter (1959), and Swan (1955).

■ *Chapter 30* ■

Two Debates: Exchange-Rate Systems and Policy Co-ordination

30.1 Introduction
30.2 Fixed versus floating exchange rates: the traditional approach
30.3 Fixed versus floating exchange rates: modern approaches

30.4 International co-ordination of macroeconomic policy
30.5 Conclusions

■ 30.1 Introduction

In this chapter we shall focus on two 'debates' in macroeconomic policy. The first, on the relative merits of fixed, pegged and floating exchange-rate systems, is of long standing. As we have noted earlier, there have been various exchange-rate systems, of which the most important have been the gold standard, the Bretton Woods pegged rate system, and floating exchange rates.[1] The era of the Bretton Woods system in particular generated much controversy over the costs and benefits of fixed and floating exchange rates, an issue that has not been, and perhaps never can be, resolved.

For convenience we shall discuss the choice between fixed, pegged and floating exchange rates under two headings: the 'traditional' and the 'modern' approach (although the distinction between the two is more blurred than is implied by this categorisation). The former concentrates on the trade-offs between a range of issues, such as the discipline imposed on policy-makers by different regimes, the impact of exchange-rate uncertainty on trade and capital flows, and the effects of speculation. Many of the arguments used are difficult to prove or disprove, and the weights given to them differ between economists, so that no clear conclusion has been reached. Partly in reaction to this, the modern approach focuses on the ability of governments to achieve domestic macroeconomic stability under the various regimes. This may be done by using one of the standard macroeconomic models, such as the Mundell–Fleming model. Alternatively, it may involve optimising some specific

643

governmental objective function within an algebraic macroeconomic model, or the specification of a macroeconomic model based on microeconomic foundations. The optimising models are more suited to texts dealing specifically with macroeconomic policy, and we shall treat them briefly.

The second, and more recent, debate is on the gains and losses that may come from international co-operation in the setting of macroeconomic policy. This debate to some extent subsumes the first, in that agreement on the exchange-rate system is one element in international co-operation, while the system used is one of the factors determining the costs and benefits of that co-operation. International policy co-operation is a wider debate in that it embodies arguments on the co-ordination of monetary and fiscal policy.

30.2 Fixed versus floating exchange rates: the traditional approach

Exchange-rate uncertainty, trade and investment

It is often argued that floating exchange rates create uncertainty and instability, and that this will inhibit foreign trade and international investment. This argument has more strength in the short than the long term. In the short term the exchange rate may change in the interval between an exporter shipping his goods to a foreign market and his receiving payment. If the payment has been agreed in terms of the foreign currency then, as we saw in Chapter 24, the exporter will make a 'windfall' gain or loss in terms of his domestic currency, depending on how the exchange rate moves. Such uncertainty may lead a risk-averse exporter/importer to reduce his trade volume. However, as we also saw in Chapter 24, an exporter/importer can insure against this risk by hedging in the forward exchange market. Such hedging however adds to the costs of international trade, and so may be expected to reduce trade flows. A similar argument obviously applies to importers, and to international investment.

The purchasing power parity (PPP) doctrine suggests that in the long run a floating exchange rate will decrease the risks associated with foreign trade and investment. For example, suppose that an American exporter currently sells goods in Britain for £100, and that the exchange rate is £1 = $2, so that he receives $200. Now suppose that the price level in the United States increases by 50 per cent compared to that in Britain, that his costs increase in line with this inflation, and that if he wishes to sell in Britain he can still only charge £100. Under a fixed exchange-rate system he would once again receive $200, and his profits would be reduced accordingly. Under a flexible exchange-rate system however the difference in inflation would in the long run change the exchange rate to £1 = $3, he would earn $300 from his exports, and his revenue would have increased in line with the general level of US prices.

Ultimately, whether exchange-rate variability reduces international trade flows is an empirical question. There is evidence that the move to floating exchange rates has increased uncertainty, and that this has had some effect on reducing both the level of international trade and its rate of growth.[2]

☐ *The effects of speculation*

A common argument against floating exchange rates is that the activities of speculators may destabilise the rate: that is, push it away from its equilibrium value. An early response to this criticism was by Friedman,[3] who argued that destabilising speculation would be irrational and could not persist. The essence of his argument was that such speculation would involve buying a currency when it was expensive, and selling it when it was cheap, which would necessarily result in speculators *as a whole* making losses. The corollary is that private speculation may be expected to be a stabilising influence, with speculators tending to buy (sell) currencies when they are below (above) their equilibrium value, so pushing the exchange rate towards equilibrium.

It is not however clear that speculation is always (or even mostly) rational. An obvious example of persistent and irrational speculation is given by the 'band-wagon' effect. The effect of new information ('news') about, say, some change in government policy or the state of the balance of payments may produce a change in the exchange rate in the appropriate direction due to the actions of some speculators. If other speculators are more responsive to the actions of the first group (or to the exchange rate) than to the original news then the exchange rate may be driven beyond its appropriate level. The likelihood of irrational speculation will be higher if there is a regular turnover of speculators in the market. Those that operate in the market on a regular basis may be expected to learn from their experience, and so to behave rationally. Those that are infrequent participants and so have acquired only limited knowledge may be more prone to such band-wagon effects. A further dimension may have been added by the adoption of 'rules of thumb', often implemented through computer programs: if the same 'rules' are used by a significant number of traders then there may be strong cumulative effects.

More recent analyses however have suggested that there may be circumstances in which speculation is both rational (to the speculator) and destabilising. For example, speculators might have a 'model' of exchange-rate determination that differs from the 'true' model. If they act upon their incorrect model then they may push the exchange rate towards the value predicted by their model rather its true value. If the exchange rate then moves in the direction predicted by their model, as it may do if the majority of speculators adhere to the same model, this may reinforce their belief in it. One problem with this is, of course, that if exchange rates are continually determined by the actions of people using the 'wrong' model then it may be argued that it becomes in effect the 'true' model!

Another counter to the argument that speculation is destabilising under floating exchange rates, and so is a powerful argument against their use, is the observation that, under certain circumstances, speculation may have equally undesirable effects under a pegged exchange-rate system. In general there will be little speculative activity with a pegged exchange rate provided that the rate stays within its prescribed bounds, and is expected to do so. Since the range of variation of the exchange rate is limited there is little scope for speculators to make profits, and little incentive for a movement out of the currency. Suppose however that the exchange rate is at the bottom of its prescribed band, and that there is thought to be some probability that it will be devalued (perhaps because the reserves have been seriously depleted by past intervention). Speculators are now faced with a clear probability of making a profit if the currency is devalued, coupled with the prospect of limited losses since the par value of the currency is most unlikely to be increased, so that the worst that can happen is that it goes to the top of the prescribed band. Moreover, speculators can afford to take a reasonably long view, since if the currency is devalued then the change is likely to be large compared to the cost of the speculation (the difference between interest rates in the country concerned and the rest of the world).

Exchange-rate regimes and macroeconomic policy

Proponents of pegged exchange rates have argued that they impose some discipline upon policy-makers. The pursuit of an inappropriate domestic policy, such as excessive monetary or fiscal expansion, will lead to downward pressure on the exchange rate, which will force intervention in the exchange markets and a fall in the reserves. If the government persists with its domestic policy then it will ultimately have to devalue the currency. This possibility should then restrain governments from pursuing such inappropriate policies, at least in the longer run, since devaluation would be interpreted as evidence of mismanagement.

On the other hand, there are various arguments that macroeconomic policy is better conducted under floating exchange rates. The most obvious is that with floating rates the balance of payments is always in equilibrium, so that governments do not have to direct economic policy towards maintaining external balance. Other arguments are based on the superior ability of a floating exchange rate to absorb 'shocks' in the system. For example, an increase in the price level in the rest of the world will not be transmitted to an increase in domestic prices if the exchange rate is free to adjust to changing price levels. Friedman has argued that while a floating exchange rate tends to move freely in either direction, domestic prices tend to be sticky, particularly downwards.[4] It is, he suggests, more efficient to allow the exchange rate to change while maintaining stable domestic prices than to hold the exchange rate constant and use deflationary policies to force price changes. Finally, and in clear contrast to the discipline argument, it has been argued that one of the major benefits of a floating exchange-rate system is that it allows countries to operate independent monetary policies, whereas pegged exchange rates constrain countries to maintain similar rates of inflation, so that they must follow broadly similar policies.

▌ 30.3 Fixed versus floating exchange rates: modern approaches

The subject of concern in the 'modern' approach is the stability of the domestic economy, usually interpreted in terms of the response of the domestic price level and income to external and internal shocks and the ability of the domestic authorities to counter those shocks if necessary. One way of analysing the problem is by constructing a macroeconomic model and investigating its behaviour under various conditions. We shall discuss how this may be done in terms of the Mundell–Fleming model developed in the preceding chapters. An alternative is to consider the optimisation of an explicit objective function, an approach we shall discuss subsequently.[5]

☐ *Economic stability in the Mundell–Fleming model*

We know from our earlier analysis of this model that the effects of monetary and fiscal policies on income are very dependent upon the exchange-rate regime, and on the degree of international capital mobility. We may summarise our earlier results as:

(a) under floating exchange rates, fiscal policy will be more effective with low capital mobility than with high mobility, and is completely ineffective when capital is perfectly mobile;

(b) under fixed exchange rates, fiscal policy will be more effective with high capital mobility than with low mobility, and is completely ineffective if capital is completely immobile;

(c) under high capital mobility, fiscal policy is more effective with fixed exchange rates than with floating rates;

(d) under floating exchange rates, monetary policy is more effective with high capital mobility than with low mobility, and is effective even with complete immobility;

(e) under fixed exchange rates, monetary policy will be ineffective regardless of the degree of capital mobility (assuming that changes in the reserves are not sterilised).

These results are equally applicable to the analysis of domestic 'shocks'. For example, suppose that there is an autonomous increase in investment. This shifts the *IS* schedule to the right, as would a fiscal expansion. If there is complete capital immobility then there will be an increase in income and/or prices under floating exchange rates, but not under fixed exchange rates. At the other extreme, if capital is perfectly mobile then there will be an increase in income and/or prices under fixed exchange rates, but not under floating exchange rates. An autonomous change in the *LM* schedule will have no effect on income and/or prices under fixed exchange rates, unless the authorities sterilise the consequent change in the foreign exchange reserves, but will have an effect under floating exchange rates, even if capital is completely immobile. Assuming that there is capital mobility (as there is at present), the Mundell–Fleming model offers us no clear ranking of fixed and floating exchange rates: fixed rates are preferable in the event of a domestic monetary shock, but floating rates are preferable when there is an expenditure shock.

We may also use the Mundell–Fleming model to examine the effects of external shocks. Suppose that there is an autonomous increase in exports, perhaps due to a change in foreign tastes. This will generate a balance-of-payments surplus and an expansion in income and/or an increase in prices. With floating exchange rates these effects will be countered by an appreciation of the currency, so that the domestic economy will be insulated from the foreign shock. With a pegged exchange rate the increase in the reserves brought about by maintaining the par value will lead to an increase in the money supply, so that the full effect of the foreign shock will pass through to the domestic economy. A floating exchange rate is therefore better than a pegged rate in insulating the domestic economy from a foreign expenditure shock.

Suppose, on the other hand, that there is a foreign monetary shock that reduces the foreign rate of interest, and that there is capital mobility. This will generate a surplus on the capital account and put pressure on the exchange rate to appreciate. The effect under a pegged exchange rate of maintaining the par value of the currency will be to expand the domestic money supply and to increase income and/or prices. With a floating exchange rate however the appreciation will result in a current account deficit and a reduction in income. There is no unambiguous ranking of the two exchange-rate regimes. If however we believe that a foreign demand expansion is likely to be accompanied by a foreign monetary expansion then the floating exchange rate would probably be superior, since the income-reducing effect of the monetary expansion would tend to offset the income-increasing effect of the expenditure expansion, whereas with a pegged exchange rate the two effects would be mutually reinforcing.

The results obtained from such an analysis are often inconclusive: floating exchange rates are superior to fixed exchange rates in some respects, but are inferior in others. The choice between them is then a matter of the trade-offs between the various attributes of the two systems. These trade-offs are essentially subjective, but may be defined in terms of an explicit objective function.

☐ *Introducing a government objective function*

The introduction of a objective function, which the government seeks to optimise by choosing appropriate values of the available policy instruments, may allow an unambiguous ordering of different exchange-rate systems. The specification of the objective function encompasses those targets assumed to concern the government. For example, when studying the effectiveness of fiscal and monetary policy in stabilising an economy, we might specify a function such as that in equation (30.1)

$$O(Y, P) = w(Y - Y_n)^2 + (1 - w)(P - P_n)^2 \tag{30.1}$$

where $0 \leq w \leq 1$. Y_n is the target (or natural) domestic real income and P_n is the target (or natural) domestic price level, while Y and P are the actual values of those variables. The government is assumed to seek to minimise the value of $O(Y, P)$. The w parameter determines the weight given to each objective: the higher is w, the greater the weight attached to the stability of real income, and the lower the weight given to price stability. Note that this particular objective function treats deviations of each variable from its target value symmetrically: the 'cost' of a given positive deviation of $Y(P)$

from its target value is the same as the cost of a negative deviation of the same magnitude.

In order to use the objective function to obtain an *unambiguous* ordering of two regimes, such as floating and real exchange rates, we must first specify numerical values for the target values and the weight, w. The objective function is then linked to an algebraic macroeconomic model that specifies the relationship between the actual values of real income and the price level and the policy instruments. The model used could be a formal version of the Mundell–Fleming model (allowing for the possibility of price changes), or a monetarist model, or whatever.[6] The only restriction is that Y and P must be independent functions of the policy instruments.

Such an approach does not of course remove the subjective element in the ranking of the two regimes: we have chosen the target values, the functional form of the objective function, and the parameter(s) of that function, and our choices will reflect our subjective assessments. What the approach does do is bring our assumptions into the open, so that they may be questioned, and allow us to analyse the sensitivity of our rankings to differences in the weights, the target values and so on.

☐ *Optimising macromodels*

Several of the recent contributions to the literature on stabilisation policy have used macroeconomic models that are founded on the microeconomics of individual optimising behaviour. Some of the models follow the Walrasian market-clearing tradition, others allow for market disequilibria. A model introduced by Cuddington, Johansson and Lofgren provides an insight into the approach.[7]

The model assumes a small open economy producing and consuming one (composite) traded good and one non-traded good. The goods are perishable (non-storable). Labour is mobile, but capital is sector-specific. Households are assumed to choose the amount of labour they supply, the quantities of the goods they consume, and their planned savings in order to maximise their welfare (which also depends on their wealth). Firms are assumed to choose their labour inputs (and hence their outputs) in order to maximise their profits, and those profits are then distributed to households (so adding to their wealth).

Disequilibrium is introduced by assuming that the demand for non-traded goods is deficient, so that producers of those goods must cut their demand for labour. This then restricts household expenditure, and we have a state of Keynesian unemployment.

Some of the results from this model are consistent with those from the Mundell–Fleming model. For example, assuming perfect capital mobility, both show that fiscal policy will increase output and worsen the balance of trade under a fixed exchange rate, and will lead to an appreciation of the exchange rate if it is floating. They also agree that monetary policy will have no effect on either output or the balance of trade under a fixed exchange rate, but will increase output when there is a floating rate. On the other hand, whereas the Mundell–Fleming model predicts that fiscal policy will have no effect on output under a flexible exchange rate, and that both fiscal and monetary policy will worsen the balance of trade under either exchange-rate regime, the Cuddington *et al.* model indicates that the effects are indeterminate.

Perhaps more importantly, the new optimising macroeconomic models do not resolve the debate about the two exchange-rate regimes. They confirm some of the results of the more traditional models, but not others, and do not lead to an unambiguous ranking. It may of course be argued that the new models are very much in their infancy, and that future developments may remove some of the ambiguities.

▌ 30.4 International co-ordination of ▌ macroeconomic policy

It should be clear from much of what has been argued in earlier chapters that the macroeconomic policies followed by one country will, if it is 'large', have an effect upon the economies of other countries. We considered this explicitly in Chapter 25, when we derived the income multipliers for two large open economies, but it is implicit in much of the discussion elsewhere. If an economy is large then any change in its output, price level and/or exchange rate must have an effect on its trading partners. Similarly, unless capital is perfectly immobile, a change in its rate of interest must be transmitted to other countries.

If the large country trades only with (relatively) small countries then it may logically ignore the effects of its domestic policies on other countries, since they are powerless to retaliate in any way. The only constraints upon domestic policy-making in the only large country may then be altruism or a belief that the effects of its policies will be so pervasive and so strong that it will experience an automatic (rather than policy-based) feed-back from the rest of the world. It may be argued that the United States was in this position for much of the period from the end of the Second World War until fairly recently. Some economists have suggested that the tendency of most post-war American economics textbooks to concentrate their discussion of macroeconomic policy on the closed economy case reflected this position!

Currie has argued that policy 'spillovers' from one country to others are prevalent, and provide the general argument for policy co-ordination.[8] He suggests four prime examples of such spillovers and their consequences:

(1) Governments may be unwilling to expand unilaterally because of the consequent balance-of-payments and exchange-rate effects: this may lead to a deflationary bias in the world economy.

(2) Governments may tend to combat inflationary pressures by a combination of monetary contraction and exchange-rate appreciation while using an expansionary fiscal policy to counter the reduction in output due to reduced competitiveness: this may result in high real interest rates and an inappropriate mix of monetary and fiscal policies at the world level.

(3) Governments may, quite reasonably, assume that their own policy actions will have little effect on the prices of traded goods, but if the majority of governments change their policies in the same way then the overall effect may be inappropriate.

(4) Governments may have inconsistent objectives about their desired current-account balance (all, for example, may seek to maintain a surplus), and attempts to achieve their objectives may be disruptive at the world level.

☐ *The gains from policy co-ordination*

The possibility of mutual gains from policy co-ordination may be demonstrated by the use of the *Hamada diagram*,[9] which is essentially an extension of the reaction curve technique that we have previously used in our analysis of intra-industry trade.

Figure 30.1 shows the derivation of the reaction curve for one country (A) in the case where, for simplicity, it is assumed that each country has only one policy instrument at its disposal. The government of A is assumed to have an objective function (or a welfare function) that may be written in terms of the values taken by the two policy instruments,[10] shown as I_A for country A, and I_B for country B. Point M_A is the optimum point for country A. That is, if A and B set their policy instruments at I_A^0 and I_B^0 respectively then the objective function of A's government is maximised.

The government's objective function is represented by a family of indifference curves, of which three are shown in Figure 30.1.[11] Indifference curve U_A^2 shows a lower level of welfare than U_A^1, and so on. Note that if

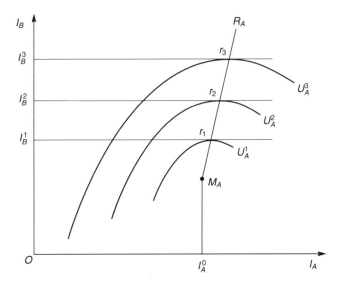

Figure 30.1 *Deriving the reaction curve for country* A

there were no spillovers then the indifference curves would be a set of
vertical straight lines, since welfare in country A would depend only on the
value of I_A.

The *reaction curve* for country A shows the level of A's policy
instrument that will give the maximum welfare for any given policy in B.
Suppose that B sets its policy instrument at I_B^1. The highest welfare that A
can obtain in this case is where an indifference curve is tangential to the
horizontal line drawn through I_B^1: that is, at point r_1. Similarly, if B's policy
is set at I_B^2 then A's (constrained) optimum point is r_2, and if B's policy is I_B^3
then A's optimum is at r_3. The locus of all points such as r_1, r_2, and r_3 (i.e.
where an A indifference curve is horizontal) is A's reaction curve, shown in
Figure 30.1 as R_A.[12]

Figure 30.2 shows the reaction curves for both countries. B's reaction
curve, R_B, is derived in the same way as A's, being the locus of all points at
which B indifference curves are vertical.

Points such as e_1, e_2, and e_3, where a country A indifference curve is
tangential to a country B indifference curve, are Pareto-efficient: once at
such a point it is only possible to increase one country's welfare by
reducing the other country's welfare. The contract curve $M_A M_B$ is the
locus of such points. By co-ordinating their policies the governments could
move to a point on the contract curve. Which point they would move to
would depend on their relative bargaining powers.

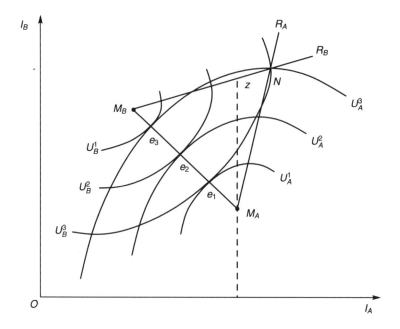

Figure 30.2 *The gains from policy co-ordination*

Unco-ordinated policy-making will lead the countries to the intersection of the two reaction curves, at point N. Suppose that they are initially at point M_A. A obviously has no incentive to move, but B may increase its welfare. The best position it can achieve given A's policy is at point z on its reaction curve. This however reduces A's welfare, and its best response given B's new policy is to move to the appropriate point on its reaction curve (horizontally to the right from z). The ensuing process will move the two countries to point N.[13]

Starting from point N, it is obvious that both countries will gain if they can agree on a joint revision of policies that will take then to any point on the contract curve $M_A M_B$ that is between e_1 and e_3. That is, co-ordination in policy-making leads to a mutually beneficial outcome.

Note that there is no requirement that the two countries agree on their policy objectives. One may wish to pursue a higher inflation/lower unemployment position than the other, for example, without either forgoing the benefits of co-operation. What is required for co-ordination to be beneficial is that one country's policies affect the other country. If this were not the case (if there were no spillovers) then A's welfare maximum would be achieved anywhere along the vertical line through M_A, and B's optimum would be anywhere on the horizontal line through M_B . Each can then attain its maximum welfare independently.

Some problems associated with policy co-operation

An obvious complication is that a country may be able to gain by *reneging* on a policy agreement, or by *free riding* (enjoying the benefits of an agreement between other countries without joining the group itself). Suppose that agreement has been reached to co-ordinate policy at point e_2. Provided that country A believes that B will continue to pursue its part of the agreed policy package then it has an incentive to change its own policy (by moving horizontally from e_2 to its own reaction curve).

Whereas this may be infeasible for one of a pair of countries (since the change in policy may be observed and will produce a policy reaction), it may be more feasible for one country within a group of co-operating countries, since the other countries may have more to lose by breaking their agreements with each other than they would gain by retaliating individually against the reneging country. On the other hand, it may be possible for the remainder of the group to agree on a common policy that will put pressure on the reneging country to rejoin the group (or draw in a free rider), or to issue a 'threat' that will bring the reneging party back into the agreement; such a threat must of course be credible.

It has been suggested that in some circumstances international policy co-operation may be welfare-decreasing. For example, Rogoff identifies the possibility that a government may, in the absence of policy co-ordination and with a floating exchange rate, be deterred by the prospect of a consequent depreciation from using unexpected monetary expansions to procure increases in output in the private sector.[14] He suggests that international co-operation in pegging exchange rates may then reduce the disincentives to the use of such monetary expansions.

Co-ordination may be welfare-reducing if it is concerned only with *some* aspects of economic policy. Currie, for example, argues that agreement on nominal-exchange-rate targets without a parallel agreement on the adjustment of monetary and fiscal policy may be welfare-reducing if the targeted exchange rates are inconsistent with the fundamental state of the economy.[15]

Given the apparent benefits from policy co-ordination (with the exception of the type of negative effects just discussed), the obvious question is why governments seem unwilling to negotiate on policy measures and their timing. A simplistic answer is that the realisation that national policies interact may bring with it the realisation that such interaction can provide an excuse for avoiding policy changes that may, in the political long run, be embarrassing. For example, a government faced with the problem of deciding whether or not to maintain deflationary policies at the cost of sustained unemployment may prefer to shift the blame for the current state of affairs on to other governments: 'we can do nothing until the government of A expands its economy' is a not atypical political plea.

☐ *'Rules' versus 'one-off' negotiations*

A more sophisticated argument relates to the difficulties inherent in formulating 'optimal' economic policies. Typically, governments find it difficult to design and implement complex policies, and optimal policies are almost invariably relatively complex (as we saw in the discussion of the 'targets and instruments' literature in earlier chapters). As Currie comments: 'It is plausible to suggest that policies that are to be implemented in practice should be relatively simple in formulation (however complex the calculations that may be used in their design). If this is so, then it applies with greater force to internationally agreed co-ordinated policies'.[16] That is, simple rules or guidelines may be the best way to establish policy co-ordination and to encourage belief in such policies among the rest of the community. Such simplicity will reduce the gain from co-ordination, but provided there is still a net gain then the *expected* gain from co-ordination with simple rules may exceed that from complex rules.

Rules may be either 'target-based' or 'instrument-based'. Under the former, agreement is reached on the targets that each co-operating party should attain (e.g. 2 per cent inflation), but each party has freedom in the choice of instruments used to meet that target. An instrument-based set of rules however will specify the values of policy instruments (e.g. 3 per cent money supply growth). Negotiation on target-based rules may be the easier option when there is no consensus on the 'true' economic model among the co-operating parties.

A further benefit from a rules-based system is that it may encourage the contracting governments to take a longer-term view of co-ordination. In the absence of rules, any 'crisis' sufficient to trigger international concern will have to be dealt with at a special meeting of the governments concerned (so-called 'discretionary co-ordination').[17] If such meetings focus only on the current issue, which will have its own peculiar characteristics, then the solution obtained is unlikely to have any general applicability, so that the next crisis will have to resolved in similar manner. Moreover, the outcome of one such meeting may set a precedent for subsequent meetings, although the procedures adopted at the first may be inappropriate for the problems leading to the second. Such one-off procedures are likely to reduce the gains from policy co-ordination compared with a more general set of rules designed to deal with a wide range of circumstances.

It has also been argued that an agreed set of rules may be beneficial if it imposes some external discipline on government policy. This presupposes that some governments are likely to 'mismanage' the economy in search of a short-term political gain, or that they are weak, so that an appeal to the need to meet external obligations will enable them to carry through an unpopular policy.

An important *caveat* in the formulation of rules is that, to be viable in the long term, they should be symmetrical in the obligations they impose on the contracting parties. This is not to say that they will in practice operate symmetrically. As we shall argue in Chapter 31, the Bretton Woods rules on exchange rates were designed to be symmetrical, although in practice the United States' role became asymmetric. However, it is difficult to envisage a set of rules that applies different rules to different members operating smoothly in the long term. An example of an asymmetric agreement is the GATT, which differentiates between developed and less-developed countries (LDCs). There has been pressure in recent years to 'graduate' some LDCs to the developed group, so removing their preferential treatment, and considerable debate on whether preferential treatment should be continued.

Arguments in favour of discretionary co-ordination stress the loss of sovereignty inherent in a rules-based system, and the flexibility of decision-making in meetings held to resolve specific issues. One consequence of maintaining sovereignty is, of course, that no agreement may be made to which all countries are prepared to subscribe. The process of discretionary co-ordination may be helped if the (potentially) interested parties meet on a reasonably regular basis to discuss a range of matters, as with the 'Group of 3' and 'Group of 7' countries.[18] However, the experience of the EC countries with the Exchange Rate Mechanism (ERM) shows that, even where a group of countries is prepared to agree on policy co-operation over a wide range of issues, and to abide by agreed rules in some areas, it may be difficult to obtain agreement in all areas.

■ 30.5 Conclusions

We have given some consideration to two continuing and related debates: whether pegged exchange rates are superior or inferior to floating rates, and whether there are net gains to be made from co-operation in, and co-ordination of, macroeconomic policy, and if so, how such co-operation should be organised. As we might expect from the fact that the debates are continuing, there are acceptable arguments to be made on each side. There also seems to be little prospect of economics being able to offer firm evidence in favour of one side or the other in either debate. This contrasts with the state of affairs in international trade, where the majority of economists would argue forcefully in favour of a free-trade regime.

☐ *Notes*

1   See McKinnon (1993) for a succinct summary of the history of exchange rate systems.
2   See Perée and Steinherr (1989) and De Grauwe (1987).
3   Friedman (1953).
4   Friedman (1953).
5   For a more detailed account, see Kearney (1990), on which this section is based.
6   See Pilbeam (1992) for a model that uses the objective function defined in equation (30.1).
7   Cuddington, Johansson and Lofgren (1984). This model is discussed in Kearney (1990).
8   Currie (1990). This section draws upon Currie's analysis.
9   Hamada (1985).
10   The basic objective function will be written in terms of target variables, such as output, the price level, and so on. However, we may use the underlying macroeconomic model to express each target variable in terms of the policy instrument, and substitution then allows us to write the objective function in terms of that instrument.
11   Strictly, the indifference curves enclose the optimum or 'bliss' point. However in the analysis presented here only a portion of each curve is relevant to the argument.
12   The reaction curve exists below M_A, but for simplicity we have omitted this section of the curve.
13   N is the Nash equilibrium point.
14   Rogoff (1985). Rogoff is concerned with the case where governments lack *reputation*. This might occur if a government had a record of trying to 'trick' the electorate. An often-quoted example is that of a short-sighted government that persuades the electorate to believe that there will low inflation in order subsequently to reduce unemployment by a 'surprise' increase in inflation. In the long run this behaviour will be detected, and the government will lose its reputation. See Artis and Lewis (1991), Chapter 5, for a more detailed discussion.
15   Currie (1990).
16   Currie (1990), p. 135.
17   Such as the 'Plaza' agreement (1985) on the management of a depreciation of the US dollar. This will be discussed in the following chapter.
18   The 'Group of 3' (G3) countries are the United States, Germany and Japan; the 'Group of 7' (G7) countries are the G3 countries plus the United Kingdom, France, Italy and Canada.

■ *Chapter 31* ■

The International Monetary System

■ *31.1* Introduction

The international monetary system, certainly as defined by the 'rules of the game', has gone through many incarnations since the start of the century.[1] In broad terms, the system has moved from the fixed exchange rates of the gold standard (ending in 1914), through a period when there was no maintained universal system, but which saw both a brief return to the gold standard and a period of floating exchange rates (1914–45), into the Bretton Woods pegged exchange-rate system (1945–1973), and finally into the current 'managed floating' system. Over the same period the dominant currency has changed, from the pound sterling at the start of the century to the US dollar in the Bretton Woods system, culminating in the present dollar/yen/Deutschmark troika.

The present international monetary system cannot be said to be either universal or in a stable state. While many countries allow their currencies to float, albeit with a degree of management designed to smooth short-term fluctuations, others peg their currencies against some target currency (or basket of currencies).[2] Moreover, some groups of countries are attempting to establish their own exchange-rate subsystems, usually in a pegged exchange-rate format. The most important example of this, at least in terms of its possible impact on the rest of the world, is the European Monetary System (EMS).

We shall discuss briefly the considerations that underlay the formulation of the Bretton Woods system. In the course of that discussion we shall gain some understanding of the reasons for the departure from the gold standard and for the suspicion with which freely floating exchange rates are regarded by many policy-makers. We shall then consider the factors that contributed to the eventual collapse of the pegged exchange-rate regime. There are two reasons for doing this. First, it is always informative to examine the weaknesses in any system, particularly one which attempts to manage a market.[3] Second, there may be lessons to be learnt from the collapse of one pegged exchange-rate system which we can apply to the prospects of another (the EMS).

■ 31.2 Some basic concepts

☐ *The consistency problem*

An international monetary system must, if it is to be successful, have some 'rules of the game' (whether explicit or implicit) that are generally accepted and by which members of the system will abide.[4] Central to the formulation and operation of any set of rules is recognition of what is known variously as the 'consistency', 'redundancy' and '$n-1$' problem.

The essence of the problem is that the sum of balance-of-payments surpluses and deficits in the world as a whole must be zero. It follows from this that in a world consisting of n countries, at most $n-1$ of those countries can determine their balance-of-payments positions independently.[5] This implies that either the nth country must accept (passively) whatever balance-of-payments position is forced upon it by the other countries,[6] or that there must be some mechanism that brings about consistency between the external objectives of the full set of n countries.[7]

Llewellyn has argued that there are five broad mechanisms for structuring an international monetary system:[8]

> (i) automatic market mechanisms such as floating exchange rates or non-sterilisation of balance of payments induced changes in the money supply; (ii) the $(n-1)$ approach, whereby one country in the system agrees not to have an external target; (iii) *ex ante* policy co-ordination designed to ensure consistent targets and compatible means of securing them; (iv) an agreement to a precise set of policy rules which indicate what is required of policymakers in specified circumstances; (v) a multilateral approach, whereby some supranational authority indicates (and enforces?) policy measures which have been calculated to ensure consistency and stability in the system. In practice, actual arrangements in the international monetary system are likely to be a hybrid of the above mechanisms.

Note that the last four options involve the surrender of sovereignty to some degree. Whether a floating exchange-rate regime does so is still a matter of debate. According to one view there is no loss of sovereignty, but the counter-argument is that changes in the exchange rate may force changes in planned policy.

☐ *Political will, hegemony and seigniorage*

No system will survive if the members of the system do not have the political will to ensure its survival. The automatic market mechanism necessary to the operation of the first option given above may be set aside by a country that is unwilling to accept the costs imposed by the economic adjustments required of the system. Should only one or even a few (small) countries do this then the system will probably survive, but should many countries do so then the system may well collapse. Similarly, options (iii), (iv) or (v) will fail if a significant group of countries renege on the agreement.

More importantly, in the light of the eventual failure of the Bretton Woods system, the *n*th country identified in option (ii) may be unwilling to accept the passive role required of it. It is interesting to consider this question briefly in general, since both the United Kingdom and the United States have played this role in the past, and Germany's role within the EMS has some elements of the *n*th-country position.

The central question is why any country would be prepared to forego control over its external balance and to accept some loss of autonomy in its control over its internal balance. One possible answer is that a country may be in an *hegemonic* position, without necessarily having sought that state. Typically, hegemony arises because the country concerned is economically and politically dominant, and is willing to accept the responsibilities that go with that dominance. This willingness may be reinforced by the gains that may come from having such a position, particularly when the dominant country's currency becomes the reserve currency. These gains, usually referred to as *seigniorage*, arise when other countries are prepared to accept short-term debt issued by the reserve currency country. Since the interest rate on short-term debt is usually relatively low, this allows the reserve-currency country to borrow cheaply from others, and to use those borrowings to finance the acquisition of more productive long-term assets in other countries. Other countries will prefer to hold their reserves in the reserve currency since they receive a higher return than would be obtained from holding them in gold. It does not of course follow that all of them will regard these seigniorage transfers as a reasonable price to pay for the reserve-currency country playing its designated role.

■ *31.3* The Bretton Woods system
□ *The background*

The pre-First-World-War gold standard was an example of an international system operating under the first of the options identified by Llewellyn. Countries played by the rules, in particular by not sterilising the domestic effects of inflows and outflows of gold.[9] It was universal, in the sense that the major industrial nations and many smaller countries maintained convertibility between their currencies and gold, or between their currencies and one that was convertible into gold,[10] and allowed free exporting and importing of gold, from 1879 to 1914 and briefly from 1927 to 1931.[11]

The first era of the full gold standard ended with the suspension of convertibility into gold by many countries soon after the outbreak of the First World War.[12] The economic situation after the war prevented the immediate restoration of convertibility into gold, and currencies exchanged at floating rates. However, re-establishment of the gold standard became an established aim of economic policy, particularly in the United Kingdom.

The structure of the international economy was markedly different after the war. The United Kingdom's position was much weaker than before, her gold reserves were seriously depleted, and she was no longer able to act as the world's banker. The United States, on the other hand, was now much more powerful economically, and held substantial reserves, but was unwilling to take over the central role previously played by the United Kingdom. The war-reparation payments imposed on Germany by the Allies contributed to the distortion of the post-war international order. Moreover, the post-war boom led to inflation, but at different rates. The UK rate of inflation was particularly high, yet the UK's economic policy was directed at maintaining the pre-war exchange rate against the dollar.

The United Kingdom returned to the gold standard in 1925 (at the pre-war rate), and most major currencies were convertible into gold by 1927.[13] The system however proved impossible to sustain. It is still a matter of debate whether the re-introduction of the gold standard triggered the slump of the 1930s and the financial problems that came with it, but it is certain that it was those problems that forced the United Kingdom to abandon convertibility into gold and depreciate the exchange rate in 1931. The devaluation of the dollar in 1933 was the final blow to the gold standard. A contributing factor to the collapse of the gold standard was the failure of some countries to 'play by the rules' as they had done before 1914. The United States in particular chose to sterilise the inflow of gold generated by its balance-of-payments surplus in order to reduce its inflationary impact, so inhibiting the workings of the adjustment mechanism within the United States, and increasing the burden of adjustment in other countries.

After the abandonment of the gold standard there was no generally accepted exchange-rate regime. Some countries formed themselves into 'currency blocs', most notably the sterling area (the United Kingdom plus the Commonwealth, but excluding Canada, Egypt, some Scandinavian countries, and for some time Japan), and a 'dollar bloc' centred on the United States. Attempts to maintain exchange rates were hampered by the low levels of reserves following the crises of the early 1930s. The situation was exacerbated by the depression, which led to a sequence of competitive devaluations as governments attempted to stimulate aggregate demand and so reduce unemployment.

The creation of the International Monetary Fund

Plans for an international institution that would organise the international monetary system circulated among the Allied powers during the Second World War. A conference in 1944 of 44 nations at Bretton Woods, New Hampshire, led among other things to the creation of the International Monetary Fund (IMF). The Bretton Woods system that the IMF was to supervise rested on two pillars: the maintenance of stable exchange rates and a multilateral credit system. The IMF would organise the system, consult with member countries about exchange-rate changes, and create international liquidity when needed.

The experience with floating exchange rates in the inter-war years, and in particular their perceived volatility, had convinced economists and policy-makers of the dangers of such a system.[14] On the other hand, the problems faced in the attempted return to the gold standard had made it evident that an attempt to maintain a fixed exchange rate at an unrealistic level was futile. The compromise adopted was that the members of the IMF should keep their exchange rates within 1 per cent of agreed par values, but that a member could propose a change in the par value of its currency if it had a 'fundamental disequilibrium' in its balance of payments. The procedure used to maintain a currency within the agreed range was that described in Chapter 24: the government was to buy or sell its domestic currency on the foreign-exchange markets as appropriate.

If the proposed change in the par value of a currency was less than 10 per cent then the IMF could not object. If however a larger change was proposed then the member country had to seek the Fund's permission. The IMF could not veto an adjustment of the exchange rate if it were made to correct a fundamental disequilibrium, but it might however object to the economic and social policies pursued in the country. The philosophy behind these rules was that exchange-rate changes should take place in an orderly manner and for justifiable economic reasons.

In principle, the IMF peg was to gold. However, in practice, countries pegged their currencies to the US dollar (which was itself pegged to gold). The dollar became the medium for intervention in the foreign exchange markets, and countries held a substantial part of their reserves in dollars. The IMF system thus has strong elements of Llewellyn's second option, with the passive role played by the United States, although there were elements of the third, fourth and fifth options.

The second pillar of the IMF was the arrangement for creating international liquidity. Each member had a right to borrow from the Fund in order to help it maintain its exchange rate within the specified range in the face of a *temporary* external deficit. This was intended, *inter alia*, to meet the possibility that, although in a fundamentally sound long-run position, a country might have to cease intervening in the foreign-exchange market in support of its currency because of a shortage of foreign-currency reserves. The borrowing would augment those reserves and allow the exchange rate to be maintained until the deficit problem had passed. The funds for such borrowing were provided by each member country placing with the Fund a 'quota', 25 per cent of which was gold and the remainder its own currency. The quota was broadly related to the country's economic importance as indicated by the value of its international trade.

Each country had an automatic right to 'borrow' up to 25 per cent of its quota, but any borrowing above that required that it agree to abide by conditions set by the IMF (relating to its macroeconomic policies), with the conditions becoming more onerous as the level of borrowing increased. (This latter procedure is often referred to as 'IMF Conditionality'.) Borrowing consisted of a country purchasing reserve assets by depositing its own currency with the IMF, and the usual requirement was that the borrowing country repurchase its currency within a 3- to 5-year period.

The quota also determined the voting rights of each country, and so its power within the Fund. This made the United States the dominant member, since its initial quota constituted 36 per cent of the IMF's then total holdings; subsequent changes in quotas did little to weaken this position.

☐ *The IMF in the 1950s and 1960s*

The IMF began its operations in 1947.[15] Initially it played a conservative role, fearing that its resources would be used to finance post-war reconstruction rather than for overcoming short-term balance-of-payments problems. This led it to take a rather passive stance in its early years, actually approving the devaluations made by the United Kingdom and most other Western European countries in 1949.

In later years the Fund took the view that changes in the par values of major currencies were undesirable. The implicit policy prescription was that temporary balance-of-payments deficits should be financed by the use of a country's own reserves and/or by its automatic borrowing right, while more persistent but not 'fundamental' imbalances should be dealt with through (expenditure-reducing) fiscal and monetary policy. Only when the imbalance was incontrovertibly 'fundamental' could a change in the par value be approved.

The IMF view was echoed by governments, particularly those of the developed nations. Borrowing from the Fund was seen as an admission that the government was not managing the economy effectively, while borrowing to such an extent that IMF Conditionality was invoked, and so sovereignty over domestic policy compromised, was to be avoided if at all possible. Devaluation however was viewed as an even clearer admission of failure. A consequence of this was that exchange-rate adjustments tended to be delayed, and that expenditure-reducing policies bore the brunt of adjustments in external imbalances.

The liberalisation of international capital movements[16] (discussed in section 31.4) further complicated the changing of a currency's par value. As Artis and Lewis note:[17]

> Speculators were able to bet against the ability and willingness of the authorities to sustain the parity. To make matters worse, the method of changing rates discontinuously in large discrete jumps ... made obvious the direction of change, allowing speculators the luxury of anticipating change with facility and virtually no risk. A government contemplating an adjustment to parity had to take cognizance of the likelihood that a change would merely encourage speculators to expect that it would be altered again in response to future payments difficulties, so making matters worse 'next time round'. Future policy credibility and the avoidance of increasingly large and destabilizing speculation pointed to the desirability of using the adjustable peg provisions of the IMF system as seldom as possible.

Giving prior notice to the IMF of an intended change in the par value of a currency, as required under the Bretton Woods system, would of course have provided speculators with the clearest possible indication of which way to bet! Not surprisingly, this encouraged governments contemplating a devaluation to deny vehemently that such was their intention, to not give prior notice to the IMF, and to announce the devaluation when the foreign exchange markets were closed. When they were made, devaluations were often larger than would have been needed had they been made when appropriate, and often followed a period of intense downward pressure on the exchange rate that had seriously depleted the country's reserves.

☐ *International liquidity: the 'Triffin Dilemma'*

The main critic of the Bretton Woods system in its early years was Robert Triffin.[18] The core of his argument was that the expansion of international trade (and the accompanying economic growth) could only be maintained by a parallel expansion of international liquidity, but that the existing mechanism for expanding liquidity could not be sustained in the long run.

At that time the US dollar was the main component in the currency reserves of the rest of the world, and those reserves had been expanding as a consequence of the United States running a continued balance-of-payments deficit, and of the rest of the world being willing to hold the increased supply of dollars as their reserves, rather than converting them into gold. Conversion of dollars into gold would of course merely change the distribution of the increasing reserves between countries, rather than increasing them. The problem was that if the short-run dollar liabilities of the United States continued to increase in relation to its holdings of gold then belief in the credibility of the US commitment to convert dollars into gold at the fixed price ($35 per ounce) would be eroded. If central banks ceased to believe that the United States would maintain its commitment then they would have an overpowering incentive to convert their existing dollar holdings into gold, and that would in turn force the United States to abandon its commitment.

This then was the 'Triffin Dilemma'. Either the United States would eliminate its balance-of-payments deficit, so that there would be a shortage of international liquidity and world growth would be curtailed, or the US deficit would continue and international liquidity would expand, but there would eventually be a crisis of confidence.[19]

Triffin's prescription (the 'Triffin Plan') was that the IMF should be turned into a 'deposit bank' for central banks.[20] His argument was that a mechanism had to be created that would allow the total growth in reserves to be brought under international control while avoiding crises in confidence. His solution was that each member country should undertake to hold a specified proportion of its reserves on deposit with the IMF, and that the IMF should have the capacity to increase international reserves by giving loans or by buying securities. A new 'reserve asset' was to be created that was to be under the control of the IMF, and at the same time the supply of alternative forms of reserves, such as the dollar, was to be controlled.

The Triffin Plan was not the only proposal for reform of the international system. Alternatives in the 'Reform Debate' encompassed a return to gold (at a higher price),[21] floating exchange rates, a system based exclusively on the dollar, and the substitution of a 'crawling peg' system for the existing 'adjustable peg'.[22] Nevertheless, it was the Triffin Plan that dominated official thinking in the 1960s.

☐ *The introduction of Special Drawing Rights*

Special Drawing Rights (SDRs) were introduced in 1967 with the intention of increasing the stock of international reserves. SDRs were originally defined in terms of gold, with 1 'unit of account' equal to 1/35th of an ounce (which was of course the gold value of the US dollar at that time). In 1974 the SDR was redefined in terms of a basket of 16 currencies, the US dollar being the dominant currency. In 1981 it was redefined again, this time in terms of a weighted basket of the US dollar, Deutschmark, yen, French franc and pound sterling.

The SDR has the characteristics of an international currency. It is not backed by gold or by any other national currency. It derives its strength from IMF members being willing to use it as a reserve currency and to use it as a means of payment between central banks in exchange for national currencies. The original instalments of SDRs were distributed to member countries according to their quota in the Fund. All members of the Fund are required to accept SDRs in exchange for their national currencies up to a limit of three times their quota, and receive interest (now a market rate of interest) on their excess holdings.

A member can draw upon its SDR account if it has balance-of-payments problems or if it wishes to augment its reserves, subject to the requirement that over a 5-year period its average SDR balance with the Fund must not fall below 15 per cent of its allocation. It does not have to consult with the IMF before doing so, and SDR drawings are not subject to IMF Conditionality. Countries that draw on their SDRS have to pay interest (again at a market rate under present arrangements).

The volume of SDRs is controlled by the IMF members. It cannot be increased unless 80 per cent of IMF votes are cast in favour of the increase.[23] Note however that no attempt has been made to control the supply of other forms of international liquidity (one of the elements in the Triffin Plan). Deciding on the appropriate expansion of international liquidity is therefore not a simple matter. In the period from 1970 to 1972 over $10 billion of SDRs were issued in anticipation of a shortage of other reserve assets. In the event, world reserves increased by nearly $70 billion over the same period, creating an 'overhang' of dollars held by central banks, firms and institutions. In the following five years no new SDRS were issued.

The breakdown of the Bretton Woods system: 1967–73

The beginning of the events that lead to the breakdown of the Bretton Woods system is usually identified as the devaluation of the pound sterling in 1967, which could not be averted even with substantial help from the United States and other countries. This increased doubts about America's commitment to maintain the dollar price of gold, and so to a flight from the dollar into gold in early 1968. The response was to create a two-tiered gold market, with official transactions between central banks maintained at $35 per ounce but with the private market price of gold allowed to be free. One consequence of this was to encourage the movement of gold from the public to the private sector, so that its importance as a reserve asset diminished sharply. Doubts about the US commitment to maintain the official gold price were not however overcome by the establishment of the two-tier system, and in August 1971, to the evident annoyance of the US authorities, the United Kingdom asked for a guarantee of the gold value of its holdings of dollars. Within a few days (on 15 August 1971) the United States decided to sever the link between the dollar and gold.[24]

The Smithsonian Agreement

After the suspension of gold convertibility by the United States, the major countries had little option but to allow their currencies to float, a circumstance they viewed with considerable disfavour. The 'Group of Ten' countries met at the Smithsonian Institution in Washington in December 1971 with the intention of re-instituting a system of stable exchange rates at new par values.[25] The realignments resulting from the 'Smithsonian Agreement' centred on an 8 per cent devaluation of the dollar, and revaluations of the yen and the Deutschmark by 17 and 14 per cent respectively.

The Agreement also widened the permissible band of movements of the exchange rates to 2.25 per cent above or below the new 'central rates'. The hope was that the wider band would reduce the pressure on deficit countries' reserves and possibly allow exchange rates to play a rather greater part in adjustment.

The Smithsonian Agreement lasted only 14 months. The 'overhang' of dollars made the new system potentially very unstable. The UK government decided to allow sterling to float in June 1972 following further balance-of-payments difficulties. There was speculation against the dollar in the following months, and in early 1973 first the Swiss franc and then the yen were allowed to float against the dollar. Finally the major countries tacitly accepted that the Bretton Woods system was at an end, and what has been called the 'non-system' came into being in March 1973.

By that time many countries viewed the breakdown of the Bretton Woods system with some favour.[26] It eliminated the *seigniorage* enjoyed by the United States through possession of the major reserve currency, which had irritated the French in particular.[27] Countries with low rates of inflation (such as Germany) were relieved of the necessity to combat 'imported inflation'. The United Kingdom felt it would be able to abandon stop–go policies and pursue a faster rate of growth. Finally, the United States seemed relieved to be free of the burdens imposed by the reserve currency status of the dollar.

The 'non-system' was legalised in 1976 by revisions of the IMF Articles. Countries are now free to choose whether to float their currencies or to peg them (to a single currency, a basket of currencies, or to the SDR). There are no rules governing pegged rates (either on the permissible range of fluctuation or on the nature of adjustments to the peg), and no *de facto* supervision of floating exchange rates. Most major industrial countries, and a few developing countries, have chosen to float their currencies, although a subgroup of the EC countries have chosen to peg their currencies to each other, while allowing them to float against other currencies (the EMS, discussed in section 31.5). A sizeable group of countries peg their currencies to the dollar, and a smaller group to the French franc. Others have elected to peg against a basket of currencies, and a small number peg against the SDR.

International reserves are held in various forms. The US dollar is still the dominant element in international foreign currency reserves, but the Deutschmark, yen, pound sterling, Swiss franc, French franc and the guilder are also widely used. A high proportion of these reserves is held in the Euromarkets (see section 31.4). Countries still maintain holdings in the IMF which, together with SDRs, make up the bulk of non-currency reserves. Many central banks still hold gold and declare it as part of their reserves, even though it seems most unlikely that they would use gold to support their currencies.

The international monetary system since the demise of Bretton Woods

Any hopes of a swift return to the pegged exchange-rate system following the events of 1973 were dampened by the oil price increase of 1973–74 (which followed a general rise in commodity prices between 1970 and 1972). The oil-importing countries experienced both a major deterioration of their terms of trade and substantial deficits on current account. These effects were not however uniform across countries, and policy responses also differed, so that inflation rates diverged. The second oil price shock of 1978 was met by greater determination to avoid the possible inflationary consequences, but only at the cost of a deeper depression that before.

In the first half of the 1980s, the US dollar appreciated strongly against other currencies. It has been argued that the main source of this appreciation was that the US authorities ran a budget deficit accompanied by a restrictive monetary policy, whereas the European countries were pursuing tight policies on both fronts. As a consequence, real interest rates in the United States rose relative to those in Europe, attracting the funds that more than financed the US's increasing current account deficit, and stimulated the appreciation of the dollar.

The dollar's appreciation however reduced the competitiveness of US industries, and this lead to an upsurge of protectionist sentiment in the US Congress. Whereas the US authorities regarded the strength of the dollar as reflecting the strength of the US economy, the Japanese and Europeans argued that it was the consequence of the US budget deficit, and should be cured by a tightening of fiscal policy in the United States. Despite, or perhaps because of, these differences in opinion, concern about the problem was instrumental in bringing about a meeting of the 'G-5' countries.[28]

The meeting, held at the Plaza Hotel in New York in September 1985, resulted in the *Plaza Accord*. The agreed plan was that the dollar should be forced down in order to improve the US trade balance, and that this should be done by co-ordinated interventions in the foreign-exchange markets and the pursuit of appropriate macroeconomic policies. The announcement of the Accord had an immediate effect on expectations, and the dollar began to fall before intervention had begun. Subsequently, substantial sales of dollars by the authorities in all the G-5 countries, but in particular those of the United States and Japan, led to a substantial depreciation of the dollar.

By early 1987, however, concerns were being expressed that the dollar was now undervalued. Following a G-7 meeting in Paris in February 1987, the *Louvre Accord* was issued.[29] This announced that the G-7 governments thought that exchange rates were now 'broadly consistent with underlying economic fundamentals', and that the G-7 governments had agreed to co-operate in keeping exchange rates around their then-current levels. The Louvre Accord was successful in stabilising exchange rates for the rest of the year. Since then there seems to have been a consensus that exchange rates should be broadly stabilised, but there is little overt co-operation.

■ *31.4* The Eurocurrency markets

We referred in Section 31.3 to the liberalisation of international capital markets. The evolution of the Eurocurrency markets (the first of which was the Eurodollar market) played a major part in this liberalisation.

Technically, an Eurodollar deposit is a (time) deposit denominated in dollars but made with a bank outside the jurisdiction of the United States. Banks that accept such deposits will of course seek use them to make loans to other customers, these being called for obvious reasons Eurodollar loans. The prefix 'Euro' has become standard, reflecting the fact that the first such deposits were made with European banks. Dollars are however no longer the only currency used for such transactions, though they dominate the Eurocurrency markets: the Euroyen, Euromark, Eurofranc (the Swiss franc) and Eurosterling markets are also significant. Moreover, the markets are no longer confined to Europe: Singapore, Hong Kong, Tokyo and some Caribbean countries are also important markets in which deposits are taken and loans made in currencies other than that of the country in which the market is situated. Because of the spread of these markets, some commentators prefer to call them 'offshore' markets.

The essence of such markets is, as we noted above, that the banks taking the deposits, and making the loans based on those deposits, are outside the political jurisdiction of the country in whose currency the transactions are denominated. The banks concerned may well however be subsidiaries or branches of banks that are themselves subject to such jurisdiction. For example, many US banks have established subsidiaries in Europe that engage in dollar-denominated transactions.

A particular advantage enjoyed by offshore branches/subsidiaries is that they are usually not subject to many of the regulations governing their parent banks, such as reserve ratios and interest rate controls. Indeed, the increased regulation of US banks in the 1960s provided a major stimulus both for the growth of the Eurodollar market and for the establishment of branches in Europe by those banks in order to circumvent those regulations. A consequence of this freedom from regulation is, as Artis and Lewis argue, that:[30]

> The banks are . . . able to transact more cheaply than from their home bases. International traders are thus able to hold balances of the major currencies used in international trade, and to cover forward exchange commitments, more cheaply and more effectively than by means of traditional foreign banking. Clearly, this particular competitive advantage of Eurocurrency business would be lost if the domestic rules and regulations were removed. In this respect the [Eurocurrency] markets are a classic example of a regulation product.

Eurocurrency transactions are now dominant: traditional foreign banking now comprises only some 11 per cent of international banking. The interesting question is why Eurocurrency transactions have not supplanted traditional foreign banking transactions completely. One explanation is that the transactions costs associated with a Eurocurrency market may well be greater than those faced when dealing with a domestic bank, particularly for small transactions. Another is that a Eurocurrency transaction may be perceived as more risky.[31] To the normal risks associated with a given transaction in a given currency must be added the risks associated with the country in which the transaction is effected; for example, the government of the country in which the transaction is made might decide to impose new banking regulations or exchange controls.

■ 31.5 The European Monetary System[32]

The long-term aim of the European Community, as embodied in the Werner Report of 1972, is the establishment of an *European Monetary Union* (EMU). The original target date for EMU was set in that Report at 1980, but the accession of Denmark, Eire and the United Kingdom in 1973 necessarily delayed any steps towards implementing the Report, and the disturbances that followed the demise of the Bretton Woods, differential inflation rates among the EC countries, and the break-up of the *Exchange Rate Mechanism* in 1992 (see later) have meant that EMU seems unlikely to be achieved in the near future.

Monetary union has two main elements: members should fix (not peg) their exchange rates to one another (some would argue that ideally there should be just one currency), and there should be complete integration of the capital markets in the member countries. This has several implications for other policies. In particular, if individual currencies are to be retained then exchange rates can only remain fixed if there is harmonisation of monetary policy.

The costs and benefits associated with monetary union compared with a system of floating exchange rates are in many respects those discussed in Chapter 30. There is however one obvious difference between the two cases, and that is that a monetary union is formed by a subset of countries. Some guidance on the desirability of forming a monetary union is given by the *theory of optimum currency areas*. This branch of economics is concerned with the criteria that determine the optimal coverage of a single currency. Should it cover one country, a group of countries, or the whole world?

There is no commonly agreed set of criteria, but work in this area has identified a variety of relevant factors. Work by Mundell suggests that the benefits to be gained from a system of pegged exchange rates, or in the extreme a common currency, increase with the mobility of factors within the union.[33] The essence of the argument is that high factor mobility provides the basis for adjustment to changes in the relative economic circumstances of members of the union. This in turn reduces the pressure for changes in the exchange rate if it is pegged, or for a country to secede from a common currency arrangement. McKinnon has argued that membership of a currency union will be more beneficial the more open is the economy.[34] The basis of this argument is that in a relatively open economy the impact of exchange-rate changes will be mainly on the price level rather on the composition of expenditure. Kenen's subsequent analysis suggests that membership of a union is more viable for countries that have a diversified range of exports and imports, since that would imply greater stability in its balance-of-payments position and so less pressure for changes in exchange rates.[35] Various authors have suggested that monetary union is only feasible if the members have approximately the same rates of inflation. This certainly appears to be the view of some EC policy-makers when considering European monetary union, although, as we shall see later, there is a counter-argument that membership of a monetary union may promote convergence of inflation rates. However Kindleberger, and subsequently Goodhart, have argued that political and social cohesion may be more important, both as a prerequisite and as a consequence, than narrow economic considerations.[36] It seems reasonable to argue that the decision on whether to form, or to join, a monetary union should be based on a detailed study that takes into account all these factors.

The Werner Report did lead to the institution of a scheme aimed at reducing the fluctuations between the currencies of the EC members. The original version of the scheme, known as the 'snake in the tunnel', required that the members restrict fluctuations between their own currencies to ± 1.125 per cent of their par values, but subject to that constraint each was allowed to fluctuate against the dollar by the full ±2.25 per cent allowed by the Smithsonian Agreement. The 'tunnel' was abandoned when the members decided to float against the dollar, the system then being known as the 'snake'. The 'snake' did not have a happy or a long life, with various countries withdrawing (some to rejoin later), and numerous currency realignments, and effectively came to an end in 1979.

The establishment of the intended successor to the snake, the *European Monetary System* (EMS), was the consequence of decisions taken at the Bremen Conference in June 1978. The Community's policy-makers were concerned that the increasing divergence between the members and the fluctuations in their exchange rates with one another would undermine the growth of free trade within the Community.

The EMS began its operations in March 1979. It has four main features: the *Exchange Rate Mechanism* (ERM), the *European currency unit* (ECU), financing facilities, and a (proposed) *European Monetary Fund* (EMF). All members of the EC are *de facto* members of the EMS, but not all participate in the ERM.

The essence of the ERM is that each participant has an allowed range within which its currency may fluctuate against the others. The 'norm' is ±2.25 per cent, but Italy (initially), Spain and the United Kingdom are permitted a band of ±6 per cent. Intervention to keep a currency within the prescribed range may be in terms of either members' currencies or (normally) the dollar. If a boundary is reached then the two members concerned are obliged either to intervene in the foreign exchange markets or to take other policy action. Any changes in the 'grid' of central rates require 'mutual agreement'.

The ECU is a weighted basket of the various EMS currencies, and is used as an 'indicator of divergence'. The basic idea is to forestall any dispute about which of the two members involved should be expected to act when a boundary is reached. That is, should the country whose currency is at the bottom of the range be required to intervene in the exchange markets and/or change its policies, or should that be the responsibility of the country whose currency is at the top of the range? Under the ECU-based system a divergence between a country's currency and the ECU that exceeds the specified boundaries leads to the presumption (but not the requirement) that the country will take remedial action.

EMS members have access to credit facilities intended to help deficit countries to manage transitory problems and defend their exchange-rate parities. These facilities, which come under three headings (covering very short-term, short-term, and medium-term requirements) are operated by the central banks of the members.

☐ *The record and prospects of the EMS*

The EMS (or more strictly participation in the ERM) is intended to reduce the volatility of nominal exchange rates among its members (compared with non-members). There is evidence that the EMS has been successful both in this and in reducing the (comparative) volatility of real effective exchange rates as well.[37]

A further benefit that it was hoped would come with membership of the ERM was that high inflation members would find it easier to reduce inflation, both by influencing private expectations and behaviour and by giving the authorities an incentive to bring inflation under control. For some countries, membership of the ERM has effectively meant pegging their currencies to the Deutschmark, which has been the lowest-inflation currency among the members. They are essentially trying to 'borrow' some of the Bundesbank's renowned credibility. Empirical studies of whether the anti-inflation effect has actually operated give no clear picture.

Membership of the ERM is not yet complete. Britain and Italy are, at the time of writing, no longer members. A major problem with joining such a system is that the appropriate parity rate is difficult to determine yet is crucial to successful membership. This is of course the problem that arose when countries attempted to rejoin the gold standard in the late 1920s. The official reason given for Britain's recent withdrawal from the ERM was that it had joined at an inappropriate parity.

The EMS bears, of course, a strong resemblance to the Bretton Woods system. Currencies are pegged to one another, but exchange rates are not fixed. This must raise the possibility of destabilising speculation against currencies in the ERM (the 'one-way bet' discussed earlier). Germany plays a role that is in some ways similar to that undertaken by the United States under Bretton Woods. The essential difference of course is that Germany is not the 'nth country', since the members of the ERM may run a collective surplus or deficit with the rest of the world. Rather than passively accepting the outcome of the policies of other countries, as the United States did for so long, Germany can play an active role in determining the policy stance of the EMS members.

■ 31.6 The international debt crisis

As noted earlier, the international capital market has become increasingly liberalised and integrated, particularly with the abandonment of exchange controls and the development of new technologies for processing, transmitting and storing information. Policy-makers in the major developed nations view this development as being largely beneficial. Those in less-developed countries (LDCs) however do not necessarily share that view. The 'debt crisis' of recent years has forced many LDCs, particularly those in the 'middle-income' group, to take costly policy measures that they would have preferred to avoid.[38]

LDCs may borrow privately (i.e. from banks and similar institutions) for a variety of reasons. Eaton and Gersovitz have suggested a useful classification: borrowing for consumption, for adjustment, and for investment.[39] Borrowing for consumption is undertaken to smooth the path of consumption over time, an important consideration for countries, such as primary commodity exporters, that face instability in their export revenue. Borrowing for adjustment is undertaken to permit the gradual introduction of policy measures that may be required as a consequence of changes in economic conditions. Borrowing for investment is, if rational, concerned with obtaining funds from foreign sources at real rates of interest that are lower than the real rates of return on the projects that are to be financed; such borrowing would then be self-financing.

Countries that borrow 'prudently' should not experience difficulty in servicing their debts (i.e. making interest payments and repaying the principal). It has been argued however that many middle-income LDCs, and in particular some Latin American countries, did not in practice borrow prudently. This is usually linked with another argument: that such countries did not use appropriate economic policies. The source of such joint imprudence is often identified as political instability and/or political will, usually manifested in the form of budgetary and balance-of-payments deficits, high inflation and overvalued exchange rates.

Imprudent borrowers should not however be able to obtain loans from prudent lenders. Analyses of the operation of loan markets suggest however that prudent lending may be difficult to achieve.[40] Lenders rarely have full information on the intentions of the borrowers, and are also exposed to the risk that the borrower will default on the loan. Most of the loans to LDCs however were either made to governments or were guaranteed by them, and lenders are (or at least were) inclined to believe that governments would not repudiate those debts.

Private lending to LDCs expanded markedly in the 1970s. The first OPEC oil-price hike of 1973 drove many LDCs into balance of payments difficulties, both through the direct effect on their import bills and through the reduction in their export revenues as a result to the recession in the developed countries. This created a potential demand for foreign borrowing. At the same time the OPEC countries, unable to absorb all the increase in their revenues, placed large volumes of 'petrodollars' on the London and New York money markets. Real interest rates were low (or even negative) in the developed countries as a consequence of the inflation and recession induced by the oil-price hike. Bankers seem to have taken the view that Latin American countries had good growth prospects, and so the petrodollars were 'recycled' through heavy lending to these countries in particular, and to LDCs in general. The loans were made at variable rates of interest, which meant that the risk of interest rate increases was carried proximately by the borrowers (but ultimately by lenders unable to extract debt service).

The second oil-price hike of 1979 triggered another series of balance of payments deficits and increased borrowing by oil-importing countries. The already indebted LDCs might however have been able to cope with this new shock had the reactions of the developed countries been the same as in 1973. Unfortunately for the LDCs, the developed countries reacted to the new situation by using restrictive monetary policies in an attempt to deal with the inflationary impact of the rise in oil prices. The consequence was a sharp increase in nominal and real interest rates (particularly in the United States, where the budget deficit increased substantially), which both drove up the cost to the LDCs of servicing their existing debt and raised the cost of new borrowings. At the same time, LDCs' export earnings on trade with the developed countries fell sharply. Nevertheless, the LDCs continued to increase their borrowing, nearly doubling their international indebtedness between 1978 and 1982.

The breaking of the debt crisis is usually dated to Mexico's announcement in August 1982 of a moratorium on its debt repayments until new arrangements had been negotiated with its creditors. Since the Mexican difficulties were not unique, this triggered a fear in the international banking community that other heavily-indebted countries would follow suit. Many banks, particularly in the United States, had a very heavy exposure to LDCs' lending, and there was a fear that a loan default by any of the major borrowers (Argentina, Brazil, Mexico and Venezuela) would trigger a run of banking failures in the developed countries.

The banks have attempted to deal with the debt crisis on an individual basis, usually by extending the maturity of their loans ('rescheduling'), and have been generally reluctant to make new loans. At the same time, governments in the developed countries have put pressure on the LDCs to at least maintain their interest payments (in order to forestall a banking crisis), and the IMF has offered loans to the heavily-indebted countries under stringent conditionality requirements. Official plans to deal with the crisis, most notably the Baker and Brady Plans, seem to have achieved little.[41] The international debt crisis is still with us, although it receives rather less publicity today as prospects in Latin America generally improve.

◾ *31.7* Summary and conclusions

International monetary arrangements are obviously not immutable. The last 100 years or so have seen a variety of systems, ranging from the fixed exchange rates of the gold standard, through the Bretton Woods pegged rate system, and into the current 'non-system' of managed floating. Changes in arrangements have usually come about as a consequence of major disturbances, but most arrangements have managed to survive at least some of the disturbances they have faced. There seems to be no consensus among commentators on whether the present system is itself transitory. It is difficult not to believe that many policy-makers have a bias towards fixed or at least managed exchange rates; the attempts to establish an EC-wide pegged exchange-rate system are an obvious example. Nevertheless, there seems little sign of an universal wish to change the current system on a global basis. It seems safest to conclude that floating exchange rates, perhaps intermingled with currency blocs, will continue, at least until the next major crisis.

☐ *Notes*

1   See McKinnon (1993) for an illuminating commentary on the rules of the game and how they have changed since 1879. McKinnon uses the distinction drawn by Mundell between a monetary *order* and a monetary *system*. In Mundell's words 'A monetary order is to a monetary system somewhat like a constitution is to a political or electoral system. We can think of the monetary system as the *modus operandi* of the monetary order' (Mundell, 1972, p. 92). This chapter will not draw such a clear distinction, and will use the term 'monetary system' to encompass both.

2   For example, many former French colonies peg their currencies to the French franc and hold their reserves in that currency, and accept the exchange-rate policies of the French authorities. The former sterling area operated in a similar manner.

3   Note that a fixed exchange-rate regime based on a commodity need not be managed; see Artis and Lewis (1991) for a discussion of commodity-based exchange rate systems.

4   The rules may be 'market-based'.

5   This is of course another way of looking at the policy co-ordination problem discussed in Chapter 30.

6   In this case the nth country must be sufficiently large to absorb the changes demanded of it by adjustment to the policies of the other countries.

7   The $n - 1$ problem is not of course unique to balance-of-payments problems. In an n-country world where the total volume of assets was fixed, there is only scope for $n - 1$ countries to determine independently their own net balance of assets. Similarly, there are only $n - 1$ possible exchange rates (relative prices) in an n-country world.

8   Llewellyn (1990), p.221.

9   See McKinnon (1993) for a discussion of the rules of the gold standard.

10   Only the United States, United Kingdom and Germany maintained full convertibility. Many others were members of various 'monetary unions', while India and China were on a silver standard.

11   See Artis and Lewis (1991) and McKinnon (1993) for detailed analyses of the operation of the gold standard. Note that there is some disagreement between authors on whether the first gold standard came to an end in 1913 or 1914.

12   Britain did not suspend convertibility during the war.

13   Since many countries held their reserves in a 'gold convertible' foreign currency (such as the US dollar and sterling), rather than in gold itself, some

writers refer to the 1927–31 system as a *gold exchange standard*. Others have applied this term to the Bretton Woods system, on the basis of the United States having been willing to exchange dollars for gold at a fixed price.

14 For example, Nurkse argued in a book written for the League of Nations in 1944 that the inter-war experience showed that floating exchange rates were inherently unstable (Nurkse, 1944). Later studies however have suggested that in fact the volatility of exchange rates largely reflected the volatility of inflation rates differentials between countries, and that floating exchange rates had played an important role in absorbing some of the shocks from macroeconomic policy. The story is complicated by the use of competitive 'beggar thy neighbour' devaluations by some countries. A good survey of the inter-war exchange rate regimes is given by Yeager (1976).

15 Tew (1982) provides an excellent discussion of the operations and the development of the Bretton Woods system.

16 Complete freedom of capital movements had not been envisaged by the architects of the Bretton Woods system.

17 Artis and Lewis (1991), p. 40.

18 See for example Triffin (1960). Others, such as Friedman, objected to the monetary *order* (see n. 1).

19 International liquidity could have been expanded by increasing the price of gold, but this was politically unacceptable, if only because the then Soviet Union and South Africa were major exporters of gold. Another alternative would have been to deflate the world economy, but this too was politically unacceptable.

20 The original 'Keynes Plan' for the Bretton Woods agreement had certain similarities.

21 A return to the gold standard was espoused in particular by France (under de Gaulle). See also n. 18.

22 The 'crawling peg' system is essentially one in which the exchange rate is adjusted at regular intervals but remains fixed in the intervening periods.

23 The number of votes a country has is determined by the size of its quota.

24 See Houthakker (1977) and Williamson (1977) for descriptions and analyses of these events.

25 The Group of Ten are Belgium, Canada, France, Germany, Great Britain, Italy, Japan, the Netherlands, Sweden and the United States.

26 See Goodhart (1984).

27 President de Gaulle referred to the seigniorage enjoyed by the United States as an 'exorbitant privilege'.

28 France, (West) Germany, Japan, the United Kingdom and the United States. These are the countries whose currencies make up the SDR 'basket'.

29 The G-7 countries are the G-5 group plus Canada and Italy.

30 Artis and Lewis (1991), p.245. Chapter 9 of Artis and Lewis covers the Eurocurrency markets in more detail than here, as does Chapter 12 of Pilbeam (1992).

31 And indeed may be more risky, as shown by the treatment of Iranian and Iraqi deposits in the United States.

32   See Pilbeam (1992), Chapter 14, and Artis and Lewis (1991), Chapter 8, on which this section is based, for a fuller discussion of the EC's monetary arrangements.
33   Mundell (1961).
34   McKinnon (1963).
35   Kenen (1969).
36   Goodhart (1975). Goodhart provides a useful survey of the optimum currency area debate.
37   See Artis and Taylor (1988).
38   See Snowden (1990), on which this account is based, for detailed analysis of international debt. Pilbeam (1992), Chapter 15, also provides a useful discussion.
39   Eaton and Gersovitz (1981).
40   See for example Stiglitz and Weiss (1981).
41   See Pilbeam (1992), p. 431, for a description of the Baker and Brady Plans.

Further Reading

There are today many books of 'readings' – collections of the classic papers in a particular area – and of 'surveys – sets of specially commissioned articles on particular aspects of international economics. Students should take advantage of both these sources.

Good recent books of survey articles include:

Greenaway, D. (ed.) (1985) *Current Issues in International Trade* (London: Macmillan).

Greenaway, D. and Winters, L. A. (eds) (1993) *Surveys in International Trade* (Oxford: Blackwell).

Llewellyn, D. T. and Milner, C. R. (eds) (1990) *Current Issues in International Monetary Economics* (London: Macmillan).

Milner, C. R. (ed.) (1990) *Export Promotion Strategies* (Hemel Hempstead: Harvester Wheatsheaf).

Collections of readings that are referred to often in the text are:

Bhagwati, J. N. (ed.) (1987) *International Trade: Selected Readings* (Cambridge, MA.: MIT Press).

Caves, R. E. and Johnson, H. G. (eds) (1968) *A.E.A. Readings in International Economics* (London: Allen & Unwin).

Ellis, H. S. and Metzler, L. A. (eds) (1950) *Readings in the Theory of International Trade* (Homewood, ILL.: Irwin).

Bibliography

Some of the papers cited have either been reprinted in books of readings or have appeared in collections of surveys. The books in which such papers appear are indicated by the following codes:

CIIT   – Greenaway, D. (ed.) (1985) *Current Issues in International Trade* (London: Macmillan).

CIIME – Llewellyn, D.T. and Milner, C.R. (eds) (1990) *Current Issues in International Monetary Economics* (London: Macmillan).

ITSR – Bhagwati, J.N. (ed.) (1987) *International Trade: Selected Readings* (Cambridge, MA.: MIT Press).

RIE   – Caves, R.E. and Johnson, H.G. (eds) (1968) *A.E.A. Readings in International Economics* (London: Allen & Unwin).

RTIT – Ellis, H.S. and Metzler, L.A. (eds) (1950) *Readings in the Theory of International Trade* (Homewood, ILL.: Irwin).

Acheson, A.L.K., Chant, J.F. and Prachowny, M.F.J. (eds) (1972) *Bretton Woods Revisited* (Toronto: University of Toronto Press).

Alexander, S.S. (1952) 'Effects of a Devaluation on a Trade Balance', *IMF Staff Papers*, reprinted in *RIE*.

Aquino, A. (1981) 'Changes Over Time in the Pattern of Comparative Advantage in Manufactured Goods: An Empirical Analysis of the Period 1962–74', *European Economic Review*, 15, 41–62.

Arrow, K.J. and Debreu, G. (1954) 'Existence of an Equilibrium for a Competitive Economy', *Econometrica*, 22, 265–90.

Arrow, K.J., Chenery, H.B., Minhas, B.S. and Solow, R.M. (1961) 'Capital–Labor Substitution and Economic Efficiency', *Review of Economics and Statistics*, 43, 225–50.

Artis, M.J. and Lewis, M.K. (1991) *Money in Britain* (London: Philip Allan).

Artis, M.J. and Taylor, M.P. (1988) 'Exchange Rates, Interest Rates, Capital Controls and the European Monetary System: Assessing the Track Record', in Giavazzi *et al.* (eds) (1988).

Balassa, B. (1963) 'An Empirical Demonstration of Classical Comparative Cost Theory', *Review of Economics and Statistics*, 45, 231–8.

Balassa, B. (1964) 'The Purchasing Power Parity Doctrine: A Reappraisal', *Journal of Political Economy*, 72, 584–96.

Balassa, B. (1965) 'Tariff Protection in Industrial Countries: An Evaluation', *Journal of Political Economy*, 73, 573–94.

Balassa, B. (1966) 'Tariff Reductions and Trade in Manufactures among Industrial Countries', *American Economic Review*, 56, 466–73.

Balassa, B. (1975) *European Economic Integration* (Amsterdam: North-Holland).

Balassa, B. (1986a) 'Intra-Industry Trade among Exporters of Manufactured Goods', in Greenaway and Tharakan (eds) (1986).

Balassa, B. (1986b) 'The Determinants of Intra-Industry Specialisation in US Trade', *Oxford Economic Papers*, 38, 220–33.

Balassa, B. (1986c) 'Intra-Industry Specialisation: A Cross-Country Analysis', *European Economic Review*, 30, 27–42.

Balasubramanyam, V. N. (1985) 'Foreign Direct Investment and the International Transfer of Technology', in *CIIT*.

Balasubramanyam, V. N. (1991) 'International Trade in Services: The Real Issues', in Greenaway *et al.* (eds) (1991).

Balasubramanyam, V. N. and Basu, D. R. (1990) 'India: Export Promotion Policies and Export Performance', in Milner (ed.) (1990).

Baldwin, R. E. (1971) 'Determinants of the Commodity Structure of U. S. Trade', *American Economic Review*, 61, 126–46.

Baldwin, R. E. (1976) 'Trade and Employment Effects in the US of a Multilateral Tariff Reduction', *American Economic Review*, 66, 142–8.

Baldwin, R. E. (1985) 'Ineffectiveness of Protection in Promoting Social Goals', *The World Economy*, 8, 109–18.

Baldwin, R. E. (1986), *The Political Economy of US. Import Policy* (Cambridge, MA.: MIT Press).

Baldwin, R. E. and Murray, T. (1977) 'M.F.N. Tariff Reductions and L.D.C. Benefits under the G.S.P.', *Economic Journal*, 87, 30–46.

Baran, P. (1957) *The Political Economy of Growth* (New York: Monthly Review Press).

Baran, P. and Sweezey, P. (1966) *Monopoly Capital* (New York: Monthly Review Press).

Beenstock, M. (1990) 'Exchange Rate Dynamics', in *CIIME*.

Behrman, J. (1978) *Development, the International Economic Order, and Commodity Agreements* (Reading, MA.: Addison-Wesley).

Bergsten, C. F. and Williamson, J. (1983) 'Exchange Rates and Trade Policy', in Cline, W. R. (ed.) *Trade Policy in the 1980s* (Washington, DC: Institute for International Economics).

Bergstrand, J. H. (1983) 'Measurement and Determinants of Intra-Industry International Trade', in Tharakan (ed.) (1983).

Bhagwati, J. N. (1955) 'Immiserizing Growth: A Geometrical Note', *Review of Economic Studies*, 25, 201–5, reprinted in *RIE*.

Bhagwati, J. N. (1964) 'The Pure Theory of International Trade: A Survey', *Economic Journal*, 74, 1–84.

Bhagwati, J. N. (1978) *Foreign Trade Regimes and Economic Development: Anatomy and Consequences of Exchange Control Regimes* (Cambridge MA.: Ballinger, for NBER).

Bhagwati, J. N. (1979) 'International Factor Movements and National Advantage', *Indian Economic Review*, October.

Bhagwati, J. N. (1982a) 'Directly Unproductive Profit-Seeking (DUP) Activities', *Journal of Political Economy*, 90, 988–1002.

Bhagwati, J. N. (1982b) 'Shifting Comparative Advantage, Protectionist Demands, and Policy Response', in Bhagwati (ed.) *Import Competition and Response* (Chicago: Chicago University Press).

Bhagwati, J. N. (1983) *International Economic Theory, vol. II: International Factor Mobility* (Cambridge, MA.: MIT Press).

Bhagwati, J. N. (1987) 'Trade in Services and the Multilateral Trade Negotiations', *The World Bank Economic Review*, 1, 549–69.

Bhagwati, J. N. (1990) 'Export-Promoting Trade Strategy: Issues and Evidence', in Milner (ed.) (1990).

Bhagwati, J. N. (1992) 'The Threats to the World Trading System', *The World Economy*, 15, 443–56.

Bhagwati, J. N. and Ramaswami, V. K. (1963) 'Domestic Distortions, Tariffs and the Theory of Optimum Subsidy', *Journal of Political Economy*, 71, 44–50.

Bhagwati, J. N. and Srinavasan, T. N. (1975) *Foreign Trade Regimes and Economic Development* (New York: Columbia University Press, for NBER).

Bhagwati, J. N. et al. (eds) (1971) *Trade, Balance of Payments and Growth: Essays in Honor of C. P. Kindleberger* (Amsterdam: North-Holland).

Bhandari, J. S. and Putnam, B. H. (eds) (1984) *Economic Interdependence and Flexible Exchange Rates* (Cambridge, MA.: MIT Press).

Bilson, J. F. O. (1978) 'Rational Expectations and the Exchange Rate', in Frenkel and Johnson (eds) (1978).

Black, J. and MacBean, A. (eds) (1989) *Causes of Changes in the Structure of International Trade, 1960–85* (London: Macmillan).

Bleaney, M. F. and Greenaway, D. (1993) 'Long-run Trends in the Relative Price of Primary Commodities and in the Terms of Trade of Developing Countries', *Oxford Economic Papers*, 45, 349–63.

Brander, J. A. and Spencer, B. (1985) 'Export Subsidies and Market Share Rivalry', *Journal of International Economics*, 18, 83–100.

Brander. J. A. and Krugman, P. R. (1983) 'A "Reciprocal Dumping" Model of International Trade', *Journal of International Economics*, 15, 313–21.

Branson, W. H. and Buiter, W. (1983) 'Monetary and Fiscal Policy with Flexible Exchange Rates', in Bhandari and Putnam (eds) (1983).

Branson, W. H. and Monoyios, N. (1977) 'Factor Inputs in US Trade', *Journal of International Economics*, 7, 111–31.

Brash, D. T. (1966) *American Investment in Australian Industry* (Cambridge, MA.: Harvard University Press).

Brown, D. K. and Stern, R. M. (1989) 'Computable General Equilibrium Estimates of the Gains from US–Canadian Trade Liberalisation', in Greenaway et al. (eds) (1989).

Brown, F. and Whalley, J. (1980) 'Equilibrium Evaluations of Tariff Cutting Proposals in the Tokyo Round and Comparisons with More Extensive Liberalisations of World Trade', *Economic Journal*, 90, 838–66.

Buchanan, N. S. (1955) 'Lines on the Leontief Paradox', *Economia Internazionale*, 8, 791–4.

Buckley, P. J. and Casson, M. (1976) *The Future of Multinational Enterprises* (London: Macmillan).

Cassell, G. (1928) *Post-War Monetary Stabilization* (New York: Columbia University Press).

Cassing, J. H. and Hillman, A. L. (1985) 'Political Influence Motives and the Choice Between Tariffs and Quotas', *Journal of International Economics*, 19, 279–90.

Caves, R. E. (1974) 'The Causes of Direct Investment: Foreign Firms' Shares in Canadian and UK Manufacturing Industry', *Review of Economics and Statistics*, 56, 279–93.

Caves, R. E. (1976) 'Economic Models of Political Choice: Canada's Tariff Structure', *Canadian Journal of Economics*, 9, 278–300.

Caves, R. E. (1981) 'Intra-Industry Trade and Market Structure in the Industrial Countries', *Oxford Economic Papers*, 33, 203–23.

Caves, R. E. (1982) *Multinational Enterprise and Economic Analysis* (Cambridge: Cambridge University Press).

Caves, R. E. and Jones, R. W. (1985) *World Trade and Payments* (Boston: Little-Brown).

Cheh, J. (1974) 'United States Concessions in the Kennedy Round and Short-Run Labour Adjustment Costs', *Journal of International Economics*, 4, 323–40.

Cheng, L. (1984) 'International Trade and Technology: A Brief Survey of the Recent Literature', *Weltwirtschaftliches Archiv*, 120, 165–89.

Cohen, B. J. (1973) *The Question of Imperialism: The Political Economy of Dominance and Dependence* (New York: Basic Books).

Congdon, T. (1990) 'Export promotion and trade liberalisation in Latin America', in Milner (ed.) (1990).

Cooper, C. A. and Massell B. F. (1965) 'A New Look at Customs Union Theory', *Economic Journal*, 75, 742–7.

Corden, W. M. (1971) *The Theory of Protection* (Oxford: Oxford University Press).

Corden, W. M. (1972) 'Economies of Scale and Customs Union Theory', *Journal of Political Economy*, 80, 465–75, reprinted in Jacquemin and Sapir (eds) (1989).

Corden, W. M. (1974) *Trade Policy and Economic Welfare* (Oxford: Oxford University Press).

Corden, W. M. (1990) 'Strategic Trade Policy. How New? How Sensible?', *PRE Working Paper*, WPS 396 (Washington, DC: World Bank).

Corden, W. M. and Neary, J. P. (1982) 'Booming Sector and De-Industrialisation in a Small Open Economy', *Economic Journal*, 92, 825–48.

Cox, D. and Harris, R. G. (1992) 'North American Free Trade and its Implications for Canada: Results from a CGE Model of North American Trade', *The World Economy*, 15, 31–44.

Crafts, N. F. R. and Thomas, M. (1986) 'Comparative Advantage in U.K. Manufacturing Trade, 1910–1935', *Economic Journal*, 96, 629–45.

Cuddington, J. J., Johansson, P. O. and Lofgren, K. G. (1984) *Disequilibrium Macroeconomics in Open Economies* (Oxford: Blackwell).

Cuddington, J. T. and Urzula, C. M. (1989) 'Trends and Cycles in the Net Barter Terms of Trade: A New Approach', *Economic Journal*, 99, 426–42.

Culem, C. and Lundberg, L. (1983) 'The Product Pattern of Intra-Industry Trade: Stability among Countries and over Time', *Weltwirtschaftliches Archiv*, 122, 113–30.

Currie, D. (1990) 'International Policy Coordination', in *CIIME*.

De Grauwe, P. (1987) 'Exchange Rate Variability and the Slow Down of International Trade', *IMF Staff Papers*, 35, 63–84.

Deaton, A. (1975) *Models and Projections of Demand in Post-War Britain* (London: Chapman & Hall).

Diaz-Alejandro, C. E. (1970) *Essays on the Economic History of the Argentine Republic* (New Haven: Yale University Press).

Dinwiddy, C. L. and Teal, F. J. (1988) *The Two-Sector General Equilibrium Model: A New Approach* (Oxford: Philip Allan).

Dixit, A. K. and Norman, V. (1980) *Theory of International Trade* (Cambridge: Cambridge University Press).

Dornbusch, R. (1976) 'Expectations and Exchange Rate Dynamics', *Journal of Political Economy*, 84, 1161–76.

Dornbusch, R. (1990) 'Exchange Rate Economics', in *CIIME*.

Dunning, J. (1977) 'Trade, Location of Economic Activity and the MNE: A Search for an Eclectic Approach', in Ohlin *et al.* (eds) (1977).

Eaton, J. and Gersovitz, M. (1981) 'Poor Country Borrowing in Private Financial Markets and the Repudiation Issues', *Princeton Studies in International Finance*, 47 (Princeton: Princeton University).

Eaton, J. and Grossman, G. M. (1986) 'Optimal Trade and Industrial Policy under Oligopoly', *Quarterly Journal of Economics*, 101, 383–406.

Edgeworth, F. Y. (1884) 'The Theory of International Values', *Economic Journal*, 4, 35–50.

Eglin, R. (1987) 'Surveillance of Balance-of-Payments Measures in the GATT', *The World Economy*, 10, 1–26.

El-Agraa, A. M. (1985) 'International Economic Integration', in *CIIT*.

Ennew, C. T., Greenaway, D. and Reed, G. V. (1990) 'Further Evidence on Effective Tariffs and Effective Protection', *Oxford Bulletin of Economics and Statistics*, 52, 69–78.

Ethier, W. (1982) 'National and International Returns to Scale in the Modern Theory of International Trade', *American Economic Review*, 72, 389–405.

Ethier, W. and Horn, H. (1984) 'A New Look at Economic Integration', in Kierzkowski (ed.) (1984), reprinted in Jacquemin and Sapir (eds) (1989).

Falvey, R. E. (1981) 'Commercial Policy and International Trade', *Journal of International Economics*, 11, 495–511.

Falvey, R. E. (1993) 'The Theory of International Trade', in Greenaway and Winters (eds) (1993).

Falvey, R. E. and Kierzkowski, H. (1987) 'Product Quality, Intra-Industry Trade and Imperfect Competition', in Kierzkowski (ed.) (1987).

Finger, J. M. (1975) 'Trade Overlap and Intra-Industry Trade', *Economic Enquiry*, 13, 581–9.

Finger, J. M. (1981) 'Policy Research', *Journal of Political Economy*, 89, 581–589.

Finger, J. M. and de Rosa, D. A. (1980) 'The Compensatory Finance Facility and Export Instability', *Journal of World Trade Law*, 14, 14–22.

Finger, J. M. and Olechowski, A. (1987) *The Uruguay Round: A Handbook for the Multilateral Trade Negotiations* (Washington, DC: World Bank).

Fleming, J. M. (1962) 'Domestic Financial Policies Under Fixed and Floating Exchange Rates', *IMF Staff Papers*, 9, 369–80.

Forsyth, D. J. and Docherty, K. (1972) *The United States Investment in Scotland* (New York: Praeger).

Forsyth, P. J. and Kay, J. A. (1980) 'The Economic Implications of North Sea Oil Revenues', *Fiscal Studies*, 1, 1–28.

Frankel, J. A. and Froot, K (1985) 'Using Survey Data to Test Some Standard Propositions Regarding Exchange Rate Expectations', *NBER Working Paper*, **1672**.

Frenkel, J. A. (1976) 'A Monetary Approach to the Exchange Rate: Doctrinal Aspects and Empirical Evidence', *Scandinavian Journal of Economics*, 78, 169–71.

Frenkel, J. A. and Johnson, H. G. (eds) (1976) *The Monetary Approach to the Balance of Payments* (Toronto: University of Toronto Press).

Frenkel, J. A. and Johnson, H. G. (eds) (1978) *The Economics of Exchange Rates* (Reading, MA.: Addison-Wesley).

Frenkel, J. A., Gylfason, T. and Helliwell, J. E. (1980) 'Synthesis of Monetary and Keynesian Approaches to Short-run Balance-of-Payments Theory', *Economic Journal*, 90, 582–92.

Frey, B. (1985) 'The Political Economy of Protection', in *CIIT*.

Frey, B. S., Pommerehne, W. W., Schneider, F. and Gilbert, G. (1984) 'Consensus and Dissension Among Economists: An Empirical Enquiry', *American Economic Review*, 74, 986–94.

Friedman, M. (1953) 'The Case for Flexible Exchange Rates', in Friedman, M., *Essays in Positive Economics* (Chicago: University of Chicago Press).

Gardner, B. (1991) 'Agricultural Protection in Industrial Countries', in Greenaway *et al.* (eds) (1991).

GATT (1979) *The Tokyo Round of Multinational Trade Negotiations* (Geneva: GATT).

Giavazzi, F., Miscossi, S. and Miller, M. (eds) (1988) *The European Monetary System* (Cambridge, Cambridge University Press).

Goodhart, C. A. E. (1975) *Money, Information and Uncertainty* (London: Macmillan).

Goodhart, C. A. E. (1984) *Monetary Theory and Practice: the UK Experience* (London: Macmillan).

Grandmont, I. M. and McFadden, D. (1972) 'A Technical Note on Classical Gains from Trade', *Journal of International Economics*, 2, 109–25.

Granger, C. W. J. (1969) 'Investigating Causal Relationships by Econometric Models and Cross Spectral Methods', *Econometrica*, 37, 424–38.

Greenaway, D. (1982) 'Identifying the Gains from Pure Intra-Industry Trade', *Journal of Economic Studies*, 9, 40–56.

Greenaway, D. (1983) *International Trade Policy: From Tariffs to the New Protectionism* (London: Macmillan).

Greenaway, D. (1985) 'Clothing from Hong Kong and Other Developing Countries', in Greenaway, D. and Hindley, B., *What Britain Pays for Voluntary Export Restraints: Thames Essay,* **43** (London: Trade Policy Research Centre).

Greenaway, D. (1991) 'Why Are We Negotiating on TRIMS?', in Greenaway *et al.* (eds) (1991).

Greenaway, D. and Milner, C. R. (1984) 'A Cross-Section Analysis of Intra-Industry Trade in the UK', *European Economic Review,* 25, 319–44.

Greenaway, D. and Milner, C. R. (1986)   *The Economics of Intra-Industry Trade* (Oxford: Blackwell).

Greenaway, D. and Milner, C. R. (1989) 'The Growth and Significance of Intra-Industry Trade' in Black and MacBean (eds) (1989).

Greenaway, D. and Milner, C. R. (1990) 'Determinants of the Structure of Import Protection in the UK', paper given to the Royal Economic Society Conference, 1990.

Greenaway, D. and Nam, C.-H. (1988) 'Industrialisation and Macroeconomic Performance in Developing Countries under Alternative Liberalisation Scenarios', *Kyklos,* 41, 419–35.

Greenaway, D. and Reed, G. V. (1990)   'Empirical Evidence on Trade Orientation and Economic Performance in Developing Countries', in Milner (ed.) (1990).

Greenaway, D. and Shaw, G. K. (1986)   *Macroeconomics* (Oxford: Blackwell).

Greenaway, D. and Tharakan, P. K. M. (eds) (1986)   *Imperfect Competition and International Trade: Policy Aspects of Intra-Industry Trade* (Brighton: Wheatsheaf).

Greenaway, D. and Winters, L. A. (eds) (1993)   *Surveys in International Trade* (Oxford: Blackwell).

Greenaway, D., Hine, R. C., O'Brien, A. P. and Thornton, R. J. (eds) (1991)   *Global Protectionism* (London: Macmillan).

Greenaway, D., Hyclak, T. and Thornton, R. J. (eds) (1989)   *Economic Aspects of Regional Trading Arrangements* (Hemel Hemstead: Harvester Wheatsheaf).

Grilli, E. R. and Yang, M. C. (1988) 'Primary Commodity Prices, Manufactured Goods Prices, and the Terms of Trade of Developing Countries: What the Long Run Shows', *World Bank Economic Review,* 2, 1–48.

Gros, D. (1987) 'Protectionism in a Framework with Intra-Industry Trade', *IMF Staff Papers,* 34, 86–114.

Grossman, G. M. (1984) 'The Gains from International Factor Movements', *Journal of International Economics,* 17, 73–83.

Grubel, H. G. and Lloyd, P. J. (1975), *Intra-Industry Trade* (London: Macmillan).

Gruber, W. H. and Vernon, R. (1970) 'The Technology Factor in a World Trade Matrix', in Vernon (ed.) (1970).

Hamada, K. (1985)   *The Political Economy of International Monetary Interdependence* (Cambridge, MA.: MIT Press).

Hamilton, C. (1985) 'Economic Aspects of Voluntary Export Restraints', in *CIIT.*

Harris, R. (1984) 'Applied General Equilibrium Analysis of Small Open Economies with Scale Economies and Imperfect Competition', *American Economic Review,* 74, 1016–32.

Havrylyshyn, O. (1983) 'The Increasing Importance of Newly-Industrialised Countries in World Trade', paper presented to a Symposium on Intra-Industry Trade at the European Institute of Advanced Studies in Management, Brussels, May.

Havrylyshyn, O. and Civan, E. (1983) 'Intra-Industry Trade and the Stage of Development: A Regression Analysis of Industrial and Developing Countries', in Tharakan (ed.) (1983).

Heckscher, E. F. (1919) 'Utrikeshandelns verkan på inkomstfödelningen', *Ekonomisk Tidskrift*, 21, 1–32, reprinted in English translation in *RTIT*.

Herrman, R., Burger, K. and Smit, H. P. (1990) 'Commodity Policy: Price Stabilisation versus Financing', in Winters and Sapsford (eds) (1990).

Hicks, J. R. (1932) *The Theory of Wages* (London: Macmillan).

Hill, T. (1977) 'On Goods and Services', *Review of Income and Wealth*, 23, 315–38.

Hindley, B. and Smith, A. (1984) 'Comparative Advantage and Trade in Services', The *World Economy*, 7, 377–81.

Hine, R. C. (1985) *The Political Economy of European Trade* (Brighton: Wheatsheaf).

Hirsch, S. (1967) *Location of Industry and International Competitiveness* (Oxford: Oxford University Press).

Hirsch, S. (1974) 'Capital or Technology? Confronting the Neo-Factor Proportions and Neo-Technology Accounts of International Trade', *Weltwirtschaftliches Archiv*, 90, 535–63.

Houthakker, H. S. (1977) 'The Breakdown of Bretton Woods', *Discussion Paper* **543**, Harvard Institute of Economic Research.

Hufbauer, G. C. (1970) 'The Impact of National Characteristics and Technology on the Commodity Composition of Trade in Manufactured Goods', in Vernon (ed.) (1970).

Hufbauer, G. C. and Schott, J. (1985) *Trading for Growth: The Next Round of Trade Negotiations* (Washington, DC: Institute for International Economics).

Hughes, H. and Seng, Y. P. (1969) *Foreign Investment and Industrialization in Singapore* (Madison: University of Wisconsin Press).

Hymer, S. H. (1976) *The International Operations of National Firms: A Study of Direct Foreign Investment* (Cambridge, MA.: MIT Press).

Isard, P. (1977) 'How Far Can We Push the Law of One Price?', *American Economic Review*, 67, 942–8.

Jacquemin, A. and Sapir, A. (eds) (1989) *The European Internal Market* (Oxford: Oxford University Press).

Johnson, H. G. (1953) 'Optimum Tariffs and Retaliation', *Review of Economic Studies*, 22, 142–53.

Johnson, H. G. (1957) 'Factor Endowments, International Trade and Factor Prices', *Manchester School*, 25, 270–83, reprinted in *RIE*.

Johnson, H. G. (1959) 'Economic Development and International Trade', *Nationaløkonomisk Tidsskrift*, 97, 253–72, reprinted in *RIE*.

Jones, R. W. (1956) 'Factor Proportions and the Heckscher–Ohlin Theorem', *Review of Economic Studies*, 24, 1–10.

Jones, R. W. (1969) 'Tariffs and Trade in General Equilibrium: Comment', *American Economic Review*, 59, 418–24.

Jones, R. W. (1971) 'A Three Factor Model in Theory, Trade and History', in Bhagwati *et al.* (eds) (1971).

Jung, W. S. and Marshall, P. J. (1985) 'Exports, Growth and Causality in Developing Countries', *Journal of Development Economics*, 18, 1–13.

Katrak, H. (1977) 'Multinational Monopolies and Commercial Policy', *Oxford Economic Papers*, 29, 283–91.

Kearney, C. (1990) 'Stabilisation Policy with Flexible Exchange Rates', in *CIIME*.

Keesing, D. B. (1966) 'Labor Skills and Comparative Advantage', *American Economic Review*, 61, 249–58.

Kemp, M. C. (1970) 'The Mills–Bastable Infant-Industry Dogma', *Journal of Political Economy*, 68, 65–7.

Kemp, M. C. and Wan, H. (1976) 'An Elementary Proposition Concerning the Formation of Customs Unions', *Journal of International Economics*, 6, 95–97.

Kenen, P. B. (1965) 'Nature, Capital and Trade', *Journal of Political Economy*, 73, 437–60.

Kenen, P. B. (1969) 'The Theory of Optimum Currency Areas: An Eclectic View', in Mundell and Swoboda (eds) (1969).

Kenen, P. B. and Voivodas, C. S. (1972) 'Export Instability and Economic Growth', *Kyklos*, 25, 791–805.

Kidron, K. (1965) *Foreign Investment in India* (London: Oxford University Press).

Kierzkowski, H. (ed.) (1984) *Monopolistic Competition in International Trade* (Oxford: Oxford University Press).

Kierzkowski, H. (ed.) (1987) *Protection and Competition in International Trade* (New York: Blackwell).

Kindleberger, C. P. (1969) *American Business Abroad: Six Lectures on Direct Investment* (New Haven: Yale University Press).

Kopitz, G. F. (1976) 'Taxation and Multinational Firm Behaviour: A Critical Survey', *IMF Staff Papers*, 23, 624–73.

Kouri, P. J. K. and Porter, M. G. (1974) 'International Capital Flows and Portfolio Equilibrium', *Journal of Political Economy*, 82, 443–67.

Krauss, M. B. (ed.) (1973) *The Economics of Integration* (London: Allen & Unwin).

Kravis, I. B. (1956) 'Wages and Foreign Trade', *Review of Economics and Statistics*, 38, 14–30.

Kravis, I. B. and Lipsey, R. G. (1978) 'Price Behaviour in the Light of Balance of Payments Theory', *Journal of International Economics*, 8, 193–246.

Krueger, A. O. (1974) 'The Political Economy of the Rent-Seeking Society', *American Economic Review*, 64, 291–303, reprinted in *ITSR*.

Krueger, A. O. (1978) *Foreign Trade Regimes and Economic Development: Liberalization Attempts and Consequences* (Cambridge MA.: Ballinger, for NBER).

Krugman, P. R. (1979) 'Increasing Returns, Monopolistic Competition, and International Trade', *Journal of International Economics*, 9, 469–79.

Krugman, P. R. (1984) 'Import Protection as Export Promotion: International Competition in the Presence of Oligopoly and Economies of Scale', in Kierzkowski (ed.) (1984).

Krugman, P. R. (1992) 'Does the New Trade Theory Require a New Trade Policy?', *The World Economy*, 15, 423–41.

Lall, S. (1973) 'Transfer Pricing by Multi-national Manufacturing Firms', *Oxford Bulletin of Economics and Statistics*, 35, 173–95.

Lall, S. (1975) *Foreign Private Manufacturing Investment and Multinational Corporations: An Annotated Bibliography* (New York: Praeger).

Lancaster, K. J. (1957) 'The Heckscher–Ohlin Trade Model: A Geometric Treatment', *Economica*, 24, 19–39.

Lancaster, K. J. (1980) 'Intra-Industry Trade Under Perfect Monopolistic Competition', *Journal of International Economics*, 10, 151–75.

Lary, H. B. (1968) *Imports of Manufactures from Less Developed Countries* (New York: Columbia Press).

Lawrence, C. and Spiller, P. T. (1986) 'Product Diversity, Economies of Scale, and International Trade', *Quarterly Journal of Economics*, 98, 63–83.

Leamer, E. (1974) 'The Commodity Composition of International Trade: An Empirical Analysis', *Oxford Economic Papers*, 26, 351–74.

Leamer, E. (1980) 'The Leontief Paradox Reconsidered', *Journal of Political Economy*, 88, 495–503, reprinted in *ITSR*.

Leontief, W. W. (1953) 'Domestic Production and Foreign Trade: the American Capital Position Re-examined', *Economia Internazionale*, 7, 3–32, reprinted in *RIE*.

Leontief, W. W. (1956) 'Factor Proportions and the Structure of American Trade: Further Theoretical and Empirical Analysis', *Review of Economics and Statistics*, 38, 386–407.

Leontief, W. W. (1964) 'An International Comparison of Factor Cost and Factor Use', *American Economic Review*, 54, 335–45.

Lerner, A. P. (1936) 'The Symmetry Between Import and Export Taxes', *Economica*, 3, 306–13, reprinted in *RIE*.

Lim, D. (1976) 'Export Instability and Economic Growth: A Return to Fundamentals', *Oxford Bulletin of Economics and Statistics*, 38, 311–22.

Lipsey, R. E. (1976) 'Review of H. G. Grubel and P. J. Lloyd's Intra-Industry Trade', *Journal of International Economics*, 6, 312–4.

Lipsey, R. G. (1960) 'The Theory of Customs Unions: A General Survey', *Economic Journal*, reprinted in *RIE*.

List, F. (1841) *Das Nationale System der Politischen Oekonomie* (Jena) (Translated by S. S. Lloyd (1924) as *The National System of Political Economy* (New York: Longmans, Green)).

Little, I., Scitovsky, T. and Scott, M. (1970) *Industry and Trade in Some Developing Countries: A Comparative Study* (London: Oxford University Press).

Llewellyn, D. T. (1990) 'The International Monetary System', in *CIIME*.

Llewellyn, D. T. and Milner, C. R. (eds) (1990) *Current Issues in International Monetary Economics* (London: Macmillan).

Loeb, G. A. (1954) 'A Estrutura do comercio Exterior da America do Norte', *Revista Brasileira de Economia*, 8.

Loertscher, R. and Wolter, F. (1980) 'Determinants of Intra-Industry Trade: Among Countries and Across Industries', *Weltwirtschaftliches Archiv*, 116, 281–93.

Lundberg, L. (1982) 'Intra-Industry Trade: The Case of Sweden', *Weltwirtschaftliches Archiv*, 118, 302–16.

MacBean, A. I. (1966)   *Export Instability and Economic Development* (London: Allen & Unwin).

MacBean, A. I. and Nguyen, D. T. (1987)   *Commodity Policies: Problems and Prospects* (London: Croom Helm).

MacBean, A. I. and Snowden, P. N. (1981)   *International Institutions in Trade and Finance* (London: Allen & Unwin).

MacDonald, R. (1985)   'Do Deviations of the Real Effective Exchange Rate Follow a Random Walk?', *Economic Notes*, 14, 63–9.

MacDonald, R. (1988)   *Floating Exchange Rates: Theories and Empirical Evidence* (London: Unwin Hyman).

MacDonald, R. (1990)   'Empirical Studies of Exchange Rate Determination', in *CIIME*.

MacDougall, G. D. A. (1951a)   'British and American Exports: A Study Suggested by the Theory of Comparative Costs', *Economic Journal*, 61, 697–724, reprinted in *RIE*.

MacDougall, G. D. A. (1951b)   'British and American Exports: A Study Suggested by the Theory of Comparative Costs', *Economic Journal*, 62, 487–521.

Machlup F. (1955)   'Relative Prices and Aggregate Spending in the Analysis of Devaluation', *American Economic Review*, 65, 255–78.

Magdoff, H. (1969)   *The Age of Imperialism* (New York: Monthly Review Press).

Mandel, E. (1968)   *Marxist Economic Theory, Vol. 2* (London: Monthly Review Press).

Manzur, M. (1990)   'An International Comparison of Prices and Exchange Rates: a New Test of Purchasing Power Parity', *Journal of International Money and Finance*, 9, 75–91.

Mayer, W. (1974)   'Short-run and Long-run Equilibrium for a Small Open Economy', *Journal of Political Economy*, 82, 955–68.

Mayes, D. G. (1978)   'The Effects of Economic Integration on Trade', *Journal of Common Market Studies*, 17, 1–25, reprinted in Jacquemin and Sapir (eds) (1978).

McKinnon, R. I. (1963)   'Optimum Currency Areas', *American Economic Review*, 53, 717–24.

McKinnon, R. I. (1993)   'The Rules of the Game: International Money in Historical Perspective', *Journal of Economic Literature*, 31, 1–44.

Meade, J. E. (1951)   *The Theory of International Economic Policy, Vol. 1: The Balance of Payments* (London: Oxford University Press).

Meade, J. E. (1952)   *A Geometry of International Trade* (London: George Allen & Unwin).

Meade, J. E. (1955)   *The Theory of Customs Unions* (Amsterdam: North-Holland).

Meade, J. E. (1964)   'International Commodity Agreements', *Lloyds Bank Review*, 73, 28–42.

Meerhaeghe, M. A. G. van (1992) *International Economic Institutions* (London: Kluwer).

Messerlin, P. A. (1990) 'Anti-Dumping Regulations or Pro-Cartel Law? The EC Chemical Cases', *The World Economy*, 13, 465–92.

Metzler, L. A. (1949a) 'Tariffs, the Terms of Trade, and the Distribution of National Income', *Journal of Political Economy*, 57, 1–29.

Metzler, L. A. (1949b) 'Tariffs, International Demand, and Domestic Prices', *Journal of Political Economy*, 57, 345–51.

Milner, C. R. (1985) 'Empirical Analysis of the Welfare Effects of Commercial Policy', in *CIIT*.

Milner, C. R. (1991) 'Graduation and Reciprocity', in Greenaway *et al.* (eds) (1991).

Milner, C. R. (ed.) (1990) *Export Promotion Strategies* (Hemel Hempstead: Harvester Wheatsheaf).

Minhas, B. S. (1963) *An International Comparison of Factor Costs and Factor Use* (Amsterdam: North-Holland).

Morrall, J. F. (1972) *Human Capital, Technology and the Role of the United States in International Trade* (Gainesville: University of Florida Press).

Morton, K. and Tulloch, P. (1977) *Trade and Developing Countries* (London: Croom Helm).

Mundell, R. A. (1957) 'International Trade and Factor Mobility', *American Economic Review*, 47, 321–35.

Mundell, R. A. (1961a) 'Flexible Exchange Rates and Employment Policy', *Canadian Journal of Economic and Political Science*, 27, 509–17.

Mundell, R. A. (1961b) 'A Theory of Optimum Currency Areas', *American Economic Review*, 51, 509–17.

Mundell, R. A. (1962) 'The Appropriate Use of Monetary and Fiscal Policy for Internal and External Stability', *IMF Staff Papers*, 9, 70–9.

Mundell, R. A. (1963) 'Capital Mobility and Stabilization Policy Under Fixed and Floating Exchange Rates', *Canadian Journal of Economic and Political Science*, 29, 475–85.

Mundell, R. A. (1964) 'Tariff Preferences and the Terms of Trade', *Manchester School of Economic and Social Studies*, 32, 1–13.

Mundell, R. A. (1972) 'The Future of the International Financial System', in Acheson *et al.* (eds) (1972).

Mundell, R. A. and Swoboda, A. K. (eds) (1969) *Monetary Problems of the International Economy* (Chicago: University of Chicago Press).

Murray, T. (1977) *Trade Preferences for Developing Countries* (New York: Wiley).

Mussa, M. (1974) 'Tariffs and the Distribution of Income: The Importance of Factor Specificity, Substitutability, and Intensity in the Short and Long Run', *Journal of Political Economy*, 82, 1191–204.

Mussa, M. (1976) 'The Exchange Rate, the Balance of Payments, and Monetary and Fiscal Policy Under a Regime of Controlled Floating', *Scandinavian Journal of Economics*, 78, 229–48.

Mussa, M. (1978) 'Dynamic Adjustment to Relative Price Changes in the Heckscher–Ohlin–Samuelson Model', *Journal of Political Economy*, 86, 775–91.

Nam, C. -H. (1990)   'Export Promotion Strategy and Economic Development in Korea', in Milner (ed.) (1990).

Neary, J.P. (1978)   'Short-run Capital Specificity and the Pure Theory of International Trade', *Economic Journal*, 88, 488–510.

Neary, J.P. (1985)   'Theory and Policy of Adjustment in an Open Economy', in *CIIT*.

Nurkse, R. (1944)   *International Currency Experience* (Geneva: League of Nations).

Nurkse, R. (1962)   *Patterns of Trade and Development* (Oxford: Blackwell).

Ohlin, B. (1933)   *Interregional and International Trade* (Cambridge, MA.: Harvard University Press).

Ohlin, B., Hesselborn, P.O. and Wijkman, P.K. (eds) (1977)   *The International Allocation of Economic Activity* (London: Macmillan).

Olson, M. (1965)   *The Logic of Collective Action* (Cambridge, MA.: Harvard University Press).

Pagoulatos, E. and Sorensen, R. (1975)   'Two-Way International Trade: An Econometric Analysis', *Weltwirtschaftliches Archiv*, 111, 454–65.

Patterson, G. (1966)   *Discrimination in International Trade: The Policy Issues* (Princeton: Princeton University Press).

Perée, E. and Steinherr, A. (1989)   'Exchange Rate Uncertainty and Foreign Trade', *European Economic Review*, 33, 1241–64.

Pilbeam, K. (1992)   *International Finance* (London: Macmillan).

Pincus, J. (1975)   'Pressure Groups and the Pattern of Tariffs', *Journal of Political Economy*, 83, 757–78.

Pomfret, R. (1986)   'The Theory of Preferential Trading Arrangements', *Welwirtschaftliches Archiv*, 122, reprinted in Jacquemin and Sapir (eds) (1989).

Posner, M.V. (1961)   'International Trade and Technical Change', *Oxford Economic Papers*, 13, 323–41.

Prebisch, R. (1950)   *The Economic Development of Latin America and Its Principal Problems* (New York: United Nations).

Prebisch, R. (1959)   'The Role of Commercial Policies in Underdeveloped Countries', *American Economic Review*, 49, 251–6.

Prebisch, R. (1984)   'Five Stages in My Thinking about Development', in Bauer, P., Meier, G. and Seers, D. (eds)   *Pioneers in Development* (Oxford: Oxford University Press).

Ray, E.J. (1981)   'Tariff and Non-tariff Barriers to Trade in the United States and Abroad', *Review of Economics and Statistics*, 63, 161–8.

Ray, E.J. (1987)   'The Impact of Special Interests on Preferential Tariff Concessions by the United States', *Review of Economics and Statistics*, 69, 187–93.

Rayner, A.J., Ingersent, K.A. and Hine, R.C. (1993)   'Agriculture in the Uruguay Round: An Assessment, *Economic Journal*, 103, 1513–27.

Rayner, A.J. and Reed, G.V. (1979)   'Domestic Price Stabilisation, Trade Restrictions and Buffer Stock Policy: A Theoretical Policy Analysis with Reference to E.E.C. Agriculture', *European Review of Agricultural Economics*, 5, 102–28.

Ricardo, D. (1817)   *Principles of Political Economy and Taxation.*, reprinted as vol. 1 of Sraffa, P. (ed.) (1951).

Riedel, J. (1977) 'Tariff Concessions in the Kennedy Round and the Structure of Protection in West Germany: an Econometric Assessment', *Journal of International Economics*, 7, 133–44.

Robinson, E. A. G. (ed.) (1960) *Economic Consequences of the Size of Nations: Proceedings of a Conference held by the International Economics Association* (London: Macmillan).

Robson, P. (ed.) (1972) *International Economic Integration* (Harmondsworth: Penguin).

Rogoff, K. (1985) 'Can International Policy Coordination be Counter-productive?', *Journal of International Economics*, 18, 199–217.

Rybczynski, T. M. (1955) 'Factor Endowment and Relative Commodity Prices', *Economica*, 22, 336–41.

Safarian, A. E. (1966) *Foreign Ownership of Canadian Industry* (Toronto: Toronto University Press).

Salter, W. E. G. (1959) 'Internal and External Balance: the Role of Price and Expenditure Effects', *Economic Record*, 35, 226–38.

Sampson, G. P. and Snape, R. H. (1985) 'Identifying the Issues in Trade and Services', *The World Economy*, 8, 171–82.

Samuelson, P. A. (1939) 'The Gains from International Trade', *Canadian Journal of Economics and Political Science*, 5, 195–205.

Samuelson, P. A. (1948) 'International Trade and the Equalization of Factor Prices', *Economic Journal*, 58, 163–84.

Samuelson, P. A. (1949) 'International Factor Price Equalization Once Again', *Economic Journal*, 59, 181–97, reprinted in *RIE* and in *ITSR*.

Samuelson, P. A. (1953) 'Prices of Factors and Goods in General Equilibrium', *Review of Economic Studies*, 21, 1–20.

Samuelson, P. A. (1962) 'The Gains from International Trade Once Again', *Economic Journal*, 72, 820–9.

Samuelson, P. A. (1964) 'Theoretical Notes on Trade Problems', *Review of Economics and Statistics*, 46, 145–54.

Sanyal, K. and Jones, R. W. (1982) 'The Theory of Trade in Middle Products', *American Economic Review*, 72, 16–31.

Sapsford, D. (1985) 'The Statistical Debate on the Net Barter Terms of Trade between Primary Commodities and Manufactures: A Comment and Some Additional Evidence', *Economic Journal*, 95, 781–88.

Savosnick, K. M. (1958) 'The Box Diagram and the Production-Possibility Curve', *Ekonomisk Tidskrift*, 60, 183–97.

Schweinberger, A. G. (1975) 'Non-traded Intermediate Products and the Measurement of Protection', *Oxford Economic Papers*, 27, 215–31.

Scitovsky, T. (1958) *Economic Theory and Western European Integration* (London: Allen & Unwin).

Shaked, A. and Sutton, J. (1984) 'Natural Oligopolies and International Trade', in Kierzkowski (ed.) (1984).

Shoven, J. B. and Whalley, J. (1992) *Applying General Equilibrium* (Cambridge: Cambridge University Press).

Singer, H. W. (1950) 'The Distribution of Gains between Investing and Borrowing Countries', *American Economic Review*, 40, 473–85.

Singer, H. W. (1988) 'The World Development Report 1987 on the Blessings of Outward Orientation: A Necessary Correction', *Journal of Development Studies*, 24, 232–6.

Smith, A. (1766) *The Wealth of Nations*, reprinted as Cannan, E. (ed.) (1961) (London: Methuen)).

Snowden, N. (1990) 'The Analysis of International Debt', in *CIIME*.

Södersten, B. and Vind, K. (1968) 'Tariffs and Trade in General Equilibrium', *American Economic Review*, 58, 394–408.

Södersten, B. and Vind, K. (1969) 'Tariffs and Trade in General Equilibrium: Reply', *American Economic Review*, 59, 424–6.

Spraos, J. (1980) 'The Statistical Debate on the Net Barter Terms of Trade between Primary Commodities and Manufactures', *Economic Journal*, 90, 107–28.

Sraffa, P. (ed.) (1951) *The Works and Correspondence of David Ricardo* (London: Cambridge University Press).

Stern, R. M. (1962) 'British and American Productivity and Comparative Costs in International Trade', *Oxford Economic Papers*, 14, 275–96.

Stern, R. M. and Maskus, K. E. (1981) 'Determinants of the Structure of US Foreign Trade, 1958–76', *Journal of International Economics*, 11, 207–24.

Stern, R. M. and Hoekman, B. M. (1987) 'Issues and Data Needs for GATT Negotiations on Services', *The World Economy*, 10, 39–60.

Stigler, G. J. (1974) 'Free Riders and Collective Action', *Bell Journal of Economics*, 5, 359–65.

Stiglitz, J. E. and Weiss, A. (1981) 'Credit Rationing in Markets with Imperfect Information', *American Economic Review*, 71, 393–410.

Stolper, W. F. and Samuelson, P. A. (1941) 'Protection and Real Wages', *Review of Economic Studies*, 9, 58–73.

Swan, T. (1955) 'Longer Run Problems in the Balance of Payments', reprinted in *RIE*.

Swerling, B. C. (1954) 'Capital Shortage and Labor Surplus in the United States', *Review of Economics and Statistics*, 36, 286–9.

Tew, J. H. B. (1982) *The Evolution of the International Monetary System: 1945–81* (London: Hutchinson).

Tharakan, P. K. M. (1984) 'Intra-Industry Trade between the Industrial Countries and the Developing World', *European Economic Review*, 26, 213–27.

Tharakan, P. K. M. (1985) 'Empirical Analyses of the Commodity Composition of Trade', in *CIIT*.

Tharakan, P. K. M. (ed.) (1983) *Intra-Industry Trade: Empirical and Methodological Aspects* (Amsterdam: North-Holland).

Tinbergen, J. (1952) *On the Theory of Economic Policy* (Amsterdam: North-Holland).

Toh, K. (1982) 'A Cross-Section Analysis of Intra-Industry Trade in US Manufacturing Industries', *Weltwirtschaftliches Archiv*, 118, 281–300.

Torrens, R. (1821) *Essay on the External Corn Trade* (London).

Tower, E. (1992) 'Domestic Resource Cost', *Journal of International Economic Integration*, 7, 20–44.

Trela, I. and Whalley, J. (1990) 'Global Effects of Developed Country Trade Restrictions on Textiles and Apparel', *Economic Journal*, 100, 1190–1205.

Triffin, R. (1960) *Gold and the Dollar Crisis* (New Haven: Yale University Press).

Truman, M. (1969) 'The European Economic Community: Trade Creation and Trade Diversion', *Yale Economic Essays*, 9, 201–57.

Valavanis-Vail, S. (1954) 'Leontief's Scarce Factor Paradox', *Journal of Political Economy*, 52, 523–8.

Vanek, J. (1965) *General Equilibrium of International Discrimination: The Case of Customs Unions* (Cambridge, Ma., Harvard University Press).

Vanek, J. F. (1959) 'The Natural Resource Content of Foreign Trade 1870–1955 and the Relative Abundance of Natural Resources in the United States', *Review of Economics and Statistics*, 41, 146–53.

Venables, A. J. (1984) 'Multiple Equilibria in the Theory of International Trade with Monopolistically Competitive Commodities', *Journal of International Economics*, 16, 103–122.

Verdoorn, P. J. (1960) 'The Intra-Bloc Trade of Benelux', in Robinson (ed.) (1960).

Vernon, R. (1966) 'International Investment and International Trade in the Product Cycle', *Quarterly Journal of Economics*, 80, 190–207.

Vernon, R. (1971) *Sovereignty at Bay: The Multinational Spread of U.S. Enterprises* (London: Basic Books).

Vernon, R. (1977) *Storm Over Multinationals: The Real Issues* (Cambridge, MA.: Harvard University Press).

Vernon, R. (ed.) (1970) *The Technology Factor in International Trade* (New York: NBER).

Viner, J. (1953) *The Customs Union Issue* (New York: Carnegie Endowment for International Peace).

Vousden, N. (1990) *The Economics of Trade Protection* (Cambridge: Cambridge University Press).

Vylder, S. de (1974) *Chile 1970–73: The Political Economy of the Rise and Fall of the Unidad Popular* (Stockholm: Unga Filosofers Forlag).

Warr, P. (1990) 'Export Processing Zones', in Milner (ed.) (1990).

Wicksell, K. (1908) *Föreläsningar i national ekonomi*, translated as *Lectures on Political Economy* (London: Routledge, 1934–5).

Widstrand, C. (ed.) (1975) *Multinational Firms in Africa* (Uppsala: Almqvist & Wiksell).

Williamson, J. (1977) *The Failure of World Monetary Reform 1971–74* (London: Nelson).

Williamson, J. and Bottrill, A. (1971) 'The Impact of Customs Unions on Trade in Manufactures', *Oxford Economic Papers*, 23, 323–51.

Williamson, J. and Miller, M. (1987) *Targets and Indicators: a Blueprint for the International Coordination of Economic Policy* (Washington, DC: Institute for International Economics).

Winham, G. R. (1986) *International Trade and the Tokyo Round Negotiations* (Princeton: Princeton University Press).

Winters, L. A. (1987) 'Britain in Europe: A Survey of Quantitative Trade Studies', *Journal of Common Market Studies*, 28, reprinted in Jacquemin and Sapir (eds) (1989).

Winters, L. A. (1990) 'The Road to Uruguay', *Economic Journal*, 100, 1288–1303.

Winters, L. A. and Sapsford, D. (eds) (1990) *Primary Commodity Prices: Economic Models and Policy* (Cambridge: Cambridge University Press).

Wolf, B. M. (1977) 'Industrial Diversification and Internationalisation: Some Empirical Evidence', *Journal of Industrial Economics*, 26, 177–91.

Wonnacott, G. P. and Wonnacott, R. J. (1981) 'Is Unilateral Tariff Reduction Preferable to a Customs Union? The Curious Case of the Missing Foreign Tariffs', *American Economic Review*, 71, 704–14.

Yeager, L. B. (1976) *International Monetary Relations: Theory, History and Policy* (New York: Harper & Row).

Author Index

Subject Index

absolute advantage *see* trade
absorption
    as approach to devaluation 620
    real balance effect 622–3
adjustment mechanism
    imbalances 525–7
    important factors in 525–7
    national income 539
    under the gold standard 613
agriculture
    Common Agricultural Policy 299,
        369
    discrimination by import
        substitution 418–19
    and new technology in
        less-developed countries 250
    tax on 247, 418
    see also United States
aid
    to less-developed countries 380,
        500
    tied 500
    US 357
Allende government 479, 486
arbitrage
    commodity 8
    interest 528–9
Argentina 416, 418–19, 421, 423–5,
    677
Asia 87
assignment problem 627–8
autarky 6

balance of payments
    autonomous and accommodating
        items in 505–6
    basic balance 507
    book-keeping 498–504
    capital account *see* capital account
    current account *see* current
        account

deficit *see* deficit
defined 497
definition of surplus and deficit
    in 504–8
disequilibrium of *see*
    disequilibrium
economic policy 614
effects of investments on 482–3
equilibrium *see* equilibrium
external balances for 550–3,
    624–30
external equilibrium *see*
    equilibrium
flow and stock transfers in 555–63
internal equilibrium *see*
    equilibrium
monetary approach *see* monetary
    approach
official settlements, concept
    of 507–8
policy for 497, 660
problems 356–7
reasons for surplus in 553
remaining items in 502–4
surplus *see* surplus
balance of trade
    effect of innovation on 83–4
    equilibrium of 522
'band proposal' 668, 670, 674
Bangladesh 433
Bastable's test for infant
    industries 258–9
Belgium 174, 480
Bolivia 396
book-keeping, balance of
    payments 498–504
box diagram 51–5, 91–2
brain drain 462
Brazil 366, 367, 382, 384, 396, 412,
    416, 417–19, 423–4, 429, 434, 490,
    677